January 16–20, 2013
Adelaide, Australia

Association for
Computing Machinery

Advancing Computing as a Science & Profession

FOGA XII

Proceedings of the Twelfth ACM Workshop on

Foundations of Genetic Algorithms

Sponsored by:

ACM SIGEVO

Supported by:

The University of Adelaide and SolveIT Software

Association for
Computing Machinery

Advancing Computing as a Science & Profession

The Association for Computing Machinery
2 Penn Plaza, Suite 701
New York, New York 10121-0701

ISBN: 978-1-4503-1990-4 (Digital)
ISBN: 978-1-4503-2274-4 (Print)

Additional copies may be ordered prepaid from:

ACM Order Department
PO Box 30777
New York, NY 10087-0777, USA

Phone: 1-800-342-6626 (USA and Canada)
+1-212-626-0500 (Global)
Fax: +1-212-944-1318
E-mail: acmhelp@acm.org
Hours of Operation: 8:30 am – 4:30 pm ET

ACM Order Number: 910134

Printed in the USA

Foreword

The twelfth meeting of the conference on the Foundations of Genetic Algorithms was held at the University of Adelaide in Australia on January 17–20, 2013. In addition, there were two satellite workshops held on January 16th. This series of meetings was first held in 1990 at Indiana University with the purpose of encouraging further research in the theoretical aspects of genetic algorithms, and has continued with biennial meetings ever since. Although the name of the conference reflects its historical origins within the genetic algorithms community, the scope has broadened to include foundational work in all forms of evolutionary algorithms, and that broader scope is clearly reflected in the papers that were presented and discussed this year.

The organization of FOGA is similar to that of a symposium or workshop. It is deliberately kept small to allow for a single, plenary session, and to encourage a lot of interaction and discussion. In addition, the page limits on the papers are significantly larger than a typical conference, allowing for a more complete presentation of ideas. Finally, the formal proceedings of FOGA are produced after the conference, giving the authors an opportunity to incorporate feedback received at the conference into their final published versions.

In addition to the sixteen papers that were presented and included in these proceedings, Professor Toby Walsh gave a keynote address titled "Constrainedness of Search". His slides are not included in the proceedings, but are available from him upon request.

The conference was sponsored by ACM SIGEVO, The University of Adelaide, and SolveIT Software. Their generous support allowed us to offer student travel grants and gave us the flexibility to organize a high quality and enjoyable conference program.

We hope you find these papers as stimulating as we did. We fully expect them to act as a catalyst for the next FOGA meeting in 2015. Enjoy!

Frank Neumann
FOGA 2013 Co-organizer
The University of Adelaide

Kenneth De Jong
FOGA 2013 Co-organizer
George Mason University

Table of Contents

FOGA 2013 Organization vii

FOGA 2013 Sponsor & Supporters viii

Full Papers

- **Objective Improvement in Information-Geometric Optimization** 1
  Youhei Akimoto *(INRIA Saclay & University Paris-Sud)*, Yann Ollivier *(CNRS & University Paris-Sud)*
- **Controlling Population Size and Mutation Strength by Meta-ES under Fitness Noise** 11
  Hans-Georg Beyer, Michael Hellwig *(Vorarlberg University of Applied Sciences)*
- **Finite Satisfiability of Propositional Interval Logic Formulas with Multi-Objective Evolutionary Algorithms** 25
  Davide Bresolin *(University of Verona)*,
  Fernando Jiménez, Gracia Sánchez, Guido Sciavicco *(University of Murcia)*
- **Explaining Optimization in Genetic Algorithms with Uniform Crossover** 37
  Keki M. Burjorjee *(Zite Inc.)*
- **When Do Evolutionary Algorithms Optimize Separable Functions in Parallel?** 51
  Benjamin Doerr *(Max-Planck-Institut für Informatik)*, Dirk Sudholt *(University of Sheffield)*,
  Carsten Witt *(Technical University of Denmark)*
- **Optimizing Expected Path Lengths with Ant Colony Optimization Using Fitness Proportional Update** 65
  Matthias Feldmann *(Saarland University)*, Timo Kötzing *(Max Planck Institute for Informatics)*
- **Introducing Graphical Models to Analyze Genetic Programming Dynamics** 75
  Erik Hemberg *(Massachusetts Institute of Technology)*, Constantin Berzan *(Tufts University)*,
  Kalyan Veeramachaneni, Una-May O'Reilly *(Massachusetts Institute of Technology)*
- **Approximating Vertex Cover Using Edge-Based Representations** 87
  Thomas Jansen *(Aberystwyth University)*, Pietro S. Oliveto, Christine Zarges *(University of Birmingham)*
- **A Runtime Analysis of Simple Hyper-Heuristics: To Mix or Not to Mix Operators** 97
  Per Kristian Lehre, Ender Özcan *(University of Nottingham)*
- **A Measure-Theoretic Analysis of Stochastic Optimization** 105
  Alan J. Lockett, Risto Miikkulainen *(University of Texas at Austin)*
- **Runtime Analysis of Mutation-Based Geometric Semantic Genetic Programming on Boolean Functions** 119
  Alberto Moraglio, Andrea Mambrini *(University of Birmingham)*, Luca Manzoni *(University of Milano-Bicocca)*
- **A Further Generalization of the Finite-Population Geiringer-like Theorem for POMDPs to Allow Recombination Overarbitrary Set Covers** 133
  Boris Mitavskiy, Jun He *(Aberystwyth University)*
- **A Feature-Based Comparison of Local Search and the Christofides Algorithm for the Travelling Salesperson Problem** 147
  Samadhi Nallaperuma, Markus Wagner, Frank Neumann *(The University of Adelaide)*,
  Bernd Bischl, Olaf Mersmann, Heike Trautmann *(TU Dortmund University)*
- **Single- and Multi-Objective Genetic Programming: New Bounds for Weighted ORDER and MAJORITY** 161
  Anh Nguyen *(The University of Adelaide)*, Tommaso Urli *(Università degli Studi di Udine)*,
  Markus Wagner *(The University of Adelaide)*
- **Triple and Quadruple Comparison-Based Interactive Differential Evolution and Differential Evolution** 173
  Yan Pei, Hideyuki Takagi *(Kyushu University)*
- **Noisy Optimization Complexity Under Locality Assumption** 183
  Jérémie Decock, Olivier Teytaud *(Inria Saclay & Université Paris-Sud)*

Author Index 190

FOGA 2013 Organization

General Chairs: Frank Neumann *(The University of Adelaide, Australia)*
Kenneth De Jong *(George Mason University, USA)*

Program Committee: Auger Anne *(INRIA, France)*
Dirk Arnold *(Dalhousie University, Canada)*
Hans-Georg Beyer *(Vorarlberg University of Applied Sciences, Austria)*
Christian Blum *(University of the Basque Country, Spain)*
Jürgen Branke *(University of Warwick, UK)*
Dimo Brockhoff *(INRIA, France)*
Kalyanmoy Deb *(Michigan State University, USA)*
Benjamin Doerr *(Max Planck Institute, Saarbrücken, Germany)*
Tobias Friedrich *(University of Jena, Germany)*
Marcus Gallagher *(The University of Queensland, Australia)*
Thomas Jansen *(Aberystwyth University, UK)*
William Langdon *(University College London, UK)*
Per Kristian Lehre *(The University of Nottingham, UK)*
Xiaodong Li *(RMIT University, Australia)*
Una-May O'Reilly *(MIT, USA)*
Pietro Oliveto *(The University of Birmingham, UK)*
Riccardo Poli *(University of Essex, UK)*
Jonathan Rowe *(The University of Birmingham, UK)*
Günter Rudolph *(TU Dortmund University, Germany)*
Marc Schoenauer *(INRIA, France)*
Jonathan Shapiro *(University of Manchester, UK)*
Thomas Stützle *(Université Libre de Bruxelles, Belgium)*
Dirk Sudholt *(University of Sheffield, UK)*
Andrew Sutton *(Colorado State University, USA)*
Lothar Thiele *(ETH Zurich, Switzerland)*
Heike Trautmann *(TU Dortmund University, Germany)*
Darrell Whitley *(Colorado State University, USA)*
Paul Wiegand *(University of Central Florida, USA)*
Carsten Witt *(Technical University of Denmark)*

FOGA 2013 Sponsor & Supporters

Sponsor:

Supporters:

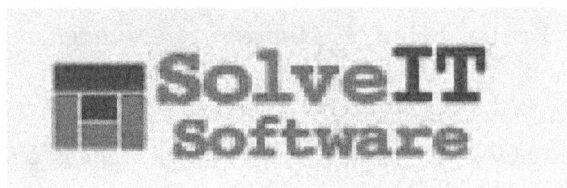

Objective Improvement in Information-Geometric Optimization

Youhei Akimoto
Project TAO – INRIA Saclay
LRI, Bât. 490, Univ. Paris-Sud
91405 Orsay, France
Youhei.Akimoto@lri.fr

Yann Ollivier
CNRS & Univ. Paris-Sud
LRI, Bât. 490
91405 Orsay, France
yann.ollivier@lri.fr

ABSTRACT

Information-Geometric Optimization (IGO) is a unified framework of stochastic algorithms for optimization problems. Given a family of probability distributions, IGO turns the original optimization problem into a new maximization problem on the parameter space of the probability distributions. IGO updates the parameter of the probability distribution along the natural gradient, taken with respect to the Fisher metric on the parameter manifold, aiming at maximizing an adaptive transform of the objective function. IGO recovers several known algorithms as particular instances: for the family of Bernoulli distributions IGO recovers PBIL, for the family of Gaussian distributions the pure rank-μ CMA-ES update is recovered, and for exponential families in expectation parametrization the cross-entropy/ML method is recovered.

This article provides a theoretical justification for the IGO framework, by proving that any step size not greater than 1 guarantees monotone improvement over the course of optimization, in terms of q-quantile values of the objective function f. The range of admissible step sizes is independent of f and its domain. We extend the result to cover the case of different step sizes for blocks of the parameters in the IGO algorithm. Moreover, we prove that expected fitness improves over time when fitness-proportional selection is applied, in which case the RPP algorithm is recovered.

Categories and Subject Descriptors

G.1.6 [**Mathematics of Computing**]: Numerical Analysis—*Optimization*

General Terms

Theory

Keywords

Information-Geometric Optimization, Natural Gradient, Quantile Improvement, Step Size, Black Box Optimization

1. INTRODUCTION

Information-Geometric Optimization (IGO) [5] is a unified framework of model based stochastic search algorithms for any optimization problem. As typified by Estimation of Distribution Algorithms (EDA) [15], model based randomized search algorithms build a statistical model P_θ on the search space X to generate search points. The parameters θ of the statistical model are updated over time so that the probability distribution hopefully concentrates around the minimum of the objective function. In most model based algorithms such as EDAs and Ant Colony Optimization (ACO) algorithms [10], parameter calibration is based on the maximum likelihood principle or other intuitive ways. IGO, unlike them, performs a natural gradient ascent of θ in the parameter space Θ, having first adaptively transformed the objective function into a function on Θ. This construction offers maximal robustness guarantees with respect to changes in the representation of the problem (change of parametrization of the search space, of the parameter space, and of the fitness values).

Importantly, the IGO framework recovers several known algorithms [5, Section 4]. When IGO is instantiated using the family of Bernoulli distributions on $\{0,1\}^d$, one obtains the *population based incremental learning* (PBIL) algorithm [6]. When using the family of Gaussian distributions on $\mathbb{R}^d$, IGO instantiates as a variant of *covariance matrix adaptation evolution strategies* (CMA-ES), the so-called pure rank-μ CMA-ES update [11]. Moreover, when using an exponential family with the expectation parameters, the IGO instance is equivalent to the cross-entropy method for optimization [7]. Of course, the IGO framework not only provides information-theoretic derivations for existing algorithms but automatically offers new algorithms for possibly complicated optimization problems. For instance, the IGO update rule for the parameters of restricted Boltzmann machines has been derived [5].

Theoretical justification of the IGO framework, therefore, is important both to provide a theoretical basis for the recovered algorithms and to make the design principle for future algorithms more reliable. Here we focus on providing a measure of "progress" over the course of IGO optimization, in terms of quantile values of the objective function.

Parameter updates by gradient ascent are somewhat justified in general, at least for infinitesimally small steps, because the gradient points to the direction of steepest ascent of a function. However, this argument does not apply to the IGO algorithm: as the objective function is adaptively transformed in a time-dependent way, the function on which the gradient is computed changes over time, so that its increase does not necessarily mean global improvement. Still, the IGO framework comes with a guarantee that an infinitesimally small IGO step along the natural gradient leads to monotone improvement of a specified quantity, for any objective function f [5, Proposition 5]: a result from [5] is that the *q-quantile value* of the objective function monotonically improves along the natural gradient. This result is limited to the exact IGO flow, i.e., an infinite number of sample points is considered and the step size of the gradient ascent is infinitesimal. Still this ensures that the randomized algorithm with large sample size stays close to the deterministic trajectory with infinite samples with high probability, provided the step size is sufficiently small. Now the question arises whether actual, non-infinitesimal step sizes still ensure monotone q-quantile improvement.

In this article, we prove that *any* step size not greater than 1 guarantees monotone q-quantile value improvement in the IGO algorithm for an exponential family with a finite step size (Theorem 6), thus extending the previous result from infinitesimal steps with continuous time to more realistic algorithmic situations. For instance, this ensures monotone q-quantile improvement in PBIL (using uniform weights, see below), or in the cross-entropy method for exponential families in expectation parameters. Interestingly, our results show that the admissible step sizes in IGO are *independent of the objective function* f, at least for large population sizes (this stems from the many invariance properties built into IGO).

We further extend the result by defining *blockwise* updates in IGO where different blocks of parameters are adjusted one after another with different step sizes. Our motivation is that in practice the pure rank-μ update CMA-ES updates the mean vector and the covariance matrix with different learning rates. We show that the blockwise update rule recovers the pure rank-μ CMA-ES update using different learning rates for the mean vector and the covariance matrix (Proposition 9). We prove that *any* distinct step sizes less than 1 guarantee monotone q-quantile improvement, which justifies the parameter setting used for the CMA-ES in practice (Theorem 10).

Other examples fitting into this framework are the Relative Payoff Procedure (RPP, also known as expectation-maximization for reinforcement learning) [9, 12], or situations where fitness-proportional selection is applied using exponential families (Theorem 12). The RPP is considered as an alternative to gradient based methods that allows to use relatively large learning rates. As it turns out, the RPP can be described as a natural gradient based algorithm with step size 1, and our result is an extension of the proof of its monotone improvement to generic natural gradient algorithms.

The article is organized as follows. In Section 2, we explain the IGO framework and its implementation in practice. IGO-maximum likelihood (IGO-ML), a variant of IGO as a maximum likelihood, is presented, followed by the relation between the IGO algorithm, IGO-ML and the cross-entropy method for optimization, for exponential families of distributions. In Section 3, we prove monotone q-quantile improvement in IGO-ML. The result is extended by defining blockwise IGO-ML, and q-quantile improvement in blockwise IGO-ML is proved. We also provide a result with finite but large population sizes. Section 4 is devoted to the natural gradient algorithm with fitness-proportional selection scheme, where monotone improvement of expected fitness is proven. A short discussion in Section 5 closes the article.

2. INFORMATION-GEOMETRIC OPTIMIZATION

In this article, we consider an objective function $f : X \to \mathbb{R}$ to be minimized over any search space X. The search space X may be continuous or discrete, finite or infinite.

Let $\{P_\theta\}$ be a family of probability distributions on X parametrized by $\theta \in \Theta$ and let p_θ be the probability density function induced by P_θ w.r.t. an arbitrary reference measure $\mathrm{d}x$ on X, namely, $P_\theta(\mathrm{d}x) = p_\theta(x)\mathrm{d}x$. Given a family of probability distributions, IGO [5] evolves the probability distribution P_{θ^t} at each time t so that higher probabilities are assigned to better regions. To do so, IGO transforms the objective function $f(x)$ into a new one $W^f_{\theta^t}(x)$, defines a function on Θ to be maximized: $J(\theta \mid \theta^t) := \mathbb{E}_{P_\theta}[W^f_{\theta^t}(x)]$, and performs the steepest gradient ascent of $J(\theta \mid \theta^t)$ on Θ. Hopefully, after some time the distribution P_{θ^t} concentrates around minima of the objective function.

IGO is designed to exhibit as many invariance properties as possible [5, Section 2]. The first property is invariance under strictly increasing transformations of f. For any strictly increasing g, IGO minimizes $g \circ f$ as easily as f. This property is realized by a quantile based mapping of f to $W^f_{\theta^t}$ at each time. The second property is invariance under a change of coordinates in X, provided that this coordinate change globally preserves the family of probability distributions $\{P_\theta\}$. For example, the IGO algorithm for Gaussian distributions on $\mathbb{R}^d$ is invariant under any affine transformation of the coordinates whereas the IGO algorithm for isotropic Gaussian distribution is only invariant under any translation and rotation. Invariance under X-coordinate transformation is one of the key properties for the success of the CMA-ES. The last property is invariance under reparametrization of θ. At least for infinitesimal steps of the gradient ascent, IGO follows the same trajectory on the parameter space whatever the parametrization for θ is. This property is obtained by considering the intrinsic (Fisher) metric on the parameter space Θ and defining the steepest ascent on Θ w.r.t. this metric, i.e., by using a natural gradient.

The study of the intrinsic metric on the parameter space of the probability distribution, called a *statistical manifold*, is the main topic of *information geometry* [4]. The most widely used divergence between two points on the space of probability distributions is the Kullback–Leibler divergence (KL divergence)

$$D_{\mathrm{KL}}(P_\theta \,\|\, P_{\theta'}) := \int \ln \frac{p_\theta(x)}{p_{\theta'}(x)} P_\theta(\mathrm{d}x) \enspace .$$

The KL divergence is, by definition, independent of the parametrization θ. Let $\theta' = \theta + \delta\theta$. Then, the KL divergence between P_θ and $P_{\theta+\delta\theta}$ expands [13] as

$$D_{\mathrm{KL}}(P_\theta \,\|\, P_{\theta+\delta\theta}) = \frac{1}{2}\delta\theta^{\mathrm{T}} \mathcal{I}_\theta \delta\theta + O(\|\delta\theta\|^3) \enspace , \qquad (1)$$

where $\|\cdot\|$ is the Euclidean norm and $\mathcal{I}_\theta$ is the Fisher information matrix at θ defined as

$$(\mathcal{I}_\theta)_{ij} := \int \frac{\partial \ln p_\theta(x)}{\partial \theta_i} \frac{\partial \ln p_\theta(x)}{\partial \theta_j} P_\theta(\mathrm{d}x) = -\int \frac{\partial^2 \ln p_\theta(x)}{\partial \theta_i \partial \theta_j} P_\theta(\mathrm{d}x) \ .$$

The expansion (1) follows from the well-known fact that the Fisher information matrix is the Hessian of KL divergence. By using the KL divergence, we have the following property of the steepest ascent direction (see [3], Theorem 1, or [5], Proposition 1).

STATEMENT 1. *Let g be a smooth function on the parameter space Θ. Let $\theta \in \Theta$ be a nonsingular point where $\nabla_\theta g(\theta) \neq 0$. Then the steepest ascent direction of g is given by the so-called natural gradient $\tilde{\nabla}_\theta g(\theta) := \mathcal{I}_\theta^{-1} \nabla_\theta g(\theta)$. More precisely,*

$$\frac{\tilde{\nabla}_\theta g(\theta)}{\|\tilde{\nabla}_\theta g(\theta)\|} = \lim_{\epsilon \to 0} \frac{1}{\epsilon} \mathop{\arg\max}_{\substack{\delta\theta \text{ such that} \\ D_{\mathrm{KL}}(P_\theta \| P_{\theta+\delta\theta}) \leq \epsilon^2/2}} g(\theta + \delta\theta) \ .$$

Since KL divergence does not depend on parametrization, the natural gradient is invariant under reparametrization of θ. Hence, the natural gradient step—steepest ascent step w.r.t. the Fisher metric—is invariant at least for an infinitesimal step size [5, Section 2.4].

2.1 Algorithm Description

For completeness, we include here a short description of the IGO algorithm. We refer to [5] for a more complete presentation.

First, IGO transforms the objective function into an adaptive weighted preference by a quantile based approach. This results in a rank based algorithm, invariant under increasing transformations of the objective function. Define the lower and upper P_θ-f-quantiles of $x \in X$ as

$$q_\theta^<(x) := P_\theta[y : f(y) < f(x)]$$
$$q_\theta^\leq(x) := P_\theta[y : f(y) \leq f(x)] \ .$$

The lower quantile value $q_\theta^<(x)$ is the probability of sampling strictly better points than x under the current distribution P_θ, while the upper quantile value $q_\theta^\leq(x)$ is the probability of sampling points better than or equivalent to x. Given a weight function (selection scheme) $w : [0,1] \to \mathbb{R}$ that is non-increasing, the weighted preference $W_\theta^f(x)$ is defined as

$$W_\theta^f(x) := \begin{cases} w(q_\theta^\leq(x)) & \text{if } q_\theta^<(x) = q_\theta^\leq(x), \\ \frac{1}{q_\theta^\leq(x) - q_\theta^<(x)} \int_{q_\theta^<(x)}^{q_\theta^\leq(x)} w(u)\,\mathrm{d}u & \text{otherwise.} \end{cases} \tag{2}$$

This way, the quality of a point is measured by a function of the P_θ-quantile in which it lies. A typical choice of the selection scheme w is $w(u) = \mathbb{1}_{[u \leq q]}/q$, $0 < q < 1$. We call it the *q-truncation* selection scheme. Using q-truncation amounts, in the final IGO algorithm, to giving the same positive weight to a fraction q of the best samples in a population, and weight 0 to the rest, as is often the case in practice.

Next, IGO turns the original objective function f on the search space X into a function $J(\theta \,|\, \theta^t)$ on the statistical manifold Θ by defining

$$J(\theta \,|\, \theta^t) := \mathbb{E}_{P_\theta}[W_{\theta^t}^f(x)] \ . \tag{3}$$

Note that $J(\theta \,|\, \theta^t)$ depends on the current position θ^t. Then, the gradient of $J(\theta \,|\, \theta^t)$ is computed as

$$\begin{aligned} \nabla_\theta J(\theta \,|\, \theta^t) &= \nabla_\theta \mathbb{E}_{P_\theta}[W_{\theta^t}^f(x)] \\ &= \nabla_\theta \int W_{\theta^t}^f(x)\, p_\theta(x)\,\mathrm{d}x \\ &= \int W_{\theta^t}^f(x)\, p_\theta(x)\, \nabla_\theta \ln p_\theta(x)\,\mathrm{d}x \\ &= \mathbb{E}_{P_\theta}[W_{\theta^t}^f(x)\, \nabla_\theta \ln p_\theta(x)] \ . \end{aligned} \tag{4}$$

Here we have used the relation $\nabla p_\theta(x) = p_\theta(x) \nabla \ln p_\theta(x)$.

Finally, IGO uses natural gradient ascent on the parameter space. The natural gradient on the statistical manifold $(\Theta, \mathcal{I})$ equipped with the Fisher metric $\mathcal{I}$ is given by the product of the inverse of the Fisher information matrix, $\mathcal{I}_\theta^{-1}$, and the vanilla gradient. That is, the natural gradient of $J(\cdot \,|\, \theta^t)$ at θ is written as $\tilde{\nabla}_\theta J(\theta \,|\, \theta^t) = \mathcal{I}_\theta^{-1} \nabla_\theta J(\theta \,|\, \theta^t)$. According to (4), we can rewrite the natural gradient as

$$\tilde{\nabla}_\theta J(\theta \,|\, \theta^t) = \mathbb{E}_{P_\theta}[W_{\theta^t}^f(x)\, \tilde{\nabla}_\theta \ln p_\theta(x)] \ . \tag{5}$$

Introducing a finite step size δt, IGO finally updates the parameter as follows

$$\theta^{t+\delta t} = \theta^t + \delta t\, \tilde{\nabla}_\theta J(\theta \,|\, \theta^t)\big|_{\theta = \theta^t} \ . \tag{6}$$

2.2 Implementation and Recovering Algorithms

When implementing IGO in practice, it is necessary to estimate the expectation in (5). The approximation is done by the Monte Carlo method using λ samples taken from P_{θ^t}. Let $x_1, \ldots, x_\lambda$ be independent samples from P_{θ^t}.

First, we need to approximate $W_{\theta^t}^f(x_i)$ for each $i = 1, \ldots, \lambda$. Define

$$\mathrm{rk}^<(x_i) := \#\{j, f(x_j) < f(x_i)\}$$
$$\mathrm{rk}^\leq(x_i) := \#\{j, f(x_j) \leq f(x_i)\} \ ,$$

let

$$\bar{w}_i := \int_{(i-1)/\lambda}^{i/\lambda} w(q)\,\mathrm{d}q, \quad \forall i \in [\![1, \lambda]\!],$$

and set

$$\widehat{w}_i = \frac{1}{\mathrm{rk}^\leq(x_i) - \mathrm{rk}^<(x_i)} \sum_{j = \mathrm{rk}^<(x_i)+1}^{\mathrm{rk}^\leq(x_i)} \bar{w}_j \ . \tag{7}$$

Then $\lambda \widehat{w}_i$ is a consistent estimator of $W_{\theta^t}^f(x_i)$, in other words, $\lim_{\lambda \to \infty} \lambda \widehat{w}_i = W_{\theta^t}^f(x_i)$ with probability one. (See the proof of Theorem 4 in [5].) If there are no ties in our sample, i.e. $f(x_i) \neq f(x_j)$ for any $i \neq j$, then $\mathrm{rk}^\leq(x_i) = \mathrm{rk}^<(x_i) + 1$ and (7) simply reads $\widehat{w}_i = \bar{w}_{\mathrm{rk}^\leq(x_i)}$, but (7) is a mathematically neater definition of rank based weights accounting for possible ties. In practice we just design the λ weight values $\bar{w}_1, \ldots, \bar{w}_\lambda$, instead of the selection scheme w.

In the rest of this article, we assume for simplicity that the selection weights $\bar{w}_i$ are non-negative and sum to 1. This is the case, for instance, if the selection scheme w is q-truncation as above.

Next, Monte Carlo sampling is applied to the expectation (5), using $\widehat{w}_i$ and x_i. Replacing the expectation with a sample average $\frac{1}{\lambda}\sum_{i=1}^{\lambda}$ and $W_{\theta^t}^f(x_i)$ with $\lambda\widehat{w}_i$, we get

$$G^t := \sum_{i=1}^{\lambda} \widehat{w}_i \, \tilde{\nabla}_\theta \ln p_\theta(x_i)|_{\theta=\theta^t} \ . \tag{8}$$

Again, G^t is a consistent estimator of the IGO step at θ^t, i.e., of $\tilde{\nabla}_\theta J(\theta \,|\, \theta^t)|_{\theta=\theta^t}$. See Theorem 4 in [5].

Now the practical IGO algorithm implementation can be written in the form of a black-box search algorithm as

1. Sample x_i, $i = 1, \dots, \lambda$, independently from P_{θ^t};
2. Evaluate $f(x_i)$ and compute $\mathrm{rk}^{\leq}(x_i)$ and $\mathrm{rk}^{<}(x_i)$;
3. Evaluate $G^t = \sum_{i=1}^{\lambda} \widehat{w}_i \, \tilde{\nabla}_\theta \ln p_\theta(x_i)|_{\theta=\theta^t}$;
4. Update the parameter: $\theta^{t+\delta t} = \theta^t + \delta t \cdot G^t$.

Finally, to obtain an explicit form of the parameter update equation, we need to know the explicit form of the natural gradient of the log-likelihood, which depends on a family of probability distributions and its parametrization. Explicit forms of $\tilde{\nabla}_\theta \ln p_\theta(x)$ are known for some specific families of probability distributions with specific parametrizations, and the above algorithm sometimes coincides with several known algorithms.

Example 1. The family of Bernoulli distributions on $X = \{0,1\}^d$ is defined as $P_\theta(x) = \prod_{j=1}^{d} \theta_j^{x_j}(1-\theta_j)^{1-x_j}$. The natural gradient of the log-likelihood is readily computed as $\tilde{\nabla}_\theta \ln p_\theta(x) = x - \theta$ (Section 4.1 in [5]). The natural gradient update reads

$$\theta^{t+\delta t} = \theta^t + \delta t \sum_{i=1}^{\lambda} \widehat{w}_i \left(x_i - \theta^t\right) \ .$$

This is equivalent to so-called PBIL (population based incremental learning, [6]).See Section 4.1 in [5] for details.

Example 2. The probability density function of a multivariate Gaussian distribution on $X = \mathbb{R}^d$ with mean vector m and covariance matrix C, is defined as

$$p_\theta(x) = \left(\det(2\pi C)\right)^{-1/2} \exp\left(-(x-m)^{\mathrm{T}} C^{-1}(x-m)/2\right) \ .$$

When $\theta = (m, C)$, the explicit form of $\tilde{\nabla} \ln p_\theta(x)$ is known to be $\tilde{\nabla} \ln p_\theta(x) = \left[\begin{smallmatrix} x-m \\ (x-m)(x-m)^{\mathrm{T}} - C \end{smallmatrix}\right]$ (see [2]). Then, the natural gradient update reads

$$\theta^{t+\delta t} = \theta^t + \delta t \sum_{i=1}^{\lambda} \widehat{w}_i \begin{bmatrix} x - m^t \\ (x-m^t)(x-m^t)^{\mathrm{T}} - C^t \end{bmatrix} \ .$$

This is equivalent to the pure rank-μ CMA-ES update [11]

$$m^{t+1} = m^t + \eta_m \sum_{i=1}^{\lambda} \widehat{w}_i (x_i - m^t)$$
$$C^{t+1} = C^t + \eta_C \sum_{i=1}^{\lambda} \widehat{w}_i \left((x_i - m^t)(x_i - m^t)^{\mathrm{T}} - C^t\right)$$

except that $\eta_m = \eta_C = \delta t$ in the natural gradient update.

2.3 Maximum likelihood, IGO-ML, and cross-entropy

In the sequel, we prove monotone improvement of the objective function for a variant of IGO known as IGO-maximum likelihood (IGO-ML, introduced in [5, Section 3]). The result is then transferred to IGO because the two algorithms exactly coincide in an important class of cases, namely, exponential families using mean value parametrization.

The IGO-ML algorithm [5, Section 3] updates the current parameter value θ^t by taking a weighted maximum likelihood of the current distribution and the best sampled points. Assume as above that $\sum \widehat{w}_i = 1$. Then the *IGO-ML update* is defined as

$$\theta^{t+\delta t} = \arg\max_\theta \left\{ (1-\delta t)\, \mathbb{E}_{P_{\theta^t}} \left[\ln p_\theta(x)\right] + \delta t \sum_i \widehat{w}_i \ln p_\theta(x_i) \right\} \tag{9}$$

where we note that the first part is the cross-entropy of P_{θ^t} and P_θ, and thus, taken alone, is maximized for $\theta = \theta^t$. Taking the limit $\lambda \to \infty$, we also define the *infinite-population IGO-ML update* as

$$\theta^{t+\delta t} = \arg\max_\theta \left\{ (1-\delta t)\, \mathbb{E}_{P_{\theta^t}} \left[\ln p_\theta(x)\right] + \delta t H_t(\theta) \right\} \tag{10}$$

where we set

$$H_t(\theta) := \mathbb{E}_{P_{\theta^t}} \left[W_{\theta^t}^f(x) \ln p_\theta(x)\right]$$

a "weighted cross-entropy" of θ and θ^t.

Note that the finite- and infinite-population IGO-ML updates only make sense when there is a unique maximizer θ in (9) and (10), respectively. This assumption is always satisfied, for instance, for exponential families of probability distributions, as considered below (Statement 2).

The IGO-ML update is compatible with the IGO update, in the sense that for $\delta t \to 0$ the direction and magnitude of these updates coincide [5, Section 3].

The IGO-ML method is also related to the cross-entropy (CE) or maximum-likelihood (ML) method for optimization [7], which can be written as

$$\theta^{t+1} = \arg\max_\theta \sum_{i=1}^{\lambda} \widehat{w}_i \ln p_\theta(x_i)$$

and its smoothed version which reads [7]

$$\theta^{t+\delta t} = (1-\delta t)\theta^t + \delta t \arg\max_\theta \sum_{i=1}^{\lambda} \widehat{w}_i \ln p_\theta(x_i) \ . \tag{11}$$

Note that IGO-ML is parametrization-independent whereas for $\delta t \neq 1$ the smoothed CE/ML method is not. Consequently, in general these updates will differ.

2.4 IGO and IGO-ML for Exponential Families

An *exponential family* is a set $\{p_\theta; \theta \in \Theta\}$ of probability density functions p_θ with respect to an arbitrary measure $\mathrm{d}x$ on X defined as

$$p_\theta(x) = \frac{1}{Z(\theta)} \exp\left(\sum_{i=1}^{n} \beta_i(\theta) T_i(x) \right) \ , \tag{12}$$

where $\beta = (\beta_i)_{1 \leq i \leq n}$ is the so-called *natural* (i.e. canonical) *parameter*; each T_i, $1 \leq i \leq n$ is a map $T_i : X \to \mathbb{R}$ such that $\{T_1, \dots, T_n, x \mapsto 1\}$ are linearly independent; $Z(\theta)$ is the normalization factor. This linear independence ensures that the manifold of the exponential family is nonsingular. Many probability models, including multivariate Gaussian distributions, are expressed as exponential families. See [4, Section 2.3] for examples.

If we define

$$\eta(\theta) := \mathbb{E}_{P_\theta}[T(x)] = \int T(x)\, p_\theta(x)\, \mathrm{d}x \ , \qquad (13)$$

$\eta = (\eta_i)_{1\le i\le n}$ is the so-called *expectation parameter.* For example, the expectation parameter for the multivariate Gaussian distribution encodes the first moment $\mathbb{E}_{P_\theta}[x]$ and the second moment $\mathbb{E}_{P_\theta}[xx^{\mathrm{T}}]$. Other examples can be found in [4, Section 3.5].

We will repeatedly and implicitly make use of the following well-known fact for exponential families.

STATEMENT 2. *Let $x_1, \dots, x_k$ be k points in X and let $\alpha_1, \dots, \alpha_k$ be non-negative numbers with $\sum \alpha_i = 1$. Then the value θ of the parameter such that the associated expectation parameter satisfies $\eta(\theta) = \sum \alpha_i T(x_i)$, if it belongs to the statistical manifold, is the unique maximizer of the weighted log-likelihood: $\theta = \arg\max \sum \alpha_i \ln p_\theta(x_i)$. An analogous statement holds if the finite sum is replaced with an integral or a combination of both.*

(Uniqueness boils down to strict concavity of $\ln p_\theta(x)$ as a function of θ. The restriction placed on η to belong to the statistical manifold is necessary: for instance, for Gaussian distributions, if the number of points k is not greater than the dimension of the ambient space, a degenerate distribution θ will result.)

The following statement from [5] shows that the natural gradient of a function in the expectation parametrization is given by the vanilla gradient of the function w.r.t. the normal parameter, and vice versa.

STATEMENT 3 (PROPOSITION 22 IN [5]). *Let g be a function on the statistical manifold of an exponential family as above. Then the components of the natural gradient w.r.t. the expectation parameters are given by the vanilla gradient w.r.t. the natural parameters and vice versa, that is,*

$$\tilde{\nabla}_{\eta_i} g = \frac{\partial g}{\partial \beta_i} \quad \text{and} \quad \tilde{\nabla}_{\beta_i} g = \frac{\partial g}{\partial \eta_i} \ .$$

According to Statement 3, each component of the natural gradient of the log likelihood $\ln p_\theta(x)$ under the exponential parametrization $\theta = \eta$ is equivalent to each component of the vanilla gradient, i.e.,

$$\tilde{\nabla}_{\eta_i} \ln p_\theta(x) = \frac{\partial \ln p_\theta(x)}{\partial \beta_i} = T_i(x) - \eta_i \ , \qquad (14)$$

where the latter equality is well-known, e.g., [4, (2.33)]. The IGO update (6) under the expectation parametrization thus reads

$$\eta^{t+\delta t} = \eta^t + \delta t\, \mathbb{E}_{P_{\theta^t}}[W^f_{\theta^t}(x)(T(x) - \eta^t)] \qquad (15)$$

and the natural gradient update with finite sample size reads

$$\eta^{t+\delta t} = \eta^t + \delta t \sum_{i=1}^{\lambda} \widehat{w}_i \left(T(x_i) - \eta^t\right) \ . \qquad (16)$$

Suppose as above that the selection weights sum to one: $\mathbb{E}_{P_\theta}[W^f_\theta(x)] = \int_0^1 w(q)\mathrm{d}q = 1$ and thus $\sum \widehat{w}_i = 1$. Then, IGO has a close relation with the CE/ML for optimization. As is stated in Theorem 15 in [5], for an exponential family the CE/ML method (11) and the IGO instance (16), when expressed with the expectation parametrization ($\theta = \eta$), coincide with IGO-ML (9).

STATEMENT 4 (THEOREM 15 IN [5]). *For optimization using an exponential family $\{P_\theta\}$, these three algorithms coincide: IGO-ML; the IGO expressed in expectation parameters; the CE/ML expressed in expectation parameters. That is, for an exponential family with the expectation parametrization, for $0 \le \delta t \le 1$ we have (writing in turn IGO, CE/ML and IGO-ML)*

$$\begin{aligned} \theta^{t+\delta t} &= \theta^t + \delta t \sum_{i=1}^{\lambda} \widehat{w}_i \left(T(x_i) - \theta^t\right) \\ &= (1-\delta t)\theta^t + \delta t \arg\max_\theta \sum_{i=1}^{\lambda} \widehat{w}_i \ln p_\theta(x_i) \\ &= \arg\max_\theta \Big\{ (1-\delta t)\mathbb{E}_{P_{\theta^t}}[\ln p_\theta(x)] \\ &\qquad + \delta t \sum_{i=1}^{\lambda} \widehat{w}_i \ln p_\theta(x_i) \Big\} \ . \end{aligned} \qquad (17)$$

In the limit of infinite sample size $\lambda \to \infty$ this rewrites

$$\begin{aligned} \theta^{t+\delta t} &= \theta^t + \delta t\, \mathbb{E}_{P_{\theta^t}}\left[W^f_{\theta^t}(x)\left(T(x) - \theta^t\right)\right] \\ &= (1-\delta t)\theta^t + \delta t \arg\max_\theta H_t(\theta) \\ &= \arg\max_\theta \Big\{ (1-\delta t)\mathbb{E}_{P_{\theta^t}}[\ln p_\theta(x)] + \delta t H_t(\theta) \Big\} \end{aligned} \qquad (18)$$

where we recall that $H_t(\theta) = \mathbb{E}_{P_{\theta^t}}\left[W^f_{\theta^t}(x) \ln p_\theta(x)\right]$.

Remark 1. Malagò et al. [16] study information-geometric aspects of exponential families for optimization. One difference from the IGO framework is that the optimization problem is defined as the minimization of the expectation of the objective function over P_θ, namely

$$\min_\theta \mathbb{E}_{P_\theta}[f(x)],$$

which they call the stochastic relaxation of the original optimization problem. They study this for an exponential family on a discrete search space with the natural parametrization ($\theta = \beta$) and propose the natural gradient descent algorithm. Note that this requires computation of the empirical Fisher information matrix to perform natural gradient descent. However, if the algorithm is modified to use the expectation parameters instead, one can compute the natural gradient descent directly as

$$\eta^{t+\delta t} = \eta^t - \delta t \sum_{i=1}^{\lambda} f(x_i)\left(T(x_i) - \eta^t\right) \ . \qquad (19)$$

We study this algorithm in Section 4.

3. QUANTILE IMPROVEMENT

One possible way to provide theoretical backing for an optimization algorithm is to show monotonic improvement at each step of the algorithm (although this is by no means necessary: e.g., for stochastic algorithms, this is not expected to hold at each step). For example, consider the sphere function $f : x \mapsto \|x\|^2$. Then, it is easy to show that the gradient steps $x^{t+\delta t} = x^t - \delta t\, \nabla_x f(x^t)$ generate a monotonically decreasing sequence $\{f(x^t)\}_{t\ge 0}$ provided $0 < \delta t \le 1/2$. For any smooth function, infinitesimal gradient steps are guaranteed to improve the objective function values; but in general the admissible step size strongly depends on the function and has to be adjusted by the user.

When it comes to the counterpart in IGO, however, we follow the gradient of the function $J(\theta \mid \theta^t)$, which depends on θ^t, so that step-by-step improvement in the objective, $J(\theta^{t+1} \mid \theta^t) > J(\theta^t \mid \theta^t)$, does not necessarily mean improvement. (It might happen that $J(\theta^t \mid \theta^{t+1}) > J(\theta^{t+1} \mid \theta^{t+1})$ and $J(\theta^{t+1} \mid \theta^t) > J(\theta^t \mid \theta^t)$ at the same time.)

A key feature of the IGO framework is its invariance under changing the objective function f by an increasing transformation (e.g. optimizing f^3 instead of f). Thus, any measure of progress that is not compatible with such transformations (e.g. the expectation $\mathbb{E}_{P_{\theta^t}} f$) is not a good candidate to always improve over the course of IGO optimization.

As a measure of improvement, Arnold et al. [5] use the notion of *q-quantile of f*. The q-quantile $Q^q_P(f)$ of f under a probability distribution P is any number m such that $P[x : f(x) \leq m] \geq q$ and $P[x : f(x) \geq m] \geq 1 - q$. For instance, $Q^q_P(f)$ is the median value of f under P if $q = 1/2$. For smooth distributions and continuous f there is only one such number m, but in general the set of such m may be a closed interval, for instance if f has "jumps". For the sake of definiteness let us use the largest such value:

$$Q^q_P(f) := \sup \{ m \in \mathbb{R} : P[x : f(x) \leq m] \geq q \text{ and } P[x : f(x) \geq m] \geq 1 - q \} \ .$$

(This is because we want to minimize the objective function f; when IGO is used for maximization instead, Theorem 6 has to be written using an infimum in the definition of $Q^q_P(f)$ instead.)

It is proven in [5] that when using the q-truncation selection scheme, the q-quantile value of f monotonically decreases along infinitesimal IGO steps.

STATEMENT 5 (PROPOSITION 5 IN [5]). *Consider the q-truncation selection scheme $w(u) = \mathbb{1}_{[u \leq q]}/q$ where $0 < q < 1$ is fixed. Then each infinitesimal IGO step (6) where δt is infinitesimal leads to monotonic improvement in the q-quantile of f: $Q^q_{P_{\theta^{t+\delta t}}}(f) \leq Q^q_{P_{\theta^t}}(f)$.*

3.1 Quantile Improvement in IGO-ML

In practice, explicit algorithms do not use continuous time with infinitesimal time steps: the time step δt may be quite large and its calibration may be an important issue. It is more interesting and important to see how long steps we can take along the natural gradient, i.e. how large a δt we can choose while guaranteeing q-quantile improvement.

When using IGO-ML (and thus when using IGO or CE/ML on an exponential family with the expectation parametrization), we can obtain such a conclusion; the size of the steps may even be chosen independently of the objective function.

THEOREM 6. *Let the selection scheme be $w(u) = \mathbb{1}_{[u \leq q]}/q$ where $0 < q < 1$. Assume that the $\arg\max$ defining the IGO-ML step (10) is uniquely determined. Then for $0 < \delta t \leq 1$, each infinite-population IGO-ML step (10) leads to q-quantile improvement: $Q^q_{P_{\theta^{t+\delta t}}}(f) \leq Q^q_{P_{\theta^t}}(f)$.*

Moreover, equality can hold only if $P_{\theta^{t+\delta t}} = P_{\theta^t}$ or if $P_{\theta^{t+\delta t}}[x : f(x) = Q^q_{P_{\theta^t}}(f)] > 0$.

COROLLARY 7. *For exponential families written in expectation parameters, on any search space, the same holds for the CE/ML method and for the IGO algorithm.*

Note that the first condition for equality means the algorithm has reached a stable point.

The second condition for equality typically happens for discrete search spaces: on such spaces, the q-quantile evolves in time by discrete jumps even when θ^t moves smoothly, so we cannot expect strict quantile improvement at each step. On the other hand, with continuous distributions on continuous search spaces, the second equality condition can only occur if the objective function has a plateau (a level set with non-zero measure).

PROOF. If $P_{\theta^{t+\delta t}} = P_{\theta^t}$, obviously $Q^q_{P_{\theta^{t+\delta t}}}(f) = Q^q_{P_{\theta^t}}(f)$. Hereunder, we assume $P_{\theta^{t+\delta t}} \neq P_{\theta^t}$.

Consider the function $J(\theta \mid \theta^t)$ defining the expected P_{θ^t}-adjusted fitness of a random point under P_θ:

$$J(\theta \mid \theta^t) = \mathbb{E}_{P_\theta}\left[W^f_{\theta^t}(x)\right]$$

and remember that $J(\theta^t \mid \theta^t) = 1$. The idea is as follows: letting Y be the set of points with $P_{\theta^t}(Y) = q$ at which the objective function f is smallest (the sublevel set of f with P_{θ^t}-mass q), then with our choice of w, $W^f_{\theta^t}(x)$ is (up to technicalities) equal to $1/q$ on Y and 0 elsewhere, so that $J(\theta \mid \theta^t)$ represents $1/q$ times the P_θ-probability of falling into Y (hence $J(\theta^t \mid \theta^t) = 1$). Thus $J(\theta \mid \theta^t) > 1$ will mean that the P_θ-probability of falling into Y is larger than q, so that P_θ improves over P_{θ^t} and the q-quantile has decreased.

We are going to prove that the IGO-ML update satisfies $J(\theta^{t+\delta t} \mid \theta^t) > 1$ if $P_{\theta^t} \neq P_{\theta^{t+\delta t}}$. More precisely we prove that

$$J(\theta^{t+\delta t} \mid \theta^t) > \exp\left(\frac{1 - \delta t}{\delta t} D_{\mathrm{KL}}(P_{\theta^t} \,\|\, P_{\theta^{t+\delta t}})\right) \ .$$

This will imply quantile improvement, thanks to the following lemma, the proof of which is postponed.

LEMMA 8. *Let the selection scheme w be as above. If $J(\theta^{t+\delta t} \mid \theta^t) > 1$, then $Q^q_{P_{\theta^{t+\delta t}}}(f) \leq Q^q_{P_{\theta^t}}(f)$. If moreover $P_{\theta^{t+\delta t}}[x : f(x) = Q^q_{P_{\theta^t}}(f)] = 0$, then $Q^q_{P_{\theta^{t+\delta t}}}(f) < Q^q_{P_{\theta^t}}(f)$.*

The lower bound on $J(\theta^{t+\delta t} \mid \theta^t)$ is obtained as follows. Since $\int W^f_{\theta^t}(x) p_{\theta^t}(x) \mathrm{d}x = 1$ and $W^f_{\theta^t}(x) p_{\theta^t}(x) \geq 0$ for any x, $W^f_{\theta^t}(x) p_{\theta^t}(x)$ can be viewed as a probability density function. Since ln is concave, by Jensen's inequality we have

$$\begin{aligned} \ln J(\theta \mid \theta^t) &= \ln \int \frac{p_\theta(x)}{p_{\theta^t}(x)} W^f_{\theta^t}(x) p_{\theta^t}(x) \mathrm{d}x \\ &\geq \int \ln\left(\frac{p_\theta(x)}{p_{\theta^t}(x)}\right) W^f_{\theta^t}(x) p_{\theta^t}(x) \mathrm{d}x \qquad (20) \\ &= H_t(\theta) - H_t(\theta^t) \ . \end{aligned}$$

Thus, if $H_t(\theta) > H_t(\theta^t)$ we have $J(\theta \mid \theta^t) > 1$.

Now, according to (10), $\theta^{t+\delta t}$ uniquely maximizes the quantity $(1 - \delta t)\mathbb{E}_{P_{\theta^t}}\left[\ln p_\theta(x)\right] + \delta t H_t(\theta)$. Therefore, if $\theta^{t+\delta t} \neq \theta^t$, we have

$$(1 - \delta t)\mathbb{E}_{P_{\theta^t}}\left[\ln p_{\theta^{t+\delta t}}(x)\right] + \delta t H_t(\theta^{t+\delta t}) > (1 - \delta t)\mathbb{E}_{P_{\theta^t}}\left[\ln p_{\theta^t}(x)\right] + \delta t H_t(\theta^t)$$

and rearranging we get

$$\begin{aligned} H_t(\theta^{t+\delta t}) - H_t(\theta^t) \\ > \frac{1-\delta t}{\delta t}\left(\mathbb{E}_{P_{\theta^t}}\left[\ln p_{\theta^t}(x)\right] - \mathbb{E}_{P_{\theta^t}}\left[\ln p_{\theta^{t+\delta t}}(x)\right]\right) \\ = \frac{1-\delta t}{\delta t} D_{\mathrm{KL}}(P_{\theta^t} \,\|\, P_{\theta^{t+\delta t}}) \ . \end{aligned} \quad (21)$$

The right-hand side of this inequality is non-negative for $0 < \delta t \leq 1$.

This will prove the theorem once Lemma 8 is proved, which we now proceed to do. □

PROOF OF LEMMA 8. Hereunder, we abbreviate m for the q-quantile value $Q^q_{P_{\theta^t}}(f)$ of f under P_{θ^t}.

Let us compute the weighted preference $W^f_{\theta^t}(x)$. Since the selection scheme w satisfies $0 \leq w(u) \leq 1/q$ for all $u \in [0;1]$, we have $0 \leq W^f_{\theta^t}(x) \leq 1/q$ for any x.

We claim that $f(x) > m$ implies $W^f_{\theta^t}(x) = 0$. Indeed, suppose that x is such that $f(x) > m$. Since by definition m is the largest value such that $P_{\theta^t}[y : f(y) \geq m] \geq 1-q$, we must have $P_{\theta^t}[y : f(y) \geq f(x)] < 1-q$. Hence $P_{\theta^t}[y : f(y) < f(x)] > q$, i.e., $q^<_{\theta^t}(x) > q$. Now this implies $W^f_{\theta^t}(x) = 0$ for our choice of selection scheme w.

Thus $W^f_{\theta^t}(x)$ is at most $1/q$ and vanishes if $f(x) > m$. For any probability distribution P_θ, this implies that

$$J(\theta \,|\, \theta^t) = \mathbb{E}_{P_\theta}[W^f_{\theta^t}(x)] \leq \frac{1}{q} P_\theta[x : f(x) \leq m] \ .$$

Therefore,

$$\begin{aligned} J(\theta \,|\, \theta^t) > 1 &\Longrightarrow P_\theta[x : f(x) \leq m] > q \\ &\Longrightarrow Q^q_{P_\theta}(f) \leq m \ . \end{aligned}$$

If moreover $P_\theta[x : f(x) = m] = 0$, we have $P_\theta[x : f(x) \leq m] = P_\theta[x : f(x) < m]$ hence

$$\begin{aligned} J(\theta \,|\, \theta^t) > 1 &\Longrightarrow P_\theta[x : f(x) < m] > q \\ &\Longleftrightarrow P_\theta[x : f(x) \geq m] < 1-q \\ &\Longrightarrow Q^q_{P_\theta}(f) < m \ . \end{aligned}$$

Altogether, $J(\theta^{t+\delta t} \,|\, \theta^t) > 1$ implies quantile improvement $Q^q_{P_{\theta^{t+\delta t}}}(f) \leq Q^q_{P_{\theta^t}}(f)$. Moreover, if $P_{\theta^{t+\delta t}}[x : f(x) = m] = 0$, we have strict quantile improvement $Q^q_{P_{\theta^{t+\delta t}}}(f) < Q^q_{P_{\theta^t}}(f)$. □

This completes the proof of Theorem 6.

Example 3. Bernoulli distributions constitute an exponential family where the sufficient statistics $T_i(x)$ are x_i. The parameter θ used in PBIL (Example 1) is indeed the expectation parameter. Thus, PBIL is an instance of IGO-ML and can be viewed as a CE/ML method at the same time. Hence, by Theorem 6, each infinite-population PBIL step leads to q-quantile improvement if we employ q-truncation selection, which is not the same as the exponential weights introduced in [6].

Remark 2. The proof of the theorem is quantitative: the Kullback–Leibler divergence $D_{\mathrm{KL}}(P_{\theta^t} \,\|\, P_{\theta^{t+\delta t}})$ indicates how much progress was made. More precisely (assuming for simplicity a continuous situation with no plateaus), while the probability under P_{θ^t} to fall into the best q percent of points for P_{θ^t} is q by definition, the probability under $P_{\theta^{t+\delta t}}$ to fall into the best q percent of points for P_{θ^t} is at least $q \exp\left(\frac{1-\delta t}{\delta t} D_{\mathrm{KL}}(P_{\theta^t} \,\|\, P_{\theta^{t+\delta t}})\right)$.

3.2 Blockwise IGO-ML

The expectation parameter is not always the most obvious one. When it comes to multivariate Gaussian distributions, the expectation parameter is the mean vector and second moment, $(m,\ mm^{\mathrm{T}} + C)$. Meanwhile, the CMA-ES and the CE/ML method for continuous optimization parametrize the mean vector and covariance matrix, hence they differ from the IGO-ML algorithm. Moreover, sometimes different step sizes (learning rates) are employed for each parameter, which makes the direction of parameter update different from that of the natural gradient. Here, we justify some of these settings by guaranteeing q-quantile improvement in an extended framework.

We define an extension of IGO-ML, *blockwise IGO-ML*, that recovers the pure rank-μ CMA-ES update with different learning rates for m and C.

Definition 1. Let $\theta = (\theta_1, \ldots, \theta_k)$ be any decomposition of the parameter θ into k blocks, and let $\{\delta t_1, \ldots, \delta t_k\}$ be a step size for each block. For $1 \leq j \leq k$, define the *j-th block partial IGO-ML update* with step size δt_j as the map sending a parameter value θ to $\Phi_j(\theta)$ where

$$\Phi_j(\theta) := \underset{\substack{\theta^* \\ \theta^*_i = \theta_i \text{ for all } i \neq j}}{\arg\max} \left\{ (1-\delta t_j)\mathbb{E}_{P_\theta}\left[\ln p_{\theta^*}(x)\right] + \delta t_j \sum_i \widehat{w}_i \ln p_{\theta^*}(x_i) \right\} \ . \quad (22)$$

The *blockwise IGO-ML* updates the parameter θ as follows. Given a current parameter value θ^t, update the first block of θ^t, then the second block, etc., in that order; explicitly, set

$$\theta^{t+1} := (\Phi_k \circ \cdots \circ \Phi_2 \circ \Phi_1)(\theta^t) \ , \quad (23)$$

where we note that the same Monte Carlo sample $\{x_i\}$ from P_{θ^t} is used throughout the whole range of block updates $\Phi_1, \ldots, \Phi_k$.

The infinite-population step ($\lambda = \infty$) reads the same with

$$\Phi_j(\theta) := \underset{\substack{\theta^* \\ \theta^*_i = \theta_i \text{ for all } i \neq j}}{\arg\max} \left\{ (1-\delta t_j)\mathbb{E}_{P_\theta}\left[\ln p_{\theta^*}(x)\right] + \delta t_j\, \mathbb{E}_{P_{\theta^t}}\left[W^f_{\theta^t}(x) \ln p_{\theta^*}(x)\right] \right\} \ . \quad (24)$$

As before, the finite- and infinite-population blockwise IGO-ML updates only make sense if the arg max in (22) or (24) is uniquely determined.

Note that the blockwise IGO-ML depends on the decomposition of the parameters into blocks and their update order, while it is independent of the parametrization inside each block. Blockwise IGO-ML is not necessarily equivalent to IGO-ML even when all δt_i are equal to δt.

PROPOSITION 9. *The pure rank-μ CMA-ES update (Example 2) is an instance of blockwise IGO-ML for Gaussian distributions, with parameter decomposition $\theta = (\theta_1, \theta_2)$ where $\theta_1 = C$, the covariance matrix, and $\theta_2 = m$, the mean vector.*

PROOF. Given $\theta^t = (C^t, m^t)$, blockwise IGO-ML first updates C as follows:

$$C^* = \arg\max_C \left\{ (1-\delta t_C)\mathbb{E}_{P_{(C^t,m^t)}}\left[\ln p_{(C,m^t)}(x)\right] + \delta t_C \sum_i \widehat{w}_i \ln p_{(C,m^t)}(x_i) \right\} . \quad (25)$$

Considering $\{P_{(C,m^t)}\}$ as an exponential family of Gaussian distributions whose mean vector is fixed to m^t, (25) can be viewed as an ordinary IGO-ML step for this restricted model. Then, since (after shifting the origin of the coordinate system to m^t) C is the expectation parameter of the restricted model, the update is given by (17) namely

$$C^* = C^t + \delta t_C \sum_{i=1}^{\lambda} \widehat{w}_i\left((x_i - m^t)(x_i - m^t)^{\mathrm{T}} - C^t\right) .$$

Next, m is updated as

$$m^* = \arg\max_m \left\{ (1-\delta t_m)\mathbb{E}_{P_{(C^*,m^t)}}\left[\ln p_{(C^*,m)}(x)\right] + \delta t_m \sum_i \widehat{w}_i \ln p_{(C^*,m)}(x_i) \right\} .$$

To derive m^*, let us differentiate the inside of arg max w.r.t. m and derive the zero point of the derivative. Seeing that $\nabla_m \ln p_{(C^*,m)}(x) = (C^*)^{-1}(x-m)$, we find the condition

$$(1-\delta t_m)(C^*)^{-1}(m^t - m^*) + \delta t_m \sum_i \widehat{w}_i (C^*)^{-1}(x_i - m^*) = 0 ,$$

which holds if and only if

$$m^* = m^t + \delta t_m \sum_{i=1}^{\lambda} \widehat{w}_i (x_i - m^t) .$$

This is equivalent to the pure rank-μ CMA-ES update. □

Quantile improvement as in Theorem 6 readily extends to this setting as follows.

THEOREM 10. *Let the selection scheme be $w(u) = \mathbb{1}_{[u \le q]}/q$ where $0 < q < 1$. Assume that the* arg max *defining each partial infinite-population IGO-ML update (24) is uniquely determined. Then for $0 < \delta t_j \le 1$ ($j \in [\![1;k]\!]$), each infinite-population blockwise IGO-ML step (23) leads to q-quantile improvement: $Q^q_{P_{\theta^{t+1}}}(f) \le Q^q_{P_{\theta^t}}(f)$.*

Moreover, equality can hold only if $P_{\theta^{t+1}} = P_{\theta^t}$ or if $P_{\theta^{t+1}}[x : f(x) = Q^q_{P_{\theta^t}}(f)] > 0$.

Consequently, each infinite-population step of the pure rank-μ CMA-ES update guarantees q-quantile improvement. Indeed, from Proposition 9 this variant of the CMA-ES is an instance of blockwise IGO-ML. Moreover, if each level set of f has zero Lebesgue measure, which often holds for continuous optimization, we have strict q-quantile improvement.

PROOF. If $P_{\theta^{t+1}} = P_{\theta^t}$, obviously $Q^q_{P_{\theta^{t+1}}}(f) = Q^q_{P_{\theta^t}}(f)$. We assume $P_{\theta^{t+1}} \ne P_{\theta^t}$ in the following.

Set $\theta^{t,0} := \theta^t$ and $\theta^{t,j} := \Phi_j(\theta^{t,j-1})$ so that $\theta^{t+1} = \theta^{t,k}$. According to Lemma 8, to prove quantile improvement it is enough to show that $J(\theta^{t+1} \,|\, \theta^t) > 1$. Moreover, this implies strict quantile improvement provided $P_{\theta^{t+1}}[x : f(x) = Q^q_{P_{\theta^t}}(f)] = 0$.

According to (20), if $H_t(\theta^{t+1}) > H_t(\theta^t)$ we have that $J(\theta^{t+1} \,|\, \theta^t) > 1$. To show that $H_t(\theta^{t+1}) > H_t(\theta^t)$ we decompose $H_t(\theta^{t+1}) - H_t(\theta^t)$ into the sum of partial differences, namely,

$$H_t(\theta^{t+1}) - H_t(\theta^t) = \sum_{j=1}^{k} H_t(\theta^{t,j}) - H_t(\theta^{t,j-1}) ,$$

and we will prove that each term is non-negative. Moreover, if $P_{\theta^{t,j}} \ne P_{\theta^{t,j-1}}$ for some $j \in [\![1;k]\!]$, we will have $H_t(\theta^{t,j}) - H_t(\theta^{t,j-1}) > 0$ for this j. Since $P_{\theta^{t+1}} \ne P_{\theta^t}$ implies $P_{\theta^{t,j}} \ne P_{\theta^{t,j-1}}$ for at least one $j \in [\![1;k]\!]$, we will have that $H_t(\theta^{t+1}) - H_t(\theta^t) > 0$, resulting in $J(\theta^{t+1} \,|\, \theta^t) > 1$.

We proceed as in Theorem 6. Since $\theta^{t,j} = \Phi_j(\theta^{t,j-1})$ is the only maximizer of (24), we have

$$(1-\delta t_j)\mathbb{E}_{P_{\theta^{t,j-1}}}\left[\ln p_{\theta^{t,j}}(x)\right] + \delta t_j H_t(\theta^{t,j}) \ge (1-\delta t_j)\mathbb{E}_{P_{\theta^{t,j-1}}}\left[\ln p_{\theta^{t,j-1}}(x)\right] + \delta t_j H_t(\theta^{t,j-1})$$

with equality holding if and only if $\theta^{t,j} = \theta^{t,j-1}$. Rearranging, we get

$$H_t(\theta^{t,j}) - H_t(\theta^{t,j-1}) > \frac{1-\delta t_j}{\delta t_j} D_{\mathrm{KL}}(P_{\theta^{t,j-1}} \,\|\, P_{\theta^{t,j}})$$

if $\theta^{t,j} \ne \theta^{t,j-1}$, and $H_t(\theta^{t,j}) = H_t(\theta^{t,j-1})$ if $\theta^{t,j} = \theta^{t,j-1}$. The right-hand side of the above inequality is non-negative for $0 < \delta t \le 1$. Therefore, $H_t(\theta^{t,j}) - H_t(\theta^{t,j-1}) \ge 0$ for all $j \in [\![1;k]\!]$. Moreover, since $P_{\theta^{t+1}} \ne P_{\theta^t}$, for at least one $j \in [\![1;k]\!]$ we have $\theta^{t,j} \ne \theta^{t,j-1}$ and thus $H_t(\theta^{t,j}) - H_t(\theta^{t,j-1}) > 0$ for this j, implying that $H_t(\theta^{t+1}) - H_t(\theta^t) > 0$. This completes the proof. □

3.3 Finite Population Sizes

The results above are valid for "ideal" updates with infinite sample size. With finite sample size, the update (9) defines a stochastic sequence (depending on the random sample $\{x_i\}$) and so one cannot expect monotone q-quantile improvement at each step. Still, we can expect q-quantile improvement with high probability when the population size is sufficiently large.

We provide an analogue of Theorem 6 for finite but large population size. A similar statement holds for blockwise IGO-ML. The proof follows a standard probabilistic approximation argument.

PROPOSITION 11. *Let $w(\cdot)$ be the q-truncation selection scheme: $w(u) = \mathbb{1}_{[u \le q]}/q$ where $0 < q < 1$. Let $\{P_\theta\}$ be an exponential family of probability distributions, parametrized by its expectation parameter. Assume that the* arg max *defining the infinite-population IGO-ML step (10) is uniquely defined.*

Assume that for all $\theta \in \Theta$, the derivative $\partial \ln P_\theta(x)/\partial\theta$ exists for P_θ-almost all $x \in X$ and has finite second moment: $\mathbb{E}_{P_\theta}\left[|\partial \ln P_\theta(x)/\partial\theta|^2\right] < \infty$.

Let $0 < \delta t \le 1$. Let $\theta^{t+\delta t}_{\lambda}$ be the IGO-ML update (9) with sample size λ, and let $\theta^{t+\delta t}_{\infty}$ be the infinite-population IGO-ML update (10). Assume that $\theta^{t+\delta t}_{\infty} \ne \theta^t$.

Then, with probability tending to 1 as $\lambda \to \infty$, the finite-population update $\theta^{t+\delta t}_{\lambda}$ results in q-quantile improvement:

$$Q^q_{P_{\theta^{t+\delta t}_{\lambda}}}(f) \le Q^q_{P_{\theta^t}}(f) .$$

Consequently, the same holds for the CE/ML method and the IGO algorithm when they are applied to an exponential family using the expectation parameters.

Note the assumption that the *ideal* dynamics has not reached equilibrium yet: $\theta_\infty^{t+\delta t} \neq \theta^t$. If $\theta_\infty^{t+\delta t} = \theta^t$, the finite-population dynamics will just randomly wander around this equilibrium value with some noise, resulting in either improvement or deterioration at each step.

Also note that the population size λ needed may depend on the current location θ^t in parameter space, as well as the objective function f. For instance, highly oscillating functions f likely require higher population sizes for a consistent estimation of the IGO-ML update.

PROOF. For exponential families, the IGO and IGO-ML updates coincide. Under the conditions of the theorem, the finite-population IGO update (8) is a consistent estimator of the infinite-population IGO update (5) [5, Proposition 18], implying that $\theta_\lambda^{t+\delta t}$ converges with probability one to $\theta_\infty^{t+\delta t}$. Under our regularity assumptions on P_θ, this implies pointwise convergence of $p_{\theta_\lambda^{t+\delta t}}$ to $p_{\theta_\infty^{t+\delta t}}$, which, since $W_{\theta^t}^f(x)$ is bounded, leads to

$$\begin{aligned} J(\theta_\lambda^{t+\delta t} \mid \theta^t) &= \mathbb{E}_{P_{\theta_\lambda^{t+\delta t}}}[W_{\theta^t}^f(x)] \\ &\to \mathbb{E}_{P_{\theta_\infty^{t+\delta t}}}[W_{\theta^t}^f(x)] = J(\theta_\infty^{t+\delta t} \mid \theta^t) \quad \text{as } \lambda \to \infty. \end{aligned}$$

Now the right-hand side is greater than 1 for $0 < \delta t \leq 1$ unless $\theta_\infty^{t+\delta t} = \theta^t$, as we have shown in the proof of Theorem 6. Thus, we have $J(\theta_\lambda^{t+\delta t} \mid \theta^t) > 1$ with high probability for sufficiently large λ. Thus Lemma 8 entails q-quantile improvement with high probability. □

4. FITNESS-PROPORTIONAL SELECTION

These results carry over to the use of a composite $g \circ f$ of a function g with the objective function f, as a selection weight instead of $W_{\theta^t}^f$ in the IGO framework. This covers, for instance, fitness-proportional selection ($g = \mathrm{Id}$). We prove that, when considering the natural gradient ascent for an exponential family (12) using the expectation parameter (13), we can guarantee monotone $\mathbb{E}_{P_\theta}[g \circ f(x)]$-value improvement for updates of step size inversely proportional to $\mathbb{E}_{P_\theta}[g \circ f(x)]$. More precisely,

THEOREM 12. *Assume $g \circ f$ is non-negative and not almost everywhere 0. Consider the update*

$$\theta^{t+\delta t} = \theta^t + \delta t\, \mathbb{E}_{P_{\theta^t}}\left[\frac{g \circ f(x)}{\mathbb{E}_{P_{\theta^t}}[g \circ f(x)]}\left(T(x) - \theta^t\right)\right], \quad (26)$$

where $\theta = \eta$ is the expectation parameter of the exponential family $\{P_\theta\}$.

Then for $0 < \delta t \leq 1$, we have

$$\mathbb{E}_{P_{\theta^{t+\delta t}}}[g \circ f(x)] \geq \mathbb{E}_{P_{\theta^t}}[g \circ f(x)] \ .$$

Moreover, equality can occur only if $P_{\theta^{t+\delta t}} = P_{\theta^t}$.

Gradient based methods with fitness-proportional selection are often employed, especially in reinforcement learning, e.g. *policy gradient with parameter based exploration* (PGPE) [17]. One disadvantage of gradient based methods is that the step size has to be calibrated by the user depending on the problem at hand. Alternative methods such as *expectation-maximization* [9], including the RPP below, are sometimes employed to avoid this issue. Theorem 12, however, ensures that each natural gradient step improves the expected fitness for $0 < \delta t \leq 1$ when an exponential family is used with its expectation parameters.

Example 4. The Relative Payoff Procedure (RPP) [12] is a reinforcement learning algorithm, also known as expectation-maximization (EM) algorithm for reinforcement learning [9]. The RPP expresses a policy on the action space $X = \{0, 1\}^d$ by a Bernoulli distribution $P_\theta(x)$ parametrized by the expectation parameter. The objective to be maximized is the expectation $\mathbb{E}_{P_\theta}[r(x)]$ of non-negative reward $r(x)$ after taking action $x \in X$. The RPP updates the parameters to

$$\theta^{t+1} = \frac{\mathbb{E}_{P_{\theta^t}}[xr(x)]}{\mathbb{E}_{P_{\theta^t}}[r(x)]} \ .$$

Remember the sufficient statistics $T(x)$ for Bernoulli distributions are $T_i(x) = x_i$. Thus the RPP is equivalent to (26) with $g \circ f(x) = r(x)$ and $\delta t = 1$ and can be viewed as a natural gradient ascent with large step.

The RPP is known from [9] to monotonically improve expected reward, thanks to its expectation-maximization interpretation. Theorem 12 can be thought of as an extension of this result, and also shows monotone improvement for the smoothed RPP, where a step size $0 < \delta t \leq 1$ is introduced.

PROOF. Most of the proof of Theorem 6 carries over. Replacing $W_{\theta^t}^f$ in (18) with $g \circ f / \mathbb{E}_{P_{\theta^t}}[g \circ f(x)]$, (18) still holds and we have

$$\begin{aligned} \theta^{t+\delta t} &= \theta^t + \delta t\, \mathbb{E}_{P_{\theta^t}}\left[\frac{g \circ f(x)}{\mathbb{E}_{P_{\theta^t}}[g \circ f(x)]}\left(T(x) - \theta^t\right)\right] \\ &= \arg\max_\theta \left\{(1 - \delta t)\mathbb{E}_{P_{\theta^t}}[\ln p_\theta(x)] \right. \quad (27) \\ &\quad \left. + \delta t \mathbb{E}_{P_{\theta^t}}\left[\frac{g \circ f(x)}{\mathbb{E}_{P_{\theta^t}}[g \circ f(x)]} \ln p_\theta(x)\right]\right\} \end{aligned}$$

Thanks to Jensen's inequality, we have the counterpart of (20) as

$$\begin{aligned} &\ln \mathbb{E}_{P_\theta}[g \circ f(x)] - \ln \mathbb{E}_{P_{\theta^t}}[g \circ f(x)] \\ &\geq \frac{\mathbb{E}_{P_{\theta^t}}[g \circ f(x) \ln p_\theta(x)]}{\mathbb{E}_{P_{\theta^t}}[g \circ f(x)]} - \frac{\mathbb{E}_{P_{\theta^t}}[g \circ f(x) \ln p_{\theta^t}(x)]}{\mathbb{E}_{P_{\theta^t}}[g \circ f(x)]} \ . \end{aligned} \quad (28)$$

Because of the second equality of (27), we have the counterpart of (21) as

$$\begin{aligned} &\frac{\mathbb{E}_{P_{\theta^t}}[g \circ f(x) \ln p_{\theta^{t+\delta t}}(x)]}{\mathbb{E}_{P_{\theta^t}}[g \circ f(x)]} - \frac{\mathbb{E}_{P_{\theta^t}}[g \circ f(x) \ln p_{\theta^t}(x)]}{\mathbb{E}_{P_{\theta^t}}[g \circ f(x)]} \\ &\qquad \geq \frac{1 - \delta t}{\delta t} D_{\mathrm{KL}}(P_{\theta^t} \,\|\, P_{\theta^{t+\delta t}}), \end{aligned}$$

and moreover, since the maximizer in (27) is unique, the inequality is strict unless $\theta^t = \theta^{t+\delta t}$. Hence, since the right-hand side is non-negative, by (28) we have $\ln \mathbb{E}_{P_\theta}[g \circ f(x)] \geq \ln \mathbb{E}_{P_{\theta^t}}[g \circ f(x)]$ with equality only if $P_{\theta^t} = P_{\theta^{t+\delta t}}$. This completes the proof. □

Remark 3. As mentioned in Remark 1, Malagò et al. [16] propose the natural gradient algorithm for discrete optimization using exponential distributions. However, as they parametrize the exponential distributions by the natural parameters $\theta = \beta$, Theorem 12 does not guarantee expected fitness improvement for their algorithms, whereas it does so for the algorithm (19) using the expectation parameters.

5. FURTHER DISCUSSION

These results contribute to bringing theory closer to practice, by waiving the need for infinitesimal step sizes in gradient ascent. Still, they cover only the "ideal" situation with infinite population size, as well as finite but very large population sizes (by a standard probabilistic approximation argument). Finite population sizes lead to stochastic behavior and so monotone objective improvement at each step occurs only with high probability.

In practice, population sizes used can be quite small, $\lambda \leq 10$, with medium to small step sizes [6,11]. It has been shown in [1, Remark 2] that when population size does not tend to infinity, the expectation of the natural gradient estimate (8) is the natural gradient (5) with a *different* selection scheme w. So using the truncation weight $w(u) = \mathbb{1}_{[u\geq q]}$ with a small population size and very small step sizes will result, by the machinery of stochastic approximation [8, 14], in simulating an infinite-population IGO step with another selection scheme, a situation outside the scope of this article. Our results, on the contrary, suggest using larger populations and larger step sizes instead.

Finally, let us stress that objective improvement is not, by itself, a sufficient guarantee that optimization performs well: in situations of premature convergence, the objective still improves at each step. Premature convergence can occur for large values of the learning rate in some instantiations of IGO and IGO-ML (see the study in [5]); our results say nothing about this phenomenon.

6. REFERENCES

[1] Y. Akimoto, A. Auger, and N. Hansen. Convergence of the continuous time trajectories of isotropic evolution strategies on monotonic $\mathcal{C}^2$-composite functions. In *Parallel Problem Solving from Nature - PPSN XII, 12th International Conference*, number 7491 in Lecture Notes in Computer Science, pages 42–51, Taormina, Italy, September 1–5 2012. Springer.

[2] Y. Akimoto, Y. Nagata, I. Ono, and S. Kobayashi. Bidirectional relation between CMA evolution strategies and natural evolution strategies. In R. Schaefer, C. Cotta, J. Kolodziej, and G. Rudolph, editors, *Parallel Problem Solving from Nature - PPSN XI, 11th International Conference*, volume 6238 of *Lecture Notes in Computer Science*, pages 154–163, Kraków, Poland, September 11–15 2010. Springer.

[3] S.-i. Amari. Natural gradient works efficiently in learning. *Neural Computation*, 10(2):251–276, 1998.

[4] S.-i. Amari and H. Nagaoka. *Methods of Information Geometry*. Translations of Mathematical Monographs vol. 191. American Mathematical Society, 2000.

[5] L. Arnold, A. Auger, N. Hansen, and Y. Ollivier. Information-Geometric Optimization algorithms: A unifying picture via invariance principles. *arXiv:1106.3708v1*, 2011.

[6] S. Baluja and R. Caruana. Removing the genetics from the standard genetic algorithm. In *Proceedings of the 12th International Conference on Machine Learning*, pages 38–46, 1995.

[7] P.-T. D. Boer, D. P. Kroese, S. Mannor, and R. Y. Rubinstein. A tutorial on the cross-entropy method. *Annals of Operations Research*, (134):19–67, 2005.

[8] V. S. Borkar. Stochastic approximation: a dynamical systems viewpoint. Cambridge University Press, 2008.

[9] P. Dayan and G. E. Hinton. Using expectation-maximization for reinforcement learning. *Neural Computation*, 9(2):271–278, 1997.

[10] M. Dorigo, V. Maniezzo, and A. Colorni. The ant system: Optimization by a colony of cooperating agents. *IEEE Transactions on Systems, Man, and Cybernetics - part B*, 26(1):1–13, 1996.

[11] N. Hansen, S. D. Muller, and P. Koumoutsakos. Reducing the time complexity of the derandomized evolution strategy with covariance matrix adaptation (CMA-ES). *Evolutionary Computation*, 11(1):1–18, 2003.

[12] G. E. Hinton. Connectionist learning procedures. *Artificial Intelligence*, 40(1-3):185–234, 1989.

[13] S. Kullback. *Information theory and statistics.* Dover Publications Inc., Mineola, NY, 1997. Reprint of the second (1968) edition.

[14] H. J. Kushner and G. G. Yin. *Stochastic approximation and recursive algorithms and applications.* Springer Verlag, 2nd edition, 2003.

[15] P. Larrañaga and J. A. Lozano. *Estimation of Distribution Algorithms: A New Tool for Evolutionary Computation.* Estimation of Distribution Algorithms: A New Tool for Evolutionary Computation. Kluwer Academic Publishers, 2002.

[16] L. Malagò, M. Matteucci, and G. Pistone. Towards the geometry of estimation of distribution algorithms based on the exponential family. In H.-G. Beyer and W. B. Langdon, editors, *FOGA '11: Proceedings of the 11th workshop proceedings on Foundations of genetic algorithms*, pages 230–242. ACM, 2011.

[17] F. Sehnke, C. Osendorfer, T. Rückstieß, A. Graves, J. Peters, and J. Schmidhuber. Parameter-exploring policy gradients. *Neural Networks*, 23(4):551–559, 2010.

Controlling Population Size and Mutation Strength by Meta-ES under Fitness Noise

Hans-Georg Beyer
Research Center PPE
Vorarlberg University of Applied Sciences
Dornbirn, Austria
Hans-Georg.Beyer@fhv.at

Michael Hellwig
Research Center PPE
Vorarlberg University of Applied Sciences
Dornbirn, Austria
Michael.Hellwig@fhv.at

ABSTRACT

This paper investigates strategy parameter control by Meta-ES using the noisy sphere model. The fitness noise considered is normally distributed with constant noise variance. An asymptotical analysis concerning the mutation strength and the population size is presented. It allows for the prediction of the Meta-ES dynamics. An expression describing the asymptotical growth of the normalized mutation strength is calculated. Finally, the theoretical results are evaluated empirically.

Categories and Subject Descriptors

I.2.8 [**Problem Solving, Control Methods, and Search**]: Control theory

Keywords

Adaptation, Evolution Strategies, Meta-ES, Mutation Strength, Population Size, Sphere Model, Fitness Noise

1. INTRODUCTION

In the field of Evolution Strategies (ESs) hierarchical organized ESs also referred to as Meta-ESs have proven themselves useful for learning the optimal strategy parameters depending on the underlying optimization problem. According to Rechenberg [8], a Meta-ES is formally defined by generalizing the ES bracket notation to

$$[\mu'/\rho', \lambda'(\mu/\rho, \lambda)^\gamma]\,. \qquad (1)$$

In (1), λ' offspring populations conducting $(\mu/\rho, \lambda)$-ESs run parallelly over a number of γ generations. Each of these ESs is realized in isolation from the others and holds different initial strategy parameters. Selection on the upper level then chooses those μ' populations for recombination which are identified to have the best strategy parameters w.r.t. a previously defined fitness criterion. Proceeding this way the Meta-ES is expected to direct the strategy parameters to optimality.

FOGA'13, January 16-20, 2013, Adelaide, Australia.

Systematic investigations on the dynamics of Meta-ES are still rare. First results were obtained by Herdy [7] who investigated Meta-ES on a set of test functions. Furthermore he was the first to provide evidence that Meta-ES can direct the inner ES to optimal performance. After some years without theoretical research on the topic Arnold [3] presented an analysis of the mutation strength adaptation by $[1, 2(\mu/\mu_I, \lambda)^\gamma]$-Meta-ES on the class of ridge functions. While his analysis concerned a wide class of ridge functions, however, it excluded the sharp ridge function. The latter has been investigated by Beyer and Hellwig in [6]. In [5], Beyer et al. also analyzed the performance of the $[1, 2(\mu/\mu_I, \lambda)^\gamma]$-Meta-ES on the sphere model $F(\mathbf{y}) = f(\|\mathbf{y} - \hat{\mathbf{y}}\|)$ considering a simple Meta-ES which controls the mutation strength and the parental population size to (near) optimality.

This paper is going to pick up on that analysis of Meta-ES on the sphere model. It extends the investigated Meta-ES algorithm and considers additionally the sphere model with fitness noise. The paper aims at learning about the ability of the specific Meta-ES to deal with the noisy optimization problem. A Meta-ES variant which simultaneously controls two strategy parameters is considered. Carrying out the theoretical analysis we expect to develop a more thorough understanding of the interactions between the different dynamics. In the following sections we analyze the behavior of Meta-ESs in the fitness environment defined by the N-dimensional sphere model under the influence of fitness noise with constant variance, i.e., *constant noise* for short

$$\tilde{F}(\mathbf{y}) = \sum_{j=1}^{N} y_j^2 + \mathcal{N}(0, \sigma_\epsilon^2). \qquad (2)$$

The constant fitness noise in (2) is modeled by means of an additive normally distributed term with mean zero and constant standard deviation σ_ϵ. Note, that σ_ϵ will be referred to as the noise strength. Fitness noise affects the selection mechanism of the Meta-ES algorithm. That is, the measured fitness $\tilde{F}(\mathbf{y})$ of a candidate solution $\mathbf{y}$ will not longer comply with the ideal fitness $F(\mathbf{y})$ but it is normally distributed with mean $F(\mathbf{y})$ and standard deviation σ_ϵ. As a consequence this may lead to the selection of inferior solutions based on their measured fitness while superior solutions are eliminated.
We will particularly focus on the control of the mutation strength σ as well as the parental population size μ. Considering constant fitness noise throughout the search space, it is not possible to determine the exact location of the optimizer with a regular ES on the spherical fitness environment, see [1]. After a number of generations the distance to the optimizer will fluctuate around a nonzero mean which increases with increasing noise strength. This residual distance can only be decreased by increasing the population size of the ES. As we will see, considering the idealized mean value

dynamics, at first priority the Meta-ES will increase the population size up to a predefined maximal value and subsequently the strategy constantly decreases the mutation strength while keeping the population size constant at its maximal value. Consequently this leads to a permanent approach to the final residual distance.

The paper is organized as follows: In Sec. 2 we present a simple $[1, 4(\mu/\mu_I, \lambda)^\gamma]$-Meta-ES which is intended to control σ and μ at the same time. Sec. 3 then builds the basis of our theoretical analysis by describing the dynamics of the inner ES and providing useful approximations. Subsequently in Sec. 4 we investigate the dynamics of the population sizes μ and λ with fixed truncation ratio ν. Afterwards, the theoretical analysis of the σ-dynamics follow in Sec. 5. A comparison with real Meta-ES runs is presented in Sec. 6. Finally, Sec. 7 provides a summary of the results and gives an outlook into future research opportunities.

2. THE [1,4]-META-ES ALGORITHM

In this section we introduce the $[1, 4(\mu/\mu_I, \lambda)^\gamma]$-Meta-ES algorithm. Using a deterministic adaptation rule the outer ES controls the population sizes μ, and λ as well as the mutation strength σ. The outer strategy is presented in Fig. 1.

$[1, 4(\mu/\mu_I, \lambda)^\gamma]$-ES	Line
Initialize($\mathbf{y_p}, \sigma_p, \alpha, \beta, \mu_p, \nu, \gamma_p, N$);	1
$d \leftarrow \gamma_p \mu_p$;	2
$t \leftarrow 0$;	3
Repeat	4
$\tilde{\sigma}_1 \leftarrow \sigma_p \alpha$; $\tilde{\sigma}_2 \leftarrow \sigma_p/\alpha$;	5
Select case μ_p	6
case $\mu_p = 1$: $\tilde{\mu}_1 \leftarrow \mu_p \beta$; $\tilde{\mu}_2 \leftarrow 1$;	7
case $\mu_p = d$: $\tilde{\mu}_1 \leftarrow d$; $\tilde{\mu}_2 \leftarrow \mu_p/\beta$;	8
case Else: $\tilde{\mu}_1 \leftarrow \mu_p \beta$; $\tilde{\mu}_2 \leftarrow \mu_p/\beta$;	9
End Select	10
$\tilde{\lambda}_1 \leftarrow \tilde{\mu}_1/\nu$; $\tilde{\lambda}_2 \leftarrow \tilde{\mu}_2/\nu$;	11
$\tilde{\gamma}_1 \leftarrow d/\tilde{\mu}_1$; $\tilde{\gamma}_2 \leftarrow d/\tilde{\mu}_2$;	12
$[\tilde{\mathbf{y}}_1, \tilde{F}_1, \sigma_1, \mu_1] \leftarrow \mathrm{ES}(\tilde{\mu}_1, \tilde{\lambda}_1, \tilde{\gamma}_1, \tilde{\sigma}_1, \mathbf{y_p})$;	13
$[\tilde{\mathbf{y}}_2, \tilde{F}_2, \sigma_2, \mu_2] \leftarrow \mathrm{ES}(\tilde{\mu}_1, \tilde{\lambda}_1, \tilde{\gamma}_1, \tilde{\sigma}_2, \mathbf{y_p})$;	14
$[\tilde{\mathbf{y}}_3, \tilde{F}_3, \sigma_3, \mu_3] \leftarrow \mathrm{ES}(\tilde{\mu}_2, \tilde{\lambda}_2, \tilde{\gamma}_2, \tilde{\sigma}_1, \mathbf{y_p})$;	15
$[\tilde{\mathbf{y}}_4, \tilde{F}_4, \sigma_4, \mu_4] \leftarrow \mathrm{ES}(\tilde{\mu}_2, \tilde{\lambda}_2, \tilde{\gamma}_2, \tilde{\sigma}_2, \mathbf{y_p})$;	16
$\mathbf{y_p} \leftarrow \tilde{\mathbf{y}}_{1;4}$;	17
$\sigma_p \leftarrow \sigma_{1;4}$;	18
$\mu_p \leftarrow \mu_{1;4}$;	19
$t \leftarrow t+1$;	20
Until(termination condition)	21

Figure 1: Pseudo code of the [1, 4]-Meta-ES. The Code of the inner ES is displayed in Fig. 2.

In Line 2 the parameter d is defined as the product of the initial isolation length γ_p and the initial population size μ_p. It is used as an upper bound for these two strategy parameters and kept constant. The algorithm is running four competing inner $[(\mu/\mu_I, \lambda)^\gamma]$-ESs which start at the same initial $\mathbf{y_p}$ (parental $\mathbf{y}$) but differ in the choice of the population size and the mutation strength. Two offspring mutation strength parameters $\tilde{\sigma}_1$ and $\tilde{\sigma}_2$ are generated in Line 5 by increasing and decreasing the parental mutation strength σ_p by a factor α. From Line 6 up to Line 11 we create the new population size parameters. At first two parameters $\tilde{\mu}_1$ and $\tilde{\mu}_2$ are computed by increasing/decreasing the parental μ_p by a factor β. If μ_p has already reached its lower bound, i.e. $\mu_p = 1$, or its upper bound d, μ_p is only modified in one direction, i.e. increased or decreased, respectively, and kept constant for the other parameter. Dividing the new parental population sizes $\tilde{\mu}_j$ by the fixed truncation ratio ν leads to the corresponding offspring population size parameters $\tilde{\lambda}_1$ and $\tilde{\lambda}_2$.
The isolation length parameters $\tilde{\gamma}_1$ and $\tilde{\gamma}_2$ are defined depending on $\tilde{\mu}_1$ and $\tilde{\mu}_2$ in Line 12, always complying with the condition [1]

$$d = \gamma\mu \quad \Leftrightarrow \quad d/\nu = \lambda\gamma. \tag{3}$$

Identifying $\lambda\gamma$ with the number of function evaluations during a single inner ES run, the way of controlling γ in (3) keeps the number of function evaluations over all observed isolation periods equal. Each combination of the two different population sizes $(\tilde{\mu}_j, \tilde{\lambda}_j)$ with corresponding isolation length $\tilde{\gamma}_j$ and the two mutation strength parameters $\tilde{\sigma}_j$ (j=1, 2) serves as strategy parameter set and is held constant within the inner ES. After having evolved over their associated isolation length, each inner ES returns the centroid of its final parental population $\mathbf{y_k}$ and its corresponding fitness value $F_k = F(\mathbf{y_k})$, $k = 1, \ldots, 4$. Finally the selection in the [1, 4]-Meta-ES is performed in Lines 17 to 19 using the standard notation "$m; \lambda'$" indicating the m-th best population out of λ' populations with respect to the fitness value generated by the respective inner $(\mu/\mu, \lambda)$-ES. That is, the strategy parameters of the best inner population are used as parental parameters in the outer ES.
The termination criterion can be specified as a fixed number of isolation periods t, or function evaluations respectively.

Function: ES($\mu, \lambda, \gamma, \sigma, \mathbf{y}$)
$g \leftarrow 1$;
While $g \le \gamma$
For $l = 1$ To λ
$\tilde{\mathbf{y}}_l \leftarrow \mathbf{y} + \sigma\mathcal{N}_l(0, \mathbf{I})$;
$\tilde{F}_l \leftarrow F(\tilde{\mathbf{y}}_l)$;
End For
$\mathbf{y} \leftarrow \frac{1}{\mu}\sum_{m=1}^{\mu} \tilde{\mathbf{y}}_{m;\lambda}$;
$g \leftarrow g + 1$;
End While
Return $[\mathbf{y}, F(\mathbf{y}), \sigma, \mu]$;

Figure 2: The inner $(\mu/\mu_I, \lambda)^\gamma$-ES

The inner ES, see Fig. 2, generates a population of $\lambda = \mu/\nu$ offspring by adding a σ mutation strength scaled vector of independent, standard normally distributed components to the centroid $\mathbf{y}$ of the parental generation. The μ best candidates in terms of their function values $\tilde{F}_l$ are chosen out of these λ offspring and used to build the new parental centroid $\mathbf{y}$. Proceeding this way over γ generations, the inner ES returns the tuple $[\mathbf{y}, F(\mathbf{y}), \sigma, \mu]$.

3. THEORETICAL ANALYSIS REGARDING CONSTANT NOISE

In this section we are going to investigate the dynamics of the inner $(\mu/\mu, \lambda)$-ES assuming that the observed fitness is disturbed by a noise term with constant noise strength σ_ϵ. Beginning with the distance to the optimizer $R(g)$ in generation g we are interested in finding a prediction of the distance $R^{(g+\gamma)}$ at the end of a single isolation period of γ generations. The starting point of the theoretical analysis is the normalized progress rate in the limit of infinite

[1] In order to always obtain integer values for μ, λ, and γ, the initial μ_p, γ_p and β, $1/\nu$ are chosen as powers of two.

search space dimensionality

$$\varphi^*(\sigma^*, \sigma^*_\epsilon) = \frac{c_{\mu/\mu,\lambda}\sigma^{*2}}{\sqrt{\sigma^{*2} + \sigma^{*2}_\epsilon}} - \frac{\sigma^{*2}}{2\mu}. \tag{4}$$

The normalized quantities used in Eq. (4) are given by

$$\sigma^* = \sigma\frac{N}{R}, \quad \sigma^*_\epsilon = \sigma_\epsilon\frac{N}{2R^2}, \text{ and } \quad \varphi^* = \varphi\frac{N}{R}. \tag{5}$$

For a precise mathematical derivation of φ^* we refer to [2, 1]. The definition of the progress coefficient $c_{\mu/\mu,\lambda}$ can be found in [4]. Note that according to (4) positive progress will only be achieved if the condition

$$\sigma^{*2} + \sigma^{*2}_\epsilon < (2\mu c_{\mu/\mu,\lambda})^2 \tag{6}$$

holds. That directly indicates an upper bound of $2\mu c_{\mu/\mu,\lambda}$ for the normalized mutation strength σ^* and the normalized noise strength σ^*_ϵ as well.
Applying the re-normalizations to Eq. (4) and taking into account the φ definition

$$\varphi^{(g)} = R^{(g)} - R^{(g+1)} \tag{7}$$

we obtain the difference equation

$$R^{(g)} - R^{(g+1)} = \frac{2c_{\mu/\mu,\lambda}R\sigma^2}{\sqrt{4R^2\sigma^2 + {\sigma_\epsilon}^2}} - \frac{N\sigma^2}{2\mu R}. \tag{8}$$

Equation (8) indicates the expected change in the distance to the optimizer between two consecutive generations.
On the basis of (8) we compute the expected steady state distance $\tilde{R}_\infty(\sigma, \sigma_\epsilon)$. It predicts the residual distance to the optimizer which can be reached by the inner ES if the ES runs for a infinite number of generations given a fixed mutation strength σ and constant population sizes μ and λ. Solving $0 = \varphi(\sigma, \sigma_\epsilon, \tilde{R}_\infty)$ for $\tilde{R}_\infty$, we obtain

$$\tilde{R}_\infty(\sigma, \sigma_\epsilon) = \sqrt{\frac{N^2\sigma^2 + \sqrt{4\mu^2 c^2_{\mu/\mu,\lambda}N^2\sigma^2_\epsilon + N^4\sigma^4}}{8\mu^2 c^2_{\mu/\mu,\lambda}}} \tag{9}$$

$$\tilde{R}_\infty(\sigma, \sigma_\epsilon) = R_\infty(\sigma)\sqrt{\frac{1}{2}\left(1 + \sqrt{1 + \frac{\vartheta^2}{R_\infty(\sigma)^2}}\right)} \tag{10}$$

with noise-to-signal ratio $\vartheta = \dfrac{\sigma_\epsilon}{\sigma}$ and the noise-free steady state distance

$$R_\infty(\sigma) = \frac{N\sigma}{2\mu c_{\mu/\mu,\lambda}}. \tag{11}$$

Considering small mutation strength sizes, i.e. $\sigma \to 0$, Eq. (9) is becoming

$$\hat{R}_\infty = \sqrt{\frac{N\sigma_\epsilon}{4\mu c_{\mu/\mu,\lambda}}} \tag{12}$$

which is already known as a good approximation of the expected steady state distance $\tilde{R}_\infty$ in the vicinity of small mutation strengths, see [1].
Because we are not able to find a closed analytical solution of the nonlinear difference equation (8) for $R^{(g+1)}$ we search for a good approximation. Approximating (8) is formally done by switching to the continuous time limit and expanding $R(g+1)$ in a Taylor series at g. Identifying $R(g+1)$ with $R^{(g+1)}$ and $R(g)$ with $R^{(g)}$ then yields

$$R^{(g+1)} - R^{(g)} = \frac{dR}{dg}1 + \dots . \tag{13}$$

Thus, by applying Eq. (8) one obtains a nonlinear differential equation which approximates the progress dynamics

$$\frac{dR}{dg} = \frac{N\sigma^2}{2\mu R} - \frac{2c_{\mu/\mu,\lambda}R\sigma^2}{\sqrt{4R^2\sigma^2 + {\sigma_\epsilon}^2}}. \tag{14}$$

However, even (14) is rather difficult to be solved. Therefore, we are searching for a linear approximation describing the dynamics towards $\tilde{R}_\infty$. Expanding (14) into a Taylor series about $\tilde{R}_\infty$, we get

$$\frac{dR}{dg} \approx \left(\frac{8c_{\mu/\mu,\lambda}\tilde{R}^2_\infty\sigma^4}{\sqrt{\left(\sigma^2_\epsilon + 4\tilde{R}^2_\infty\sigma^2\right)^3}} - \frac{N\sigma^2}{2\tilde{R}^2_\infty\mu} - \frac{2c_{\mu/\mu,\lambda}\sigma^2}{\sqrt{\sigma^2_\epsilon + 4\tilde{R}^2_\infty\sigma^2}}\right)(R - \tilde{R}_\infty) \tag{15}$$

$$= \left(\frac{8c_{\mu/\mu,\lambda}\tilde{R}^2_\infty\sigma^4}{\sqrt{\left(\sigma^2_\epsilon + 4\tilde{R}^2_\infty\sigma^2\right)^3}} - \frac{N\sigma^2}{2\tilde{R}^2_\infty\mu} - \frac{2c_{\mu/\mu,\lambda}\sigma^2(\sigma^2_\epsilon + 4\tilde{R}^2_\infty\sigma^2)}{\sqrt{\left(\sigma^2_\epsilon + 4\tilde{R}^2_\infty\sigma^2\right)^3}}\right)(R - \tilde{R}_\infty) \tag{16}$$

$$= -\left(\frac{N\sigma^2}{2\tilde{R}^2_\infty\mu} + \frac{2c_{\mu/\mu,\lambda}\sigma^2\sigma^2_\epsilon}{(\sigma^2_\epsilon + 4\tilde{R}^2_\infty\sigma^2)^{\frac{3}{2}}}\right)(R - \tilde{R}_\infty). \tag{17}$$

Inserting Eq. (17) in (13) we finally obtain

$$R^{(g)} - R^{(g+1)} \approx \left(\frac{N\sigma^2}{2\tilde{R}^2_\infty\mu} + \frac{2c_{\mu/\mu,\lambda}\sigma^2\sigma^2_\epsilon}{(\sigma^2_\epsilon + 4\tilde{R}^2_\infty\sigma^2)^{\frac{3}{2}}}\right)(R^{(g)} - \tilde{R}_\infty) \tag{18}$$

as a linear approximation of the difference equation (8). For reasons of clarity and comprehensibility we define

$$a := \frac{N\sigma^2}{2\tilde{R}^2_\infty\mu} \quad \text{and} \quad b := \frac{2c_{\mu/\mu,\lambda}\sigma^2\sigma^2_\epsilon}{(\sigma^2_\epsilon + 4\tilde{R}^2_\infty\sigma^2)^{\frac{3}{2}}}. \tag{19}$$

Thus, Eq. (18) reads

$$R^{(g+1)} = \left(R^{(g)} - \tilde{R}_\infty\right)(1 - (a + b)) + \tilde{R}_\infty. \tag{20}$$

Computing

$$R^{(g+2)} = \left(R^{(g+1)} - \tilde{R}_\infty\right)(1 - (a + b)) + \tilde{R}_\infty \tag{21}$$

$$= \left(R^{(g)} - \tilde{R}_\infty\right)(1 - (a + b))^2 + \tilde{R}_\infty \tag{22}$$

and continuing this way yields the following equation for the expected distance $R^{(g+\gamma)}$ after one isolation period of γ generations

$$R^{(g+\gamma)} = \left(R^{(g)} - \tilde{R}_\infty\right)(1 - (a + b))^\gamma + \tilde{R}_\infty. \tag{23}$$

Assuming that the sum $a + b$ is sufficiently small one can apply the approximation

$$(1 - x)^k \approx 1 - kx \quad \forall x \text{ with } |x| \ll 1. \tag{24}$$

The assumption $a + b \approx 0$ is valid considering sufficiently small mutation sizes σ, see also (19) for $\sigma \to 0$. Using (24) we obtain an even simpler approximation for the distance to the optimizer after a single inner ES isolation period

$$R^{(g+\gamma)} = R^{(g)}(1 - (a + b)\gamma) + \tilde{R}_\infty(a + b)\gamma. \tag{25}$$

In order to confirm the good compliance between the original Meta-ES dynamics resulting from Eq. (8) and their approximations, see Eq. (23) and Eq. (25), we check the iteratively generated dynamics against each other. The iteration proceeds the following way: Four pairs of strategy parameters are computed from the initial parameters. These are $(\beta\mu, \alpha\sigma)$, $(\beta\mu, \sigma/\alpha)$, $(\mu/\beta, \alpha\sigma)$, and $(\mu/\beta, \sigma/\alpha)$. For each combination of strategy parameters the theoretical equations are iterated over a single isolation period. The length of the isolation period depends on the chosen population size, i.e. it is $\gamma = d/(\beta\mu)$ or $\gamma = (d\beta)/\mu$) respectively. The best of the four independent runs by means of the generated fitness value is selected.

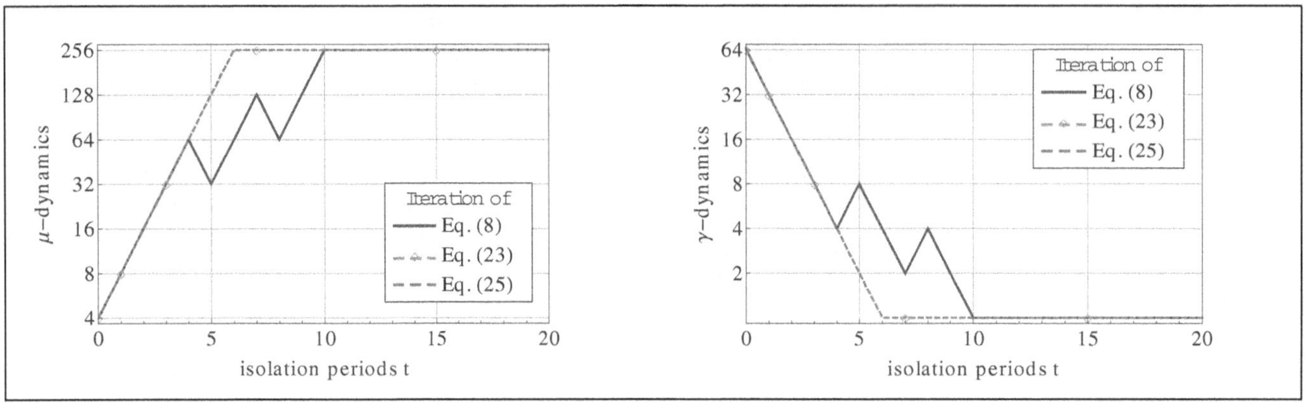

Figure 3: Illustration of the iteratively computed μ- and γ-dynamics resulting from Eq. (8) and from its approximations in Eq. (23) and Eq. (25), respectively. To point out the slight differences only the results of the first 20 of 1000 isolation periods are presented.

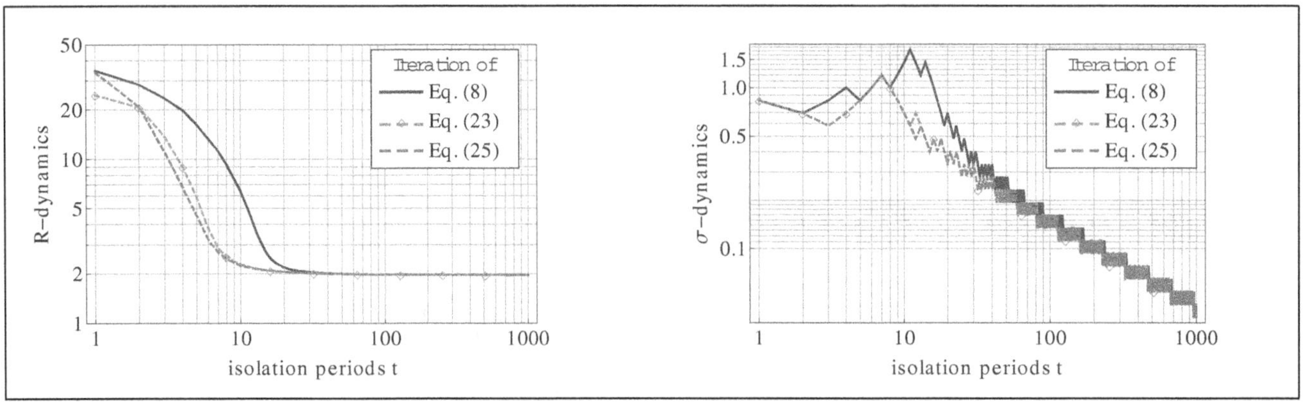

Figure 4: On the lhs the comparison of the distance R to the optimizer between the iterative results of Eq. (8) and its approximations in Eq. (23) and Eq. (25) is depicted per isolation period, or per d/v = 1024 function evaluations respectively. The figure on the rhs shows the corresponding mutation strength σ.

Its strategy parameters as well as its generated distance R are used as initial strategy parameters of the next iteration step. All results are computed from the same initial values. Figures 3 and 4 display the dynamics. We have chosen a search space dimensionality of $N = 1000$. The initial mutation strength is $\sigma_p = 1$ and the constant noise strength is set to $\sigma_\epsilon = 5$. The initial population sizes are $\mu_p = 4$ and $\lambda_p = 16$, respectively. This is due to the truncation ratio of $v = 1/4$. $\gamma_p = 64$ is the initial isolation length. The adjustment parameters are $\alpha = 1.2$ and $\beta = 2$.

In Fig. 3 we present the μ-dynamics in the graph on the lhs and the γ-dynamics on the rhs. The strategy increases the population size μ up to its initially defined maximal value $d = 256$. Consequently by construction the corresponding γ-dynamics show the converse behavior. That is, the isolation length of the inner ES is reduced to 1 by the selection mechanism of the outer ES. The μ-dynamics as well as the γ-dynamics of the approximations, (23) and (25), perfectly match while they differ slightly from the dynamics of Eq. (8) which is represented by the solid blue line. But these differences can only be observed during the first few isolation periods. All three dynamics overlap after each has finally reached its maximal population size, and minimal isolation length respectively, and remain in this state until the algorithm terminates.

The R-dynamics as well as the σ-dynamics are illustrated in Fig. 4. Again we compare the iteratively computed results of equations (8), (23), and (25). In both cases we notice a similar pattern of the original dynamics and its approximations. After a couple of isolation periods the dynamics almost match. On the rhs the Meta-ES reduces the mutation strength. During the decline the σ-dynamics show an oscillating behavior. Note that this oscillation phases grow with decreasing σ. While the oscillations slow down the decrease of the mutation strength, the Meta-ES gradually reduces σ and by implication σ^*, too. A more detailed investigation of this oscillation behavior will be provided in Sec. 5.

Taking a look at the distance R to the optimizer on the lhs of Fig. 4 we observe the dynamics approaching the residual steady state distance $\tilde{R}_\infty$. In fact, since the σ-dynamics converge to zero the R-dynamics approach the approximated steady state distance $\hat{R}_\infty = 1.961$, see Eq. (12).

The good agreement between the dynamics resulting from Eq. (8) and the dynamics iterating its approximations justifies the use of the approximations in the further theoretical investigation of the Meta-ES.

4. THE POPULATION SIZE DYNAMICS

This section focuses on the μ-dynamics of the Meta-ES. Since all iterations in the previous section show the strategy's behavior to increase the parental population size μ to its maximum we are interested in a theoretical analysis. Note that in our considerations $d := \mu\gamma$ is defined as the upper bound of the parameter μ, or γ respectively.

In the first step we assume a noise free fitness environment ($\sigma_\epsilon = 0$) throughout Sec. 4.1. Afterwards in Sec. 4.2 we include fitness noise into our considerations. In the noise-free case the results from Sec. 3 allow for a rather simple examination of the strategy's population adaptation behavior. Of course, the investigations assuming a noisy fitness landscape are more complicated.

4.1 Noise-free Fitness Environment

Since the approximation (25) corresponds well with Eq. (8) and its application simplifies the analysis considerably, we will use (25) as the starting point of the following investigations. Assuming $\sigma_\epsilon^* = 0$, Eq. (25) transforms into

$$R^{(g+\gamma)} = R^{(g)}(1 - a\gamma) + \tilde{R}_\infty a\gamma. \tag{26}$$

With $\tilde{R}_\infty(\sigma, 0) = \dfrac{N\sigma}{2\mu c_{\mu/\mu,\lambda}}$, see Eq. (9), and $a = \dfrac{2\mu c^2_{\mu/\mu,\lambda}}{N}$ this yields

$$R^{(g+\gamma)} = R^{(g)}\left(1 - \frac{2c^2_{\mu/\mu,\lambda}}{N}d\right) + c_{\mu/\mu,\lambda}\sigma\gamma. \tag{27}$$

The first addend does no longer depend on either the population size parameter μ^2 or on the mutation strength parameter. This simplifies the following calculations significantly.

After each isolation period the outer ES computes two new parental population sizes μ by increasing and decreasing the parental population size of the best inner strategy by the parameter $\beta > 1$. In the same manner the algorithm builds two new mutation strengths σ by varying the mutation strength of the best inner strategy by the parameter α. Thus we obtain the four new strategy parameters which will establish the next four inner ESs

$$\mu_+ := \mu\beta \quad \text{and} \quad \mu_- := \mu/\beta, \tag{28}$$

as well as

$$\sigma_+ := \sigma\alpha \quad \text{and} \quad \sigma_- := \sigma/\alpha. \tag{29}$$

Note that $\mu_\pm$, and $\sigma_\pm$ correspond to $\tilde{\mu}_1$ and $\tilde{\mu}_2$, and $\tilde{\sigma}_1$ and $\tilde{\sigma}_2$ respectively, which have been mentioned in Sec. 2.

In this section we apply the following simplification for the progress coefficients

$$c_{\mu/\mu,\lambda} \approx c_{\mu_+/\mu_+,\lambda_+} \approx c_{\mu_-/\mu_-,\lambda_-}. \tag{30}$$

This assumption is valid because in the asymptotic limit case the progress coefficient $c_{\mu/\mu,\lambda}$ only depends on the truncation ratio $\nu = \mu/\lambda$, see also [4].

In the following we identify $R_{+-}^{(g+\gamma)}$ with the expected distance realized by the inner ES that operates with μ_+ and σ_- over a single isolation period. The expected distances of the three other inner strategies $R_{++}^{(g+\gamma)}$, $R_{-+}^{(g+\gamma)}$, and $R_{--}^{(g+\gamma)}$ are defined analogously. Consequently using Eq. (27) we get

$$R_{++}^{(g+\gamma)} = R^{(g)}\left(1 - \frac{2c^2_{\mu/\mu,\lambda}}{N}d\right) + c_{\mu/\mu,\lambda}\sigma\alpha\frac{\gamma}{\beta}, \tag{31}$$

$$R_{+-}^{(g+\gamma)} = R^{(g)}\left(1 - \frac{2c^2_{\mu/\mu,\lambda}}{N}d\right) + c_{\mu/\mu,\lambda}\frac{\sigma}{\alpha}\frac{\gamma}{\beta}, \tag{32}$$

$$R_{-+}^{(g+\gamma)} = R^{(g)}\left(1 - \frac{2c^2_{\mu/\mu,\lambda}}{N}d\right) + c_{\mu/\mu,\lambda}\sigma\alpha\gamma\beta, \tag{33}$$

$$R_{--}^{(g+\gamma)} = R^{(g)}\left(1 - \frac{2c^2_{\mu/\mu,\lambda}}{N}d\right) + c_{\mu/\mu,\lambda}\frac{\sigma}{\alpha}\gamma\beta. \tag{34}$$

The algorithm chooses the strategy parameter of the inner ES which generates the smallest distance R to the optimizer. That is, by comparing two expected distances the sign of their difference indicates which strategy is preferred by the Meta-ES. Thus in order to compare all four inner strategies against each other we have to consider six different cases.

At first we examine the four cases which differ in the population parameter μ. Remembering the condition $1 < \alpha < \beta$ we get

$$R_{++}^{(g+\gamma)} - R_{-+}^{(g+\gamma)} = c_{\mu/\mu,\lambda}\sigma\gamma\frac{(\alpha - \alpha\beta^2)}{\beta} < 0, \tag{35}$$

$$R_{++}^{(g+\gamma)} - R_{--}^{(g+\gamma)} = c_{\mu/\mu,\lambda}\sigma\gamma\frac{(\alpha^2 - \beta^2)}{\alpha\beta} < 0, \tag{36}$$

$$R_{+-}^{(g+\gamma)} - R_{-+}^{(g+\gamma)} = c_{\mu/\mu,\lambda}\sigma\gamma\left(\frac{1}{\alpha\beta} - \alpha\beta\right) < 0, \tag{37}$$

$$R_{+-}^{(g+\gamma)} - R_{--}^{(g+\gamma)} = c_{\mu/\mu,\lambda}\sigma\gamma\frac{(\alpha - \alpha\beta^2)}{\alpha^2\beta} < 0. \tag{38}$$

It can be observed that the Meta-ES favors the inner ESs with the higher population size μ. Thus the Meta-ES is expected to permanently increase the parental population size μ after each isolation period of γ generations until finally the upper bound d is reached. Consequently the strategy decreases the isolation length γ down to 1. Now we consider the two remaining cases

$$R_{++}^{(g+\gamma)} - R_{+-}^{(g+\gamma)} = c_{\mu/\mu,\lambda}\sigma\gamma\frac{(\alpha^2\beta - \beta)}{\alpha\beta^2} > 0, \tag{39}$$

$$R_{-+}^{(g+\gamma)} - R_{--}^{(g+\gamma)} = c_{\mu/\mu,\lambda}\sigma\gamma\frac{(\alpha^2\beta - \beta)}{\alpha} > 0. \tag{40}$$

We observe that the Meta-ES prefers the strategies which operate with the decreased mutation strength σ_-.

Thus $R_{+-}^{(g+\gamma)}$ dominates the other three expected distances. That is, the Meta-ES is to be expected to choose the inner strategy which increases the population size μ and simultaneously decreases the mutation strength σ. That is, in the absence of fitness noise the μ- and σ-dynamics can be characterized by

$$\mu^{(g+\gamma)} = \mu^{(g)}\beta \quad \text{and} \tag{41}$$

$$\sigma^{(g+\gamma)} = \sigma^{(g)}/\alpha \tag{42}$$

until the upper bound d of the population size parameter is reached. After that, the population size μ remains in its maximum while the mutation strength σ is decreased further on. An illustration of the μ and σ dynamics in the noise-free fitness case is given in Fig. 5. The dynamics are generated by iteration of Eq. (25). Except for the noise strength ($\sigma_\epsilon = 0$) all initial parameters agree with their choices in Sec. 3. That is, we chose $N = 1000$, $\mu_p = 4$, $\nu = 1/4$, $\lambda_p = 16$, $\beta = 2$, $\gamma_p = 64$, $\sigma_p = 1$ and $\alpha = 1.2$.

According to our predictions, see (41) and (42), the population size μ is increased until it reaches its maximal value d. Furthermore

[2] Assuming a sufficiently large population size such that $c_{\mu/\mu,\lambda}$ depends only on the truncation ratio μ/λ.

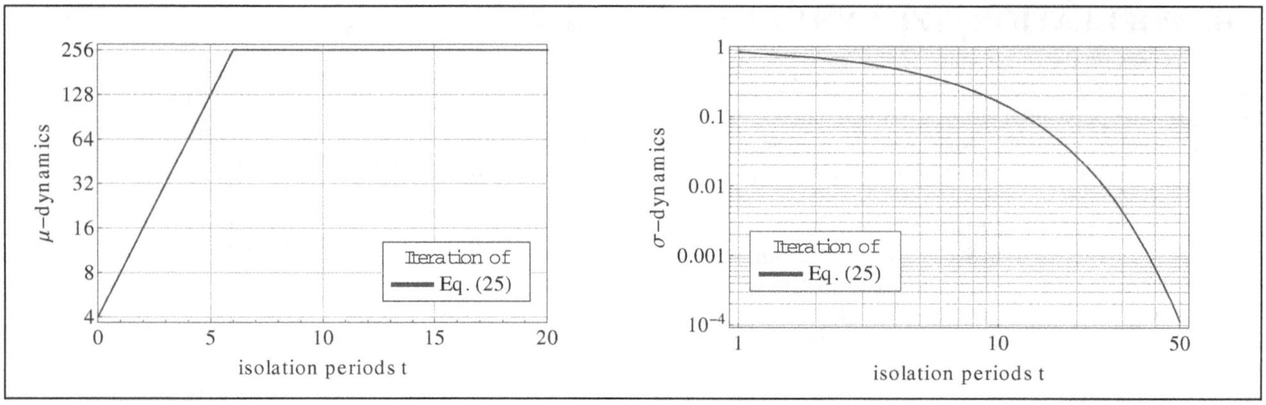

Figure 5: On the left hand side the μ-dynamic resulting from the iteration of Eq. (25) is shown. The noise strength is $\sigma_\epsilon = 0$. The right hand side presents the respective σ dynamics. The initial population size is $\mu = 4$ and the initial isolation length is $\gamma = 64$, i.e. their upper bound is set to $d = 256$.

the Meta-ES steadily decreases the mutation strength σ over the observed isolation periods.

4.2 μ-Dynamics Considering Fitness Noise

The next step includes fitness noise into our considerations. We already know that the choice of a higher population size allows for a lower residual distance in standard ESs [1]. That is why, in the presence of fitness noise with constant noise strength σ_ϵ, we conclude that the Meta-ES increases the population size μ to its maximum d just like in the noise-free case. Operating at maximal population size, the isolation inside the algorithm only proceeds over one generation, i.e. $\gamma = 1$. Therefore, it is possible to analyze the μ dynamics easily. Moreover, considering sufficiently small σ, the change in the mutation strength between two consecutive isolation periods is neglectable. Using Eq. (4) and (5) we get

$$R^{(g+1)} = R^{(g)} - \varphi^* \frac{R^{(g)}}{N}. \tag{43}$$

Remembering (28) and ignoring the σ adaptation at this point, we write $R_+^{(g+1)}$ and $R_-^{(g+1)}$ for the expected distance which is realized by the inner ES that operates with μ_+ and μ_-, respectively. Hence the two expected distances at the end of the isolation period are

$$R_+^{(g+1)} = R^{(g)} - \left(\frac{c_{\mu/\mu,\lambda}\sigma^{*2}}{\sqrt{\sigma_\epsilon^{*2} + \sigma^{*2}}} - \frac{\sigma^{*2}}{2\beta\mu} \right) \frac{R^{(g)}}{N}, \tag{44}$$

$$R_-^{(g+1)} = R^{(g)} - \left(\frac{c_{\mu/\mu,\lambda}\sigma^{*2}}{\sqrt{\sigma_\epsilon^{*2} + \sigma^{*2}}} - \frac{\beta\sigma^{*2}}{2\mu} \right) \frac{R^{(g)}}{N}. \tag{45}$$

Again the sign of their difference determines which strategy parameters are chosen in the outer ES. Thus, we consider

$$R_+^{(g+1)} - R_-^{(g+1)} = \left(\frac{\sigma^{*2}}{2\beta\mu} - \frac{\beta\sigma^{*2}}{2\mu} \right) \frac{R^{(g)}}{N} = \left(\frac{1}{\beta} - \beta \right) \frac{\sigma^{*2}}{2\mu} \frac{R^{(g)}}{N}. \tag{46}$$

Because of the condition $\beta > 1$ this difference is always negative

$$R_+^{(g+1)} - R_-^{(g+1)} < 0. \tag{47}$$

That is, once the Meta-ES has reached its minimal isolation length $\gamma = 1$, the algorithm permanently increases the population size μ up to its maximum $\mu = d$ and maintains this state for the remaining isolation periods. This behavior has also been observed in Sec. 3, see Fig. 3.

5. INVESTIGATING THE MUTATION STRENGTH DYNAMICS

Due to the results of the iterated dynamics in Sec. 3 and our theoretical observations in Sec. 4, the $[1, 4(\mu, \lambda)^\gamma]$-Meta-ES is regarded to continuously increases the parental population μ to its maximal value $d = \mu\gamma$. As a consequence, the isolation length γ reduces to 1 respectively. In this section we assume that the strategy has already reached its maximal population size and remains in this state according to Sec. 4.2. Therefore, we investigate the σ-dynamics regarding an $[1, 4(\mu, \lambda)^1]$-Meta-ES with $\beta = 1$. That is, neither the population size μ nor the isolation length $\gamma = 1$ will be changed by the outer ES. In the first step, Sec. 5.1 aims at a qualitative description of the σ dynamics. This allows for an interpretation of the σ dynamics observed in Sec. 3, Fig 4. Then in Sec. 5.2 we are going to investigate the dynamics of the normalized mutation strength. We provide a description of the σ^* dynamics' asymptotic growth.

5.1 Explaining the σ-Dynamics

The outer ES generates two new σ-values from the parental mutation strength $\sigma^{(t)}$ (t being the generation counter of the outer ES)

$$\sigma_+ := \alpha\sigma^{(t)} \quad \text{and} \quad \sigma_- := \sigma^{(t)}/\alpha. \tag{48}$$

Remembering Eq. (8), and writing σ instead of $\sigma^{(t)}$, this results in two expected distances $R^{(t+1)}$ at the end of isolation period $t + 1$

$$R_+^{(t+1)} = R^{(t)} - \frac{\alpha\sigma c_{\mu/\mu,\lambda}}{\sqrt{1 + \frac{\sigma_\epsilon^2}{4R^{(t)2}\alpha^2\sigma^2}}} + \frac{\alpha^2\sigma^2 N}{2\mu R^{(t)}}, \tag{49}$$

$$R_-^{(t+1)} = R^{(t)} - \frac{\sigma c_{\mu/\mu,\lambda}}{\alpha\sqrt{1 + \frac{\alpha^2\sigma_\epsilon^2}{4R^{(t)2}\sigma^2}}} + \frac{\sigma^2 N}{2\alpha^2\mu R^{(t)}}. \tag{50}$$

Note that in contrast to Sec. 4, $R_+^{(t+1)}$ and $R_-^{(t+1)}$ now refer to the inner ES which operates with σ_+ and σ_-, respectively.
The algorithm chooses the parameters of the strategy which generates the smaller distance to the optimizer. That is, the sign of the difference $R_+^{(t+1)} - R_-^{(t+1)}$ determines whether the Meta-ES increases or decreases the mutation strength σ

$$\begin{aligned} R_+^{(t+1)} - R_-^{(t+1)} < 0 \quad &\Rightarrow \quad \sigma^{(t+1)} = \sigma^{(t)}\alpha \\ R_+^{(t+1)} - R_-^{(t+1)} > 0 \quad &\Rightarrow \quad \sigma^{(t+1)} = \sigma^{(t)}/\alpha. \end{aligned} \tag{51}$$

Combining (49) and (50), the difference $R_+^{(t+1)} - R_-^{(t+1)}$ reads

$$\frac{\alpha^2\sigma^2 N}{2\mu R^{(t)}} - \frac{\alpha\sigma c_{\mu/\mu,\lambda}}{\sqrt{1+\frac{\sigma_\epsilon^2}{4R^{(t)^2}\alpha^2\sigma^2}}} - \frac{\sigma^2 N}{2\alpha^2\mu R^{(t)}} + \frac{\sigma c_{\mu/\mu,\lambda}}{\alpha\sqrt{1+\frac{\alpha^2\sigma_\epsilon^2}{4R^{(t)^2}\sigma^2}}} \quad (52)$$

$$= \frac{\sigma^2 N}{2\mu R^{(t)}}\left(\alpha^2 - \frac{1}{\alpha^2}\right) - \left(\frac{\alpha\sigma c_{\mu/\mu,\lambda}}{\sqrt{1+\frac{\sigma_\epsilon^2}{4R^{(t)^2}\alpha^2\sigma^2}}} - \frac{\sigma c_{\mu/\mu,\lambda}}{\alpha\sqrt{1+\frac{\alpha^2\sigma_\epsilon^2}{4R^{(t)^2}\sigma^2}}}\right), \quad (53)$$

and considering the normalizations, see Eq. (5), it can be transformed into

$$\sigma\left[\frac{\sigma^*}{2\mu}\left(\alpha^2 - \frac{1}{\alpha^2}\right) - c_{\mu/\mu,\lambda}\left(\frac{\alpha}{\sqrt{1+\frac{\sigma_\epsilon^{*2}}{\alpha^2\sigma^{*2}}}} - \frac{1}{\alpha\sqrt{1+\frac{\alpha^2\sigma_\epsilon^{*2}}{\sigma^{*2}}}}\right)\right] \quad (54)$$

$$= \sigma\left[\frac{(\alpha^4-1)\sigma^*}{2\mu\alpha^2} - \frac{c_{\mu/\mu,\lambda}\sigma^*}{\alpha^2}\left(\frac{\alpha^4}{\sqrt{\alpha^2\sigma^{*2}+\sigma_\epsilon^{*2}}} - \frac{1}{\sqrt{\frac{\sigma^{*2}}{\alpha^2}+\sigma_\epsilon^{*2}}}\right)\right]. \quad (55)$$

Defining Δ by the term in the square brackets of Eq. (55)

$$\boxed{\Delta := \frac{(\alpha^4-1)\sigma^*}{2\mu\alpha^2} - \frac{c_{\mu/\mu,\lambda}\sigma^*}{\alpha^2}\left(\frac{\alpha^4}{\sqrt{\alpha^2\sigma^{*2}+\sigma_\epsilon^{*2}}} - \frac{1}{\sqrt{\frac{\sigma^{*2}}{\alpha^2}+\sigma_\epsilon^{*2}}}\right)} \quad (56)$$

the σ-dynamic depends only on the sign of Δ, i.e.,

$$\begin{aligned} \Delta < 0 \quad &\Rightarrow \quad \sigma^{(t+1)} = \sigma^{(t)}\alpha, \\ \Delta > 0 \quad &\Rightarrow \quad \sigma^{(t+1)} = \sigma^{(t)}/\alpha. \end{aligned} \quad (57)$$

Note that Δ depends on the normalized mutation strength σ^* as well as the normalized noise strength σ_ϵ^*. With $\Delta(\sigma^*, \sigma_\epsilon^*)$ we have found the evolution equation for σ

$$\boxed{\sigma^{(t+1)} = \sigma^{(t)}\alpha^{-\mathrm{sign}(\Delta(\sigma^{*(t)}, \sigma_\epsilon^{*(t)}))}.} \quad (58)$$

The sign of Δ is plotted depending on σ^* and σ_ϵ^* in Fig. 6. The values of σ^* and σ_ϵ^* are varied within their range of positive progress from zero to $2\mu c_{\mu/\mu,\lambda}$, see Eq. (6). Negative values of $\Delta(\sigma^*, \sigma_\epsilon^*)$ are represented by the yellow region, and positive ones by the red region respectively. For example, if the strategy operates with a combination of σ^* and σ_ϵ^* values from the yellow region ($\Delta < 0$) it will increase the mutation strength after the isolation period.

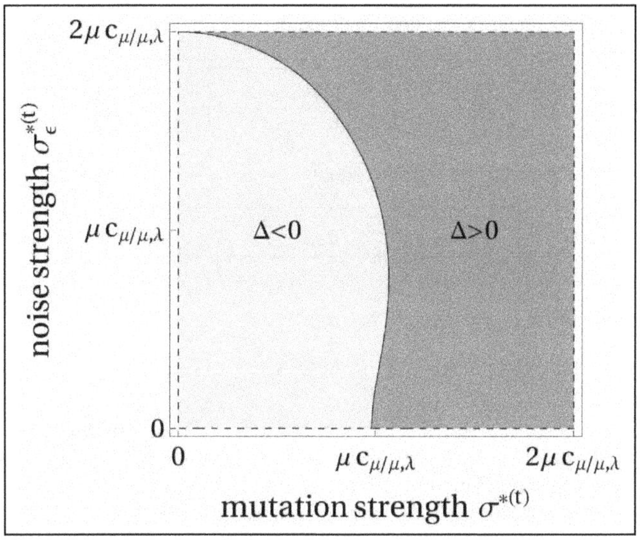

Figure 6: On the sign of Δ depending on σ^* and σ_ϵ^*. The remaining parameters are $\mu = 256$, $\nu = 1/4$, and $\alpha = 1.2$

We are interested in the critical value $\sigma_0^* > 0$ around which the sign of $\Delta(\sigma^*, \sigma_\epsilon^*)$ changes. According to the combination of σ^* and σ_ϵ^* in Fig. 6 this critical value can be found on the black line between the two colored regions. Computing σ_0^* from Eq. (56) leads directly to the condition

$$\frac{(\alpha^4-1)}{2\mu c_{\mu/\mu,\lambda}} \stackrel{!}{=} \frac{\alpha^4}{\sigma_\epsilon^*\sqrt{1+\frac{\alpha^2\sigma^{*2}}{\sigma_\epsilon^{*2}}}} - \frac{1}{\sigma_\epsilon^*\sqrt{1+\frac{\sigma^{*2}}{\alpha^2\sigma_\epsilon^{*2}}}}. \quad (59)$$

This must be solved for σ^*. Finding an analytical expression for σ_0^* of (59) is demanding. Therefore, we apply the following approximation

$$\sqrt{1+\frac{\sigma^{*2}}{\sigma_\epsilon^{*2}}} \approx 1 + \frac{\sigma^{*2}}{2\sigma_\epsilon^{*2}}, \quad (60)$$

assuming that $\sigma^{*2}/\sigma_\epsilon^{*2} < 1$ holds when the Meta-ES has reached a certain vicinity to its steady state $\hat{R}_\infty$, see Eq. (12). Thus we can rewrite (59)

$$\frac{(\alpha^4-1)\sigma_\epsilon^*}{2\mu c_{\mu/\mu,\lambda}} \simeq \frac{\alpha^4}{1+\frac{\alpha^2\sigma^{*2}}{2\sigma_\epsilon^{*2}}} - \frac{1}{1+\frac{\sigma^{*2}}{2\alpha^2\sigma_\epsilon^{*2}}}. \quad (61)$$

Converting the fractions to a common denominator, we get

$$\frac{(\alpha^4-1)\sigma_\epsilon^*}{2\mu c_{\mu/\mu,\lambda}} \simeq \frac{(\alpha^4-1)}{1+\frac{\sigma^{*2}}{2\alpha^2\sigma_\epsilon^{*2}}+\frac{\alpha^2\sigma^{*2}}{2\sigma_\epsilon^{*2}}+\frac{\sigma^{*4}}{4\sigma_\epsilon^{*4}}}. \quad (62)$$

Rearranging the terms leads to

$$\frac{2\mu c_{\mu/\mu,\lambda}}{\sigma_\epsilon^*} \simeq 1 + \frac{\sigma^{*2}}{2\alpha^2\sigma_\epsilon^{*2}} + \frac{\alpha^2\sigma^{*2}}{2\sigma_\epsilon^{*2}} + \frac{\sigma^{*4}}{4\sigma_\epsilon^{*4}}, \quad (63)$$

and with further transformations we get a quadratic equation in σ^{*2}

$$\sigma^{*4} + 2\frac{\alpha^4+1}{\alpha^2}\sigma_\epsilon^{*2}\sigma^{*2} + 4\sigma_\epsilon^{*4}\left(1 - \frac{2\mu c_{\mu/\mu,\lambda}}{\sigma_\epsilon^*}\right) \simeq 0. \quad (64)$$

Solving (64) for σ^{*2} yields

$$\sigma_0^{*2} \simeq -\frac{\alpha^4+1}{\alpha^2}\sigma_\epsilon^{*2} + \sqrt{\sigma_\epsilon^{*4}\left[\left(\frac{\alpha^4+1}{\alpha^2}\right)^2 + 4\left(\frac{2\mu c_{\mu/\mu,\lambda}}{\sigma_\epsilon^*} - 1\right)\right]}. \quad (65)$$

Taking the square root, one finally gets

$$\sigma_0^* \simeq \sigma_\epsilon^* \sqrt{\sqrt{\left(\frac{\alpha^4+1}{\alpha^2}\right)^2 + 4\left(\frac{2\mu c_{\mu/\mu,\lambda}}{\sigma_\epsilon^*} - 1\right)} - \left(\frac{\alpha^4+1}{\alpha^2}\right)}. \tag{66}$$

Dividing Eq. (66) by σ_ϵ^*, one obtains

$$\frac{\sigma_0^*}{\sigma_\epsilon^*} \simeq \sqrt{\sqrt{\left(\frac{\alpha^4+1}{\alpha^2}\right)^2 + 4\left(\frac{2\mu c_{\mu/\mu,\lambda}}{\sigma_\epsilon^*} - 1\right)} - \left(\frac{\alpha^4+1}{\alpha^2}\right)}. \tag{67}$$

Note that for $\sigma_\epsilon = const.$, it holds

$$\sigma_\epsilon^* = \frac{\sigma_\epsilon N}{2R^2} \overset{R \to \hat{R}_\infty}{\longrightarrow} 2\mu c_{\mu/\mu,\lambda}. \tag{68}$$

Taking (68) into account, one sees that in (67) the critical value σ_0^* in relation to the normalized noise strength σ_ϵ^* is decreasing to zero in the asymptotic limit. Figure 7 displays this behavior. A continuous increase of σ_ϵ^* to its maximal value $2\mu c_{\mu/\mu,\lambda}$ drives $\sigma_0^*/\sigma_\epsilon^*$ and σ_0^* to zero.
Taking up the σ_0^* behavior, we can continue with the qualitative analysis of the σ-dynamics. Equation (57) becomes

$$\begin{aligned} \sigma^* < \sigma_0^* \quad &\Rightarrow \quad \sigma^{(t+1)} = \sigma^{(t)}\alpha, \\ \sigma^* > \sigma_0^* \quad &\Rightarrow \quad \sigma^{(t+1)} = \sigma^{(t)}/\alpha. \end{aligned} \tag{69}$$

According to these equations, the Meta-ES adapts σ so that the normalized mutation strength σ^* reaches a certain vicinity to its point of discontinuity σ_0^*. In this region the σ dynamics enter a limit cycle. This corresponds to the oscillatory behavior of the σ dynamics which was already observed in Sec. 3, Fig. 4. The limit cycle will only be left if the point of discontinuity σ_0^* changes. Notice that σ_0^* still depends on the normalized noise strength σ_ϵ^*. As long as the Meta-ES reduces the distance R to the optimizer, σ_ϵ^* approaches its saturation value $2\mu c_{\mu/\mu,\lambda}$. Since the critical value σ_0^* decreases tendentially, the strategy is able to leave the current σ limit cycle and decrease the mutation strength until it enters the next limit cycle. This behavior explains the σ dynamics in Sec. 3 where we observed a rather slow mutation strength decrease in stepwise limit cycles.

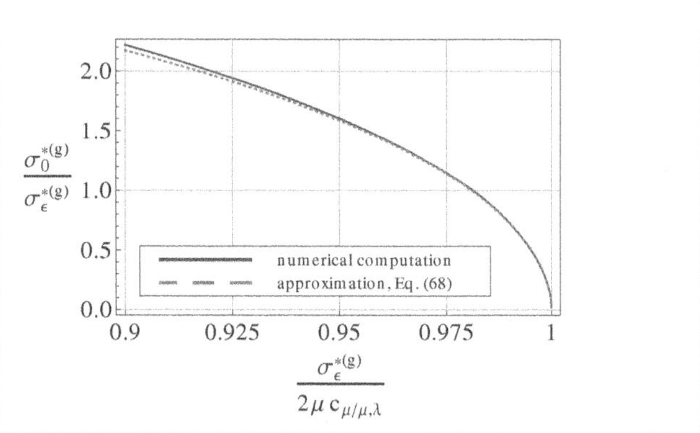

Figure 7: The dashed red line shows the results of the approximation $\sigma_0^*/\sigma_\epsilon^*$, see Eq. (67). It is compared to the numerically computed root of Eq. (56) which is plotted with regard to σ_ϵ^* and represented by the solid blue line. The graph presents the results for $\sigma_\epsilon^*/2\mu c_{\mu/\mu,\lambda} \in [0.9, 1]$. One observes a good compliance between the numerical results and the approximation for σ_ϵ^* values in the vicinity of $2\mu c_{\mu/\mu,\lambda}$.

5.2 Calculating the σ^*-Dynamics

Now we consider the evolution of the normalized mutation strength σ^* in order to analyze the steady state behavior of the Meta-ES. Remembering Eq. (5), Eq. (58), and taking into account

$$R^{(t+1)} = R^{(t)}\left(1 - \frac{1}{N}\varphi^*(\sigma^{*(t)}\alpha^{-\mathrm{sign}(\Delta(\sigma^{*(t)},\sigma_\epsilon^{*(t)}))}, \sigma_\epsilon^{*(t)})\right), \tag{70}$$

see Eq. (8), finally yields

$$\boxed{\sigma^{*(t+1)} = \sigma^{*(t)} \frac{\alpha^{-\mathrm{sign}(\Delta(\sigma^{*(t)},\sigma_\epsilon^{*(t)}))}}{1 - \frac{1}{N}\varphi^*(\sigma^{*(t)}\alpha^{-\mathrm{sign}(\Delta(\sigma^{*(t)},\sigma_\epsilon^{*(t)}))}, \sigma_\epsilon^{*(t)})}.} \tag{71}$$

Our goal is the computation of the expected normalized mutation strength dynamics σ^* around which the ES oscillates in its steady state. At this point it should be noticed that the σ^*-dynamic directly interacts with the σ_ϵ^*-dynamic. The latter determines the critical value σ_0^* and thereby the strategy's behavior to increase or decrease the (normalized) mutation strength. That is, we have to solve an iterative mapping depending on $\sigma^{*(t)}$ and $\sigma_\epsilon^{*(t)}$

$$\sigma^{*(t+1)} = f_\sigma(\sigma^{*(t)}, \sigma_\epsilon^{*(t)}; \alpha, \mu, N). \tag{72}$$

With Eq. (5), and (8) we also derive the iterative mapping of the σ_ϵ^*-dynamics

$$\boxed{\sigma_\epsilon^{*(t+1)} = \frac{\sigma_\epsilon^{*(t)}}{\left(1 - \frac{1}{N}\varphi^*(\sigma^{*(t)}\alpha^{-\mathrm{sign}(\Delta(\sigma^{*(t)},\sigma_\epsilon^{*(t)}))}, \sigma_\epsilon^{*(t)})\right)^2}.} \tag{73}$$

In order to calculate the asymptotic dynamics one has to apply various asymptotically exact simplifications. First, consider the progress rate

$$\varphi^*(\sigma^*, \sigma_\epsilon^*) = \frac{c_{\mu/\mu,\lambda}\sigma^{*2}}{\sqrt{\sigma_\epsilon^{*2} + \sigma^{*2}}} - \frac{\sigma^{*2}}{2\mu} \tag{74}$$

which asymptotically ($\sigma^*/\sigma_\epsilon^* \to 0$) can be expressed by

$$\begin{aligned} \varphi^*(\sigma^*, \sigma_\epsilon^*) &= \frac{c_{\mu/\mu,\lambda}\sigma^{*2}}{\sigma_\epsilon^*\sqrt{1 + \frac{\sigma^{*2}}{\sigma_\epsilon^{*2}}}} - \frac{\sigma^{*2}}{2\mu} & (75) \\ &\simeq \sigma^{*2}\left(\frac{c_{\mu/\mu,\lambda}}{\sigma_\epsilon^*} - \frac{1}{2\mu}\right) & (76) \\ &= \underbrace{\frac{\sigma^{*2}}{2\mu\sigma_\epsilon^*}\left(2\mu c_{\mu/\mu,\lambda} - \sigma_\epsilon^*\right)}_{=:\, \tilde{\varphi}^*(\sigma^*, \sigma_\epsilon^*)}. & (77) \end{aligned}$$

As a consequence one obtains a simpler σ_ϵ^*-dynamics. Writing σ^* and σ_ϵ^* instead of $\sigma^{*(t)}$ and $\sigma_\epsilon^{*(t)}$, it reads

$$\sigma_\epsilon^{*(t+1)} \simeq \frac{\sigma_\epsilon^*}{\left(1 - \frac{2}{N}\tilde{\varphi}^*(\sigma^*\alpha^{-\mathrm{sign}(\Delta(\sigma^*,\sigma_\epsilon^*))}, \sigma_\epsilon^*)\right)}. \tag{78}$$

Considering small progress in the asymptotic limit one can apply

$$\frac{1}{1-x} \approx 1 + x \quad \forall\, x \text{ with } |x| \ll 1 \tag{79}$$

resulting in

$$\sigma_\epsilon^{*(t+1)} \simeq \sigma_\epsilon^{*(t)}\left(1 + \frac{2}{N}\tilde{\varphi}^*(\sigma^{*(t)}\alpha^{-\mathrm{sign}(\Delta(\sigma^{*(t)},\sigma_\epsilon^{*(t)}))}, \sigma_\epsilon^{*(t)})\right). \tag{80}$$

Using $\tilde{\varphi}^*$, Eq. (77), one obtains

$$\sigma_\epsilon^{*(t+1)} \simeq \sigma_\epsilon^* + \frac{\sigma^{*2}\alpha^{-2\mathrm{sign}(\Delta(\sigma^*,\sigma_\epsilon^*))}}{\mu N}\left(2\mu c_{\mu/\mu,\lambda} - \sigma_\epsilon^*\right). \tag{81}$$

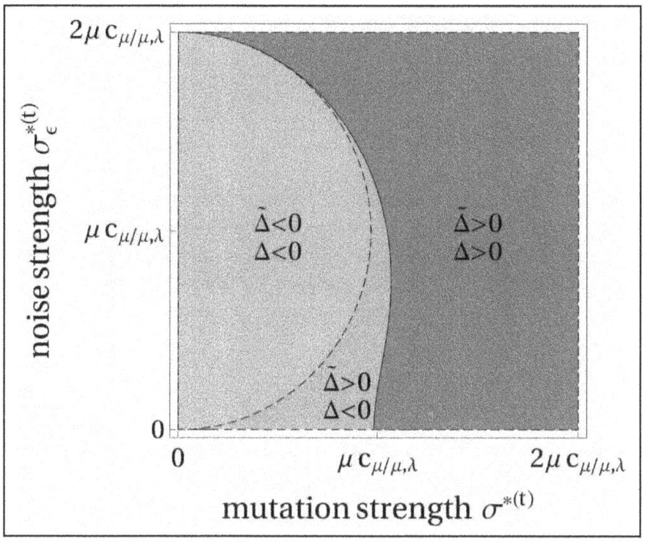

Figure 8: Illustration of the trade-off between Δ, Eq. (56) and its approximation $\tilde{\Delta}$, Eq. (87).

As a next step an approximation for $\Delta(\sigma^*, \sigma_\epsilon^*)$, Eq. (56) is needed. Assuming $\sigma^*/\sigma_\epsilon^* \to 0$, one finds the following asymptotical approximation

$$\frac{\sigma^*}{2\mu}\frac{\alpha^4-1}{\alpha^2} - \frac{\sigma^* c_{\mu/\mu,\lambda}}{\alpha^2\sigma_\epsilon^*}\left(\frac{\alpha^4}{\left(1+\frac{\alpha^2\sigma^{*2}}{2\sigma_\epsilon^{*2}}\right)} - \frac{1}{\left(1+\frac{\sigma^{*2}}{2\alpha^2\sigma_\epsilon^{*2}}\right)}\right). \tag{82}$$

This can further be transformed into

$$\frac{\sigma^*}{\alpha^2}\left[\frac{(\alpha^4-1)}{2\mu} - \frac{c_{\mu/\mu,\lambda}}{\sigma_\epsilon^*}\left(\frac{(\alpha^4-1)}{1+\frac{\alpha^4+1}{\alpha^2}\frac{\sigma^{*2}}{2\sigma_\epsilon^{*2}}+\frac{\sigma^{*4}}{4\sigma_\epsilon^{*4}}}\right)\right] \tag{83}$$

$$= \frac{\sigma^*(\alpha^4-1)}{\alpha^2}\left(\frac{1}{2\mu} - \frac{4c_{\mu/\mu,\lambda}\sigma_\epsilon^{*3}}{4\sigma_\epsilon^{*4}+\sigma^{*4}+2\frac{\alpha^4+1}{\alpha^2}\sigma_\epsilon^{*2}\sigma^{*2}}\right). \tag{84}$$

The term σ^{*4} in the denominator of the subtrahend can be neglected considering small mutation strengths, i.e. $\sigma \to 0$. Thus, one obtains

$$\frac{\sigma^*(\alpha^4-1)}{\alpha^2}\left(\frac{1}{2\mu} - \frac{c_{\mu/\mu,\lambda}\sigma_\epsilon^*}{\sigma_\epsilon^{*2}+\frac{\alpha^4+1}{2\alpha^2}\sigma^{*2}}\right) \tag{85}$$

$$= \frac{\sigma^*(\alpha^4-1)}{2\mu\alpha^2\left(\sigma_\epsilon^{*2}+\frac{\alpha^4+1}{2\alpha^2}\sigma^{*2}\right)}\underbrace{\left(\sigma_\epsilon^{*2}+\frac{\alpha^4+1}{2\alpha^2}\sigma^{*2}-2\mu c_{\mu/\mu,\lambda}\sigma_\epsilon^*\right)}_{=:\,\tilde{\Delta}(\sigma^*,\sigma_\epsilon^*)}. \tag{86}$$

The sign of Δ and, by implication, the decision inside the Meta-ES to increase or decrease the mutation strength σ or σ^*, respectively, by the factor α is now only depending on

$$\boxed{\tilde{\Delta}(\sigma^*, \sigma_\epsilon^*) = \frac{\alpha^4+1}{2\alpha^2}\sigma^{*2} - \sigma_\epsilon^*\left(2\mu c_{\mu/\mu,\lambda} - \sigma_\epsilon^*\right).} \tag{87}$$

In Fig. 8 $\Delta(\sigma^*, \sigma_\epsilon^*)$, see Eq. (56), and its approximation $\tilde{\Delta}(\sigma^*, \sigma_\epsilon^*)$ are compared. The gray region ($\tilde{\Delta} > 0, \Delta < 0$) represents the trade-off between exact Δ and its approximation. Especially in the asymptotically interesting region of small σ^* values and $\sigma_\epsilon^* \approx 2\mu c_{\mu/\mu,\lambda}$, the approximation shows a good agreement with Δ.
The results of the iterative computations of the original dynamics (71) and (73) lead to the conclusion that the σ^*-dynamics mainly depend on the α term. That is, the term $(1 - \varphi^*/N)$ in (71) can be neglected and by combination with Eq. (87) this yields the following approximation of the σ^*-dynamics

$$\boxed{\sigma^{*(t+1)} = \sigma^{*(t)}\alpha^{-\mathrm{sign}(\tilde{\Delta}(\sigma^{*(t)},\sigma_\epsilon^{*(t)}))}.} \tag{88}$$

A conclusive asymptotic approximation of the σ_ϵ^*-dynamics is found by inserting Eq. (87) into Eq. (81)

$$\boxed{\sigma_\epsilon^{*(t+1)} \simeq \sigma_\epsilon^{*(t)} + \frac{\left(\sigma^{*(t)}\alpha^{-\mathrm{sign}(\tilde{\Delta}(\sigma^{*(t)},\sigma_\epsilon^{*(t)}))}\right)^2}{\mu N}\left(2\mu c_{\mu/\mu,\lambda} - \sigma_\epsilon^{*(t)}\right).} \tag{89}$$

Note, if σ^* is in the vicinity of σ_0^*, i.e. $\tilde{\Delta} \approx 0$, the analysis of the Meta-ES suggests an oscillatory behavior in the σ^* values. Actually, such a behavior is observed, see Fig. 9. The actual σ^* dynamics have a globally decreasing tendency superimposed by local oscillations. In Fig. 9 and Fig. 10 we validate the approximations (88) and (89) by comparing them with the original σ^* and σ_ϵ^* dynamics from Eq. (71) and Eq. (73), respectively. The normalized noise strength is depicted in relation to its saturation value $2\mu c_{\mu/\mu,\lambda}$. Both dynamics are iterated over one million isolation periods of $\gamma = 1$ generation using a population size of $\mu = 10$ and a truncation ratio $\nu = 1/4$. The search space dimension is $N = 100$ and the adjustment parameter is set to $\alpha = 1.05$. The iterations start with $\sigma_\epsilon^* = 2\mu c_{\mu/\mu,\lambda} - 0.1$ and $\sigma^* = \sqrt{(2\mu c_{\mu/\mu,\lambda})^2 - \sigma_\epsilon^{*2}}$ to ensure the compliance with condition (6). In both figures the original dynamics are illustrated by solid blue lines while the dashed red lines represent the approximations. Notice the oscillating behavior of the normalized mutation strength dynamics in Fig. 9. With the continuous decrease of the difference $2\mu c_{\mu/\mu,\lambda} - \sigma_\epsilon^*$ in Fig. 10 also the critical value σ_0^* slowly decreases, see Eq. (66). This way the σ^* dynamics are able to leave their limit cycles from time to time which leads to the observable stepwise descent. Note that the phases of oscillation grow with decreasing σ^*. It can be observed that in both cases the slopes of the approximations and the original dynamics match after having evolved over a sufficiently large number of isolation periods. Therefore, one can use the approximation in order to compute the rate at which the mutation strength dynamics descent. To this end, combine the σ^*-, Eq. (88), and σ_ϵ^*-dynamics from Eq. (89). Introduce the quantity $\delta^{(t)}$

$$\delta^{(t)} = 2\mu c_{\mu/\mu,\lambda} - \sigma_\epsilon^{*(t)}, \tag{90}$$

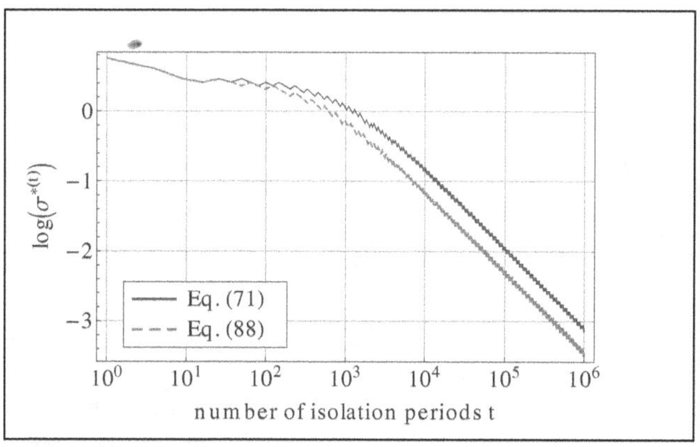

Figure 9: The comparison of the iterated σ^*-dynamic from Eq. (71) represented by the blue line and its asymptotic approximation from Eq. (88) depicted as the red dashed line.

that measures the deviation of the normalized noise strength σ^*_ϵ from its saturation value $2\mu c_{\mu/\mu,\lambda}$. Inserting (90) into (89), one obtains

$$\delta^{(t+1)} = \left(1 - \frac{\sigma^{*(t)^2}}{\mu N}\alpha^{-2\text{sign}(\tilde{\Delta}(\sigma^{*(t)},\sigma_\epsilon^{*(t)}))}\right)\delta^{(t)}. \quad (91)$$

As one can see in Fig. 9, there are periods in the σ^* evolution where the σ^* values exhibits oscillatory behavior. This is reflected in the oscillatory change in the sign of $\tilde{\Delta}$. Since σ^*_0 corresponds to $\tilde{\Delta} = 0$ one has to mathematically treat the behavior at $\tilde{\Delta} = 0$, i.e. $\text{sign}(\tilde{\Delta}) = \text{sign}(0) = 0$. This immediately leads to (92).

$$\delta^{(t+1)} = \left(1 - \frac{\sigma^{*(t)^2}}{\mu N}\right)\delta^{(t)} \quad (92)$$

$$= \left(1 - \frac{\sigma^{*(t)^2}}{\mu N}\right)^{t+1}\delta^{(0)}. \quad (93)$$

With Eq. (93) we are able to simplify Eq. (87) in order to make a prediction about the asymptotic behavior of the σ^*-dynamics. In a first step Eq. (90) is inserted into (87) yielding

$$\tilde{\Delta}(\sigma^*, \delta^{(t)}) = \frac{\alpha^4+1}{2\alpha^2}\sigma^{*2} - 2\mu c_{\mu/\mu,\lambda}\delta^{(t)} + \delta^{(t)^2}. \quad (94)$$

Applying (93), the rhs becomes

$$\frac{\alpha^4+1}{2\alpha^2}\sigma^{*2} - 2\mu c_{\mu/\mu,\lambda}\left(1-\frac{\sigma^{*2}}{\mu N}\right)^t\delta^{(0)} + \left(\left(1-\frac{\sigma^{*2}}{\mu N}\right)^t\delta^{(0)}\right)^2 \quad (95)$$

$$= \frac{\alpha^4+1}{2\alpha^2}\sigma^{*2} - 2\mu c_{\mu/\mu,\lambda}\left(1-\frac{\sigma^{*2}}{\mu N}\right)^t\delta^{(0)} + \left(1-\frac{\sigma^{*2}}{\mu N}\right)^{2t}\delta^{(0)^2}. \quad (96)$$

Taking advantage of $\left(1-\frac{\sigma^{*2}}{\mu N}\right)^t \simeq \left(1 - t\frac{\sigma^{*2}}{\mu N}\right)$ for $\frac{\sigma^{*2}}{\mu N} \ll 1$ one finds the asymptotical approximation of $\tilde{\Delta}(\sigma^*, \delta^{(0)})$

$$\frac{\alpha^4+1}{2\alpha^2}\sigma^{*2} - 2\mu c_{\mu/\mu,\lambda}\left(1 - t\frac{\sigma^{*2}}{\mu N}\right)\delta^{(0)} + \left(1 - 2t\frac{\sigma^{*2}}{\mu N}\right)\delta^{(0)^2}. \quad (97)$$

By further transformation one obtains

$$\left[\frac{\alpha^4+1}{2\alpha^2} + \left(\frac{2\delta^{(0)}(\mu c_{\mu/\mu,\lambda} - \delta^{(0)})}{\mu N}\right)t\right]\sigma^{*2} - 2\mu c_{\mu/\mu,\lambda}\delta^{(0)} + \delta^{(0)^2}. \quad (98)$$

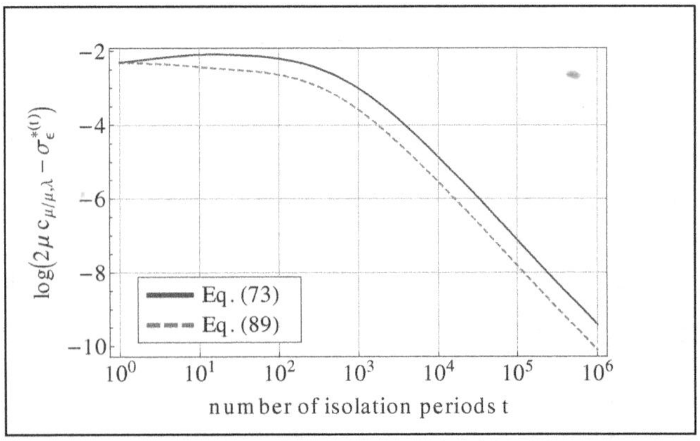

Figure 10: The difference of the iterated σ^*_ϵ-dynamic from Eq. (73) to the saturation value $2\mu c_{\mu/\mu,\lambda}$ (blue line) is compared to its asymptotic approximation given by the dynamics of Eq. (89), which are represented by the dashed red line.

The root σ^*_0 of Eq. (98) can easily be found by solving $\tilde{\Delta} \overset{!}{=} 0$ resulting in

$$\sigma^*_0 \simeq \sqrt{\frac{(2\mu c_{\mu/\mu,\lambda} - \delta^{(0)})\delta^{(0)}}{\frac{\alpha^4+1}{2\alpha^2} + \left(\frac{2\delta^{(0)}(\mu c_{\mu/\mu,\lambda}-\delta^{(0)})}{\mu N}\right)t}}. \quad (99)$$

That is, in the asymptotic limit the point of discontinuity σ^*_0 can be approximated by Eq. (99). The mutation strength dynamics oscillate around σ^*_0. Thus, we have found a description of the asymptotic σ^*-dynamics which only depends on the initial deviation $\delta^{(0)}$ of σ^*_ϵ from $2\mu c_{\mu/\mu,\lambda}$ and on the number of isolation periods t. In the next step we consider

$$\frac{(\alpha^4+1)}{2\alpha^2}\frac{1}{t} \xrightarrow{t\to\infty} 0 \quad (100)$$

in order to develop an even simpler expression describing the asymptotic growth rate:

$$\boxed{\sigma^*_0 \simeq \frac{\tau}{\sqrt{t}}.} \quad (101)$$

Here, we have substituted

$$\tau := \sqrt{\frac{\mu N(2\mu c_{\mu/\mu,\lambda} - \delta^{(0)})}{2\mu c_{\mu/\mu,\lambda} - 2\delta^{(0)}}}. \quad (102)$$

After a sufficiently large number of isolation periods, the descent of σ^*_0 is described by Eq. (101). It decreases obeying a square root law proportional to τ. Since the σ^* dynamics oscillate around σ^*_0 they consequently decrease with the same rate. That is, having evolved over a large number of isolation periods, the normalized mutation strength dynamics of the Meta-ES approach zero. In order to illustrate the compliance of this results we refer to the illustration in Fig. 11.

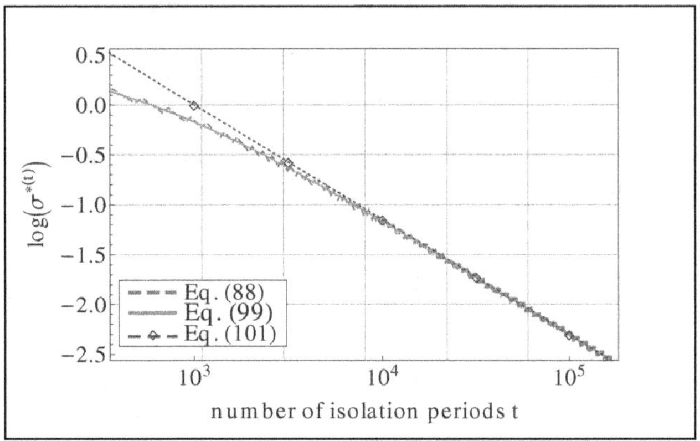

Figure 11: Combination of the results from Fig. 9 with the prediction of Eq. (99) depicted by the solid green line which overlaps with the red dotted curve representing Eq. (88). The dashed blue line with markers represents the result of Eq. (101).

The solid green line in Fig. 11 depicts the approximation of σ^*_0 from Eq. (99). Equation (101) is represented by the dashed blue line. One observes that the growth characteristics overlap in the asymptotic limit. It can be seen that the dashed red line, which asymptotically approximates the σ^*-dynamics, see Eq. (88), oscillates perfectly around the point of discontinuity σ^*_0.
At this point one can draw the following conclusion concerning the

asymptotic growth rate of the σ-dynamics. First note that the distance to the optimizer R is nearly constant in the vicinity of the steady state distance $\hat{R}_\infty$. Considering $R \to \hat{R}_\infty$ and (5) one obtains

$$\sigma^* = \frac{N}{R}\sigma \simeq \sqrt{\frac{4\mu c_{\mu/\mu,\lambda}N}{\sigma_\epsilon}}\sigma. \tag{103}$$

Thus in the asymptotic limit the σ-dynamics exhibits a similar behavior as the σ^*-dynamics: The mutation strength oscillates around a critical value σ_0 which asymptotically decreases with t according to

$$\boxed{\sigma_0 \simeq \frac{\tilde{\tau}}{\sqrt{t}}.} \tag{104}$$

Similar to σ_0^*, it decreases according to a square root law, however, with a different time constant $\tilde{\tau}$. The calculation of $\tilde{\tau}$ is beyond the scope of this paper.

6. SIMULATIONS

This section focuses on a comparison of the analytical investigations from the previous sections with the experimental runs of the $[1, 4(\mu/\mu_I, \lambda)^\gamma]$-Meta-ES algorithm presented in Sec. 2. This way we check the compliance of the results of the experiments with our theoretical predictions. The algorithm, see also Fig. 1 and Fig. 2, is initialized with parental population size $\mu_p = 2$ and truncation ratio $\nu = 1/4$ yielding $\lambda_p = 8$. The adjustment parameter of the population size is $\beta = 2$. We consider a search space dimensionality of $N = 1000$. The initial isolation time is set to $\gamma_p = 128$ which leads to an upper bound of $d = 256$ for the μ and γ dynamics. The mutation strength is initialized at $\sigma_p = 1$ with adjustment parameter $\alpha = 1.05$. As the starting point of the algorithm we choose $(\mathbf{y_p})_i = 10$, $i = 1, \dots, N$. This allows for a better observation of the point at which the influence of the constant fitness noise gains in importance. The noise strength is set to $\sigma_\epsilon = 5$. The algorithm is terminated after evolving over 10000 isolation periods.

The theoretical results are obtained by the iteration of Eq. (8) on the basis of the same initial values. The iteration proceeds as described at the end of Sec. 3. In the figures the results are displayed by the solid blue lines. Note that the iterated dynamics rely on the knowledge of the ideal fitness values in the selection process of the best inner ES. Whereas the selection in the experiments is based on the observed noisy fitness of the centroids returned by the inner strategies. This leads to deviations between iteratively generated and experimental results. In order to decrease the deviations we consider multiple experiments. Averaged over 20 independent runs of the algorithm the experimental results are presented as dashed red lines in Fig. 12 to Fig. 14.

Figure 12 depicts the R-dynamics of the Meta-ES. During the first 10 isolation periods the iterative and the experimental dynamics nearly match. Then the effects of the fitness noise can be observed. The iteratively computed R-dynamics approaches its expected residual steady state distance $\hat{R}_\infty$. The decrease of the experimentally obtained R values decelerates. This results from the reduction of the isolation time γ, which is induced by increasing the population size. Regarding the population size dynamics in Fig. 13, we observe a good agreement provided that the strategy is able to increase the population size μ. After having reached the maximal value $d = 256$, the corresponding isolation time is $\gamma = 1$. In this state the μ-dynamics can either remain in its maximum or decrease again. Unlike our theoretical predictions suggest, the experimental μ-dynamics leaves the state of maximal population size. Despite the population size fluctuates under the influence of noise, we can

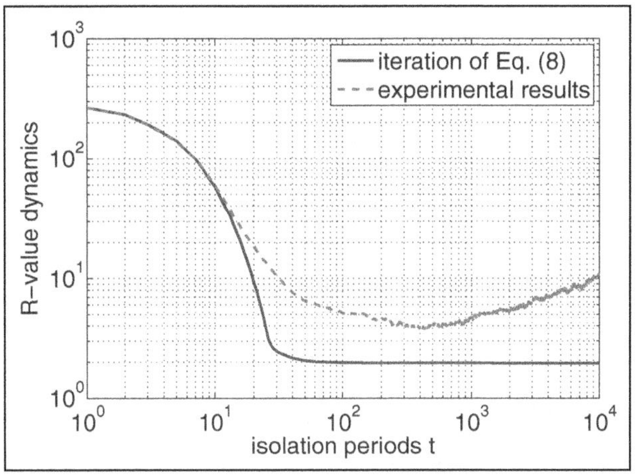

Figure 12: Comparison of the distance to the optimizer, obtained by iteration of Eq. (8), with the results of the average of 20 independent experimental runs of the Meta-ES.

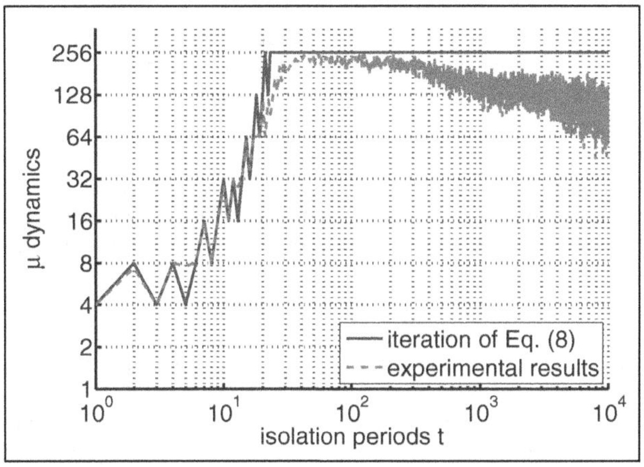

Figure 13: The parental population size dynamics resulting from the experiment are depicted by the dashed red line. The iteratively computed dynamics resulting from Eq. (8) is represented by the solid blue line.

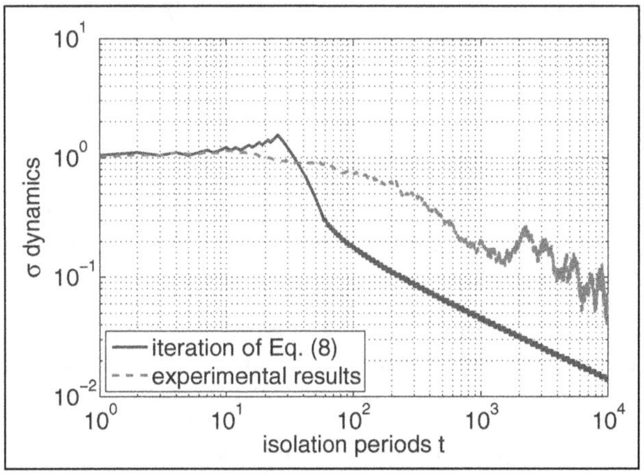

Figure 14: The σ dynamics resulting from Eq. (8) is compared to the experimental results. The mutation strength adjustment parameter is set to α = 1.05.

measure the strategy's tendency to favor greater population sizes. Considering the small isolation time and the influence of the fitness noise, we are able to explain the fluctuations. The smaller the fitness value the more it is affected by the noise. As the strategy approaches its residual steady state distance $\tilde{R}_\infty$ the noise disturbs the selection process. That is, the algorithm may select an inner strategy which decreases the population size, because it has the best observed noisy fitness. This leads the Meta-ES to leave its maximal population size $\mu = 256$ which directly influences the steady state distance $\tilde{R}_\infty$. Decreasing μ values cause $\tilde{R}_\infty$ to rise and consequently the R-dynamics increase, see Fig. 12. Since the population size is adjusted by the factor $\beta = 2$ this changes in the steady state distance can be relatively large. In Fig. 14 the σ-dynamics are displayed. Again one observes a good agreement of both dynamics during the first isolation periods.

At the point where the population size reaches its maximum the empirically generated results reveal significant deviations from the theoretical predictions. However, both dynamics show the same tendency to decrease the mutation strength σ. One can reduce the deviation by increasing the α factor, e.g. $\alpha = 1.2$. While this ensures a faster adaptation of the σ values and thus getting closer to the theoretical σ curve, the general deviation tendency does not change. The rather large deviations observed are due to the noisy fitness information which has not been included in the modeling of the selection process of the outer ES.

The theoretical analysis neglects the influence of fitness noise on the selection process of the outer ES. The dynamics resulting from the iteration of the theoretical equations rely on the knowledge of the expected ideal fitness values returned by the inner ESs. Whereas the selection in the experiments is based on the observed noisy fitness of the final parental centroids. This leads to significant deviations between theoretical and experimental dynamics. In order to confirm this explanation the following experiment has been conducted.

The real Meta-ES run can be emulated by adding noise to the fitness values of the theoretical predictions. In each isolation period a simulated noise term is added to the four iteratively generated fitness values resulting from the inner ESs. Selection within the iteration is then performed by choosing the best of these four "noisy" fitness values. The inner ES corresponding to the best observed fitness value provides its strategy parameters to the next iteration step. The noise term is modeled by a normally distributed random number with mean 0. Its variance is varying with the isolation period. For each isolation period this variance is determined by measuring the empirical variance of the four function values in the according isolation period of the real Meta-ES run. The empirical variances are averaged over 20 independent simulations. Also the iterative dynamics incorporating noise are averaged over 20 independent runs. Note, that the experimental dynamics are generated as explained in the beginning of this section. The initialization is maintained as well.

The iteration of Eq. (8) equipped with noise in the selection process of the outer ES is referred to as noisy iteration. The corresponding dynamics are illustrated by the solid blue lines in Fig. 15 to Fig. 17. The experimental dynamics are represented by dashed red lines.

Regarding the distance to the optimizer in this situation both dynamics fail to approach the minimal residual steady state distance $\hat{R}_\infty(d)$, see Fig. 15. $\hat{R}_\infty(d) = \sqrt{\frac{N\sigma_\epsilon}{4dc_{d/d,\lambda}}}$ corresponds to the maximal parental population size $\mu = d$ realizable by the Meta-ES algorithm.

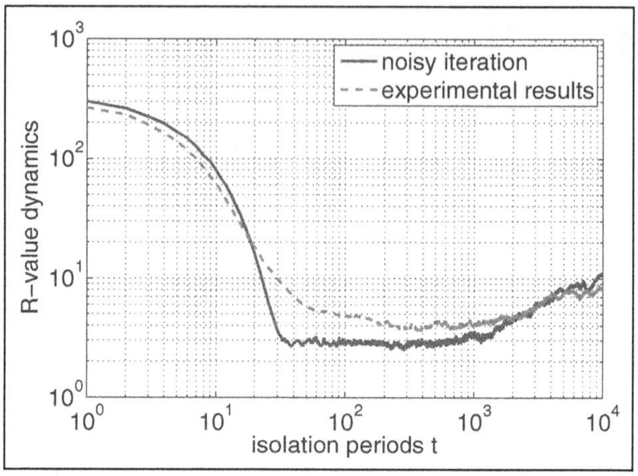

Figure 15: Dynamics of the distance to the optimizer, obtained by iteration of Eq. (8) provided with noise, and the results of the experimental run of the Meta-ES.

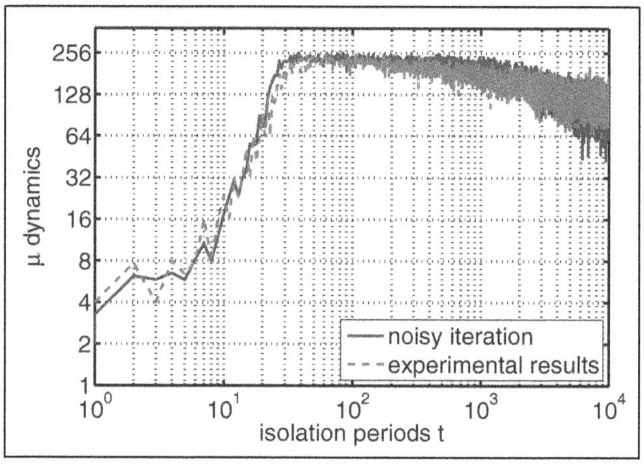

Figure 16: The parental population size dynamics resulting from the experiment compared to the noisy iteration dynamics using Eq. (8).

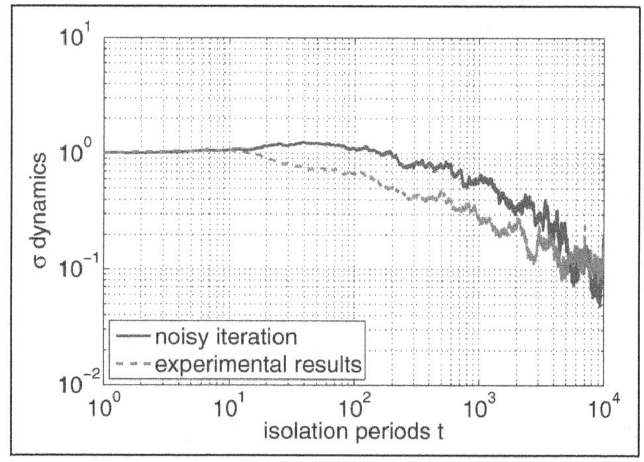

Figure 17: The mutation strength dynamics resulting from Eq. (8) equipped with noise is compared to the experimental results.

The deviations are a result of the fluctuations in the μ dynamics illustrated in Fig. 16. The noisy iteration as well as the experimental dynamics show larger deviations from the maximal parental population size $\mu = d$ with increasing number of isolation periods t. This behavior is resulting from the influence of fitness noise while selecting the best observed inner ES. Additionally, in Fig. 17 an improved agreement of the two mutation strength dynamics is observable.

In each case the iterative and the experimental dynamics show a similar behavior. Thus the behavior of the experimental dynamics can be reconstructed better by considering noise disturbances in the selection process of the theoretical model. This indicates that the deviations are - at least partially - a result of the disregard of selection noise in the theoretical modeling.

7. CONCLUSIONS AND OUTLOOK

In this paper we investigated the ability of a $[1, 4(\mu/\mu_I, \lambda)^\gamma]$-Meta-ES to simultaneously control the population size μ and the mutation strength σ on the sphere model in particularly under the influence of fitness noise with constant variance. A theoretical analysis of the strategy's adaptation behavior has been presented. Considering asymptotically exact approximations we were able to calculate the general behavior of the μ- as well as the σ-dynamics. While the μ-dynamics increases μ exponentially fast up to the predefined μ-bound, the σ-dynamics exhibits a square root law when approaching the steady state. That means that the approach to the steady state is rather slow.

The derivations presented assumed an error-free selection process in the meta strategy. In that point, the analysis deviates from the real Meta-ES. This deviation is the main reason for the deviations observed when comparing the theoretical results with real Meta-ES experiments.

One might consider to incorporate the noisy selection process of the outer ES in the analysis. This way the theoretical model would gain accuracy in reproducing the experimental dynamics. However, this is not really the direction of research we regard as a meaningful next step. The results rather indicate that the Meta-ES considered is not well suited for this noisy optimization problem. This leads to the question how to change the Meta-ES algorithmically such that it exhibits a better long-term behavior. That is, the selection process of the outer ES must be improved. One may think of various measures how to improve the selection process. For example, one could use $\gamma > 1$ runs to obtain more reliable fitness values (moving average). Investigations dealing with such questions will be next on our agenda.

8. ACKNOWLEDGMENTS

This work was supported by the Austrian Science Fund (FWF) under grant P22649-N23.

9. REFERENCES

[1] D. V. Arnold. *Noisy Optimization with Evolution Strategies.* Kluwer, 2002.

[2] D. V. Arnold and H.-G. Beyer. Local Performance of the $(\mu/\mu_I, \lambda)$-ES in a Noisy Environment. In *W. Martin and W. Spears, editors, Foundations of Genetic Algorithms, 6*, pages 127–141. Morgan Kaufmann, 2001.

[3] D. V. Arnold and A. MacLeod. Step length adaption on ridge functions. *Evolutionary Computation*, 16:151–184, 2008.

[4] H.-G. Beyer. *The Theory of Evolution Strategies.* Natural Computing Series, Springer, Heidelberg, 2001.

[5] H.-G. Beyer, M. Dobler, C. Hämmerle, and P. Masser. On Strategy Parameter Control by Meta-ES. GECCO-2009: Proceedings of the Genetic and Evolutionary Computation Conference, pages 499–506. ACM, 2009.

[6] H.-G. Beyer, M. Hellwig. Mutation Strength Control by Meta-ES on the Sharp Ridge. GECCO-2012: Proceedings of the Genetic and Evolutionary Computation Conference, pages 305–312. ACM, 2012.

[7] M. Herdy. Reproductive Isolation as Strategy Parameter in Hierarchically Organized Evolution Strategies. In *R. Männer and B. Manderick, editors, Parallel Problem Solving from Nature 2*, pages 207–217. Elsevier, 1992.

[8] I. Rechenberg. *Evolutionsstrategie '94.* Frommann-Holzboog Verlag, Stuttgart, 1994.

Finite Satisfiability of Propositional Interval Logic Formulas with Multi-Objective Evolutionary Algorithms

Davide Bresolin
Dept. of Computer Science
University of Verona, Italy
davide.bresolin@univr.it

Fernando Jiménez
Dept. of Information Engineering and Communications
University of Murcia, Spain
fernan@um.es

Gracia Sánchez
Dept. of Information Engineering and Communications
University of Murcia, Spain
gracia@um.es

Guido Sciavicco
Dept. of Information Engineering and Communications
University of Murcia, Spain
guido@um.es

ABSTRACT

Interval temporal logics provide a natural framework for temporal reasoning about interval structures over linearly ordered domains, where intervals are taken as the primitive ontological entities. Despite being relevant for a broad spectrum of application domains, ranging from temporal databases to artificial intelligence and verification of reactive systems, interval temporal logics still misses algorithms and tools capable of supporting them in an efficient way. In this paper, we approach the finite satisfiability problem for the simplest meaningful interval temporal logic (which is NEXPTIME-complete), namely A (also known as Right Propositional Neighborhood Logic), by means of a multi-objective combinatorial optimization model solved with three different multi-objective evolutionary algorithms. As a result we obtain a decision procedure that, although incomplete, turns out to be unexpectedly suitable and easy to implement with respect to classical complete algorithms. Moreover, this approach allows one to effectively search for the minimal model that satisfy a set of A-formulas without using any kind of normal form.

Categories and Subject Descriptors

I.2 [**Artificial Intelligence**]: Knowledge Representation Formalisms and Methods

General Terms

Theory, Algorithms

Keywords

Evolutionary Algorithms, Modal and Temporal Logics

1. INTRODUCTION

Interval temporal logics provide a natural framework for temporal reasoning about interval structures over linearly (or partially) ordered domains. They take time intervals as the primitive ontological entities and define truth of formulae relative to time intervals, rather than time points. Interval logics feature modal operators that correspond to various relations between pairs of intervals. In particular, the well-known logic HS, introduced by Halpern and Shoham in [17] features a set of modal operators that makes it possible to express all Allen's interval relations [2]. Interval-based formalisms have been extensively used in various areas of AI, such as planning and plan validation, theories of action and change, natural language processing, and constraint satisfaction problems. Most of them make severe syntactic and semantic restrictions that considerably weaken their expressive power. Interval temporal logics relax these restrictions allowing one to cope with much more complex application domains and scenarios, but many of them, including HS and the majority of its fragments, turned out to be undecidable ([3, 17]). In general, decidability and complexity of HS-fragments depend, among other, on the class of linearly ordered sets on which they are interpreted, and the set of Allen's relations captured by the modal operators. Among the few decidable cases in the finite case, we mention the fragments $\mathsf{A}\overline{\mathsf{A}}$ (that features modal operator for the relations *meets* and *met by*, and it is also known as Propositional Neighborhood Logic) and its fragment A [7, 6], both NEXPTIME-complete, $\mathsf{AB}\overline{\mathsf{B}}\overline{\mathsf{L}}$ (*meets*, *starts*, *started by*, and *later*), which is EXPSPACE-complete [8], $\mathsf{A}\overline{\mathsf{A}}\mathsf{B}\overline{\mathsf{B}}$ (*meets*, *starts* and their inverses), which is non-primitive recursive, and $\mathsf{B}\overline{\mathsf{B}}$ [24], which is NP-complete [15]; a comprehensive study can be found in [23]. In all such cases an implementable deduction method has been provided (usually based on tableaux), and their completeness and termination are guaranteed by suitable model-theoretic properties that allow one to limit the search for a model. Even in the

Relation	Operator	Formal definition
meets	$\langle A\rangle$	$[a,b]R_A[c,d] \Leftrightarrow b=c$
before	$\langle L\rangle$	$[a,b]R_L[c,d] \Leftrightarrow b<c$
started-by	$\langle B\rangle$	$[a,b]R_B[c,d] \Leftrightarrow a=c, d<b$
finished-by	$\langle E\rangle$	$[a,b]R_E[c,d] \Leftrightarrow b=d, a<c$
contains	$\langle D\rangle$	$[a,b]R_D[c,d] \Leftrightarrow a<c, d<b$
overlaps	$\langle O\rangle$	$[a,b]R_O[c,d] \Leftrightarrow a<c<b<d$

Table 1: Allen's interval relations and the corresponding HS modalities.

simplest significative cases of $\mathsf{A}\overline{\mathsf{A}}$ and its fragment A (the NP-complete fragment $\mathsf{B}\overline{\mathsf{B}}$ is so weak that it can be reduced to temporal logics based on points, such as LTL[F,P] [12]) the high complexity of the satisfiability problem makes it quite difficult to be used in practice; this, on the contrary, it is not the case for point-based temporal logics, whose complexity is usually NP or PSPACE [12]. We therefore believe that there is room for a different approach to satisfiability checking in the interval-based case.

In this paper we explore an alternative solution approach, in which a multi-objective combinatorial optimization problem is identified and solved by using metaheuristics. Metaheuristics have been shown to be effective for difficult combinatorial optimization problems appearing in various industrial, economical, and scientific domains. Prominent examples of metaheuristics for combinatorial optimization are evolutionary algorithms, which have been found very powerful for satisfiability problems [1, 11, 16, 21, 22, 28]. We consider here the simplest meaningful pure interval temporal logic, that is A (a.k.a RPNL), studied in [7], interpreted over finite linear models. This interval temporal logic extends classical propositional logic with a single modal operators, denoted $\langle A\rangle$, which is interpreted as the relation *meets* from Allen's repository (see Tab. 1). We propose a multi-objective evolutionary approach to test the finite satisfiability of a set of A-formulas. Obviously, completeness of the algorithm is no longer guaranteed, as we need to put a bound on the number of (fitness) evaluations of the algorithm on a given input. But our aim is to show that evolutionary algorithms are more efficient on the practical side: they somehow imitate the thinking process during model searching, and, therefore, should such model exist, they should be able to find it in a quicker way. Moreover, by means of a multi-objective search, we can also solve a (satisfiability related) problem which has received practically no attention in the literature, that is, the problem of finding the minimal model that satisfies a (set of) formula(s).

2. RELATED WORK

The study of satisfiability of logical formulas by means of evolutionary algorithms has not been studied very deeply in the literature. Let us summarize here some relevant work.

The first pure logical problem to which an evolutionary approach has been attempted is SAT, that is, propositional satisfiability. Among the work in the field of the evolutionary computation for SAT, we can mention the rather complete studies [11, 16]; in particular, in [16] the authors conclude that the so-called bit-string representation shows the most promising results. Such a representation has been also applied in [22] to solve 3-SAT instances. Moreover, in [21] the authors present a hybrid algorithm that embeds a tabu search procedure into the evolutionary framework, and it is characterized by specialized crossover operators and their interaction. Another hybrid method has been proposed in [1], where greedy local search is incorporated into the evolutionary approach. Finally, an adaptive evolutionary algorithm that dynamically adapts the search strategy by using information on the best solutions found in the recent past has been proposed in [28].

The natural successive step from pure propositional satisfiability is that of modal satisfiability. An example in this sense is given in [30], where a first structured study of modal satisfiability via local search has been done. In that paper, the authors consider a very simple example from the classical modal repository, that is, the modal logic S5. This is the modal logic of equivalence relations, and the reason for this choice is the simplicity and regularity of S5 structures, that make them feasible for an initial study. Their approach consists of transforming the initial S5-formula into a S5-CNF formula (conjunctive normal form), equi-satisfiable to the original one, and with modal depth no more than 1. Then, they adapt the classical propositional evolutionary algorithm to modal clauses in order to look for a solution.

It is worth noticing that, to the best of our knowledge, there exists practically no literature about propositional temporal logic satisfiability with evolutionary approach. The present paper, therefore, is a first attempt to tackle the satisfiability problem for a modal temporal logic using evolutionary algorithms.

3. PRELIMINARIES

Let $\mathbb{D} = \langle D, <\rangle$ be a finite linearly ordered set. An *interval* over $\mathbb{D}$ is an ordered pair $[a,b]$, where $a,b \in D$ and $a<b$. In this paper we choose to exclude intervals of the type $[a,a]$ (called *point intervals*), even though all the results presented here can be easily generalized to include them. There are 12 different non-trivial relations (excluding the equality) between two strict intervals in a linear order, often called *Allen's relations* [2]: the six relations depicted in Tab. 1 and the inverse relations. We treat interval structures as Kripke structures and Allen's relations as accessibility relations in them, thus associating a modal operator $\langle X\rangle$ with each Allen's relation R_X. For each operator $\langle X\rangle$, its *transpose*, denoted by $\langle\overline{X}\rangle$, corresponds to the inverse relation $R_{\overline{X}}$ of R_X (that is, $R_{\overline{X}} = (R_X)^{-1}$).

Halpern and Shoham's logic HS is a multi-modal logic with formulae built over a set $\mathcal{AP}$ of propositional letters, the propositional connectives $\vee$ and $\neg$, and a set of modal operators associated with all Allen's relations. With every subset $\{R_{X_1},\ldots,R_{X_k}\}$ of these relations, we associate the fragment $\mathsf{X}_1\mathsf{X}_2\ldots\mathsf{X}_k$ of HS, whose the formulae are defined by the grammar:

$$\varphi ::= p \mid \neg\varphi \mid \varphi\vee\psi \mid \langle X_1\rangle\varphi \mid \ldots \mid \langle X_k\rangle\varphi.$$

The other propositional connectives, $\wedge$ and $\rightarrow$, and the dual operators $[X]$ are defined as usual, e.g., $[X]\varphi \equiv \neg\langle X\rangle\neg\varphi$. The semantics of HS is given in terms of *interval models* $M = \langle\mathbb{I}(\mathbb{D}), V\rangle$, where $\mathbb{I}(\mathbb{D})$ is the set of all (strict) intervals over $\mathbb{D}$. The *valuation function* $V : \mathcal{AP} \mapsto 2^{\mathbb{I}(\mathbb{D})}$ assigns to every $p \in \mathcal{AP}$ the set of intervals $V(p)$ on which p holds. The *truth* of a formula on a given interval $[a,b]$ in an interval model M is defined by structural induction on formulae:

- $M, [a, b] \Vdash p$ iff $[a, b] \in V(p)$, for all $p \in \mathcal{AP}$;
- $M, [a, b] \Vdash \neg\psi$ iff it is not the case that $M, [a, b] \Vdash \psi$;
- $M, [a, b] \Vdash \psi \vee \xi$ iff $M, [a, b] \Vdash \psi$ or $M, [a, b] \Vdash \xi$;
- $M, [a, b] \Vdash \langle X \rangle \psi$ iff there exists an interval $[c, d]$ such that $[a, b] R_X [c, d]$ and $M, [c, d] \Vdash \psi$, where R_X is any of Allen's relations.

The remaining propositional connectives, as well as the propositional constants $\top$ and $\bot$, can be considered as abbreviations, and *validity* of a formula is defined as standard.

In the rest of the paper, we focus our attention on the problem of *finite satisfiability* of the HS-fragment A. Therefore, to every purpose, $\mathbb{D} = \{0, 1, \ldots, N-1\}$ will be always a finite set (with at least two distinct points), and formulas of the logic will be generated by using, among all the modal operators, only $\langle A \rangle$:

$$\varphi ::= p \mid \neg\varphi \mid \varphi \vee \psi \mid \langle A \rangle \varphi.$$

This logic is one of the simplest, yet meaningful, propositional interval temporal logics, that has been studied in the recent literature (see, e.g. [7]). Its (finite) satisfiability problem has been shown to be NEXPTIME-complete, and a deterministic, sound, complete and terminating tableau method for it has been devised and implemented. In particular, finite satisfiability can be reduced to satisfiability in the class of models based on the set of (prefixes of) natural numbers by simply observing that finiteness can be forced with the constant A-formula $\langle A \rangle [A] \bot$; in turn, as it has been noticed in [7], satisfiability can be reduced to *initial satisfiability*, that is, for every $\varphi \in$ A, φ is (finitely) satisfiable if and only if it is finitely satisfiable over the interval $[0, 1]$. Therefore, from now on, we will limit our attention to finite initial satisfiability ($FSAT_{\mathsf{A}}$, for short).

The fragment A, seen as a sub-logic of $\mathsf{A}\bar{\mathsf{A}}$ (PNL) and therefore also of its metric version (MPNL [5]), is interesting from the practical point of view. Expressiveness and (potential) applications of these languages have been extensively discussed in [4, 5]: we refer the reader to such a publication for details. Here, we provide a short summary of its outcomes. First, it has been shown that MPNL is expressive enough to encode classical point-based temporal operators, like 'sometimes in the future' and 'sometimes in the past', as well as to define a metric version of the 'until' operator. Moreover, it has been proved that almost all Allen's relations (but the relation *during*), over bounded intervals, can be expressed in MPNL, by making use of the universal and the difference modalities (both expressible in pure PNL). Finally, a set of application examples, ranging from formal specification of complex systems (like a gas burner or a railway signaling system) to medical guidelines and ambient intelligence, has been given. Most (although not all) of the above considerations are still valid when we restrict our attention to the simple fragment A.

4. MULTI-OBJECTIVE EVOLUTIONARY APPROACH FOR FINITE SATISFIABILITY

A multi-objective optimization model. In this section, we give the basic notions of multi-objective optimization, and we show how $FSAT_{\mathsf{A}}$ can be formulated in this context.

DEFINITION 1. *An (unconstrained)* multi-objective combinatorial optimization problem *($\mathcal{MO}$) can be formulated in terms of integer mathematical programming as a minimization/maximization problem of a tuple of* objective *functions $f_1(\bar{x}), f_2(\bar{x}), \ldots, f_n(\bar{x})$, each one of which has codomain $\mathbb{R}$ (in the most general case), where $\bar{x}$ is a vector of integer parameters, and where, for each $1 \leq i \leq s$, $x_i \in [l_i, u_i]$ for some integer values $l_i \leq u_i \in \mathbb{Z}$. We denote by $\mathcal{F}$ the set of vectors $\bar{x}$ that satisfy the above constraint (*solutions*).*

When solving a $\mathcal{MO}$, one aims to simultaneously optimize the value of the objective functions $f_1, f_2, \ldots, f_n$. We are not interested in all possible solutions, but only those that are optimal, as defined below.

DEFINITION 2. *Given a $\mathcal{MO}$, the set $\mathcal{F}$ of its solutions, and a solution $\bar{x} \in \mathcal{F}$, we say that $\bar{x}$ is* not dominated *(or* Pareto optimal*) if and only if there is no $\bar{y} \in \mathcal{F}$ such that 1) $f_i(\bar{y})$ is not worse than $f_i(\bar{x})$ for each $1 \leq i \leq n$, and 2) there exists $1 \leq i \leq n$ for which $f_i(\bar{y})$ improves $f_i(\bar{x})$. The subset $\mathcal{F}' \subseteq \mathcal{F}$ of all $\bar{x}$ which are not dominated is called* Pareto set.

We want to show now that $FSAT_{\mathsf{A}}$ can be seen as a $\mathcal{MO}$ with $n = 2$. Given a finite model $M = \langle \mathbb{I}(\mathbb{D}), V \rangle$ and a set of A-formulas $\Phi = \{\varphi_1, \ldots, \varphi_k\}$, we define:

$$f_1^{\Phi}(M) = \left(\Sigma_i^k f_{\Vdash}(M, [0, 1], \varphi_i) \right) / k \text{ and } f_2^{\Phi}(M) = N,$$

where $f_{\Vdash}(M, [0, 1], \varphi_i)$ is 1 (resp., 0) if and only if $M, [0, 1] \Vdash \varphi_i$ (resp., $M, [0, 1] \nVdash \varphi_i$), and where $N = |\mathbb{D}|$.

To complete the encoding of $FSAT_{\mathsf{A}}$, we have to show how to represent $M = \langle \mathbb{I}(\mathbb{D}), V \rangle$ as a vector of integer variables. First of all, given a set of A-formulas Φ, let $\mathcal{AP} = \{p_1, \ldots p_\nu\}$ be the set of different propositional letters that appear in formulas of Φ. Since each propositional letter is either true or false over every interval in $\mathbb{I}(\mathbb{D})$, we can uniquely represent the valuation of an interval $[a, b]$ by a ν-digit binary number $b_1, \ldots b, \nu$, where $b_i = 1$ if and only if $[a, b] \in V(p_i)$. Hence, every interval in $\mathbb{I}(\mathbb{D})$ is represented by a natural number from 0 to $2^\nu - 1$, and the complete model M is encoded by a vector $(m_1, \ldots, m_s)$ of variables such that, for each l, $m_l \in [0, 2^\nu - 1]$, and m_l represents a given interval on M. In this way, if $|\mathbb{D}| = N$, then $s = (N \cdot (N-1))/2$.

With a little notational abuse, and using M to denote the vector $(m_1, \ldots, m_s)$, we can define our multi-objective combinatorial optimization problem as follows:

$$FSAT_{\mathsf{A}}(\Phi) = \begin{cases} \max f_1^{\Phi}(M) \\ \min f_2^{\Phi}(M) \end{cases}$$

namely, to maximize the number of formulas from Φ that are satisfied (objective function f_1), minimizing the length of the model (objective function f_2).

Multi-objective evolutionary computation. Evolutionary algorithms (EAs) are particularly suitable for multi-objective optimization [9, 10], as they search in parallel multiple optimal solutions. An EA is capable of finding a set of optimal solutions in its final population from a single run. Once we have the set of optimal solutions, we can choose the most satisfactory one by applying a preference criterion. Three multi-objective Pareto-based evolutionary approaches have been used to solve $FSAT_{\mathsf{A}}$, namely, Preselection with niches (PSN), ENORA and NSGA-II; they differ from each other in the selection mechanism. PNS was initially developed in [14] for function approximation and dynamic modeling with TSK fuzzy models. ENORA was proposed in [20] for multi-objective constrained real parameter optimization. Finally, NSGA-II is the well known technique proposed in [10], and it was initially developed for real parameter optimization in multi-objective constrained optimization problems.

The three algorithms have been adapted in this work to solve $FSAT_{\mathsf{A}}$, with the following common characteristics: 1) They are all Pareto-based: in a single run, they find multiple non-dominated solutions; 2) They are all *elitist*, i.e., the fitness value of the best individual in a generation T does not get worse w.r.t. the generation $T-1$; 3) They have variable length integer representation; 4) The initial population is generated randomly with a uniform distribution within the boundaries of the search space; 5) The variation operators act on integer numbers. A *uniform crossover* and three types of mutation, namely, *change mutation*, *add mutation*, and *reduce mutation*, have been used, and parameter values are dynamically adapted.

Representation and initial population. Our algorithm is based on a variable length integer representation $M = (m_1, \ldots, m_s)$ of size $s = (N \cdot (N-1))/2$, where $s \geq 1$ and $N = |\mathbb{D}|$. Nevertheless, for the sake of convenience to the fitness evaluation and to the design of the variation operators, we use a $(N \times N)$ matrix representation, as follows:

$$FSAT_{\mathsf{A}}(\Phi) = \begin{cases} \max f_1^{\Phi}(M) \\ \min f_2^{\Phi}(M) \end{cases}$$

namely, to maximize the number of formulas from Φ that are satisfied (objective function f_1), minimizing the length of the model (objective function f_2).

Multi-objective evolutionary computation. Evolutionary algorithms (EAs) are particularly suitable for multi-objective optimization [9, 10], as they search in parallel multiple optimal solutions. An EA is capable of finding a set of optimal solutions in its final population from a single run. Once we have the set of optimal solutions, we can choose the most satisfactory one by applying a preference criterion. Three multi-objective Pareto-based evolutionary approaches have been used to solve $FSAT_{\mathsf{A}}$, namely, Preselection with niches (PSN), ENORA and NSGA-II; they differ from each other in the selection mechanism. PNS was initially developed in [14] for function approximation and dynamic modeling with TSK fuzzy models. ENORA was proposed in [20] for multi-objective constrained real parameter optimization. Finally, NSGA-II is the well known technique proposed in [10], and it was initially developed for real parameter optimization in multi-objective constrained optimization problems.

The three algorithms have been adapted in this work to solve $FSAT_{\mathsf{A}}$, with the following common characteristics: 1) They are all Pareto-based: in a single run, they find multiple non-dominated solutions; 2) They are all *elitist*, i.e., the fitness value of the best individual in a generation T does not get worse w.r.t. the generation $T-1$; 3) They have variable length integer representation; 4) The initial population is generated randomly with a uniform distribution within the boundaries of the search space; 5) The variation operators act on integer numbers. A *uniform crossover* and three types of mutation, namely, *change mutation*, *add mutation*, and *reduce mutation*, have been used, and parameter values are dynamically adapted.

Representation and initial population. Our algorithm is based on a variable length integer representation

```
proc Initialization (popsize, N_max)
  for all 1 ≤ i ≤ popsize
    let N random ∈ [1, N_max];
    POP_i ← InizialInd (N);
  return POP;
```

```
proc InitialInd (N)
  for all 1 ≤ i ≤ N − 1
    for all i + 1 ≤ j ≤ N
      let R random ∈ [0, 2^ν − 1]
      m_ij ← R;
  return M';
```

Figure 1: Pseudo-code for setting the initial population.

$$g_{\Vdash}^{T}(M,[a,b],p) = \begin{cases} 0 & \text{if } [a,b] \in V(p) \\ 1 & \text{otherwise} \end{cases}$$

$$g_{\Vdash}^{F}(M,[a,b],p) = \begin{cases} 1 & \text{if } [a,b] \in V(p) \\ 0 & \text{otherwise} \end{cases}$$

$$g_{\Vdash}^{T}(M,[a,b],\neg\psi) = g_{\Vdash}^{F}(M,[a,b],\psi)$$

$$g_{\Vdash}^{F}(M,[a,b],\neg\psi) = g_{\Vdash}^{T}(M,[a,b],\psi)$$

$$g_{\Vdash}^{T}(M,[a,b],\psi \vee \xi) = min\left(g_{\Vdash}^{T}(M,[a,b],\psi), g_{\Vdash}^{T}(M,[a,b],\xi)\right)$$

$$g_{\Vdash}^{F}(M,[a,b],\psi \vee \xi) = g_{\Vdash}^{F}(M,[a,b],\psi) + g_{\Vdash}^{F}(M,[a,b],\xi)$$

$$g_{\Vdash}^{T}(M,[a,b],\langle A\rangle\psi) = \begin{cases} min_{c=b+1}^{N-1} g_{\Vdash}^{T}(M,[b,c],\psi) & \text{if } b < N-1 \\ 1 & \text{otherwise} \end{cases}$$

$$g_{\Vdash}^{F}(M,[a,b],\langle A\rangle\psi) = \begin{cases} \Sigma_{c=b+1}^{N-1} g_{\Vdash}^{T}(M,[b,c],\psi) & \text{if } b < N-1 \\ 0 & \text{otherwise} \end{cases}$$

Figure 2: Definition of the functions $g_{\Vdash}^{T}$ and $g_{\Vdash}^{F}$.

$M = (m_1, \ldots, m_s)$ of size $s = (N \cdot (N-1))/2$, where $s \geq 1$ and $N = |\mathbb{D}|$. Nevertheless, for the sake of convenience to the fitness evaluation and to the design of the variation operators, we use a $(N \times N)$ matrix representation, as follows:

$$M' = \begin{bmatrix} m'_{11} & m'_{12} & \ldots & m'_{1N} \\ m'_{21} & m'_{22} & \ldots & m'_{2N} \\ \vdots & \vdots & \vdots & \vdots \\ m'_{N1} & m'_{N2} & \ldots & m'_{NN} \end{bmatrix}$$

where $0 \leq m'_{ij} \leq 2^{\nu} - 1$ and $1 \leq i, j \leq N$. Of all values of M' only the elements m'_{ij} such that $i < j$ are relevant for the problem, as they correspond to intervals on the model we are searching for, and we can safely ignore the values of the elements m'_{ij} such that $i \geq j$. Thus, the vector M corresponds to the upper triangle of M': $M = (m_1, m_2, \ldots, m_s) = (m'_{12}, m'_{13}, \ldots, m'_{1N}, m'_{23}, \ldots, m'_{2N}, \ldots)$.

We recall that the value of a given m'_{ij} corresponds to the binary representation $m'_{ij} = b_{ij1}, b_{ij2} \ldots, b_{ij\nu}$ of the propositional letters that are true over the interval $[i-1, j-1]$. In this way, we can easily check if the k-th propositional letter of the language is true over a given interval $[i-1, j-1]$, by simply computing $b_{ijk} = \frac{m'_{ij}}{2^{k-1}}$ mod 2. Given a population size *popsize* and the maximum dimension N_{max} of the model, the pseudo-code for the procedures used to set the initial population is specified in Fig. 1.

Fitness functions. As $FSAT_{\mathsf{A}}$ has been defined as an optimization problem, we already know the objective function. One of the main ingredients in EAs is, though, the *fitness* function, used to guide the algorithm towards the objective. Our objective is constituted by two functions f_1^{Φ} and f_2^{Φ}; thus, we are after two fitness functions F_1^{Φ}, F_2^{Φ}. Since f_2^{Φ} is defined as the length of the underlying domain, the choice of using f_2 as a fitness function ($F_2^{\Phi} = f_2^{\Phi}$) turned out to be perfectly adequate. In the case of the objective function f_1, our first approach was to do the same, and use f_1^{Φ} as fitness function ($F_1^{\Phi} = f_1^{\Phi}$). However, the initial experiments discovered that this choice presents a problem, due to the particular definition of the objective function f_1. Indeed, given a single A-formula φ, and a set of tentative models $M_1, M_2, \ldots$, the value of $f_1(M_i)$ can either be 0 or 1, and this does not give us any useful indication: if, by chance, one of the models returns 1, we are done, but, otherwise, we do not know which models to select in order to guide the searching for better ones. This problem is therefore particularly evident when $|\Phi|$ is relatively small (or even 1, that is, when we check the satisfiability of a single formula).

To improve the performances of the algorithms, we explored the use of a different fitness function, whose value depends not only on the truth value of a formula on the initial interval $[0,1]$, but also on the truth value of its subformulas on the entire model, with the goal to measure how much the current model is far from satisfying the complete formula. Formally, we define a pair of functions $g_{\Vdash}^T$ and $g_{\Vdash}^F$. Intuitively, $g_{\Vdash}^T(M,[a,b],\varphi)$ measures the number of mistakes that we have done in designing M to satisfy φ over $[a,b]$, while $g_{\Vdash}^F(M,[a,b],\varphi)$ measures the number of mistakes that we have done in designing M to *not* satisfy φ over $[a,b]$. The definition of the two functions are given in Fig. 2, and are guided by the semantics of A-formulas. For example, suppose that we want to know whether or not a given $M = \langle \mathbb{I}(\mathbb{D}), V\rangle$ satisfies $\varphi = \langle A\rangle\psi$ over the interval $[a,b]$, and suppose that $\mathbb{D} = \{0,1,\ldots,N-1\}$. To compute the number of mistakes that M presents for φ over $[a,b]$, we evaluate $g_{\Vdash}^T(M,[b,c],\psi)$, where c ranges between $b+1$ and $N-1$, and we take the minimum of them. So, bigger models that do not satisfy $\langle A\rangle\psi$ are considered to be worse than smaller ones, following, so to say, the intuition: if M is very big, and we still cannot find an interval $[b,c]$ that satisfies ψ, we are probably looking in the wrong direction. The definition of $g_{\Vdash}^T$ and $g_{\Vdash}^F$ are sound, in the sense that if φ is satisfied over $M,[a,b]$ then $g_{\Vdash}^T(M,[a,b],\varphi) = 0$, while when $\neg\varphi$ is satisfied over $M,[a,b]$, $g_{\Vdash}^F(M,[a,b],\varphi) = 0$.

THEOREM 3. *Suppose that φ is a A-formula, $M = \langle \mathbb{I}(\mathbb{D}), V\rangle$ such that $\mathbb{D} = \{0,1,\ldots,N-1\}$, and that $[a,b]$ is an interval. Then the following two properties hold: (i) $M,[a,b] \Vdash \varphi$ if and only if $g_{\Vdash}^T(M,[a,b],\varphi) = 0$, and (ii) $M,[a,b] \nVdash \varphi$ if and only if $g_{\Vdash}^F(M,[a,b],\varphi) = 0$.*

PROOF. We first consider claim *(i)*, and we proceed by structural induction on φ. The base case $\varphi = p$ is straightforward. If $\varphi = \psi \vee \xi$, we have that $M,[a,b] \Vdash \psi \vee \xi$ if and only if $M,[a,b] \Vdash \psi$ or $M,[a,b] \Vdash \xi$. By inductive hypothesis, $M,[a,b] \Vdash \psi$ (resp., $M,[a,b] \Vdash \xi$) if and only if $g_{\Vdash}^T(M,[a,b],\psi) = 0$ (resp., $g_{\Vdash}^T(M,[a,b],\xi) = 0$), that is, if and only if the minimum among $g_{\Vdash}^T(M,[a,b],\psi)$ and $g_{\Vdash}^T(M,[a,b],\xi)$ is 0, which, by definition, happens if and only if $g_{\Vdash}^T(M,[a,b],\psi \vee \xi) = 0$. Negation can be dealt with by observing that $M,[a,b] \Vdash \neg\xi$ if and only if $M,[a,b] \nVdash \xi$. By claim *(ii)*, this is happens if and only if $g_{\Vdash}^F(M,[a,b],\xi) = 0$, and thus (by the definition of $g_{\Vdash}^T$), if and only if $g_{\Vdash}^T(M,[a,b],\neg\xi) = 0$. Finally, when $\varphi = \langle A\rangle\psi$, we have that $M,[a,b] \Vdash \langle A\rangle\psi$ if and only if there exists c such that $b < c <= N-1$, and that $M,[b,c] \Vdash \psi$. By inductive hypothesis, this happens if and only if $g_{\Vdash}^T(M,\psi,[b,c]) = 0$. Since $b < N-1$, we have that $min_{c=b+1}^{N-1}\left(g_{\Vdash}^T(M,[b,c],\psi)\right) = 0$, and, by definition, $g_{\Vdash}^T(M,\langle A\rangle\psi,[a,b]) = 0$ as required. □

Now, we are ready to define the alternative fitness function as follows:

$$G_1^{\Phi}(M) = -\Sigma_i^k g_{\Vdash}^T(M,[0,1],\varphi_i).$$

The reason for G_1^{Φ} being defined as a negative function is that, in this way, maximizing the fitness function corresponds to the objective of maximizing f_2, as required by the optimization problem.

Variation operators. We propose five variation operators: *interval crossover*, *logical crossover*, *change mutation*, *add mutation*, and *reduce mutation*. Let us analyze the pseudo-code for each one of them.

The *crossover*, given two individuals $M'_1 = \left\{m'^{1}_{ij}\right\}$, where $1 \le i < j \le N'_1$, and and $M'_2 = \left\{m'^{2}_{ij}\right\}$, where $1 \le i < j \le N'_2$, such that $N'_1 \ge N'_2$, by crossing M'_1 and M'_2 generates two offsprings $M'_3 = \left\{m'^{3}_{ij}\right\}$, where $1 \le i < j \le N'_1$, and $M'_4 = \left\{m'^{4}_{ij}\right\}$ with $1 \le i < j \le N'_2$, as specified in Fig. 3(a). Crossover operators use a binary crossover mask [9]. In the *logical* version, the one shown above, crosses between the parents are performed bit-to-bit, while, in the *interval* version of this operator, they are made at the level of an entire interval m_{ij}.

In the case of the *change mutation* operator (Fig. 3(b)), from $M'_1 = \left\{m'^{1}_{ij}\right\}$ of dimension N'_1, we produce an offspring $M'_2 = \left\{m'^{2}_{ij}\right\}$, of dimension $N'_2 = N'_1$, in which every truth value has been switched with probability α, where α is a dynamically adapted parameter.

Finally, mutation operators work by adding or removing points from the model. If $M'_1 = \left\{m'^{1}_{ij}\right\}$, where $1 \le i < j \le N'_1$, and such that $N'_1 < N_{max}$, the *add mutation* (Fig. 3(c)) operator generates a $M'_2 = \left\{m'^{1}_{ij}\right\}$, with $1 \le i < j \le N'_2$, where $N'_2 = N'_1 + 1$, and, for every $1 \le i < j \le N'_1$, $m'^{2}_{ij} = m'^{1}_{ij}$, while the last column of the new matrix is filled with random values. This corresponds to extending the candidate model of exactly one point at the end, keeping all the information of the old candidate. The *reduce mutation* (Fig. 3(d)), to be applied under the assumption $N'_1 > 2$, corresponds to deleting the last point of the model. Both operators are, in general, called a random number of times to produce increments and reductions of several points each.

5. TESTING

In this section we approach the problem of generating a test set of A-formulas over which we can compare the performance of our algorithm. In particular, we want to compare the three selection mechanisms PSN, ENORA, and NSGA-II, and the two fitness functions F_1^{Φ} and G_1^{Φ}, in order to establish which combinations works best for the problem at hand.

Rule	Formula	Transformed	Side conditions
1	$X \to \xi \vee \psi$	$(X \to Y \vee \xi) \wedge (Y \to \psi)$	ψ is not a literal, and Y is a new symbol
2	$X \to \neg(\psi \vee \xi)$	$(X \to \neg\psi) \wedge (X \to \neg\xi)$	–
3	$X \to (\xi \wedge \psi)$	$(X \to \xi) \wedge (X \to \psi)$	–
4	$X \to \neg(\xi \wedge \psi)$	$(X \to Y \vee \neg\xi) \wedge (Y \to \neg\psi)$	ψ is not a literal, and Y is a new symbol
5	$X \to (\xi \to \psi)$	$(X \to \neg\xi \vee \psi)$	–
6	$X \to \neg(\xi \to \psi)$	$(X \to \xi) \wedge (X \to \neg\psi)$	–
7	$X \to \neg\neg\xi$	$(X \to \xi)$	–
8	$X \to \langle A\rangle\psi$	$(X \to \langle A\rangle Y) \wedge (Y \to \psi)$	ψ is not a literal, and Y is a new symbol
9	$X \to [A]\psi$	$(X \to [A]Y) \wedge (Y \to \psi)$	ψ is not a literal, and Y is a new symbol
10	$X \to \neg\langle A\rangle\psi$	$(X \to [A]Y) \wedge (Y \to \neg\psi)$	Y is a new symbol
11	$X \to \neg[A]\psi$	$(X \to \langle A\rangle Y) \wedge (Y \to \neg\psi)$	Y is a new symbol

Table 2: Transformation rules into A-clauses

Generating a test set is not an easy task, and even more so considering that test set generation is a problem that has been studied for propositional logic and classical modal logic, but not for interval temporal logic. In the modal case, the literature include, among others, DLP [26], FACT [18], *SAT [13], and MSPASS [19]. A comprehensive analysis of the various techniques and methods can be found in [27]. Some of the desirable qualities of a test generator include [27]: 1. *Representativeness*: the ideal test set should represent a significant sample of the whole input space, and a good empirical test set should at least cover a large area of inputs; 2. *Difficulty*: a good empirical test set should provide a sufficient level of difficulty for the system(s) being tested; 3. *Termination*: to be of practical use, the tests should terminate and provide information within a reasonable amount of time (if the inputs are too hard, then the system may not be able to provide answers within the established time: this inability of the system is of interest, but can make system comparison impossible or insignificant); 4. *Scalability*: the difficulty of problems should scale up, as comparing absolute performances may be less significant than comparing how performances scale up with problems of increasing difficulty; 5. *Valid vs. not-valid balance*: in a good test set, valid and not-valid problems should be more or less equal both in number and in difficulty, and the maximum uncertainty regarding the solution of the problems is desirable; 6. *Reproducibility*: a good test set should allow for easily reproducing the results; 7. *Parameterization*: parameterized inputs with sufficient parameters and degrees of freedom allow the inputs to range over a large portion of the input space; 8. *Control*: in particular, it is very useful to have parameters that control monotonically the key features of the input test set, like the average difficulty and the "valid vs. non-valid" rate; 9. *Modal vs. propositional balance*: reasoning in modal logics involves alternating between two orthogonal search efforts, that is, pure modal reasoning and pure propositional reasoning: a good test set should be challenging from both viewpoints.

In view of these considerations, we now develop a normal form for A-formulas for the purpose of testing the various algorithms. We show that every A-formula can be equivalently transformed into a set of clauses, and each clause can, in turn, be reduced to a 3-elements clause. We have already observed that we can restrict our attention to initial satisfiability: let us call τ_1 the corresponding transformation. In the following we will present a transformation τ_2 in 3-elements clauses by means of which we conclude that: a A-formula is finitely satisfiable if and only if $\tau_1(\varphi)$ is initially and finitely satisfiable if and only if $\tau_2(\tau_1(\varphi))$ is initially and finitely satisfiable. This means that we can restrict our attention to problems in the form of conjunctions of clauses and still respect criterium number 1 above (representativeness).

Clauses and normal form. Let us start with defining a *universal operator* $[U]\varphi$ that ensures that φ holds on every interval of the model. Assuming $[U]\varphi$ is evaluated over $[0,1]$, we have that:

$$[U]\varphi \equiv \varphi \wedge [A]\varphi \wedge [A][A]\varphi.$$

Now, under the assumption that φ is based on a set of propositional letters $\mathcal{AP}$, we introduce an extended set $\mathcal{AP}^+ = \mathcal{AP} \uplus \{X_0, X, Y, \ldots\}$. The symbol X_0 is supposed to be true exactly over the initial interval.

Definition 4. *A* A*-formula is said to be a* A-clause *if and only if it has one of the following forms: 1. $X_0 \to X$; 2. $X \to \bigvee_{i=1}^{n} L_i$; 3. $X \to \bigvee_{i=1}^{n} KL_i$, where K has the form $\langle A\rangle$, $[A]$, $\neg\langle A\rangle$, or $\neg[A]$ (*modal prefix*), and for all i, L_i is a literal (i.e., a propositional letter from the set $\mathcal{AP}^+$ or its negation).*

As middle step to define the transformation τ_2, we want to prove that every A-formula can be transformed into a conjunction of A-clauses, possibly universally quantified. This is done as follows. Let φ be any A-formula. The *transformed formula* $X_0 \wedge [U](\bigwedge_{i=1}^{t} C_i)$ is obtained by applying the transformation rules given in in Tab. 2 to the formula $X_0 \wedge [U](X_0 \to \varphi)$, until no rule is applicable anymore. The corresponding *set of* A*-clauses* is $C_1, \ldots, C_t$. We have to show that this step is sound and complete, that is, we have to show that if φ is an initially satisfiable A-formula, then so is the transformed formula (soundness) and, conversely, that if the transformed formula is initially satisfiable, then φ is also initially satisfiable (completeness).

Lemma 5 (Soundness). *Let φ be any initially satisfiable* A*-formula. Then, the corresponding transformed formula $X_0 \wedge [U](\bigwedge_{i=1}^{t} C_i)$ is initially satisfiable.*

Proof. Suppose that φ is an initially satisfiable formula, and that M is a model such that $M, [0,1] \Vdash \varphi$. To prove the

```
proc LogicalCrossover (M'_1, M'_2)
  for all 1 ≤ i ≤ N'_2 − 1
    for all i + 1 ≤ j ≤ N'_2
      for all 1 ≤ k ≤ ν
        let R random ∈ {0, 1};
        if R = 0
          then b'^3_ijk ← b'^1_ijk , b'^4_ijk ← b'^2_ijk;
          else b'^3_ijk ← b'^2_ijk , b'^4_ijk ← b'^1_ijk;
  for all N'_2 ≤ i ≤ N'_1 − 1
    for all i + 1 ≤ j ≤ N'_1
      m'^3_ij ← m'^1_ij;
  return (M'_3, M'_4);
```

(a) Crossover operator

```
proc Change (M'_1, α)
  M'_2 = M'_1;
  N'_2 = N'_1;
  for all 1 ≤ i ≤ N'_2 − 1
    for all i + 1 ≤ j ≤ N'_2
      for all 1 ≤ k ≤ μ
        let R random ∈ [0, 1];
        if R < α
          then b'^2_ijk = b'^2_ijk ⊕ 1;
  return M'_2;
```

(b) Change operator

```
proc AddMutation (M'_1)
  for all 1 ≤ i ≤ N'_1 − 1
    for all i + 1 ≤ j ≤ N'_1
      m'^2_ij ← m'_1;
  N'_2 ← N'_1 + 1;
  for all 1 ≤ i ≤ N'_2 − 1
    let R random ∈ [0, 2^ν − 1]
    m'^2_i(N'_2−1) ← R;
  return M'_2;
```

(c) Add mutation operator

```
proc ReduceMutation (M'_1)
  for all 1 ≤ i ≤ N'_1 − 2
    for all i + 1 ≤ j ≤ N'_1 − 1
      m'^2_ij ← m'_1;
  N'_2 ← N'_1 − 1;
  return M'_2;
```

(d) Reduce mutation operator

Figure 3: Pseudo-code for the variation operators.

claim we extend M to a new model $M' = \langle \mathbb{I}(\mathbb{D}), V' \rangle$ over the set of propositional letters $\mathcal{AP}^+$ as follows: for every rule $X \rightarrow \psi$ that is applied in the transformation of φ, we put $V'(X) = \{[a,b] : M,[a,b] \Vdash \psi\}$. The valuation of the propositional letters that belongs to $\mathcal{AP}$ remains unchanged.

To complete the proof it suffices to show that $M',[0,1] \Vdash X_0 \wedge [U](\bigwedge_{i=1}^{t} C_i)$. We proceed by induction on the application of the rules, starting from the initial formula $\varphi_0 = X_0 \wedge [U](X_0 \rightarrow \varphi)$. By the definition of M' we have that $M',[0,1] \Vdash \varphi$ and $V'(X_0) = \{[a,b] : M,[a,b] \Vdash \varphi\}$. This implies that $M',[0,1] \Vdash X_0$ and $M',[0,1] \Vdash [U](X_0 \rightarrow \varphi)$, as required.

For the inductive case, suppose that $\varphi_i = X_0 \wedge [U](\bigwedge_{j=1}^{t} C_j^i)$ is the formula obtained at the i-th step and that $M',[0,1] \Vdash \varphi_i$. Without loss of generality, we can assume that at the $(i+1)$-th step a rule is applied to the clause C_1^i (if this is not the case we can renumber the clauses), we distinguish between different cases, based on the rule applied to C_1^i.

- If rule 1 is applied, then $C_1^i = X \rightarrow \xi \vee \psi$ and the resulting formula is $\varphi_{i+1} = X_0 \wedge [U]((X \rightarrow Y \vee \xi) \wedge (Y \rightarrow \psi) \wedge \bigwedge_{j=2}^{t} C_j^i)$. By the definition of M', we have that $V'(Y) = \{[a,b] : M,[a,b] \Vdash \psi\}$, and thus that for every interval $[a,b]$, $M',[a,b] \Vdash (X \rightarrow \psi)$. Consider now an interval $[c,d]$ such that $M',[c,d] \Vdash X$: by definition of M', this implies that $M',[c,d] \Vdash \xi \vee \psi$. By the semantics, we have that $M',[c,d] \Vdash \xi$ or $M',[c,d] \Vdash \psi$. By the definition of M', we can conclude that $M',[c,d] \Vdash Y$ if and only if $M',[c,d] \Vdash \psi$, and thus that $M',[c,d] \Vdash Y \vee \xi$, as required.
- The other boolean cases (rules 2–7) are similar and can be proved in a similar way.
- If rule 8 is applied, then $C_1^i = X \rightarrow \langle A \rangle \psi$ and the resulting formula is $\varphi_{i+1} = X_0 \wedge [U]((X \rightarrow \langle A \rangle Y) \wedge (Y \rightarrow \psi) \wedge \bigwedge_{j=2}^{t} C_j^i)$. By the definition of M', we have that $V'(Y) = \{[a,b] : M,[a,b] \Vdash \psi\}$, and thus that for every interval $[a,b]$, $M',[a,b] \Vdash (X \rightarrow \psi)$. Consider now an interval $[c,d]$ such that $M',[c,d] \Vdash X$: by definition of M', this implies that $M',[c,d] \Vdash \langle A \rangle \psi$. By the semantics, we have that there exists $e > d$ such that $M',[d,e] \Vdash \psi$. By the definition of M', this implies that $M',[d,e] \Vdash Y$, and thus that $M',[c,d] \Vdash \langle A \rangle Y$, as required.
- The remaining cases (rules 8–11) are similar to the case of rule 8 and thus skipped.

This concludes the proof. □

LEMMA 6 (COMPLETENESS). *Consider any* A*-formula* φ*. If the transformed formula* $X_0 \wedge [U](\bigwedge_{i=1}^{t} C_i)$ *is initially satisfiable, then* φ *is initially satisfiable.*

PROOF SKETCH. The proof is similar to the one of Lemma 5, and thus we only sketch it without entering in the details. In this case we start by assuming that the transformed formula $X_0 \wedge [U](\bigwedge_{i=1}^{t} C_i)$ is initially satisfiable and, by going backward with respect to the application of the rules, we show that the initial formula $\varphi_0 = X_0 \wedge [U](X_0 \rightarrow \varphi)$ is also initially satisfiable, using an induction argument similar to the one in the soundness proof. Once this is done, initial satisfiability of φ is trivial: given any model M for φ_0, we have that $M,[0,1] \Vdash X_0$. From the clause $X_0 \rightarrow \varphi$ we can conclude that $M,[0,1] \Vdash \varphi$ and thus that M is the model for φ we are looking for. □

THEOREM 7. *The transformation of* A*-formulas is sound and complete.*

At this point, we can complete the transformation τ_2 into clauses of three elements. This is quite straightforward. Consider any A-clause $(X \rightarrow L_1 \wedge L_2 \wedge \ldots \wedge L_n)$, where $L_1, \ldots, L_n$ are either literals or modal prefixes followed by a literal: it can be turned into a conjunction of two smaller clauses by simply substituting it by $(X \rightarrow L_1 \wedge Y) \wedge (Y \rightarrow L_2 \wedge \ldots \wedge L_n)$. By repeatedly applying this technique, and by eliminating the use of $\rightarrow$, we can finally state the following theorem.

THEOREM 8. *Given any* A*-formula* φ*, we have that the formula* $\tau_1(\tau_2(\varphi)) = X_0 \wedge [U](\bigwedge_{i=1}^{t} C_i)$ *is such that: 1. Each*

	$P^{F_1}_{\Phi_1}$			$P^{G_1}_{\Phi_1}$			$P^{G_1}_{\Phi_2}$		
	PSN	**NSGA-II**	**ENORA**	**PSN**	**NSGA-II**	**ENORA**	**PSN**	**NSGA-II**	**ENORA**
Minimum	0.1167	0.1000	0.0833	0.1167	0.1167	0.0833	0.5000	1.0000	0.5000
Maximum	0.1583	0.2083	0.1583	0.1667	0.2083	0.1583	1.0000	1.0000	1.0000
Mean	0.1401	0.1632	0.1060	0.1421	0.1640	0.1048	0.9950	1.0000	0.8050
S.D.	0.0193	0.0224	0.0160	0.0193	0.0272	0.0500	0.0500	0.0000	0.2193
C.I. Low	0.1363	0.1587	0.1028	0.1383	0.1586	0.1016	0.9851	1.0000	0.7615
C.I. High	0.1439	0.1676	0.1092	0.1459	0.1694	0.1079	1.0049	1.0000	0.8485

S.D = Standard Deviation of Mean   C.I. = Confidence Interval for the Mean (90%)

Table 3: Statistics for the Hypervolume obtained with 100 runs of algorithms for $P^{F_1}_{\Phi_1}$, $P^{G_1}_{\Phi_1}$, and $P^{G_1}_{\Phi_2}$.

C_i is a formula of the type $(L_1 \vee L_2 \vee L_3)$, where L_1, L_2, L_3 are either literals or modal prefixes followed by a literal; 2. φ is satisfiable if and only if $\tau_1(\tau_2(\varphi))$ is initially satisfiable.

Concluding, if we limit ourselves to problems in the form of conjunctions of three-elements A-clauses we still have a representative set of problems; moreover, the problem is scalable in nature, as it suffices to increase the number of clauses and the cardinality of the set of propositional letters to have bigger problems. The "valid vs. non-valid" balance is maintained by simply modulating two parameters: the more propositional letters, the easier is the problem (keeping the number of clauses fixed), and orthogonally, the more clauses, the more difficult it is (keeping the number of propositional letter fixed). So the problem set is parameterized by these two numbers, plus the probability of having a negative literal and the probability of having a modal one, to allows us also to control the "modal vs. non-modal" balance. It is important to stress that the introduction of a normal form only serves to the purpose of testing the algorithm, which instead is able to work with formulas of any kind written in the grammar of A.

Example. Consider the following (unsatisfiable) formula $\varphi = [A](p \to q) \wedge \langle A \rangle p \wedge [A]\neg q$. The transformation steps are the following:

1. $[A](p \to q) \wedge \langle A \rangle p \wedge [A]\neg q$;
2. $X_0 \wedge [U](X_0 \to ([A](p \to q) \wedge \langle A \rangle p \wedge [A]\neg q))$ (initial formula);
3. $X_0 \wedge [U]((X_0 \to [A](p \to q)) \wedge (X_0 \to (\langle A \rangle p \wedge [A]\neg q)))$ (rule 3);
4. $X_0 \wedge [U]((X_0 \to [A]Y) \wedge (Y \to (p \to q)) \wedge (X_0 \to (\langle A \rangle p \wedge [A]\neg q)))$ (rule 9);
5. $X_0 \wedge [U]((X_0 \to [A]Y) \wedge (Y \to (\neg p \vee q)) \wedge (X_0 \to (\langle A \rangle p \wedge [A]\neg q)))$ (rule 5);
6. $X_0 \wedge [U]((X_0 \to [A]Y) \wedge (Y \to (\neg p \vee q)) \wedge (X_0 \to \langle A \rangle p) \wedge (X_0 \to [A]\neg q))$ (rule 3);
7. $X_0 \wedge [U]((\neg X_0 \vee [A]Y) \wedge (\neg Y \vee \neg p \vee q) \wedge (\neg X_0 \vee \langle A \rangle p) \wedge (\neg X_0 \vee [A]\neg q))$ (reduction and elimination of $\to$).

As a final step, we translate $[U]$ into the original language, obtaining a set of 13 clauses (three clauses for every universally quantified clause) for this example.

6. EXPERIMENTAL RESULTS

In this section, we provide a report on the experimental results that we have obtained, with the aim of comparing the three selection mechanisms that have been used, namely, ENORA, NSGA-II, and PSN. We have separated the testing into two successive phases. We first focused our attention on a single, relatively complex, test problem, given in two different forms, and, second, as we have explained in the previous section, we focused on generating a meaningful set of problems in the form of universally quantified clauses.

Phase 1: evaluation of the algorithms' performance. We considered a single formula in two different forms. The first one, Φ_1, is composed by 15 formulas, over a set $\mathcal{AP}$ of seven propositional letters $p_0 \dots p_6$, and, as explained, we have been looking for the smallest model that satisfies the conjunction of all them. The second one, Φ_2, is the conjunction of the 15 formulas into a single one. Obviously, the two problems are logically equivalent, but, as we will see, they behave differently from the evolutionary point of view. The formulas used for this test are:

1. $\langle A \rangle p_i$, for every $i \in \{1, \dots, 4\}$;
2. $[A]\neg(p_i \wedge p_j)$, for every $i \neq j \in \{1, \dots, 4\}$;
3. $[A](p_3 \to [A]\bot)$;
4. $[A](p_2 \to \langle A \rangle p_5)$;
5. $[A]((p_0 \vee p_1) \to [A]\neg p_5)$;
6. $[A](p_1 \to \langle A \rangle p_6)$;
7. $[A](p_0 \to [A]\neg p_6)$,

Moreover, we have run the selection mechanisms with both the fitness functions F_1 and G_1, in order to analyze the different behaviors; in the following, we denote by P^F_Φ the problem $FSAT_A(\Phi)$ ($\Phi \in \{\Phi_1, \Phi_2\}$) solved by using the fitness function F ($F \in \{F_1, G_1\}$). The three selection mechanisms have been run 100 times each, with dynamically adapted parameters [29]; moreover, the number of evaluation has been set to 10000, while N (number of points in a candidate solution) ranges between 2 and 10, and the number of individuals in each population has been set to 100. In Tab. 3 we show the statistical values of the obtained *hypervolume*, that is, the fraction of the solution space that is not dominated by any of the solutions (see [10]), computed over the 100 runs for three of the four problems: $P^{F_1}_{\Phi_2}$ does not show significant values (and therefore it is not shown), and this means that none of the three algorithm was able to evolve, as the fitness function F_1 has not enough information to help the evolution when the number of formulas is too low (as explained in Section 4); this information is also graphically shown in Fig. 5. Fig. 4 shows the evolution of the mean hypervolume in the meaningful cases. These results justified the introduction of the fitness function G_1.

To perform a statistical comparison of the results obtained by the three algorithms (PSN, NSGA-II and ENORA) a confidence interval of 90% has been used for the mean ob-

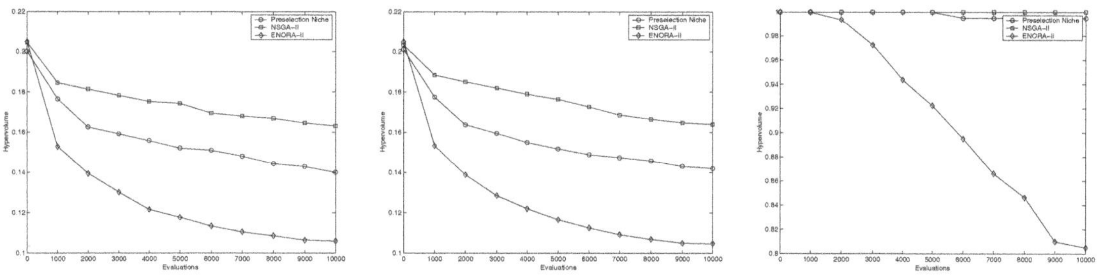

(a) (b) (c)

Figure 4: Mean hypervolume evolution for$P^{F_1}_{\Phi_1}$ (a), $P^{G_1}_{\Phi_1}$ (b), and $P^{G_1}_{\Phi_2}$ (c).

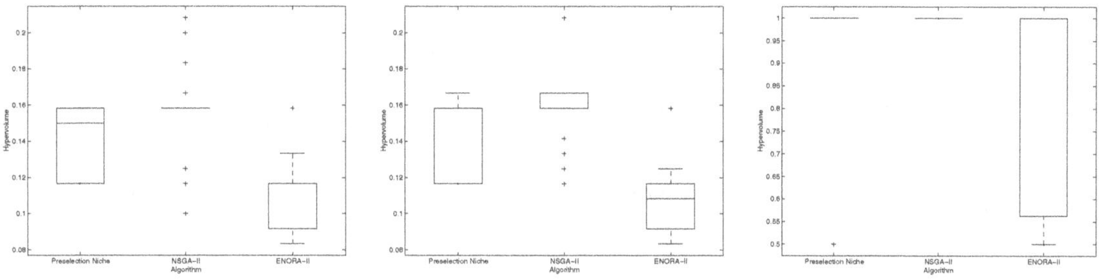

(a) (b) (c)

Figure 5: Box plot of the hypervolume for $P^{F_1}_{\Phi_1}$ (a), $P^{G_1}_{\Phi_1}$ (b), and $P^{G_1}_{\Phi_2}$ (c).

tained with a pair-wise *t-test* [25], as there is no dependency among the populations involved. As a result of the pair-wise comparisons, we can conclude that ENORA provides lower values than PSN and NSGA-II, and, in particular:

- Problem Φ_1 with fitness function F_1 ($P^{F_1}_{\Phi_1}$): 1. ENORA performs better than PSN; 2. ENORA performs better than NSGA-II; 3. PSN performs better than NSGA-II.
- Problem Φ_1 with fitness function G_1 ($P^{G_1}_{\Phi_1}$): 1. ENORA performs better than PSN; 2. ENORA performs better than NSGA-II; 3. PSN performs better than NSGA-II;
- Problem Φ_2 with fitness function G_1 ($P^{G_1}_{\Phi_2}$): 1. ENORA performs better than PSN 2. ENORA performs better than NSGA-II 3. PSN and NSGA-II have no significative statistical difference.

Explicit multiway test (e.g., Fisher LSD or Tukey Means) are being considered for comparisons in future works. The confidence intervals obtained show that ENORA provides lower values than PSN and NSGA-II. Therefore, the approximations obtained with ENORA are better, according to the hypervolume indicator. The t-test is robust with samples of more than 30 individuals [25] (we have 100), and so the results are significant, leading us to conclude that the differences between the hypervolume values obtained with the algorithms are statistically significant. The statistical analysis shows that, for the type of multi-objective problems being considered, a Pareto search based on the partition of the search space into radial slots is more efficient than general search strategies based solely on diversity functions, such as NSGA-II, or diversity schemes involving the explicit formation of niches, such as PSN.

From the practical point of view, a typical satisfiability problem consists of a set of requirements to be satisfied in conjunction (such as Φ_1), and, given the results obtained, we would choose the set of solutions given by ENORA by using G_1. The Pareto front (recall that F_1 ranges from 0 - not satisfied, to 1 - satisfied, while G_1 ranges over $\mathbb{N}$, where 0 is satisfied) in this case is given in Fig. 6(a). Among all solution, we choose the minimal one that satisfies all formulas on the interval [0, 1], and such a solution, depicted in Fig. 6(b), corresponds to the boldface values. Concluding, ENORA is the best algorithm for this particular problem, and G_1 behaves better than F_1, as it was able to give a result in a case in which F_1 was not.

Phase 2: evaluation of the algorithms' robustness. As we have detailed in the previous section, we generated a set of problems in terms of universally quantified clauses. We generated 72 problems. The first (easy) 36 problems have been defined with a number of propositional letters from 3 to 8, and with a number of clauses from 3 to 8 as well; so, for example, the first one has 3 letters and 3 clauses, the sixth has 8 letters and 3 clauses, and so on. In terms of difficulty of a single problem, as we have explained, we expected to see harder problems as the number of clauses goes up (for a fixed number of propositional letters), and simpler ones as the number of letters goes up (for a fixed number of clauses). The second set of 36 (harder) problems have been defined in the same way, whereas the number of letters goes from 10 to 15, and the number of clauses from 20 to 23. The other two parameters, namely, the probability of negation and the the probability of modal literal, have been maintained fixed, respectively, to 0.5 and 0.3. The results of this test are shown in Tab. 4 and Tab. 5. For every problem, we showed the best values of F_1 and G_2 over the 100 executions, and its corresponding N (dimension of the model); the symbol # indicates the ordering number of the problem (from 1 to 72), NV indicates the number

$\mathbf{P}^{G_1}_{\Phi_1}$	$\mathbf{P}^{F_1}_{\Phi_1}$	N
−4.000000	0.733333	2
−3.000000	0.800000	3
−2.000000	0.866667	4
−1.000000	0.933333	5
0.000000	**1.000000**	**6**

(a)

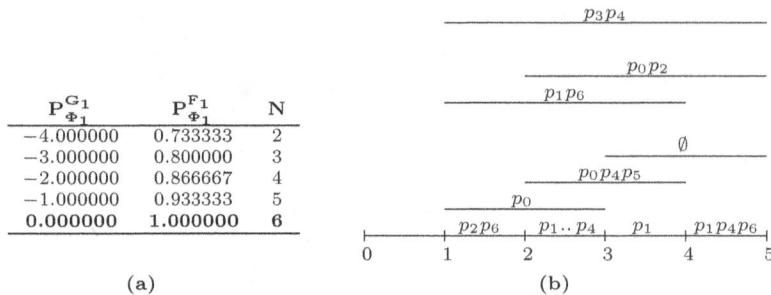

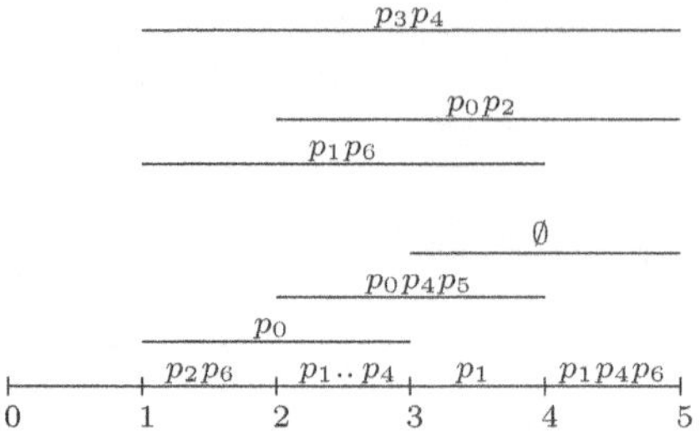

(b)

Figure 6: Pareto front obtained by ENORA w.r.t. G_1 and N (a), and solution (b).

of propositional variables, NC the number of universally quantified clauses, and NF the corresponding number of formulas (notice that, obviously, $NF = NC * 3 + 1$) Even if the problems have been generated in a randomly fashion, they turn out to be mostly satisfiable on very short models. There are, though, some cases in which our algorithms were not able to find a solution: as we expected, the more complex the problem is, the less likely is to see the problem solved. Now, we know that this approach is not complete, which means that, in the negative cases, we cannot ensure that the problem has no solution. On the other hand, for a single problem the fact that 100 evaluations were all negatives gives us a clear indication that most probably such a solution does not exist. We were able to see that, at least in the case of problem number 25, there is, as a matter of fact, no solution, and, therefore, the evolutionary approach gave us a correct answer. To see this, let us look into the details of problem number 25; it contains 19 formulas, that correspond to 6 universal clauses plus the initial one:

1. p_0;
2. $[U](\neg p_2 \vee \neg p_2 \vee \neg p_1)$;
3. $[U](p1 \vee p_2 \vee \neg[A]p_1)$;
4. $[U](\neg[A]p_0 \vee [A]p_0 \vee p_2)$;
5. $[U](p_1 \vee p_0 \vee p_0)$;
6. $[U](\langle A\rangle p_2 \vee p_1 \vee \neg[A]p_2)$;
7. $[U]([A]p_0 \vee \neg[A]p_2 \vee p_0)$.

If we try to satisfy this problem on a finite model of a single interval $[0, 1]$, we have that clause 4 (resp., 6) forces p_2 (resp., p_1) to be true on it, while clause 2 forbids both of them to hold on it, and we have a contradiction. Hence, any model for the formula will contain at least three points. Now, suppose that such a model exists, and consider the interval $[1, N-1]$, where N is dimension of the model. Clauses 4 and 6 force p_2 and p_1 to hold over $[1, N]$, in contradiction with clause 2. This implies that a finite model for this set of formulas cannot exists.

7. DISCUSSION AND CONCLUSIONS

Concluding, in this paper we identified a multi-objective optimization model for the problem $FSAT_A$, and we adapted three (elitist, Pareto-based, multi-objective) well-known algorithms (namely, NSGA-II, PSN, and ENORA) to solve it, proposing 5 specialized operators and two different fitness functions, F_1 (that we can call 'intuitive' version), and G_1 ('specialized' version). We compared the performances of the three algorithms by means of a statistical analysis on the hypervolume metric for a meaningful test problem (given in two different forms); we found that ENORA is the best algorithm for the considered problem, and that G_1 behaves better than F_1, as it was able to give a result in a case in which F_1 was not. Then, we tested the robustness of the algorithms by running it on a set of 72 randomly generated problems. The generation technique was adapted from the current available literature on random generation of logical formulas. Even so, most problem were actually satisfiable, and, therefore, the "valid vs. non-valid" balance was not as accurate as it should have been. Nevertheless, we found that this rate tends to 50% as the complexity of the problems raises up. In particular, observe that, on the one side, we could choose to modulate in a different way the two fixed parameters, namely, the probability of negation and of modal literal, but, most probably, the best solution is to design a formula schema in such a way that it is satisfiable over models no smaller than a given N, and scale it. Finally, we plan to compare these results with the available deterministic algorithms for satisfiability checking of A-formulas, and to explore this line of research in more expressive and complex interval temporal logic, for which classical decision algorithm are particularly difficult to implement and whose complexities are particularly high.

8. ACKNOWLEDGMENTS

We acknowledge the support from the Spanish fellowship program *'Ramon y Cajal' RYC-2011-07821* (G. Sciavicco).

9. REFERENCES

[1] L. Aksoy and E. Gunes. An evolutionary local search algorithm for the satisfiability problem. In *Proc. of the 14th Turkish conference on Artificial Intelligence and Neural Networks*, pages 185–193. Springer, 2006.

[2] J. F. Allen. Maintaining knowledge about temporal intervals. *Communications of the ACM*, 26(11):832–843, 1983.

[3] D. Bresolin, D. Della Monica, V. Goranko, A. Montanari, and G. Sciavicco. Decidable and Undecidable Fragments of Halpern and Shoham's Interval Temporal Logic: Towards a Complete Classification. In *Proc. of 15th Int. Conf. on Logic for Programming, Artificial Intelligence, and Reasoning*, volume 5330 of *LNCS*, pages 590–604. Springer, 2008.

[4] D. Bresolin, D. Della Monica, V. Goranko, A. Montanari, and G. Sciavicco. Metric propositional neighborhood logic: Expressiveness, decidability, and undecidability. In *Proc. of the 19th European Conference on Artificial Intelligence (ECAI)*, pages 695–700. IOS Press, 2010.

				PSN			NSGA-II			ENORA		
#	NV	NC	NF	F_1	G_1	N	F_1	G_1	N	F_1	F_2	N
1	3	2	7	0	1.000000	2	0	1.000000	2	0	1.000000	2
2	4	2	7	0	1.000000	2	0	1.000000	2	0	1.000000	2
3	5	2	7	0	1.000000	2	0	1.000000	2	0	1.000000	2
4	6	2	7	0	1.000000	2	0	1.000000	2	0	1.000000	2
5	7	2	7	0	1.000000	2	0	1.000000	2	0	1.000000	2
6	8	2	7	0	1.000000	2	0	1.000000	2	0	1.000000	2
7	3	3	10	0	1.000000	3	0	1.000000	3	0	1.000000	3
8	4	3	10	0	1.000000	2	0	1.000000	2	0	1.000000	2
9	5	3	10	0	1.000000	2	0	1.000000	2	0	1.000000	2
10	6	3	10	0	1.000000	2	0	1.000000	2	0	1.000000	2
11	7	3	10	0	1.000000	2	0	1.000000	2	0	1.000000	2
12	8	3	10	0	1.000000	2	0	1.000000	2	0	1.000000	2
13	3	4	13	0	1.000000	2	0	1.000000	2	0	1.000000	2
14	4	4	13	0	1.000000	2	0	1.000000	2	0	1.000000	2
15	5	4	13	0	1.000000	2	0	1.000000	2	0	1.000000	2
16	6	4	13	0	1.000000	2	0	1.000000	2	0	1.000000	2
17	7	4	13	0	1.000000	2	0	1.000000	2	0	1.000000	2
18	8	4	13	0	1.000000	2	0	1.000000	2	0	1.000000	2
19	3	5	16	0	1.000000	3	0	1.000000	3	0	1.000000	3
20	4	5	16	0	1.000000	2	0	1.000000	2	0	1.000000	2
21	5	5	16	0	1.000000	2	0	1.000000	2	0	1.000000	2
22	6	5	16	0	1.000000	2	0	1.000000	2	0	1.000000	2
23	7	5	16	0	1.000000	2	0	1.000000	2	0	1.000000	2
24	8	5	16	0	1.000000	2	0	1.000000	2	0	1.000000	2
25	3	6	19	−1	0.947368	2	−1	0.947368	2	−1	0.947368	2
26	4	6	19	0	1.000000	2	0	1.000000	2	0	1.000000	2
27	5	6	19	0	1.000000	3	0	1.000000	3	0	1.000000	3
28	6	6	19	0	1.000000	2	0	1.000000	2	0	1.000000	2
29	7	6	19	0	1.000000	2	0	1.000000	2	0	1.000000	2
30	8	6	19	0	1.000000	2	0	1.000000	2	0	1.000000	2
31	3	7	22	−1	0.954545	2	−1	0.954545	2	−1	0.954545	2
32	4	7	22	0	1.000000	2	0	1.000000	2	0	1.000000	2
33	5	7	22	0	1.000000	2	0	1.000000	2	0	1.000000	2
34	6	7	22	0	1.000000	2	0	1.000000	2	0	1.000000	2
35	7	7	22	0	1.000000	2	0	1.000000	2	0	1.000000	2
36	8	7	22	0	1.000000	3	0	1.000000	3	0	1.000000	3

Table 4: Results of the experiment for the 36 "easy" problems.

[5] D. Bresolin, D. Della Monica, V. Goranko, A. Montanari, and G. Sciavicco. Metric propositional neighborhood logics on natural numbers. *Software and Systems Modeling*, pages 1–20, 2011. 10.1007/s10270-011-0195-y.

[6] D. Bresolin, V. Goranko, A. Montanari, and G. Sciavicco. Propositional interval neighborhood logics: Expressiveness, decidability, and undecidable extensions. *Annals of Pure and Applied Logic*, 161(3):289 – 304, 2009.

[7] D. Bresolin, A. Montanari, and G. Sciavicco. An optimal decision procedure for Right Propositional Neighborhood Logic. *Journal of Automated Reasoning*, 38(1-3):173–199, 2007.

[8] D. Bresolin, P. Sala, and G. Sciavicco. On begins, meets, and before. *International Journal on Foundations of Computer Science*, 3(23):559–583, 2012.

[9] C. C. Coello, D. V. Veldhuizen, and G. Lamont. *Evolutionary Algorithms for Solving Multi-Objective Problems (Genetic Algorithms and Evolutionary Computation)*. Springer, 2002.

[10] K. Deb. *Multi-Objective Optimization Using Evolutionary Algorithms*. Wiley, 2001.

[11] H. Ellerweg. *A Study of Evolutionary Algorithms for the Satisfiability Problem*. PhD thesis, University of Paderborn, 2004.

[12] E. A. Emerson. Temporal and modal logic. In J. van Leeuwen, editor, *Handbook of Theoretical Computer Science*, volume B: Formal Models and Semantics, pages 995–1072. MIT Press, 1990.

[13] E. Giunchiglia, A. Tacchella, and F. Giunchiglia. Sat-based decision procedures for classical modal logics. *Journal of Automed Reasoning*, 28(2):143–171, 2002.

[14] A. Gómez-Skarmeta, F. Jiménez, and G. Sánchez. Improving interpretability in approximative fuzzy models via multiobjective evolutionary algorithms. *International Journal of Intelligent Systems*, 22(9):943–969, 2007.

[15] V. Goranko, A. Montanari, and G. Sciavicco. A road map of interval temporal logics and duration calculi. *Journal of Applied Non-Classical Logics*, 14(1–2):9–54, 2004.

[16] J. Gottlieb, E. Marchiori, and C. Rossi. Evolutionary algorithms for the satisfiability problem. *Evolutionary Computation*, 10(1):35–50, 2002.

[17] J. Halpern and Y. Shoham. A propositional modal logic of time intervals. *Journal of the ACM*, 38(4):935–962, 1991.

[18] I. Horrocks. Using an expressive description logic:

				PSN			NSGA-II			ENORA		
#	NV	NC	NF	F_1	G_1	N	F_1	G_1	N	F_1	F_2	N
37	10	20	61	−1	0.983607	2	−1	0.983607	2	−1	0.983607	2
38	11	20	61	0	1.000000	2	0	1.000000	2	0	1.000000	2
39	12	20	61	0	1.000000	2	0	1.000000	2	0	1.000000	2
40	13	20	61	0	1.000000	2	0	1.000000	2	0	1.000000	2
41	14	20	61	0	1.000000	2	0	1.000000	2	0	1.000000	2
42	15	20	61	0	1.000000	3	0	1.000000	3	0	1.000000	3
43	10	21	64	0	1.000000	2	0	1.000000	2	0	1.000000	2
44	11	21	64	0	1.000000	2	0	1.000000	2	0	1.000000	2
45	12	21	64	0	1.000000	2	0	1.000000	2	0	1.000000	2
46	13	21	64	0	1.000000	2	0	1.000000	2	0	1.000000	2
47	14	21	64	−1	0.984375	2	−1	0.984375	2	−1	0.984375	2
48	15	21	64	−1	0.984375	2	−1	0.984375	2	−1	0.984375	2
49	10	22	67	−1	0.985075	3	−1	0.985075	3	−1	0.985075	3
50	11	22	67	−1	0.985075	2	−1	0.985075	2	−1	0.985075	2
51	12	22	67	0	1.000000	2	0	1.000000	2	0	1.000000	2
52	13	22	67	0	1.000000	2	0	1.000000	2	0	1.000000	2
53	14	22	67	0	1.000000	3	0	1.000000	3	0	1.000000	3
54	15	22	67	0	1.000000	2	0	1.000000	2	0	1.000000	2
55	10	23	70	0	1.000000	2	0	1.000000	2	0	1.000000	2
56	11	23	70	0	1.000000	2	0	1.000000	2	0	1.000000	2
57	12	23	70	0	1.000000	2	0	1.000000	2	0	1.000000	2
58	13	23	70	0	1.000000	2	0	1.000000	2	0	1.000000	2
59	14	23	70	0	1.000000	2	0	1.000000	2	0	1.000000	2
60	15	23	70	−1	0.985714	2	−1	0.985714	2	−1	0.985714	2
61	10	24	73	−1	0.986301	2	−1	0.986301	2	−1	0.986301	2
62	11	24	73	0	1.000000	2	0	1.000000	2	0	1.000000	2
63	12	24	73	0	1.000000	2	0	1.000000	2	0	1.000000	2
64	13	24	73	0	1.000000	2	0	1.000000	2	0	1.000000	2
65	14	24	73	−1	0.986301	2	−1	0.986301	2	−1	0.986301	2
66	15	24	73	0	1.000000	2	0	1.000000	2	0	1.000000	2
67	10	25	76	0	1.000000	3	0	1.000000	3	0	1.000000	3
68	11	25	76	−1	0.986842	2	−1	0.986842	2	0	1.000000	3
69	12	25	76	0	1.000000	2	0	1.000000	2	0	1.000000	2
70	13	25	76	0	1.000000	3	0	1.000000	3	0	1.000000	3
71	14	25	76	0	1.000000	2	0	1.000000	2	0	1.000000	2
72	15	25	76	−1	0.986842	2	−1	0.986842	2	−1	0.986842	2

Table 5: Results of the experiment for the 36 "hard" problems.

Fact or fiction? In *Proc. of the 6th International Conference on Principles of Knowledge Representation and Reasoning (KR)*, pages 636–649, 1998.

[19] U. Hustadt and R. Schmidt. An empirical analysis of modal theorem provers. *Journal of Applied Non-Classical Logics*, 9(4):479–522, 1999.

[20] F. Jiménez, G. Sánchez, J. Cadenas, A. Gómez-Skarmeta, and J. Verdegay. Nonlinear optimization with fuzzy constraints by multi-objective evolutionary algorithms. In *Proc. of the 8th Computational Intelligence, Theory and Applications International Conference Fuzzy Days*, pages 713–722. Springer, 2004.

[21] H. Jin-Kao, F. Lardeux, and F. Saubion. Evolutionary computing for the satisfiability problem. In *Proc. of the 3rd European Workshop on Evolutionary Computation in Combinatorial Optimization*, volume 2611 of *LNCS*, pages 258–268. Springer, 2003.

[22] J. Koza, editor. *Solving Satisfiability Problems with Genetic Algorithms*, pages 206–213. Stanford Bookstore, 2000.

[23] D. D. Monica, D. Bresolin, A. Montanari, and G. Sciavicco. Interval temporal logics over finite linear orders:the complete picture. In *Proc. of the 20th European Conference on Artificial Intelligence (in publication)*, 2012.

[24] A. Montanari, G. Puppis, and P. Sala. Maximal decidable fragments of Halpern and Shoham's modal logic of intervals. In *ICALP (2)*, pages 345–356, 2010.

[25] M. O'Mahony. *Sensory Evaluation of Food: Statistical Methods and Procedures.* CRC Press, 1986.

[26] P. Patel-Schneider. Dlp system description. In *Proc. of the 11th Description Logics Workshop (DL)*, pages 87–89, 1998.

[27] P. Patel-Schneider and R. Sebastiani. A new general method to generate random modal formulae for testing decision procedures. *Journal of Artificial Intelligence Research*, 18:351–389, 2003.

[28] C. Rossi, E. Marchiori, and J. Kok. An adaptive evolutionary algorithm for the satisfiability problem. In *Proc. of the ACM symposium on Applied computing*, volume 1, pages 463–469. ACM, 2000.

[29] M. Srinivas and P. L.M. Adaptive probabilities of crossover and mutation in genetic algorithms. *IEEE Transactions on Systems, Man and Cybernetics*, 4(24):656–667, 1994.

[30] M. Stol and M. D. Rijke. Modal logic and local search. In *Proc. of the KI-2001 Workshop on Modal Logic and Artificial Intelligence*, 2001.

Explaining Optimization In Genetic Algorithms with Uniform Crossover

Keki M Burjorjee
Zite, Inc.
487 Bryant St.
San Francisco, CA 94107
kekib@cs.brandeis.edu

ABSTRACT

Hyperclimbing is an intuitive, general-purpose, global optimization heuristic applicable to discrete product spaces with rugged or stochastic cost functions. The strength of this heuristic lies in its insusceptibility to local optima when the cost function is deterministic, and its tolerance for noise when the cost function is stochastic. Hyperclimbing works by *decimating* a search space, i.e., by iteratively fixing the values of small numbers of variables. The *hyperclimbing hypothesis* posits that genetic algorithms with uniform crossover (UGAs) perform optimization by implementing *efficient* hyperclimbing. Proof of concept for the hyperclimbing hypothesis comes from the use of an analytic technique that exploits algorithmic symmetry. By way of validation, we present experimental results showing that a simple tweak inspired by the hyperclimbing hypothesis dramatically improves the performance of a UGA on large, random instances of MAX-3SAT and the Sherrington Kirkpatrick Spin Glasses problem. An exciting corollary of the hyperclimbing hypothesis is that a form of *implicit parallelism* more powerful than the kind described by Holland underlies optimization in UGAs. The implications of the hyperclimbing hypothesis for Evolutionary Computation and Artificial Intelligence are discussed.

Categories and Subject Descriptors

I.2.8 [**Computing Methodologies**]: Artificial Intelligence—*Problem Solving, Control Methods, and Search*; F.2 [**Theory of Computation**]: Analysis of Algorithms And Problem Complexity—*Miscellaneous*

General Terms

Algorithms; Theory

Keywords

Genetic Algorithms; Uniform Crossover; Hyperclimbing ; MAXSAT; Spin Glasses; Global Optimization; Decimation

1. INTRODUCTION

Optimization in genetic algorithms with uniform crossover (UGAs) is one of the deep mysteries of Evolutionary Computation. The use of uniform crossover causes genetic loci to be unlinked, i.e. recombine freely. This form of recombination was first used by Ackley [1] in 1987, and was subsequently studied by Syswerda [29], Eshelman et al. [8], and Spears & De Jong [28, 7], who found that it frequently outperformed crossover operators that induce tight linkage between genetic loci (e.g. one point crossover). It is generally acknowledged that the efficacy of uniform crossover, a highly disruptive form of variation, cannot be explained within the rubric of the *building block hypothesis* [11, 25, 9], the beleaguered, but still influential explanation for optimization in genetic algorithms with strong linkage between loci. Yet, no alternate, scientifically rigorous explanation for optimization in UGAs has been proposed. The hypothesis presented in this paper addresses this gap. This hypothesis posits that UGAs perform optimization by implicitly and efficiently implementing a global search heuristic called *hyperclimbing*.

Hyperclimbing is a *global decimation heuristic*, and as such is in good company. Global decimation heuristics are currently the state of the art approach to solving large instances of the Boolean Satisfiablity Problem (SAT) close to the SAT/UNSAT threshhold (i.e. hard instances of SAT) [18]. Conventional global decimation heuristics—e.g. Survey Propagation [20], Belief Propagation, Warning Propagation [3]—use message passing algorithms to compile statistical information about the space being searched. This information is then used to irrevocably fix the values of one, or a small number, of search space attributes, effectively reducing the size of the space. The decimation heuristic is then recursively applied to the resulting search space. Survey Propagation, perhaps the best known global decimation strategy, has been used along with *Walksat* [27] to solve instances of SAT with upwards of a million variables. The hyperclimbing hypothesis posits that in practice, UGAs also perform optimization by decimating the search spaces to which they are applied. Unlike conventional decimation strategies, however, a UGA obtains statistical information about the search space implicitly and efficiently by means other than message passing.

We stress at the outset that our main concern in this paper is scientific rigor in the Popperian tradition [24], not mathematical proof within a formal axiomatic system. To be considered scientifically rigorous, a hypothesis about an evolutionary algorithm should meet at least the following two criteria: First, it should be based on weak assumptions about the distribution of fitness induced by the ad-hoc representational choices of evolutionary algorithm users. This is nothing but an application of Occam's Razor to the domain of Evolutionary Computation. Second, the hypothesis should predict unexpected behavior. (Popper noted that the predictions that lend the most credence to a scientific hypothesis are the ones that augur phenomena that would not be expected in the absence of the hypothesis—e.g. gravitational lensing in the case of Einstein's theory of General Relativity)

The criteria above constitute the most basic requirements that a hypothesis should meet. But one can ask for more; after all, one has greater control over evolutionary algorithms than one does over, say, gravity. Recognizing this advantage, we specify two additional criteria. The first is upfront proof of concept. Any predicted behavior must be demonstrated unambiguously, even if it is only on a contrived fitness function. Requiring upfront proof of concept heads off a situation in which predicted behavior fails to materialize in the setting where it is most expected (cf. Royal Roads experiments [21]). Such episodes tarnish not just the hypothesis concerned but the scientific approach in general—an approach, it needs to be said in light of the current slant of theoretical research in evolutionary computation—that lies at the foundation of many a vibrant field of engineering. The second criterion is upfront validation of unexpected behavior on a non-contrived fitness function. Given the control we have over an evolutionary algorithm, it is reasonable to ask for a prediction of unexpected behavior on a real-world fitness function, and to require upfront validation of this prediction.

The hyperclimbing hypothesis, we are pleased to report, meets all of the criteria listed above. The rest of this paper is organized as follows: Section 2 provides an informal description of the hyperclimbing heuristic and lists the underlying assumptions about the distribution of fitness. A more formal description of the hyperclimbing heuristic appears in Appendix A. Section 3 outlines symmetries of uniform crossover and length independent mutation that we subsequently exploit. Section 4, presents proof of concept, i.e. it describes a stochastic fitness function—the Royal Roads of the hyperclimbing hypothesis—on which a UGA behaves as described. Then, by exploiting the symmetries of uniform crossover and length independent mutation, we argue that the adaptive capacity of a UGA scales extraordinarily well as the size of the search space increases. We follow up with experimental tests that validate this conclusion. In section 5 we make a prediction about the behavior of a UGA, and validate this prediction on large, randomly generated instances of MAX-3SAT and the Sherrington Kirkpatric Spin Glasses problem. We conclude in Section 6 with a discussion about the generalizability of the hyperclimbing hypothesis and its implications for Evolutionary Computation.

2. THE HYPERCLIMBING HEURISTIC

For a sketch of the hyperclimbing heuristic, consider a search space $S = \{0,1\}^\ell$, and a (possibly stochastic) fitness function that maps points in S to real values. Given some index set $\mathcal{I} \subseteq \{1,\ldots,\ell\}$, $\mathcal{I}$ partitions S into $2^{|\mathcal{I}|}$ subsets called *schemata* (singular schema) [21] as in the following example: suppose $\ell = 4$, and $\mathcal{I} = \{1,3\}$, then $\mathcal{I}$ partitions S into the subsets $\{0000, 0001, 0100, 0101\}$, $\{0010, 0011, 0110, 0111\}$, $\{1000, 1001, 1100, 1101\}$, $\{1010, 1011, 1110, 1111\}$. Partitions of this type are called *schema partitions.* Schemata and schema partitions can also be expressed using templates, for example, $0*1*$ and $\#*\#*$ respectively. Here the symbol $*$ stands for 'wildcard', and the symbol $\#$ denotes a defined bit. The *order* of a schema partition is simply the cardinality of the index set that defines the partition. Clearly, schema partitions of lower order are coarser than schema partitions of higher order. The *effect* of a schema partition is defined to be the variance of the expected fitness of the constituent schemata under sampling from the uniform distribution over each schema. So for example, the effect of the schema partition $\#*\#* = \{0*0*\,, 0*1*\,, 1*0*\,, 1*1*\}$ is

$$\frac{1}{4}\sum_{i=0}^{1}\sum_{j=0}^{1}(F(i*j*) - F(****))^2$$

where the operator F gives the expected fitness of a schema under sampling from the uniform distribution.

A hyperclimbing heuristic starts by sampling from the uniform distribution over the entire search space. It subsequently identifies a coarse schema partition with a non-zero effect, and limits future sampling to a schema in this partition with above average expected fitness. In other words the hyperclimbing heuristic fixes the *defining bits* [21] of this schema in the population. This schema constitutes a new (smaller) search space to which the hyperclimbing heuristic is recursively applied. Crucially, the act of fixing defining bits in a population has the potential to "generate" a detectable non-zero effects in schema partitions that previously might have had a negligible effects. For example, the schema partition $*\#***\#$ may have a negligible effect, whereas the schema partition $1\#*0*\#$ has a detectable non-zero effect. This observation is essential to understanding the hyperclimbing heuristic's capacity for optimization. A fitness distribution in which this structure is recursively repeated is said to have *staggered conditional effects.* The assumption that a fitness function induces staggered conditional effects is a weak assumption. In comparison, the building block hypothesis assumes unstaggered unconditional effects, and even this only when the defining bits of building blocks can be unlinked. This is a much stronger assumption because there are vastly more ways for effects to be staggered and conditional than unstaggered and unconditional. A more formal description of the hyperclimbing heuristic can be found in Appendix A, and a simple realization of a fitness function with staggered conditional effects appears in Section 4

At each step in its progression, hyperclimbing is sensitive, not to the fitness value of any individual point, but to the sampling means of relatively coarse schemata. This heuristic is, therefore, *natively* able to tackle optimization problems with stochastic cost functions. Considering its simplicity, the hyperclimbing heuristic has almost certainly been lighted upon by other researchers in the general field of discrete optimization. In all likelihood it was set aside each time because of the seemingly high cost of implementation for all but the smallest of search spaces or the coarsest of schema partitions. Given a search space comprised of ℓ binary variables, there are $\binom{\ell}{o}$ schema partitions of order o. For any fixed value of o, $\binom{\ell}{o} \in \Omega(\ell^o)$ [6]. The exciting finding presented in this paper is that UGAs can implement hyperclimbing cheaply for large values of ℓ, and values of o that are small, but greater than one.

3. SYMMETRIES OF A UGA

A genetic algorithm with a finite but non-unitary population of size N (the kind of GA used in practice) can be modeled by a Markov Chain over a state space consisting of all possible populations of size N [22]. Such models tend to be unwieldy [13] and difficult to analyze for all but the most trivial fitness functions. Fortunately, it is possible to avoid this kind of modeling and analysis, and still obtain precise results for non-trivial fitness functions by exploiting some simple symmetries introduced through the use of uniform crossover and length independent mutation.

A homologous crossover operator between two chromosomes of length ℓ can be modeled by a vector of ℓ random binary variables $\langle X_1, \ldots, X_\ell\rangle$ from which crossover masks are sampled. Likewise, a mutation operator can be modeled by a vector of ℓ random binary variables $\langle Y_1, \ldots, Y_\ell\rangle$ from which mutation masks are sampled. Only in the case of uniform crossover are the random variables $X_1, \ldots, X_\ell$ independent and identically distributed. This absence of *positional bias* [8] in uniform crossover constitutes a symmetry. Essentially, permuting the bits of all chromosomes using some permutation π before crossover, and permuting the bits back using π^{-1} after crossover has no effect on the dynamics of a UGA. If, in addition, the random variables $Y_1, \ldots, Y_\ell$ that model the mutation operator are independent and identically distributed (which is typical), and (more crucially) independent of the value of ℓ, then in the event that the values of chromosomes at some locus i are immaterial during fitness evaluation, the locus i can be "spliced out" without affecting allele dynamics at other loci. In other words, the dynamics of the UGA can be *coarse-grained* [4].

These conclusions flow readily from an appreciation of the symmetries induced by uniform crossover and length independent mutation. While the use of symmetry arguments is uncommon in EC research, symmetry arguments form a crucial part of the foundations of physics and chemistry. Indeed, according to the theoretical physicist E. T. Jaynes "almost the only known exact results in atomic and nuclear structure are those which we can deduce by symmetry arguments, using the methods of group theory" [16, p331-332]. Note that the conclusions above hold true regardless of the selection scheme (fitness proportionate, tournament, truncation, etc), and any fitness scaling that may occur (sigma scaling, linear scaling etc). "The great power of symmetry arguments lies just in the fact that they are not deterred by any amount of complication in the details", writes Jaynes [16, p331]. An appeal to symmetry, in other words, allows one to cut through complications that might hobble attempts to reason within a formal axiomatic system.

Of course, symmetry arguments are not without peril. However, when used sparingly and only in circumstances where the symmetries are readily apparent, they can yield significant insight at low cost. It bears emphasizing that the goal of foundational work in evolutionary computation is not pristine mathematics within a formal axiomatic system, but insights of the kind that allow one to a) explain optimization in current evolutionary algorithms on real world problems, and b) design more effective evolutionary algorithms.

4. PROOF OF CONCEPT

Providing unambiguous evidence that a UGA can behave as described in the hyperclimbing hypothesis is one of the explicit goals of this paper. To achieve this aim we introduce the *staircase function*, a "Royal Roads" for the hyperclimbing heuristic, and provide experimental evidence that a UGA can perform hyperclimbing on a particular parameterization of this function. Then, using symmetry arguments, we conclude that the running time and the number of fitness queries required to achieve equivalent results scale surprisingly well with changes to key parameters. An experimental test validates this conclusion.

Algorithm 1:
A staircase function with descriptor $(h, o, \delta, \sigma, \ell, L, V)$

Input: g is a chromosome of length ℓ

```
x ← some value drawn from the distribution N(0, 1)
for i ← 1 to h do
    if Ξ_{L_i:}(g) = V_i1 ... V_io then
        x ← x + δ
    else
        x ← x − (δ/(2^o − 1))
        break
    end
end
return x
```

Definition 1. *A staircase function descriptor is a 6-tuple $(h, o, \delta, \ell, L, V)$ where h, o and ℓ are positive integers such that $ho \leq \ell$, δ is a positive real number, and L and V are matrices with h rows and o columns such that the values of V are binary digits, and the elements of L are distinct integers in $\{1, \ldots, \ell\}$.*

For any positive integer ℓ, let $[\ell]$ denote the set $\{1, \ldots, \ell\}$, and let $\mathfrak{B}_\ell$ denote the set of binary strings of length ℓ. Given any k-tuple, x, of integers in $[\ell]$, and any binary string $g \in \mathfrak{B}_\ell$, let $\Xi_x(g)$ denote the string $b_1, \ldots, b_k$ such that for any $i \in [k]$, $b_i = g_{x_i}$. For any $m \times n$ matrix M, and any $i \in [m]$, let $M_{i:}$ denote the n-tuple that is the ith row of M. Let $\mathcal{N}(a, b)$ denote the normal distribution with mean a and variance b. Then the function, f, described by the staircase function descriptor $(h, o, \delta, \ell, L, V)$ is the stochastic function over the set of binary strings of length ℓ given by Algorithm 1. The parameters h, o, δ, and ℓ are called the *height, order, increment* and *span*, respectively, of f. For any $i \in [h]$, we define *step* i of f to be the schema $\{g \in \mathfrak{B}_\ell | \Xi_{L_{i:}}(g) = V_{i1} \ldots V_{io}\}$, and define *stage* i of f to be the schema $\{g \in \mathfrak{B}_\ell | (\Xi_{L_{1:}}(g) = V_{11} \ldots V_{1o}) \wedge \ldots \wedge (\Xi_{L_{i:}}(g) = V_{i1} \ldots V_{io})\}$.

The stages of a staircase function can be visualized as a progression of nested *hyperplanes*[1], with hyperplanes of higher order and higher expected fitness nested within hyperplanes of lower order and lower expected fitness. By choosing an appropriate scheme for mapping a high-dimensional hypercube onto a two dimensional plot, it becomes possible to visualize this progression of hyperplanes in two dimensions (Appendix B).

A step of the staircase function is said to have been *climbed* when future sampling of the search space is largely limited to that step. Just as it is hard to climb higher steps of a physical staircase without climbing lower steps first, it

[1]A hyperplane, in the current context, is just a geometrical representation of a schema [10, p 53].

Algorithm 2: Pseudocode for the UGA used. The population size is an even number, denoted N, the length of the chromosomes is ℓ, and for any chromosomal bit, the probability that the bit will be flipped during mutation (the per bit mutation probability) is p_m. The population is represented internally as an N by ℓ array of bits, with each row representing a single chromosome. GENERATE-UX-MASKS(x, y) creates an x by y array of bits drawn from the uniform distribution over $\{0, 1\}$. GENERATE-MUT-MASKS(x, y, z) returns an x by y array of bits such that any given bit is 1 with probability z.

```
pop ← INITIALIZE-POPULATION(N,ℓ)
while some termination condition is unreached do
    fitnessValues ← EVALUATE-FITNESS(pop)
    adjustedFitVals ← SIGMA-SCALE(fitnessValues)
    parents ← SUS-SELECTION(pop, adjustedFitVals)
    crossMasks ←GENERATE-UX-MASKS(N/2, ℓ)
    for i ← 1 to N/2 do
        for j ← 1 to ℓ do
            if crossMasks[i, j] = 0 then
                newPop[i, j] ← parents[i, j]
                newPop[i + N/2, j] ← parents[i + N/2, j]
            else
                newPop[i, j] ← parents[i + N/2, j]
                newPop[i + N/2, j] ← parents[i, j]
            end
        end
    end
    mutMasks ←GENERATE-MUT-MASKS(N, ℓ, p_m)
    for i ← 1 to N do
        for j ← 1 to ℓ do
            newPop[i, j] ← XOR(newPop[i, j],
            mutMasks[i, j])
        end
    end
    pop ← newPop
end
```

can be computationally expensive to identify higher steps of a staircase function without identifying lower steps first (Theorem 1, Appendix C). The difficulty of climbing step $i \in [h]$ *given* stage $i-1$, however, is non-increasing with respect to i (Corollary 1, Appendix C). We conjecture that staircase functions capture a feature— *staggered conditional effects*— that is widespread within the fitness functions resulting from the representational choices of GA users.

4.1 UGA Specification

The pseudocode for the UGA used in this paper is given in Algorithm 2. The free parameters of the UGA are N (the size of the population), p_m (the per bit mutation probability), and EVALUATE-FITNESS (the fitness function). Once these parameters are fixed, the UGA is fully specified. The specification of a fitness function implicitly determines the length of the chromosomes, ℓ. Two points deserve further elaboration:

1. The function SUS-SELECTION takes a population of size N, and a corresponding set of fitness values as inputs. It returns a set of N parents drawn by fitness proportionate *stochastic universal sampling* (SUS). Instead of selecting N parents by spinning a roulette wheel with one pointer N times, stochastic universal sampling selects N parents by spinning a roulette wheel with N equally spaced pointers just once. Selecting parents this way has been shown to reduce sampling error [2, 21].

2. When selection is fitness proportionate, an increase in the average fitness of the population causes a decrease in selection pressure. The UGA in Algorithm 2 combats this ill-effect by using sigma scaling [21, p 167] to adjust the fitness values returned by EVALUATE-FITNESS. These adjusted fitness values, not the raw ones, are used when selecting parents. Let $f_x^{(t)}$ denote the raw fitness of some chromosome x in some generation t, and let $\overline{f^{(t)}}$ and $\sigma^{(t)}$ denote the mean and standard deviation of the raw fitness values in generation t respectively. Then the *adjusted fitness* of x in generation t is given by $h_x^{(t)}$ where, if $\sigma^{(t)} = 0$ then $h_x^{(t)} = 1$, otherwise,

$$h_x^{(t)} = \min(0, 1 + \frac{f_x^{(t)} - \overline{f^{(t)}}}{\sigma^{(t)}})$$

The use of sigma scaling also causes negative fitness values to be handled appropriately.

4.2 Performance of a UGA on a class of Staircase Functions

Let f be a staircase function with descriptor $(h, o, \delta, \ell, L, V)$, we say that f is *basic* if $\ell = ho$, $L_{ij} = o(i-1) + j$, (i.e. if L is the matrix of integers from 1 to ho laid out row-wise), and V is a matrix of ones. If f is known to be basic, then the last three elements of the descriptor of f are fully determinable from the first three, and its descriptor can be shortened to (h, o, δ). Given some staircase function f with descriptor $(h, o, \delta, \ell, L, V)$, we define the *basic form* of f to be the (basic) staircase function with descriptor (h, o, δ).

Let ϕ^* be the basic staircase function with descriptor $(h = 50, o = 4, \delta = 0.3)$, and let U denote the UGA defined in section 4.1 with a population size of 500, and a per bit mutation probability of 0.003 (i.e, $p_m = 0.003$). Figure 1a shows that U is capable of robust optimization when applied to ϕ^* (We denote the resulting algorithm by U^{ϕ^*}). Figure 1c shows that under the action of U, the first four steps of ϕ^* go to fixation[2] in ascending order. When a step gets fixed, future sampling will largely be confined to that step—in effect, the hyperplane associated with the step has been climbed. Note that the UGA does not need to "fully" climb a step before it begins climbing the subsequent step (Figure 1c). Animation 1 in the online appendix[3] shows that the hyperclimbing behavior of U^{ϕ^*} continues beyond the first four steps.

[2]The terms 'fixation' and 'fixing' are used loosely here. Clearly, as long as the mutation rate is non-zero, no locus can ever be said to go to fixation in the strict sense of the word.

[3]Online appendix available at http://bit.ly/QFHNAk

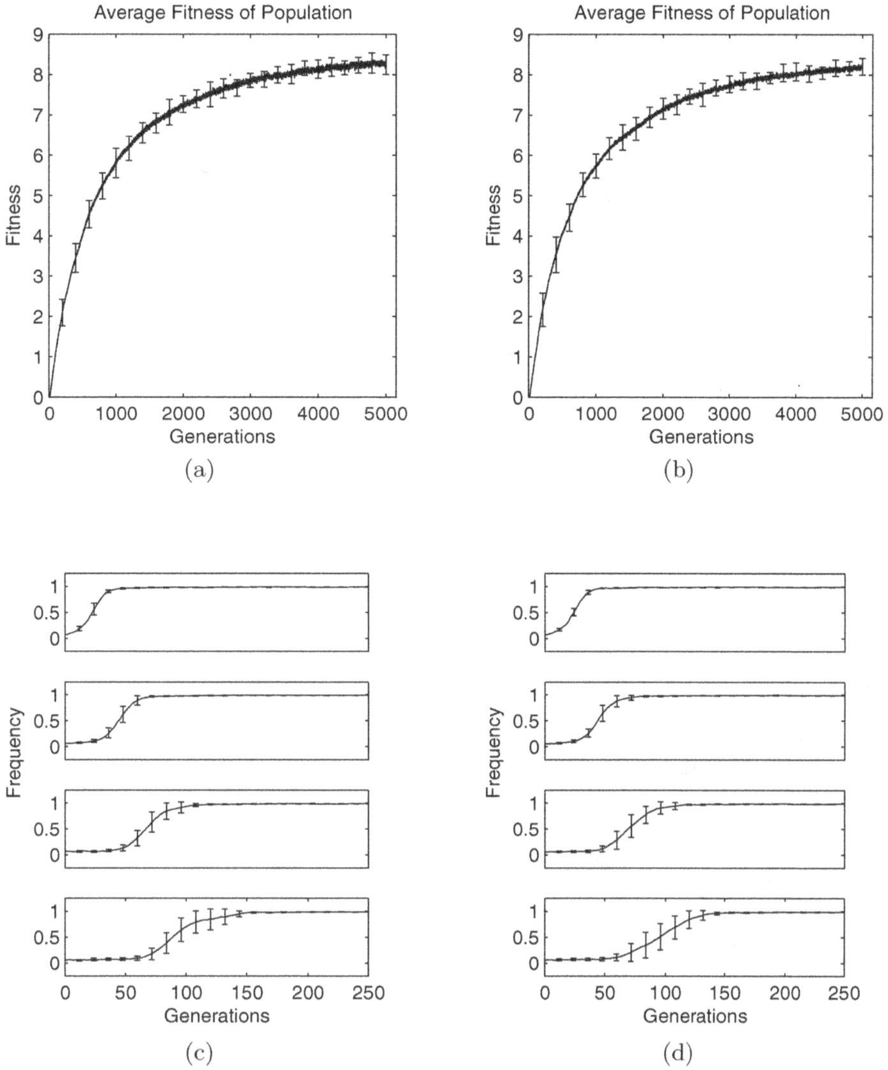

Figure 1: (a) The mean, across 20 trials, of the average fitness of the population of U^{ϕ^*} in each of 5000 generations. The error bars show five standard errors above and below the mean every 200 generations. (c) Going from the top plot to the bottom plot, the mean frequencies, across 20 trials, of the first four steps of the staircase function U^{ϕ^*} in each of the first 250 generations. The error bars show three standard errors above and below the mean every 12 generations. (b,d) Same as the plots on the left, but for U^{ϕ}

4.3 Symmetry Analysis and Experimental Confirmation

Let W be some UGA. For any staircase function f, and any $x \in [0,1]$, let $p^{(t)}_{(W^f,i)}(x)$ denote the probability that the frequency of *stage* i of f in generation t of W^f is x. Let f^* be the basic form of f. Then, by appreciating the symmetries between the UGAs W^f and W^{f^*} one can conclude the following:

Conclusion 1. *For any generation t, any $i \in [h]$, and any $x \in [0,1]$, $p^{(t)}_{(W^f,i)}(x) = p^{(t)}_{(W^{f^*},i)}(x)$*

This conclusion straightforwardly entails that to raise the average fitness of a population by some attainable value,

1. The expected number of generations required is *constant* with respect to the span of a staircase function (i.e., the query complexity is constant)
2. The running time[4] scales *linearly* with the span of a staircase function
3. The running time and the number of generations are unaffected by the last two elements of the descriptor of a staircase function

Let f be some staircase function with basic form ϕ^* (defined in Section 4.2). Then, given the above, the application of U to f should, discounting deviations due to sampling,

[4]Here, we mean the running time in the conventional sense, not the number of fitness queries.

produce results identical to those shown in Figures 1a and 1c. We validated this "corollary" by applying U to the staircase function ϕ with descriptor $(h = 50, o = 4, \delta = 0.3, \ell = 20000, L, V)$ where L and V were randomly generated. The results are shown in Figures 1b and 1d. Note that gross changes to the matrices L and V, and an increase in the span of the staircase function by two orders of magnitude did not produce any statistically significant changes. It is hard to think of another algorithm with better scaling properties on this non-trivial class of fitness functions.

5. VALIDATION

Let us pause to consider a curious aspect of the behavior of U^{ϕ^*}. Figure 1 shows that the growth rate of the average fitness of the population of U^{ϕ^*} decreases as evolution proceeds, and the average fitness of the population plateaus at a level that falls significantly short of the maximum expected average population fitness of 15. As discussed in the previous section, the difficulty of climbing step i given stage $i-1$ is non-increasing with respect to i. So, given that U successfully identifies the first step of ϕ^*, why does it fail to identify all remaining steps? To understand why, consider some binary string that belongs to the ith stage of ϕ^*. Since the mutation rate of U is 0.003, the probability that this binary string will still belong to stage i *after* mutation is 0.997^{io}. This entails that as i increases, U^{ϕ^*} is less able to "hold" a population within stage i. In light of this observation, one can infer that as i increases the sensitivity of U to the conditional fitness signal of step i given stage $i-1$ will decrease. This loss in sensitivity explains the decrease in the growth rate of the average fitness of U^{ϕ^*}. We call the "wastage" of fitness queries described here *mutational drag.*

To curb mutational drag in UGAs, we conceived of a very simple tweak called *clamping*. This tweak relies on parameters `flagFreqThreshold` $\in [0.5, 1]$, `unflagFreqThreshold` $\in [0.5,$ `flagFreqThreshold`$]$, and the positive integer `waitingPeriod`. If the *one-frequency* or the *zero-frequency* of some locus (i.e. the frequency of the bit 1 or the frequency of the bit 0, respectively, at that locus) at the beginning of some generation is greater than `flagFreqThreshold`, then the locus is flagged. Once flagged, a locus remains flagged as long as the one-frequency or the zero-frequency of the locus is greater than `unflagFreqThreshold` at the beginning of each subsequent generation. If a flagged locus in some generation t has remained constantly flagged for the last `waitingPeriod` generations, then the locus is considered to have passed our fixation test, and is not mutated in generation t. This tweak is called clamping because it is expected that in the absence of mutation, a locus that has passed our fixation test will quickly go to strict fixation, i.e. the one-frequency, or the zero-frequency of the locus will get "clamped" at one for the remainder of the run.

Let U_c denote a UGA that uses the clamping mechanism described above and is identical to the UGA U in every other way. The clamping mechanism used by U_c is parameterized as follows: `flagFreqThreshold` $= 0.99$, `unflagFreqThreshold` $= 0.9$, `waitingPeriod=200`. The performance of $U_c^{\phi^*}$ is displayed in figure 2a. Figure 2b shows the number of loci that the clamping mechanism left unmutated in each generation. These two figures show that the clamping mechanism effectively allowed U_c to climb all the stages of ϕ^*. Animation 2 in the online appendix shows the

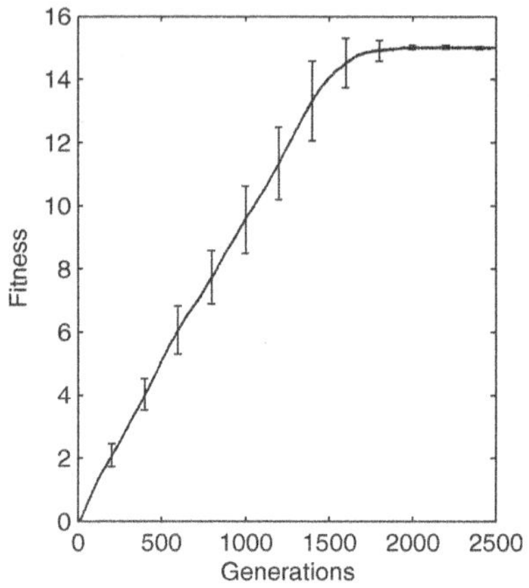

(a)

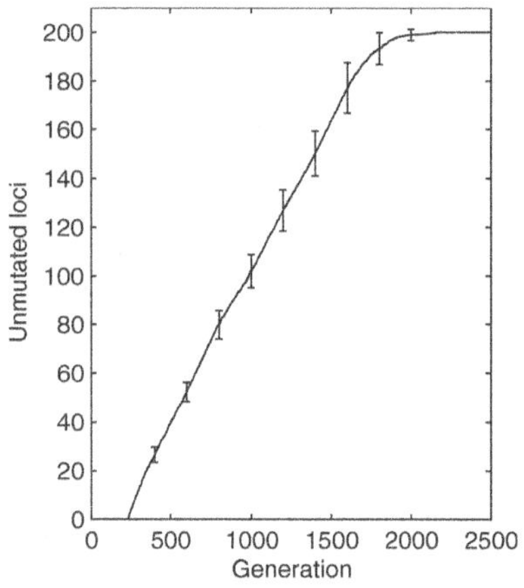

(b)

Figure 2: *(Top)* The mean (across 20 trials) of the average fitness of the UGA U_c on the staircase function ϕ^*. Errorbars show five standard errors above and below the mean every 200 generations. *(Bottom)* The mean (across 20 trials) of the number of loci left unmutated by the clamping mechanism. Errorbars show three standard errors above and below the mean every 200 generations

one-frequency dynamics, across 500 generations, of a single run of $U_c^{\phi^*}$. The action of the clamping mechanism can be seen in the absence of 'jitter' in the one-frequencies of loci that have been at fixation for 200 or more generations.

If the hyperclimbing hypothesis is accurate, then mutational drag is likely to be an issue when UGAs are applied to other problems, especially large instances that require the use of long chromosomes. In such cases, the use of clamping should improve performance. We now present the results of experiments where the use of clamping clearly improves the performance of a UGA on large instances of MAX-3SAT and the Sherrington Kirkpatrik Spin Glasses problem.

5.1 Validation on MAX-3SAT

MAX-kSAT [14] is one of the most extensively studied combinatorial optimization problems. An instance of this problem consists of n boolean variables, and m clauses. The *literals* of the instance are the n variables and their negations. Each clause is a disjunction of k of the total possible $2n$ literals. Given some MAX-kSAT instance, the value of a particular setting of the n variables is simply the number of the m clauses that evaluate to *true*. In a *uniform random* MAX-kSAT problem, the clauses are generated by picking each literal at random (with replacement) from amongst the $2n$ literals. Generated clauses containing multiple copies of a variable, and ones containing a variable and its negation, are discarded and replaced.

Let Q denote the UGA defined in section 4.1 with a population size of 200 ($N = 200$) and a per bit mutation probability of 0.01 (i.e., $p_m = 0.01$). We applied Q to a randomly generated instance of the Uniform Random 3SAT problem, denoted *sat*, with 1000 binary variables and 4000 clauses. Variable assignments were straightforwardly encoded, with each bit in a chromosome representing the value of a single variable. The fitness of a chromosome was simply the number of clauses satisfied under the variable assignment represented. Figure 3a shows the average fitness of the population of Q^{sat} over 7000 generations. Note that the growth in the maximum and average fitness of the population tapered off by generation 1000.

The UGA Q was applied to *sat* once again; this time, however, the clamping mechanism described above was activated in generation 2000. The resulting UGA is denoted Q_c^{sat}. The clamping parameters used were as follows: `flagFreqThreshold` $= 0.99$, `unflagFreqthreshold` $= 0.8$, `waitingPeriod` $= 200$. The average fitness of the population of Q_c^{sat} over 7000 generations is shown in Figure 3b, and the number of loci that the clamping mechanism left unmutated in each generation is shown in Figure 3c. Once again, the growth in the maximum and average fitness of the population tapered off by generation 1000. However, the maximum and average fitness began to grow once again starting at generation 2200. This growth coincides with the commencement of the clamping of loci (compare Figures 3b and 3c).

5.2 Validation on an SK Spin Glasses System

A Sherrington Kirkpatrick Spin Glasses system is a set of coupling constants J_{ij}, with $1 \leq i < j \leq \ell$. Given a configuration of "spins" $(\sigma_1, \ldots, \sigma_\ell)$, where each spin is a value in $\{+1, -1\}$, the "energy" of the system is given by

$$E(\sigma) = -\sum_{1 \leq i < j \leq \ell} J_{ij}\sigma_i\sigma_j$$

The goal is to find a spin configuration that minimizes energy. By defining the fitness of some spin configuration σ to be $-E(\sigma)$ we remain true to the conventional goal in genetic algorithmics of maximizing fitness. The coupling constants in J may be drawn from the set $\{-1, 0, +1\}$ or from the gaussian distribution $\mathcal{N}(0, 1)$. Following Pelikan et al. [23], we used coupling constants drawn from $\mathcal{N}(0, 1)$. Each chromosome in the evolving population straightforwardly represented a spin configuration, with the bits 1 and 0 denoting the spins $+1$ and -1 respectively[5]. The UGAs Q and Q_c (described in the previous subsection) were applied to a randomly generated Sherrington Kirkpatrik spin glasses system over 1000 spins, denoted *spin*. The results obtained (Figures 3d, 3e, and 3f) were similar to the results described in the previous subsection.

It should be noted that clamping by itself does not cause decimation. It merely enforces strict fixation once a high degree of fixation has already occurred along some dimension. In other words, clamping can be viewed as a decimation "lock-in" mechanism as opposed to a decimation "forcing" mechanism. Thus, the occurrence of clamping shown in Figure 3 entails the prior occurrence of decimation.[6]

The effectiveness of clamping demonstrated in this section lends considerable support to the hyperclimbing hypothesis. The method followed is out of Popper's Logic of Scientific Discovery [24]. A *scientific* theory allows one to make testable predictions of the form "if experiment X is executed, outcome Y will be observed". One is free to choose any X and Y as long as X entails Y given the theory. If the test is successful, the theory gains credibility in proportion to the extent to which Y is unanticipated in the absence of the theory. More support of this kind can be found in the work of Huifang and Mo [15] where the use of clamping improved the performance of a UGA on a completely different problem—optimizing the weights of a quantum neural network.

6. CONCLUSION

Simple genetic algorithms with uniform crossover (UGAs) perform optimization by implicitly exploiting the structure of fitness distributions that arise in practice through the ad-hoc representational choices of users. Two key questions are i) What is the nature of this structure? and ii) How is this structure exploited by the UGA? This paper offers a hypothesis that answers these and other questions about UGA behavior. The submitted hypothesis satisfies two basic requirements that one might expect any scientific hypothesis to meet—it relies only on assumptions that are weak, and it predicts an unexpected phenomenon. The hypothesis meets two additional requirements specific to the domain of evolutionary computation: It is accompanied by upfront proof of concept, and upfront validation. Section 4 unambiguously showed that a UGA can behave as described in the hyperclimbing hypothesis, and in Section 5, we predicted behavior that would not be expected in the absence of the hyperclimbing hypothesis, and validated this behavior on two non-contrived fitness functions: MAX-3SAT and the Sherrington Kirkpatrick Spin Glasses Problem.

An exciting corollary of the hyperclimbing hypothesis is that *implicit parallelism is real*. To be sure, what we mean

[5]Given an $n \times \ell$ matrix P representing a population of n spin configurations, each of size ℓ, the energies of the spin configurations can be expressed compactly as $-PJ^TP^T$ where J is an $\ell \times \ell$ upper triangular matrix containing the coupling constants of the SK system.

[6]A cautionary note: It may be tempting, based on the results obtained, to speculate that mutation hurts UGA performance, either on the fitness functions examined, or in general. After all, if one stops using mutation altogether, then the problem described at the beginning of Section 5—the problem addressed by clamping—disappears. We stress that this would be an incorrect conclusion to draw. A rigorous treatment of the specific roles played by mutation and uniform crossover in the implementation of hyperclimbing is beyond our current scope. We emphasize, however, that they *both* have parts to play. Briefly, mutation prevents the strict fixation of loci that have lost entropy to random drift, and uniform crossover allows hyperclimbing to proceed in parallel [5, Chapter 4].

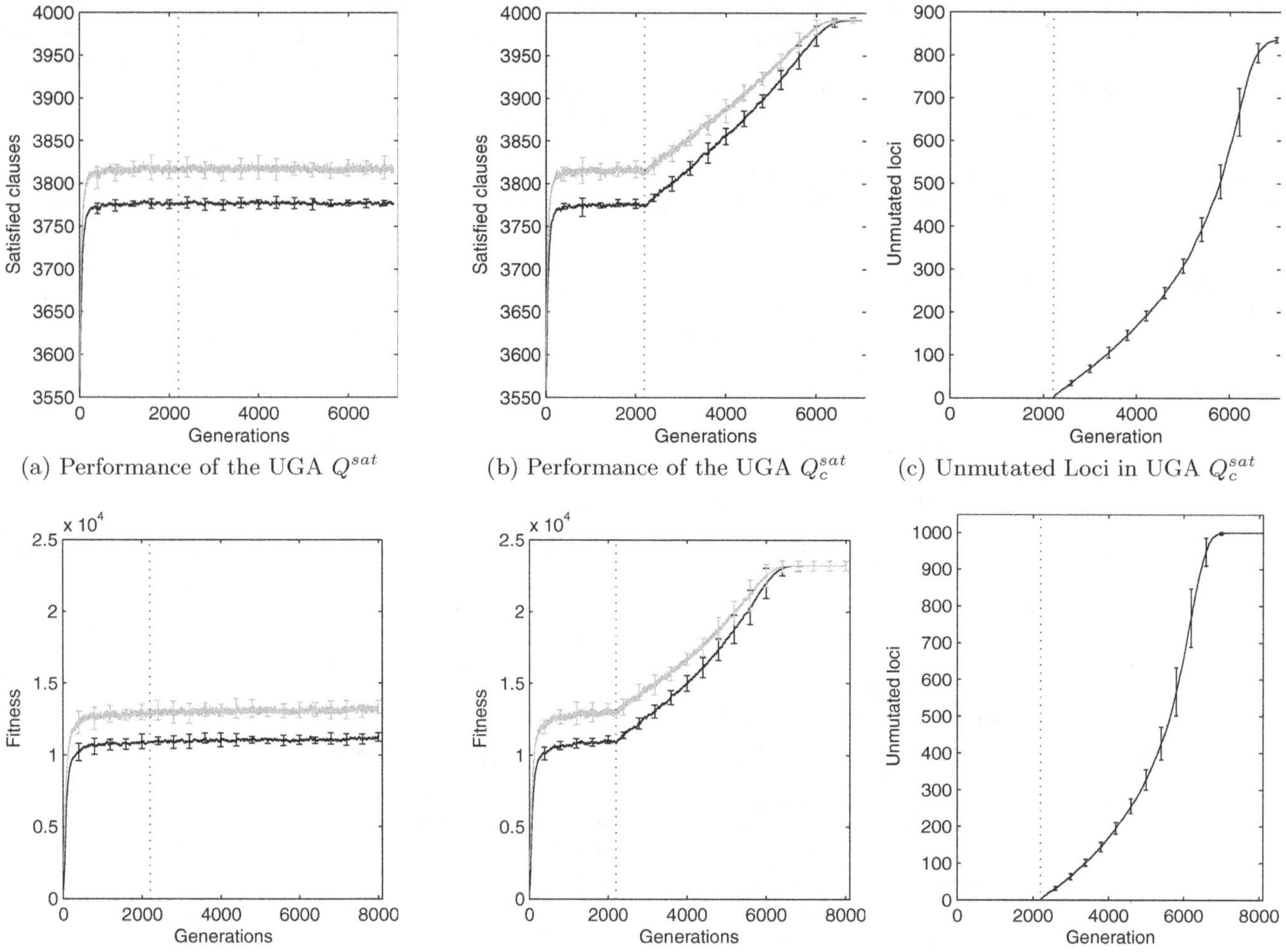

(a) Performance of the UGA Q^{sat} (b) Performance of the UGA Q_c^{sat} (c) Unmutated Loci in UGA Q_c^{sat}

(d) Performance of the UGA Q^{spin} (e) Performance of the UGA Q_c^{spin} (f) Unmutated Loci in UGA Q_c^{spin}

Figure 3: *(a,b)* The performance, over 10 trials, of the UGAs Q and the UGA Q_c on a randomly generated instance of the Uniform Random 3SAT problem with 1000 variables and 4000 clauses. The mean (across trials) of the average fitness of the population is shown in black. The mean of the best-of-population fitness is shown in blue. Errorbars show five standard errors above and below the mean every 400 generations. *(c)* The mean number of loci left unmutated by the clamping mechanism used by Q_c. Errorbars show three standard errors above and below the mean every 400 generations. The vertical dotted line marks generation 2200 in all three plots.*(d,e,f)* Same as above, but but for a randomly generated Sherrington Kirkpatrick Spin Glasses System over 1000 spins (see main text for details)

by implicit parallelism differs somewhat from what Holland meant. It is not the average fitness of coarse schemata that gets evaluated and acted upon in parallel, but the effects of vast numbers of coarse schema *partitions*. Significantly, the defining length of the schemata in these partitions need not be low. The implicit parallelism described in this paper is thus of a more powerful kind than that described by Holland. Readers seeking additional evidence of implicit parallelism in UGAs are referred to Chapter 3 of [5].

A second corollary is that the idea of a *hyperscape* is much more helpful than the idea of a landscape [30, 17] for understanding UGA behavior. Landscapes and hyperscapes are both just ways of geometrically conceptualizing fitness functions. Landscapes draw one's attention to the interplay between fitness and neighborhood structure, whereas hyperscapes focus one's attention on the *statistical* fitness properties of individual hyperplanes, and the spatial relationships between hyperplanes—lower order hyperplanes can *contain* higher order hyperplanes, hyperplanes can *intersect* each other, and disjoint hyperplanes belonging to the same hyperplane partition can be regarded as *parallel.* The use of hyperscapes for understanding GA dynamics originated with Holland [12] and was popularized by Goldberg [10]. Unfortunately, the use of hyperscapes tends to be associated with belief in the building block hypothesis. With the building block hypothesis falling into disrepute [9, 25], hyperscapes no longer enjoy the level of attention and interest they once did. The hyperclimbing hypothesis resurrects the hyperscape as a legitimate object of study, and posits that a hyperscape feature called *staggered conditional effects* is the key to understanding the UGA's capacity for optimization.

We see this paper as a foray into a new and exciting area of research. Much work remains:

- The hyperclimbing hypothesis needs to be fleshed out. Understanding the roles played by mutation and crossover in the implementation of hyperclimbing and understanding when a UGA will be deceived by a hyperscape are important goals.
- Predicting unexpected phenomena and validating them should be an ongoing activity. In the interest of making progress, scientists sacrifice certainty, and strike a bargain in which doubt can only be diminished, never eliminated. "Eternal vigilance" [26], in other words, becomes the cost of progress. This means that the work of the scientist, unlike that of the mathematician, is never quite done.
- Useful as it may be as an explanation for optimization in UGAs, the ultimate value of the hyperclimbing hypothesis lies in its *generalizability*. In a previous work [5], the notion of a unit of inheritance—i.e., a gene—was used to generalize this hypothesis to account for optimization in genetic algorithms with strong linkage between chromosomal loci (including genetic algorithms that do not use crossover). It may be possible for the hyperclimbing hypothesis to be generalized further to account for optimization in other kinds of evolutionary algorithms. whose search spaces consist of real valued vectors, trees, graphs, and instances of other data structures, as well as evolutionary algorithms that use complex variation operators (i.e. probabilistic model building genetic algorithms).
- The field's inability to identify a computation of some kind that evolutionary algorithms perform efficiently is a big reason why Evolutionary Computation remains a niche area within Artificial Intelligence. The realization that implicit parallelism is real has the potential to address this shortcoming. The field of Machine Learning, in particular, stands to benefit from advances in EC. Most machine learning problems reduce to optimization problems, so a new appreciation of how large-scale, general-purpose global optimization can be efficiently implemented should be of interest to researchers in this field. Reaching out to this and other sub-communities in ways that resonate is a priority.
- Last and most importantly, the numerous implications of the hyperclimbing hypothesis for the construction of more effective representations and evolutionary algorithms needs to be explored. The simplicity of the hyperclimbing hypothesis has us particularly excited. Staggered conditional effects and implicit parallelism are easy concepts to grasp, and offer a rich set of avenues to explore (branching and backtracking in hyperspace are two immediate ideas). We are curious to see what folks come up with.

The online appendix is available at `http://bit.ly/QFHNAk`

7. REFERENCES

[1] D.H. Ackley. *A connectionist machine for genetic hillclimbing*. Kluwer Academic Publishers, 1987.

[2] James E. Baker. Adaptive selection methods for genetic algorithms. In John J. Grefenstette, editor, *Proceedings of the First International Conference on Genetic Algorithms and Their Applications*. Lawrence Erlbaum Associates, Publishers, 1985.

[3] Alfredo Braunstein, Marc Mézard, and Riccardo Zecchina. Survey propagation: an algorithm for satisfiability. *CoRR*, cs.CC/0212002, 2002.

[4] Keki Burjorjee. Sufficient conditions for coarse-graining evolutionary dynamics. In *Foundations of Genetic Algorithms 9 (FOGA IX)*, 2007.

[5] K.M. Burjorjee. *Generative Fixation: A Unifed Explanation for the Adaptive Capacity of Simple Recombinative Genetic Algorithms*. PhD thesis, Brandeis University, 2009.

[6] T. H. Cormen, C. H. Leiserson, and R. L. Rivest. *Introduction to Algorithms*. McGraw-Hill, 1990.

[7] Kenneth A De Jong and William M Spears. A formal analysis of the role of multi-point crossover in genetic algorithms. *Annals of Mathematics and Artificial Intelligence*, 5(1):1–26, 1992.

[8] L.J. Eshelman, R.A. Caruana, and J.D. Schaffer. Biases in the crossover landscape. *Proceedings of the third international conference on Genetic algorithms table of contents*, pages 10–19, 1989.

[9] D. B. Fogel. *Evolutionary Computation : Towards a New Philosophy of Machine Intelligence*. IEEE press, 2006.

[10] David E. Goldberg. *Genetic Algorithms in Search, Optimization & Machine Learning*. Addison-Wesley, Reading, MA, 1989.

[11] David E. Goldberg. *The Design Of Innovation*. Kluwer Academic Publishers, 2002.

[12] John H. Holland. *Adaptation in Natural and Artificial Systems: An Introductory Analysis with Applications to Biology, Control, and Artificial Intelligence*. MIT Press, 1975.

[13] John H. Holland. Building blocks, cohort genetic algorithms, and hyperplane-defined functions. *Evolutionary Computation*, 8(4):373–391, 2000.

[14] Holger H. Hoos and Thomas Stützle. *Stochastic Local Search: Foundations and Applications*. Morgan Kaufmann, 2004.

[15] Li Huifang and Li Mo. A new method of image compression based on quantum neural network. In *International Conference of Information Science and Management Engineering*, pages p567 – 570, 2010.

[16] E.T. Jaynes. *Probability Theory: The Logic of Science*. Cambridge University Press, 2007.

[17] S.A. Kauffman. *The Origins of Order: Self-Organization and Selection in Evolution*. Biophysical Soc, 1993.

[18] L. Kroc, A. Sabharwal, and B. Selman. Message-passing and local heuristics as decimation strategies for satisfiability. In *Proceedings of the 2009 ACM symposium on Applied Computing*, pages 1408–1414. ACM, 2009.

[19] J. T. Langton, A. A. Prinz, and T. J. Hickey. Combining pixelization and dimensional stacking. In *Advances in Visual Computing*, pages II: 617–626, 2006.

[20] M. Mézard, G. Parisi, and R. Zecchina. Analytic and algorithmic solution of random satisfiability problems. *Science*, 297(5582):812–815, 2002.

[21] Melanie Mitchell. *An Introduction to Genetic Algorithms*. The MIT Press, Cambridge, MA, 1996.

[22] A.E. Nix and M.D. Vose. Modeling genetic algorithms with Markov chains. *Annals of Mathematics and Artificial Intelligence*, 5(1):79–88, 1992.

[23] Martin Pelikan. Finding ground states of sherrington-kirkpatrick spin glasses with hierarchical boa and genetic algorithms. In *GECCO 2008: Proceedings of the 10th annual conference on Genetic and Evolutionary Computation Conference*, 2008.

[24] Karl Popper. *The Logic Of Scientific Discovery*. Routledge, 2007.

[25] C.R. Reeves and J.E. Rowe. *Genetic Algorithms: Principles and Perspectives: a Guide to GA Theory*. Kluwer Academic Publishers, 2003.

[26] Alexander Rosenbluth and Norbert Wiener. Purposeful and non-purposeful behavior. *Philosophy of Science*, 18, 1951.

[27] B. Selman, H. Kautz, and B. Cohen. Local search strategies for satisfiability testing. *Cliques, coloring, and satisfiability: Second DIMACS implementation challenge*, 26:521–532, 1993.

[28] William M. Spears and Kenneth De Jong. On the virtues of parameterized uniform crossover. In R. K. Belew and L. B. Booker, editors, *Proc. of the Fourth Int. Conf. on Genetic Algorithms*, pages 230–236, San Mateo, CA, 1991. Morgan Kaufmann.

[29] G. Syswerda. Uniform crossover in genetic algorithms. In J. D. Schaffer, editor, *Proceeding of the Third International Conference on Genetic Algorithms*. Morgan Kaufmann, 1989.

[30] Sewall Wright. The roles of mutation, inbreeding, crossbreeding and selection in evolution. In *Proceedings of the Sixth Annual Congress of Genetics*, 1932.

APPENDIX

A. THE HYPERCLIMBING HEURISTIC: FORMAL DESCRIPTION

Introducing new terminology and notation where necessary, we present a formal description of the hyperclimbing heuristic. For any positive integer ℓ, let $[\ell]$ denote the set $\{1,\ldots,\ell\}$, and let $\mathfrak{B}_\ell$ denote the set of all binary strings of length ℓ. For any binary string g, let g_i denote the ith bit of g. For any set X, let $\mathbb{P}^{\mathrm{X}}$ denote the power set of X. Let $\mathbb{S}_\ell$ and $\mathbb{SP}_\ell$ denote the set of all schemata and schema partitions, respectively, of the set $\mathfrak{B}_\ell$. We define the *schema model set of* ℓ, denoted $\mathbb{SM}_\ell$, to be the set $\{h : D \to \{0,1\} | D \in \mathbb{P}^{[l]}\}$. Each each member of this set is a mapping from the defining bits of a schema to their values.

Given some schema $\gamma \subset \mathfrak{B}_\ell$, let $\pi(\gamma)$ denote the set $\{i \in [\ell] \,|\, \forall x, y \in \gamma, x_i = y_i\}$. We define a *schema modeling function* $\mathbf{SMF}_\ell : \mathbb{S}_\ell \to \mathbb{SM}_\ell$ as follows: for any $\gamma \in \mathbb{S}_\ell$, $\mathbf{SMF}_\ell$ maps γ to the function $h : \pi(\gamma) \to \{0,1\}$ such that for any $g \in \gamma$ and any $i \in \pi(\gamma)$, $h(i) = g_i$. We define a *schema partition modeling function* $\mathbf{SPMF}_\ell : \mathbb{SP}_\ell \to \mathbb{P}^{[\ell]}$ as follows: for any $\Gamma \in \mathbb{SP}_\ell$, $\mathbf{SPMF}_\ell(\Gamma) = \pi(\gamma)$, where $\gamma \in \Gamma$. As $\pi(\psi) = \pi(\xi)$ for all $\psi, \xi \in \Gamma$, the schema partition modeling function is well defined. It is easily seen that $\mathbf{SPF}_\ell$ and $\mathbf{SPMF}_\ell$ are both bijective. For any schema model $h \in \mathbb{SM}_\ell$, we denote $\mathbf{SMF}_\ell^{-1}(h)$ by $[\![h]\!]_\ell$. Likewise, for any "schema partition model" $S \in \mathbb{P}^{[\ell]}$ we denote $\mathbf{SPMF}_\ell^{-1}(S)$ by $[\![S]\!]_\ell$. Going in the forward direction, for any schema $\gamma \in \mathbb{S}_\ell$, we denote $\mathbf{SMF}_\ell(\gamma)$ by $\langle\gamma\rangle$. Likewise, for any schema partition $\Gamma \in \mathbb{SP}_\ell$, we denote $\mathbf{SPMF}_\ell(\Gamma)$ by $\langle\Gamma\rangle$. We drop the ℓ when going in this direction, because its value in each case is ascertainable from the operand. For any schema partition Γ, and any schema $\gamma \in \Gamma$, the *order* of Γ, and the *order* of γ is $|\langle\Gamma\rangle|$.

For any two schema partitions $\Gamma_1, \Gamma_2 \in \mathbb{SP}_\ell$, we say that Γ_1 and Γ_2 are *orthogonal* if the models of Γ_1 and Γ_2 are disjoint (i.e., $\langle\Gamma_1\rangle \cap \langle\Gamma_2\rangle = \emptyset$). Let Γ_1 and Γ_2 be orthogonal schema partitions in $\mathbb{SP}_\ell$, and let $\gamma_1 \in \Gamma_1$ and $\gamma_2 \in \Gamma_2$ be two schemata. Then the concatenation $\Gamma_1\Gamma_2$ denotes the schema partition $[\![\langle\Gamma_1\rangle \cup \langle\Gamma_2\rangle]\!]_\ell$, and the concatenation $\gamma_1\gamma_2$ denotes the schema $[\![h : \langle\Gamma_1\rangle \cup \langle\Gamma_2\rangle \to \{0,1\}]\!]_\ell$ such that for any $i \in \langle\Gamma_1\rangle$, $h(i) = \langle\gamma_1\rangle(i)$, and for any $i \in \langle\Gamma_2\rangle$, $h(i) = \langle\gamma_2\rangle(i)$. Since $\langle\Gamma_1\rangle$ and $\langle\Gamma_2\rangle$ are disjoint, $\gamma_1\gamma_2$ is well defined. Let Γ_1 and Γ_2 be orthogonal schema partitions, and let $\gamma_1 \in \Gamma_1$ be some schema. Then $\gamma.\Gamma_2$ denotes the set $\{\gamma\xi \in \Gamma_1\Gamma_2 \,|\, \xi \in \Gamma_2\}$.

Given some (possibly stochastic) fitness function f over the set $\mathfrak{B}_\ell$, and some schema $\gamma \in \mathbb{S}_\ell$, we define the fitness of γ, denoted $F_\gamma^{(f)}$, to be a random variable that gives the fitness value of a binary string drawn from the uniform distribution over γ. For any schema partition $\Gamma \in \mathbb{SP}_\ell$, we define the *effect* of Γ, denoted $\mathbf{Effect}[\Gamma]$, to be the variance[7] of the expected fitness values of the schemata of Γ. In other words,

$$\mathbf{Effect}[\Gamma] = 2^{-|\langle\Gamma\rangle|} \sum_{\gamma\in\Gamma} \left(\mathbf{E}[F_\gamma^{(f)}] - 2^{-|\langle\Gamma\rangle|} \sum_{\xi\in\Gamma} \mathbf{E}[F_\xi^{(f)}] \right)^2$$

Let $\Gamma_1, \Gamma_2 \in \mathbb{SP}_\ell$ be schema partitions such that $\langle\Gamma_1\rangle \subset \langle\Gamma_2\rangle$. It is easily seen that $\mathbf{Effect}[\Gamma_1] \leq \mathbf{Effect}[\Gamma_2]$. With equality if and only if $F_{\gamma_2}^{(f)} = F_{\gamma_1}^{(f)}$ for all schemata $\gamma_1 \in \Gamma_1$ and $\gamma_2 \in \Gamma_2$ such that $\gamma_2 \subset \gamma_1$. This condition is unlikely to arise in practice; therefore, for all practical purposes, the effect of a given schema partition decreases as the partition becomes coarser. The schema partition $[\![\,[l]\,]\!]_\ell$ has the maximum effect. Let Γ and Ψ be two orthogonal schema partitions, and let $\gamma \in \Gamma$ be some schema . We define the conditional effect of Ψ *given* γ, denoted $\mathbf{Effect}[\Psi|\gamma]$, as follows:

$$\mathbf{Effect}[\Psi|\gamma] = 2^{-|\langle\Psi\rangle|} \sum_{\psi\in\Psi} \left(\mathbf{E}[F_{\gamma\psi}^{(f)}] - 2^{-|\langle\Psi\rangle|} \sum_{\xi\in\Psi} \mathbf{E}[F_{\gamma\xi}^{(f)}] \right)^2$$

A hyperclimbing heuristic works by evaluating the fitness of samples drawn initially from the uniform distribution over the search space. It finds a coarse schema partition Γ with a non-zero effect, and limits future sampling to some schema γ of this partition whose average sampling fitness is greater than the mean of the average sampling fitness values of the schemata in Γ. By limiting future sampling in this way, the heuristic raises the expected fitness of all future samples. The heuristic limits future sampling to some schema

[7] We use variance because it is a well known measure of dispersion. Other measures of dispersion may well be substituted here without affecting the discussion

by fixing the defining bits [21] of that schema in all future samples. The unfixed loci constitute a new (smaller) search space to which the hyperclimbing heuristic is then recursively applied. Crucially, coarse schema partitions orthogonal to Γ that have undetectable *unconditional* effects, may have detectable effects when conditioned by γ.

B. VISUALIZING STAIRCASE FUNCTIONS

The following addressing scheme allows us to project a high dimensional fitness function onto a two dimensional plot.

DEFINITION 2. *A* refractal addressing system *is a tuple* (m, n, X, Y), *where* m *and* n *are positive integers and* X *and* Y *are matrices with* m *rows and* n *columns such that the elements in* X *and* Y *are distinct positive integers from the set* $[2mn]$, *such that for any* $k \in [2mn]$, k *is in* $X \iff k$ *is not in* Y *(i.e. the elements of* $[2mn]$ *are evenly split between* X *and* Y*).*

A refractal addressing system (m, o, X, Y) determines how the set $\mathfrak{B}_{2mn}$ gets mapped onto a $2^{mn} \times 2^{mn}$ grid of pixels. For any bitstring $g \in \mathfrak{B}_{2mn}$ the xy-address (a tuple of two values, each between 1 and 2^{mn}) of the pixel representing g is given by Algorithm 3.

Example: Let $(h = 4, o = 2, \delta = 3, \ell = 16, L, V)$ be the descriptor of a staircase function f, such that

$$V = \begin{bmatrix} 1 & 0 \\ 0 & 1 \\ 0 & 0 \\ 1 & 1 \end{bmatrix}$$

Let $A = (m = 4, n = 2, X, Y)$ be a refractal addressing system such that $X_{1:} = L_{1:}$, $Y_{1:} = L_{2:}$, $X_{2:} = L_{3:}$, and $Y_{2:} = L_{4:}$. A *refractal plot*[8] of f is shown in Figure 4a.

This image was generated by querying f with all 2^{16} elements of $\mathfrak{B}_{16}$, and plotting the fitness value of each bitstring as a greyscale pixel at the bitstring's refractal address under the addressing system A. The fitness values returned by f have been scaled to use the full range of possible greyscale shades.[9] Lighter shades signify greater fitness. The four stages of f can easily be discerned.

Suppose we generate another refractal plot of f using the same addressing system A, but a different random number generator seed; because f is stochastic, the greyscale value of any pixel in the resulting plot will then most likely differ from that of its homolog in the plot shown in Figure 4a. Nevertheless, our ability to discern the stages of f would not be affected. In the same vein, note that when specifying A, we have not specified the values of the last two rows of X and Y; given the definition of f it is easily seen that these values are immaterial to the discernment of its "staircase structure".

On the other hand, the values of the first two rows of X and Y are highly relevant to the discernment of this structure. Figure 4b shows a refractal plot of f that was obtained using a refractal addressing system $A' = (m = 4, n = 2, X', Y')$ such that $X'_{4:} = L_{1:}$, $Y'_{4:} = L_{2:}$, $X'_{3:} = L_{3:}$, and $Y'_{3:} = L_{4:}$. Nothing remotely resembling a staircase is visible in this plot.

[8]The term "refractal plot" describes the images that result when *dimensional stacking* is combined with *pixelation* [19].
[9]We used the Matlab function `imagesc()`

Algorithm 3: The algorithm for determining the (x, y)-address of a chromosome under the refractal addressing system (m, n, X, Y). The function BIN-TO-INT returns the integer value of a binary string.

Input: g is a chromosome of length $2mn$

$granularity \leftarrow 2^{mn}/2^n$
$x \leftarrow 1$
$y \leftarrow 1$
for $i \leftarrow 1$ *to* m **do**
  $x \leftarrow x + granularity * \text{BIN-TO-INT}\ (\Xi_{X_{i:}}(g))$
  $y \leftarrow y + granularity * \text{BIN-TO-INT}\ (\Xi_{Y_{i:}}(g))$
  $granularity \leftarrow granularity/2^n$
end
return x, y

The lesson here is that the discernment of the fitness staircase inherent within a staircase function depends critically on how one 'looks' at this function. In determining the 'right' way to look at f we have used information about the descriptor of f, specifically the values of h, o, and L. This information will not be available to an algorithm which only has query access to f.

Even if one knows the right way to look at a staircase function, the discernment of the fitness staircase inherent within this function can still be made difficult by a low value of the increment parameter. Figure 5 lets us visualize the decrease in the salience of the fitness staircase of f that accompanies a decrease in the increment parameter of this staircase function. In general, a decrease in the increment results in a decrease in the 'contrast' between the stages of that function, and an increase the amount of computation required to discern these stages.

C. ANALYSIS OF STAIRCASE FUNCTIONS

Let ℓ be some positive integer. Given some (possibly stochastic) fitness function f over the set $\mathfrak{B}_\ell$, and some schema $\gamma \subseteq \mathfrak{B}_\ell$ we define the *fitness signal* of γ, denoted $S(\gamma)$, to be $\mathbf{E}[F_\gamma^{(f)}] - \mathbf{E}[F_{\mathfrak{B}_\ell}^{(f)}]$. Let $\gamma_1 \subseteq \mathfrak{B}_\ell$ and $\gamma_2 \subseteq \mathfrak{B}_\ell$ be schemata in two orthogonal schema partitions. We define the *conditional fitness signal of* γ_1 *given* γ_2, denoted $S(\gamma_1 \,|\, \gamma_2)$, to be the difference between the fitness signal of $\gamma_1\gamma_2$ and the fitness signal of γ_2, i.e. $S(\gamma_1 \,|\, \gamma_2) = S(\gamma_1\gamma_2) - S(\gamma_2)$. Given some staircase function f we denote the ith step of f by $\lfloor f \rfloor_i$ and denote the ith stage of f by $\lceil f \rceil_i$.

Let f be a staircase function with descriptor $(h, o, \delta, \ell, L, V)$. For any integer $i \in [h]$, the fitness signal of $\lfloor f \rfloor_i$ is one measure of the difficulty of "directly" identifying step i (i.e., the difficulty of determining step i without first determining any of the preceding steps $1, \ldots, i-1$). Likewise, for any integers i, j in $[h]$ such that $i > j$, the conditional fitness signal of step i given stage j is one measure of the difficulty of directly identifying step i given stage j (i.e. the difficulty of determining $\lfloor f \rfloor_i$ given $\lceil f \rceil_j$ without first determining any of the intermediate steps $\lfloor f \rfloor_{j+1}, \ldots, \lfloor f \rfloor_{i-1}$).

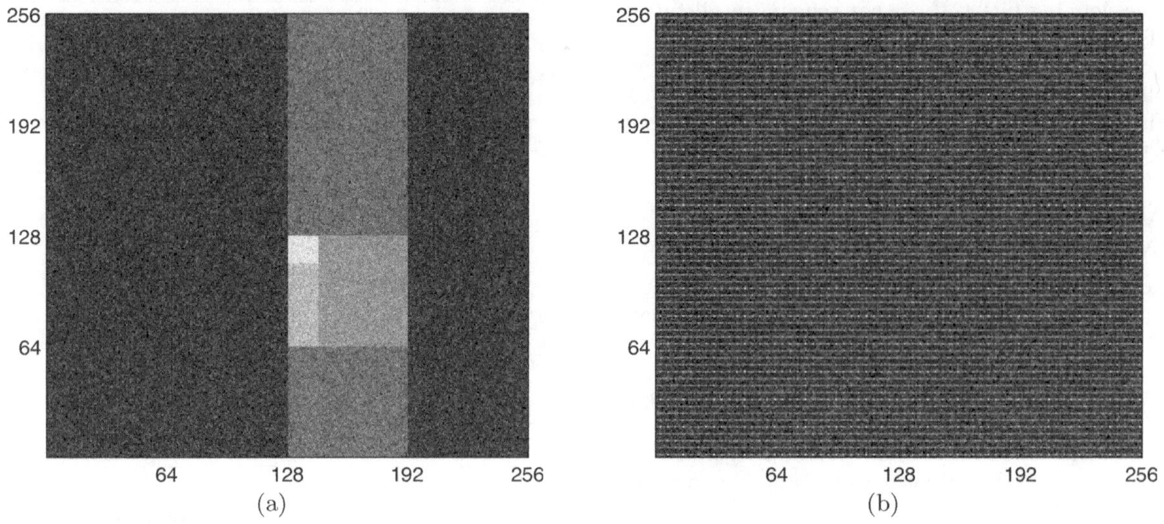

Figure 4: A refractal plot of the staircase function f under the refractal addressing systems A (*left*) and A' (*right*).

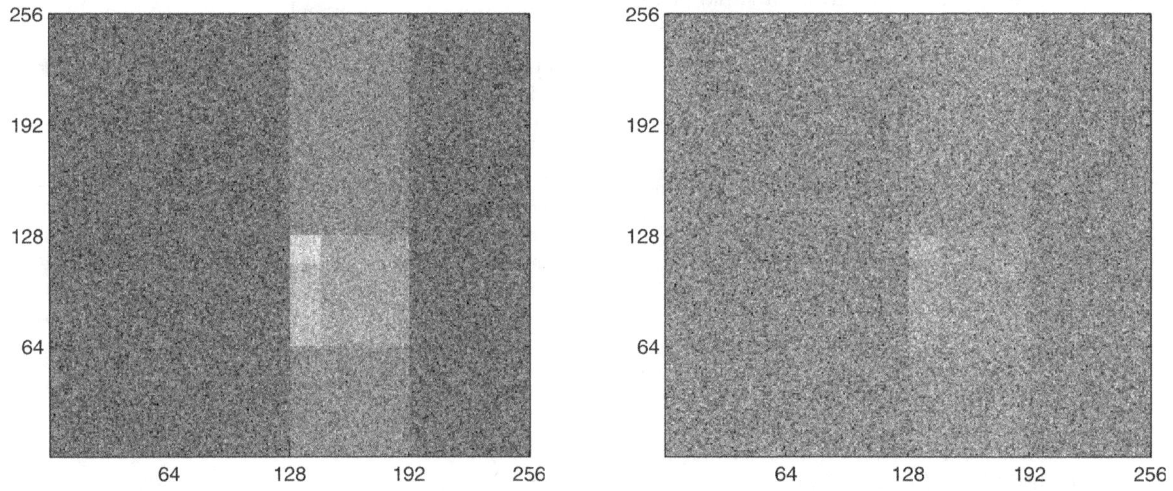

Figure 5: Refractal plots under A of two staircase functions, which differ from f only in their increments—1 *(left plot)* and 0.3 *(right plot)* as opposed to 3.

By Theorem 1 (Appendix C), for any $i \in [h]$, the unconditional fitness signal of step i is

$$\frac{\delta}{2^{o(i-1)}}$$

This value decreases exponentially with i and o. It is reasonable, therefore, to suspect that the direct identification of step i of f quickly becomes infeasible with increases in i and o. Consider, however, that by Corollary 1, for any $i \in \{2, \ldots, h\}$, the *conditional* fitness signal of step i *given* stage $(i-1)$ is δ, a *constant* with respect to i. Therefore, if some algorithm can identify the first step of f, one should be able to use it to iteratively identify all remaining steps in time and fitness queries that scale linearly with the height of f.

LEMMA 1. *For any staircase function f with descriptor $(h, o, \delta, \ell, L, V)$, and any integer $i \in [h]$, the fitness signal of stage i is $i\delta$.*

PROOF: Let x be the expected fitness of $\mathfrak{B}_\ell$ under uniform sampling. We first prove the following claim:

CLAIM 1. *The fitness signal of stage i is $i\delta - x$*

The proof of the claim follows by induction on i. The base case, when $i = h$ is easily seen to be true from the definition of a staircase function. For any $k \in \{2, \ldots, h\}$, we assume that the hypothesis holds for $i = k$, and prove that it holds for $i = k-1$. For any $j \in [h]$, let $\Gamma_j \in \mathbb{SP}_\ell$ denote the schema partition containing step i. The fitness signal of stage $k-1$

is given by

$$\frac{1}{2^o}\left(S(\lceil f\rceil_k) + \sum_{\psi \in \Gamma_k\setminus\{\lfloor f\rfloor_k\}} S(\lceil f\rceil_{k-1}\psi)\right)$$

$$= \frac{k\delta - x}{2^o} + \frac{2^o-1}{2^o}\left(\delta(k-1) - \frac{\delta}{2^o-1} - x\right)$$

where the first term of the right hand side of the equation follows from the inductive hypothesis, and the second term follows from the definition of a staircase function. Manipulation of this expression yields

$$\frac{k\delta + (2^o-1)\delta(k-1) - \delta - 2^o x}{2^o}$$

which, upon further manipulation, yields $(k-1)\delta - x$.

This completes the proof of the claim. To prove the lemma, we must prove that x is zero. By claim 1, the fitness signal of the first stage is $\delta - x$. By the definition of a staircase function then,

$$x = \frac{\delta - x}{2^o} + \frac{2^o-1}{2^o}\left(-\frac{\delta}{2^o-1}\right)$$

Which reduces to

$$x = -\frac{x}{2^o}$$

Clearly, x is zero. □

COROLLARY 1. *For any $i \in \{2,\ldots,h\}$, the conditional fitness signal of step i given stage $i-1$ is δ*

PROOF The conditional fitness signal of step i given stage $i-1$ is given by

$$\begin{aligned} &S(\lfloor f\rfloor_i \mid \lceil f\rceil_{i-1}) \\ &= S(\lceil f\rceil_i) - S(\lceil f\rceil_{i-1}) \\ &= (i\delta - (i-1)\delta) \\ &= \delta \ \Box \end{aligned}$$

THEOREM 1. *For any staircase function f with descriptor $(h, o, \delta, \sigma, \ell, L, V)$, and any integer $i \in [h]$, the fitness signal of step i is $\delta/2^{o(i-1)}$.*

PROOF: For any $j \in [h]$, let $\Lambda_j \in \mathbb{SP}_\ell$ denote of the partition containing stage j, and let $\Gamma_j \in \mathbb{SP}_\ell$ denote of the partition containing step j. We first prove the following claim

CLAIM 2. *For any $i \in [h]$,*

$$\sum_{\xi \in \Lambda i\setminus\{\lceil f\rceil_i\}} S(\xi) = -i\delta$$

The proof of the claim follows by induction on i. The proof for the base case ($i = 1$) is as follows:

$$\sum_{\xi \in \Lambda_1\setminus\{\lceil f\rceil_1\}} S(\xi) = (2^o-1)\left(\frac{-\delta}{2^o-1}\right) = -\delta$$

For any $k \in [h-1]$ we assume that the hypothesis holds for $i = k$, and prove that it holds for $i = k+1$.

$$\sum_{\xi \in \Lambda_{k+1}\setminus\{\lceil f\rceil_{k+1}\}} S(\xi)$$

$$= \sum_{\psi\in\Gamma_{k+1}\setminus\{\lfloor f\rfloor_{k+1}\}} S(\lceil f\rceil_k\psi) + \sum_{\xi \in \Lambda_k\setminus\{\lceil f\rceil_k\}} \sum_{\psi \in \Gamma_{k+1}} S(\xi\psi)$$

$$= \sum_{\psi \in \Gamma_{k+1}\setminus\{\lceil f\rceil_{k+1}\}} S(\lceil f\rceil_k\psi) + \sum_{\psi \in \Gamma_{k+1}} \sum_{\xi \in \Lambda_k\setminus\{\lceil f\rceil_k\}} S(\xi\psi)$$

$$= (2^o-1)S(\lceil f\rceil_k) + 2^o\left(\sum_{\xi \in \Lambda_k\setminus\{\lceil f\rceil_k\}} S(\xi)\right)$$

where the first and last equalities follow from the definition of a staircase function. Using Lemma 1 and the inductive hypothesis, the right hand side of this expression can be seen to equal

$$(2^o-1)\left(k\delta - \frac{\delta}{2^o-1}\right) - 2^o k\delta$$

which, upon manipulation, yields $-\delta(k+1)$.

For a proof of the theorem, observe that step 1 and stage 1 are the same schema. So, by Lemma 1, $S(\lfloor f\rfloor_1) = \delta$. Thus, the theorem holds for $i = 1$. For any $i \in \{2,\ldots,h\}$,

$$S(\lfloor f\rfloor_i) = \frac{1}{(2^o)^{i-1}}\left(S(\lceil f\rceil_i) + \sum_{\xi \in \Lambda_{i-1}\setminus\{\lceil f\rceil_{i-1}\}} S(\xi\lfloor f\rfloor_k)\right)$$

$$= \frac{1}{(2^o)^{i-1}}\left(S(\lceil f\rceil_i) + \sum_{\xi \in \Lambda_{i-1}\setminus\{\lceil f\rceil_{i-1}\}} S(\xi)\right)$$

where the last equality follows from the definition of a staircase function. Using Lemma 1 and Claim 2, the right hand side of this equality can be seen to equal

$$\frac{i\delta - (i-1)\delta}{(2^o)^{i-1}}$$

$$= \frac{\delta}{2^{o(i-1)}} \quad \Box$$

When Do Evolutionary Algorithms Optimize Separable Functions in Parallel?

Benjamin Doerr
Max-Planck-Institut für Informatik
66123 Saarbrücken, Germany

Dirk Sudholt
Dept. of Computer Science
University of Sheffield
Sheffield S1 4DP, UK

Carsten Witt
DTU Compute
Technical University of Denmark, Denmark

ABSTRACT

Separable functions are composed of subfunctions that depend on mutually disjoint sets of bits. These subfunctions can be optimized independently, however in black-box optimization this direct approach is infeasible as the composition of subfunctions may be unknown. Common belief is that evolutionary algorithms make progress on all subfunctions in parallel, so that optimizing a separable function does not take not much longer than optimizing the hardest subfunction—subfunctions are optimized "in parallel."

We show that this is only partially true, already for the simple (1+1) evolutionary algorithm ((1+1) EA). For separable functions composed of k Boolean functions indeed the optimization time is the maximum optimization time of these functions times a small $O(\log k)$ overhead. More generally, for sums of weighted subfunctions that each attain non-negative integer values less than $r = o(\log^{1/2} n)$, we get an overhead of $O(r \log n)$. However, the hoped for parallel optimization behavior does not always come true. We present a separable function with $k \leq \sqrt{n}$ subfunctions such that the (1+1) EA is likely to optimize many subfunctions sequentially. The reason is that standard mutation leads to interferences between search processes on different subfunctions. Under mild assumptions, we show that such a sequential optimization behavior is worst possible.

Categories and Subject Descriptors

F.2.2 [**Analysis of Algorithms and Problem Complexity**]: Nonnumerical Algorithms and Problems

General Terms

Algorithms, Performance, Theory

Keywords

Separable functions, linear functions, pseudo-Boolean optimization, runtime analysis, theory

FOGA'13, January 16–20, 2013, Adelaide, Australia.

1. INTRODUCTION

A function $f : \{0,1\}^n \to \mathbb{R}$ is called separable if it can be written as sum $f = \sum_{i=1}^{k} f_i$ of functions $f_1, \dots, f_k$ which depend on disjoint sets of bits. That is, there are pairwise disjoint sets $I_1, \dots, I_k \subseteq \{1, \dots, n\} =: [n]$ such that $f_i(x) = f_i(y)$ whenever x and y are identical on bit-positions outside I_i.

Separability is an important property in optimization. If f is separable as above, then x is an optimum of f if and only if it is an optimum of each f_i. Moreover, since the f_i depend on distinct sets of input variables, one can find an optimum of f by optimizing each f_i and combining the solutions.

Black-box optimization methods like evolutionary algorithms and other bio-inspired search heuristics cannot directly profit from separability, since they do not have access to an explicit problem description. Note that this problem-independence is one of the reasons why evolutionary algorithms are used a lot in practice. This raises the question of how well separable functions can be optimized via evolutionary methods.

Not having access to an explicit problem description does not outrule a priori that evolutionary algorithms easily optimize separable functions. Evolutionary algorithms could benefit from separability as random mutations have a chance to optimize several subfunctions "in parallel". Separability implies that mutation can make improvements on several non-optimized subfunctions. In fact, one could hope that evolutionary algorithms optimize f in roughly the same time as they would need to optimize all f_i in parallel. The time for optimizing all f_i is generally larger than the time for optimizing the hardest f_i as we are looking at the time until the *last* subfunction is optimized. This may lead to a small overhead, a factor in the expected running time that may grow slowly with k, the number of subfunctions.

For simple separable functions, such an optimization behavior has indeed been observed. For the simplest separable function OneMax defined by $\text{OneMax} : \{0,1\}^n \to \mathbb{R}; x \mapsto \sum_{i \in [n]} x_i$, it is relatively easy to see that both the randomized local search heuristic (RLS) and the (1+1) evolutionary algorithm ((1+1) EA, see Section 2 for formal definitions) find the optimum in $\Theta(n \log n)$ iterations. Note that with $f_i : \{0,1\}^n \to \mathbb{R}; x \mapsto x_i$ we have $\text{OneMax} = \sum_{i \in [n]} f_i$ and each f_i depends only on the ith bit. Hence OneMax is indeed separable. Both heuristics need an expected number of $\Theta(n)$ iterations to find the optimum of each f_i. Consequently, the optimization time for f is not much more than the one of each f_i. The additional $\log n$ factor describes the above-mentioned overhead. Roughly speaking, it stems from the fact that while most of the f_i are optimized in parallel (and thus in time $O(n)$), there will be few outliers that need $\Theta(n \log n)$ iterations to receive a bit-flip in their domain. This relates to the well-known coupon collector theorem [17].

The same results are true for arbitrary linear functions $f : \{0,1\}^n \to \mathbb{R}; x \mapsto \sum_{i \in [n]} w_i x_i$. This innocent-looking result was proven first by Droste, Jansen and Wegener in their seminal work [7, 8], but it took a series of publications to obtain a true understanding of this optimization process [10, 11, 5, 4, 26]. Again, this result might indicate that separable functions are easily optimized via randomized search heuristics in time not much above the time needed to optimize the separable components.

There are many other well-known separable functions where subfunctions depend on more than one bit—functions that have had a significant impact on academic research and the development of evolutionary algorithms. The De Jong Test Suite [2] has been used as a standard for testing evolutionary algorithms for decades, and many functions therein are separable [25]. Modern benchmarks contain a well-balanced mixture of separable and non-separable functions [21]. Royal Road functions [15], defined in an attempt to demonstrate the usefulness of crossover, are also separable. Despite separable functions playing a central role in our field, there is no rigorous analysis focused on the performance of evolutionary algorithms optimizing separable functions.

In this work, we make progress towards a more general understanding of how evolutionary algorithms optimize separable functions. We investigate when and under what conditions evolutionary algorithms optimize subfunctions of a separable functions "in parallel", in a sense that the expected optimization time equals the time for optimizing the hardest subfunction, with a reasonable overhead. Note that in the presence of global search operators we never observe a truly parallel search process as the search processes on different subfunctions interfere. In particular, even elitist evolutionary algorithms can be driven to accept a search point where the value of single subfunctions is decreased—so long as the fitness of the composite fitness function does not decrease. We will demonstrate rigorously that these interferences can have negligible effects, or lead to a drastic change in the optimization process—moving from parallel optimization to a rather sequential optimization process.

Like many previous theoretical works, we regard the simple (1+1) EA only. This seems to be a fair compromise between overly simplistic heuristics like randomized local search and mutation-based evolutionary algorithms having larger populations. The theoretical work done so far indicates that many general phenomena of mutation-based evolutionary algorithms can already be observed for the (1+1) EA [8, 19, 26]. As usual, we measure the performance of this heuristic via the expected optimization time, that is, the expected number of function evaluations performed in one run of the algorithm.

1.1 Our Results

If only local variation operators are used, e. g., mutation flipping only a single bit, it is easy to see that then subfunctions in a separable function are optimized independently and in parallel. We make this precise for randomized local search (RLS) in Section 2.3. For global operators like standard mutation the situation is more complicated, so we focus on the (1+1) EA in the remainder.

We first show that if f is the separable sum of Boolean functions (that is, the f_i take the values zero and one only), then again we observe that the (1+1) EA optimizes the f_i mostly in parallel. More precisely, if T^* is an upper bound for the expected times needed to optimize any of the f_i starting at an arbitrary search point, then the expected optimization time of f is $O(T^* \log k)$. This result naturally extends the classic analysis for the OneMax function, and it significantly improves the best known running time bound for Royal Road functions (see the end of Section 3).

Surprisingly, the optimization behavior drastically changes for the general case of separable functions. For all $k = O(\sqrt{n})$ we prove that already a weighted sum of k LeadingOnes functions depending on (disjoint) sets of n/k bits has an expected optimization time of $\Theta(n^2)$. Since each subfunction has an expected optimization time of $\Theta(n^2/k)$, the one of f is larger by a factor of $\Theta(k)$. The proof reveals what could be guessed from these numbers, namely that here indeed the subfunctions are optimized sequentially roughly in order of decreasing weights.

We give two fairly general upper bounds to deal with these and more general separable functions. Via the well-established fitness level method [22] we show a general upper bound (Theorem 12 in Section 5) that in many situations, including the functions constructed in the previous paragraph, can be used to show that the expected optimization time of a separable function is bounded by sum of the expected optimization times of the subfunctions. Our result extends Theorem 5.2 in [23], which is a general bound for separable functions not allowing to take into account additional knowledge about the subfunctions.

We then extend our initial result on unweighted Boolean functions towards weighted sums of subfunctions and larger fitness ranges. Via adaptive drift analysis [4], we show an upper bound (Theorem 14 in Section 6) that roughly speaking shows that if the subfunctions only take integer values in $[0, r]$, where $r = o(\log^{1/2} n)$, then the expected optimization time of f is at most of order $rT^* \log n$, where again T^* is the maximum expected optimization time among the subfunctions, starting from arbitrary search points. Hence apart from the dependence on r, we observe a parallel-type optimization behavior. This bound can be seen as a natural extension of the analysis of linear functions [8, 6]. The $\log n$ term in our bound probably cannot be replaced by $\log k$.

1.2 Related Work

The question whether evolutionary algorithms can optimize parts of the problem in parallel has been discussed already in the early days of evolutionary computation. The notion of "implicit parallelism" reflects the hypothesis that evolutionary algorithms optimize multiple schemata in parallel [9]. This hypothesis has been heavily criticized (see, e. g., Wright, Vose and Rowe [27]) and nowadays the notion of "implicit parallelism" has been abandoned.

While "implicit parallelism" is doubtful in general, it seems plausible when considering schemata induced by subfunctions in a separable function. After all, here all subfunctions represent "building blocks" of the composite function by definition. But our results show that still subfunctions (and therefore schemata/building blocks) are not always optimized in parallel, even for simple separable functions. This is further evidence that the notion of "implicit parallelism" is misguided, even under sensible and favorable conditions implied by separability.

Separability has also been considered in the context of cooperative coevolution [18]. The idea is that multiple evolutionary algorithms each optimize disjoint parts of a problem, and all parts are assembled to perform a fitness evaluation. For a long time separability was thought to be a key factor in the success of cooperative coevolution. But Jansen and Wiegand [12] showed rigorously for a cooperative coevolutionary (1+1) EA that separability does not imply good performance, and neither is inseparability a sufficient factor for bad performance. They also showed that the cooperative coevolutionary (1+1) EA can outperform the classical (1+1) EA, if the former is tailored towards the partitioning of the bit string. In other words, in their setting the coevolutionary algorithms are set up so that each algorithm optimizes a single subfunction. In this work we do not assume any knowledge about the partition of the bit string into subfunctions, as this knowledge is rarely available in black-box optimization.

2. PRELIMINARIES AND NOTATION

In this section, we make the definition of separability precise, introduce the algorithms regarded, and prove that the (non-evolutionary) randomized local search (RLS) heuristic always optimizes separable functions in parallel.

2.1 Separability

Throughout this paper, we regard *pseudo-Boolean* functions $f : \{0,1\}^n \to \mathbb{R}$, that is, functions defined on bit-strings of length n. We call n the *dimension* of the *search space* $\{0,1\}^n$.

Let $I \subseteq [n] := \{1, \dots, n\}$. We say that f *only depends on the bit-positions in* I if

$$\forall x, y \in \{0,1\}^n : (\forall i \in I : x_i = y_i) \implies (f(x) = f(y))$$

is satisfied. A function $f : \{0,1\}^n \to \mathbb{R}$ is *separable* if there are $k \in \mathbb{N}_{\geq 2}$, $f_1, \dots, f_k : \{0,1\}^n \to \mathbb{R}$, and disjoint sets $I_1, \dots, I_k \subseteq [n]$ such that $f = \sum_{i=1}^k f_i$ and for all $i \in [k]$, f_i depends only on the bit-positions in I_i. We also say that f is the separable sum of the f_i.

In the remainder of this paper, when talking about a separable function f, we shall always (implicitly) assume that we also introduced k, the f_i and the I_i as above.

Note that the definition of separability implies that if we alter a search point x only on bit-positions in some I_i, then the change of the f-value is fully determined by (and in fact equal to) the one of f_i.

FACT 1. *Let f be separable as above. Let $x, y \in \{0,1\}^n$ such that $x_i = y_i$ for all $i \in [n] \setminus I_i$. Then*

$$f(y) - f(x) = f_i(y) - f_i(x).$$

2.2 The (1+1) Evolutionary Algorithm

Being the simplest mutation-based algorithm that deserved the adjective "evolutionary", in this work we shall concentrate on the so-called (1+1) EA. This algorithm maintains a population of size 1. In each generation it creates a single offspring by independently flipping each bit in the current search point with the standard mutation probability $1/n$. The new search point replaces the old one in case its f-value is not worse.

(1+1) EA with mutation probability $1/n$

Initialization: Choose $x \in \{0,1\}^n$ uniformly at random.
repeat forever
  Create $y \in \{0,1\}^n$ by copying x.
  Mutation: Flip each bit in y independently with probability $1/n$.
  Selection: **if** $f(y) \geq f(x)$ **then** $x := y$.

In this theoretical work, we are interested in the time needed until the (1+1) EA finds an optimal search point. For this reason, we did not specify a termination criterion. As usual in this research field, we measure time by counting the number of f-evaluations until an optimum is found. For the (1+1) EA, apart from an additive deviation of one, this is equal to the number of iterations of the repeat loop.

2.3 Randomized Local Search Optimizing Separable Functions

If we replace the standard bit mutation (flipping each bit independently with probability $1/n$) in the (1+1) EA by flipping a single, randomly chosen bit, we obtain another well-studied randomized search heuristic called *randomized local search* (RLS). It is usually not considered an evolutionary algorithm, among others, because it lacks the property that the mutation operator can transform any individual to any other (though with very small probability when the individuals are not similar). One consequence is that RLS can get stuck in local optima, and that convergence to an optimal solution is not guaranteed.

Still RLS can be a useful heuristic in practice, possibly together with restart strategies. RLS has also been studied by the theory community, among others for the reason that it often behaves similar to the (1+1) EA, but is easier to analyze (see, e. g., again the linear functions problem).

When optimizing separable functions, as we will see in this work, significant differences exist. In particular, we now show that RLS always optimizes the different subfunctions of a separable function in parallel, resulting in an optimization time that is at most the maximum of the ones of the subfunctions times a logarithmic factor.

Note that this does not mean that RLS is generally better suited to optimize separable functions than the (1+1) EA. Since the result below takes into account the optimization times of RLS on the subfunctions, such a conclusion is only admissible when RLS is also competitive on all the subfunctions.

THEOREM 2. *Let f be a separable function composed of k subfunctions. Let T^* be such that the expected optimization time of RLS started with an arbitrary initial search point is at most T^* for each of the subfunctions. Then the expected optimization time of RLS on f is $O(T^* \log k)$.*

PROOF. Let $i \in [k]$. Consider a run of RLS on f_i, let $y^{(0)}, y^{(1)}, \dots$ denote the (random) sequence of search points generated by this. By assumption, for all $t \geq 0$ and independent of the value of $y^{(t)}$, the probability that $y^{(t+2T^*)}$ is not optimal, is at most $1/2$, using Markov's inequality. A simple induction shows that $y^{(2\ell T^*)}$ is not optimal with probability at most $2^{-\ell}$.

Consider now a run of RLS on f, let $x^{(0)}, x^{(1)}, \ldots$ denote the (random) sequence of search points generated by this. Since RLS chooses the initial search point uniformly at random, $x^{(0)}_{|I_i}$ and $y^{(0)}_{|I_i}$, that is, the search points restricted to the entries with index in I_i, are identically distributed. Assume that for some $t \geq 0$, $x^{(t)}_{|I_i}$ and $y^{(t)}_{|I_i}$ are identically distributed. Since each application of the mutation operator changes one bit only, it in particular changes either (i) only bits in I_i or (ii) no bits in I_i. In the first case, by Fact 1, acceptance of the offspring is identical for optimizing f and f_i; consequently, $x^{(t+1)}_{|I_i}$ and $y^{(t+1)}_{|I_i}$ are identically distributed. In Case (ii), trivially $x^{(t+1)}_{|I_i}$ and $y^{(t+1)}_{|I_i}$ are identically distributed. By induction, for all $t \geq 0$, $x^{(t)}_{|I_i}$ and $y^{(t)}_{|I_i}$ are identically distributed.

By the argument of the first paragraph, the probability that $x^{(2\ell T^*)}$ is not optimal for f_i, is at most $2^{-\ell}$. A simple union bound argument shows that with probability at most $k2^{-\ell}$, $x^{(2\ell T^*)}$ is not optimal for some f_i, $i \in [k]$, and consequently, is not an optimum of f. Hence the first-hitting time $T := \min\{t \geq 0 \mid x^{(t)} \text{ optimal for } f\}$, which is one less than the optimization time of f, satisfies $\Pr(T \geq t) \leq k2^{-\lfloor t/(2T^*) \rfloor} \leq 2k2^{-t/(2T^*)}$.

We finally use the elementary estimate $E(T) \leq \sum_{t=1}^{\infty} \Pr(T \geq t)$, see, e.g., Lemma 1 in [3]. Splitting the sum appropriately, we compute

$$
\begin{aligned}
E(T) &\leq \sum_{t=1}^{\infty} \Pr(T \geq t) \\
&\leq 2T^* \log(2k) + \sum_{t=\lceil 2T^* \log(2k) \rceil}^{\infty} 2k2^{-t/(2T^*)} \\
&\leq 2T^* \log(2k) + \sum_{t=0}^{\infty} 2^{-t/(2T^*)} \\
&= O(T^* \log k) + O(T^*),
\end{aligned}
$$

where the last estimate stems from a standard geometric series argument $\sum_{t=0}^{\infty} 2^{-t/(2T^*)} = 1/(1-2^{-1/(2T^*)})$ and the estimate $f(x)-f(y) \geq (y-x)\min\{|f'(\xi)| \mid \xi \in [x,y]\}$, valid for all differentiable, strictly decreasing functions $f\colon [x,y] \to \mathbb{R}$, here applied to $f\colon \xi \mapsto 2^{-\xi}$, $x = 0$ and $y = 1/(2T^*)$. □

3. SUMS OF BOOLEAN FUNCTIONS ARE OPTIMIZED IN PARALLEL

We now investigate a simple setting where all subfunctions are unweighted Boolean functions, i.e., each subfunction only has fitness values 0 or 1. This function class includes OneMax and Royal Road functions [15], amongst others. The result demonstrates our basic proof technique; it will be generalized towards weighted sums of subfunctions in Section 6.

Theorem 3. *Assume $f = \sum_{i=1}^{k} f_i$ where $f_i\colon \{0,1\}^n \to \{0,1\}$ and all f_i depend on pairwise disjoint sets of bits. Suppose for each f_i and for every initial configuration x_i, we have that the expected optimization time of the (1+1) EA working on f_i is bounded by T^*. Then the expected optimization time of the (1+1) EA working on f is bounded by*

$$T^* \cdot 4e^2(1 + \ln k) = T^* \cdot O(\log k).$$

We first show in how far the (1+1) EA working on the composite function f simulates the (1+1) EA working on subfunctions f_i only. We upper bound the time until the (1+1) EA working on f finds an optimum of f_i for the first time. This time is by a factor of $e = \exp(1)$ larger than the time for optimizing f_i in isolation. The reason is that when optimizing the composite function f mutation can flip bits that are irrelevant for f_i, but lead to a smaller f-value and hence a rejected offspring. Note that after the (1+1) EA has found an optimum on f_i, this optimum may be lost again if improvements are found on other subfunctions at the same time.

Lemma 4. *Consider a function $f = \sum_{i=1}^{k} f_i$ over pairwise disjoint sets of bits, where $f_i\colon \{0,1\}^n \to \{0,1\}$. Let T_i^* be the random optimization time of the (1+1) EA with mutation probability $1/n$ working on f_i. Let T^* be the first generation where the (1+1) EA working on f has found a solution x with $f_i(x) = 1$. Then*

$$E(T^*) \leq e \cdot E(T_i^*).$$

Proof. Abbreviate $f_{\neq i} = f - f_i$. Let $\{X\}_{t \geq 0}, X_t \in \{0,1\}^n$ denote the trajectory of current search points in the (1+1) EA working on f, i.e., search points after mutation and selection. Define $T_X^* := \inf\{t \mid f(X_t) = 1\}$. We now pessimistically consider a modified (1+1) EA, leading to a slightly pessimistic process $\{Y\}_{t \geq 0}$. We assume that whenever mutation creates a search point Y'_t out of Y_t where $f_{\neq i}(Y_t) > f_{\neq i}(Y'_t)$ that then the outcome is rejected automatically and $Y_{t+1} = Y_t$. This avoids the case that outside the bits of f_i the fitness is decreased by 1, but the result is accepted nevertheless because f_i is increased by 1 at the same time. Now on $\{Y\}_{t \geq 0}$ we have that a mutation of Y_t is accepted if and only if $f_{\neq i}$ is not decreased. It is obvious that $\Pr(T_X^* \geq t) \leq \Pr(T_Y^* \geq t)$ for all $t \in \mathbb{N}$, where T_Y^* is defined analogously to T_X^*.

Further define $\{Z\}_{t \geq 0}$ as the trajectory of the (1+1) EA working on f_i. Now Y can be regarded as a lazy version of Z: for all $t, t' \in \mathbb{N}$, whenever $Y_{t'} = Z_t$, we have the following. Let $t'' > t'$ be the first generation after t' where mutation does not decrease $f_{\neq i}$. Then $Y_{t''}$ and Z_{t+1} have the same distribution. The mentioned event is independent of Z_t, and it has probability at least $(1 - 1/n)^{n-1} \geq 1/e$. Therefore, $E(T_X^*) \leq E(T_Y^*) \leq e \cdot E(T_Z^*) = e \cdot E(T_i^*)$. □

Using Lemma 4 we now prove Theorem 3. As mentioned, subfunctions that are optimized can lose their optima if other subfunctions are being optimized in the same generation. However, as we are considering unweighted Boolean functions, the number of optimized subfunctions can never decrease.

Proof of Theorem 3. Let N_t denote the number of non-optimized subfunctions at time t. We claim that $E(N_t - N_{t+2eT^*} \mid N_t) \geq 1/(2e) \cdot N_t$. Fix an arbitrary subfunction i that is not optimized at time t. By Lemma 4 the (1+1) EA on f simulates the (1+1) EA on f_i, up to a slowdown of e: the expected time until the (1+1) EA on f first finds an optimum on f_i is at most eT^*. By Markov's inequality, we have a probability of at least 1/2 that this happens in $2eT^*$ generations.

Assume that this happens, and that no other subfunction finds an optimum in the same generation. For the (1+1) EA working on f this means the following. If no bit outside of x_i is flipped, f is increased by 1 in generation t'. This happens with probability at least $(1-1/n)^{n-1} \geq 1/e$. Hence N_t is decreased by 1 with probability at least $1/e$ (conditional on optimizing the subfunction within $2eT^*$ generations). The expected decrease of N_t per subfunction is thus $1/(2e)$. The same holds in case $m > 1$ subfunctions are optimized in the same generation; then we only need to assume that no bits in other subfunctions are flipped and get an expected decrease of N_t of even $m/(2e)$.

The claim then follows from an application of the multiplicative drift theorem (see Theorem 19 in the appendix) to the number of non-optimized subfunctions after periods of $2eT^*$ generations, each. Initially $N_0 \leq k$, hence we get an upper bound of

$$T^* \cdot 4e^2(1+\ln k). \quad \square$$

Applications

As a first application, consider n subfunctions $f_1, \dots, f_n$ on single bits, where each f_i is the identity function. In other words, $f(x) = \sum_{i=1}^{n} x_i$ is the well-known function OneMax.

We clearly have that the expected optimization time of the (1+1) EA on some fixed function f_i is at most $T^* := n$ as flipping the i-th bit is sufficient for finding the optimum. Theorem 3 then gives an upper bound of $4e^2n(1+\ln n) = O(n \log n)$.

Corollary 5. *The expected optimization time of the (1+1) EA on* OneMax *is* $O(n \log n)$.

Note that this bound is by a factor of $(1+o(1)) \cdot 4e$ larger than the actual expected optimization time [19, 26].

Our reasoning extends to Royal Road functions [15] defined as follows. Let $f_i := \prod_{j=1}^{d} x_{(i-1)d+j}$, where $d = n/k$, i. e., f_i is a monomial of degree d, and let $f := \sum_{i=1}^{k} f_i$. Since the (1+1) EA optimizes monomials of degree d in an expected time $O((n/d) \cdot 2^d))$ (see Theorem 3.1 in [24]), we obtain from Theorem 3 the upper bound $O((n/d)(\log n) \cdot 2^d)$.

Corollary 6. *The expected optimization time of the (1+1) EA on Royal Road functions on* n/d *disjoint blocks of size* d *is* $O((n/d)(\log n) \cdot 2^d)$.

The previous best known bound was $O((n/d)^2 \cdot 2^d)$ (Theorem 7.2 in [24]); it relied on optimizing all subfunctions sequentially. Furthermore, it was restricted to $d \leq 2\log n - 2\log\log n - O(1)$. This restriction does not apply to our result.

4. AN EXAMPLE FOR SEQUENTIAL OPTIMIZATION

We now show that under more general conditions the (1+1) EA can be forced to optimize all subfunctions (or a constant fraction thereof) sequentially. For the sake of simplicity and readability, we aim at keeping the subfunctions as simple as possible. In fact, with mild conditions on the block size and appropriate weights, the simple subfunction LeadingOnes$(x) := \sum_{i=1}^{n} \prod_{j=1}^{i} x_j$ serves this purpose.

Define $w\text{CLOB}_{\ell,k}$ (concatenated LeadingOnes with blocks and weights) as follows. Given a number of blocks k and block length ℓ, denote $x = x_1 x_2 \dots x_k$ with $x_i = x_{i,1} x_{i,2} \dots x_{i,\ell} \in \{0,1\}^\ell$. Then

$$w\text{CLOB}_{\ell,k}(x) := \sum_{i=1}^{k} (\ell+1)^{k-i} \cdot \text{LeadingOnes}(x_i).$$

The function is inspired by a function $\text{CLOB}_{\ell,k}$ due to Jansen and Wiegand [12]. However, their function has uniform weights and it encourages bits not part of leading ones to attain value 0. The weights in our function ensure that for each $1 \leq i \leq k$ each operation that changes the LeadingOnes-value in block i completely dominates all effects on blocks $i+1, i+2, \dots, k$. Hence "heavy" blocks are optimized independently of lighter blocks.

The main idea of this construction is as follows. Whenever the (1+1) EA makes an improvement in one of the first i blocks, every mutation on blocks $i+1, i+2, \dots, k$ is accepted. If such a mutation destroys many leading ones in some block $j > i$, the (1+1) EA has to rediscover these leading ones. Under certain conditions made precise in the following, these disruptive mutations happen frequently. Then we are in a situation where, whenever a new block has been optimized, one of the heaviest non-optimized blocks has a low number of leading ones. So the (1+1) EA still needs to spend $\Omega(\ell n)$ generations optimizing this block. Loosely speaking, the (1+1) EA optimizes many blocks in the order of decreasing weights. This then implies a time bound of $\Theta(k\ell n)$, which reflects (up to constant factors) the expected time for optimizing k blocks sequentially.

Theorem 7. *The expected optimization time of the (1+1) EA on the function* $w\text{CLOB}_{\ell,k}$ *for* $k \leq c\sqrt{n}$ *blocks of length* $\ell = \lfloor n/k \rfloor$, $c > 0$ *an arbitrary constant, is* $\Theta(k\ell n) = \Theta(n^2)$.

A major obstacle in this analysis is the following. Imagine a disruptive mutation destroys a long prefix of leading ones by flipping a 1-bit to 0. The reader might be tempted to think that then the (1+1) EA could easily rediscover this prefix since flipping this bit back to 1 re-creates the prefix of leading ones. Even if this does not happen immediately, we could expect many bits following the first 0-bit to be set to 1, so that the (1+1) EA can make rapid progress towards the previous LeadingOnes-value once the first 0-bit is flipped. This is in stark contrast to the original setting of the (1+1) EA on LeadingOnes as there all bits following the first 0-bit are distributed uniformly at random [8].

However, this intuition is wrong. In fact, the (1+1) EA is likely to flip many of these tailing 1-bits in a random fashion before the first 0-bit is flipped. Even stronger, we find that tailing 1-bits have a negligible effect on the optimization process. We show in the following that with high probability the (1+1) EA quickly "forgets" about bits following the first 0-bit, and the progress is similar to the setting where these bits are distributed uniformly at random in the first place.

We first cite the following lemma from [14], stating that when a bit is subjected to random mutations, the random bit value quickly approaches a uniform random distribution.

Lemma 8 (Lässig and Sudholt [14]). *Let* $x^0, x^1, \dots, x^t$ *be a sequence of random bit strings such that* x^{j+1} *results from* x^j *by flipping each bit in* x^j *independently with probability* $1/n$. *Then for* $t \in \mathbb{N}$, *every* $x^* \in \{0,1\}^n$, *and every* $i \in [n]$

$$\left|\Pr(x_i^t = x_i^*) - \frac{1}{2}\right| = \frac{1}{2}\left(1-\frac{2}{n}\right)^t.$$

This implies

$$\Pr(x_i^t = 1) \leq \frac{1}{2}\left(1+\left(1-\frac{2}{n}\right)^t\right).$$

Using this, we obtain the following bound on the progress of evolutionary algorithms on the function LEADINGONES. Instead of considering the (1+1) EA only, we generalize this result to an algorithm $\mathcal{A}$ that potentially accepts worse offspring as well. This means that this lemma will be applicable to the process observed on light blocks as there worse offspring can be accepted in case heavier blocks lead to a fitness improvement.

The lemma makes use of the *principle of deferred decision* [16, page 9] with respect to bits to the right of the first 0-bit. These bits are initially random, and they are subjected to random mutations as long as they are irrelevant for the fitness. Instead of tracking their random values over time, we only determine their random values at the time they do become important for the fitness evaluation.

Note that the situation of these bits having a random value re-occurs whenever these bits have been subjected to random mutations for some time (cf. Lemma 8). The lemma assumes that there is some probability bound $p^* \geq 1/2$ for these bits having value 1 at the time we determine their random value.

LEMMA 9. *Consider an evolutionary algorithm $\mathcal{A}$ with population size 1 and the following property: whenever $\mathcal{A}$ creates an offspring x' out of the current search point x, then x' surely becomes the new search point when $f(x') \geq f(x)$ and potentially (according to an arbitrary scheme) when $f(x') < f(x)$.*

Consider $\mathcal{A}$ on LEADINGONES, starting with a LEADINGONES-value of i. Let Δ_t denote the random increase of the LEADINGONES-value in t generations. Suppose there is some value $p^* \geq 1/2$ such that $\mathcal{A}$ has the following property. Whenever $\mathcal{A}$ increases the best-so-far LO-value from j to some larger value, then the probability of bit $j+a$, where $a \geq 2$, being 1 is at most p^*, irrespective of other bits. Then for all $0 < \delta < 1$ we have

$$\Pr\left(\Delta_t > \left(1-\frac{1}{n}\right)^i \cdot \frac{t}{n} \cdot \frac{(1+\delta)^2}{1-p^*}\right) \leq 2\exp\left(-\Omega(\delta^2 \cdot t/n)\right).$$

PROOF. The event from the claim implies that either

1. $\mathcal{A}$ has increased the LEADINGONES-value more than $\alpha := \frac{(1+\delta)(1-1/n)^i \cdot t}{n}$ times or
2. in no more than α increases of the best LEADINGONES-value more than $\alpha \cdot (1+\delta) \cdot \left(\frac{1}{1-p^*} - 1\right)$ free riders are gained.

The reason is that, if neither of these events happens, the total increase of the best LEADINGONES-value is at most $\alpha + \alpha \cdot (1+\delta) \cdot \left(\frac{1}{1-p^*} - 1\right) \leq \alpha \cdot (1+\delta) \cdot \frac{1}{1-p^*}$, which is the stated progress bound.

The probability of increasing the LEADINGONES-value in one generation from a value $j \geq i$ is $(1-1/n)^j \cdot 1/n \leq (1-1/n)^i \cdot 1/n$. The reason is that $\mathcal{A}$ has to flip the first 0-bit, which happens with probability $1/n$. In addition, the first j bits must not flip, which happens with probability $(1-1/n)^j$. We pessimistically assume that the probability of increasing the LEADINGONES-value always equals $(1-1/n)^i \cdot 1/n$ (a formal argument justifying this is, e.g., Lemma 1.18 from [1]). This enables us to apply Chernoff bounds as then we are dealing with i. i. d. variables. The probability of the first event is at most $\exp(-\Omega(\delta^2 \cdot t/n))$.

The number of free riders in one improvement is one less than a geometric distribution with parameter $1-p^*$, whose expectation is $1/(1-p^*)$. By Theorem 1.14 in [1], the total number of free riders in α improvements is at most $\alpha(1+\delta) \cdot (1/(1-p^*)-1)$ with probability at most $\exp(-\Omega(\delta^2 \cdot \alpha)) = \exp(-\Omega(\delta^2 \cdot t/n))$.

Taking the union bound for the two events proves the claim. □

Now we are ready to show the following progress bound, where the progress is independent of the configuration of bits after the first 0-bit. For time spans t not too large, this matches the progress of the (1+1) EA with uniform random configurations for these bits, up to small-order terms (cf. [14, Corollary 1] or [13, Theorem 8]).

LEMMA 10. *For every $0 < \varepsilon \leq 1/2$ the following holds. Consider $\mathcal{A}$ defined as in Lemma 9 starting with an arbitrary bit string with LEADINGONES-value i. With probability at least $1 - n^{-\varepsilon} - O(1/n)$ after t generations, $t = \Omega(n \log n)$, the LEADINGONES-value is no more than*

$$i + \left(1-\frac{1}{n}\right)^i \cdot \frac{2t}{n} + O(n^\varepsilon \log n) + O\left(\sqrt{(t \log n)/n}\right) + O(t/n^2).$$

PROOF. We state the following conditions that together are sufficient conditions for the LEADINGONES-value being bounded as claimed.

1. During the first $t_1 := n^{1-\varepsilon}$ generations, the algorithm never flips the bit at position $i+1$.
2. In addition, during the following $t_2 := c_2 n \ln n$ generations after that, c_2 a large enough positive constant specified later, the LEADINGONES-value does not rise above $i + O(n^\varepsilon \log n)$.
3. In addition, during the next $t_3 := t - t_1 - t_2$ generations after the above, the algorithm gains less than $\left(1-\frac{1}{n}\right)^i \cdot \frac{2t}{n} + O(\sqrt{(t \log n)/n}) + O(t/n^2)$ further leading ones.

The probability of the first event is, by Bernoulli's inequality,

$$\left(1-\frac{1}{n}\right)^{n^{1-\varepsilon}} \geq 1 - n^{-\varepsilon}.$$

Within these t_1 generations, irrespective of the first event, each generation leads to an accepted search point with probability at least $(1-1/n)^i$. We assume $i \leq n-1$ as otherwise the claim is trivial, hence $(1-1/n)^i \geq (1-1/n)^{n-1} \geq 1/e$. By Chernoff bounds, with probability $1 - \exp(-\Omega(n^\varepsilon)) \geq 1 - O(1/n)$ $\mathcal{A}$ has evolved a search point that resulted from a sequence of at least $t_1/3$ mutations, starting with the initial search point. Assuming that this happens, then at any point in time after t_1 generations, whenever a bit is first considered for fitness evaluation, the probability of it having value 1 is bounded by (using $e^x \leq 1 + x/2$ for $-1 \leq x \leq 0$)

$$\frac{1}{2} \cdot \left(1 + \left(1-\frac{2}{n}\right)^{t_1/3}\right) \leq \frac{1}{2} \cdot (1 + \exp(-2n^{-\varepsilon}/3))$$
$$\leq \frac{1}{2} \cdot \left(2 + \frac{-n^{-\varepsilon}}{3}\right) = 1 - \frac{n^{-\varepsilon}}{6}.$$

by Lemma 8, regardless of its initial value. Using Lemma 9 with $p^* := 1 - \frac{n^{-\varepsilon}}{6}$, $\delta := 1/2$, and $t_2 = c_2 n \ln n$ generations, for a sufficiently large constant c_2, we get that with probability at least $1-1/n$ we have progress at most $O(t_2/n \cdot n^{\varepsilon}) = O(n^{\varepsilon} \log n)$.

For the third event we apply Lemma 9 again. After t_2 generations, if c_2 is large enough, we have at least $t_2/3$ accepted generations, with probability at least $1 - O(1/n)$. Then we are in a situation where $p^* \leq 1/2 + 1/n$. Further put $\delta := \sqrt{(n \log n)/t}$ and assume $c_2 \geq 1$, so that $\delta \leq 1$. Consider a time span of t generations, using $t_3 \leq t$. Then by Lemma 9, with probability at least $1 - 1/n$ the progress in t generations is bounded by

$$\left(1-\frac{1}{n}\right)^i \cdot \frac{t}{n} \cdot \frac{(1+\delta)^2}{1/2-1/n}.$$

Now we have $(1+\delta)^2 = 1 + 2\delta + \delta^2 \leq 1 + 3\delta$ and $\frac{1}{1/2-1/n} \geq 2 + 5/n$ for $n \geq 10$. Combining this with the above, we get a progress bound of

$$\left(1-\frac{1}{n}\right)^i \cdot \frac{t}{n} \cdot \left(1+3\sqrt{\frac{n \log n}{t}}\right)\left(2+\frac{5}{n}\right)$$
$$\leq \left(1-\frac{1}{n}\right)^i \cdot \frac{t}{n} \cdot \left(2+6\sqrt{\frac{n \log n}{t}}+\frac{20}{n}\right)$$
$$\leq \left(1-\frac{1}{n}\right)^i \cdot \frac{2t}{n} + 6\sqrt{\frac{t \log n}{n}} + \frac{20t}{n^2}.$$

Adding this to the previous progress bound of $O(n^{\varepsilon} \log n)$ and taking the union bound for failure probabilities proves the claim. □

The next lemma shows that blocks are easily "reset" to a small LeadingOnes-value. With constant probability, this makes the (1+1) EA spend time $\Omega(\ell n)$ on this block.

Lemma 11. *Consider the (1+1) EA on $w\text{CLOB}_{\ell,k}$ with block length $\ell = \Omega(\sqrt{n})$. For $1 \leq j \leq k$ let T_j be the stopping time at which the j most heavy blocks are optimized for the first time. Fix a non-optimized block i. Assume that during the last $\ell n/12$ generations before T_{i-1} the (1+1) EA has found at least $\ell/36$ improvements. Then there is an event that only depends on mutations within block i, occurs with probability $\Omega(1)$, and implies that $T_i \geq T_{i-1} + \ell n/6$, i. e. the (1+1) EA needs at least $\ell n/6$ generations to optimize block i.*

Proof. The process of the (1+1) EA optimizing $w\text{CLOB}_{\ell,k}$ can be split into several different processes optimizing LeadingOnes on different blocks of the function. For the heaviest non-optimized block, the (1+1) EA operating on $w\text{CLOB}_{\ell,k}$ simulates the (1+1) EA on that block. In particular, this process is independent of smaller blocks. On less heavy blocks the following holds. In generations where the (1+1) EA operating on $w\text{CLOB}_{\ell,k}$ accepts a new offspring, it simulates an algorithm $\mathcal{A}$ on the considered block that has the following properties. If the LeadingOnes-value on the block has not worsened, it accepts the new offspring. But it can accept a worse offspring under certain conditions, i. e., if a heavier block has generated an improvement. This matches the definition of $\mathcal{A}$ from Lemma 9. In generations where the (1+1) EA on $w\text{CLOB}_{\ell,k}$ rejects, block i remains unchanged, hence we can safely ignore these steps when considering $\mathcal{A}$ operating on block i.

Consider the (1+1) EA on $w\text{CLOB}_{\ell,k}$ before the mentioned $\ell/36$ improvements in heavier blocks happen. During each of these steps every mutation in block i is accepted. Consider the first $\ell/3$ bits in block i. If all these bits are set to 1 initially, the probability that one of these bits is flipped to 0 at least once in the mentioned steps is at least $1-(1-1/n)^{\ell/3 \cdot \ell/36} \geq 1 - \exp(-\ell^2/(108n)) \geq \Omega(1)$ using $\ell = \Omega(\sqrt{n})$. If not, we have a 0-bit from the beginning.

Starting from a solution with one of the first $\ell/3$ bits set to 0, the (1+1) EA operating on $w\text{CLOB}_{\ell,k}$ simulates at most $\ell n/4$ generations of the algorithm $\mathcal{A}$ on block i, as in $\ell n/4$ generations we clearly have at most $\ell n/4$ accepted steps. We apply Lemma 10 to $\mathcal{A}$ with $\varepsilon := 1/4$, starting from the search point mentioned above. We use a time span of $\ell n/4$ generations and note that the above mutation happens at a time index at least $T_i - \ell n/12$. Lemma 10 yields that at time $T_i + \ell n/6$, hence within a total number of at most $\ell n/4$ generations, the LeadingOnes-value in block i is no more than $\ell/3 + \ell/2 + O(n^{1/4} \log n) + O(\sqrt{\ell \log n}) + O(\ell/n) < \ell$ if n is large enough. This proves the claim. □

Finally, we assemble all the pieces to prove the main result of this section.

Proof of Theorem 7. The upper bound follows from considering all blocks sequentially; the expected time to gather ℓ leading ones is $O(\ell n)$ [14, Lemma 4].

It is easy to see, reusing previous arguments or [14, Lemma 4], that with probability $1 - 2^{-\Omega(\ell)}$ the (1+1) EA needs at least $\ell n/12$ generations to optimize the first, heaviest block. Defining T_j as in Lemma 11 we therefore assume $T_1 \geq \ell n/12$.

Note that at every point in time and for every non-optimal current search point the probability of the (1+1) EA generating an improvement is at least $1/n \cdot (1-1/n)^{n-1} \geq 1/(en)$. The expected number of improvements in any fixed time period of $\ell n/12$ generations is at least $\ell/(12e)$. By Chernoff bounds, with probability $1 - 2^{-\Omega(\ell)}$ we have at least $\ell n/36$ improvements. By the union bound, the probability that this holds for every time period up to generation n^2 is at least $1 - n^2 \cdot 2^{-\Omega(\ell)} = 1 - 2^{-\Omega(\ell)+2\log n} = 1 - 2^{-\Omega(\ell)}$. Then it holds in particular for every $1 \leq j \leq k$ that in the $\ell n/12$ generations preceding T_j we have had at least $\ell n/36$ improvements (unless $T_j > n^2$, in which case we are done anyway).

This means that the preconditions of Lemma 11 are fulfilled for every block. All events mentioned in Lemma 11 only concern mutations in the respective block, hence they are mutually independent between blocks. For each block we have that with probability $\Omega(1)$ the (1+1) EA spends at least $\ell n/12$ generations on the block. This establishes the lower bound $\Omega(k\ell n)$. This bound still holds when taking into account the union bound for all failure probabilities mentioned in this proof. □

5. UPPER BOUNDS BY FITNESS LEVELS

Now we show that the expected optimization time of any separable function is always bounded by the sum of expected optimization times for all subfunctions, at least asymptotically. For the ease of presentation, in this section we assume that the minimum of each f_i is zero, and that our goal is to maximize the objective value.

Throughout this section, we assume that the f_i fulfill the following *strong fitness level assumptions*. In simple words, they say that for each f_i the search space can be partitioned into fitness ranges of non-increasing thickness such that the

(1+1) EA optimizing f_i with probability at least p mutates the current individual into one with fitness larger by at least the thickness of the current level.

ASSUMPTION 1. *For each $i \in [k]$, let f_i fulfill the following assumptions. There are $\ell_i \in \mathbb{N}$ and $0 = a_{i0} < a_{i1} < \ldots < a_{i\ell_i} = \max\{f_i(x) \mid x \in S\}$. For all $j \in [\ell_i]$, let $d_{ij} := a_{ij} - a_{ij-1}$. Assume that $d_{ij} \geq d_{ij+1}$ for all $j \in [\ell_i - 1]$. Let $A_{ij} := \{x \in S \mid a_{ij-1} \leq f_i(x) < a_{ij}\}$ for all $j \in [\ell_i + 1]$, where $a_{i\ell_i+1} := \infty$. Assume that for all $j \in [\ell_i]$ and all $x \in A_{ij}$, the (1+1) EA optimizing f_i with current search point equal to x with probability p in one iteration finds a search point y with $f_i(y) \geq f_i(x) + d_{ij}$.*

THEOREM 12. *If the f_i fulfill the above strong fitness level assumptions, then the expected optimization time of the (1+1) EA on f is at most $e(1/p)\sum_{i\in[k]} \ell_i$.*

PROOF. Let $L = \{(i,j) \mid i \in [k], j \in [\ell_i]\}$ and $\ell = |L| = \sum_{i\in[k]} \ell_i$. Let $(i_1,j_1),(i_2,j_2),\ldots,(i_\ell,j_\ell)$ be an enumeration of L sorted according to decreasing d-values, that is, such that $d_{i_m,j_m} \geq d_{i_{m+1},j_{m+1}}$ for all $m \in [\ell-1]$. Let $b_0 := 0$, $b_m := \sum_{q\in[m]} d_{i_q,j_q}$ for all $m \in [\ell]$, and $b_{\ell+1} := \infty$. Let $B_m := \{x \in S \mid b_{m-1} \leq f(x) < b_m\}$ for all $m \in [\ell+1]$. Then the B_m form an f-based partition of S. Note that, by construction, $\max B_m - \min B_m < b_m - b_{m-1} = d_{i_m,j_m}$. Hence the "thickness" of these levels is non-increasing with m.

In the following, we shall show that for all $m \in [\ell]$ and $x \in B_m$, the (1+1) EA optimizing f with current search point equal to x has a probability of at least p/e to improve x in one iteration to a search point y with fitness at least $f(x) + d_{i_m,j_m}$. In particular, $y \in B_{m+1} \cup \ldots \cup B_{\ell+1}$. From this, the classical fitness level argument ([22] or Lemma 2.7 in [23]), immediately yields an expected optimization time of at most $e\ell(1/p)$.

Hence let $m \in [\ell]$ and $x \in B_m$. Then $f(x) < b_m$. For $i \in [k]$, let m_i be the number of (i_q, j_q) with $q \in [m]$ such that $i_q = i$. Note that $m = \sum_{i\in[k]} m_i$ and $b_m = \sum_{q\in[m]} d_{i_q,j_q} = \sum_{i\in[k]}\sum_{j\in[m_i]} d_{ij} = \sum_{i\in[k]}\sum_{j\in[m_i]}(a_{ij} - a_{ij-1}) = \sum_{i\in[k]} a_{im_i}$. Here the second equality stems from the fact that $(d_{i_m,j_m})_m$ is a non-increasing sequence containing the members of the, by assumption non-increasing, sequences $(d_{ij})_j$ for all i. Since

$$\sum_{i\in[k]} f_i(x) = f(x) < b_m = \sum_{i\in[k]} a_{im_i},$$

by the pigeon hole principle, there is an $i^* \in [k]$ such that $f_{i^*}(x) < a_{i^*m_{i^*}}$. Let $j^* \in [m_{i^*}]$ be such that $x \in A_{i^*,j^*}$.

Let us regard one iteration of the (1+1) EA optimizing f with current search point x. With probability $(1-1/n)^{n-|B_{i^*}|} \geq (1-1/n)^{n-1} > 1/e$, only bits in B_i are flipped in the mutation step. Conditional on this, the (1+1) EA optimizing f behaves identical to the (1+1) EA optimizing f_{i^*}. In particular, with probability at least p, we find a search point y with $f_{i^*}(y) \geq f_{i^*}(x) + d_{i^*,j^*}$. Since by construction $d_{i^*,j^*} \geq d_{i_m,j_m}$, this y is in $B_{m+1} \cup \ldots \cup B_{\ell+1}$. The total probability of the (1+1) EA finding such a y in one iteration is at least $(1/e)p$ as desired. □

The result described by Theorem 12 is at its core a very general statement as the proof relies almost exclusively on the assumed probabilities for improvements. The only "genotypic" (space-dependent) aspect is the factor e: the inverse $1/e$ is a lower bound on the probability that the (1+1) EA on f simulates a step on f_i and thereby does not alter any solution components irrelevant to f_i. This lends itself to being generalized to a general probability bound q instead of $1/e$, and arbitrary product spaces as search space. One example where the former might be useful is the consideration of mutation rates greater than $1/n$. Moreover, the result extends beyond the (1+1) EA to arbitrary Markovian black-box search algorithms $\mathcal{A}$[1] where we have a lower bound on the probability that the fitness of a best-so-far search point is increased as stated in Assumption 1. Note that for population-based heuristics this condition implies that $\mathcal{A}$ must always keep a current best search point in the population.

The following corollary summarizes these considerations.

COROLLARY 13. *Theorem 12 extends towards an upper bound of $1/(pq)\sum_{i\in[k]} \ell_i$ for an arbitrary Markovian black-box search algorithm $\mathcal{A}$ on an arbitrary product space $S = D_1 \times \cdots \times D_n$ of discrete sets $D_1, \ldots, D_n$ (f being separable on S in the obvious way) if*

1. *Assumption 1 holds with regard to $\mathcal{A}$ and x being any best-so-far point found by $\mathcal{A}$ and*
2. *for every $i \in [k]$ and in every iteration, independently with probability at least q, $q > 0$, $\mathcal{A}$ optimizing f simulates an iteration of $\mathcal{A}$ optimizing f_i where no component irrelevant to f_i is being changed.*

6. UPPER BOUNDS BY DRIFT ANALYSIS

In Section 3, we showed for unweighted sums of Boolean subfunctions a kind of parallel optimization. As a generalization, we now consider weighted separable functions of the kind $f = \sum_{i=1}^{k} w_i f_i$ for weights $w_i \in \mathbb{Z}$, and assume for simplicity that also $f_i\colon \{0,1\}^n \to \mathbb{Z}$ for $1 \leq i \leq k$. The aim is to base an analysis generalizing Section 3 on the largest range of the subfunctions, whereas the weights surprisingly do not seem to play any significant role in this context. Let $r_i := \max\{f_i(x) \mid x \in \{0,1\}^n\} - \min\{f_i(x) \mid x \in \{0,1\}^n\}$ denote the range of f_i, i. e., the difference of its largest and smallest value. We now let $r := \max_{i=1}^{k}\{r_i\}$ denote the largest range of the subfunctions and study the optimization time depending on r.

If r is sufficiently small, then the (1+1) EA on f behaves similarly as on a (generalized) linear function [6] and we obtain a runtime behavior that is similar to parallel optimization of the subfunctions, regardless of the weights w_i. More precisely, we obtain the following bound, where the number of variables only accounts for a logarithmic factor, whereas r appears as a linear factor.

THEOREM 14. *Assume $r = o(\log^{1/2} n)$ and let T^* be an upper bound on the expected optimization time of the*

[1]A black-box search algorithm can be described as a strategy for iteratively querying search points and their function values. If search points $x_0, \ldots, x_t$ have been queried, the algorithm queries another point x_{t+1} and its fitness $f(x_{t+1})$ based on $x_0, \ldots, x_t$ and $f(x_0), \ldots, f(x_t)$. A Markovian black-box search algorithm is a black-box search algorithm, which is also a Markov chain. As such, it has a current state and transition probabilities to other states only depend on the current state.

(1+1) EA that holds on every f_i, $1 \leq i \leq k$, for every initial search point. Then the expected optimization time of the (1+1) EA on $f = \sum_{i=1}^{k} w_i f_i$ is at most $(1+o(1))(4e^2 r T^* \ln n)$.

Applications

Theorem 14 allows us to analyze the optimization time of (1+1) EA on weighted generalizations of the Royal Road functions defined in Section 3. Taking over the definitions from there, we let $f := \sum_{i=1}^{k} w_i f_i$ for weights $w_i \in \mathbb{R}^+$, i. e., we obtain the unweighted Royal Road functions if $w_i = 1$ for all i. Since the (1+1) EA optimizes monomials of degree d in an expected time $O((n/d)2^d))$ (see Theorem 3.1 in [24]), we obtain from Theorem 14 the following generalization of Corollary 6.

COROLLARY 15. *The expected optimization time of the (1+1) EA on arbitrarily weighted Royal Road functions on n/d disjoint blocks of size d is $O((n/d)(\log n) \cdot 2^d)$.*

If $d = 1$, we are dealing with linear functions, where T^* equals $1/n$, i. e., the expected time for a single bit to flip. Hence, we obtain the following bound, which is only by a factor $(1 + o(1))4e$ larger than the actual optimization time [26]. At the same time, it generalizes Corollary 5.

COROLLARY 16. *The expected optimization time of the (1+1) EA on an arbitrary linear function is at most $(1 + o(1))(4e^2 n \ln n)$.*

Proof

To prove Theorem 14, we follow the techniques developed in [26] and [6] by applying drift analysis using a potential function $g(x)$ defined below. The aim is to analyze the potential $X^{(t)} := g(x^{(t)})$ of the random search point $x^{(t)}$ maintained by the (1+1) EA on f at time t. We first bound its expected one-step change $E(X^{(t)} - X^{(t+1)})$, i. e., the expected decrease of distance from time t to time $t + 1$, under certain conditions. This will allow us to bound the drift in a phase of length $2T^*$. The following lemma states this bound as well as a bound on the maximum value of the potential function, which is required in the multiplicative drift theorem (Theorem 19).

LEMMA 17.

1. *$E(X^{(t)} - X^{(t+2T^*)} \mid X^{(t)}) \geq \frac{X^{(t)}}{2e^2 r} \cdot (1 - \alpha^{-1}(n))$ for every arbitrarily slowly increasing function $\alpha(n) = \omega(1)$.*
2. *$\ln(X^{(t)}) \leq (1 + o(1)) \ln n$.*

Plugging this into Theorem 19 (formally switching over to the process $\{X_{2T^* \cdot t}\}$, $t \geq 0$) yields the upper bound from Theorem 14.

The proof of Lemma 17 relies on the analysis of the one-step drift of the potential function $g\colon \{0,1\}^n \to \mathbb{R}$. We now introduce the setup required to define $g(x)$. To ease the presentation, we make the following standard assumptions that hold without loss of generality. We imagine the variables $x_n, \ldots, x_1$ and subfunctions $f_k, \ldots, f_1$ be sorted decreasingly from left to right with decreasing significance, i. e., we call f_k and x_n the leftmost subfunction resp. variable and f_1 and x_1 the rightmost one and assume that $w_k \geq w_{k-1} \geq \cdots \geq w_1 > 0$. Moreover, we assume that the subsets are intervals, more precisely, that there are k indices $m_1 = 1, \ldots, m_k$ such that f_i only depends on the variables with index $\{m_i, \ldots, m_{i+1} - 1\}$, where $m_{k+1} = n + 1$. Since the (1+1) EA is ranking-based, i. e., does not change behavior when adding constant terms to the objective function, we may w. l. o. g. assume that $\min\{f_i(x) \mid x \in \{0,1\}^n\} = 0$ and $f_i^{\max} := \max\{f_i(x) \mid x \in \{0,1\}^n\} = r_i$. Hence, $f_i(x) \in \{0, \ldots, r_i\}$. Let $f^{\max} := \sum_{i=1}^{k} f_i^{\max}$. Recall that the aim is to maximize f, which is equivalent to finding a search point maximizing every single f_i.

DEFINITION 1. *Given a search point x and the function $f = \sum_{i=1}^{k} w_i f_i$, we write $a_i := f_i(x)$. We define the following sequence over $i \in \mathbb{N}$:*

$$\phi_i := \left(1 + \frac{r^2 \alpha(n)}{n(1 - 1/n)^{n-1}}\right)^{i-1}.$$

From this, we establish the sequence of weights g_i as follows:

$$\gamma_i := \phi_{m_i},$$

$$g_i := \min\left\{\gamma_i, g_{i-1} \cdot \frac{w_i}{w_{i-1}}\right\}$$

for all $1 < i \leq k$ and $g_1 := \gamma_1 := \phi_1 := 1$. Through this we obtain the potential function

$$g : \{0,1\}^n \to \mathbb{R}, \quad x \mapsto f^{\max} - \sum_{i=1}^{n} g_i a_i.$$

For any $i \in \{1, \ldots, n\}$, we further define the following terms

- *$\kappa(i) := \max\{j \leq i \mid g_j = \gamma_j\}$, the most significant index right of i (possibly i itself) capping according to the sequence γ_i,*
- *$L(i) := \{k, \ldots, \kappa(i)\}$, the indices left from $\kappa(i)$,*
- *$R(i) := \{\kappa(i) - 1, \ldots, 1\}$, the indices right from $\kappa(i)$.*

The idea of the potential function, reflected by the minimum operator in the definition of g_i, is to cap the original weights at γ_i in case they are "too steeply increasing" and to rebuild the slope of original weights otherwise by letting $g_i/g_{i-1} = w_i/w_{i-1}$. The variable $\kappa(i)$ is intuitively a "breaking point" and denotes the most significant subfunction right of i where g_j equals γ_j. The intuition is that the potential function will underestimate the progress made in all subfunctions being at least as significant as $f_{\kappa(i)}$ (which are the functions in $L(i)$), in particular an assumed progress made on f_i will be underestimated. In all less significant subfunctions (those in $R(i)$), we will pessimistically assume that they contribute a loss, and the choice of $\kappa(i)$ guarantees that this loss is overestimated.

Observe that the potential function g describes a distance from the optimum function value, and that $g(x) = 0$ if and only if $f(x) = f^{\max}$. As mentioned above, we are going to analyze the stochastic process $X_{t \geq 0}^{(t)}$ where $X^{(t)} = g(x^{(t)})$ for all t, and define $\Delta_t := X^{(t)} - X^{(t+1)}$. The one-step drift $E(\Delta_t)$ of the distance function will be worked out conditioned on certain events, which reflect the most significant subfunction changing its value. The following notions prepare the definition of these events.

DEFINITION 2. *Given two search points $x^{(t)}$ and $x^{(t+1)}$, we define*

- $\delta(i) := a_i^{(t)} - a_i^{(t+1)}$, *which is the change of distance w. r. t. subfunction i.*
- $I_D := \{i \in I \mid \delta(i) > 0\}$ *the subfunctions decreasing distance (good) .*
- $I_F := \{i \in I \mid \delta(i) < 0\}$ *those increasing distance (further away/bad).*
- $I_0 := \{i \in I \mid \delta(i) = 0\}$ *those with unchanged distance.*

Note that the three sets I_D, I_F and I_0 partition the set of indices I and that the indices in I_0 contribute nothing to our expected change of Δ_t.

Obviously, for $\Delta_t \neq 0$ it is necessary that $x^{(t+1)} \neq x^{(t)}$. We fix an arbitrary search point $x^{(t)}$ and let A be the event that $x^{(t+1)} \neq x^{(t)}$. The event A is equivalent to

$$I_D \neq \emptyset \text{ and } \sum_{j \in I_D} \delta(j) w_j + \sum_{j \in I_F} \delta(j) w_j \geq 0.$$

Hence, for event A to occur it is necessary that for at least one $i \in I_D$

$$\sum_{j \in I_D} \delta(j) w_j + \sum_{j \in I_F \cap L(i)} \delta(j) w_j \geq 0,$$

since we only ignore the loss due to the functions in $R(i)$. We decompose the event A according to the leftmost function decreasing distance.

DEFINITION 3. *The event A_i, $1 \leq i \leq k$, occurs iff the following two conditions hold simultaneously.*

1. $i = \max I_D$.
2. $\sum_{j \in I_D} \delta(j) w_j + \sum_{j \in I_F \cap L(i)} \delta(j) w_j \geq 0$.

Note that the event A is the *disjoint* union of the events A_i. The key inequality used to bound the one-step drift is stated in the following lemma, where we write $a_i^{(t)} = f_i(x^{(t)})$.

LEMMA 18. $E(\Delta_t \mid A_i) \geq \frac{a_i^{(t)} \cdot g_i}{er} \cdot (1 - \alpha^{-1}(n))$ *for all* $1 \leq i \leq k$ *and all* $t \geq 0$.

Before we prove Lemma 18, let us show how it can be used to prove Lemma 17.

PROOF OF LEMMA 17. We still fix an arbitrary search point $x^{(t)}$, denote by $X^{(t)} = g(x^{(t)})$ its potential and investigate the following $2T^*$ steps. As observed above, in each of these steps the potential remains either unchanged or a certain event A_i occurs. Let $A_i(t')$ be the event that A_i occurs at time t', i. e., with respect to mutation of the random search point $x^{(t')}$. The total drift within $2T^*$ steps can then be expressed as

$$E(X^{(t)} - X^{(t+2T^*)}) = \sum_{t'=t}^{t+2T^*} \sum_{i=1}^{k} E(\Delta_{t'} \mid A_i(t')) \cdot \Pr(A_i(t')).$$

Since $E(\Delta_{t'} \mid A_i(t')) \geq 0$ for any i by Lemma 18, we can concentrate on a subset of functions to bound the drift from below. Using $I := \{i \mid a_i^{(t)} < f_i^{\max}\}$, i. e., the subfunctions which do not take their optimum on $x_i^{(t)}$, we obtain

$$E(X^{(t)} - X^{(t+2T^*)}) \geq \sum_{t'=t}^{t+2T^*} \sum_{i \in I} E(\Delta_{t'} \mid A_i(t')) \cdot \Pr(A_i(t')).$$

Using Lemma 18 again, the last bound is at least

$$\sum_{i \in I} \frac{a_i^{(t)} \cdot g_i}{er} \cdot \left(1 - \frac{1}{\alpha(n)}\right) \sum_{t'=t}^{t+2T^*} \Pr(A_i(t')).$$

Note that $\sum_{i \in I} a_i^{(t)} g_i = X^{(t)}$. Hence, if the claim $\sum_{t=t'}^{t+2T^*} \Pr(A_i(t')) \geq 1/(2e)$ can be proven, we get

$$E(X^{(t)} - X^{(t+2T^*)} \mid X^{(t)}) \geq \frac{X^{(t)}}{2e^2 r} \cdot \left(1 - \frac{1}{\alpha(n)}\right),$$

which proves the first statement of Lemma 17. To prove the missing claim, we use the fact that T^* is a bound on the expected optimization time, and therefore, in particular, a bound on the expected time for an improvement, valid on every subfunction for every initial search point. With probability at least $(1 - 1/n)^{n-1} \geq e^{-1}$, a step of the (1+1) EA does only flip bits belonging to the subfunction under consideration. Hence, the expected number of steps until it improves the subfunction is at most eT^*, and by Markov's inequality the improvement takes place after at most $2eT^*$ steps with probability at least 1/2.

For the second statement of Lemma 17, we use that for every t it holds $X^{(t)} \leq \sum_{i=1}^{k} r\gamma_i \leq \sum_{i=1}^{n} r\phi_i$. Using the geometric series and the inequality $1 + x \leq e^x$, the latter is at most

$$\frac{r\left(1 + \frac{r^2\alpha(n)}{e^{-1}n}\right)^n}{\frac{r^2\alpha(n)}{e^{-1}n}} \leq \frac{e^{-1}n \cdot e^{enr^2\alpha(n)/n}}{r\alpha(n)} \leq \frac{ne^{er^2\alpha(n)}}{r\alpha(n)}.$$

From this we obtain

$$\ln(X^{(0)}) \leq er^2\alpha(n) + \ln(n) - \ln(r^2\alpha(n)) = (1 + o(1)) \ln n,$$

where the final statement follows from the assumption $r = o(\log^{1/2} n)$ and the fact that $\alpha(n)$ is arbitrarily slowly increasing (assuming large enough n such that $\alpha(n) \geq 1$). □

The still outstanding proof of Lemma 18 requires a careful analysis of the one-step drift, taking into account the specific structure of the drift function.

PROOF OF LEMMA 18. Recall that we condition on the event A_i (Definition 3), which is based on the leftmost subfunction improving value. Moreover, recall the notions introduced in Definitions 1 and 2. Let

$$\Delta_L(i) := \sum_{j \in I_D} \delta(j) g_j + \sum_{j \in I_F \cap L(i)} \delta(j) g_j,$$

$$\Delta_R(i) := \sum_{j \in I_F \cap R(i)} \delta(j) g_j.$$

Clearly, we have $\Delta_t = \Delta_L(i) + \Delta_R(i)$. By the linearity of expectation, we obtain

$$E(\Delta_t \mid A_i) = E(\Delta_L(i) \mid A_i) + E(\Delta_R(i) \mid A_i). \quad (1)$$

We first show that $(\Delta_L(i) \mid A_i)$ is a nonnegative random variable, i. e., the probability of any negative outcome is 0. To prove this assume that A_i holds, which means that no subfunction left of f_i decreases distance. Furthermore, note that by definition

$$g_j / g_{\kappa(i)} \leq w_j / w_{\kappa(i)} \text{ for } k \geq j > i, \quad (2)$$

$$g_j / g_{\kappa(i)} = w_j / w_{\kappa(i)} \text{ for } i \geq j \geq \kappa(i), \quad (3)$$

$$g_j / g_{\kappa(i)} \geq w_j / w_{\kappa(i)} \text{ for } \kappa(i) > j \geq 1 \,. \quad (4)$$

Hence,

$$\begin{aligned}
&(\Delta_L(i) \mid A_i) \\
&= \sum_{j\in I_D} \delta(j)g_j + \sum_{j\in I_F\cap L(i)} \delta(j)g_j \\
&\geq \sum_{j\in I_D} \delta(j)g_{\kappa(i)} \cdot \frac{w_j}{w_{\kappa(i)}} + \sum_{j\in I_F\cap L(i)} \delta(j)g_{\kappa(i)} \cdot \frac{w_j}{w_{\kappa(i)}} \\
&= \frac{g_{\kappa(i)}}{w_{\kappa(i)}} \left(\sum_{j\in I_D} \delta(j)w_j + \sum_{j\in I_F\cap L(i)} \delta(j)w_j \right) \geq 0,
\end{aligned}$$

where the first inequality uses (3) and (4) to bound the first sum and (2) to bound the second one. The last inequality stems from the definition of A_i.

Now let S_i be the event that $|I_F \cap L(i)| = 0$, that is, that no function in $L(i)$ is increasing distance. We have

$$\begin{aligned}
&E(\Delta_L(i) \mid A_i) = \\
&E(\Delta_L(i) \mid A_i \cap S_i)\cdot \Pr(S_i \mid A_i) + E(\Delta_L(i) \mid A_i \cap \bar{S}_i)\cdot \Pr(\bar{S}_i \mid A_i)
\end{aligned}$$

by the law of total probability. Since the random variable $(\Delta_L(i) \mid A_i)$ cannot have any negative outcomes, all these conditional expectations are non-negative as well. From (1) we thus derive

$$E(\Delta_t \mid A_i) \geq E(\Delta_L(i) \mid A_i \cap S_i)\cdot \Pr(S_i \mid A_i) + E(\Delta_R(i) \mid A_i). \tag{5}$$

We will bound this central inequality furthermore to obtain our result. For $(S_i \mid A_i)$ to occur, it is sufficient that all functions of index $j \in L(i) \setminus \{i\}$ are not increasing the distance from their respective optimum (since A_i already demands that f_i is not increasing distance). These functions together are defined on the variables with index in $\{m_{\kappa(i)}, \ldots, n\} \setminus \{m_i, \ldots, m_{i+1} - 1\}$, i. e., at most $n - m_{\kappa(i)}$ variables. Consequently, $\Pr(S_i \mid A_i) \geq (1 - 1/n)^{n - m_{\kappa(i)}} \geq (1 - 1/n)^{n-1}$. We pessimistically assume that $\delta(i) = 1$, i. e., function f_i decreases distance from its optimum by only 1. We estimate $E(\Delta_L(i) \mid A_i \cap S_i) \geq 1 \cdot g_i \geq (a_i^{(t)}/r) \cdot g_i$.

We also pessimistically assume that every function of index $j \in R(i)$ that is touched by a mutation increases distance by the maximum possible value, i. e., $\delta(j) = -r$. By the linearity of expectation, the expected loss with respect to f_j, which is dependent on the variables of index $m_j, \ldots, m_{j+1} - 1$, is bounded from below by

$$(1/n) \sum_{q=m_j}^{m_{j+1}-1} -rg_j \geq -(r/n) \sum_{q=m_j}^{m_{j+1}-1} \phi_q$$

since $g_j \leq \phi_{m_j}$. Taking together the variables for all functions in $R(i)$, we obtain $E(\Delta_R(i) \mid A_i) \geq -(r/n) \cdot \sum_{j=1}^{m_{\kappa(i)}-1} \phi_j$. These estimates and (5) yield

$$\begin{aligned}
E(\Delta_t \mid A_i) &\geq (1 - 1/n)^{n-1} \frac{a_i^{(t)} g_i}{r} - (r/n) \sum_{j=1}^{m_{\kappa(i)}-1} \phi_j \\
&= (1 - 1/n)^{n-1} \frac{a_i^{(t)} g_i}{r g_{\kappa(i)}} \gamma_{\kappa(i)} - (r/n) \sum_{j=1}^{m_{\kappa(i)}-1} \phi_j.
\end{aligned}$$

Plugging in the definition of ϕ_j in the geometric series, the last sum is estimated by

$$\begin{aligned}
\sum_{j=1}^{m_{\kappa(i)}-1} \phi_j &= \frac{\left(1 + \frac{r^2\alpha(n)}{n(1-1/n)^{n-1}}\right)^{m_{\kappa(i)}} - 1}{\frac{r^2\alpha(n)}{n(1-1/n)^{n-1}}} \\
&\leq \frac{\phi_{m_{\kappa(i)}}}{\frac{r^2\alpha(n)}{n(1-1/n)^{n-1}}} = \frac{\gamma_{\kappa(i)} n(1-1/n)^{n-1}}{r^2\alpha(n)}.
\end{aligned}$$

Hence,

$$\begin{aligned}
E(\Delta_t \mid A_i) &\geq (1 - 1/n)^{n-1} \frac{a_i^{(t)} g_i}{r g_{\kappa(i)}} \gamma_{\kappa(i)} - (1 - 1/n)^{n-1} \frac{\gamma_{\kappa(i)}}{r\alpha(n)} \\
&\geq (1 - 1/n)^{n-1} \frac{a_i^{(t)} g_i}{r g_{\kappa(i)}} \gamma_{\kappa(i)} \left(1 - \frac{1}{\alpha(n)}\right) \\
&= (1 - 1/n)^{n-1} \frac{a_i^{(t)} g_i}{r} \left(1 - \frac{1}{\alpha(n)}\right).
\end{aligned}$$

The last inequality stems from (2), which gives $g_i/g_{\kappa(i)} \geq 1$, as well as from the fact that $a_i^{(t)} \geq 1$. The last equality uses $g_{\kappa(i)} = \gamma_{\kappa(i)}$ from (3). Since $(1 - 1/n)^{n-1} \geq e^{-1}$, the lemma has been proved. □

One might wonder whether the factor $\ln n$ in Theorem 14 could be improved to a factor $\ln k$, which appears in Theorem 3, i. e., the bound for the case of unweighted, Boolean subfunctions covered in Section 3. However, we do not think this is possible in general. To support this conjecture, consider the following function f. We divide the set of variables into $k = \log^{1/3} n$ contiguous blocks of size $d = n/k$. Each block $x_i = \{x_{i1}, \ldots, x_{id}\}$ is then further divided into k subblocks of length n/k^2, which define the subfunctions with range $\{0, \ldots, k\}$ by counting the leading number of all-ones subblocks. The subfunctions are finally given exponentially scaled weights using ideas made precise in Section 4. Formally,

$$f := \sum_{i=1}^{k} (n+1)^{k-i} \sum_{a=1}^{k} \prod_{j=1}^{an/k^2} x_{ij}.$$

Here we feel that the (1+1) EA working on f will be forced to optimize the blocks sequentially. We hypothesise that the expected optimization time per block is $\Theta(kT^*)$, where T^* is the expected optimization time per subblock, and the total expected optimization time is $\Theta(k^2T^*)$, or $\Theta(rkT^*)$ using the language of Theorem 14. Altogether, $k = \log^{1/3} n$ would appear as a linear factor, which suggests that the theorem requires a factor that is polylogarithmic in n. In this sense, the weighted case considered in this section seems to be slightly harder than the unweighted, Boolean case from Section 3.

7. CONCLUSIONS AND FUTURE WORK

We have investigated the question whether in separable functions subfunctions are optimized "in parallel" by evolutionary algorithms. This behavior seems plausible as evolutionary algorithms can make progress on all subfunctions in parallel. It relates to the notion of "implicit parallelism" discussed in the context of Schema theory and the building-block hypothesis [9]. While implicit parallelism as a general concept is disputed [27], in the favorable setting of separable functions the notion of parallelism still seems plausible.

Indeed, the simple (1+1) EA can optimize sums of k Boolean functions in time $O(T^* \log k)$, where T^* is an upper bound on the expected optimization on any subfunction from any initial search point. This general result has led to a significant improvement of the best known upper bound for Royal Road functions. We have generalized this result towards sums of weighted subfunctions, and a slightly larger fitness range for each subfunction: non-negative integers up to $r = o(\log^{1/2} n)$. This has led to an upper bound of $O(T^* r \log n)$.

On the other hand, we have shown that for a separable sum of weighted LEADINGONES-functions the (1+1) EA typically optimizes the subfunctions roughly sequentially. Mutations increasing the fitness of a subfunction with a large weight can at the same time destroy prefixes of leading ones in subfunctions with smaller weights.

Our results show that the question of whether subfunctions are optimized in parallel is more involved than previously thought. We have presented examples and conditions for "parallel" and "sequential" optimization behavior, and there may exist further functions where the optimization behavior of EAs is somewhat in between these two extremes. Also note that we required T^* to be an upper bound on the expected optimization time that holds for every initialization. This does not well reflect the expected optimization time on functions that contain hard local optima that are reached very rarely when using random initialization. We believe that using a more relaxed definition of T^*, even larger performance gaps can be created for artificial functions.

The specific results presented here have only been shown for the (1+1) EA in pseudo-Boolean search spaces. However, we are optimistic that the effects demonstrated here also occur in more sophisticated EAs and in other discrete product spaces.

As future work, we intend to apply the proof techniques developed here to obtain tight bounds for monotone polynomials. The latter consist of weighted subfunctions on potentially overlapping sets of bits; bits that are present in multiple subfunctions agree in terms of their optimal bit value. A more detailed analysis of monotone polynomials would improve results from Wegener and Witt [23]. Another direction is to analyze the impact of crossover in the context of separable functions. A recent analysis by Sudholt [20] has shown that using crossover can roughly halve the expected number of function evaluations on separable functions like ONEMAX and Royal Road functions.

8. REFERENCES

[1] A. Auger and B. Doerr. *Theory of Randomized Search Heuristics.* World Scientific, 2011.

[2] K. De Jong. *An Analysis of the Behavior of a Class of Genetic Adaptive Systems.* PhD thesis, University of Michigan, Dept. of Computer and Communication Sciences, Ann Arbor, Michigan, 1975.

[3] B. Doerr and L. Goldberg. Drift analysis with tail bounds. In *Proceedings of Parallel Problem Solving from Nature (PPSN XI), Part I,* LNCS 6238, pages 174–183. Springer, 2010.

[4] B. Doerr and L. A. Goldberg. Adaptive drift analysis. *Algorithmica,* 2012. To appear, http://dx.doi.org/10.1007/s00453-011-9585-3.

[5] B. Doerr, D. Johannsen, and C. Winzen. Multiplicative drift analysis. In *Proceedings of Genetic and Evolutionary Computation Conference (GECCO 2010),* pages 1449–1456. ACM, 2010.

[6] B. Doerr and S. Pohl. Run-time analysis of the (1+1) evolutionary algorithm optimizing linear functions over a finite alphabet. In *Proceedings of the Genetic and Evolutionary Computation Conference (GECCO 2012),* pages 1317–1324. ACM Press, 2012.

[7] S. Droste, T. Jansen, and I. Wegener. A rigorous complexity analysis of the (1+1) evolutionary algorithm for separable functions with Boolean inputs. *Evolutionary Computation,* 6(2):185–196, 1998.

[8] S. Droste, T. Jansen, and I. Wegener. On the analysis of the (1+1) evolutionary algorithm. *Theoretical Computer Science,* 276:51–81, 2002.

[9] D. E. Goldberg. *Genetic Algorithms in Search Optimization and Machine Learning.* Addison-Wesley, 1989.

[10] J. He and X. Yao. Drift analysis and average time complexity of evolutionary algorithms. *Artificial Intelligence,* 127:51–81, 2001.

[11] J. Jägersküpper. A blend of Markov-chain and drift analysis. In *Proceedings of Parallel Problem Solving from Nature (PPSN X),* LNCS 5199, pages 41–51. Springer, 2008.

[12] T. Jansen and R. P. Wiegand. The cooperative coevolutionary (1+1) EA. *Evolutionary Computation,* 12(4):405–434, 2004.

[13] T. Jansen and C. Zarges. Fixed budget computations: A different perspective on run time analysis. In *Proceedings of the Genetic and Evolutionary Computation Conference (GECCO 2012),* pages 1325–1332. ACM Press, 2012.

[14] J. Lässig and D. Sudholt. The benefit of migration in parallel evolutionary algorithms. In *Proceedings of the Genetic and Evolutionary Computation Conference (GECCO 2010),* pages 1105–1112. ACM Press, 2010.

[15] M. Mitchell, S. Forrest, and J. H. Holland. The royal road for genetic algorithms: Fitness landscapes and GA performance. In *Proceedings of the First European Conference on Artificial Life,* pages 245–254. MIT Press, 1991.

[16] M. Mitzenmacher and E. Upfal. *Probability and Computing.* Cambridge University Press, 2005.

[17] R. Motwani and P. Raghavan. *Randomized Algorithms.* Cambridge University Press, 1995.

[18] M. Potter and K. De Jong. A cooperative coevolutionary approach to function optimization. In *Parallel Problem Solving from Nature – PPSN III,* volume 866 of *LNCS,* pages 249–257. Springer, 1994.

[19] D. Sudholt. General lower bounds for the running time of evolutionary algorithms. In *Proceedings of Parallel Problem Solving from Nature (PPSN XI), Part I,* LNCS 6238, pages 124–133. Springer, 2010.

[20] D. Sudholt. Crossover speeds up building-block assembly. In *Proceedings of the Genetic and Evolutionary Computation Conference (GECCO 2012),* pages 689–696. ACM Press, 2012.

[21] K. Tăng, X. Lĭ, P. N. Suganthan, Z. Yáng, and T. Weise. Benchmark Functions for the CEC'2010

Special Session and Competition on Large-Scale Global Optimization. Technical report, University of Science and Technology of China (USTC), School of Computer Science and Technology, Nature Inspired Computation and Applications Laboratory (NICAL): Héféi, Ānhuī, China, 2010.
[22] I. Wegener. Methods for the analysis of evolutionary algorithms on pseudo-Boolean functions. In R. Sarker, X. Yao, and M. Mohammadian, editors, *Evolutionary Optimization*, pages 349–369. Kluwer, 2002.
[23] I. Wegener and C. Witt. On the analysis of a simple evolutionary algorithm on quadratic pseudo-boolean functions. *Journal of Discrete Algorithms*, 3(1):61–78, 2005.
[24] I. Wegener and C. Witt. On the optimization of monotone polynomials by simple randomized search heuristics. *Combinatorics, Probability & Computing*, 14(1-2):225–247, 2005.
[25] D. Whitley, K. Mathias, S. Rana, and J. Dzubera. Evaluating evolutionary algorithms. *Artificial Intelligence*, 85:245–276, 1996.
[26] C. Witt. Tight bounds on the optimization time of a randomized search heuristic on linear functions. *Combinatorics, Probability and Computing*, 22(2):294–318, 2013.
[27] A. H. Wright, M. D. Vose, and J. E. Rowe. Implicit parallelism. In *Proceedings of the 2003 international conference on Genetic and evolutionary computation: Part II*, GECCO'03, pages 1505–1517. Springer, 2003.

APPENDIX

THEOREM 19 (MULTIPLICATIVE DRIFT [4]). *Let $S \subseteq \mathbb{R}$ be a finite set of positive numbers with minimum 1. Let $\{X^{(t)}\}_{t\geq 0}$ be a sequence of random variables over $S \cup \{0\}$. Let T be the random first point in time $t \geq 0$ for which $X^{(t)} = 0$.*

Suppose that there exists a $\delta > 0$ such that

$$E(X^{(t)} - X^{(t+1)} \mid X^{(t)} = s) \geq \delta s$$

for all $s \in S$ with $\Pr(X^{(t)} = s) > 0$. Then for all $s_0 \in S$ with $\Pr(X^{(0)} = s_0) > 0$,

$$E(T \mid X^{(0)} = s_0) \leq \frac{\ln(s_0) + 1}{\delta}.$$

Moreover, it holds that $\Pr(T > (\ln(s_0) + t)/\delta)) \leq e^{-t}$.

Optimizing Expected Path Lengths with Ant Colony Optimization Using Fitness Proportional Update

Matthias Feldmann
Saarland University
Saarbrücken, Germany

Timo Kötzing
Max Planck Institute for Informatics
Saarbrücken, Germany

ABSTRACT

We study the behavior of a Max-Min Ant System (MMAS) on the stochastic single-destination shortest path (SDSP) problem. Two previous papers already analyzed this setting for two slightly different MMAS algorithms, where the pheromone update fitness-independently rewards edges of the best-so-far solution.

The first paper showed that, when the best-so-far solution is not reevaluated and the stochastic nature of the edge weights is due to noise, the MMAS will find a tree of edges successfully and efficiently identify a shortest path tree with minimal noise-free weights. The second paper used reevaluation of the best-so-far solution and showed that the MMAS finds paths which beat any other path in direct comparisons, if existent. For both results, for some random variables, this corresponds to a tree with minimal expected weights.

In this work we analyze a variant of MMAS that works with fitness-proportional update on stochastic-weight graphs with arbitrary random edge weights from $[0, 1]$. For δ such that any suboptimal path is worse by at least δ than an optimal path, then, with suitable parameters, the graph will be optimized after $O\left(\frac{n^3 \ln(n/\delta)}{\delta^3}\right)$ iterations (in expectation).

In order to prove the above result, the multiplicative and the variable drift theorem are adapted to continuous search spaces.

Categories and Subject Descriptors

F.2 [**Theory of Computation**]: Analysis of Algorithms and Problem Complexity

General Terms

Theory, algorithms

Keywords

Ant colony optimization, stochastic problem, single-destination shortest path, theory

FOGA'13, January 16-20, 2013, Adelaide, Australia.

1. INTRODUCTION

Ant Colony Optimization (ACO) is a randomized general purpose optimization meta heuristic with a very broad field of application and was first described in Dorigo's Ph.D. thesis [6]. ACO is inspired by swarm intelligence exhibited by ant colonies, where complex behavior emerges from the simple behavior of individual ants, using *pheromones* as an indirect communication mechanism. In particular, the idea is based on the foraging behavior of ant colonies and develops as well as stores its knowledge in the pheromones. The paper [22] presents a way of ensuring exploration of the search space by upper and lower bounds on the pheromones (resulting in so-called Max-Min Ant Systems, MMAS).

Although the single-destination shortest paths problem is one of the most natural applications of ACO, it was also used to solve many other problems, including NP-hard ones such as the Traveling Salesperson Problem (TSP) [6, 7] and more [8]. In general, ACO-algorithms are employed when a solution consists of several components; artificial ants then construct solutions by choosing components. Pheromone is added to components which are often contained in good solutions (as they hopefully carry some responsibility for the good quality of the solution), while pheromone is evaporated from others. The magnitude of the pheromone update is governed by the so-called *evaporation factor* ρ. Small ρ leads to a slower but broader search in the search space, usually resulting in better solutions at the cost of a longer running time of the algorithm.

On the theoretical side, there is a good number of analyses regarding the behavior of ACO algorithms for about a decade, starting with early convergence proofs [9,10] to more recent advances on combinatorial problems like MST [19] and TSP [16], and pseudo-Boolean functions [17]. Of particular interest to this paper is the work in [1] on the single-destination shortest path (SDSP) problem, a problem equivalent to the classical single-*source* shortest path (SSSP) problem. The authors of [1] give an elitist MMAS (which we call MMAS-el, "el" being short for "elitist") for this problem and show a good optimization behavior. We are here interested in a *stochastic* version of SDSP, and the optimization behavior of algorithms similar to MMAS-el.

Experiments have shown that in problems involving uncertainty, ACO algorithms can be particularly successful [2]. The papers [11, 12] give first formal analyses of ACO algorithms in uncertain domains and show convergence to the desired solutions. The paper [14] picks up on MMAS-el and gives a rigorous analysis of its performance on the stochastic

SDSP problem and shows under which conditions optimization is successful.

The general setting of [14] was that the stochastic nature of the path lengths is due to *noise*. The goal then was to find the edge with the best noise-less weight. In particular, from [14] we know that MMAS-el is not necessarily well-suited for finding solutions that are *optimal in expectation*, as the search is guided by the best-so-far solution.

In [4], the MMAS-el algorithm was modified by re-evaluating the best-so-far solution every iteration to avoid permanently being mislead by a single exceptionally good evaluation of a non-optimal solution. The paper shows that, in this case, the pheromones converge to the solution which has a better evaluation against any other solution in a direct comparison more than half of the time; however, such a solution need not exist, and even if it exists, it is not necessarily the solution optimal in expectation.

In this work we analyze a different variant of the MMAS-el, based on fitness proportional pheromone update (we call this algorithm MMAS-fp), on the stochastic SDSP problem; this scheme is also used in practice [22]. In difference to MMAS-el, in each iteration, the newly constructed solution always gets rewarded, but the amount of pheromone added depends on the quality of the solution; no best-so-far solution needs to be stored. This mechanism leads to an implicit averaging and we prove that (a normalizing variant of) MMAS-fp finds all shortest paths that are better than non-optimal paths by at least δ in

$$O\left(\frac{n^3 \ln(n/\delta)}{\delta^3}\right)$$

iterations.

This gives a qualitative difference to [14] and [4], where the algorithms did not favor paths that are good in expectation, but instead paths either have low weights with reasonable probability (in [14]) or paths which come out better than others in direct comparison with probability higher than 0.5 (in [4]). As an illustration, consider the following (multi-)graph with random variables A, B and C as edge weights.

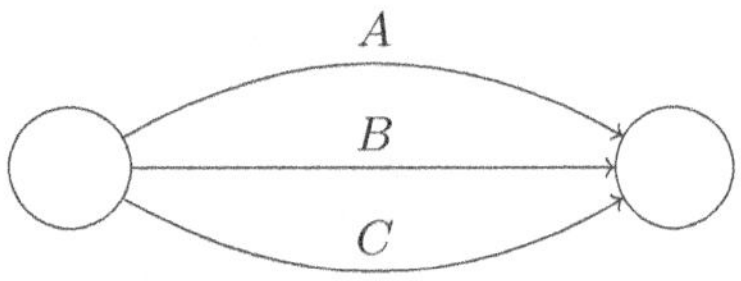

Consider A to be 0 with probability 0.01 and 200 otherwise; B to be 1 with probability 0.6 and 100 otherwise; and C to be always 10. In this setting, MMAS-el as in [14] will eventually find and converge to the edge with random weight A, as here a very low weight of 0 is possible. MMAS-el with re-evaluation as in [4] will converge to the edge with weight B, as it comes out better than any other edge with probability at least 0.6. Finally, MMAS-fp will converge to edge C, the edge best in expectation.

For the mathematical analysis we use the multiplicative and the variable drift theorem (see [5] and [15, 18], respectively), as well as well as recent improvements [4,21]. But as these drift theorems require discrete search spaces, we adapt both formally to continuous domains. This is necessary, as the pheromones are updated with the random outcome of fitness evaluations, so that uncountably many different pheromone values are possible after a single iteration. Our proofs for these adaptations make use of suitable discretizations of the search space. Note that the initial drift theorem [13] did not require finiteness of the search space; similarly, one version of the multiplicative drift theorem does not require this [3].

In Section 2 we give our continuous drift theorems; we define the problem and our algorithms formally in Section 3. Section 4 gives our results on the performance of MMAS-fp and Section 5 concludes.

2. DRIFT THEOREM ADAPTATIONS

In this chapter we first adapt the multiplicative drift theorem to continuous search spaces, which we will apply in a first runtime analysis in Section 4. Afterwards we combine the progress made in [4] and [21] on variable drift theorems to new such drift theorem, before we show in a second step that here the restriction to finite state sets is (with a minor restriction) not necessary either.

2.1 Continuous Multiplicative Drift

If we add the restriction of a finite search space in the theorem just below (i.e., S finite instead of a bounded interval), we get the known multiplicative drift theorem [5]. In a somewhat different setting, this theorem has been proven without use of other drift theorems in [3]; we give another proof here to exemplify the discretization in this simple case of the multiplicative drift theorem, so that our later application in the proof of Theorem 3 is easier to follow.

THEOREM 1. *Let $S = [s_{min}, s_{\max}] \subseteq \mathbb{R}^+$ be a set of positive numbers with minimum s_{min} and maximum $s_{\max}$. Let $(X^t)_{t\in\mathbb{N}}$ be a sequence of random variables over $S \cup \{0\}$. Let T be the random variable denoting the first point in time $t \in \mathbb{N}$ for which $X^t = 0$. Suppose that there exists a constant $\delta > 0$ such that, for all t and closed intervals $I \subseteq S$ with $P(X^t \in I) > 0$,*

$$E(X^t - X^{t+1} \mid X^t \in I) \geq \delta \min(I).$$

Then, for all closed intervals $I_0 \subseteq S$ with $P(X^0 \in I_0) > 0$, we have

$$E(T \mid X^0 \in I_0) \leq \frac{1 + \ln(\max(I_0)/s_{min})}{\delta}.$$

PROOF. Let $\varepsilon \in \mathbb{R}$ such that $0 < \varepsilon \leq \min(\delta/4, \delta s/8)$. We define a function f discretizing our search space as follows. For all x, we let

$$f(x) = \min\left(\left\lceil \frac{x}{\varepsilon} \right\rceil \varepsilon, s_{\max}\right).$$

We let $S' = \{f(x) \mid x \in S\}$ be our discretized search space. As $|S'| \leq s_{\max}/\varepsilon$, $S' \subseteq S$ is a finite set of positive numbers. Note that, for all x with $s_{min} \leq x \leq s_{\max}$, we have $|f(x) - x| \leq \varepsilon$; furthermore, since only 0 is mapped to 0, and 0 is the only pre-image of 0, we have that T is the random variable denoting the first point in time $t \in \mathbb{N}$ for which $f(X^t) = 0$. We want to apply the multiplicative drift theorem from [5] to the sequence of random variables $\left(f(X^t)\right)_{t\in\mathbb{N}}$. For all

$s \in S'$, we have

$$\begin{aligned} &E(f(X^t) - f(X^{t+1}) \mid f(X^t) = s) \\ &\quad \geq E(f(X^t) - f(X^{t+1}) \mid s - \varepsilon < X^t \leq s) \\ &\quad \geq E(X^t - X^{t+1} \mid s - \varepsilon < X^t \leq s) - 2\varepsilon \\ &\quad \geq \delta\,(s - \varepsilon) - 2\varepsilon \\ &\quad \geq s\delta\,(1 - \varepsilon/\delta - 2\varepsilon/(s\delta)). \end{aligned}$$

From the condition on ε we know that this bound is positive. Let $I_0 \subseteq S$ be a closed interval with $P(X^0 \in I_0) > 0$; thus, there is $s_0 \leq \max(I_0)$ such that $P(f(X^0) = f(s_0)) > 0$. Hence, we get

$$\begin{aligned} E(T \mid X^0 \in I_0) &\leq E(T \mid f(X^0) \leq f(\max(I_0))) \\ &\leq \frac{1 + \ln\left((\max(I_0) + \varepsilon)/s_{min}\right)}{\delta\,(1 - 1/k - \delta/k)} \end{aligned}$$

from the multiplicative drift theorem [5]. For every ε as above, we have that $b(\varepsilon) := E(T|f(X^0))$ is an upper bound on $E(T|X^0)$. Thus, $\lim_{\varepsilon \to 0} b(\varepsilon)$ is also an upper bound on $E(T|X^0)$, because for every $z > \lim_{\varepsilon \to 0} b(\varepsilon)$ an ε' can be found such that $z > b(\varepsilon')$. Thus,

$$E(T|X^0 \in I_0) \leq \lim_{\varepsilon \to 0} b(\varepsilon) = \frac{1 + \ln\left(\max(I_0)/s_{min}\right)}{\delta}.$$

This shows the claim. □

2.2 Continuous Variable Drift

The variable drift theorem presented in [15] was improved in two independent ways, once in [4] (allowing for non-monotone drift functions) and in [21] (allowing for non-differentiable drift functions).

It is easy to see that the proofs of these two drift theorems can be combined to get the combined result as follows.

THEOREM 2. *Let $(X^t)_{t\geq 0}$ be a sequence of random variables over a finite state space $0 \in S \subseteq \mathbb{R}_0^+$ and let $s_{min} := \min\{x \in S | x > 0\}$. Furthermore, let T be the random variable denoting the first point in time $t \in \mathbb{N}$ for which $X^t = 0$. Suppose that there exist $c \geq 1, d > 0$ and a function $h : \mathbb{R}^+ \to \mathbb{R}^+$ such that the function $\frac{1}{h(x)}$ is integrable on $[s_{min}, s_{\max}]$ and*

- *for all $t < T$, $E(X^t - X^{t+1} \mid X^t) \geq h(X^t)$;*
- *for all $t < T$, $P(|X^t - X^{t+1}| \leq d) = 1$; and*
- *for all $x < y$ with $y - x \leq d$, we have $h(x) \leq c\,h(y)$.*

Then

$$E(T \mid X^0) \leq c\left(\frac{s_{min}}{h(s_{min})} + \int_{s_{min}}^{X^0} \frac{1}{h(x)} dx\right).$$

For $d = s_{\max}$ and $c = 1$, Theorem 2 yields and demands as much as the theorem presented in [21]. A proof of this theorem can be found in the appendix.

We can now adapt this variable drift theorem to one with continuous search spaces much like in Theorem 1 for the case of multiplicative drift, using the same proof idea. However, we will need to add the restriction of h being continuous.

THEOREM 3. *Let $(X^t)_{t\geq 0}$ be a sequence of random variables over a state space $S = [s_{min}, s_{\max}] \cup 0 \subseteq \mathbb{R}_0^+$ and let $s_{min} > 0$. Furthermore, let T be the random variable denoting the first point in time $t \in \mathbb{N}$ for which $X^t = 0$. Suppose that there exist $c \geq 1$, $d, \delta > 0$ and a $h : \mathbb{R}^+ \to \mathbb{R}^+$ continuous such that the function $\frac{1}{h(x)}$ is integrable on $[s_{min}, s_{\max}]$ and, for all $t < T$ and closed intervals $I \subseteq S$ with $P(X^t \in I)$,*

- *$E(X^t - X^{t+1} | X^t \in I) \geq \inf_{x \in I} h(x)$;*
- *$P(|X^t - X^{t+1}| \leq d - \delta) = 1$; and*
- *for all $x < y$ with $y - x \leq d$, we have $h(x) \leq c\,h(y)$.*

Then, for all intervals I_0 with $P(X^0 \in I_0) > 0$,

$$E(T \mid X^0 \in I_0) \leq c\left(\frac{s_{min}}{h(s_{min})} + \int_{s_{min}}^{\max(I_0)} \frac{1}{h(x)} dx\right).$$

PROOF. Let $h_{min} = \inf_{s \in [s_{min}, s_{\max}]} h(s)$; elementary analysis shows $h_{min} \neq 0$. For all ε such that

$$0 < \varepsilon < \min\{h_{min}/4, d/2, \delta/2\}$$

we define f such that, for all $x \geq 0$,

$$f(x) = \max\left(\left\lfloor \frac{x}{\varepsilon} \right\rfloor \varepsilon, s_{min}\right),$$

just as in the proof of Theorem 1. Let $S' = \{0\} \cup \{f(s) \mid s \in S\}$. Clearly, S' is a finite set of positive numbers. For all $x > s_{min}$ we have $|f(x) - x| \leq \varepsilon$ and $f(s_{min}) = s_{min}$. We define a function $h' : \mathbb{R}^+ \to \mathbb{R}^+$, such that, for all x, $h'(x) = \inf_{x \leq s < x+\varepsilon} h(s) - 2\varepsilon$, and $c' := c(1 + \frac{2\varepsilon}{h_{min} - 2\varepsilon})$. We have, for all $t < T$ and $x \in S'$,

$$\begin{aligned} &E(f(X^t) - f(X^{t+1}) \mid f(X^t) = x) \\ &\quad \geq E(X^t - X^{t+1} - 2\varepsilon \mid x \leq X^t < x + \varepsilon) \\ &\quad \geq E(X^t - X^{t+1} \mid x \leq X^t < x + \varepsilon) - 2\varepsilon \\ &\quad \geq \inf_{x \leq s < x+\varepsilon} h(s) - 2\varepsilon = h'(x) \end{aligned}$$

and

$$\begin{aligned} P(f(X^t) - f(X^{t+1}) \leq d) &\geq P(X^t - X^{t+1} + 2\varepsilon \leq d) \\ &= P(X^t - X^{t+1} \leq d - 2\varepsilon) \\ &\geq P(X^t - X^{t+1} \leq d - \delta) = 1. \end{aligned}$$

For all z, let $\bar{h}(z) = \inf_{z \leq s < z+\varepsilon} h(s)$. We have, for all $x < y$ with $y - x \leq d$, using $h_{min} \leq \bar{h}(y)$, we have

$$\begin{aligned} c'h'(y) &= c\left(1 + \frac{2\varepsilon}{h_{min} - 2\varepsilon}\right)(\bar{h}(y) - 2\varepsilon) \\ &\geq c\left(1 + \frac{2\varepsilon}{\bar{h}(y) - 2\varepsilon}\right)(\bar{h}(y) - 2\varepsilon) \\ &= c\bar{h}(y) \\ &\geq c\bar{h}(y) - 2\varepsilon \\ &\geq \bar{h}(x) - 2\varepsilon \\ &= h'(x). \end{aligned}$$

Thus, we can apply Theorem 2 to the sequence of random variables $(f(X^t))_{t \in \mathbb{N}}$. Thus, for all closed intervals $I_0 \subseteq S$ with $P(X^t \in I_0)$ we have

$$\begin{aligned} &E(T \mid X^0 \in I_0) \leq E(T \mid f(X^0) \leq \max(I_0)) \\ &\leq c'\left(\frac{f(s_{min})}{h'(f(s_{min}))} + \int_{f(s_{min})}^{\max(I_0)} \frac{1}{h'(x)} dx\right) \\ &\leq c'\left(\frac{s_{min}}{\bar{h}(s_{min}) - 2\varepsilon} + \int_{s_{min}}^{\max(I_0)} \frac{1}{\bar{h}(x) - 2\varepsilon} dx\right). \end{aligned}$$

As above, we can choose ε arbitrarily small, so that c' converges to 1 and, for all x, $h'(x)$ converges to $h(x)$. As in

Theorem 1, we can take the infimum of all upper bounds as an upper bound, leading to

$$E(T \mid X^0 \in I_0) \leq c \left(\frac{s_{min}}{h(s_{min})} + \int_{s_{min}}^{\max(I_0)} \frac{1}{h(x)} dx \right).$$

This shows the claim. □

Finally, we will use a simplified continuous version of the drift theorem concerned with negative drift from [20]; note that the given proof makes no particular use of the requirement of finiteness of the search space, so that we state the following theorem without this condition.

THEOREM 4. *Let $(X^t)_{t\geq 0}$ be a sequence of random variables over a state space $S = [s_{\min}, s_{\max}] \subseteq \mathbb{R}$. Furthermore, let T be the random variable denoting the first point in time $t \in \mathbb{N}$ for which $X^t = s_{\min}$. Suppose that there is a minimal drift $\varepsilon > 0$ and a maximal step size δ such that, for all $t < T$ and closed intervals $I \subseteq S$ with $P(X^t \in I)$,*

- *$E(X^t - X^{t+1} | X^t \in I) \geq \varepsilon$; and*
- *$P(X^t - X^{t+1} \leq \delta) = 1$.*

Let $\ell = (s_{\max} - s_{\min})/\delta$. Then there is a constant $c > 0$ such that

$$P(T \leq 2^{c\ell}) = 2^{-\Omega(\ell)}.$$

This follows from [20, Theorem 4] by rescaling the search space by a factor of $1/\delta$. The second condition is here simplified: instead of requiring the probability to jump a distance of d to be inverse exponentially related to d, we just require that the probability of large jumps is 0.

3. THE ACO ALGORITHMS

In this section we first formally introduce the single-destination shortest path (SDSP) problem. Afterwards the two algorithms which we will analyze in Section 4 are presented in detail.

3.1 Problem Definition

The single-source shortest path problem is one of the most-studied problems in computer science. Given a weighted graph (V, E, w), the goal is to find a shortest path from a given source-vertex to every other vertex in the graph. In this work, we analyze the single-*destination* shortest path problem. Here, from every vertex in the graph, a shortest path has to be found to a single destination vertex. Both problems are equivalent, because one provides the optimal solution for the other if the direction of all edges are reverted. For the sake of simplicity we only deal with weakly connected directed acyclic graphs (DAGs) with a unique sink. This ensures that there is a path from every vertex to the sink, which we regard as the destination vertex.

To model the *stochastic* SDSP, we exchange the deterministic weights w of a graph with random variables X. Each edge e now carries a random variable $X_e \in [0, 1]$ that serves as stochastic weight. The deterministic version of SDSP is a special case of the stochastic SDSP, in which all random variables have variance zero.

DEFINITION 5. *Let (V, E) be a DAG (we allow for multiple parallel edges). Assume that there is a unique sink (a vertex without outgoing edges). For each edge $e \in E$, let $X_e \in [0, 1]$ be a random variable describing the stochastic length of e. We denote by $X = (X_e)_{e\in E}$ the family of all these. For any (directed) path p consisting of the edges $E_p \subseteq E$, we let $X_p = \sum_{e\in E_p} X_e$ be the* (random) length *of the path p.*

If, for each path p in G, X_p is a random variable in $[0, 1]$, then the triple $G = (V, E, X)$ is called graph with (bounded) stochastic edge weights *or simply a* stochastic-weight graph.

Note that, in a DAG with a unique sink, the sink is reachable from every other vertex. Furthermore, every graph where edge weights are random according to bounded distributions can be scaled and shifted to be a stochastic-weight graph in the sense defined above without changing the (expected) shortest path tree of this "normalized" instance (but with changes to the behavior of the algorithms in this paper); that is, if all random weights are in the interval $[a, b]$ (with $a < b$), then mapping all weights with

$$x \mapsto \frac{x - a}{b - a}$$

will lead to such normalized weights.

3.2 MMAS-fp

MMAS-fp is very similar to the ACO-algorithms for SDSP given in [1,4,14]; the key difference is the fitness proportional pheromone update, instead of pheromone update based on the best-so-far solution. The MMAS starts with a homogeneous pheromone distribution on the edges of the graph, and then iteratively updates this distribution. Every iteration, from each vertex of the graph (other than the sink) an artificial ant performs a random walk over the graph until it hits the sink, and then updates the pheromones on the edges outgoing from its start vertex. Note that, in contrast to many applications, only one ant (per vertex) is used, as opposed to sending out several ants and then (for example) choosing only the best to make an update.

The complete MMAS-fp algorithm is described in Algorithm 1 and uses other definitions from this section.

Algorithm 1 MMAS-fp

Parameters: ρ, τ_{min};
Input: DAG $G = (V, E)$;
initialize pheromones τ
while termination criterion not met **do**
    for $u \in V$ in parallel **do**
        construct simple path p_u from u to sink w.r.t. τ;
        $w \leftarrow evaluate(p_u)$;
        $E_u \leftarrow \{(u, v) \in E \mid v \in V\}$;
        for $e \in E_u$ **do**
            if e first edge in p_u **then**
                $\tau(e) \leftarrow \max((1 - \rho)\tau(e) + \rho(1 - w)), \tau_{min})$;
            else
                $\tau(e) \leftarrow \max((1 - \rho)\tau(e), \tau_{min})$;
return τ;

Path construction.

An ant constructs a path as follows. If the ant is currently in vertex v after walking the path p and v is not the sink, it randomly chooses one of the edges leaving v. The pheromones are stored in a function $\tau : E \rightarrow \mathbb{R}^+$. We let E_v

be the set of edges leaving v, and we let the probability of choosing edge $e \in E_v$ be exactly

$$P(\text{"choose edge } e\text{ "}) = \frac{\tau(e)}{\sum_{e' \in E_v} \tau(e')}.$$

Afterwards the ant traverses the chosen edge, adds its new position to the path p and further builds its path from there. Algorithm 2 specifies the path construction. At the beginning, the pheromone values of all edges coming from a vertex of out-degree m are initialized with $1/m$ to make every choice equally probable. Note that, since we will only be dealing with DAGs, the path construction does not have to consider loops.

Algorithm 2 Path Construction

1: **Input:** DAG $G = (V, E)$, start vertex u, pheromones τ;
2: $i \leftarrow 0$, $v_0 \leftarrow u$;
3: $V_1 \leftarrow \{p \in V | (v_0, v) \in E\}$;
4: **while** $V_{i+1} \neq \emptyset$ **do**
5: $\quad i \leftarrow i + 1$
6: $\quad$ choose $v_i \in V_i$ proportional to $\tau(v_{i-1}, v_i)$;
7: $\quad V_{i+1} \leftarrow \{v \in V | (v_i, v) \in E\}$;
8: **return** $(v_0, \dots, v_i)$

Pheromone Update.

After all ants have finished constructing their paths, the pheromones are updated; each ant starting from a vertex v, updates all and only the edges leaving v. To get a Max-Min Ant System, we ensure that no pheromone value drops below a predefined threshold τ_{min}. An explicit upper bound for the pheromones is not needed, because every edge loses a factor of ρ of its pheromones and can gain at most ρ, such that the highest value the pheromones can reach is 1.

For a given vertex v, let e_v be the edge that the ant starting at v chose as the first edge, and let w be the (randomly evaluated) length of its path; then, for each edge e outgoing from v, the new pheromone on e is

$$\tau'(e) = \begin{cases} \max((1-\rho)\tau(e) + \rho(1-w), \tau_{min}), & \text{if } e = e_v; \\ \max((1-\rho)\tau(e), \tau_{min}), & \text{otherwise.} \end{cases}$$

In particular, all edges evaporate some pheromone, and only the chosen edge gets rewarded, with a higher amount of pheromone the shorter the path is.

3.3 MMAS-fp with Normalization

A problem with MMAS-fp is that, for low average values of the random variables, *all* pheromone values more or less approach the lower pheromone border, which makes the influence of the value of τ_{min} too strong.

Thus, we introduce the a variant of MMAS-fp, called MMAS-fp-norm, which performs a normalization of the pheromone values at the end of each iteration (see Algorithm 3).

As we will see, for this variant of MMAS-fp we get tighter bounds on the optimization time.

4. RUNTIME ANALYSIS

In this section we analyze the algorithms from Section 3 on the stochastic SDSP. We start with an analysis of m-parallel links, multigraphs representing simple decision points for the algorithm. Afterwards, we use the results of the analysis

---

Algorithm 3 MMAS-fp-norm

1: **Parameters:** ρ, τ_{min};
2: **Input:** DAG $G = (V, E)$;
3: initialize pheromones τ
4: **while** termination criterion not met **do**
5: $\quad$ **for** $u \in V$ in parallel **do**
6: $\quad\quad$ construct simple path p_u from u to sink w.r.t. τ;
7: $\quad\quad w \leftarrow evaluate(p_u)$;
8: $\quad\quad E_u \leftarrow \{(u, v) \in E \mid v \in V\}$;
9: $\quad\quad$ **for** $e \in E_u$ **do**
10: $\quad\quad\quad$ **if** e first edge in p_u **then**
11: $\quad\quad\quad\quad \tau(e) \leftarrow \max((1-\rho)\tau(e) + \rho(1-w)), \tau_{min})$;
12: $\quad\quad\quad$ **else**
13: $\quad\quad\quad\quad \tau(e) \leftarrow \max((1-\rho)\tau(e), \tau_{min})$;
14: $\quad\quad r = \sum_{e \in E_u} \tau(e)$;
15: $\quad\quad$ **for** $e \in E_u$ **do**
16: $\quad\quad\quad \tau(e) \leftarrow \tau(e)/r$;
17: **return** τ;

---

for parallel links to give an upper bound on the expected running time of the algorithm on arbitrary graphs. But first we give some definitions.

If an edge e was constantly reinforced, its pheromone value τ would still not increase arbitrarily high, but converge to a point where the reinforcement and the loss of the evaporation cancel out. The closer τ gets to this point, the smaller is its expected gain. At the same time, other edges can be at τ_{min} and will therefore not lose any more pheromone. This motivates the following definition, which we will use as our optimization goal.

DEFINITION 6. *Let v be a vertex in a stochastic-weight graph (V, E, X). We call v β-optimized iff the probability of choosing the first edge on an optimal path from v to the sink is at least $(1 - \beta)$. We call a graph β-optimized iff all its vertices are β-optimized.*

Of course two edges with random variables that have almost identical expected value will be hard to tell apart and the relation between the pheromones on those edges will change only very slowly. The difference in the expected value of the random variables between the optimal edge(s) and the others will be an important measurement for the difficulty of the problem, which motivates the following definition.

DEFINITION 7. *Let v be a vertex of degree m in a stochastic-weight graph (V, E, X). For every outgoing edge e_i of v let ℓ_i denote the expected length of the shortest path from v to the sink using e_i. Without loss of generality we assume that $\ell_i \leq \ell_{i+1}$ for all $1 \leq i \leq n-1$. We call the vertex v δ-different iff, for all i with $2 \leq i \leq n$, we have either $\ell_i = \ell_1$ or $\ell_i - \ell_1 \geq \delta$. We call the vertex v strictly δ-different iff, for all i with $2 \leq i \leq n$, we have that $\ell_i - \ell_1 \geq \delta$. We call a graph (strictly) δ-different iff all its vertices are (strictly) δ-different.*

4.1 MMAS-fp on Parallel Links

We start our analysis with a simple case in which the ants will make only a single decision with m alternatives. A simple mathematical model for this is a graph with only two vertices, one of them the sink, and multiple parallel links towards the sink. An *m-parallel link* is a directed multigraph with two vertices and m edges $e_1, e_2, \dots e_m$ from one vertex to the sink; every edge represents one alternative. The following diagram illustrates this graph.

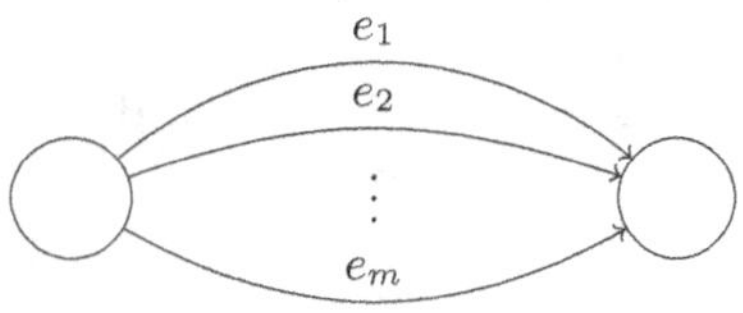

In this case, MMAS-fp simplifies a lot, as only one ant constructs a solution in every iteration, and each path constructions consists only of a single choice. This will allow us to make an easier mathematical analysis; later, we will reduce the case of general graphs to multiple applications of our findings for parallel links.

The crucial step in analyzing an algorithm with a drift theorem lies in finding a suitable potential function. At all times the potential has to decrease in expectation, for the Multiplicative Drift Theorem by at least a constant factor. Also, all states of potential 0 must be optimal states.

In every iteration, we denote with τ the pheromone of the optimal edge $e_{\max}$, and with r the sum of the pheromone on the edges. For further analysis, we choose $\phi = 1 - \tau/r$ as the potential. As $\tau \le r$, the potential lies always between zero and one. When the potential is very small, then we know that the probability of choosing the optimal edge is very high, namely $1 - \phi = \tau/r$.

As in many other analyses of ACO systems, it is interesting to see that the total pheromone r behaves very similar to the pheromones on a single edge. In particular, it loses a factor of ρ of its pheromones in every iteration as well and gets reinforced with a random variable between 0 and 1 times ρ, that is built out of the random variables of the single edges and their probability to be chosen. But as it can never get reinforced with a value grater than ρ and also ρ of its pheromones evaporate, r is bounded from above, as the next lemma proves.

LEMMA 8. *Let (V, E, X) m-parallel link; let the evaporation factor ρ be $0 < \rho < 0.5$, and $\tau_{\min} \le 1/m$. Then, after every iteration of MMAS-fp, we have $r \le 2$ and $r(1-\rho) + \tau_{\min} m\rho + \rho \le 2$.*

PROOF. We prove the statement by induction over the number of the iterations. We denote with r^t the total pheromone after t iterations. For the induction base, $r^0 \le 2$ comes directly from the choice of $1/m$ for the initial pheromone values. For the induction step we have that

$$r^{t+1} \le r^t(1-\rho) + \tau_{\min} m\rho + \rho \le r^t - r^t\rho + \rho + \rho,$$

as every X_e can evaluate only to numbers smaller 1 and $m\tau_{\min} \le 1$. Now we use the induction hypothesis and get

$$r^{t+1} \le r^t(1-\rho) + \rho + \rho \le 2(1-\rho) + \rho + \rho \le 2$$

as desired. □

Equipped with these tools we can now formally prove an upper bound on the expected number of iterations that are needed to β-optimize a strictly δ-different m-parallel link.

THEOREM 9. *Let $G = (V, E, X)$ be a strictly δ-different m-parallel link. Let β, ρ and $\tau_{\min}$ be such that $0 < \beta < 0.5$, $0 < \rho \le \frac{\beta\delta}{8}$ and $\tau_{\min} \le \rho/m$. Then, after in expectation*

$$O\left(\frac{\ln(1/\beta)}{\delta\rho\tau_{\min}}\right)$$

iterations of MMAS-fp, G is β-optimized.

PROOF. We let $e_{\max}$ be the (unique) optimal edge and let $x = 1 - E(X_{e_{\max}})$. For all $t \in \mathbb{N}$, let τ^t be the pheromone on $e_{\max}$ and r^t be the total pheromone in iteration t; furthermore, let $Y^t = \left(1 - \frac{\tau^t}{r^t}\right)$ for $1 - \frac{\tau^t}{r^t} \ge \beta$ and 0 else. Let T be the random variable describing the first point in time t such that $Y^t < \beta$. Then, for all $t < T$, we have

$$\begin{aligned} E\left(\Delta^t Y\right) &:= E\left(Y^t - Y^{t+1} \mid Y^t = 1 - \frac{\tau^t}{r^t}\right) \\ &= \left(1 - \frac{\tau^t}{r^t}\right) - E\left(1 - \frac{\tau^{t+1}}{r^{t+1}}\right) \\ &= E\left(\frac{\tau^{t+1}}{r^{t+1}}\right) - \frac{\tau^t}{r^t} \end{aligned}$$

Fix any $t < T$ and let $\tau = \tau^t$, $r = r^t$ and $\Delta Y = \Delta^t Y$. Because in the worst case m edges can be at $\tau_{\min}$ and thus not lose any pheromones and with P("$e_{\max}$ gets selected") $= \frac{\tau}{r}$ we have

$$\begin{aligned} E\left(\frac{\tau^{t+1}}{r^{t+1}}\right) \ge & \frac{\tau}{r} \frac{\tau(1-\rho) + \rho x}{(r - m\tau_{\min})(1-\rho) + m\tau_{\min} + \rho x} \\ & + \left(1 - \frac{\tau}{r}\right) \frac{\tau(1-\rho)}{(r - m\tau_{\min})(1-\rho) + m\tau_{\min} + \rho(x - \delta)}. \end{aligned}$$

To enhance readability let $A := r(1-\rho) + \rho x + \rho\tau_{\min} m - \rho\delta$; with some straightforward manipulations, we get

$$\begin{aligned} E(\Delta Y) &\ge -\frac{\tau}{r} + \frac{\tau}{r}\frac{\tau(1-\rho) + \rho x}{A + \rho\delta} + \left(1 - \frac{\tau}{r}\right)\frac{\tau(1-\rho)}{A} \\ &= \tau \frac{\rho\delta\left(1 - \frac{\tau}{r}\right)(1-\rho) - \frac{A\rho\tau_{\min} m}{r}}{A(A + \rho\delta)}. \end{aligned}$$

Because of Lemma 8 we know $A + \rho\delta \le 2$ and with $\rho x - \rho\delta < \rho$ and $r \ge \tau_{\min} m$ we have

$$E(\Delta Y) \ge \frac{\tau}{4}\left(\rho\delta\left(1 - \frac{\tau}{r}\right)(1-\rho) - 2\rho\right).$$

As $\rho < 0.5$:

$$E(\Delta Y) \ge \frac{\tau\rho}{4}\left(\left(1 - \frac{\tau}{r}\right)0.5\delta - 2\rho\right).$$

From $\rho \le \frac{\beta\delta}{8}$ and $\left(1 - \frac{\tau}{r}\right) \ge \beta$ we get $\rho < \frac{\left(1 - \frac{\tau}{r}\right)\delta}{8}$, and we get $2\rho < \left(1 - \frac{\tau}{r}\right)\delta/4$ and thus

$$\left(1 - \frac{\tau}{r}\right)0.5\delta - 2\rho \ge 0.25\left(1 - \frac{\tau}{r}\right)\delta.$$

So we have

$$E(\Delta Y) \ge \frac{\tau}{32}\left(1 - \frac{\tau}{r}\right)\rho\delta \ge \left(1 - \frac{\tau}{r}\right)\frac{\tau_{\min}\rho\delta}{32} \ge Y^t \frac{\tau_{\min}\rho\delta}{32}.$$

We have $\tau^0 = \frac{1}{m}$, so $Y^0 = \left(1 - \frac{1}{m}\right)$ and once $Y^t < \beta$, the optimization process is finished. Now we can apply the continuous multiplicative drift theorem on the the random variables Y^t, which gives

$$E(T) = O\left(\frac{\ln(1/\beta)}{\delta\rho\tau_{\min}}\right).$$

This finishes the proof. □

If we choose $\rho = \Theta(\beta\delta)$ and $\tau_{\min} = \Theta(\rho/m)$ we get an optimization time of $O\left(\frac{m\ln(1/\beta)}{\beta^2\delta^3}\right)$.

4.2 MMAS-fp-norm on Parallel Links

Now we turn to the analysis of MMAS-fp with normalization. In this case, the total pheromone is always 1, so we use as potential $1-\tau$, with τ the pheromone on the optimal edge.

Let $G=(V,E,X)$ be a strictly δ-different m-parallel link. For all $t\in\mathbb{N}$, let τ^t be the pheromones in the t-th iteration of the MMAS-fp-norm Algorithm and let $Y^t=(1-\tau^t)$ and $\Delta^t Y=Y^t-Y^{t+1}$. Let T be the random variable describing the first time when $Y^t\leq\beta$.

As the drift function we use

$$h:\mathbb{R}^+\to\mathbb{R}^+, x\to min(x,(1-x))\frac{\delta\rho}{9}.$$

Intuitively, we can show a small drift if only very little pheromone is on the desired edge (as this edge is chosen infrequently) and similarly, only a small edge when already a lot of pheromone is present (as the update rule, in this case, makes only very small updates); for medium amounts of pheromone we can expect the best drift. In the following we will prove all three conditions that are needed for the Continuous Variable Drift Theorem separately. Afterwards, we put everything together in the proof of Theorem 13.

We start with condition one, which requires that for every possible potential, the drift-function h gives a lower bound on the drift expected if given a state with that potential.

LEMMA 10. *Let $\beta,\tau_{\min}$ and ρ be such that $0<\beta<0.5$, $0<\tau_{\min}\leq\frac{\beta\delta}{2m}$ and $0<\rho\leq 0.5$. Then, for all $t<T$,*

$$E\left(\Delta^t Y \mid Y^t=1-\tau\right)\geq h\left(Y^t\right).$$

PROOF. Let $e_{\max}$ be the optimal edge. With x we denote $1-E(X_{e_{\max}})$. Let $t\in\mathbb{N}$ with $Y^t>\beta$, let $\tau:=\tau^t$ and $\Delta Y=\Delta^t Y$. Then

$$\begin{aligned}E(\Delta Y)&=(1-\tau)-E\left(1-\tau^{t+1}\mid Y^t=1-\tau\right)\\&=E\left(\tau^{t+1}\mid Y^t=1-\tau\right)-\tau.\end{aligned}$$

In the following we denote τ' as the pheromone on $e_{\max}$ before the normalization and r' as the sum of all pheromones at the same time, such that $\tau^{t+1}=\frac{\tau'}{r'}$. As, in the worst case, m edges can be at $\tau_{\min}$ and thus not lose any pheromones and with P("$e_{\max}$ gets selected") $=\tau$ we have

$$\begin{aligned}E(\tau^{t+1})\geq{}&\tau\frac{\tau(1-\rho)+\rho x}{(1-m\tau_{\min})(1-\rho)+m\tau_{\min}+\rho x}\\&+(1-\tau)\frac{\tau(1-\rho)}{(r-m\tau_{\min})(1-\rho)+m\tau_{\min}+(\rho x-\rho\delta)}\end{aligned}$$

To enhance readability, we let $A=(1-\rho)+\rho x+\rho\tau_{\min}m-\rho\delta$. Then we have

$$\begin{aligned}E(\Delta Y)&\geq-\tau+\tau\frac{\tau(1-\rho)+\rho x}{A+\rho\delta}+(1-\tau)\frac{\tau(1-\rho)}{A}\\&=\frac{\rho\delta(1-\tau)\tau(1-\rho)-\tau A(A+\rho\delta)}{A(A+\rho\delta)}\\&+\frac{A\tau(\tau(1-\rho)+\rho x)+A(1-\tau)\tau(1-\rho)}{A(A+\rho\delta)}.\end{aligned}$$

Because in every iteration r' can only gain at most ρ, we have that $A+\rho\delta\leq r'_{\max}\leq 1+\rho$ and thus $A(A+\rho\delta)\leq(1+\rho)^2$.

$$\begin{aligned}E(\Delta Y)\geq{}&\frac{\tau}{(1+\rho)^2}(\rho\delta(1-\tau)(1-\rho)+\\&A(-A-\rho\delta+\tau(1-\rho)+\rho x+(1-\tau)(1-\rho)))\\={}&\frac{\tau}{(1+\rho)^2}(\rho\delta(1-\tau)(1-\rho)-A(\rho\tau_{\min}m))\end{aligned}$$

Because in every iteration r' can only lose at most ρ, we have that $A\geq r'_{\min}\geq 1-\rho$ and thus

$$E(\Delta Y)\geq\frac{\tau\rho(1-\rho)}{(1+\rho)^2}(\delta(1-\tau)-\tau_{\min}m)$$

From $\tau_{\min}\leq\frac{\beta\delta}{2m}$ we get that $\tau_{\min}m\leq\frac{\beta\delta}{2}$. As $(1-\tau)\geq\beta$ we have $\delta(1-\tau)-\tau_{\min}m\geq\frac{\delta(1-\tau)}{2}$ and

$$E(\Delta Y)\geq\tau(1-\tau)\delta\rho\frac{(1-\rho)}{2(1+\rho)^2}.$$

As $0<\rho<0.5$ we have

$$E(\Delta Y)\geq\tau(1-\tau)\frac{\delta\rho}{9}\geq h(1-\tau)=h(Y^t)$$

as desired. □

The following lemma deals with the second condition of the Theorem 1. It gives an upper bound on how much the potential function can change in one step. The main argument is that τ can only change by ρ at most, because it either loses a factor ρ of its current value, which is never bigger than 1, or it gains $\rho X_{e_{\max}}$ with $X_{e_{\max}}$ being at most 1.

LEMMA 11. *Let $0<\rho<0.5$. For all $t<T$ we have*

$$P(|Y^t-Y^{t+1}|<4\rho)=1.$$

PROOF. Let $t<T$, $\tau_{\min}\leq\tau^t\leq(1-\beta)$ and $\tau:=\tau^t$. In the following we denote τ' as the pheromone on the optimal edge before the normalization and r' as the sum of all pheromones at the same time such that $\tau^{t+1}=\frac{\tau'}{r'}$. If $\tau^{t+1}>\tau^t$ then

$$|(1-\tau)-(1-\tau^{t+1})|\leq\frac{\tau'}{r'}-\tau\leq\frac{\tau+\rho}{1-\rho}-\tau<4\rho$$

and if $\tau^{t+1}\leq\tau^t$

$$|(1-\tau)-(1-\tau^{t+1})|\leq\tau-\frac{\tau'}{r'}\leq\tau-\frac{\tau(1-\rho)}{1+\rho}<4\rho.$$

This finishes the proof. □

With the following lemma we give a factor by which the drift function may decrease at most in one step for increasing potential.

LEMMA 12. *For all $x,y\in\mathbb{R}^+$ with $\tau_{\min}\leq x<y\leq 1-\tau_{\min}$ and $y-x\leq 4\rho$, we have $h(x)\leq\left(1+\frac{4\rho}{\tau_{\min}}\right)h(y)$.*

PROOF. For $y\leq 0.5$ we have $h(y)=y\frac{\rho\delta}{9}$, which is monotonous and therefore we have $h(x)\leq ch(y)$ for every $c\geq 1$. For $y\geq 0.5$ we have $h(y)=(1-y)k$, with $k=\delta\rho/9$. We have

$$\frac{h(x)}{h(y)}=\frac{1-x}{1-y}\leq\frac{1-y+4\rho}{1-y}\leq 1+\frac{4\rho}{\tau_{\min}}$$

as desired. □

Now we put the pieces together and apply the variable drift theorem, which will give us the desired upper bound on the runtime of MMAS-fp-norm on parallel links.

THEOREM 13. *Let $\beta, \tau_{\min}$ and ρ be such that $0 < \beta < 0.5$, $0 < \tau_{\min} \leq \frac{\beta\delta}{2m}$ and $0 < \rho \leq 0.5$. Then, after in expectation*

$$O\left(\frac{\ln(1/(\tau_{\min}\beta))}{\delta \min(\rho, \tau_{\min})}\right)$$

iterations of MMAS-fp-norm, the strictly δ-different m-parallel link G is β-optimized.

PROOF. For all $t \in \mathbb{N}$, we change Y^t to 0 if $\tau < \beta$ (this can only increase drift). Lemmas 10 to 12 show that with $d = 4\rho$ and $c = 1 + \frac{4\rho}{\tau_{\min}}$ for h all conditions of the continuous variable drift theorem are fulfilled. Thus, we get

$$\begin{aligned} E(T \mid Y_0) &\leq c\left(\frac{s_{\min}}{h(s_{\min})} + \int_{s_{\min}}^{Y_0} \frac{1}{h(x)} dx\right) \\ &= c\left(\frac{\beta}{\beta\rho\delta/9} + \int_{\beta}^{1-\tau_{\min}} \frac{1}{h(x)} dx\right) \\ &= c\frac{9}{\rho\delta}\left(1 + \int_{\beta}^{0.5} \frac{1}{x} dx + \int_{0.5}^{1-\tau_{\min}} \frac{1}{1-x} dx\right). \end{aligned}$$

This equals

$$\begin{aligned} &c\frac{9}{\rho\delta}\left(1 + \int_{\beta}^{0.5} \frac{1}{x} dx + \int_{\tau_{\min}}^{0.5} \frac{1}{y} dy\right) \\ &= \left(1 + \frac{4\rho}{\tau_{\min}}\right)\frac{9}{\rho\delta}\left(1 + 2\ln 0.5 - \ln(\tau_{\min}) - \ln\beta\right) \\ &= O\left(\frac{\ln(1/(\tau_{\min}\beta))}{\min(\tau_{\min}, \rho)\delta}\right). \end{aligned}$$

This finishes the proof. □

Recall that, for MMAS-fp, Theorem 9 gives a bound of

$$O\left(\frac{\ln(1/\beta)}{\delta\rho\tau_{\min}}\right).$$

The bound of Theorem 13 improves on the denominator, as it now only included the smaller of $\tau_{\min}$ and ρ; however, the numerator as an addition $\log(1/\tau_{\min})$, which is comparatively small.

Especially for the next section, we are also interested in how long an edge stays optimized. As we have drift in the right direction and a small step size, an application of the negative drift theorem [20] gives us an answer.

THEOREM 14. *Let $\beta, \tau_{\min}$ and ρ be such that $0 < \beta < 0.5$, $0 < \tau_{\min} \leq \frac{\beta\delta}{2m}$ and $0 < \rho \leq 0.5$. Then, once G is β-optimized, there is a constant c such that, for all s, G stays $(\beta + s\rho)$-optimized for 2^{cs} iterations with probability $1 - 2^{-\Omega(s)}$.*

PROOF. In Lemma 10 we proved a strictly positive drift towards being β-optimized. From Lemma 11 we know that the step-size of the potential is in $O(\rho)$. Now the drift theorem concerned with negative drift from Oliveto and Witt [20] in the simplified form stated in Theorem 4 gives the desired result. □

Theorem 14 allows for the following interpretation of small pheromone update factor ρ: the MMAS does not quickly adapt to unlucky evaluations of random variables, but conservatively stays with the medium-term best option.

4.3 MMAS-fp-norm on SDSP

In this section we extend our analysis to arbitrary graphs. We suppose our graphs to be δ-different and give an upper bound on the expected runtime on the algorithm to β-optimize the graph. Note that every graph is δ-different for some $\delta > 0$, but usually this δ is not known beforehand, which makes it hard to set the parameters right. To avoid confusion we first introduce vocabulary that will help us talk about the length of paths more clearly.

DEFINITION 15. *Let v be a vertex in the directed stochastic-weight graph. We define* OEPL(v) *(optimal expected path length) as the expected length of the in path from v to the sink which is shortest in expectation.*

The main idea in the following proofs is to start with the sink, which is of course always optimized, and then gradually widen the circle of optimized vertices until the whole graph is optimized, as was done previously in many other papers.

Whenever a decision making process in a vertex has to be analyzed, a parallel link is constructed to simulate this process such that Theorem 13 can be applied. This step is performed in Lemma 16.

LEMMA 16. *Let v be a vertex of degree m in a δ-different stochastic-weight graph $G = (V, E, X)$ without parallel edges. Suppose that all vertices on a shortest path from v to the sink except for v be $\delta/(2n)$-optimized and stay so optimized for any polynomial number of rounds. Then, with parameters ρ and $\tau_{\min}$ such that $\frac{\delta^2}{16n^2} = \tau_{\min} \leq \rho \leq 0.5$, after in expectation $O\left(\frac{\ln(n/\delta)}{\delta\tau_{\min}}\right)$ iterations of MMAS-fp-norm, v is $\delta/(4n)$-optimized.*

PROOF. Let p be a shortest path from v to the sink such that every vertex other than v is $\delta/(2n)$-optimized; let v' be the second vertex on p (right after v). Thus, an ant starting from v using the edge to v' and then walking randomly according to the construction procedure construct a path of expected length x with

$$\begin{aligned} x &\leq \mathrm{OEPL}(v) + 1 - (1 - \delta/(2n))^n \\ &\leq \mathrm{OEPL}(v) + \delta/2 \end{aligned}$$

as we deviate from the optimal path with probability at most $1 - (1 - \delta/(2n))^n$, and this gives a path of length at most 1 (this uses the definition of stochastic-weight graph, which requires all path lengths to be random variables in $[0, 1]$); the second inequality uses Bernoulli's inequality. All paths not using the edge (v, v') can in the worst case have an expected length y of at least

$$y \geq \mathrm{OEPL}(v) + \delta$$

as G is δ-different. Let m be the out-degree of v in G. Now we can simulate the optimization of v by constructing a parallel link G' consisting of v and the sink. We use m edges from v to the sink with random variables $X_1, \ldots X_m \in [0, 1]$ with expected values $E(X_1) = \mathrm{OEPL}(v) + \delta/2$ and $E(X_i) = \mathrm{OEPL}(v) + \delta$ for all i with $2 \leq i \leq m$; thus, we have

$$E(X_i) - E(X_1) \geq \frac{\delta}{2}.$$

Thus, the constructed parallel link G' is a strictly $\delta' := \delta/2$-different stochastic-weight graph. As G has no parallel edges, the out-degree m of v is bounded by n. The optimization time of G' gives an upper bound on the time until v in G is optimized: X_1 represents all the (in expectation) shortest paths, the other X_i represent the other choices. We apply Theorem 13 with $\beta = \delta/(2n)$ such that the crucial inequality

$$\tau_{\min} = \frac{\delta^2}{16n^2} = \frac{\delta}{4n}\frac{\delta}{2}\frac{1}{2n} \leq \frac{\beta\delta'}{2m}$$

is fulfilled. The theorem yields that after

$$O\left(\frac{\ln(1/(\tau_{\min}\beta))}{\delta'\tau_{\min}}\right) = O\left(\frac{\ln(1/(\tau_{\min}\delta))}{\delta\tau_{\min}}\right)$$

iterations of MMAS-fp-norm G' is $\delta/(4n)$-optimized. □

Now all that is left to do is applying Lemma 16 to every vertex in an order such that the lemma is always applied to vertices the shortest expected paths of which use only vertices that are already optimized. Note that this Theorem applies to a limited range of ρ, for which a good bound is derivable.

THEOREM 17. *Let $G = (V, E, X)$ be a δ-different stochastic-weight graph. Let $\tau_{\min}$ and ρ be such that*

$$\tau_{\min} \leq \frac{\delta^2}{16n^2} \text{ and } \tau_{\min} \leq \rho \leq \frac{\delta}{4n(\log n)^2}.$$

Then, after in expectation

$$O\left(\frac{n\ln\left(1/(\tau_{\min}\delta)\right)}{\delta\tau_{\min}}\right)$$

iterations of MMAS-fp-norm the graph is $\delta/2$-optimized.

PROOF. We apply Theorem 14 with $s = (\log n)^2$ and Lemma 16 once for each vertex going backwards in a topological sorting of all vertices. This gives a high probability of success within the stated time bound; using a standard restart argument, we get the desired bound on the expectation. □

If we plug $\tau_{\min}$ into the runtime formula, we get an expression dependent only on the graph-size n and the difference δ:

$$O\left(\frac{n^3\ln\left(n/\delta\right)}{\delta^3}\right).$$

Note that a very similar proof would also work with the MMAS-fp algorithm.

5. SUMMARY

In this work we saw that MMAS-fp (with or without normalization) is well suited for solving the stochastic SDSP problem for stochastic-weight graphs: in contrast to other algorithms, it optimizes the expected path length, as opposed to "winning paths" (paths which come out shorter than any other path with a probability of at least 50%) like in [4] for an elitist MMAS.

On the downside, a parameter δ has to be estimated upfront in order to set the parameters right. An upper bound for the expected optimization time of the algorithm then depends on this constant δ and the size of the graph n: $O\left(\frac{n^3\ln(n/\delta)}{\delta^3}\right)$. In future works, one could try to make the parameters dependent of an approximation factor instead of the not very practical value δ. It would also be interesting to see how MMAS-fp behaves for δ too small; we conjecture that, in this case, the algorithm would converge to some "robust" solution, a solution which has very good expected value even when deviating from it randomly.

For the analysis we used drift theorems on the continuous pheromone-values; in particular, for the algorithms we considered, the state of the algorithm is a random element of an uncountable set, if the random variables used have uncountable support. Thus, we cannot restrict ourselves to a finite state space, which drift theorems usually demand. In order to be able to use drift analysis, we showed that the finiteness-condition is mostly superfluous: we proved that a multiplicative and a variable drift theorem are true for an interval in $\mathbb{R}$ as the search space. It will be interesting to see if the conditions of the theorem can be further weakened, making drift analysis an even more universal and handy tool.

Acknowledgments

The authors are thankful to the anonymous reviewers, which helped improve this version a lot. Also, we are indebted to Benjamin Doerr for several fruitful discussions.

6. REFERENCES

[1] N. Attiratanasunthron and J. Fakcharoenphol. A running time analysis of an ant colony optimization algorithm for shortest paths in directed acyclic graphs. *Information Processing Letters*, 105:88–92, 2008.

[2] L. Bianchi, M. Dorigo, L. M. Gambardella, and W. J. Gutjahr. A survey on metaheuristics for stochastic combinatorial optimization. *Natural Computing*, 8:239–287, 2009.

[3] B. Doerr and L. Goldberg. Adaptive drift analysis. *Algorithmica*, 2011.

[4] B. Doerr, A. Hota, and T. Kötzing. Ants easily solve stochastic shortest path problems. In *Proceedings of the Conference on Genetic and Evolutionary Computation (GECCO'12)*, pages 17–24. ACM, 2012.

[5] B. Doerr, D. Johannsen, and C. Winzen. Multiplicative drift analysis. In *Proceedings of the Conference on Genetic and Evolutionary Computation (GECCO'10)*, pages 1449–1456. ACM, 2010.

[6] M. Dorigo. *Optimization, Learning and Natural Algorithms (in Italian)*. PhD thesis, Dipartimento di Elettronica, Politecnico di Milano, Milan, Italy, 1992.

[7] M. Dorigo, V. Maniezzo, and A. Colorni. Ant system: optimization by a colony of cooperating agents. *IEEE Transactions on Systems, Man, and Cybernetics, Part B*, 26:29–41, 1996.

[8] M. Dorigo and T. Stützle. *Ant colony optimization.* MIT Press, 2004.

[9] W. J. Gutjahr. A graph-based ant system and its convergence. *Future Generation Comper Systems*, 16:873–888, 2000.

[10] W. J. Gutjahr. ACO algorithms with guaranteed convergence to the optimal solution. *Information Processessing Letters*, 82:145–153, 2002.

[11] W. J. Gutjahr. A converging ACO algorithm for stochastic combinatorial optimization. In *Proceedings of the Symposium on Stochastic Algorithms: Foundations and Applications (SAGA'03)*, pages 10–25, 2003.

[12] W. J. Gutjahr. S-ACO: An ant-based approach to combinatorial optimization under uncertainty. In *Proceedings of the ANTS Conference (ANTS'04)*, pages 238–249. Springer, 2004.

[13] B. Hajek. Hitting-time and occupation-time bounds implied by drift analysis with applications. *Advances in Applied Probability*, 14:502–525, 1982.

[14] C. Horoba and D. Sudholt. Ant colony optimization for stochastic shortest path problems. In *Proceedings of the Conference on Genetic and Evolutionary Computation (GECCO'10)*, pages 1465–1472. ACM, 2010.

[15] D. Johannsen. *Random Combinatorial Structures and Randomized Search Heuristics.* PhD thesis, Universität des Saarlandes, 2010. Available online at http://scidok.sulb.uni-saarland.de/volltexte/2011/3529/pdf/Dissertation_3166_Joha_Dani_2010.pdf.

[16] T. Kötzing, F. Neumann, H. Röglin, and C. Witt. Theoretical analysis of two ACO approaches for the traveling salesman problem. *Swarm Intelligence*, 6:1–21, 2012.

[17] T. Kötzing, F. Neumann, D. Sudholt, and M. Wagner. Simple max-min ant systems and the optimization of linear pseudo-boolean functions. In *Proceedings of Foundations of Genetic Algorithms (FOGA'11)*, pages 209–218. ACM, 2011.

[18] B. Mitavskiy, J. E. Rowe, and C. Cannings. Preliminary theoretical analysis of a local search algorithm to optimize network communication subject to preserving the total number of links. In *Proceedings of the IEEE Congress on Evolutionary Computation (CEC'08)*, pages 1484–1491, 2008.

[19] F. Neumann and C. Witt. Ant colony optimization and the minimum spanning tree problem. *Theoretical Computer Science*, 411:2406–2413, 2010.

[20] P. S. Oliveto and C. Witt. Simplified drift analysis for proving lower bounds in evolutionary computation. *Algorithmica*, 59:369–386, 2011.

[21] J. E. Rowe and D. Sudholt. The choice of the offspring population size in the $(1, \lambda)$ EA. In *Proceedings of the Conference on Genetic and Evolutionary Computation (GECCO'12)*, pages 1349–1356, 2012.

[22] T. Stützle and H. H. Hoos. MAX-MIN ant system. *Future Generation Computer Systems*, 16:889–914, 2000.

Introducing Graphical Models to Analyze Genetic Programming Dynamics

Erik Hemberg
MIT CSAIL
hembergerik@csail.mit.edu

Constantin Berzan
Department of Computer Science
Tufts University
cberzan@gmail.com

Kalyan Veeramachaneni
MIT CSAIL
kalyan@csail.mit.edu

Una-May O'Reilly
MIT CSAIL
unamay@csail.mit.edu

ABSTRACT

We propose graphical models as a new means of understanding genetic programming dynamics. Herein, we describe how to build an unbiased graphical model from a population of genetic programming trees. Graphical models both express information about the conditional dependency relations among a set of random variables and they support probabilistic inference regarding the likelihood of a random variable's outcome. We focus on the former information: by their structure, graphical models reveal structural dependencies between the nodes of genetic programming trees. We identify graphical model properties of potential interest in this regard – edge quantity and dependency among nodes expressed in terms of family relations. Using a simple symbolic regression problem we generate a graphical model of the population each generation. Then we interpret the graphical models with respect to conventional knowledge about the influence of subtree crossover and mutation upon tree structure.

Categories and Subject Descriptors

D.1.2 [**Programming Techniques**]: Automatic Programming

General Terms

Algorithms

Keywords

genetic programming, graphical models, Bayesian network

1. INTRODUCTION

We begin by noting that the population of a GP run can be regarded as observed stochastic samples of a set of random variables where the stochasticity injected into the samples changes over time (generations) due to the evolutionary operators of selection, mutation and crossover. Alternatively, but equivalently, the GP population each generation can be regarded as observed samples of a different statistical population. Generally, a GP run is the outcomes from a set of random variables, spaced in time at the interval of generations.

The population dynamics of genetic programming are still not completely understood (15), i.e. how the dependencies between the solutions vary in the population and how they changes over time (generations). Using the insight that each genetic population of a GP generation is a set of samples, our aim is to model the statistical population from which they are drawn as a distribution of random variables. We will then analyze the changes in each distribution as the generations proceed. Previously, analyzing a GP run's dynamics has focused on studying the distribution of tree size, tree depth or solution fitness as probability distributions or simply calculating the moments of this distribution like mean and standard deviation (17). In contrast, our method is a probabilistic statistical approach.

We examine how to build a multivariate distribution Π which is represented by a set of samples (a generation) of GP trees. We use a prototype tree which is the size and shape of the largest possible GP tree for the problem. Each node of the prototype tree represents a random variable. GP trees are mapped onto the prototype tree to become samples of the multivariate distribution, see Fig. 1. We use a probabilistic graphical model to represent this multivariate distribution. (In a graphical model a directed acyclical graph denotes the conditional dependences between random variables.) To efficiently build Π requires accommodating GP trees which are of variable sizes and shape, identifying the best possible representation of the graphical model (GM) given a set of trees, and devising computational efficiencies which allow the building of the graphical model to be tractable.

In the last two decades building graphical models and associated inference engines has been addressed by numerous researchers (7; 11). We explored a variety of techniques (which lead to different graphical models) from this body of literature to address the challenges graphical model building in the GP context specifically poses. We present one technique in Section 3. It is chosen because it is unbiased with respect to any assumptions about variable dependency.

FOGA'13, January 16-20, 2013, Adelaide, Australia.

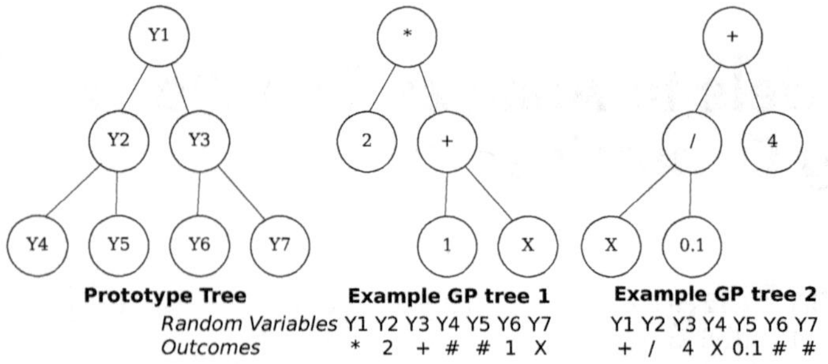

Figure 1: A prototype tree of depth d = 2, two example GP trees, and, as a result of alignment with the prototype tree, their random variable outcomes. Note that we do not show # *(null)* nodes.

Once we describe computationally efficient means to build a probabilistic graphical model we proceed to analyze how the generational graphical models transition over the course of a run as a result of selection and crossover. Specifically, we set up a very simple GP symbolic regression problem (Pagie-2D (16)) to execute over a fixed number of generations. Then we execute experiments composed of GP runs which vary the presence or absence of different operators. For each set of runs with a particular variation operator (only crossover or only mutation), we then aggregate all the trees of a generation and treat this as a set of samples from which we build a graphical model. We analyze the changes in the resulting graphical models as we process one generation after another.

The paper's contributions are:

1. Use of probabilistic graphical models for modeling structural dynamics of a population of GP trees

2. Description of an efficient technique to build graphical models. The technique needs to be fast because our aim is to to build graphical models for the population from every generation. The technique further needs to be unbiased to permit the data to be as accurately reflected as possible.

3. Analyzes of GP tree dynamics in different variational operator scenarios with respect to structural dependencies mapped from graphical models.

We proceed in the following manner: In Section 2 we present an overview of current techniques that analyze GP populations. In Section 3 we present how we resolve the issues arising in how to build a graphical model for a GP population. We also present how we have used a genetic algorithm to efficiently learn the structure of a Bayesian network from a fully observed data set. In Section 4 we present the results for a first set of statistical analyzes that reference generational graphical models. We present our conclusions and future work in Section 5. The Appendix describes the building of the graphical model in more detail.

2. BACKGROUND

Many different statistics have been used to study GP. Widely used and reported, "conventional" analyzes include a time series plot, per generation, of mean, standard deviation, maximum and minimum size of structure (e.g. tree, graph or other executable representation) or population fitness. Tomassini et al. (21) study fitness distance correlation as a difficulty measure in genetic programming. Langdon and Poli (12) analyze the behavior of GP on a wide range of problems, e.g. artificial ant and the Max Problem using schema analysis and Price's covariance and selection theorem.

Nearly all visualizations of structure have been for illustrative purposes according to Daida et al. (5), who visualized tree structures in GP. This new way of "seeing" can afford a potentially rich way of understanding dynamics that underpin GP. Almal et al. (2) perform a population based study of evolutionary dynamics in GP and show that heat maps are a useful tool for exploring the dynamics of genetic programming. The visualization allows the user to draw conclusions from data. We expand on this by inducing a graphical model to both visualize and explain the structure and content of a GP tree.

Daida et al. (6) study phase transitions in GP search to support a statistical mechanics approach where GP would be quantitatively compared to a broad range of other systems rigorously described by phase transitions. In order to identify subtrees that carry out similar semantic tasks, Wolfson et al. (22) perform post-evolutionary analysis of GP by defining a functionality-based similarity score between expressions. Similar sub-expressions are clustered from a number of independently-evolved fit solutions, thus identifying important semantic building blocks lodged within the hard-to-read GP trees.

Raidl and Gottlieb (18) empirically investigate locality, heritability and heuristic bias in Evolutionary Algorithms by generating individuals with static measurements based on randomly created solutions. This is done in order to quantify and visualize specific properties, and shed light onto the complex behavior of the system. Here, we take a different approach and we investigate the structure and contents of a GP tree by creating a graphical model from a population of GP trees.

In a paper by McPhee and Hopper (13) they analyze genetic diversity through population history by size and showed that the genetic diversity was low. They measure the number of different nodes in the population based on if the nodes begin at the root or non-root. Our study differs by investigating the dependencies between the nodes in the solutions based on a graphical model from the solution. Thus, we do not need to identify any relationships between individual solutions in the population, instead we take a statistical approach and learn a model of the population.

3. GRAPHICAL MODELS FOR GP

Our goal is to model the multivariate distribution of the trees in the GP population in generation t. We denote this by Π_t. The following issues are resolved in order to build a multivariate distribution for the population:

GP trees are of variable size: Because a population's trees vary in size and structure and GP's representation is not homologous, the question of defining the random variables is open to question. We choose a prototype tree based approach in which each node in a tree with a maximum size is a random variable and its support is all possible functions and terminals that could be at its position. We present more details in Section 3.1.

Defining the random variables in this manner provides us with a fixed set of variables for the multivariate distribution.

Modeling the multivariate distribution: Our representation of the multivariate distribution needs to allow us to gain insight from it. We choose a Bayesian network based representation which allows us to identify directed dependencies between the nodes of GP trees. We provide more details in Section 3.2.

Efficient building of the distribution: Given our choices of a prototype tree for the random variable set and a Bayesian network model, a further challenge is to build the distribution efficiently.

3.1 GP trees to random variables

To define the random variables for the modeling distribution we adopt a prototype tree based approach, see Fig. 1. Prototype trees have been used to represent GP trees when developing estimation of distribution based GP (EDA-GP), e.g. Salustowicz and Schmidhuber (19) and Hasegawa and Iba (8). A prototype tree is the size and shape of the largest (i.e. completely full) tree in the GP experiment. Each node in the prototype tree designates a random variable whose support (possible outcomes) depends on its position in the tree. That is, the root of the prototype tree, which can assume any function, is a random variable with its support being the problem's function set because each function is a possible outcome for the root's random variable. Each leaf of the prototype tree, which can only assume a terminal, is a random variable with support comprising the problem's terminal set (because each terminal is a possible outcome of a leaf's random variable). For each interior node, support is the set of all functions and terminals because each terminal or function is a possible outcome of an interior node's random variable. Because any GP tree may be smaller than the experiment's prototype tree, an extra outcome, *null*, is added to the support at every node except the root.

For example, for a symbolic regression problem with function set $\{+, -, /, *\}$ and terminal set $\{x_1, x_2\}$, prototype tree leaves have a support of two terminals and *null*, the root has a support of four functions, and all the intermediate nodes have a support of six outcomes (function set, terminals and *null*). The number of random variables in the multivariate distribution at time t, Π_t depends on the size of the prototype tree. The fundamental challenge in using a prototype tree based representation is supporting a large prototype tree so that every possible size or shape of a GP tree within a run can align with the prototype tree.

The GP tree population at a generation is a set of samples. To transform a tree to a sample, it is aligned with the prototype tree from the root downwards. Each function or terminal of the sample is counted as an outcome of the random variable onto which it maps in the prototype tree. Where the sample tree has no nodes, *null* outcomes are assumed. Figure 1 illustrates the transformation of a set of GP trees to outcome statistics of the prototype tree's random variables. As a graphical model for Π_t is built for each generation, the population of GP trees is transformed to samples by alignment with the prototype tree, and the outcomes of the random variables are statistically accumulated from each sample.

We choose a Bayesian network representation for the graphical model because it allows us to analyze the changes in the multivariate distribution via its graphical properties. Next, we describe this representation.

3.2 Bayesian networks as a graphical model

We can associate the population in standard GP with an implicit probability distribution over the random variables in the prototype tree. We want to explicitly model this distribution, and examine the dependency structure that emerges between nodes in the prototype tree. Our modeling tool of choice is the Bayesian network, consult (11) for an introduction to Bayesian networks. A Bayesian network $\mathcal{B} = \langle \mathcal{G}, \theta \rangle$ is a probabilistic graphical model that represents a joint probability distribution over a set of random variables $Y_1, \ldots, Y_n$. The Bayesian network representation has two components. A directed acyclic graph (DAG) $\mathcal{G}$ encodes (conditional) independence relations between random variables. More precisely, a missing edge encodes an independence relationship. Each random variable is a node in this graph. A set of local probability models θ defines the conditional probability distribution of each node given its parents in the graph. Let Pa_Y denote the parents of node Y in $\mathcal{G}$. Then the network $\mathcal{B}$ encodes the following probability distribution:

$$P(Y_1, \ldots, Y_n) = \prod_{i=1}^{n} P(Y_i \mid \mathrm{Pa}_{Y_i}).$$

Learning Bayesian networks from data has received much attention in the machine learning community (11). The space of all possible DAGs for n nodes is super-exponential in n, and finding the optimal network for a given data set is in general NP-hard (11). Learning algorithms for Bayesian networks loosely fit in two categories: constraint-based approaches, which use statistical tests to determine whether an edge is present or not, and search-and-score techniques, which define a scoring function and then search for a high scoring network. The scoring function prefers network structures that model the data set well, while penalizing structures that are too complex.

3.3 Learning network structure

Some search-and-score techniques, such as the *K2* algorithm (4), require that we prepare an edge order for learning the parameters of the nodes. Given an order, an edge can appear between nodes A and B only if A precedes B in the order. In our case of prototype trees for GP, specifying an accurate node order is not obvious. For example, if we impose a left-to-right depth-first search order, then a node in the graphical model cannot have an edge from its right sibling or its right uncle. In GP terms, this implies we would not sample relationships among the functions and terminals which are parameters of a parent function, in a right to left order. In Fig. 2 the possible dependencies in left-to-right depth-first order is shown, the dashed arrows are impossible dependencies given the ordering. If we impose a left-to-right breadth-first search order, a node in the graphical model cannot have an edge from any node to its right (at the same height) or below it. *K2* is commonly used in EDA-GP (8) where the node order is assumed to be depth-first search yet its assumptions are not necessarily valid.

Because we wanted to discover the true dependency structure in a population's distribution, we aimed to impose as

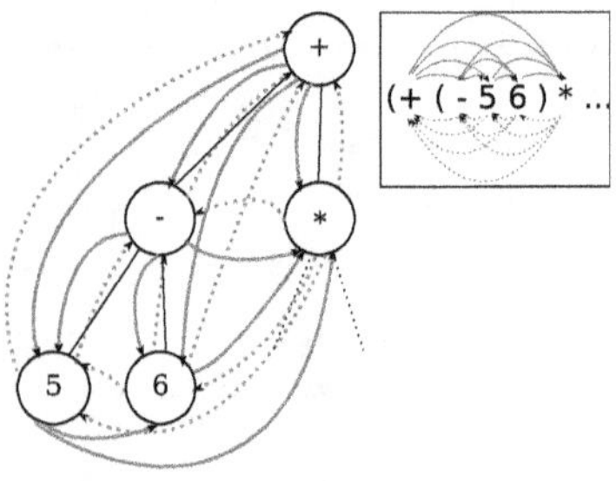

Figure 2: Shows order bias, with possible dependencies in left-to-right depth-first order depicted by the arrows, the dashed arrows are impossible dependencies given the ordering. In the square the string representation of the tree, with the same possible and impossible dependencies, is shown.

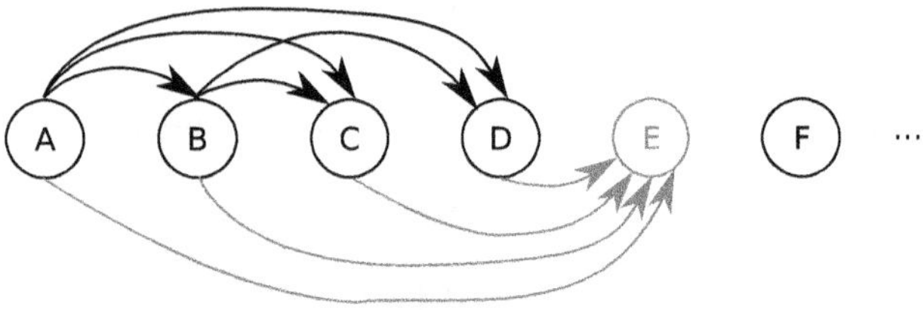

Figure 3: Possible structure with known node order. Suppose the node order is $A, B, C, D, E, F, \ldots$. This means that every edge in the network must go from left to right. Suppose we have already found the best parent sets for nodes A, B, C, and D, and are now considering node E. Each of E's parents must precede E in the order. We can add any of the edges shown in red without introducing a cycle. Furthermore, the parents we choose for E will not limit the choice of parents for nodes F and beyond.

few restrictions as possible on the type of graphical model structure we could learn. Thus, we opted for a search-and-score algorithm that did not require a node order as input (1). This algorithm uses an evolutionary algorithm in a search-and-score approach to propose and search for node orders leading to an optimal network structure. For each order the EA proposes, the algorithm then identifies an optimal network structure. This requires evaluating every structure that is consistent with that order. Since in our approach each individual is an order, this identification occurs during the evaluation of an individual's fitness. While the identification is computationally expensive, the number of structures (DAGs) that are consistent with the order is finite. In Section A, we present a scalable approach to systematically overcome the computational burden.

When learning the order of a DAG, parents of any node Y must precede Y in the ordering. In other words, given a node ordering R, such that for any nodes X and Y, if $X \overset{R}{<} Y$ (X precedes Y in R), then any edge between X and Y must be directed from X to Y. The ordering constraint R allows the choice of parents for one node to be independent of the other nodes' parents. This is because any combination of edges consistent with the ordering R produces an acyclic graph. Figure 3 illustrates this observation.

With a decomposable score this makes the choice of parents for any node X independent of the choice of parents for any other node Y. A decomposable score allows us to evaluate parent sets for each node independently and select the best one for each node and total score of the entire network is the total sum of all the scores for each node. It is apparent that the minimum across each node's family score minimizes the overall score as well. This means that now we can search for each node's parent set independently. If we limit the indegree (number of parents) of every node to a constant $k < n/2$, then there are at most

$$1 + \binom{n-1}{1} + \ldots + \binom{n-1}{k} = O\left(k \cdot \binom{n-1}{k}\right) = O(n^k)$$

possible parent sets for each node, where n is the number of nodes in the network. Finding the optimal parent set for all nodes thus requires at most

$$n \cdot O(n^k) = O(n^{k+1})$$

parent sets to be evaluated, which is polynomial in n, for a fixed k. This means that we can exhaustively search over the space of networks that are consistent with an ordering R and have an indegree of at most k.

Of course, an $O(n^{k+1})$-time exhaustive search is only reasonable if k is small (up to about 3 or 4). This restriction is not as bad as it seems, because we cannot learn Bayesian networks with large parent sets anyway, unless we have an extremely large training set. To see why, consider a Bayesian network where all variables are binary. If a variable X has no parents, then to compute the Bayesian score we only need two counts from the training set: $M[X = 0]$ and $M[X = 1]$. If X has one parent Y, then we need four counts: $M[X = 0, Y = 0]$, $M[X = 0, Y = 1]$, $M[X = 1, Y = 0]$, and $M[X = 1, Y = 1]$. If X has two parents, we need eight counts, and so on. In general, if X has k parents, we need a total of 2^{k+1} counts. As the number of parents Pa_X increases, it becomes less and less likely to find representative counts for all possible assignments $M[\mathrm{Pa}_X = \mathrm{pa}_X, X = x]$ in the training set. This phenomenon of *data fragmentation* means that we can only learn networks where each node has a small numbers of parents. Thus, setting the maximum indegree k to a small value is justified.

4. EXPERIMENTS

In this section we start by describing our choice of demonstration problem (Section 4.1), our procedure for transforming population data into graphical models (Section 4.2) and how we set up a number of experiments (Section 4.3) for which we build a graphical model every at generation. By their structure, graphical models reveal structural dependencies between the nodes of genetic programming trees. In Section 4.2 we identify graphical model properties of potential interest in this regard – edge quantity and dependency among nodes expressed in terms of family relations. We then interpret each experiment in light of the operator it has used and the information the graphical model conveys. This section contains an extended analysis of experiments initially done in (9) and (10).

4.1 Demonstration Problem

Because our goal is to figure out the nature of insights a graphical model offers in terms of its dependency struc-

Table 1: Parameters for the GP runs in ECJ. *XO* is crossover, *Mut* is mutation, *No ops* is selection without variational operators and *No Sel* is crossover with random selection.

Parameter	*XO*	*Mut*	*No ops*	*No Sel*
Crossover	0.9	0.0	0.0	0.9
Mutation	0.0	1.0	0.0	0.0
Selection	Tournament size 7			Random
Population size	10,000			
Generations	40			
Initialization	Ramped Half-Half			
Max Depth	5			
Language	Symbolic Regression			
Functions ($\mathcal{F}$)	$\{+, -, *, \%\}$			
Terminal ($\mathcal{T}$)	{x,y, 0.1, 1.0}			

ture, for our experiments we choose Pagie-2D (16) which is a simple but sufficiently realistic symbolic regression problem with a modestly sized set of functions and terminals. The problem is to regress an expression matching the target function $1/(1 + x^{-4}) + 1/(1 + y^{-4})$ over 676 fitness cases in $[-5, 5]^2$, and fitness is calculated as the mean squared error. The GP parameters are summarized in Table 1, and % is protected division. We run standard GP on the Pagie-2D problem using tournament selection with a tournament size of 7 and ramped half-half initialization. We employ a prototype tree of depth 5, which has 63 nodes implying an equivalent maximum tree size for the Pagie-2D runs. Our runs execute for 40 generations, using ECJ[1], with a population size of 10,000.

4.2 Graphical Model Building Procedure

After each generation, we store the entire population to disk so we can build its corresponding graphical model. We start by converting each population into a data set $\mathcal{D}$ with one row for every tree and 63 columns, one per outcome of the 63 random variables. We represent each tree as a row of 63 outcomes, by aligning it to the prototype tree, starting from the root, with a depth-first order traversal and substituting *null* for any node of the tree not in the prototype tree.

The root can take any outcome from the set of functions: $S_{\text{root}} = \{+, -, *, \%\}$. The leaves can take any outcome from the set of terminals, as well as *null*: $S_{\text{leaf}} = \{x, y, 0.1, 1.0, \textit{null}\}$. Intermediary nodes can take any outcome from the set of functions and terminals, as well as *null*: $S_{\text{intermediary}} = \{+, -, *, \%, x, y, 0.1, 1.0, \textit{null}\}$. Thus, our data set $\mathcal{D}$'s columns are 63 random variables $Y = \{Y_1, Y_2, \ldots Y_{63}\}$. Each variable is discrete, and its support is either S_{root}, S_{leaf}, or $S_{\text{intermediary}}$. We then learn, as described in Section 3, a graphical model for the distribution $P(Y_1, Y_2 \ldots Y_{63}|\mathcal{D})$.

4.3 Experiment Definition and Method

We define three experiments which vary in terms of GP operator in order to detect differences in this respect:

No variational operators Neither crossover nor mutation is used, selection only acts on the population.

Crossover Single point subtree crossover is the only variational operator and it is used in combination with selection.

Mutation Subtree mutation is the only variational operator and it is used in combination with selection.

No selection Single point subtree crossover is the only variational operator and selection is random.

Each experiment consists of 30 independent runs. For each run we build a graphical model each generation. This results in 1200 graphical models per experiment and 4800 graphical models overall.

4.4 Study of Graphical Model Properties

This section outlines the properties of the graphical model which is studied as well as the results from the different experimental setups. The aim is to identify properties which can explain the dynamics of GP populations.

4.4.1 Edge Quantity

Fig. 4 shows an example graphical model for a GP population at generation 25 (G_{25}), taken from a run using crossover. In addition to studying graphical models at different generations directly, a graphical model structural property worthy of attention is the number of edges in the graph. In graphical model terms, because an edge from Node A to Node B implies that the likelihood of random variable B depends on random variable A, edge quantity reveals the degree of variable inter-dependence. Edge quantity conveys different information from previous work in GP where, by simple counting, the frequency of symbols is determined or even the frequency of symbols in specific tree locations is determined. Simple counting does not reflect dependencies which the graphical modeling mines from the population by treating it as samples and using max-likelihood estimation. Given that a graphical model supplies dependency information, these dependencies should then be mapped back to the prototype tree to provide interpretation in a GP context. That is, each random variable of a graphical model maps to a node of a prototype tree which in turn maps to the symbol set, i.e. the function and terminal sets, of a GP experiment.

We can formulate one simple hypothesis: a random population of GP trees would result in a graphical model where there are arbitrary dependencies (i.e. edges) between nodes compared to a population evolved later in a run. The later population has been "shaped" by selection and variation so it will be reflected by a structure in the dependencies. These dependencies will reflect the complex mapping between genotype and phenotype, i.e. the direct representation of the solution and its behavior. Fig. 5(a), with data aggregated over each of the four experiments, shows the change in edge quantity over generations. It provides one unit of evidence for the hypothesis. In the initial populations' graphical model there are few edges, then, due to selection, the number sharply rises regardless of whether variation is employed. When a variational operator is employed, subsequently the edge quantity diminishes and eventually tapers. This can also be seen for the run without selection, where the rise is significantly smaller. We speculate that this dynamic will generally remain the same with other problems due to the macro-influences of the operators but will vary in detail due to the unique fitness landscape of every problem.

[1] `http://cs.gmu.edu/~eclab/projects/ecj/`

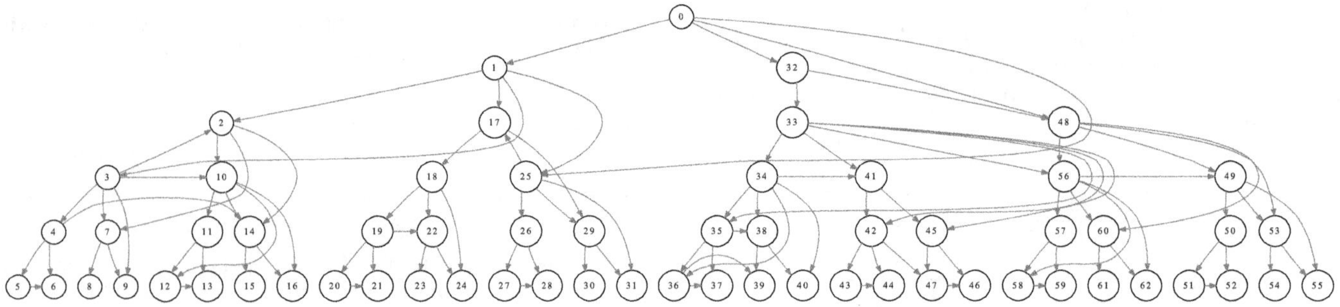

Figure 4: A graphical model for generation 25 from a run of the crossover only experiment.

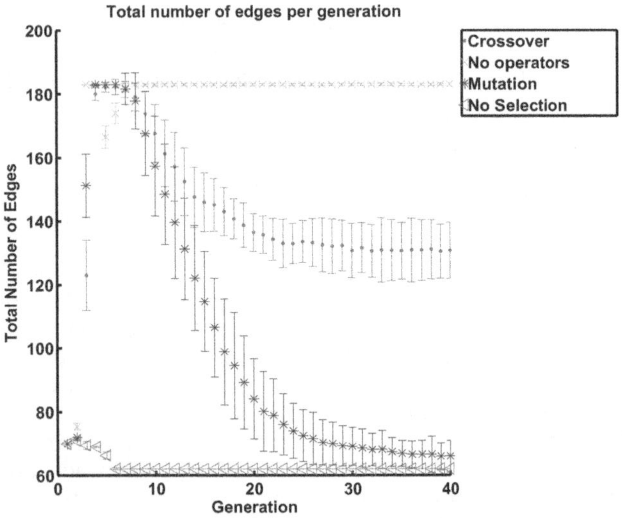

(a) Edge quantity per generation, average of 30 runs.

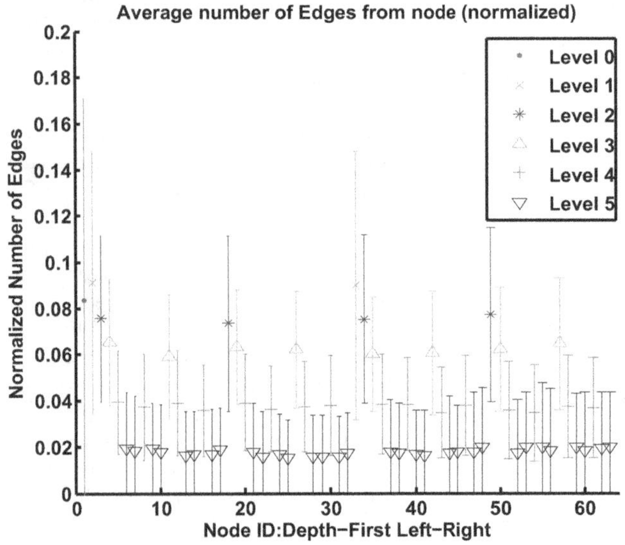

(b) Average edges per node, color sorted by depth level. Nodes are ordered in depth-first left-right.

Figure 5: Edge quantity plots

Edge quantity can be studied further. Fig. 5(b) indicates how many edges there are at each depth level of the prototype tree by showing the average number of edges per node, with error bars, for a run which used crossover. The nodes are ordered depth-first left-right. The coloring shows the depth level of the node and the number of edges are normalized according to the possible number of edges, 62. We observe more edges at lower depth levels.

4.4.2 Edge Type

While a random population's graphical model edges will generally span, in GP terms, between a node and its parent, we would hypothesize that an evolved population's edges would span between a node and its sibling and even, to higher ancestral generations (in tree structure terms), to its uncles and grandparents or farther. This leads us to investigate the ancestral property of edges.

We therefore also perform a basic enumeration of different types of edges. We define parent, sibling, grand-parent, grand-grand-parent, grand-grand-grand-parent, grand-grand-grand-grand-parent, uncle, and unclassified types. Sibling edges are one direction only: a sibling is the rightmost child of a parent but not the leftmost child of a parent. The edge types are illustrated in Fig. 6(a) using different dashes to denote each type. In Fig. 6(b) an example tree with a count of parent, left sibling, nephew and grandparent edge types is shown.

The interpretation of edges according to this structural ancestry typing is interesting. To see this, it is necessary to conceptually map between a prototype tree's (or graphical model's) edges to GP context in the following manner: A GP tree is a representation for an (executable) expression that is a nested set of functions where arguments of a function are recursively themselves functions until the recursion "bottoms out" where arguments are non-functions (variables or constants, a.k.a terminals) represented as leaves. A GP tree is evaluated (a.k.a executed or interpreted) by a preorder parse where successive arguments are recursively evaluated in preorder. The dependency edges to a leaf from nodes above it in the tree indicate which functions in the expression depend on that argument's value. If the dependency edge is reversed in direction, i.e. from a leaf to a node above it, it indicates that a function elsewhere in the tree (coming either before or after the evaluation of the terminal when the nested expression is evaluated) influences the value of the terminal (e.g. whether it is 0.1 or 1.0 in Pagie-2D).

We now proceed to analyze each experiment wherein variation differs. We start with a baseline where the GP run uses selection but no crossover or mutation.

4.4.3 No Variational Operators Experiment

When GP is run without any variation operators, selection

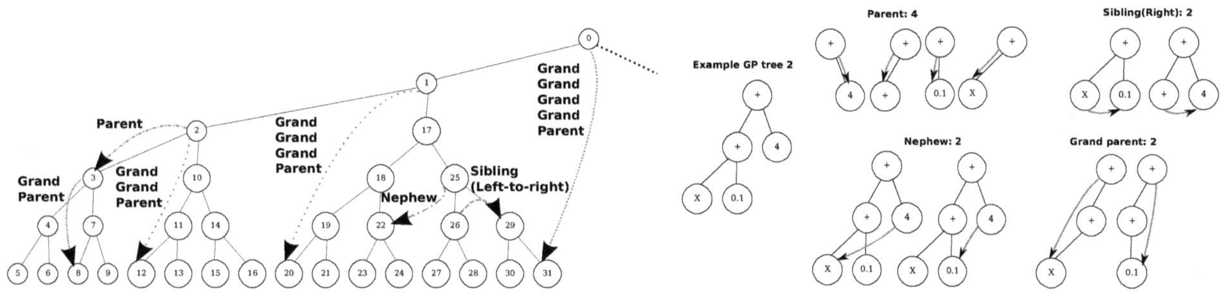

(a) Edge types (b) Number of edge types in the example tree

Figure 6: Possible edge types by ancestry. In Fig. 6(a) the edges (dependencies) in the GM which are studied are shown. Fig. 6(b) there is an example of how the edge types are counted.

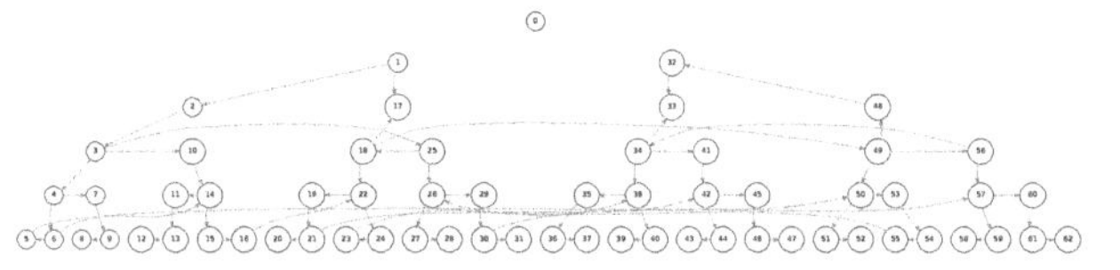

(a) Generation 0, no variational operators

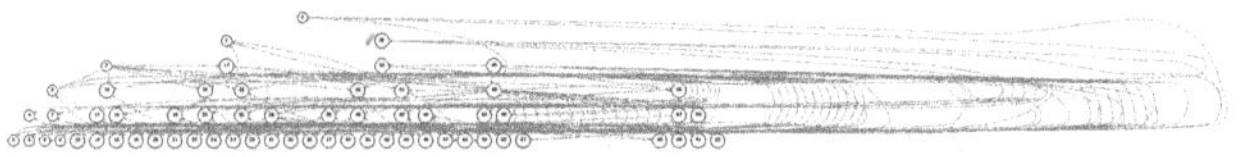

(b) Generation 13, no variational operators

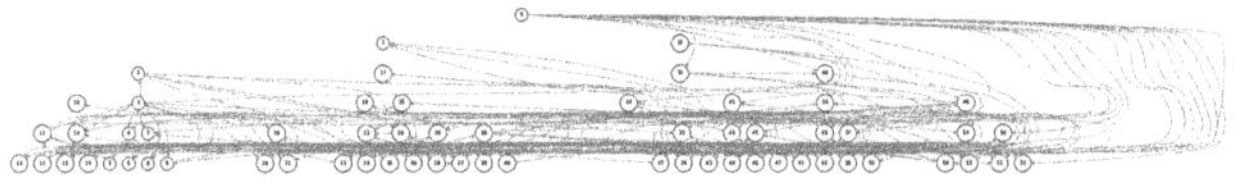

(c) Generation 40, no variational operators

Figure 7: Selection Only Experiment: graphical models for one randomly selected run at generation 0, 13 and 40.

eventually hones in on a completely homogeneous population. We find in our runs that this usually happens by generation ten. For one run, Fig. 7(a) shows a graphical model of the random population at generation 0. It has relatively fewer edges than subsequent generations. Fig. 7(b) shows a graphical model of generation 13 when the number of edges has increased. After the generation when the population has converged to a single point, any variation we observe in generational graphical models is due to the stochasticity of the EA we use to build the model.

Recall that our model building algorithm limits the number of dependency edges from a node to three. This implies that the maximum number of edges, given a prototype tree of size 63, equals 183. Which is the case at generation 40, when the population has completely converged to one GP solution, per Fig. 7(c) the graphical model has the maximum number of edges.

Next we consider edge types. The prevailing edge type is parent, as shown in Fig. 8(a). This figure is a time series plot of edge type quantity expressed as the ratio of the number of edges in the graph of the type to the total possible number of edges of the type. For example, for an edge of type parent there are 62 possible edges, a ratio of 0.5 means that there are 31 edges in the graphical model of this type. There are many different types of edges in a homogeneous population and they vary more between each generation compared to the experiments using operators. Half of the edges are unclassified, the other half is almost uniformly distributed between the edge types, except for grand grand parent. Moreover, the sibling relations are not as frequent compared to the experiments using operators. This is again likely due to the fact that the population is homogeneous and the structure finding algorithm is stochastic.

4.4.4 Mutation Only Experiment

In the experiment where GP was run only with a subtree mutation operator for variation, we examine three resulting graphical models at different generations, the quantity of edges and their ancestry type.

Mutation randomizes the population, but selection promotes the edge types associated with fit solutions. This makes later generation graphical models distinguishable from the initial population. The graphical models in Fig. 9 show a selective pruning of edges over generations.

Consulting Fig. 5(a) as to the number of edges, we observe the quantity rapidly increasing (in approximately the first 7 generations) to reach close to the maximum number of possible edges in the graphical model, before decreasing to almost the same number of edges as nodes. The edge ratios shown in Fig. 8(b) indicate the most frequent type of edge is from a parent to a child. As the number of edges decrease, the most frequent edge type is parent, then sibling and some uncles, with hardly any grand-parent dependencies. Our interpretation is that by adding new random subtrees, mutation creates new local dependence which is confined to the subtree. It disrupts any dependencies extending out of the subtree which it excises. This would imply that mutation runs have more parent edges.

4.4.5 Crossover Only Experiment

Considering the experiment where GP was run only with the subtree crossover operator for variation, we examine three resulting graphical models from different generations, the quantity of edges and their ancestry type.

The graphical models in Fig. 8(c) differ by generation and, in unshown detailed graphical model data (animated generation by generation), we observe that the change from one generation to the next is very gradual, more so than with mutation. Consulting Fig. 5(a), we observe that initially there are approximately 70 edges, while there is a peak of approximately 180 edges around generation six. Then the

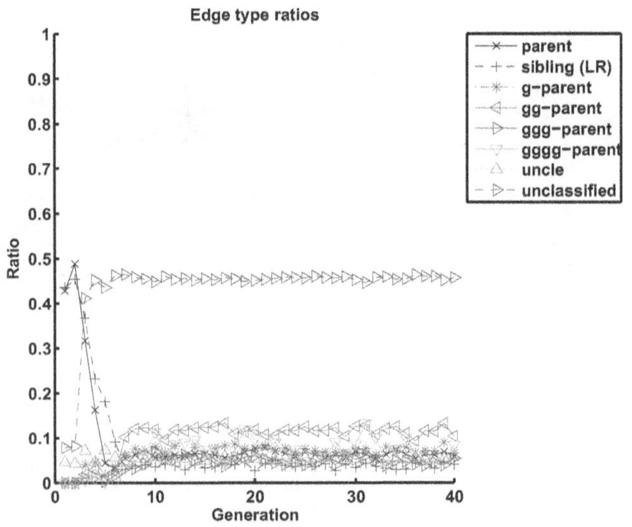

(a) Edge type ratios, no operators

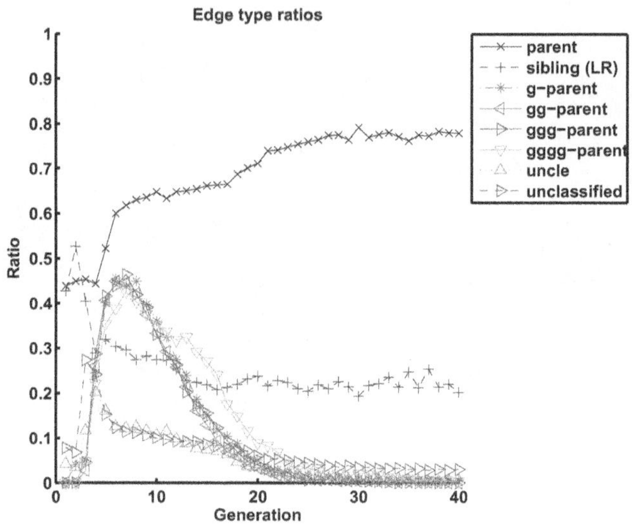

(b) Edge type ratios, mutation

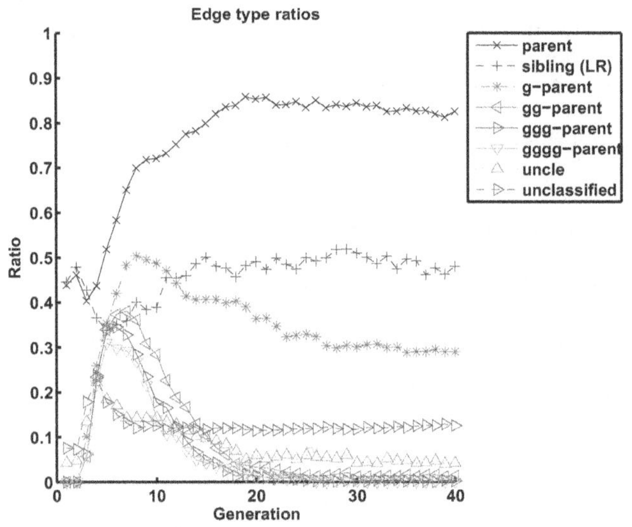

(c) Edge type ratios, crossover

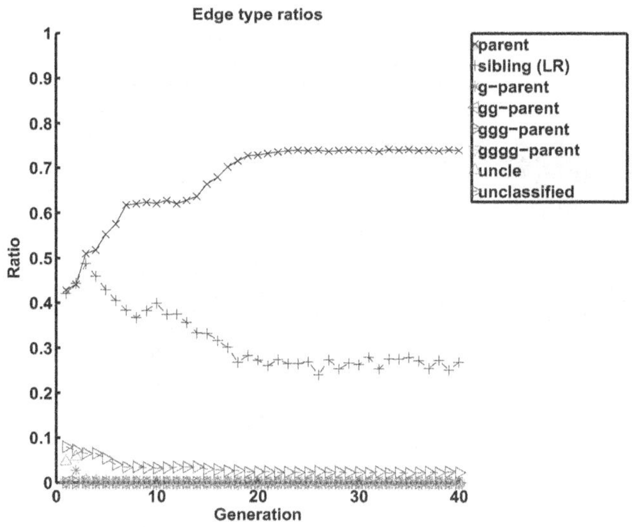

(d) Edge type ratios, no selection

Figure 8: Plot of the ratios of edges in different types. For Pagie 2D without crossover and mutation 8(a), mutation 8(b), crossover 8(c) and no selection 8(d).

number of edges tails off and stabilizes at approximately 130. When we align our animation with the fitness time series we see the tail off synchronizes with approximately the same generation when fitness stops improving and the population has started to converge.

Considering the type of edges, per Fig. 8(b), we observe that, after generation 20, almost all nodes in the graphical model have an edge with their ancestor and half have edges to their sibling. After 25 generations the ratios of the other edges have somewhat stabilized. Fig. 5(b) is an example of crossover only experiment. We see a consistency in the number of edges given the depth level of the node in the tree. As expected, the nodes at the lower depth levels have fewer edges.

Crossover is a subtree swap. This implies that it preserves more short and long range, i.e. ancestral dependencies such as parent, sibling plus grandparent and uncle. Because of the exchange, rather than the new material, it results in only a minor net change in dependency, *at the structural level.* Of course, the issue with crossover in GP is its semantic consequences while its structural behavior directly follows from its definition.

4.4.6 No Selection Experiment

For the experiment where GP was run with random selection and only the subtree crossover operator for variation, we examine the quantity of edges and their ancestry type.

The graphical models for some generation are not shown, but they have very few edges and the connections are mainly between parent and sibling, we verify this by consulting Fig. 8(d). In addition, in Fig. 5(a), we observe that initially there are approximately 70 edges and within 6 generations the number drops to the the minimum number of edges. This effect is most likely due to the effect of initialization.

The next section will further discuss the results from the different experiments.

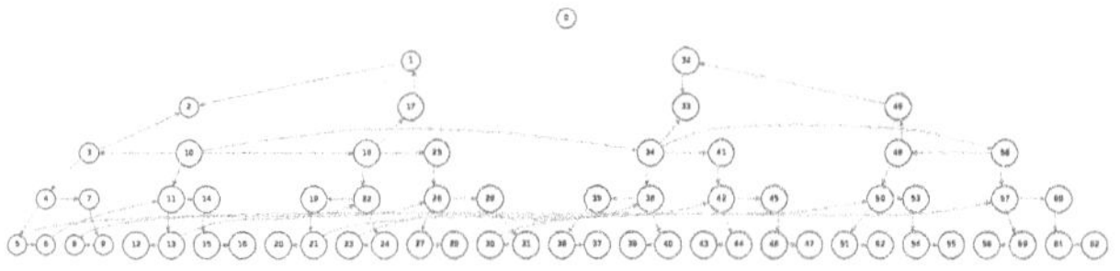

(a) Generation 0, mutation

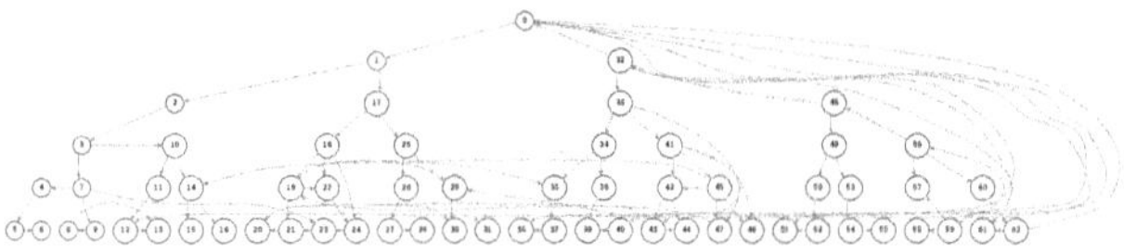

(b) Generation 13, mutation

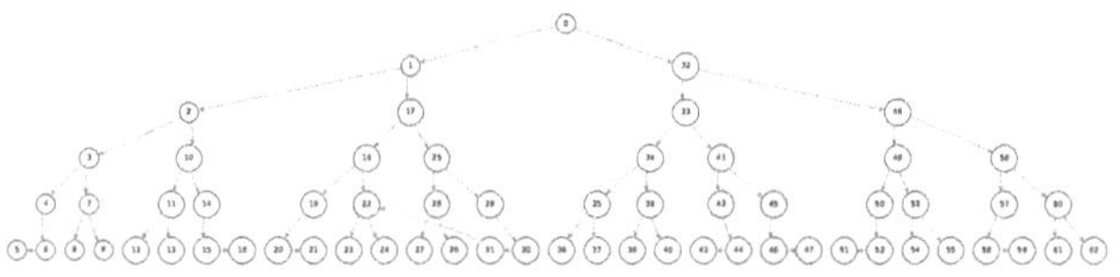

(c) Generation 40, mutation

Figure 9: Mutation Only Experiment: graphical models for one randomly selected run at generation 0, 13 and 40.

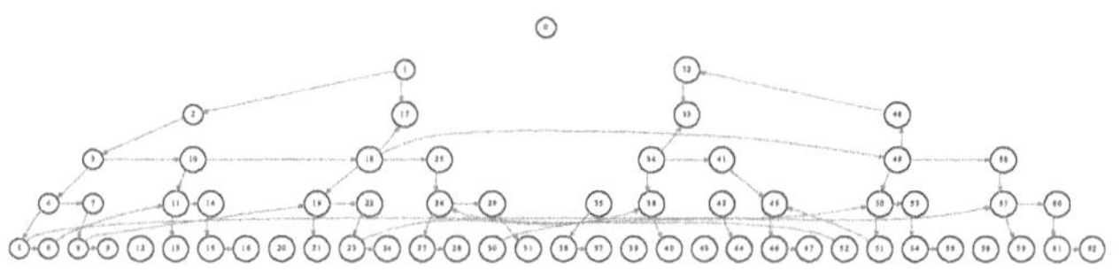

(a) Generation 0, crossover

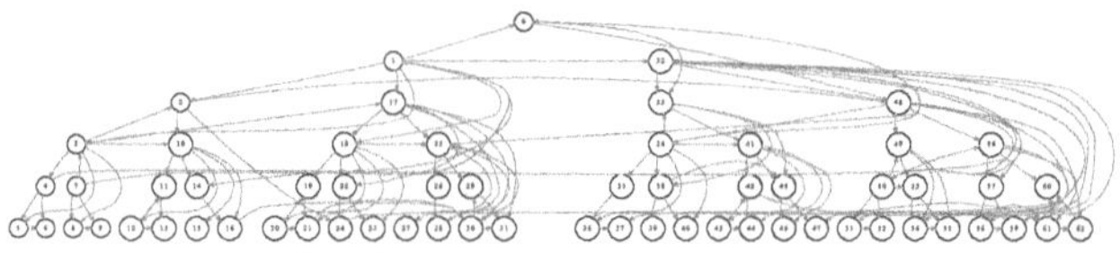

(b) Generation 13, crossover

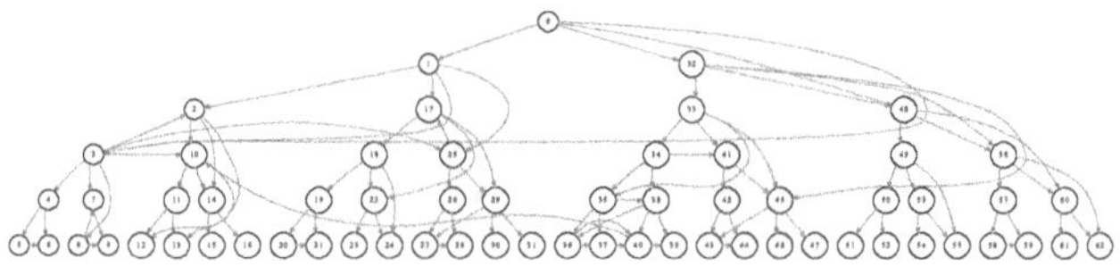

(c) Generation 40, crossover

Figure 10: Crossover Only Experiment: graphical models for one randomly selected run at at generation 0, 13, and 40

4.5 Cross Experiment Remarks

Our understanding of mutation and crossover would lead us to hypothesize that the dependencies being studied, due to their structural nature, would be different. Comparing Fig. 9 to Fig. 10 bears this out. In the crossover only experiment we can observe that crossover's graphical model in the final generation has different dependencies and more dependencies than mutation. This is interpretable: crossover is an exchange with less net disruption while mutation introduces new material while excising existing material. Both operators culminate with approximately the same quantity of parent edge types but reach this endpoint with different trajectories (compare Fig. 8(b) to Fig. 8(c)). Crossover has more siblings, and longer range dependencies with uncles and grand-parents. This is consistent with the difference between the two operators in terms of different extents of dependence preservation and disruption.

From the different experiments which differ by variation operator, we are able to distinguish distinctly different graphical models, both regarding number of edges and type of edges. For all runs, across the variation operator experiments (i.e. excluding selection only), when inspecting the fitness, the best fitness is only slightly improving during the runs. The operators manipulate the population in such a way that the dependencies between experiments differ. When comparing the number of edges and the type of edges from each experiment it can be seen that the number of edges in the crossover only experiment is higher than for a random population. The crossover operator helps to create a population that has many parent dependencies, sibling dependencies and some longer grand-parent dependencies. In contrast, for the experiments with the mutation operator the number of edges is the same as for a initial random population, but the structure is quite different from initial random. The types of edges are not the same as when crossover is used either, there are hardly any longer dependencies, such as grand-parents edges. When random selection is used there are no long distance dependencies and the only the minimum number of edges after a the effects of initialization have disappeared. Finally, the number of edges in a homogeneous setup is very high, reaching the maximum limit of edges and the variation in edges is most likely due to the stochastic learning of the graphical model.

A graphical model also provides a way to generate a GP population from its parsimonious representation. It is an approximate form of compression where a very important property of the original population is preserved - variable dependency. Further information from the graphical model could be taken into account when designing operators in GP, or reduced Bayesian network for EDA-style GP, as in Hemberg et al (9).

5. CONCLUSIONS & FUTURE WORK

We have introduced graphical models as a new means of investigating the dynamics of genetic programming populations in general and,in this work specifically, GP's operators. Graphical model based analysis is complementary to conventional statistics that are tracked across generations. The graphical model shows the dependencies between nodes in GP trees when treated as a multivariate distribution represented as prototype trees. We presented an unbiased means of deriving a graphical model and introduced an EA based algorithm for efficiently finding graphical models. Moreover, algorithm wise we only search for order of the nodes in a graphical model, unlike K2 which searches for a graphical model given an order. We exhaustively search for best graphical model for each order. For the purpose to overcome the cost of exhaustive search, we initially build a cache and ADTrees. These techniques speed up the fitness evaluation in the creation of the graphical model.

It is important to recognize that alternate kinds of graphical models could be built. Graphical models different from the one we present have the potential to emphasize different properties about GP's population distribution. We envision future investigations that would answer which are most appropriate and insightful for modeling GP dynamics. Our motivation herein was to investigate whether insight into a run's dynamics at the population, tree structure level, could be gained by observing the dependency structure graphical models reveal about the multivariate distribution associated with functions and terminals in GP trees. The graphical model information is in this form structural rather than syntax oriented.

Using Pagie-2D problems as exemplars, we take first steps in analyzing generation and inter-generation dynamics of GP runs in terms of changing graphical model structure. The experiments show that there is a distinct difference in the graphical model of a GP population when different operators are used, both in the number of edges in the graphical model and the types of edges.

For future work further problems and operators will be investigated. Other work can be combinations of edge types as well as doing inference of the outcome of the random variables from the generated graphical models. Moreover, if we correlate fitness with the graphical model we can:

- Pool all samples and take top fitness slice and learn a graphical model.
- Use fitness value as a conditional value for the graphical model.
- Align the data based on fitness to get the dependency structure of populations with similar fitness distribution

Acknowledgment

We thank the support received from General Electric Global Research Center and Li Ka Shing Foundation.

APPENDIX

A. FAST LEARNING OF THE MODEL

We use an evolutionary algorithm for learning the structure of a Bayesian network from a fully observed data set. This algorithm searches over the space of node *orders*, rather than searching over the space of DAGs. The genetic algorithm proposes an order and an optimal DAG is identified by exhaustively searching through different possible DAGs given this order. Each DAG is scored using a Bayesian score function.

A.1 Representation and Operators

In our GA over orders, we use the node order R as the genotype of an individual. We use swap mutation and cycle crossover as our operators (3). There are many networks consistent with the order R. We define the phenotype of an individual as the *best* network consistent with R, subject to a maximum indegree k, which is fixed at the start of the algorithm. This follows the setup that Teyssier and Koller (20) used for their hill-climbing algorithm over orders. The GA needs to find the best DAG for R and k.

A.1.1 The Bayesian Score

We want our scoring function to measure how well a structure fits the data. We also want it to penalize complex structures, because a simpler model makes inference more tractable. The Bayesian score is one of several scoring functions satisfying these criteria. We define a prior $P(\mathcal{G})$ over graph structures, and another prior $P(\boldsymbol{\theta}_{\mathcal{G}} \mid \mathcal{G})$ over parameters given a graph. The posterior over structures for a data set $\mathcal{D}$ is given by Bayes' rule:

$$P(\mathcal{G} \mid \mathcal{D}) = \frac{P(\mathcal{D} \mid \mathcal{G})\, P(\mathcal{G})}{P(\mathcal{D})}$$

where the denominator is a normalizing factor that does not depend on the structure we are trying to evaluate. The Bayesian score is then given by:

$$\text{score}_B(\mathcal{G} : \mathcal{D}) = \log P(\mathcal{D} \mid \mathcal{G}) + \log P(\mathcal{G}). \quad (1)$$

The second term is usually less important, because it does not grow with the size of $\mathcal{D}$. The first term is the logarithm of the marginal likelihood of the data given the structure, which averages over the choices of parameters for $\mathcal{G}$:

$$P(\mathcal{D} \mid \mathcal{G}) = \int_{\boldsymbol{\theta}_{\mathcal{G}}} P(\mathcal{D} \mid \boldsymbol{\theta}_{\mathcal{G}}, \mathcal{G})\, P(\boldsymbol{\theta}_{\mathcal{G}} \mid \mathcal{G})\, d\boldsymbol{\theta}_{\mathcal{G}},$$

where $P(\mathcal{D} \mid \boldsymbol{\theta}_{\mathcal{G}}, \mathcal{G})$ is the likelihood of the data set given the network $\langle \mathcal{G}, \boldsymbol{\theta} \rangle$, and $P(\boldsymbol{\theta}_{\mathcal{G}} \mid \mathcal{G})$ is our prior over parameters given a structure. The marginal likelihood is also known as the evidence function.

If the prior over parameters is a Dirichlet distribution where $P(\boldsymbol{\theta}_{Y_i \mid \text{pa}_{Y_i}} \mid \mathcal{G})$ has hyperparameters $\{\alpha^{\mathcal{G}}_{y_i^j \mid \boldsymbol{u}_i}\}$ for j from 1 to $|Y_i|$, which satisfies global and local parameter independence. With $\alpha^{\mathcal{G}}_{Y_i \mid \boldsymbol{u}_i} = \sum_j \alpha^{\mathcal{G}}_{y_i^j \mid \boldsymbol{u}_i}$, then the marginal likelihood can be written as follows:

$$P(\mathcal{D} \mid \mathcal{G}) = \prod_i \prod_{\boldsymbol{u}_i \in Val(\text{Pa}^{\mathcal{G}}_{Y_i})} \left[\frac{\Gamma(\alpha^{\mathcal{G}}_{Y_i \mid \boldsymbol{u}_i})}{\Gamma(\alpha^{\mathcal{G}}_{Y_i \mid \boldsymbol{u}_i} + M[\boldsymbol{u}_i])} \cdot \prod_{y_i^j \in Val(Y_i)} \frac{\Gamma(\alpha^{\mathcal{G}}_{y_i^j \mid \boldsymbol{u}_i} + M[y_i^j, \boldsymbol{u}_i])}{\Gamma(\alpha^{\mathcal{G}}_{y_i^j \mid \boldsymbol{u}_i})} \right] \quad (2)$$

This formula is simplified by choosing a reasonable prior.

Priors and Decomposability

It is desirable to have a scoring function that decomposes:

$$\text{score}(\mathcal{G} : \mathcal{D}) = \sum_i \text{FamScore}(Y_i \mid \text{Pa}^{\mathcal{G}}_i : \mathcal{D})$$

where the family score $\text{FamScore}(Y_i \mid \boldsymbol{U} : \mathcal{D})$ measures how well the variables $\boldsymbol{U}$ serve as parents of Y. With a decomposable score, local changes to the structure affect only a small number of families, and so we do not have to recompute the score of the entire network. For example, if we change the order such that we only swap the last two positions in a node ordering R we only have to search for the best parent sets for the last two nodes and only evaluate the family scores for these two nodes. Additionally, we can search for best parent sets of individual nodes independently.

To ensure that the Bayesian score decomposes, our structure and parameter priors should satisfy some conditions. The structure prior should satisfy structure modularity:

$$P(\mathcal{G}) \propto \prod_i P(\text{Pa}_{Y_i} = \text{Pa}^{\mathcal{G}}_{Y_i}),$$

where $P(\text{Pa}_{Y_i} = \text{Pa}^{\mathcal{G}}_{Y_i})$ is the probability of choosing that specific set of parents for X_i. The parameter prior should satisfy global parameter independence and parameter modularity:

$$P(\boldsymbol{\theta}_{Y_i|U} \mid \mathcal{G}) = P(\boldsymbol{\theta}_{Y_i|U} \mid \mathcal{G}')$$

for any pair of structures $\mathcal{G}$, $\mathcal{G}'$.

When we have no prior knowledge about the structure we are trying to learn, we can use a structure prior that assigns equal probability to every possible structure. In this case, we can ignore the second term ($logP(\mathcal{G})$) in the Bayesian score (equation 1), and evaluate structures solely by their marginal log-likelihood $\log P(\mathcal{D} \mid \mathcal{G})$.

In the case when we have no prior knowledge about the parameters, we can use the BDeu prior. (BDeu stands for uniform Bayesian Dirichlet prior satisfying likelihood equivalence (11).) For this prior, we only need to specify an equivalent sample size (or strength) α. Given a node Y_i and its parents Pa_{Y_i}, the BDeu prior assigns equal probabilities to all values of the node and parents:

$$\alpha_{y_i|\mathrm{pa}_{Y_i}} = \alpha \cdot \frac{1}{|\,Val(Y_i, \mathrm{Pa}_{Y_i})|}, \qquad (3)$$

where $|\,Val(Y_i, \mathrm{Pa}_{Y_i})|$ is the number of possible assignments to X_i and Pa_{Y_i}. Let $\gamma(\boldsymbol{Y}) = \alpha \cdot \frac{1}{|Val(\boldsymbol{Y})|}$ for any set of nodes $\boldsymbol{Y}$. Then the marginal log-likelihood score decomposes into a sum of terms for each family:

$$\mathrm{FamScore}(Y_i, \mathrm{Pa}_{Y_i}) = \sum_{\boldsymbol{u}_i \in Val(\mathrm{Pa}^{\mathcal{G}}_{Y_i})} \Bigg[\qquad (4)$$

$$\sum_{y_i^j \in Val(y_i)} \ln \frac{\Gamma(\gamma(Y_i, \mathrm{Pa}_{Y_i}) + M[y_i^j, \boldsymbol{u}_i])}{\Gamma(\gamma(Y_i, \mathrm{Pa}_{Y_i}))}$$

$$\ln \frac{\Gamma(\gamma(\mathrm{Pa}^{\mathcal{G}}_{Y_i}))}{\Gamma(\gamma(\mathrm{Pa}^{\mathcal{G}}_{Y_i})) + M[\boldsymbol{u}_i])} +$$

$$\sum_{y_i^j \in Val(y_i)} \ln \frac{\Gamma(\gamma(Y_i, \mathrm{Pa}_{Y_i}) + M[y_i^j, \boldsymbol{u}_i])}{\Gamma(\gamma(Y_i, \mathrm{Pa}_{Y_i}))} \Bigg]$$

A.2 Caching for Efficient Fitness Evaluation

Evaluating the fitness of an individual in our GA involves computing the Bayesian score of a network, which is an expensive operation. We use two levels of caching to speed up this computation. The first level caches sufficient statistics (counts) of the data set. The second level caches set scores.

Suppose that we had a *contingency table* for a node Y_i and its parents Pa_{Y_i}. This table contains one row for each possible assignment to Y_i and Pa_{Y_i}, and the number of times that assignment occurs in the training set. If we have this contingency table, then we can evaluate $FamScore(Y_i, \mathrm{Pa}_{Y_i})$ in time linear to the size of the contingency table, simply by performing the summation in Equation (4). We can compute contingency tables naively as follows:

- We start with a table with all zeros.
- From each row in the data set, we extract the values of Y_i and Pa_{Y_i}, and denote them y_i and $\boldsymbol{u}_i$ respectively.
- We then increment the row corresponding to $y_i, \boldsymbol{u}_i$ in the contingency table.

With this approach, computing each contingency table requires one pass over the entire data set.

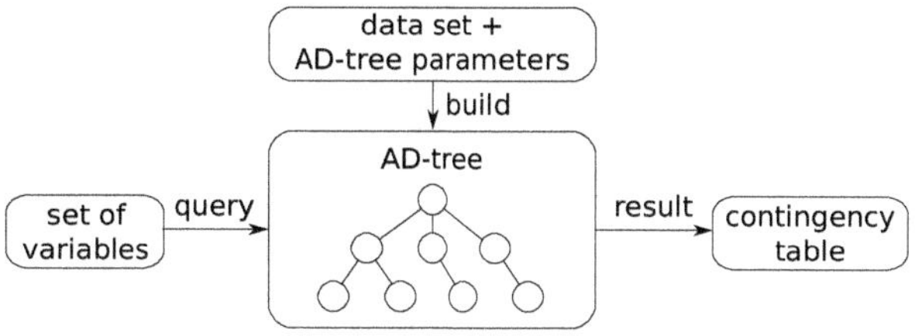

Figure 11: An AD-tree is built once and queried many times.

Our first level of caching uses the AD-tree data structure of Moore and Lee (14) to speed up the computation of contingency tables. The AD-tree saves time at the expense of using more memory. It is a tree data structure, where each node "splits" the data set according to all possible assignments to a variable. Contingency tables can be computed from the AD-tree in time that is independent of the total size of the data set. Thus, we no longer require one full pass through the data set to compute a contingency table. Figure 11 illustrates the usage of the AD-tree. For details see Moore and Lee (14).

Traditional hill-climbing methods cache family scores so that they can be retrieved again and again without being recomputed. We improve on this slightly by noticing that with the BDeu prior, the family score (equation (4)) decomposes into two set scores:

$$\mathrm{FamScore}(Y_i, \mathrm{Pa}_{Y_i}) = \mathrm{SetScore}(\mathrm{Pa}_{Y_i} \cup \{Y_i\}) - \mathrm{SetScore}(\mathrm{Pa}_{Y_i})$$

where

$$\mathrm{SetScore}(\boldsymbol{Y}) = \sum_{\boldsymbol{v}_i \in Val(\boldsymbol{Y})} \ln \frac{\Gamma(\alpha_{\boldsymbol{Y}})}{\Gamma(\alpha_{\boldsymbol{Y}} + M[\boldsymbol{v}_i])}$$

for any set of variables $\boldsymbol{Y}$, and $\alpha_{\boldsymbol{Y}} = \alpha \cdot \frac{1}{|Val(\boldsymbol{Y})|}$. Computing a family score seems to require the contingency tables of $\mathrm{Pa}_{Y_i} \cup \{Y_i\}$ and Pa_{Y_i}. But in fact, the latter contingency table can be obtained from the former by marginalizing the column Y_i. This means that only one AD-tree query is required for computing the score of a family.

Our second level of caching stores set scores instead of family scores. This results in more cache hits, because multiple families during the lifetime of the algorithm may have the same set of parents.

Additional improvements We cache sufficient statistics and set scores, as we did for our GA over graphs (section A.2). Note that we no longer need to build the full AD-tree. If the maximum indegree is k, we will never need contingency tables for more than $k+1$ variables, so we only need to build the AD-tree up to depth $k+1$.

From Teyssier and Koller (20) we use the following. Suppose our maximum indegree is k. For each node X, we compute the score of all possible parent sets of size k or less. We rank these parent sets in decreasing order by score. We then prune the set of possible parent sets as follows: if $\boldsymbol{U}' \subset \boldsymbol{U}$ and $\mathrm{FamScore}(X \mid \boldsymbol{U}') > \mathrm{FamScore}(X \mid \boldsymbol{U})$, then we remove the parent set $\boldsymbol{U}$ from consideration. For any order R, if $\boldsymbol{U}$ is a valid choice of parents for X, then $\boldsymbol{U}'$ is also valid, and has a better score. Therefore, we can safely eliminate $\boldsymbol{U}$, because we would never prefer it over $\boldsymbol{U}'$. We say that $\boldsymbol{U}$ is *dominated* by $\boldsymbol{U}'$.

To evaluate an order R, we go through every node from

first to last. For node X, we go through the ranked list of its possible parent sets, stopping at the first parent set consistent with the order R. This is the optimal parent set for X, subject to the order R and the indegree constraint. We continue until we have found the optimal parent set for each node. At this point, as we previously discussed, we have found the optimal network for the order R and the given maximum indegree.

References

[1] Berzan, C.: An Exploration of Structure Learning in Bayesian Networks. Tufts University Senior Honors Thesis, Tufts University (2012)

[2] Almal, A., MacLean, C., Worzel, W.: A population based study of evolutionary dynamics in genetic programming. Rick Riolo, Terence Soule and Bill Worzel (Eds.) (2009)

[3] Arthur Carvalho.: A cooperative coevolutionary genetic algorithm for learning bayesian network structures. GECCO 2011, 1131–1138

[4] Cooper, G. F., Herskovits, E.: A Bayesian Method for the Induction of Probabilistic Networks from Data Machine Learning, 1992, 9, 309-347

[5] Daida, J., Hilss, A., Ward, D., Long, S.: Visualizing tree structures in genetic programming. Genetic Programming and Evolvable Machines 6(1), 79–110 (2005)

[6] Daida, J., Tang, R., Samples, M., Byom, M.: Phase transitions in genetic programming search. Genetic Programming Theory and Practice IV, 237–256 (2007)

[7] Nir Friedman, Iftach Nachman, and Dana Peér.: Learning bayesian network structure from massive datasets: The "sparse candidate" algorithm. In *Uncertainty in Artificial Intelligence (UAI-99)*, 206–215, San Francisco, CA, 1999. Morgan Kaufmann.

[8] Hasegawa, Y., Iba, H.: A Bayesian network approach to program generation. IEEE Transactions on Evolutionary Computation, 12(6), 750–764 (2008)

[9] Erik Hemberg, Kalyan Veeramachaneni, James McDermott, Constantin Berzan, Una-May O'Reilly: An investigation of local patterns for estimation of distribution genetic programming. GECCO 2012: 767-774

[10] Erik Hemberg, Kalyan Veeramachaneni, Una-May O'Reilly: Graphical models and what they reveal about GP when it solves a symbolic regression problem. GECCO(Companion) 2012: 493-494

[11] Koller, D., Friedman, N.: Probabilistic Graphical Models: Principles and Techniques. MIT Press (2009)

[12] Langdon, W.B., Poli, R.: Foundations of Genetic Programming. Springer-Verlag (2002),

[13] McPhee, N., Hopper, N.: Analysis of genetic diversity through population history GECCO, 1999, 2, 1112-1120

[14] Andrew Moore and Mary Soon Lee.: Cached sufficient statistics for efficient machine learning with large datasets. *Journal of Artificial Intelligence Research*, 8:67–91, March 1998.

[15] O'Neill, Michael and Vanneschi, Leonardo and Gustafson, Steven and Banzhaf, Wolfgang.: Open issues in genetic programming *Genetic Programming and Evolvable Machines*, 11, 3:339–363, 2010

[16] Pagie, L., Hogeweg, P.: Evolutionary Consequences of Coevolving Targets. Evolutionary Computation 5, 401–418 (1997)

[17] Poli, R., Langdon, W.B., McPhee, N.F.: A field guide to genetic programming `http://lulu.com` (2008)

[18] Raidl, G., Gottlieb, J.: Empirical analysis of locality, heritability and heuristic bias in evolutionary algorithms: A case study for the multidimensional knapsack problem. Evolutionary Computation 13(4), 441–475 (2005)

[19] Salustowicz, R., Schmidhuber, J.: Probabilistic incremental program evolution. Evolutionary Computation 5(2), 123–141 (1997)

[20] M. Teyssier and D. Koller. Ordering-based search: A simple and effective algorithm for learning bayesian networks. In *Proceedings of the Twenty-first Conference on Uncertainty in AI (UAI)*, 584–590, Edinburgh, Scotland, UK, July 2005.

[21] Tomassini, M., Vanneschi, L., Collard, P., Clergue, M.: A study of fitness distance correlation as a difficulty measure in genetic programming. Evolutionary Computation 13(2), 213–239 (2005)

[22] Wolfson, K., Zakov, S., Sipper, M., Ziv-Ukelson, M.: Have your spaghetti and eat it too: evolutionary algorithmics and post-evolutionary analysis. Genetic Programming and Evolvable Machines 12(2), 121–160 (2011)

Approximating Vertex Cover Using Edge-Based Representations

Thomas Jansen
Dept. of Computer Science
Aberystwyth University
Aberystwyth SY23 3D, UK
t.jansen@aber.ac.uk

Pietro S. Oliveto
School of Computer Science
University of Birmingham
Birmingham B15 2TT, UK
P.S.Oliveto@bham.ac.uk

Christine Zarges
School of Computer Science
University of Birmingham
Birmingham B15 2TT, UK
C.Zarges@bham.ac.uk

ABSTRACT

In the literature only lower bounds are available on the approximation ratio of randomised search heuristics for vertex cover in the single-objective problem setting. These analyses are based on the natural vertex-based representation. Inspired by a well-known problem-specific approximation algorithm, we present an analysis of randomised search heuristics using edge-based representations. For the canonical objective function we prove that the performance can still be arbitrarily bad for the (1+1) EA and also RLS, even when using large search neighbourhoods. Adding slightly more information to the objective function turns RLS and the (1+1) EA into efficient 2-approximation algorithms requiring $O(m \log m)$ steps where m is the number of edges. Although equivalent in the worst case, such an upper bound on the runtime is at least a linear factor better than that of the multi-objective case for sparse graphs and for graphs with large optimal vertex covers. Furthermore RLS algorithms, that after an improvement do not flip tested bits before trying previously untested ones, guarantee 2-approximations in $O(m)$ steps.

Categories and Subject Descriptors

F.2.2 [**Analysis of Algorithms and Problem Complexity**]: Nonnumerical Algorithms and Problems

General Terms

Algorithms, Design, Performance, Theory

Keywords

runtime analysis; random local search; (1+1) EA; vertex cover; representation

1. INTRODUCTION

Vertex cover is one of the best known NP-hard combinatorial optimisation problems [29]. By itself or together with its many variants it has numerous applications in fields such as scheduling, networking and bioinformatics (see e. g. [2, 16, 30]). Given an undirected graph $G = (V, E)$, the *vertex cover* problem consists of finding a minimum subset of nodes $V_c \subseteq V$ such that every edge $e \in E$ is adjacent to at least one of the nodes in V_c. Due to its importance and difficulty, plenty of research has focused on finding algorithms that deliver good approximate solutions [17]. The most simple and popular one works as follows. As long as edges still remain, an edge is chosen uniformly at random from G, both its endpoints are inserted in the cover and removed from the graph [29]. Since each edge must be covered by at least one of its endpoints, the size of the returned vertex cover is at most twice the size of the minimum one so it guarantees a 2-approximation. The best known approximation algorithm does not perform much better, guaranteeing a solution of ratio at most $2 - \Theta(1/\sqrt{\log(n)})$ [19]. The best known result about the inapproximability of vertex cover states that in general it cannot be approximated to any constant factor smaller than 2 [21]. This result, however, depends on the unique games conjecture [20]. Under the weaker assumption P $\neq$ NP the best known lower bound for the approximation factor is 1.3606 [4].

Empirical results have suggested that evolutionary algorithms (EAs) can be competitive in practice with problem-specific approximation algorithms [12, 22]. In particular, the experiments performed by Bäck and Khuri have shown that a standard Genetic Algorithm (GA) can outperform approximation algorithms on large classes of random graphs with different edge densities [22]. The GA used the most obvious vertex-based approach for the encoding; a bit string of length $n = |V|$ where the value of each bit defined whether the corresponding node of the graph was in the cover. A penalty of size n was added for each uncovered edge to deal with infeasible solutions. Many other applications of EAs to vertex cover and related problems have also used the same encoding (see e. g. [1, 3]).

Motivated by these empirical results several theoretical analyses of EAs and other randomised search heuristics as approximation algorithms for vertex cover have been carried out using the described penalty-based node encoding [25]. However, the worst-case approximation ratios have turned out not to be competitive. Both Random Local Search (RLS) and the simple (1+1) EA deliver arbitrarily bad approximations on a complete bipartite instance class [13], while restart strategies and populations do not help much either [27, 28]. Some theoretical justification of the good performance of EAs for sparse random graphs has also

FOGA'13, January 16–20, 2013, Adelaide, Australia.

been given [33]. Concerning more complicated randomised search heuristics such as EAs using diversity mechanisms [14] with and without crossover and Artificial Immune Systems it has been shown how they can effectively optimise instances that are hard for simple EAs [27, 18]. However concerning worst-case guarantees, either no significant lower bounds on the approximation ratio are given [27] or arbitrarily bad approximation ratios are shown (i.e. for the immune inspired B-Cell algorithm with not too large population sizes [18]).

Concerning the classical multi-objective setting (i. e. one objective denotes the number of chosen vertices and the other denotes the number of uncovered edges [13]) only an upper bound of $O(OPT \cdot n^4)$ fitness function evaluations to guarantee an OPT-approximation is known [23] (where OPT denotes the size of an optimal vertex cover). If the fitness function is changed to consider the relaxed vertex cover Integer Linear Programming (ILP) for $G(x) = (V, E/E(x))$ as second objective (where x is the current set of chosen vertices) a 2-approximation can be guaranteed by a Global SEMO algorithm in time $O(n^2 \log n + OPT \cdot n^2)$ [23]. By further adding a mutation operator that flips vertices incident to uncovered edges with a probability of 1/2, the Global SEMO is a Fixed Parameter Tractable (FPT) EA for the vertex cover problem finding the optimal solution in $O(n^2 \log n + OPT \cdot n^2 + n \cdot 4^{OPT})$ steps [23].

Inspired by the problem-specific 2-approximation algorithm, (from now on referred to as *Vercov* as in [22]), in this paper we consider a simple single-objective fitness function using edge-based encodings. Vercov iteratively chooses edges until a maximal matching is constructed, thus guarantees an approximation ratio of 2. Hence, a natural question to ask is whether an EA can "learn" to construct a 2-approximate vertex cover by imitating the problem-specific algorithm.

There are several examples where the (1+1) EA or other evolutionary algorithms are able to imitate problem-specific algorithms. These include the (1+1) EA for constructing maximum matchings (by following augmenting paths) [15], the (1+1) EA for partition [32], and evolutionary algorithms imitating dynamic programming approaches [5]. All these examples are based on defining an appropriate problem encoding, i. e., an appropriate search space and a fitness function containing moderate problem knowledge. Also, it has already been shown various times how by changing the genotype representation faster algorithms can be achieved (see [25, 26] for overviews). The case of EAs for Eulerian cycles is exemplary in this sense. By carefully changing the representation the runtime of a (1+1) EA for Eulerian cycles has been reduced in a series of papers from $O(m^4)$ [24] through $\Theta(m^3)$ [6] and $\Theta(m^2 \log m)$ [10] down to $\Theta(m \log m)$ [8]. Furthermore, just switching from vertex-based to edge-based representations has already shown the potential to increase the efficiency of EAs in shortest path problems [9], where an edge-based representation is at least as natural to choose as a vertex-based one. To this end we consider simple randomised search heuristics on edge-based encodings with very little problem knowledge.

On one hand our choice for the vertex cover problem would be quite surprising (recall that we are looking for a vertex set) if not justified by the Vercov algorithm that searches in the space of edges. On the other hand, knowledge of how Vercov works might suggest that EAs with edge-based representations could easily guarantee 2-approximations. Our results show that simply giving the classical large penalty to infeasible solutions does not avoid arbitrarily bad worst-case approximation ratios for the (1+1) EA and RLS. In fact, there is a positive probability that the algorithms get stuck in local optima from which they require at least superpolynomial time to escape. However, for our worst-case instance classes such probabilities are overwhelmingly small. Hence, the efficiency of EAs with edge-based representation and the most natural fitness function is not completely ruled out. Nevertheless, with more problem knowledge one can guarantee good approximation ratios in expected polynomial time. By simply adding an extra penalty to adjacent edges in the current solution, we show that both RLS and the (1+1) EA can imitate Vercov, thus guaranteeing an approximation ratio of 2 in expected time $O(m \log m)$. Although this is equivalent to the upper bound required for the multi-objective approach in the worst case, it is at least a linear factor better both in the case of sparse graphs and of graphs with large optimal vertex covers. Furthermore RLS algorithms, that after an improvement do not flip tested bits before trying previously untested ones, guarantee 2-approximations in $O(m)$ steps.

The rest of the paper is structured as follows. In Section 2 the algorithms, the edge-based encoding and related fitness function are introduced. The negative results for RLS and neighbourhood size 1 are presented in Section 3; they are extended to larger neighbourhood sizes and the (1+1) EA in Section 4. In Section 5 we present the 2-approximation EAs for vertex cover. In the final section conclusions are drawn.

2. PRELIMINARIES

Motivated by Vercov we define the set of all edges as the search space, i. e., for a graph $G = (V, E)$ the search space is $\{0,1\}^{|E|}$. This induces a vertex cover by taking all nodes such that there is a selected incident edge. The canonical way to define an objective function based on this encoding is to use the number of vertices in the cover and add a penalty term for uncovered edges.

DEFINITION 1. *Let $G = (V, E)$ with $E = \{e_1, e_2, \ldots, e_n\}$ be a problem instance for vertex cover. We define the search space $S := \{0,1\}^n$. An $s \in S$ induces a subset of edges $E(s) = \{e_i \mid s[i] = 1\}$. This in turn induces a subset of vertices $V(s) = \{v \in V \mid \exists e \in E(s) \colon v \in e\}$. We define an objective function by means of*

$$f(s) = |V(s)| + (|V| + 1) \cdot |\{e \in E \mid e \cap V(s) = \emptyset\}| .$$

Note that in the rest of the paper n refers to the number of edges in the graph. It is easy to see that if $V(s)$ is a vertex cover, $f(s)$ equals the size of $V(s)$. Otherwise we have $f(s) > |V|$ so that non-covers have larger function values than any cover. The set of global minima induces exactly all optimal vertex covers.

We consider two simple randomised search heuristics to compute vertex covers, i. e., for the minimisation of f. One is random local search (RLS), the other a simple EA called the (1+1) EA. We describe both algorithms formally, but leave the selection of the initial candidate solution open. There are several different commonly used options for doing this. One variant that is popular in evolutionary computation is to select the initial search point uniformly at random. In

Algorithm 1 Random local search with neighbourhood N (RLS_N).

1. **Initialisation**
   Create an initial individual x.
2. **Variation**
   Select $y \in N(x)$ uniformly at random.
3. **Selection for Replacement**
   If $(f(y) \leq f(x))$ then $x := y$.
4. **Stopping**
   If stopping criterion not met continue at line 2.

Algorithm 2 The (1+1) EA.

1. **Initialisation**
   Create an initial individual x.
2. **Variation**
   a) Create y by copying x.
   b) Flip each bit in y independently with probability $1/n$.
3. **Selection for Replacement**
   If $(f(y) \leq f(x))$ then $x := y$.
4. **Stopping**
   If stopping criterion not met continue at line 2.

combinatorial optimisation, it is also common to start with a trivial feasible solution. In the case of vertex cover this is the set of all vertices (i. e., in our edge-based representation the set of all edges 1^n). We do not define stopping criteria. In our analysis we consider the algorithms as infinite random processes and analyse the first point of time when a solution with certain properties is found. Examples for such properties include being a global or local optimum or being an approximation of some quality. Time is measured as usual by the number of function evaluations.

RLS (formally defined as Algorithm 1) is defined using a search neighbourhood N. A neighbourhood $N\colon S \to \mathcal{P}(S)$ maps $s \in S$ to its neighbours $N(s) \subseteq S$. With different neighbourhoods different instantiations of RLS can be defined.

We define several common neighbourhoods for RLS in the following. We use the notation $[k] = \{1, 2, \ldots, k\}$ as an abbreviation and $\mathrm{H}(x, y) = |\{x[i] \neq y[i] \mid i \in [n]\}|$ for the Hamming distance of $x, y \in \{0,1\}^n$. The most common neighbourhood is the one bit Hamming neighbourhood N_1. We use RLS as a shorthand for RLS_{N_1}.

DEFINITION 2. *For $x \in \{0,1\}^n$ and $k \in [n]$ let the neighbourhood $N_k(x) := \{y \in \{0,1\}^n \mid H(x,y) = k\}$, and let the neighbourhood $N_{\leq k}(x) := \bigcup_{i \in [k]} N_i(x)$.*

The (1+1) EA (formally defined as Algorithm 2) is the most simple EA that has been the subject of intense studies for a long time [11]. The only difference to RLS is that instead of picking the next candidate point from a neighbourhood it defines a probability distribution over the search space and prefers points with smaller Hamming distance. Note that this probability distribution makes the (1+1) EA very different from RLS_{N_n}. In fact, it is well known that the (1+1) EA performs similar to RLS_{N_1} in many cases [7]. Here we will consider situations where this is not the case and the two algorithms perform quite differently.

3. RLS WITH NEIGHBOURHOOD SIZE 1

In this section we consider RLS with the most natural neighbourhood N_1. The edge-based representation is introduced with the hope of overcoming the limitations of the vertex-based representation [13, 27, 28]. Being inspired by Vercov one may hope that using the edge-based representation RLS is also able to guarantee a 2-approximation. But we prove that this is not the case.

THEOREM 3. *There exists a graph such that, with positive probability, RLS_{N_1} finds no solution with a better approximation ratio than $(|V|-1)/2$ with random initialisation and initialisation in the full cover. The expected time to produce a better approximation is infinite.*

PROOF. Let $i \in \mathbb{N} \setminus [2]$. We consider the following complete bipartite graph instance $G_i = (V_i, E_i)$, setting $V_i = \{b_1, b_2, a_1, a_2, \ldots, a_i\}$ and $E_i = \bigcup_{j \in [i]} \{\{b_1, a_j\}, \{b_2, a_j\}\}$ (see Figure 1 for an example). We observe that G_i has $i + 2$ nodes and $2i$ edges (thus, in our notation $n = 2i$). An optimal cover contains the nodes b_1, b_2 and has size 2. We remark that Vercov will select two edges that share no node and therefore arrives at a cover of size 4, obtaining an approximation ratio of exactly 2. One kind of local optimum for RLS_{N_1} is a vertex cover where either all edges $\{b_1, a_j\}$ (with $j \in [i]$) or all edges $\{b_2, a_j\}$ (with $j \in [i]$) are selected. This induces a vertex cover of size $i + 1$. Its approximation ratio equals $(i+1)/2 = (|V| - 1)/2$. With random initialisation the probability to initially start in such a cover equals $1/2^{n-1}$. With initialisation in the full cover 1^n RLS arrives at such a cover if all edges 'on one side' are flipped out before any edge 'of the other side' is touched. This has probability $p_1(i) := 2 \cdot i/(2i) \cdot (i-1)/(2i-1) \cdots 1/(i+1) = 2(i!)^2/((2i)!)$. □

We consider the case of initialisation with the full cover in more detail. Note that $p_1(i)$ is exponentially small in i; we have $p_1(i) = \Theta\left(\sqrt{i}/2^{2i}\right)$. This is considerably smaller than the probability for the (1+1) EA of getting trapped on a bad approximation for the bipartite instance class and vertex-based representation [13]. There this probability was bounded below by $n^{\delta - 13e}$, $\delta > 0$ a constant.

In addition to the local optima from the proof of Theorem 3 only two other kinds of local optima are present in G_i. The second type are covers that contain the edges $\{b_1, a_j\}, \{b_2, a_j\}$ for some $j \in [i]$. It induces a vertex cover of size 3, thus an approximation ratio of 3/2. Note that this is strictly better than the approximation ratio of Vercov on G_i. Given that no vertex cover of the first type is reached the probability to reach such a vertex cover equals $q_2(i) := 1/i$ for symmetry reasons. This will become clear when we consider the third and last type of vertex covers that are local optima.

This type contains the edges $\{b_1, a_{j_1}\}, \{b_2, a_{j_2}\}$ for some $j_1, j_2 \in [i]$ with $j_1 \neq j_2$. If we omit the condition $j_1 \neq j_2$ all such vertex covers have equal probability to be reached. This proves the statement for the conditional probability to reach a vertex cover of the second type and yields $q_3(i) := 1 - 1/i$ for the probability of reaching a vertex cover of the third type given that no vertex cover of the first type is reached. The vertex cover has size 4 and is of the same type and size as a vertex cover found by Vercov. Hence, with overwhelming probability RLS performs at least as well as Vercov on G_i. The same kind of result also holds for random initialisation.

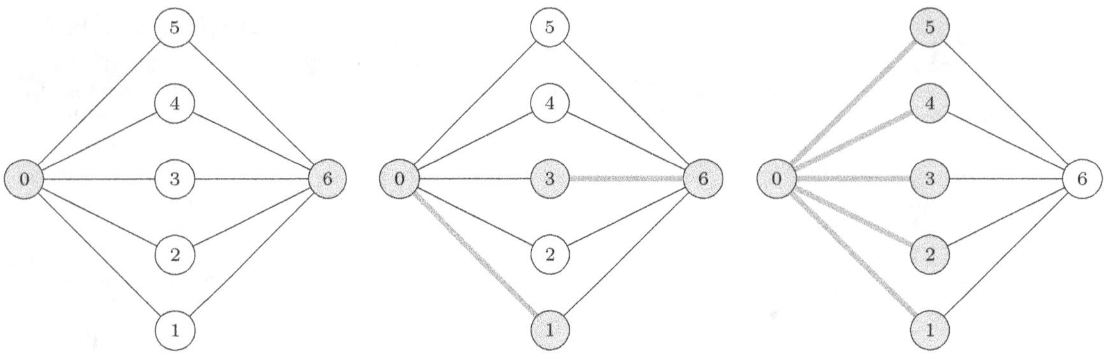

Figure 1: Three example covers for the graph instance G_i with $i = 5$: a possible optimal cover of size 2 (left), a possible solution of the approximation algorithm (middle), and a possible solution of RLS$_{N_1}$ (right).

COROLLARY 4. *With overwhelming probability $1-p_1(i) = 1-\Theta(\sqrt{n}/2^n)$ RLS$_{N_1}$ produces an approximation of at most 2 for G_i in $O(n \log n)$ steps.*

Let $p_2(i)$ and $p_3(i)$ denote the unconditional probabilities of reaching a vertex cover of types 2 or 3, respectively. We know that $p_2(i)/p_3(i) = q_2(i)/q_3(i)$ holds since $p_2(i)$ and $p_3(i)$ are the corresponding unconditional probabilities for the conditional probabilities $q_2(i)$ and $q_3(i)$. This yields $p_2(i)/p_3(i) = 1/(i-1)$. Moreover, we have $p_1(i) + p_2(i) + p_3(i) = 1$. This yields $p_3(i) = (1-p_1(i))(i-1)/i$ and $p_2(i) = (1-p_1(i))/i$.

Considering RLS on G_i we see that the expected approximation ratio that is obtained equals $((i+1)/2)p_1(i) + (3/2)p_2(i) + 2p_3(i) = 2 - 1/(2i) + \Theta(e^i/i^{i-1}) = 2 - \Theta(1/n)$ and observe that this is less than 2, i.e., the expected approximation ratio is strictly better than that of Vercov (but it converges to 2 with increasing i). Note that the expected approximation ratio is the same if we consider m independent copies of G_i as one vertex cover instance (but the probability for deviations from this expected approximation ratio becomes smaller with an increasing number of copies).

In summary, we have that with positive probability RLS may find a vertex cover that is a local optimum and almost arbitrarily bad, i.e., having approximation ratio $(|V|-1)/2$. However, we have that the expected approximation ratio on this family of problem instances is strictly better than that of Vercov.

4. RLS WITH LARGER NEIGHBOURHOOD SIZES AND THE (1+1) EA

The results from the previous section can easily be extended to larger neighbourhoods, i.e., RLS$_N$ for larger neighbourhoods N and the (1+1) EA, by extending the graph instance from Theorem 3 to graph classes $G_{k,\ell} = (V_{k,\ell}, E_{k,\ell})$ with $k \in \mathbb{N}$, $\ell \in \mathbb{N}_0$. We start with a formal definition of $G_{k,\ell}$ and depict $G_{1,\ell}$ as an example in Figure 2. A sketch of $G_{k,\ell}$ can be found in Figure 3. Note that the subgraph of $G_{1,\ell}$ induced by $b_{1,1}$ and $b_{1,2}$ together with $A_{1,\ell}$ coincides with the graph instance from Theorem 3. In order to obtain graphs $G_{k,\ell}$ for other values of k, roughly speaking, we need to extend $A_{k,\ell}$ and add more components of b, c and d nodes to $G_{1,\ell}$. The resulting $A_{k,\ell}$ and B_k form a complete bipartite graph.

DEFINITION 5. *Let $k \in \mathbb{N}$, $\ell \in \mathbb{N}_0$. The graph $G_{k,\ell} = (V_{k,\ell}, E_{k,\ell})$ is defined as follows. The set of nodes $V_{k,\ell}$ is defined by $V_{k,\ell} = A_{k,\ell} \cup B_k \cup C_k \cup D_k$ with the following node sets.*

$$A_{k,\ell} = \{a_1, a_2, \ldots, a_{5k+2+\ell}\}$$

$$B_k = \{b_0\} \cup \bigcup_{i=1}^{k} \{b_{i,1}, b_{i,2}\}$$

$$C_k = \{c_0\} \cup \bigcup_{i=1}^{k} \{c_{i,1}, c_{i,2}\}$$

$$D_k = \bigcup_{i=1}^{k} \{d_{i,1}, d_{i,2}\}$$

The set of edges $E_{k,\ell}$ is defined by

$$E_{k,\ell} = \{\{a,b\} \mid a \in A_{k,\ell}, b \in B_k\} \cup \{b_0, c_0\}$$
$$\cup \bigcup_{i=1}^{k} \Big\{\{b_{i,1}, c_{i,1}\}, \{b_{i,2}, c_{i,2}\}\Big\} \cup \bigcup_{i=1}^{k} \Big\{\{c_{i,1}, d_{i,1}\},$$
$$\{c_{i,1}, d_{i,2}\}, \{c_{i,2}, d_{i,1}\}, \{c_{i,2}, d_{i,2}\}\Big\}.$$

We observe that $G_{k,\ell}$ contains $|V_{k,\ell}| = 5k + 4 + \ell$ nodes and $|E_{k,\ell}| = 10k^2 + (15 + 2\ell)k + \ell + 3$ edges. An optimal vertex cover of size $4k+1$ contains all nodes from B_k and all nodes from C_k except for c_0. The local optimum of size $8k + \ell + 3 = 2(4k+1) + \ell + 1$ we consider contains all nodes from $A_{k,\ell}$, b_0, all nodes from C_k except for c_0 and independently for each $i \in \{1, 2, \ldots, k\}$ either $d_{i,1}$ or $d_{i,2}$. This local optimum can be selected by the randomised search heuristic by selecting all edges $\{a_i, b_0\}$ and independently for each $i \in \{1, 2, \ldots, k\}$ either the two edges $\{c_{i,1}, d_{i,1}\}$ and $\{c_{i,2}, d_{i,1}\}$ or the two edges $\{c_{i,1}, d_{i,2}\}$ and $\{c_{i,2}, d_{i,2}\}$. It has approximation ratio $2 + (\ell+1)/(4k+1)$.

In the following we prove that in order to leave this local optimum one needs to flip at least $4k$ edges simultaneously. To facilitate the argumentation, we start with an analysis for $G_{1,\ell}$.

THEOREM 6. *Consider the graph instance $G_{1,\ell}$. With positive probability RLS$_{N_{\leq 3}}$ finds no solution with a better approximation ratio than $2 + (\ell+1)/5$ with random initialisation and also with initialisation in the full cover 1^n. The expected time to produce a better approximation is infinite.*

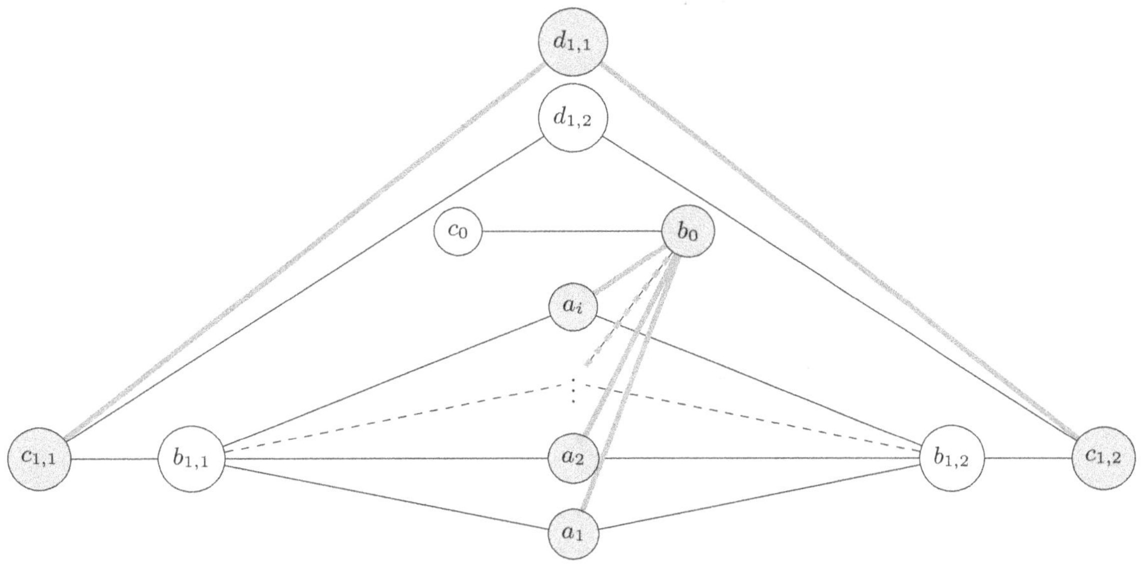

Figure 2: An example for the graph instance $G_{1,\ell}$ with $i = |A_{k,\ell}| \geq 7$: a possible optimal cover of size 5 is $V' = \{b_0, b_{1,1}, b_{1,2}, c_{1,1}, c_{1,2}\}$; a possible local optimum for $\text{RLS}_{\leq 3}$ of size $4 + i \geq 11$ is marked in grey. In this example $|V| = i + 8$ and $n = 3i + 7$.

PROOF. Similarly to Theorem 3, it is easy to see that $\text{RLS}_{N_{\leq 3}}$ constructs the local optimum depicted in Figure 2 with positive probability. As discussed before this cover has approximation ratio $2 + (\ell + 1)/5$. It remains to show, that $\text{RLS}_{N_{\leq 3}}$ is not able to escape from this local optimum. Recall, that once the algorithm has obtained a feasible solution, only feasible solutions will be accepted. Moreover, a node is in the cover if at least one of its incident edges is selected by the algorithm.

We first observe that in the considered situation it is not possible to add or delete a single edge since this would either result in a non-feasible or in a worse solution. Thus, 1-bit flips do not help $\text{RLS}_{N_{\leq 3}}$ to leave the local optimum.

Now consider a mutation where no edge incident to a node a_i is involved. The only accepted mutation removes the edges $(c_{1,1}, d_{1,1})$, $(d_{1,1}, c_{1,2})$ and inserts the edges $(c_{1,1}, d_{1,2})$, $(d_{1,2}, c_{1,2})$. All other mutations lead either to infeasible solutions or larger covers.

Next consider a mutation involving an edge incident to a node a_i. Recall that $A_{1,\ell}$ and B_1 are node sets of a complete bipartite graph. Thus, in order to have a feasible solution either all nodes in $A_{1,\ell}$ or all nodes in B_1 need to be in the cover. This implies that nodes from $A_{1,\ell}$ can only be removed from the cover if both missing nodes from B_1 are added. Adding the two missing nodes from B_1 requires two different edges to flip. In order not to increase the number of nodes in the cover, at least two other nodes need to be removed. Each such removal requires one additional edge to flip. Thus, only mutations involving at least four edges can be accepted. □

The above argumentation can be easily extended to the more general case.

THEOREM 7. *Consider the graph instance $G_{k,\ell}$ with $\ell \leq 2^k$. With positive probability $RLS_{N_{\leq 4k-1}}$ finds no solution with a better approximation ratio than $2 + (\ell + 1)/(4k + 1)$ with random initialisation and also with initialisation in the full cover 1^n. The expected time to produce a better approximation is infinite.*

With positive probability the (1+1) EA reaches a point in the search space where it needs in expectation a superpolynomial time to improve over a $2 + (\ell + 1)/(4k + 1)$ approximation.

PROOF. Reconsider the proof of Theorem 6. It is easy to see that both algorithms can construct a cover of size $8k + \ell + 3$ by keeping all edges $\{a_i, b_0\}$ and independently for each $i \in \{1, 2, \ldots, k\}$ either the two edges $\{c_{i,1}, d_{i,1}\}$ and $\{c_{i,2}, d_{i,1}\}$ or the two edges $\{c_{i,1}, d_{i,2}\}$ and $\{c_{i,2}, d_{i,2}\}$. Since this cover has an approximation ratio of $2 + (\ell + 1)/(4k + 1)$, it suffices to show, that the algorithms need to flip at least $4k$ edges simultaneously to escape from this local optimum.

Roughly speaking, the graph $G_{k,\ell}$ consists of k copies of $G_{1,\ell}$ that are connected via the nodes in $A_{k,\ell}$ (see Figure 3). Therefore, most of the arguments carry over. In particular, it is not possible to add or delete a single edge since this would either result in a non-feasible or in a worse solution. Thus, 1-bit flips do not help. For mutations where no edge incident to a node a_i is involved, in each component, the only accepted mutation removes the edges $(c_{i,1}, d_{i,1})$, $(d_{i,1}, c_{i,2})$ and inserts the edges $(c_{i,1}, d_{i,2})$, $(d_{i,2}, c_{i,2})$. This yields a symmetric situation to the considered cover. In mutations involving an edge incident to a node a_i, in order to have a feasible solution either all nodes in $A_{k,\ell}$ or all nodes in B_k need to be in the cover. This implies that nodes from $A_{k,\ell}$ can only be removed from the cover if all missing nodes from B_k are added. Adding these $2k$ nodes from B_k requires $2k$ different edges to flip. In order not to increase the number of nodes in the cover, at least $2k$ other nodes need to be removed. Each such removal requires one additional edge to flip. Thus, only mutations involving at least $4k$ edges can be accepted.

Since we have $\ell \leq 2^k$, $4k = \Omega(\ln n)$ holds. As the expected waiting time for a $4k$-bit mutation is bounded below by $(4k)!$ the result follows. □

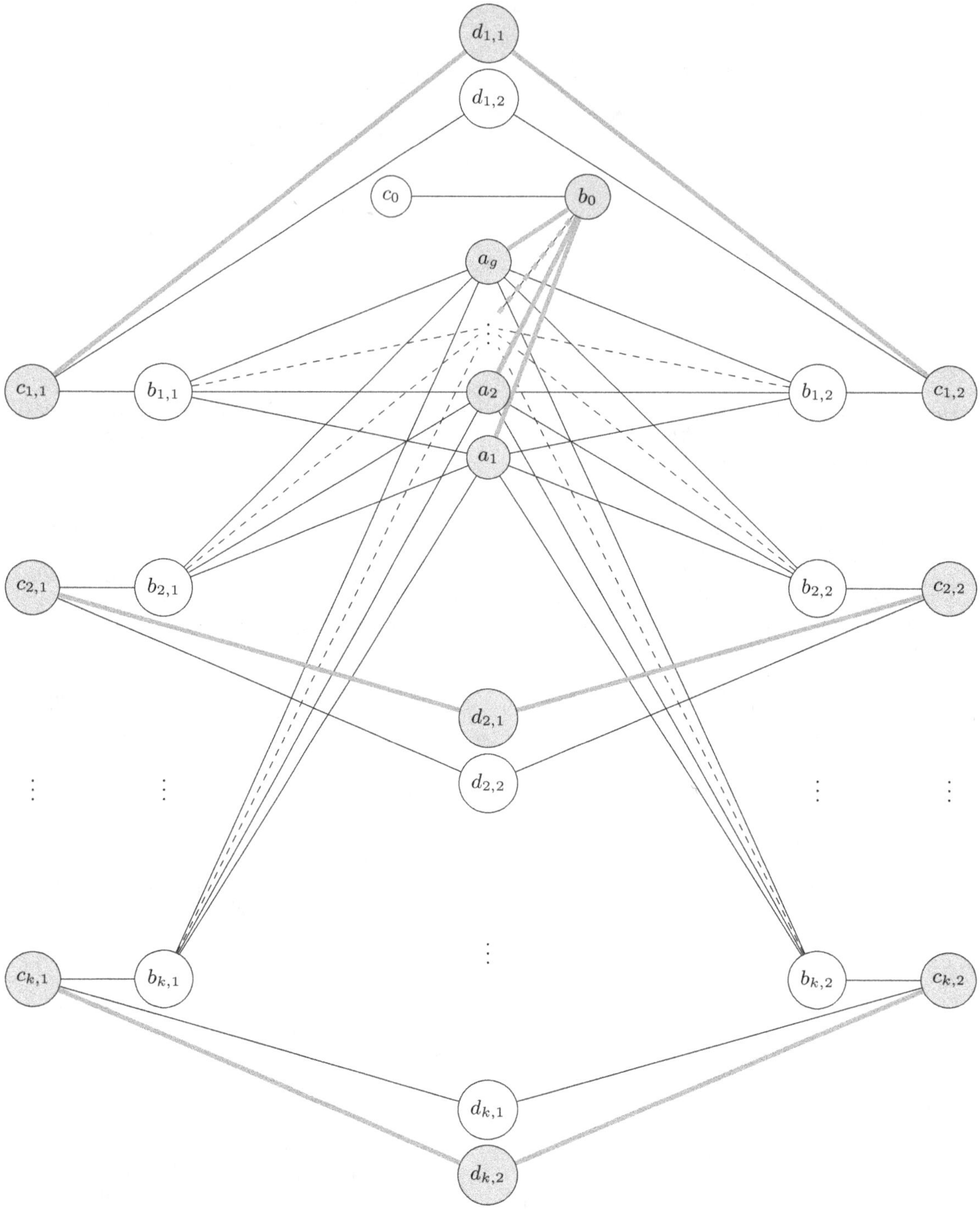

Figure 3: An example for the graph instance $G_{k,\ell}$ with $g = |A_{k,\ell}| \geq 5k + 2$: a possible optimal cover of size $4k + 1$ is $V' = \{b_0, b_{j,1}, b_{j,2}, c_{j,1}, c_{j,2} \mid j = 1, \ldots, k\}$; a possible local optimum for $\mathrm{RLS}_{N_{\leq 4k-1}}$ of size $3k + i + 1 \geq 8k + 3$ is marked in grey.

Note that with $\ell = 2^k$ Theorem 7 yields a lower bound on the approximation ratio of $\Theta(|V| / \log(|V|))$. For $\text{RLS}_{N_{4k-1}}$ we can improve this lower bound to $\Theta(|V|)$ by having k constant and ℓ grow so that $2 + (\ell+1)/(4k+1) = \Theta(|V|)$.

COROLLARY 8. *Consider the graph instance $G_{k,\ell}$ for some constant k. $RLS_{N_{\leq 4k-1}}$ finds with positive probability no solution with an approximation ratio better than*

$$2 + \frac{\ell+1}{4k+1} = \Theta(|V|)$$

with random initialisation and also with initialisation in the full cover 1^n. The expected optimisation time is infinite.

Since the probabilities of getting trapped on the bad approximations are even smaller than for G_i, the following corollary naturally follows.

COROLLARY 9. *With overwhelming probability the (1+1) EA and $RLS_{N_{\leq 4k-1}}$ produce an approximation of at most 2 for $G_{k,\ell}$ in $O(n \log n)$ steps.*

5. 2-APPROXIMATION ALGORITHMS

It was known that with a vertex-based encoding RLS and the (1+1) EA can be very inefficient on vertex cover, i. e., with positive probability they are stuck with extremely bad covers [13, 28]. Considering Vercov we switched to an edge-based representation (Definition 1). However, this alone does not improve the situation.

Solving problems by means of randomised search heuristics (like RLS or EAs) starts with defining an encoding. Such an encoding consists of two parts, the definition of the search space and the objective function. Finding an appropriate encoding is fundamental for the efficiency of a randomised search heuristic [31]. Ideally, there is a bijective mapping between the search space and the set of potential solutions. If this is not possible at least a surjective mapping from the search space to the space of potential solutions is desirable.

We observe that the vertex-based encoding allows for a bijective mapping whereas the edge-based encoding is not even surjective. It is restricted to solutions of the kind Vercov can find.

Objective functions should assign optimal function values to points which are mapped to optimal solutions. It appears to be desirable that points that map to non-feasible solutions have worse function values than points that are mapped to feasible solutions. This is the case for f. However, for the vertex cover problem using the edge-based representation introduced here, it does not seem to be advantageous to have two incident edges selected. This is reflected in our second objective function f_e defined in the following.

DEFINITION 10. *Let $G = (V, E)$ with $E = \{e_1, e_2, \ldots, e_n\}$ be a problem instance for vertex cover. We define the search space $S := \{0,1\}^n$, $E(s)$ and $V(s)$ as in Definition 1. We define an objective function by means of*

$$f_e(s) = f(s) + (|V|+1) \cdot (n+1) \cdot \left|\{(e,e') \in E(s) \times E(s) \mid e \neq e', e \cap e' \neq \emptyset\}\right|.$$

The function f_e introduces an additional penalty term that adds $(|V|+1) \cdot (n+1)$ for each pair of selected edges that share a node. Note, that such edges could also not have been chosen by Vercov. We observe that feasible solutions may have worse function values than infeasible ones. However, we prove that both, RLS and the (1+1) EA, guarantee to find a 2-approximation efficiently using f_e and the edge-based representation.

THEOREM 11. *The (1+1) EA and RLS_{N_1} using objective function f_e both find a vertex cover that is at least a 2-approximation in expected time $O(n \log n)$ regardless of the initial search point.*

PROOF. It is known that the (1+1) EA and RLS_{N_1} both find the global optimum of $\sum_{i \in [n]} x[i]$ (known as OneMax) in expected time $\Theta(n \log n)$ [11]. We consider a run of one of these algorithms in two phases. The first phase starts with initialisation and ends when $f_e(x) < (|V|+1)(n+1)$ holds for the first time. The second phase starts after the first phase and ends when $f_e(x) < |V|+1$ holds for the first time. At the end of the second phase we have $f_e(x) = |V(s)|$ and no penalty term is involved. Therefore, $V(s)$ is a vertex cover. It is based on a selection of edges that Vercov could have selected. Thus, it is a 2-approximation.

In the first phase the function value can be improved by removing an edge that shares a node with another selected edge. Removing edges until no two edges share a node is easier than minimising OneMax: it suffices to flip single bits and the number of bits that are available for flipping is proportional to the distance to a goal point. Differently from OneMax, here we have several goal points, i.e., points where this phase ends. Hence, this phase is easier than minimising OneMax and we obtain $O(n \log n)$ as a bound for the expected length of this phase.

In the second phase the function value can be improved by including an edge that is currently not covered by any node. Such an edge exists since we have

$$|V| + 1 < f_e(s) < (|V|+1)(n+1)$$

during this phase. While $f_e(s) < (|V|+1)(n+1)$ guarantees that no two selected edges share a common node $|V|+1 < f_e(s)$ guarantees that there is an uncovered edge. For this edge its two nodes do not belong to any selected edge. Hence its inclusion reduces the function value. Selecting such edges until no such edge exists is easier than minimising OneMax again implying an upper bound of $O(n \log n)$. □

The proof of Theorem 11 implies that an RLS_{N_1} algorithm, that upon an improvement does not flip again previously tested bits before flipping the untested ones, guarantees a 2-approximation in $O(n)$ steps. Hence, we have presented a randomised search heuristic that is asymptotically equivalent to Vercov.

We remark that one has to be careful when designing fitness functions with the aim of proving an algorithm to be efficient. This situation is different from trying to solve the problem at hand efficiently in practice. In the latter case we are in the area of problem-specific algorithm design and should use any useful information available. However, this only makes sense if the resulting algorithm is competitive in practice, i.e., with respect to actual run time and quality of solution, with the best known problem-specific algorithm. If, on the other hand, the main goal is to (theoretically) investigate the performance of different randomised search heuristics and their encodings, it is very important to avoid any kind of cheating in order to obtain meaningful results.

In this case, a fitness function needs to be natural and must not include too much problem knowledge since otherwise we are again in the area of algorithm design. Thus, when introducing a new encoding one needs to argue why this is still a natural way to tackle the problem by means of randomised search heuristics unless one is able to beat the best known algorithms for the problem in practice.

For example, consider a solution V' for vertex cover. We can define the fitness (that we minimise) as the Hamming distance to V'. Clearly, this turns the problem into OneMax so that RLS_{N_1} and (1+1) EA both find a solution in time $O(n \log n)$. This holds for our edge-based encoding as well as for a vertex-based encoding and is a rather trivial observation that holds for each problem. Since vertex cover is NP-hard we cannot efficiently compute an optimal V' but we can compute efficiently a V' that is a 2-approximation. Thus, obtaining a 2-approximation in time $O(n \log n)$ with RLS_{N_1} or (1+1) EA is trivial. However, this fitness function is clearly not natural any more and incorporates far too much problem knowledge such that it is inappropriate for the second purpose mentioned. It is also not appropriate in the area of algorithm design since the resulting algorithm is no improvement.

We see that one has to be careful how the fitness function is designed in order to obtain meaningful results. Fitness functions should be simple, natural, not contain too specific information and be efficient to compute. All this is the case for the fitness function f_e developed here as argued above.

6. CONCLUSIONS

EAs have been reported to be efficient heuristics for solving the NP-hard vertex cover problem. Theoretical analyses have revealed that in the worst case EAs can get stuck with almost arbitrarily bad approximations. These results hold for EAs using a vertex-based encoding and a single-objective approach. Motivated by reports of good results due to edge-based encodings for other problems and, more importantly, a problem-specific 2-approximation algorithm for vertex cover called Vercov we introduced an edge-based representation.

Using a canonical fitness function we proved that RLS with 1-bit neighbourhood may get stuck with an approximation ratio of $\Theta(|V|)$ for a graph with $|V|$ nodes. But for our worst case instance RLS finds at least a 2-approximation with probability $1 - \Theta(\sqrt{n}/2^n)$ efficiently where n is the number of edges in the graph. Using a more complex worst case instance we can generalise the bad approximation ratio of $\Theta(|V|)$ for any neighbourhood of bit strings of arbitrary constant Hamming distance. With even larger neighbourhoods with Hamming distance up to $O(\log(n)/\log\log(n))$ RLS may still be stuck with an approximation ratio as bad as $\Theta(|V|\,/\log|V|)$. This result also generalises to the (1+1) EA that allows for mutations of unlimited distance. Given that it reaches the cover that is a local optimum for RLS even the (1+1) EA is stuck with an $\Theta(|V|\,/\log|V|)$ approximation for a superpolynomial number of steps.

Using the same representation but a slightly different objective function we can prove that both, RLS and the (1+1) EA are able to obtain at least a 2-approximation in expected time $O(n \log n)$. Thus, with only slightly more information (that can easily be computed efficiently) and an edge-based representation they become efficient approximation algorithms for vertex cover. Note that although equivalent in the worst case, our upper bound is at least a linear factor better than the one known for the multi-objective approach in the case of sparse graphs and in the case of graphs with large optimal vertex covers. Furthermore RLS algorithms, that after an improvement do not flip tested bits before trying previously untested ones, guarantee 2-approximations in $O(n)$ steps.

Among the potential research directions two routes are particularly interesting. On one hand, more work on the general topic of representation should be executed. It is for example an open problem to find a simple and natural single-objective function that can be computed efficiently that
achieves similar results for RLS and the (1+1) EA using a vertex-based representation. We pointed out that there are trivial objective functions that achieve that but these are not at all natural. On the other hand, our difficult instances are based on local optima for RLS that most likely are no actual obstacle. For these instances RLS and the (1+1) EA achieve an approximation ratio 2 in polynomial time with high probability. It is a challenging open problem to prove a general constant upper bound on the expected approximation ratio for the (1+1) EA and RLS on vertex cover in the single-objective setting.

Acknowledgments

This material is based in part upon works supported by the Science Foundation Ireland under Grants No. 07/SK/I1205 and No. 05/IN/I886. The second author was supported by EPSRC under grant N. EP/H028900/1. The third author was partly supported by a postdoctoral fellowship from the German Academic Exchange Service (DAAD) while visiting the University of Warwick in Coventry, UK.

7. REFERENCES

[1] T. Bäck and S. Khuri. An evolutionary heuristic for the maximum independent set problem. In *Proceedings of the First IEEE International Conference on Evolutionary Computation (ICEC 1994)*, pages 531–535. IEEE Press, 1994.

[2] N. Bansal and S. Khot. Inapproximability of hypergraph vertex cover and applications to scheduling problems. In *Proceedings of the 37th International Colloquium Conference on Automata, Languages and Programming (ICALP 2010)*, LNCS 6198, pages 250–261. Springer, 2010.

[3] T. N. Bui and P. H. Eppley. A hybrid genetic algorithm for the maximum clique problem. In *Proceedings of the 6th International Conference on Genetic Algorithms (ICGA 1995)*, pages 478–484. Morgan Kaufmann, 1995.

[4] I. Dinur and S. Safra. On the hardness of approximating vertex cover. *Annals of Mathematics*, 162(1):439–485, 2005.

[5] B. Doerr, A. V. Eremeev, F. Neumann, M. Theile, and C. Thyssen. Evolutionary algorithms and dynamic programming. *Theoretical Computer Science*, 412(43):6020–6035, 2011.

[6] B. Doerr, N. Hebbinghaus, and F. Neumann. Speeding up evolutionary algorithms through asymmetric mutation operators. *Evolutionary Computation*, 15(4):401–410, 2007.

[7] B. Doerr, T. Jansen, and C. Klein. Comparing global and local mutations on bit strings. In *Proceedings of the Genetic and Evolutionary Computation Conference (GECCO 2008)*, pages 929–936. ACM Press, 2008.

[8] B. Doerr and D. Johannsen. Adjacency list matchings - an ideal genotype for cycle covers. In *Proceedings of the Genetic and Evolutionary Computation Conference (GECCO 2007)*, pages 1203–1210. ACM Press, 2007.

[9] B. Doerr and D. Johannsen. Edge-based representation beats vertex-based representation in shortest path problems. In *Proceedings of the Genetic and Evolutionary Computation Conference (GECCO 2010)*, pages 759–766. ACM Press, 2010.

[10] B. Doerr, C. Klein, and T. Storch. Faster evolutionary algorithms by superior graph representation. In *Proceedings of the 1st IEEE Symposium on Foundations of Computational Intelligence (FOCI 2007)*, pages 245–250. IEEE Press, 2007.

[11] S. Droste, T. Jansen, and I. Wegener. On the analysis of the (1+1) evolutionary algorithm. *Theoretical Computer Science*, 276(1–2):51–81, 2002.

[12] I. K. Evans. Evolutionary algorithms for vertex cover. In *Proceedings of 7th International Conference on Evolutionary Programming (EP 1998)*, LNCS 1447, pages 377–386. Springer, 1998.

[13] T. Friedrich, J. He, N. Hebbinghaus, F. Neumann, and C. Witt. Approximating covering problems by randomized search heuristics using multi-objective models. *Evolutionary Computation*, 18(4):617–633, 2010.

[14] T. Friedrich, P. S. Oliveto, D. Sudholt, and C. Witt. Analysis of diversity-preserving mechanisms for global exploration. *Evolutionary Computation*, 17(4):455–476, 2009.

[15] O. Giel and I. Wegener. Evolutionary algorithms and the maximum matching problem. In *Proceedings of the 20th Annual Symposium on Theoretical Aspects of Computer Science (STACS 2003)*, LNCS 2607, pages 415–426. Springer, 2003.

[16] S. Guha, R. Hassin, S. Khuller, and E. Or. Capacitated vertex covering with applications. In *Proceedings of the 13th Annual ACM-SIAM Symposium on Discrete Algorithms (SODA 2002)*, pages 858–865. SIAM Press, 2002.

[17] D. S. Hochbaum, editor. *Approximation algorithms for NP-hard problems*. PWS Publishing Company, Boston, MA, USA, 1997.

[18] T. Jansen, P. S. Oliveto, and C. Zarges. On the analysis of the immune-inspired B-cell algorithm for the vertex cover problem. In *Proceedings of the 10th International Conference on Artificial Immune Systems (ICARIS 2011)*, LNCS 6825, pages 117–131. Springer, 2011.

[19] G. Karakostas. A better approximation ratio for the vertex cover problem. *ACM Transactions on Algorithms*, 5(4):41:1–41:8, 2009.

[20] S. Khot. On the power of unique 2-prover 1-round games. In *Proceedings of the 34th Annual ACM Symposium on Theory of Computing (STOC 2002)*, pages 767–775. ACM Press, 2002.

[21] S. Khot and O. Regev. Vertex cover might be hard to approximate to within $2-\varepsilon$. *Journal of Computer and System Sciences*, 74(3):335–349, 2008.

[22] S. Khuri and T. Bäck. An evolutionary heuristic for the minimum vertex cover problem. In *KI-94 Workshops (Extended Abstracts)*, pages 86–90. Gesellschaft für Informatik, 1994.

[23] S. Kratsch and F. Neumann. Fixed-parameter evolutionary algorithms and the vertex cover problem. *Algorithmica*, 65(4):754–771, 2013.

[24] F. Neumann. Expected runtimes of evolutionary algorithms for the eulerian cycle problem. *Computers & OR*, 35(9):2750–2759, 2008.

[25] F. Neumann and C. Witt. *Bioinspired Computation in Combinatorial Optimization – Algorithms and Their Computational Complexity.* Springer, 2010.

[26] P. S. Oliveto, J. He, and X. Yao. Time complexity of evolutionary algorithms for combinatorial optimization: a decade of results. *International Journal of Automation and Computing*, 4(3):281–293, 2007.

[27] P. S. Oliveto, J. He, and X. Yao. Analysis of population-based evolutionary algorithms for the vertex cover problem. In *Proceedings of the 10th IEEE Congress on Evolutionary Computation (CEC 2008)*, pages 1563–1570. IEEE Press, 2008.

[28] P. S. Oliveto, J. He, and X. Yao. Analysis of the (1+1)-EA for finding approximate solutions to vertex cover problems. *IEEE Transactions on Evolutionary Computation*, 13(5):1006–1029, 2009.

[29] C. H. Papadimitriou and K. Steiglitz. *Combinatorial Optimization: Algorithms and Complexity.* Prentice-Hall, 1982.

[30] S. Pirzada and A. Dharwadker. Applications of graph theory. *Journal of the Korean Society for Industrial and Applied Mathematics*, 11(4):19–38, 2007.

[31] F. Rothlauf. *Representations for Genetic and Evolutionary Algorithms.* Springer, 2006.

[32] C. Witt. Worst-case and average-case approximations by simple randomized search heuristics. In *Proceedings of the 22nd Annual Symposium on Theoretical Aspects of Computer Science (STACS 2005)*, LNCS 3404, pages 44–56. Springer, 2005.

[33] C. Witt. Analysis of an iterated local search algorithm for vertex cover in sparse random graphs. *Theoretical Computer Science*, 425(1):417–425, 2012.

A Runtime Analysis of Simple Hyper-Heuristics: To Mix or Not to Mix Operators

Per Kristian Lehre
ASAP Research Group
School of Computer Science
University of Nottingham, UK
PerKristian.Lehre@nottingham.ac.uk

Ender Özcan
ASAP Research Group
School of Computer Science
University of Nottingham, UK
Ender.Ozcan@nottingham.ac.uk

ABSTRACT

There is a growing body of work in the field of hyper-heuristics. Hyper-heuristics are high level search methodologies that operate on the space of heuristics to solve hard computational problems. A frequently used hyper-heuristic framework mixes a predefined set of low level heuristics during the search process. While most of the work on such selection hyper-heuristics in the literature are empirical, we analyse the runtime of hyper-heuristics rigorously. Our initial analysis shows that mixing heuristics could lead to exponentially faster search than individual (deterministically chosen) heuristics on chosen problems. Both mixing of variation operators and mixing of acceptance criteria are investigated on some selected problems. It is shown that mixing operators is only efficient with the right mixing distribution (parameter setting). Additionally, some of the existing adaptation mechanisms for mixing operators are also evaluated.

Categories and Subject Descriptors

F.2 [**Theory of Computation**]: Analysis of Algorithms and Problem Complexity

General Terms

Theory, Algorithms

Keywords

Runtime Analysis, Hyper-heuristic, Stochastic Local Search

1. INTRODUCTION

Hyper-heuristic methodologies are learning mechanisms or search techniques that *mix* a prefixed set of user-defined heuristics (neighbourhood operators) or *generate* automatically new ones based on user-defined components [3]. This study focuses on the former type of selection hyper-heuristics. The key components in a single point based selection hyper-heuristic framework are identified as *heuristic selection* and *move acceptance* [25]. Usually, a high level hyper-heuristic aims to iteratively improve an initially generated complete solution by repeatedly selecting a low level perturbative neighbourhood operator, then using it to generate a new complete solution and finally deciding whether to accept or reject the new solution at each step. This heuristic selection process can be viewed as setting the probability of each low level operator for selection and application of a selected operator based on these probabilities to a candidate solution. A number of empirical studies indicate the success of selection hyper-heuristics which mix different heuristics when solving real world problems, ranging from Personnel Scheduling [7] to Vehicle Routing [27]. Additionally, Mısır [18] explored the behaviour of group decision making strategies which successfully mixed well known move acceptance operators and outperformed individual move acceptance operators when used as the selection hyper-heuristic components. More examples on the empirical success of hyper-heuristics can be found in [4].

Cowling et al. [7, 8] introduced hyper-heuristics as "heuristics to choose heuristics" and investigated the performance of *simple* hyper-heuristics across a set of real-world scheduling problem instances. The study focused on simple heuristic selection methods, such as, *Simple Random* and *Random Permutation.* These two methods do not learn, as they do not receive any feedback during the search process. Simple Random chooses a low level operator uniformly at random in each step, while Random Permutation uses a uniform random permutation of a given set of low level operators and successively uses a low level operator from that list. Two different types of acceptance strategies can be found in the literature: *deterministic* or *non-deterministic.* The authors used two deterministic acceptance operators which would make the same acceptance decision regardless of the given step during the search using the same current and new candidate solutions(s) in [7]: *All Moves* (AM) and *Only Improvements* (OI). AM accepts all solutions regardless of their quality (fitness), while OI accepts only improving moves and previous solution is used in the next step, when a non-improving move is made.

The learning heuristic selection methods can adapt during the search process improving their decision capability for the selection of *promising* neighbourhood operators. Nareyek [21] proposed *Reinforcement Learning* (RL) which scores each low level operator based on its individual performance. The probability of an operator being selected is updated depending on these scores. For example, roulette wheel strategy chooses a low level heuristic with a probability given by

FOGA'13, January 16-20, 2013, Adelaide, Australia.

the ratio of its individual score to the sum of scores of all low level operators. After the selected operator is applied to the current solution, the score of a low level operator is increased in the case of success indicating improvement in the quality of the new candidate solution and decreased in the case of a failure. There are many different selection hyper-heuristic components studied in the literature. Özcan et al. [26] investigated the memory length issues in reinforcement learning using a case study. Gibbs et al. [11] and Burke et al. [2] compared the performance of different reinforcement learning based heuristic selection methods when used within a selection hyper-heuristic framework for sports scheduling, examination timetabling, respectively. An overview of hyper-heuristics and more can be found in [28, 5, 4].

A significant trend in research on randomised search heuristics including evolutionary algorithms is the advent of rigorously proven results about their expected runtime [1, 22]. Runtime analyses show how the expected optimisation time of a search heuristic depends on its parameter settings and the characteristics of the optimisation problem at hand. Such analyses often provide deeper insights into the behaviour of search heuristics as compared to the empirical investigations.

There are some work on selection hyper-heuristics in the direction of gaining more insights regarding their behaviour via landscape analysis [17, 24, 23]. The theoretical work on selection hyper-heuristics is still very limited. Recently, He et al. [13] compared pure and mixed strategy (1+1) EAs using the so-called asymptotic hitting time as performance measure. A mixed strategy uses multiple mutation operators and chooses one based on a given fixed distribution, while a pure strategy uses a single mutation operator. The authors claimed that the asymptotic hitting time of a mixed strategy over a set of mutation operators O, is not worse than that of the worst pure strategy using one operator in O only.

The asymptotic hitting time considered by He et al. [13] is a different performance measure than the expected runtime, which is considered in this study. The theoretical work on the runtime analysis of selection hyper-heuristics is almost non existent. To the best knowledge of the authors, this study is one of the initial studies in the area. Our motivation is to illustrate that mixing (neighbourhood or acceptance) operators as components of a selection hyper-heuristic can be more efficient on certain problems. We perform runtime analyses of hyper-heuristics for choosing the right parameter setting for mixing low level operators. Moreover, the expected runtime of a simple reinforcement learning scheme and other mechanisms are compared.

1.1 Notation

The paper uses the following notation. For $n \geq 1$, define the set of integers $[n] := \{1, \ldots, n\}$, and $[0..n] := \{0\} \cup [n]$. Given a vector $v \in \mathbb{R}^n$ (e.g., a bitstring) and an integer $i \in [n]$, then v_i denotes the i-th element of v. The notation $X \sim D$ signifies that X is a random variable with distribution D. In particular, $D_p(a, b)$ with parameter $p \in [0, 1]$ is the distribution where $X \sim D_p(a, b)$ if and only if $\Pr[X = a] = p$ and $\Pr[X = b] = 1 - p$. The n-th harmonic number is denoted H_n. The runtime analysis uses standard notation (e.g., O, Ω and Θ) for asymptotic growth of functions (see, e.g., [6]).

2. MIXING NEIGHBOURHOOD OPERATORS

This section considers hyper-heuristics that mix neighbourhood operators (also called variation operators). The progress made in runtime analysis of evolutionary algorithms demonstrates the importance of completely understanding the simple algorithms and simple problems before proceeding to runtime analysis of more complex algorithms and more complex problems. We therefore consider a simple hyper-heuristic, Algorithm 1 below, which is a variant of the well-known (1+1) EA [9]. This algorithm is also similar to the randomised local search (RLS) variant used in Giel and Wegener [12].

Algorithm 1

1: $x \sim \text{UNIF}(\{0,1\}^n)$
2: **while** termination criteria not satisfied **do**
3:     Var $\sim D_{\bar{p}}(\text{OP}_1, \text{OP}_2, ..., \text{OP}_m)$ // Selects a neighbourhood operator.
4:     $x' \sim \text{Var}(x)$
5:     **if** $f(x') \geq f(x)$ **then** $x \leftarrow x'$.
6: **end while**

The RLS algorithm maintains a current solution x, from which a neighbouring candidate solution x' is generated in each iteration. The candidate solution replaces the current solution if it is not worse than the current solution. The (1+1) EA produces the candidate solution by flipping each bit in the current solution with probability $1/n$. In contrast, Algorithm 1 produces the candidate solution using one of the m neighbourhood operators. Based on the probability distribution $\bar{p}$, it selects and applies the operator OP_i with probability p_i, for $i \in [m]$, where $\sum_{i=1}^{m} p_i = 1$.

We will use *fitness-based partitions*, which is a well known method for runtime analysis of randomised search heuristics.

DEFINITION 1. *A tuple $(A_0, A_1, \ldots, A_\ell)$ is an f-based partition of a function $f : \{0,1\}^n \rightarrow \mathbb{R}$ if*

1. $\bigcup_{i=0}^{\ell} A_i = \{0,1\}^n$
2. $A_i \cap A_j = \emptyset$ *for* $\forall i, j$ *and* $i \neq j$
3. $f(A_i) < f(A_j)$ *for* $\forall i, j$ *and* $i < j$
4. $f(A_\ell) = \max_x f(x)$

The set A_i, $i \in [\ell]$ is referred to as the *i-th fitness level.* If the probability of leaving fitness level i is at least s_i, then the expected time to leave fitness level i is at most $1/s_i$.

THEOREM 1. *Given any f-based partition, let s_i be the minimum probability for a (1+1) EA to leave A_i towards $A_{i+1} \cup \cdots \cup A_\ell$. The expected runtime of (1+1) EA on f is bounded from above by*

$$E\left(T_{(1+1)\text{ EA},f}\right) \leq \sum_{i=0}^{\ell-1} \frac{1}{s_i}$$

Theorem 1 can also be applied to the hyper-heuristic framework in Algorithm 1. Assuming that there is a fitness based partition for a given problem, Theorem 2 shows that the upper bound on the expected runtime of an algorithm mixing a set of operators as in Algorithm 1 can be computed based on the shortest expected running time for a solution to move from one fitness level to an upper level across all levels based on a given probability distribution.

THEOREM 2. *Given a function $f : \{0,1\}^n \to \mathbb{R}$ and an f-based partition $(A_0, \ldots, A_\ell)$, let T be the runtime of Algorithm 1 with parameters $p_i > 0, \forall i$ on the function f. For each $i \in [0..\ell-1]$, let r_i^k be the minimum probability for Algorithm 1 to leave fitness level A_i towards $A_{i+1} \cup \cdots \cup A_\ell$ using the mutation operator $\textsc{Op}_k$. Then, the expected runtime of Algorithm 1, is bounded from above by*

$$E\left(T_{Algorithm\ 1,f}\right) \leq \sum_{i=0}^{\ell-1} \min_{1\leq k\leq m} \frac{1}{p_k r_i^k} \leq \min_{1\leq k\leq m} \sum_{i=0}^{\ell-1} \frac{1}{p_k r_i^k} \quad (1)$$

PROOF. Use Theorem 1, with

$$s_i = \sum_{k=1}^{m} p_k r_i^k \geq \max_{1\leq k\leq m} p_k r_i^k,$$

for $i \in [0..m-1]$, and the theorem follows. □

Algorithm 2 (HH) is a special case of Algorithm 1, where $m = 2$:

Algorithm 2

1: $x \sim \textsc{Unif}(\{0,1\}^n)$
2: **while** termination criteria not satisfied **do**
3: Var $\sim D_p(\textsc{RLSmoveOneBit}, \textsc{RLSmoveTwoBits})$ // Selects a neighbourhood operator.
4: $x' \sim \text{Var}(x)$
5: **if** $f(x') \geq f(x)$ **then** $x \leftarrow x'$.
6: **end while**

With probability p, HH applies the 1-bitflip operator RLSMOVEONEBIT which flips one uniformly chosen bit position. With probability $1-p$, HH picks the 2-bitflip operator RLSMOVETWOBITS which flips two different and uniformly chosen bit-positions.

2.1 Analysis of the ONEMAX function

The following "warm-up" analysis describes the behaviour of a simple and standard hyper-heuristic which mixes heuristics on a familiar problem. We do not expect that a hyper-heuristic performs well in a case where the optimal setting is known, since hyper-heuristics are meant to be general methodologies that could be applied to a variety of problem domains.

The ONEMAX function is a well known benchmark function which counts the number of nonzero bits in the given bitstring.

$$\textsc{OneMax}(x) := \sum_{i=1}^{n} x_i \quad (2)$$

THEOREM 3. *The expected runtime of Algorithm 2 on* ONEMAX *is*

$$E\left(T_{HH,\textsc{OneMax}}\right) \leq \begin{cases} (\frac{1}{p})n(\ln(n)+1) & \text{if } p > \frac{\ln(n)+1}{n+\ln n}, \text{ and} \\ \frac{1}{(1-p)}n^2 & \text{otherwise.} \end{cases}$$

PROOF. We apply Theorem 2 with the canonical partition $A_i := \{x \mid \textsc{OneMax}(x) = i\}$, for $i \in [0..n]$. In order for a solution to be improved to a higher fitness level, it is sufficient to flip a single 0-bit. The minimum probability for this event considering a candidate solution at the i-th fitness level is given by $r_i^1 = (n-i)/n$ or $r_i^2 = (n-i)(n-i-1)/n^2$ (assuming $i \leq n-2$, otherwise $r_i^2 = 0$) when RLSMOVEONEBIT or RLSMOVETWOBITS is selected, respectively. By Theorem 2,

$$\begin{aligned} E\left(T_{HH,\textsc{OneMax}}\right) &\leq \min\left\{\sum_{i=0}^{n-1}\frac{1}{pr_i^1}, \sum_{i=0}^{n-1}\frac{1}{(1-p)r_i^2}\right\} \\ &= \min\left\{\frac{1}{p}\sum_{i=0}^{n-1}\frac{n}{(n-i)}, \right. \\ &\qquad \left. \frac{1}{1-p}\sum_{i=0}^{n-2}\frac{n^2}{(n-i)(n-i-1)}\right\} \\ &= \min\left\{\frac{n}{p}H_n, \frac{n^2}{1-p}\sum_{j=1}^{n-1}\frac{1}{j(j+1)}\right\} \\ &\leq \min\left\{\frac{n}{p}(\ln(n)+1), \frac{n^2}{1-p}\left(1-\frac{1}{n}\right)\right\}. \end{aligned}$$

The first term on the right hand-side will be the minimum if

$$\begin{aligned} \frac{n}{p}(\ln(n)+1) &< \frac{n^2}{1-p}\left(1-\frac{1}{n}\right) \\ \frac{1}{p} - 1 &< \frac{n-1}{\ln(n)+1} \end{aligned}$$

and the theorem follows. □

2.2 Analysis of the GAPPATH function

As a simple benchmark, we use the GAPPATH function defined below.

$$\textsc{GapPath}(x) := \begin{cases} \textsc{Zm}(x) & \text{if } \textsc{Ridge}(x) \equiv 1 \pmod 3 \\ \textsc{Zm}(x) + 2n\textsc{Ridge}(x) & \text{otherwise.} \end{cases} \quad (3)$$

where $\textsc{Zm}(x) := \sum_{i=1}^{n}(1-x_i)$, and

$$\textsc{Ridge}(x) := \begin{cases} i & \text{if } x = 1^i0^{n-i} \text{ for } i \in [0..n] \\ 0 & \text{otherwise.} \end{cases}$$

In order not to unnecessarily complicate the analysis, we assume that $n = 3k$ for some integer $k \geq 1$.

The GAPPATH function is a variant of the SPI function (short path with increasing values on the path), which is a standard benchmark function in theoretical analysis of evolutionary algorithms [16, 15]. These functions feature a short path which corresponds to all search points on the form 1^i0^{n-i}. The function value of any search point outside the path is the number of 0-bits, and is inferior to the path members. The function GAPPATH differs from SPI, in that the path contains gaps where the function values are inferior to the rest of the path. The gaps correspond to all search points on the form 1^i0^{n-1} where $i \equiv 1 \pmod 3$. A typical randomised search heuristic will optimise GAPPATH by first locating the search point 0^n, then by traversing along the path while "jumping" across the gaps. Due to the gaps in the GAPPATH function, it is straightforward to see that using only a 1-bitflip operator, or only using a 2-bitflip operator will not be effective.

THEOREM 4. *If $p = 0$ or $p = 1$, then the expected runtime of Algorithm 2 on* GAPPATH *is infinite.*

PROOF. Setting $p = 0$ implies that the algorithm will only use the 2-bitflip operator. With probability $1/2^n$, the initial search point is $1^2 0^{n-2}$. All search points within Hamming distance 2 from this point have inferior function value. Hence, the algorithm will never accept any search point produced from the 2-bitflip operator. By the law of total probability, the expected runtime is therefore infinite. An analogous argument can be made for the case $p = 1$ with respect to the initial search point $1^3 0^{n-3}$ and the 1-bitflip operator. □

We will therefore consider mixing of operators, i.e., choosing $p \in (0, 1)$, and study how the choice of parameter p influences the expected runtime. We start by estimating the expected time to make a single improving step along the path.

LEMMA 1. *Let $p \in (0, 1)$. Assume that the current search point is $x = 1^j 0^{n-j}$, where $j \equiv i \pmod 3$ for $i \in \{0, 2\}$. Let T_i be the random time until a search point with strictly higher function value is obtained. Then, the expectation of T_i is*

$$E(T_i \mid p) = \begin{cases} \frac{n(n-1)}{2(1-p)}, & i = 0 \\ \frac{n}{p}, & i = 2 \end{cases}$$

PROOF. The probability that the 2-bitflip operator improves a search point where $\text{RIDGE}(x) \equiv 0 \pmod 3$ is $r_0 := (2/n)(1/(n-1))$, and the probability that a 1-bitflip operator improves a search point where $\text{RIDGE}(x) \equiv 2 \pmod 3$ is $r_2 := 1/n$. Hence,

$$E(T_0 \mid p) = \frac{1}{r_0(1-p)} = \frac{n(n-1)}{2(1-p)},$$
$$E(T_2 \mid p) = \frac{1}{r_2 p} = \frac{n}{p}.$$

□

It is now easy to calculate the expected runtime with a fixed mixing parameter p.

THEOREM 5. *The expected runtime of Algorithm 2 initialised with the search point 0^n on GAPPATH with fixed mixing parameter $p \in [0, 1]$ is $\left(\frac{n^3-3n^2}{6(1-p)} + \frac{n^2}{3(1-p)p}\right)$.*

PROOF. To obtain the optimum, it is necessary to transition from state $\text{RIDGE}(x) \equiv 0 \pmod 3$ to $\text{RIDGE}(x) \equiv 2 \pmod 3$ and back $n/3$ times. Hence, the expected runtime of the algorithm is

$$(n/3)\left(E(T_0 \mid p) + E(T_2 \mid p)\right)$$

where the expectations of T_0 and T_2 are given in Lemma 1. Hence,

$$\frac{n}{3}\left(\frac{n(n-1)}{2(1-p)} + \frac{n}{p}\right) = \frac{n^2}{3}\left(\frac{p(n-1)+2-p}{2(1-p)p}\right)$$

and the theorem follows. □

Theorem 5 implies that the expected runtime of Algorithm 2 is $O(\max\{n^2/p, n^3/(1-p)\})$. Moreover, if $p = n^{-c}$, where $c \geq 1$, then the expected runtime is $\frac{n^{c+2}}{3} + \frac{n^3}{6} + O(n^2)$. Similarly, if $p = 1 - n^{-c}$, then the expected runtime is $\frac{n^{c+3}}{6} - \frac{n^{c+2}}{6} + O(n^2)$.

We will revisit and use the GAPPATH function in Section 4.

3. MIXING ACCEPTANCE CRITERIA

This section considers hyper-heuristics that mix move acceptance operators. We show that mixing move acceptance operators can be efficient on problems where individual acceptance operators fail.

Algorithm 3

```
x ~ UNIF({0,1}^n)
while termination criteria not satisfied do
    x' ~ FLIPRANDOMBIT(x)
    ACC ~ D_p(AM, OI) // Selects an acceptance operator.
    if ACC(x, x') then x <- x'
end while
```

Algorithm 3 follows the same outline as Algorithm 2, but differs in the choice of neighbourhood operator and move acceptance operator. Algorithm 3 always uses the 1-bitflip operator as neighbourhood operator, and it mixes two different move acceptance operators. With probability p, it chooses the AM (x, x') acceptance operator (always move) which always accepts the candidate solution x'. With probability $1-p$, it uses the OI(x, x') acceptance operator (only improvement) which accepts the candidate solution x' if and only if $f(x') > f(x)$, ie., it is strictly better than the current candidate solution.

The pseudo-Boolean function RR_k, also called the *royal road function* [29], splits a bitstring of length n into $m := \lfloor n/k \rfloor$ blocks of length k. A block containing exactly i 0-bits, for $i \in [0..k]$ is called an *i-block*. The function value of a bitstring equals the number of 0-blocks in the bitstring.

$$\text{RR}_k(x) := \sum_{i=1}^{\lfloor n/k \rfloor} \prod_{j=1}^{k} x_{k(i-1)+j}.$$

The simplest case $k = 1$ equals to the well-known ONEMAX function. The problem becomes harder for larger values of k. The RR_k function is similar but not identical to, the Royal Road function defined in [19].

We will first show that it is necessary to mix the acceptance criteria, i.e. choosing $p \in (0, 1)$, in order to optimise RR_k efficiently. By setting $p = 0$, Algorithm 3 will only accept improving moves, which is problematic because RR_k with $k \geq 2$ contains large plateaus.

THEOREM 6. *If $p = 0$, then the expected optimisation time of Algorithm 3 on RR_k with $k \geq 2$ is infinite.*

PROOF. Any search point that is obtained by flipping any of the first k positions in the bitstring $x := 0^2 1^{n-2}$ has the same function value as x, and will not be accepted by the OI-operator. Any search point that is obtained by flipping any of the $n-k$ last bit positions in x will have inferior function value, and will not be accepted by the OI-operator. The initial search point is x with probability $1/2^n$. The expected runtime on RR_k is therefore infinite by the law of total probability. □

It is obvious that Algorithm 3 degenerates into a random walk over the set of bitstrings when $p = 1$. Mixing the acceptance operators is therefore necessary, and a natural question is to determine the right parameter setting for p. By intuition, if p is chosen too high, the algorithm will accept too many worsening moves. In fact, Theorem 8 which will be presented later, shows that the expected runtime is super-polynomial, even for as small parameter settings as $p = \omega(\log(n)/n)$. The following theorem shows how to set p to guarantee polynomial expected runtime.

THEOREM 7. *For any integer $k \geq 2$, let $m := \lfloor n/k \rfloor$. If $0 < p \leq 1/(6mk^k)$, then the expected runtime of Algorithm 3 on RR_k is no more than $m(1+mk^k)/p$. If additionally $p = \Omega(1/mk^k)$, then the expected runtime is $O(m^3k^{2k})$.*

PROOF. Consider the vector-valued stochastic process $X_t \in \mathbb{N}^{k+1}$, where $X_t = v$ if the current search point in iteration t consists of v_i blocks with exactly i 0-bits for all $i \in [k]$. The drift of this process will be analysed with respect to the distance function $g(v) = \sum_{i=0}^{k} f_i v_i$, where for all $i \in [0..k]$

$$f_i := \begin{cases} 0 & \text{if } i = 0 \\ \frac{k}{2m} & \text{if } i = 1 \\ \frac{k}{2m} + \sum_{j=2}^{i} k^{k+2-j} & \text{if } 2 \leq i \leq k. \end{cases}$$

Note that $f_{i+1} - f_i = k^{k+1-i}$ and $f_{i+1} - f_{i-1} = k^{k+1-i}(1+k)$ for all $i \in [2, k-1]$. Obviously, the distance function g is non-negative and bounded from above by

$$B := k/2 + mk^{k+1} > mf_k.$$

Define the random variable

$$\Delta_t(v) := (g(X_{t-1}) - g(X_t) \mid X_{t-1} = v).$$

For each pair $i, j \in [k]$, where $i \neq j$, let the random variable $M_t(i,j)$ denote the number of i-blocks in iteration $t-1$ that was turned into j-blocks in iteration t. For each $i \in [k]$, let $M_t(i,i) = 0$. Now, define the conditional random variables

$$\Delta_t^{(i)}(v) := \left(\sum_{j=0}^{k} (f_i - f_j) M_t(i,j) \mid X_{t-1} = v \right)$$

Intuitively, the random variable $\Delta_t^{(i)}$ describes the drift contribution from i-blocks, so that the total drift can be decomposed as

$$\begin{aligned} \Delta_t(v) &= \sum_{i=0}^{k} f_i v_i - \sum_{i=0}^{k} f_i X_t(i) \\ &= \sum_{i=0}^{k} f_i v_i - \sum_{i=0}^{k} f_i \left(v_i + \sum_{j=0}^{k} M_t(j,i) - \sum_{j=0}^{k} M_t(i,j) \right) \\ &= \left(\sum_{i=0}^{k} f_i \sum_{j=0}^{k} M_t(i,j) \right) - \left(\sum_{i=0}^{k} f_i \sum_{j=0}^{k} M_t(j,i) \right) \\ &= \sum_{i=0}^{k} \sum_{j=0}^{k} (f_i - f_j) M_t(i,j) = \sum_{i=0}^{k} \Delta_t^{(i)}(v). \end{aligned}$$

The drift contribution from the 0-blocks is

$$\Delta_t^{(0)}(v) = -p \cdot (v_0/m)(k/2m) \geq -pk/(2m).$$

The drift contribution from the 1-blocks is

$$\Delta_t^{(1)}(v) = \frac{v_1}{km} \left(\frac{k}{2m} - (k-1)pk^k \right) \geq \frac{v_1}{2m} \left(\frac{1}{m} - 2pk^k \right).$$

The drift contribution from the i-blocks with $i \in [2, k-1]$ is

$$\begin{aligned} \Delta_t^{(i)}(v) &= \frac{pv_i}{m} \left(\frac{i(f_i - f_{i-1})}{k} + \frac{(k-i)(f_i - f_{i+1})}{k} \right) \\ &= \frac{pv_i}{m} \left(\frac{i(f_{i+1} - f_{i-1})}{k} - (f_{i+1} - f_i) \right) \\ &= \frac{pv_i}{m} k^{k+1-i} \left(\frac{i(1+k)}{k} - 1 \right) \\ &= \frac{pv_i}{m} k^{k+1-i} \left(\frac{i}{k} \right) \geq \frac{pv_i k}{m}. \end{aligned}$$

Finally, the drift contribution from the k-blocks is

$$\Delta_t^{(k)}(v) = p\frac{v_k}{m} k^2.$$

Two cases are now distinguished. In the case when $v_1 \geq 1$,

$$\begin{aligned} \Delta_t(v) &\geq \Delta_t^{(1)}(v) + \Delta_t^{(0)}(v) \geq \frac{v_1}{2m} \left(\frac{1}{m} - 2pk^k \right) - \frac{pk}{2m} \\ &\geq \frac{1}{2m} \left(\frac{1}{m} - p(2k^k + k) \right) \\ &> \frac{1}{2m} \left(\frac{1}{m} - \frac{1}{2m} \right) = \frac{1}{4m^2}, \end{aligned}$$

using the assumption $p \leq 1/(6mk^k) < 1/(2m(2k^k + k))$.

In the second case, where $v_1 = 0$, and $v_0 \leq m - 1$, then

$$\begin{aligned} \Delta_t(v) &\geq \Delta_t^{(0)}(v) + \Delta_t^{(2)}(v) + \cdots + \Delta_t^{(k)}(v) \\ &\geq \frac{kp}{m} \left(v_2 + \cdots + v_k - \frac{1}{2} \right) \geq \frac{kp}{2m}. \end{aligned}$$

In both cases, $\Delta_t(v) \geq \Delta := kp/(2m)$ holds. Given that $g(X_t) \leq B$, it follows by the polynomial drift theorem (see eg. [14]) that the expected time until $g(X_t) = 0$ is no more than

$$B/\Delta \leq \left(k/2 + mk^{k+1} \right) (2m)/(kp) \leq m(1+mk^k)/p. \quad \square$$

We then show that if the parameter p in Algorithm 3 is chosen asymptotically larger than $\log(m)/(km)$, then the expected runtime on the RR_k problem is super-polynomial. This theorem also covers the special case $p = 1$, stating that Algorithm 3 becomes ineffective when the AM acceptance operator is used alone.

THEOREM 8. *If $p > g(m)/(km)$ for any function $g(m) \leq m/2$, then the expected runtime of Algorithm 3 on RR_k is $e^{\Omega(g(m))}$.*

PROOF. Assume optimistically that the number of 1-blocks never increases above $g(m)/2 + 1$, and that all other blocks are 0-blocks. Clearly, this will only make Algorithm 3 optimise RR_k faster. If the number of 1-blocks is no more than $g(m)/2$, then the probability of increasing the number of 1-blocks is at least $q := (3/4)p \leq (m - g(m)/2)p/m$ and the probability of decreasing the number of 1-blocks is no more than $r := (1/2)p \geq g(m)/(2km)$.

The algorithm is modelled by the stochastic process $X_t \in \mathbb{N}$ on the integers where $\Pr[X_t = X_{t-1} + 1] = q/(r+q)$ and $\Pr[X_t = X_{t-1} - 1] = r/(r+q)$. Assume that $X_0 = g(m)/2$. By the gambler's ruin problem (see [10]), it follows that the probability that the process reaches the point 0 before first reaching the point $g(m)/2 + 1$ is

$$\frac{\left(\frac{q}{r}\right) - 1}{\left(\frac{q}{r}\right)^{g(m)/2} - 1} = \frac{\frac{1}{2}}{\left(\frac{3}{2}\right)^{g(m)/2} - 1} = e^{-\Omega(g(m))}.$$

It is therefore clear, that if the algorithm at some point has $g(m)/2$ 1-blocks, then the probability that the algorithm reaches 0 1-blocks before reaching $g(m)/2+1$ 1-blocks is also $e^{-\Omega(g(m))}$. By a Chernoff bound (see eg. [20]), the number of 0-blocks in the initial search point is less than $m-g(m)/2-1 \geq (3/4)m-1$ with probability $1-e^{-\Omega(m)}$. Hence, the expected number of times the current search point has $m-g(m)/2-1$ 0-blocks before reaching the optimum is $e^{\Omega(g(m))}$, which concludes the proof. □

The result in Theorem 8 is complemented with a plot of the drift field corresponding to the number of 1-blocks and 2-blocks in the case $k=2$. With i 1-blocks, and j 2-blocks, these drifts are respectively

$$D_1(i,j) = \frac{(m-i-j)p}{m} + \frac{jp}{m} - \frac{ip}{2m}$$

$$D_2(i,j) = \frac{ip}{2m} - \frac{jp}{m}$$

When the mixing parameter p is too high, the algorithm accepts too many worsenings, and the current search point drifts towards an equilibrium point which is far from the global optimum at origin, as shown in Fig. 1.

4. ADAPTATION OF THE MIXING PARAMETER

The previous two sections have shown that mixing operators can be more efficient than each individual operator. However, the results also show that the efficiency of the mixing approach depends on having an appropriate mixing distribution. Theorems 7 and 8 tell us that the expected runtime (i.e., exponential vs polynomial) depends critically on the mixing parameter p, and that the right choice of p is problem-dependant (in the case of RR_k, it depends on parameter k).

We therefore consider mechanisms for online adaptation of the mixing parameter p in the context of neighbourhood operators. For simplicity, we assume a scenario where Algorithm 2 can choose between two parameter settings, $p=p_{\mathrm{hi}}$ or $p=p_{\mathrm{lo}}$, where $0 \leq p_{\mathrm{lo}} < 1/2 \leq p_{\mathrm{hi}} \leq 1$. Setting $p=p_{\mathrm{hi}}$ implies that the 1-bitflip operator will be chosen most often, while setting $p=p_{\mathrm{lo}}$ implies that the 2-bitflip operator will be chosen most often. The *permutation* mechanism deterministically chooses $p=p_{\mathrm{hi}}$ in even iteration numbers, and $p=p_{\mathrm{lo}}$ in odd iteration numbers. The *simple reinforcement learning* mechanism sets $p=p_{\mathrm{hi}}$ if the last improving step was made with the 1-bitflip operator, and $p=p_{\mathrm{lo}}$ if the last improving step was made with the 2-bitflip operator. The simple reinforcement approach is also commonly referred to as *random permutation gradient* hyper-heuristic in the literature [7, 4].

THEOREM 9. *The expected runtime of Algorithm 2 on* GAPPATH *with simple reinforcement learning with parameters p_{hi} and p_{lo}, starting with $p=p_{hi}$ from the search point 0^n is*

$$\frac{n}{3}\left(\frac{n(n-1)}{2(1-p_{hi})} + \frac{n}{p_{lo}}\right)$$

PROOF. Starting from $\mathrm{RIDGE}(x)=0$, the first improving step will be made by the 2-bitflip operator. In all subsequent iterations, the algorithm will choose the parameter setting $p=p_{\mathrm{hi}}$ when $\mathrm{RIDGE}(x) \equiv 0 \pmod 3$, and $p=p_{\mathrm{lo}}$ when

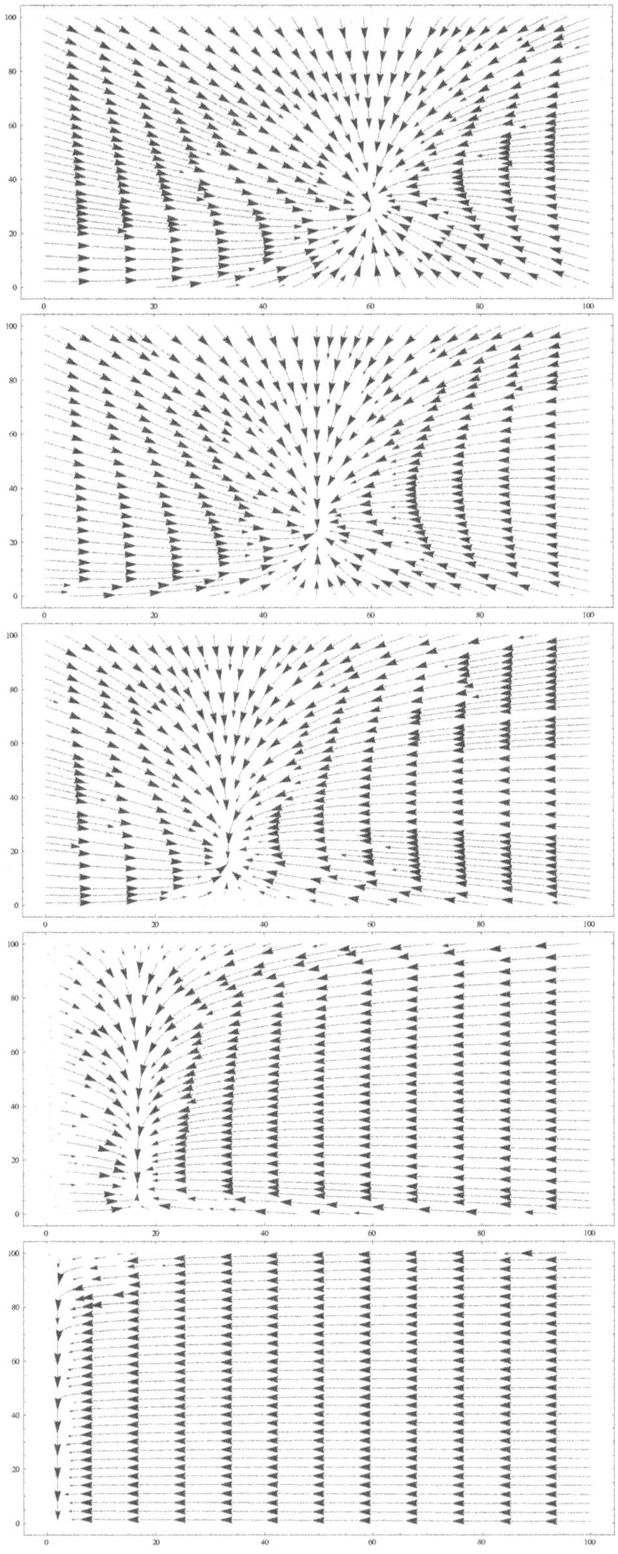

Figure 1: The drift of the number of 1-blocks (horizontal) and the number of 2-blocks (vertical) in the current search point of Algorithm 3 on the Royal Roads function (RR_k) when $k=2$, $m=100$, and (from top to bottom) $p=3/4$, $p=1/2$, $p=1/4$, $p=1/10$, and $p=1/100$. The global optimum 1^n is located at origin.

RIDGE$(x) \equiv 2 \pmod 3$. Hence, the expected optimisation time is by Lemma 1

$$\frac{n}{3}\left(E\left(T_0 \mid p = p_{\rm hi}\right) + E\left(T_2 \mid p = p_{\rm lo}\right)\right) = \frac{n}{3}\left(\frac{n(n-1)}{2(1-p_{\rm hi})} + \frac{n}{p_{\rm lo}}\right)$$

□

Finally, we have the following theorem for the permutation mechanism.

THEOREM 10. *The expected runtime of Algorithm 2 on* GAPPATH *with the permutation mechanism where* $p_{lo} = 1 - p_{hi} = 1/n$ *is no more than* $(1/3)n^3 + (1/3)n^2 + O(1)$ *when starting with the search point* 0^n.

PROOF. Let r be the probability of making an improving step, assuming that the correct mutation operator is selected. Let $q_{\rm hi}$ and $q_{\rm lo}$ be the probabilities of selecting the correct mutation operator given that $p = p_{\rm hi}$, respectively $p = p_{\rm lo}$. Since there are only two operators to choose from, it holds that

$$q_{\rm hi}q_{\rm lo} = (1 - p_{\rm lo})p_{\rm lo} = \frac{1}{n}\left(1 - \frac{1}{n}\right).$$

Starting from an even iteration number, the probability of making at least one improvement within the next two iterations is

$$q_{\rm hi}r + (1 - q_{\rm hi}r)q_{\rm lo}r = r(1 - q_{\rm hi}q_{\rm lo}r) = r(1 - O(r/n)),$$

So the expected number of iterations to make an improvement is no more than

$$(2/r)(1 + O(r/n)) = 2/r + O(1/n).$$

In the case where RIDGE$(x) \equiv 0 \pmod 3$, the probability of making an improvement with the 2-bitflip operator is $r = (2/n)(1/(n-1))$. Hence, it holds that

$$E\left(T_0\right) \leq n(n-1) + O(1/n).$$

In the case where RIDGE$(x) \equiv 2 \pmod 3$, the probability of making an improvement with the 1-bitflip operator is $r = 1/n$. Hence it holds that

$$E\left(T_2\right) \leq 2n + O(1/n).$$

Following the same argument as above, the expected runtime on the problem is no more than

$$(n/3)\left(E\left(T_0\right) + E\left(T_2\right)\right) \leq (n/3)\left(n^2 + n + O(1/n)\right) = n^3/3 + n^2/3 + O(1).$$

□

Starting from a random solution will require an additional running time to obtain 0^n (see Section 2.1). This process is exactly the same as solving ONEMAX in which the 0-bits are counted instead of 1-bits. In order to emphasise the remaining expected time, this additional runtime is omitted in Table 1.

5. CONCLUSION

Hyper-heuristic studies have been mostly empirical. This paper provides one of the first runtime analyses of selection hyper-heuristics. We have shown that mixing different neighbourhood or move acceptance operators can be more efficient than using stand-alone individual operators in some cases. However, the analysis also shows that the performance of the mixing operators rely critically on having the right mixing distribution, which is problem dependent. Table 1 shows the result of an analysis of some well-known mechanisms under certain settings. Most notably, a previous successful mechanism which reinforces the operator performs poorer than the static mixing distributions. This is just a first step towards more rigorous analysis of hyper-heuristics. Future work should consider more complex hyper-heuristics, and more complex problem scenarios.

Acknowledgements

This work was supported in part by EPSRC under grant no. grant EP/F033214/1.

6. REFERENCES

[1] A. Auger and B. Doerr. *Theory of Randomized Search Heuristics: Foundations and Recent Developments.* World Scientific Publishing Co., Inc., River Edge, NJ, USA, 2011.

[2] E. Burke, G. Kendall, M. Mısır, and E. Özcan. Monte carlo hyper-heuristics for examination timetabling. *Annals of Operations Research*, 196:73–90, 2012.

[3] E. K. Burke, M. Hyde, G. Kendall, G. Ochoa, E. Özcan, and J. R. Woodward. A classification of hyper-heuristic approaches. In M. Gendreau and J.-Y. Potvin, editors, *Handbook of Metaheuristics*, volume 146 of *International Series in Operations Research and Management Science*, pages 449–468. Springer, 2010.

[4] E. K. Burke, M. R. Hyde, G. Kendall, G. Ochoa, E. Özcan, and R. Qu. Hyper-heuristics: A survey of the state of the art. Technical Report NOTTCS-TR-SUB-0906241418-2747, School of Computer Science, University of Nottingham, 2010.

[5] K. Chakhlevitch and P. I. Cowling. Hyperheuristics: Recent developments. In *Adaptive and Multilevel Metaheuristics*, volume 136 of *Studies in Computational Intelligence*, pages 3–29. Springer, 2008.

[6] T. H. Cormen, C. E. Leiserson, R. L. Rivest, and C. Stein. *Introduction to Algorithms.* McGraw Hill, New York, NY, 2nd edition, 2001.

[7] P. Cowling, G. Kendall, and E. Soubeiga. A hyper-heuristic approach to scheduling a sales summit. In *Practice and Theory of Automated Timetabling III : Third International Conference, PATAT 2000*, volume 2079 of *LNCS*. Springer, 2000.

[8] P. Cowling, G. Kendall, and E. Soubeiga. Hyperheuristics: A tool for rapid prototyping in scheduling and optimisation. In S. Cagoni, J. Gottlieb, E. Hart, M. Middendorf, and R. Goenther, editors, *Applications of Evolutionary Computing: Proceeding of Evo Workshops 2002*, volume 2279 of *Lecture Notes in Computer Science*, pages 1–10, Kinsale, Ireland, April 3-4 2002. Springer-Verlag.

Mechanism	Expected Runtime
Simple permutation	$(1/3)n^3 + (1/3)n^2 + O(1)$
Static parameter $p = 1/n$	$(1/2)n^3 + O(n^2)$
Static parameter $p = 1 - 1/n$	$(1/6)n^4 - (1/6)n^3 + O(n^2)$
Simple reinforcement $p_{\text{lo}} = 1 - p_{\text{hi}} = 1/n$	$(1/6)n^4 + (1/6)n^3$
Static $p = 1$ or $p = 0$	∞

Table 1: Impact of parameter update mechanism on the runtime of Algorithm 2 on the GAPPATH function. The mechanisms are ordered w.r.t. increasing runtime.

[9] S. Droste, T. Jansen, and I. Wegener. On the analysis of the (1+1) Evolutionary Algorithm. *Theoretical Computer Science*, 276:51–81, 2002.

[10] W. Feller. *An Introduction to Probability Theory and Its Applications*, volume 1. Wiley, New York, 1968.

[11] J. Gibbs, G. Kendall, and E. Özcan. Scheduling english football fixtures over the holiday period using hyper-heuristics. In *Proceedings of the 11th international conference on Parallel problem solving from nature: Part I*, PPSN'10, pages 496–505, Berlin, Heidelberg, 2010. Springer-Verlag.

[12] O. Giel and I. Wegener. Maximum cardinality matchings on trees by randomized local search. In *Proceedings of the 8th annual conference on Genetic and evolutionary computation*, GECCO '06, pages 539–546, New York, NY, USA, 2006. ACM.

[13] J. He, F. He, and H. Dong. Pure strategy or mixed strategy? - an initial comparison of their asymptotic convergence rate and asymptotic hitting time. In J.-K. Hao and M. Middendorf, editors, *Evolutionary Computation in Combinatorial Optimization - 12th European Conference, EvoCOP 2012, Málaga, Spain, April 11-13, 2012. Proceedings*, volume 7245 of *Lecture Notes in Computer Science*, pages 218–229. Springer, 2012.

[14] J. He and X. Yao. A study of drift analysis for estimating computation time of evolutionary algorithms. *Natural Computing*, 3(1):21–35, 2004.

[15] T. Jansen. On the analysis of dynamic restart strategies for evolutionary algorithms. In J. J. M. Guervós, P. Adamidis, H.-G. Beyer, J. L. F.-V. Martín, and H.-P. Schwefel, editors, *Parallel Problem Solving from Nature PPSN VII*, volume 2439 of *Lecture Notes in Computer Science*, pages 33–43. Springer Berlin / Heidelberg, 2002.

[16] T. Jansen and I. Wegener. Evolutionary algorithms - how to cope with plateaus of constant fitness and when to reject strings of the same fitness. *IEEE Transactions on Evolutionary Computation*, 5(6):589–599, 2001.

[17] I. Maden, A. S. Uyar, and E. Özcan. Landscape analysis of simple perturbative hyper-heuristics. In *Mendel 2009: 15th International Conference on Soft Computing*, pages 16–22, 2009.

[18] M. Mısır. Group decision making in hyper-heuristics. Master's thesis, Department of Computer Engineering, Yeditepe University, 2008.

[19] M. Mitchell, S. Forrest, and J. H. Holland. The royal road for genetic algorithms: Fitness landscapes and GA performance. In F. J. Varela and P. Bourgine, editors, *Proceedings of the First European Conference on Artificial Life, 1991*, pages 245–254, Paris, 11–13 1992. MIT Press.

[20] R. Motwani and P. Raghavan. *Randomized Algorithms*. Cambridge University Press, 1995.

[21] A. Nareyek. Choosing search heuristics by non-stationary reinforcement learning. In M. G. C. Resende, J. P. de Sousa, and A. Viana, editors, *Metaheuristics*, pages 523–544. Kluwer Academic Publishers, Norwell, MA, USA, 2004.

[22] F. Neumann and C. Witt. *Bioinspired Computation in Combinatorial Optimization: Algorithms and Their Computational Complexity*. Springer-Verlag New York, Inc., New York, NY, USA, 1st edition, 2010.

[23] G. Ochoa, R. Qu, and E. K. Burke. Analyzing the landscape of a graph based hyper-heuristic for timetabling problems. In *Proceedings of the 11th Annual conference on Genetic and evolutionary computation*, GECCO '09, pages 341–348, New York, NY, USA, 2009. ACM.

[24] G. Ochoa, J. A. Vázquez-Rodríguez, S. Petrovic, and E. Burke. Dispatching rules for production scheduling: a hyper-heuristic landscape analysis. In *Proceedings of the Eleventh conference on Congress on Evolutionary Computation*, CEC'09, pages 1873–1880, Piscataway, NJ, USA, 2009. IEEE Press.

[25] E. Özcan, B. Bilgin, and E. E. Korkmaz. A comprehensive analysis of hyper-heuristics. *Intelligent Data Analysis*, 12:3–23, 2008.

[26] E. Özcan, M. Mısır, G. Ochoa, and E. Burke. A reinforcement learning – great-deluge hyper-heuristic for examination timetabling. *International Journal of Applied Metaheuristic Computing (IJAMC)*, 1(1):39–59, 2010.

[27] D. Pisinger and S. Ropke. A general heuristic for vehicle routing problems. *Computers and Operations Research*, 34:2403– 2435, 2007.

[28] P. Ross. Hyper-heuristics. In E. K. Burke and G. Kendall, editors, *Search Methodologies: Introductory Tutorials in Optimization and Decision Support Techniques*, chapter 17, pages 529–556. Springer, 2005.

[29] T. Storch and I. Wegener. Real royal road functions for constant population size. *Theoretical Computer Science*, 320(1):123–134, 2004.

A Measure-Theoretic Analysis of Stochastic Optimization

Alan J. Lockett
Department of Computer Science
Univers ty of Texas
Austin, TX, USA
alockett@cs.utexas.edu

Risto Miikkulainen
Department of Computer Science
University of Texas
Austin, TX, USA
risto@cs.utexas.edu

ABSTRACT

This paper proposes a measure-theoretic framework to study iterative stochastic optimizers that provides theoretical tools to explore how the optimization methods may be improved. Within this framework, optimizers form a closed, convex subset of a normed vector space, implying the existence of a distance metric between any two optimizers and a meaningful and computable spectrum of new optimizers between them. It is shown how the formalism applies to evolutionary algorithms in general. The analytic property of continuity is studied in the context of genetic algorithms, revealing the conditions under which approximations such as meta-modeling or surrogate methods may be effective. These results demonstrate the power of the proposed analytic framework, which can be used to propose and analyze new techniques such as controlled convex combinations of optimizers, meta-optimization of algorithm parameters, and more.

Categories and Subject Descriptors

I.2.6 [**Artificial Intelligence**]: Learning; I.2.m [**Artificial Intelligence**]: Miscellaneous—*evolutionary computation, theory of optimization*

Keywords

Evolutionary computation, genetic algorithms, stochastic optimization, theory of genetic algorithms, optimizer space, population-based optimizers, functional analysis

1. INTRODUCTION AND MOTIVATION

Although particular evolutionary algorithms have been studied formally in great detail, there have been relatively few attempts to provide a unified framework that would allow meaningful formal comparisons between different evolutionary techniques, leading to improved methods. The work of Vose on Random Heuristic Search (RHS) is an important exception [17, 18], but it is limited to finite, discrete spaces, is primarily algebraic in nature, and is most commonly applied to genetic algorithms. This paper outlines a new formal approach to the study of optimization algorithms more generally as mathematical objects. It accommodates arbitrary Borel-measurable spaces and applies to all iterative optimization algorithms, although the particular focus in this paper is on evolutionary algorithms optimizing static (e.g. non-dynamic, deterministic) fitness functions.

This formalization leads to several interesting conclusions. First, in the proposed analysis, a variety of algebraic operations are defined that can be used to create new algorithms; these operators also characterize the space of optimization algorithms as an infinite-dimensional vector space, complete with formal definitions of distance and continuity. Second, the framework subsumes almost all evolutionary algorithms that are commonly used for optimization; it will be demonstrated how several evolutionary algorithms can be instantiated within the framework. Third, within this framework, it is possible to prove that techniques such as meta-modeling and fitness surrogates [4, 7] should perform well for most optimizers, since most of the common evolutionary algorithms are continuous almost surely, a fundamental result that means that approximations of fitness functions or optimizers behave like the approximated quantities. This paper addresses each of these three topics in sequence below.

2. THE OPTIMIZATION PROBLEM

An optimization problem will be denoted formally as a tuple (f, X), where f is a fitness function and X is the (potentially constrained) search domain over which f is to be optimized. Without loss of generality, optimization is assumed to be synonymous with minimization; a function f can be maximized by minimizing its additive inverse $-f$. This study makes the following assumptions about the nature of the search space and the fitness function:

The search space is a topological space (X, τ) where X is the collection of possible solutions and τ is a given topology [12]. Topologies are mainly used to reason about issues such as continuity, limits, and nearness without reference to distance metrics.

In addition, the search space is a measurable space $(X, \mathcal{B}_\tau)$, where $\mathcal{B}_\tau$ is the Borel σ-algebra on the topology τ. A σ-algebra on a space X is a set of subsets of X that can be measured [2, 3, 6]. That is, they preserve certain intuitive notions about volume or area. For instance, if any two subsets of X can be measured, then so can their union, intersection, and complements. The Borel σ-algebra is the smallest σ-algebra under which the open and closed sets of the topology are measurable.

These requirements are quite broad and accommodate all familiar spaces on which optimization is performed, including binary strings, real vectors, neural networks, graphs, state machines, and programs.

The objective function is drawn from the space of real functions on X, denoted $\mathbb{R}^X$. The topology of pointwise convergence is assumed for this function space. Under this topology, a set of functions $\{f_n\}$ converges to a function f if and only if $f_n(x) \to f(x)$ for all $x \in X$. When a σ-algebra on $\mathbb{R}$ is required, the standard Borel σ-algebra for the Euclidean topology is assumed [2, 6].

The formalization below is based on measure theory. A *measure* is a set function (usually nonnegative) that assigns a volume to each set in a σ-algebra. A *probability measure* is a measure μ that additionally has $\mu(X) = 1$. Lebesgue integration over a real function with respect to a measure sums up the measure of the level sets of the function. A function f is measurable if the sets $\{x : f(x) \leq y\}$ are contained in $\mathcal{B}_\tau$ for all $y \in \mathbb{R}$. It is integrable on a measure μ if $\int_X |f|\, d\mu < \infty$ [3, 6]. For a given measure μ, the search space is a measure space, written as $(X, \mathcal{B}_\tau, \mu)$. In Euclidean space, μ is assumed to be the Lebesgue measure, the familiar measure of volume.

With this background, the space of iterative stochastic optimizers can now be defined.

3. OPTIMIZER SPACE

In order to state theorems that can encompass the vast majority of optimization methods, these methods must belong to a common mathematical space. Such a space can be found by examining the defining characteristic of iterative optimizers, namely, the iterative sequence of points they produce.

3.1 Stochastic Iterative Optimizers

At its core, an iterative optimizer follows a trajectory through the search domain. At each point in time, it observes the fitness value of each point along the trajectory so far and uses this information to propose one or more points to add to the trajectory, with the goal that later points in the trajectory should have better fitness. The internal structure of the fitness function is known only to a limited extent. Thus the iterative optimizer must propose new points to evaluate based only upon the current trajectory and its fitness evaluations. The distinguishing feature of a particular method is the mechanism that it uses in order to propose new points (e.g. how it creates new populations). Most non-analytic optimization methods follow an iterative process matching this general description.

Optimization has been studied from this perspective before in the context of No Free Lunch (NFL) theorems. Radcliffe and Surry presented such a formalization in 1995 [13], followed by Wolpert and Macready in 1997 [19]. Similar formalizations have been used broadly since that time [16, 1, 14], but always with the goal of studying NFL. With some modifications and generalizations, however, the same techniques can be used on its own in order to study theoretical questions about optimization methods.

Formally, recall that the fitness functions are drawn from the space $\mathbb{R}^X$, where X is the search domain. Let $\mathcal{T}[X]$ be the space of finite sequences with arbitrary length on X. Elements of $\mathcal{T}[X]$ will be referred to as *trajectories* or *evaluation histories*, and the entries in a trajectory will be indexed with superscripts, i.e. t^i is the ith entry in the sequence t.[1] Negative superscripts will be used to index the trajectory from right to left, e.g. t^{-1} is the last element of the trajectory t. The notation $|t|$ will be used to refer to the length of the trajectory t, and $\emptyset$ will refer to the trajectory of length zero. Let $\mathcal{P}[X] = \mathcal{P}[X, \mathcal{B}_\tau]$ be the space of probability measures on the search domain X that are measurable with respect to the Borel σ-algebra $\mathcal{B}_\tau$.

Definition 1. A *stochastic iterative optimizer* is a function $\mathcal{G} : \mathcal{T}[X] \times \mathbb{R}^X \to \mathcal{P}[X]$. Let the space of all such optimizers be denoted by $\mathcal{PF} = \mathcal{PF}[X]$ (an abbreviation for *probability-valued functions*).

To make the meaning of these formal objects clear, consider how the optimizer $\mathcal{G}$ is applied to an example optimization problem (f, X). For concreteness, suppose that $\mathcal{G}$ implements a $(1+1)$–ES, and let the search domain be the real line, $X = \mathbb{R}$. Let the $(1+1)$–ES use Gaussian mutation with a fixed variance σ^2. The first step is to sample an initial point z_1 by sampling $z_1 \sim \mathcal{G}[\emptyset, f]$. In this case $\mathcal{G}[\emptyset, f]$ is an initial distribution, for example, a standard Gaussian. Then $f(z_1)$ is observed, and a new point z_2 is sampled from $\mathcal{G}[(z_1), f]$. In particular, $\mathcal{G}[(z_1), f]$ is a Gaussian centered at z_1 with variance σ^2. The process continues iteratively, and new points $z_3, z_4, z_5, \ldots$ are sampled one at a time, with $z_n \sim \mathcal{G}[(z_1, \ldots, z_{n-1}), f]$. For the $(1+1)$–ES, $\mathcal{G}[(z_1, \ldots, z_{n-1}), f]$ is a Gaussian distribution with variance σ^2 centered at

$$\mathrm{argmax}_{x \in \{z_1, \ldots, z_{n-1}\}} f(x). \tag{1}$$

The discussion so far raises two questions about the selected formalism. First, why is the optimizer passed a full copy of the fitness function f, when in fact the $(1+1)$–ES depends only on the fitness evaluation of the points $z_1, z_2, \ldots$? Other similar formulations (e.g. [13, 19]) define an optimization algorithm to depend only on the value of the fitness function at the evaluation points thus far, e.g. $f(z_1), f(z_2), \ldots$. The more general definition here accounts for optimization methods that might look at features of the fitness evaluation other than just the fitness value, such as the derivatives of the fitness function, or statistics gathered during a simulation. Some evolutionary algorithms, such as Novelty Search [9], do indeed use such features to guide their exploration of the search domain.

The second question is how this formalization can account for evolutionary methods that use population sizes larger than one; this question is addressed in the next section.

3.2 Population-Based Optimizers

Evolutionary methods generate entire populations, not individual points, so the choice in the previous section to use probability distribution over individual points may seem unusual. However, each population is nothing more than a collection of points. A population can be generated by sampling the new set of points one at a time with the appropriate dependency relationships. It is entirely correct to approach evolutionary algorithms from a probabilistic perspective, since the underlying probability distribution governing these methods is nothing other than the mechanism

[1] The subscript notation, e.g. t_n, is reserved for sequences of trajectories, used in Section 8 to obtain continuity results.

by which the next population is created from previous populations with random variations.

A population-based optimizer $\mathcal{G}$ with population size $K > 0$ can be represented as a sequence of K separate optimizers $\mathcal{G}_1, \cdots, \mathcal{G}_K$ (not necessarily distinct), each of which is used to generate one individual per population. A trajectory can then be broken up into populations, with one optimizer assigned to each slot in the population. A population-based optimizer is given by $\mathcal{G}[t, f] = \mathcal{G}_{k(t)}[t, f]$, where $k(t) \equiv 1 + (|t| \mod K)$ is the index of the individual in the population currently being constructed. The function $k(t)$ will be used repeatedly below.

A population may be treated as an element in the product space X^K consisting of K copies of the search domain X. A trajectory $t \in \mathcal{T}[X]$ can be broken up into a history of populations $H = h^1, h^2, h^3, \cdots$ with $h^i \in X^K$ using the mapping $h^{i,k} = t^{(i-1)K+k+1}$, recalling that trajectories are indexed with superscripts. Let $H(t)$ be the history of complete populations in the trajectory t, so that $H(t)$ ignores any elements in t with index greater than $\lfloor |t|/K \rfloor$. Then $H(t)$ is a trajectory over populations, i.e. $H(t) \in \mathcal{T}\left[X^K\right]$. To complete the setup, let $\text{traj}(H)$ convert a population history $H \in \mathcal{T}\left[X^K\right]$ to a trajectory in $\mathcal{T}[X]$ via the mapping $\text{traj}(H)^j = H^{\lfloor j/K \rfloor, 1+(j \mod K)}$. Then $\text{traj}(H(t)) = t$ if and only if the length of t is a multiple of K, i.e. $|t| = K\lfloor |t|/K \rfloor$; otherwise, it truncates the end of t at the last population boundary. The notation $\mathcal{G}[H(t), f]$ may be used to mean $\mathcal{G}[\text{traj}(H(t)), f]$ when this notation is clear from the context.

A population-based optimizer is distinguished by the fact that it respects the population boundary, and new populations can only be generated based on information available from prior populations.

Definition 2. An optimizer $\mathcal{G} \in \mathcal{PF}$ is a *population-based optimizer* with population size K if $\mathcal{G}[t_1, f] = \mathcal{G}[t_2, f]$ whenever $f(t_1^{i_1}) = f(t_2^{i_2})$ for all $1 \leq i_j \leq |t_j| - k(t_j)$, where $k(t)$ is computed for population size K.

That is, to be a population-based optimizer, an optimizer must be able to evaluate points in parallel. The space of all population-based optimizers of population size K will be denoted by $\mathcal{PBO}_K$.

The simplest way for an optimizer to be population-based is if the optimizer does not depend on the objective at all.

Definition 3. An optimizer $\mathcal{G} \in \mathcal{PF}$ is *objective-agnostic* if $\mathcal{G}[t, f] = \mathcal{G}[t, g]$ for all $f, g \in \mathbb{R}^X$.

Most algorithms in evolutionary and natural computation depend on the objective only through the fitness evaluations along the evaluation history, i.e. on $f(x)$ for $x \in t$. Such an algorithms will be termed *trajectory-restricted.*

Definition 4. An optimizer $\mathcal{G} \in \mathcal{PF}$ is *trajectory-restricted* if $\mathcal{G}[t, f] = \mathcal{G}[t, g]$ whenever $f(x) = g(x)$ for all $x \in t$.

The set of trajectory-restricted optimizers corresponds directly to the set of optimizers usually studied for the NFL theorems [19, 14]. Most evolutionary algorithms are trajectory-restricted population-based optimizers. The following example will illustrate these concepts.

3.3 Example: Simulated Annealing

Simulated annealing [8] is a widely used optimization method that can be formalized as a population-based optimizer with population size 2. At each non-initial time step for simulated annealing, there is an accepted solution x, and a new solution y is proposed. The objective value $f(y)$ is computed, and y replaces x as the accepted solution with probability

$$A(y, x, f, T) = \exp\left(\frac{1}{T}\left[f(x) - f(y)\right]\right) \wedge 1, \qquad (2)$$

where T is the temperature parameter of simulated annealing and the infix operator $\wedge$ indicates the minimum of its arguments, so that y is always accepted if $f(y) < f(x)$. Clearly, simulated annealing is trajectory-restricted. For this formalization, the population for simulated annealing consists of the accepted and proposed solutions.

Simulated annealing generates the proposed solution from a space-dependent *proposal distribution.* For this example, let the search domain be the real line, $X = \mathbb{R}$, with a multivariate Gaussian as the proposal distribution, $\mathcal{N}\langle \mu, \sigma^2 \rangle$, for some fixed positive number $\sigma \in \mathbb{R}$. Let the trajectory t store the accepted solution and the proposed solution in alternation, so that each point t^n in the trajectory is the accepted solution at the $\lfloor \frac{n}{2} \rfloor^{th}$ time step if n is odd, and the proposed solution if n is even. Then set $\mu = t^{-1}$, the last accepted solution in the trajectory. Then the proposal distribution is

$$\mathcal{P}[t, f] = \mathcal{N} < t^{-1}, I > . \qquad (3)$$

Given a proposed y and an accepted solution x, simulated annealing performs a Bernoulli trial to determine whether to accept y or keep x. Let $\mathcal{B}\langle p, y, x \rangle$ be a Bernoulli distribution that produces y with probability p and x with probability $1 - p$. The acceptance step for simulated annealing is then

$$\mathcal{A}[t, f] = \mathcal{B}\langle A(t^{-1}, t^{-2}, f, T(|t|/2)), t^{-1}, t^{-2} \rangle, \qquad (4)$$

recalling that t^{-1} contains the proposal and t^{-2} the accepted solution. The temperature $T(n)$ is assumed to be a function of the length of the trajectory, commonly $T(n) = 1/\log n$.

Simulated annealing can thus be viewed as a population-based optimizer $\mathcal{SA}$ of size 2 with $\mathcal{SA}_1 = \mathcal{A}$ and $\mathcal{SA}_2 = \mathcal{P}$. The starting population (t_1, t_2) is initialized randomly, and thenceforth $\mathcal{SA}_1$ and $\mathcal{SA}_2$ are used in alternation to accept and propose solutions.

The profusion of symbols in this example may seem unnecessary at first. However, the formalism makes it possible to compare simulated annealing directly with other optimization methods in a way that pseudocode does not allow. For instance, the classic $(1+1)$–ES is formally the norm-limit of $\mathcal{SA}$ as the temperature schedule goes to zero.

In addition, the simulated annealing example makes use of several components and techniques that will be used in defining evolutionary algorithms. The proposal distribution $\mathcal{P}$ plays the role of a mutation operator in evolutionary methods, randomly altering a previously evaluated point. The acceptance optimizer $\mathcal{A}$ mirrors the role of selection in evolutionary methods. The formal elements of evolutionary algorithms will be explored further in Section 6, after some required notation is introduced in Section 3.4.

3.4 Notation and Conventions

This subsection completes the notation and conventions that will be used throughout the subsequent text. Optimizers will typically be denoted by capital cursive letters, usually by $\mathcal{G}$. The expression $\mathcal{G}[t,f]$ will be used to refer to the probability measure corresponding to a trajectory $t \in \mathcal{T}[X]$ and a fitness function $f \in \mathbb{R}^X$. Accordingly, $\mathcal{G}[t,f](A)$ indicates the probability that the next point will lie inside of a set A contained in the σ-algebra $\mathcal{B}_\tau$. The notation $\mathcal{G}[t,f](dx)$ represents a quantity that can be integrated over A in the Lebesgue sense to obtain $\mathcal{G}[t,f](A) = \int_A \mathcal{G}[t,f](dx)$.

Fitness functions $f \in \mathbb{R}^X$ are assumed to have a finite minimum, denoted by $f^* = \inf_X f(x) > -\infty$. For the purposes of the present study, unbounded functions in $\mathbb{R}^X$ may be ignored without causing a problem.

Only static, single-objective fitness functions are considered in this theory. The formalism could be expanded to accommodate either dynamic or stochastic objective functions, but these adaptations would yield separate results and would complicate the discussion that follows. Unless mentioned or otherwise clear from context, the terms *optimization* and *optimum* should be interpreted as *minimization* and *minimum* in the remainder of the paper.

As mentioned above, trajectories will be indexed using superscripts, so that t^n indicates the nth evaluation point in t, with indices starting at 1 for the initial point. Negative superscripts index the trajectory backwards, so that t^{-1} is the last point in t, t^{-2} the next to last, and so on. Subscripts on trajectories indicate a sequence of trajectories, so that e.g. t_n is not a point, but an entire sequence of points. Thus t_n^m represents a particular point within a sequence of evaluation histories. Two trajectories can be concatenated to form a longer trajectory, denoted by a union operator, e.g. $t = t_1 \cup t_2$. An element $x \in X$ can also be appended to a trajectory, denoted similarly by $t = t_1 \cup x$. The notation $t \cup \left(\bigcup_{i=1}^K x_i\right)$ indicates successive concatenation, i.e. $t \cup x_1 \cup x_2 \cup \cdots \cup x_K$. Given a sequence $(x_n)_{n=1}^\infty$, the expression $(x_n)_{n=1}^N$ represents a trajectory of length N, and $(x_n)_{n=1}^0 = \emptyset$ by convention. In addition to indexing, the notation $x \in t$ will be used to indicate that x is an arbitrary point occurring at some point in t, i.e., $x = t^n$ for some n.

As discussed in Section 3.2, the notation $H(t)$ is used to convert a trajectory in $\mathcal{T}[X]$ to a trajectory in $\mathcal{T}[X^K]$ for some fixed K that will be clear from the context. When this is done, $H(t)^n$ refers to the nth entry of $H(t)$, an element of X^K, and $H(t)^{n,k}$ refers to the kth component of the nth entry, an element of X.

Consider the process of running an optimizer $\mathcal{G} \in \mathcal{PF}$ on an objective function f. First, the trajectory is initialized to $t_0 = \emptyset$. Then, a point $x_1 \in X$ is sampled from $\mathcal{G}[t_0,f]$. This population is appended to t_0 to create $t_1 = t_0 \cup x_1$. Next, a population x_2 is sampled from $\mathcal{G}[t_1,f]$ and appended to t_1 to form $t_2 = t_1 \cup x_2$. The process continues until a stopping criterion is reached. Thus in actual practice the trajectory t is sampled progressively from the optimizer $\mathcal{G}$, and the trajectory takes on random values. This random sequence of evaluation points is a stochastic process, termed the *optimization process*, denoted by $Z = (Z_n)_{n\in\mathbb{N}}$. The process Z is said to be *generated by* $\mathcal{G}$ on f.

With the basic formalism now presented, the Sections 4 and 5 will expand these fundamentals with definitions and constructive operators that make it possible to describe more complex optimizers in Section 6 and 7 and to prove theorems about them in Section 8.

4. ALGEBRAIC OPERATIONS

Optimizers can be combined or altered algebraically to form a new optimizer in several ways. In this section, mechanisms for algebraically combining operators are discussed. These operations will be used extensively to provide formal representations of evolutionary algorithms in Section 6.

4.1 Convolution

The first operator will be termed convolution due to its similarity to the convolution of two functions. In this case, two optimizers are convolved to produce a third optimizer, and the constituent parts may or may not be practical optimizers on their own. The convolution operator, denoted by $\star$, is defined by the equation

$$(\mathcal{G}_1 \star \mathcal{G}_2)[t,f](A) \equiv \int_X \mathcal{G}_2[t \cup x, f](A)\; \mathcal{G}_1[t,f](dx). \quad (5)$$

Convolution performs the intuitive function of applying two probability distributions in sequence. First, a point is sampled from $\mathcal{G}_1$, and then a point is sampled from $\mathcal{G}_2$ given the outcome of sampling $\mathcal{G}_1$. In fact, the entire process of stochastic optimization described in the previous sections boils down to the successive application of the convolution operator, so that if $(Z_n)_{n\in\mathbb{N}}$ is generated by $\mathcal{G}$, then $(Z_{2n})_{n\in\mathbb{N}}$ is generated by $\mathcal{G}\star\mathcal{G}$. In general, $Z_n \sim (\bigstar_{m=1}^n \mathcal{G})[\emptyset, f]$ when $Z \sim \mathcal{G}_f$, where $\bigstar_{m=1}^n \mathcal{G}$ represents n successive applications of convolution. When two or more convolution operators are used, convolution is assumed to be left associative, e.g. $\mathcal{G}_1 \star \mathcal{G}_2 \star \mathcal{G}_3 = (\mathcal{G}_1 \star \mathcal{G}_2) \star \mathcal{G}_3$. Because convolution is not necessarily commutative, right association is not equal to left association, and so the postfix notation $(\mathcal{G}\bigstar_{m=1}^n)$ will indicate chained right associations, e.g. $\mathcal{G}_1 \star (\mathcal{G}_2 \star \mathcal{G}_3)$. The description of evolutionary algorithms in particular can be substantially simplified by the use of the convolution operator. For example, a genetic algorithm may be described as the convolution of selection, crossover, and mutation distributions.

4.2 Trajectory Truncation

Sometimes an optimizer will ignore one or more elements of the evaluation history. This property is particularly important for population-based optimizers, which often ignore the previously generated members of the current population. Define trajectory truncation by the symbol $\triangleleft$ so that

$$(\triangleleft\mathcal{G})[t \cup x, f] = \mathcal{G}[t,f], \quad (6)$$

with the base case $(\triangleleft\mathcal{G})[\emptyset,f] = \mathcal{G}[\emptyset,f]$. This operator can be applied to the same optimizer more than once. The notation $\triangleleft_k\mathcal{G}$ will be used to represent the optimizer resulting from $k \geq 0$ applications of trajectory truncation, with $\triangleleft_0\mathcal{G} \equiv \mathcal{G}$.

4.3 Pointwise Scalar Multiplication

Define pointwise scalar multiplication so that

$$(\alpha\mathcal{G})[t,f](A) \equiv \alpha(\mathcal{G}[t,f](A)) \quad (7)$$

for $\alpha \in \mathbb{R}$. It is clear that $\alpha\mathcal{G}$ is not a member of $\mathcal{PF}$ for $\alpha \neq 1$, since $\alpha\mathcal{G}[t,f](X) = \alpha$ and $\alpha\mathcal{G}[t,f]$ is not a probability distribution. However, $\alpha\mathcal{G}$ is a member of a larger space that will be introduced in Section 5 below.

4.4 Pointwise Addition

Define pointwise addition so that

$$(\mathcal{G}_1 + \mathcal{G}_2)[t,f](A) \equiv \mathcal{G}_1[t,f](A) + \mathcal{G}_2[t,f](A). \quad (8)$$

As with scalar multiplication, it is clear that $\mathcal{G}_1 + \mathcal{G}_2$ is not contained within $\mathcal{PF}$, but the operation is well-defined nonetheless and is used below.

4.5 Convex Combination

Optimizers can be combined convexly to form new operators using the basic operations of pointwise addition and pointwise scalar multiplication. Used by themselves, these two operations are not closed on $\mathcal{PF}$, but their convex combinations are closed.

Let $\alpha \in [0,1]$ and consider $\mathcal{G} = \alpha\mathcal{G}_1 + (1-\alpha)\mathcal{G}_2$. Then $\mathcal{G}[t,f]$ is always a probability distribution, so $\mathcal{G} \in \mathcal{PF}$. More generally, choose $\alpha_1, \dots \alpha_n$ in $[0,1]$ such that $\sum_i \alpha_i = 1$, and suppose that $\mathcal{G}_1, \dots, \mathcal{G}_n$ are optimizers. Then $\mathcal{G} = \sum_i \alpha_i \mathcal{G}_i$ is a convex combination of $\mathcal{G}_1, \dots, \mathcal{G}_n$, and $\mathcal{G} \in \mathcal{PF}$. So $\mathcal{PF}$ is closed under convex combination.

To emphasize, $\mathcal{PF}$ is a convex space, i.e. it is closed under convex combinations. For any $\mathcal{G}_1, \dots, \mathcal{G}_n$ contained in any one of these spaces, all convex combinations also lie inside the same space.

The fact that $\mathcal{PF}$ is convex is the first part of a larger result. In fact, $\mathcal{PF}$ is a closed, convex subset of a normed vector space, which means that the space of optimizers is continuous and linear. This topic is explored next.

5. A NORMED VECTOR SPACE

Iterative stochastic optimizers are vectors in an appropriate vector space under the vector operations of pointwise scalar multiplication and pointwise addition. A vector space is continuous and linear, meaning that one can make arbitrarily small perturbations of one vector in the direction of any other vector. Such spaces have a regular structure that is easily manipulated in order to prove theorems. The vector space of optimizers consists of functionals that take a trajectory and a fitness function and return a signed measure.

5.1 Vector Space

A *vector space*, also termed a *linear space*, is a space in which each element (called a *vector*) can be scaled to form a line through scalar multiplication or added to another element to obtain a third element also contained in the space. The multiplication and addition operations must satisfy certain requirements, namely: addition needs to be commutative and invertible; an identity must exist for each operation; and multiplication must distribute over addition. A *normed vector space* additionally possesses a *norm*, which assigns an absolute magnitude to each element in the space and can be used to generate a distance metric. The space of optimizers $\mathcal{PF}$ can be used to generate a normed vector space by extending it to include the closure of $\mathcal{PF}$ under scalar multiplication and pointwise addition.

5.2 Measure-Valued Functionals

For $\mathcal{G} \in \mathcal{PF}$ and $\alpha \neq 1$, the pseudo-optimizer $\alpha\mathcal{G}$ fails to be in $\mathcal{PF}$ only because $\alpha\mathcal{G}[t,f](X) = \alpha \neq 1$. Although $\alpha\mathcal{G}[t,f]$ is not a probability measure, it is a measure. A *finite signed measure* is a set-valued function defined over a σ-algebra that is additive on disjoint sets. It may take on both positive and negative values, but must be finite on every set in the σ-algebra. Denote by $\mathcal{M}[X] = \mathcal{M}[X, \mathcal{B}_\tau]$ the space of all finite signed measures on $(X, \mathcal{B}_\tau)$. The space $\mathcal{M}[X]$ is a Banach space, a complete, normed vector space. The standard norm for $\mathcal{M}[X]$ is the *total variation norm*, which is the largest absolute measure assigned to any set in the σ-algebra, $||\mu||_\mathcal{M} \equiv \sup_{A\in\mathcal{B}_\tau} |\mu(A)|$.

The space of probability measures $\mathcal{P}[X]$ is a closed, convex subset of $\mathcal{M}[X]$. Although all probability measures have a total variation norm of 1 by definition, the difference of two probability measures is well defined and non-trivial. This difference defines a distance metric on probability measures,

$$d(\mathbb{P},\mathbb{Q}) = ||\mathbb{P}-\mathbb{Q}||_\mathcal{M} = \sup_{A\in\mathcal{B}_\tau} |\mathbb{P}(A) - \mathbb{Q}(A)| \qquad (9)$$

for probability measures $\mathbb{P}$ and $\mathbb{Q}$. Intuitively, the distance between two probability measures is determined by the set to which the two measures assign the largest difference in probability mass.

Now define the functional space

$$\mathcal{MF}_0 = \mathcal{MF}_0[X] = \left\{\mathcal{G} : \mathcal{T}[X] \times \mathbb{R}^X \to \mathcal{M}[X]\right\}, \qquad (10)$$

where $\mathcal{MF}$ stands for *measure-valued functionals.* The space $\mathcal{MF}_0$ contains $\mathcal{PF}$, but it also contains many other objects as well. An element in $\mathcal{MF}_0$ is a function that produces a finite signed measure over the search space when given any finite trajectory and any fitness function. Define vector operations in $\mathcal{MF}_0$ pointwise as for $\mathcal{PF}$. These vector operations satisfy the required vector properties. The zero vector for $\mathcal{MF}_0$ is the function that returns the zero measure on all inputs. So $\mathcal{MF}_0$ is a vector space. In fact, $\mathcal{MF}_0$ is just the vector closure of $\mathcal{PF}$ under the operations of pointwise scalar multiplication and addition.

The next step is to find a norm for $\mathcal{MF}_0$ to compare the distance between optimizers. A norm can be created from

$$||\mathcal{G}||_{\mathcal{MF}} = \sup_{t\in\mathcal{T}, f\in\mathbb{R}^X} ||\mathcal{G}[t,f]||_\mathcal{M}. \qquad (11)$$

The function $||\cdot||_{\mathcal{MF}}$ satisfies all the properties of a norm with the exception that it is not bounded on $\mathcal{MF}_0$. However, the subset of $\mathcal{MF}_0$ on which it is finite forms a vector subspace $\mathcal{MF}_0$ that contains $\mathcal{PF}$. To this end, define

$$\mathcal{MF} \equiv \{\mathcal{G} \in \mathcal{MF}_0 : ||\mathcal{G}||_{\mathcal{MF}} < \infty\}.$$

THEOREM 5.1. *$\mathcal{MF}$ is a normed vector subspace of $\mathcal{MF}_0$ under $||\cdot||_{\mathcal{MF}}$.*

PROOF. The vector space structure of $\mathcal{MF}_0$ has already been discussed. To see that $||\cdot||_{\mathcal{MF}}$ is a norm, note that for $\mathcal{G} \in \mathcal{MF}$, $\alpha \in \mathbb{R}$,

$$||\alpha\mathcal{G}||_{\mathcal{MF}} = \sup_{t,f} ||\alpha\mathcal{G}||_\mathcal{M} = |\alpha|\, ||\mathcal{G}||_{\mathcal{MF}}.$$

Additionally, if $\mathcal{G} \neq 0$, there exist t, f s.t. $||\mathcal{G}[t,f]||_\mathcal{M} > 0$, so $||\mathcal{G}||_{\mathcal{MF}} > 0$ as well. For the triangle inequality,

$$||\mathcal{G}_1 + \mathcal{G}_2||_{\mathcal{MF}} = \sup_{t\in\mathcal{T}, f\in\mathbb{R}^X} ||\mathcal{G}_1[t,f] + \mathcal{G}_2[t,f]||_\mathcal{M} \qquad (12)$$

$$\leq \sup_{t\in\mathcal{T}, f\in\mathbb{R}^X} ||\mathcal{G}_1[t,f]||_\mathcal{M} + ||\mathcal{G}_2[t,f]||_\mathcal{M} \qquad (13)$$

$$\leq \sup_{t\in\mathcal{T}, f\in\mathbb{R}^X} ||\mathcal{G}_1[t,f]||_\mathcal{M} + \sup_{t\in\mathcal{T}, f\in\mathbb{R}^X} ||\mathcal{G}_2[t,f]||_\mathcal{M} \qquad (14)$$

$$= ||\mathcal{G}_1||_{\mathcal{MF}} + ||\mathcal{G}_2||_{\mathcal{MF}} < \infty. \qquad (15)$$

So $||\cdot||_{\mathcal{MF}}$ is indeed a norm.

$\mathcal{MF}$ is a vector subspace because it contains the zero vector and is closed under vector addition and scalar multiplication. □

It may be asked whether $\mathcal{MF}$ is complete and therefore Banach. The answer is no; it is easy to create sequences in $\mathcal{MF}$ with an unbounded norm in the limit. However, this fact will not be particularly restrictive for the purpose of analysis, since the iterative stochastic optimizers form a closed subset of $\mathcal{MF}$.

PROPOSITION 5.2. *$\mathcal{PF}$ is a closed, convex subset of $\mathcal{MF}$.*

PROOF. First of all, if $\mathcal{G} \in \mathcal{PF}$ then $||\mathcal{G}||_{\mathcal{MF}} = 1 < \infty$, so $\mathcal{PF} \subseteq \mathcal{MF}$. To show that $\mathcal{PF}$ is closed, let $||\mathcal{G}_n - \mathcal{G}||_{\mathcal{MF}} \to 0$ for $(\mathcal{G}_n) \subseteq \mathcal{PF}$. Then for all t, f, $||\mathcal{G}_n[t,f] - \mathcal{G}[t,f]||_{\mathcal{M}} \to 0$, and for all $A \in \mathcal{B}_{\tau}$,

$$\mathcal{G}[t,f](X) = \lim_n \mathcal{G}_n[t,f](X) = 1, \quad (16)$$

$$\mathcal{G}[t,f](A) = \lim_n \mathcal{G}_n[t,f](A) \geq 0. \quad (17)$$

That is, $\mathcal{G}[t,f]$ is a probability measure, so $\mathcal{G} \in \mathcal{PF}$.

To establish convexity, let $\mathcal{G}_1, \mathcal{G}_2 \in \mathcal{PF}$, and let $\alpha \in [0,1]$. Set $\mathcal{G} = \alpha\mathcal{G}_1 + (1-\alpha)\mathcal{G}_2$. Then for all t, f, and A,

$$\mathcal{G}[t,f](X) = \alpha\mathcal{G}_1[t,f](X) + (1-\alpha)\mathcal{G}_2[t,f](X) = 1, \quad (18)$$

$$\mathcal{G}[t,f](A) = \alpha\mathcal{G}_1[t,f](A) + (1-\alpha)\mathcal{G}_2[t,f](A) \geq 0, \quad (19)$$

and therefore $\mathcal{G} \in \mathcal{PF}$. □

Thus iterative stochastic optimizers are vectors. There is a fixed numeric distance between any two computable optimizers, and there is a an entire spectrum of computable optimizers that progressively blend between them, no matter how different the optimizers in question may be. For example, there exists a unique optimizer that is exactly halfway between conjugate gradient descent and differential evolution. This insight is surprising and opens a fundamentally new way of looking at optimization methods. A sampling of how this theory of optimizers may be used to prove theorems about optimizers is given in Section 8, after specific discussion of how evolutionary algorithms fit into the formalism.

6. EVOLUTIONARY ALGORITHMS

In this section, the basic components of evolutionary algorithms are represented in the formal framework of the previous sections. This process demonstrates the formalization and lays the ground work to prove complex theorems, as is done in Section 8.

6.1 Evolutionary Algorithms Characteristics

The core characteristics of an evolutionary algorithm include competition within a population, preferential selection of competitive individuals, reproduction among selected individuals, and random variation of selected individuals. These four processes can be realized into evaluation, selection, recombination, and mutation phases. In the case of asexual reproduction, recombination may be vacuous. In formal terms, an evolutionary algorithm can be formalized as a convolution of three components, one each for selection, recombination, and mutation processes.

Each phase of an evolutionary algorithm can be described as an optimizer, just as the acceptance phase and proposal phase of simulated annealing were separated into two different components in Section 3.3. Thus evolutionary algorithms can be formalized by defining what principles make an optimizer work as a selection rule, a recombination operator, or a mutation operator. The optimizers representing each phase are not effective optimizers by themselves. The constituent components of an evolutionary algorithm are only optimizers in a formal sense, but these components represent genetic operators that can be mixed and matched mathematically to form new optimization methods.

6.2 Selection, Recombination, and Mutation

These three phases of an evolutionary algorithm may be thought of as intermediate steps, each of which creates a full population and hands it off to the next phase. Selection chooses K points from among the previously observed points. Recombination invokes one or more additional selection rules to tack on extra parents and then merges these parents with a crossover rule. This merged output of K individuals is then handed off to the mutation operator, which alters each individual independently. These three stages will now be discussed rigorously one at a time.

6.2.1 Selection Rules

Selection in evolutionary algorithms is a filtering task, characterized as follows: Given a set of previously observed individuals, select a group of K individuals to form the basis of the next population. The selection process must place zero weight on unobserved individuals; only members of the population history can be selected. Given a trajectory $t \in \mathcal{T}$, define the previously observed individuals in t as $P(t) = \{x \in X : \exists n \text{ s.t.} x = t^n\}$. Accounting for populations, a *selection rule* is an optimizer that places zero probability on any proposed population that would expand $P(t)$.

Definition 5. An optimizer $\mathcal{S} \in \mathcal{PBO}_K$ is a *selection rule* if $\mathcal{S}[t,f](A) = 0$ whenever $\exists x \in A$ s.t. $P(t \cup x) \neq P(t)$.

It may seem strange that the selection rule is allowed to select any member of $P(t)$ and not just the members of the last population ($P(H(t)^{-1})$). But there are a number of evolutionary methods that select members of populations prior to the last population, such as those using elitist selection. Methods that store the locally best individual (such as differential evolution) also need the flexibility to select from previous generations. Furthermore, several recently proposed techniques such as Novelty Search [9], Curiosity Search [15], and Evolutionary Annealing [10] store members from each population in an archive, making them available for selection.

6.2.2 Recombination and Crossover

Recombination combines some number of selected individuals as parents to form a hybrid child. Although traditional recombination methods in genetic algorithms utilize only two parents, other methods use an arbitrary number of parents. In evolution strategies, for example, intermediate crossover averages components across several solutions. A recombination operator first selects the parents for each member of the population and then invokes a crossover rule to combine the parents. The number of selected parents (usually just two) is said to be the *order* of the crossover rule and the recombination operator. Parent selection for an nth order operator stacks n populations on top of the current trajectory. A crossover rule consumes these n populations and leaves a single merged population in their place.

The key feature of a crossover rule is that it should combine only the selected parents. It should therefore be independent of all other components of the input trajectory. It should also ignore the fitness of the selected parents, deferring such judgments to the selection operators. For the kth

member of the population the selected parents in a crossover rule of order n are just the kth members of the previous n populations in the trajectory. Define the trajectory

$$\text{parents}(t, n, k, K) \equiv \bigcup_{i=1}^{n} H(t)^{-i,k}, \qquad (20)$$

recalling that $H(t)$ is the population history of t, negative indices count backwards from the end of the history, and the double index chooses the kth member of the $-i^{th}$ population. Then parents(t, n, k, K) is the reverse ordered list of the parents available to the crossover rule.

Definition 6. An objective-agnostic optimizer $\mathcal{C} \in \mathcal{PBO}_K$ is a crossover rule of order n if there exist $\mathcal{C}_1, \ldots, \mathcal{C}_K \in \mathcal{PF}$ such that $\mathcal{C}[t, f] = \mathcal{C}_{k(t)}[t, f]$ and for all $k = 1, \ldots, K$ and all $t_1, t_2 \in \mathcal{T}$, $\mathcal{C}_k [t_1, f] = \mathcal{C}_k [t_2, f]$ whenever

$$\text{parents}(t_1, n, k, K) = \text{parents}(t_2, n, k, K).$$

That is, a crossover rule is independent of all but the selected parents.

This definition of crossover accepts a wide range of instantiations that do not necessarily match the concept of crossover in a traditional genetic algorithm. This intuition will be restored with the introduction of crossover masks in Section 7. With crossover rules defined, the definition of a recombination operator can now be given.

Definition 7. An optimizer $\mathcal{R} \in \mathcal{PBO}_K$ is a recombination operator of order n if there exists a sequence of $n-1$ selection rules $\mathcal{S}_1, \ldots, \mathcal{S}_{n-1} \in \mathcal{PBO}_K$ and a crossover rule $\mathcal{C} \in \mathcal{PBO}_K$ of order n such that

$$\mathcal{R} = \triangleleft \mathcal{S}_1 \star (\triangleleft_2 \mathcal{S}_2 \star (\cdots \star (\triangleleft_{n-1} \mathcal{S}_{n-1} \star \mathcal{C}))).$$

Operationally, each of the selection rules $\mathcal{S}_i$ are applied in order, with the previous selection hidden by the trajectory-truncation operator. Finally, the crossover rule is invoked to combine the selected points, including the first point selected by an initial selection rule outside of the recombination operator. [2] The convolution is performed with right association so that the results of selection are stacked together and not consumed until the crossover rule is reached. Note that there is only one possible recombination operator of order 1, and it vacuously reproduces the selected population, representing asexual reproduction.

6.2.3 Mutation Operators

Mutation in evolutionary algorithms alters a single member of a proposed population. Mutation must be objective-agnostic; it cannot be aware of the fitness of the point it is mutating.In addition, a mutation operator can only vary the individual member of the population that has been proposed to it. That is, a mutation operator must ignore every member of the trajectory except the one that is being mutated. Conversely, a mutation operator cannot simply ignore the individual it is mutating. Therefore, a condition is included stating that the mutation operator must depend on the object being mutated for at least some trajectories. These restrictions are added to make the definition of evolutionary algorithms in Definition 9 below meaningful; without these conditions, any optimizer would be an evolutionary algorithm.

[2]The initial selection rule could have been pushed inside the recombination operator, but keeping it outside makes the formal definition of an evolutionary algorithm more natural.

Definition 8. An optimizer $\mathcal{V} \in \mathcal{PBO}_K$ is a *mutation operator* if $\mathcal{V}$ is factorial and objective-agnostic and for all $1 \le i \le K$, the following two conditions hold:

- $\forall t_1, t_2 \in \mathcal{T}$, $\mathcal{V}_i [t_1, f] = \mathcal{V}_i [t_2, f]$ whenever $H(t_1)^{-1,i} = H(t_2)^{-1,i}$, and
- $\exists t_1, t_2 \in \mathcal{T}$ s.t. $H(t_1)^{-1,i} \neq H(t_2)^{-1,i}$ and $\mathcal{V}_i [t_1, f] \neq \mathcal{V}_i [t_2, f]$.

These definitions are constructed to be as restrictive as possible while still accounting for the full range of genetic operators commonly used in evolutionary methods. They can be assembled to form a complete algorithm using the convolution operator.

6.3 Quasi-Evolutionary Algorithms

Selection, recombination, and mutation operators can be combined to form a general schema for evolutionary algorithms. The result is slightly more general than a typical evolutionary algorithm and is termed a *quasi-evolutionary algorithm.*

Definition 9. An optimizer $\mathcal{E} \in \mathcal{PBO}_K$ is called a *quasi-evolutionary algorithm* if it is not objective-agnostic and if there exist a selection rule $\mathcal{S}$, a recombination operator $\mathcal{R}$ of order 1 or greater, and a mutation operator $\mathcal{V}$ such that $\mathcal{E} = \mathcal{S} \star \mathcal{R} \star \mathcal{V}$.

PROPOSITION 6.1. *By implication, $\mathcal{E} \in \mathcal{PBO}_K$ is also a quasi-evolutionary algorithm if it is not objective-agnostic and there is a selection rule $\mathcal{S}$ and a mutation operator $\mathcal{V}$ such that $\mathcal{E} = \mathcal{S} \star \mathcal{V}$, in which case $\mathcal{E}$ has a recombination operator of order* 1.

Intuitively, a quasi-evolutionary algorithm samples one or more selection rules to propose a new parent population from the selected individuals, then recombines the parent population to form a new child population, and finally samples a mutation operator to alter the selected individuals.

The term "quasi-evolutionary algorithm" is used because this formalism does not exclude certain non-evolutionary algorithms such as Nelder-Mead or greedy hill-climbing. In fact, many optimization methods can be formally described as "quasi-evolutionary" through the use of innovative crossover rules, despite the substantial restrictions on the definitions above. When evolutionary algorithms are described mathematically in this manner, it is not clear that there exists a single elegant description that separates traditional evolutionary algorithms from other optimization methods [11].

7. GENETIC ALGORITHMS

Modern genetic algorithms mix and match a variety of selection, crossover, and mutation components to form an optimization routine. This section will examine some of the most common among these components.

7.1 Selection in GAs

Selection in genetic algorithms is typically restricted to the members of the last population, so that a genetic algorithm unfolds as a sequence of populations each constructed solely from the previous one. An optimizer $\mathcal{G} \in \mathcal{PBO}_K$ is termed *population-Markov* if it depends only on the last population, that is, if $\mathcal{G}[t_1, f] = \mathcal{G}[t_2, f]$ whenever $H(t_1)^{-1} = H(t_2)^{-1}$. Genetic algorithms are population-Markov in general.

PROPOSITION 7.1. *A quasi-evolutionary algorithm is population-Markov if and only if its recombination operator and selection rule are, and a recombination operator is population-Markov if and only if all of its selection rules are.*

Two of the most common selection rules historically are proportional selection and tournament selection. In *proportional selection*, members of the prior population are selected independently proportional to their fitness in the previous population. Ordinarily, the fitness function is assumed to be positive, and the genetic algorithm is maximizing the fitness and so prefers larger fitness values. To use proportional selection for minimization, a *modulating function* $g > 0$ is introduced so that $g(t, y)$ is intended to be positive and increasing as $y = f(x)$ is minimized. If it is desired to maximize f and $f > 0$, then $g(t, y) = |y|$ will prefer the minimal values of $-f$. Proportional selection with this choice of modulating function will be termed *standard proportional selection* or *roulette wheel selection*. A more neutral choice is $g(t, x) = \exp(-x)$; note that this choice is similar to the acceptance probability for simulated annealing. Given a modulating function g, proportional selection is given by

$$\mathcal{PS}\langle g\rangle [t, f] (\{y\}) \propto N_{H(t)^{-1}}(y) [g(t, f(y))], \quad (21)$$

where $N_P(y)$ is the number of times the individual y appears in the population P. Then N_P is nonzero for at most K points, so the normalization can be computed by summing over the prior population $H(t)^{-1}$.

Proportional selection is highly sensitive to the magnitude of variation in the fitness function and so can become trapped in steep local minima. *Tournament selection* chooses members of the prior population according to their rank in the population in order to maintain diversity within the population. In this section only tournaments over the full population are considered. Full tournament selection chooses the best member of the last population with probability q. If the best member is not selected, the second best member is chosen with probability q, and then the third, and the fourth, and so on. If the population is exhausted, the selection wraps back around to the best individual. The parameter q is referred to as the *selection pressure* since high values of q favor the best individuals in the population. Tournament selection is given explicitly by

$$\mathcal{TS}\langle q\rangle [t, f] (\{y\}) \propto (1-q)^{R\left(y, f, H(t)^{-1}\right)}, \quad (22)$$

where $R(y, f, P) \in \mathbb{N} \cup \{\infty\}$ is the rank of the individual y in the population P under the fitness function f, with 0 being the best rank, and $R(y, f, P) = \infty$ if y does not appear in P. In case of ties among non-equal individuals, assume later members of the population are ranked higher. Again, $\mathcal{TS}$ is nonzero for at most K points so that the normalization is easily computed. Notice that the right-hand side of Equation 22 can be treated as a modulating function.

7.2 Crossover in GAs

The distinguishing characteristic of a genetic algorithm is undoubtedly recombination with two parents (sexual reproduction). Standard crossover rules of order 2 include one point crossover, multipoint crossover, and uniform crossover. The parents are selected using one or more selection rules, and then a "child" is created using the crossover rule to combine the properties of the parents.

Because crossover rules are specific to the search space, examples will only be given for the case in which the search space X is a d-dimensional vector space, $X = Y^d$, such as $X = \mathbb{R}^d$ (Euclidean space) or $X = \{0,1\}^d$ (binary space). In this case, many second-order crossover rules can be determined by a random binary vector $M \in \{0,1\}^d$ which will be termed the *crossover mask*. If $M_i = 1$, then the child copies the ith attribute of the father. If $M_i = 0$, then the child copies the ith attribute of the mother. Denote by $\mathbf{1}$ the vector in $\{0,1\}^d$ whose entries are all one, and let $x \otimes y$ be the vector that is the componentwise product of vectors x and y. For a trajectory t, let $p(t)$ be the selected father and $m(t)$ the selected mother, so that $p(t) = \text{parents}(t, 2, k(t), K)^{-1}$ and $m(t) = \text{parents}(t, 2, k(t), K)^{-2}$. Define a random variable C_t by

$$C_t = M \otimes p(t) + (\mathbf{1} - M) \otimes m(t). \quad (23)$$

Then given a distribution $\mathbb{P}_M$ over M, a *masked crossover rule* is just the distribution of C_t and can be written as

$$\mathcal{C}\langle \mathbb{P}_M\rangle [t, f](A) = \sum_{z \in \{0,1\}^d} \mathbb{P}(C_t \in A \mid M = z)\ \mathbb{P}_M(z), \quad (24)$$

Single point, multipoint, and uniform crossover can be defined by specifying $\mathbb{P}_M$. For uniform crossover, the choice of mask is uniformly random,

$$\mathcal{UC}[t, f] = \mathcal{C}\left\langle \text{Uniform}\left(\{0,1\}^d\right)\right\rangle. \quad (25)$$

For single point crossover, a random index $i \in \{1, \ldots, d\}$ is chosen, and the mask is set so that $M_j = 1$ for $j \leq i$ and $M_j = 0$ for $j > i$. In multipoint crossover, a fixed number of random indices $i_1, \ldots, i_n$ are chosen and then sorted. M then alternates between series of zeros and a series of ones, starting with ones and with switches occurring at each of the i_j. Let $\mathcal{SC}$ denote single-point crossover and let $\mathcal{MC}$ represent multipoint crossover.

7.3 Mutation Operators

Mutation operators depend on the search space and can be almost any objective-agnostic distribution. The most common mutators, however, are Bernoulli mutation in binary spaces and Gaussian mutation in Euclidean space. In discrete or combinatorial spaces, mutation distributions typically involve random structural operators.

First, consider Gaussian mutation in $X = \mathbb{R}^d$. The mean of the Gaussian is simply the point being mutated (t^{-1}) and the covariance is a function of the prior points evaluated, often a constant. Then *Gaussian mutation* with a covariance-generating function Σ is given by

$$\mathcal{N}\langle \Sigma\rangle [t, f] \quad = \quad \mathcal{N}\left(t^{-1}, \Sigma(H(t))\right), \quad (26)$$

where $\mathcal{N}(\mu, \Sigma)$ is the normal distribution and the symbol $\mathcal{N}$ is overloaded to represent Gaussian mutation as well.

When the search space is binary, $X = \{0,1\}^d$, *Bernoulli mutation* at rate p is given by

$$\mathcal{B}\langle p\rangle [t \cup z, f] (\{y\}) = \prod_j p^{|y_j - z_{i,j}|} (1-p)^{\left(1 - |y_j - z_{i,j}|\right)} \quad (27)$$

7.4 Formal Genetic Algorithms

An evolutionary algorithm can be defined as a quasi-evolutionary algorithm with a masked crossover rule. A genetic algorithm can then be identified as an evolutionary algorithm that is also population-Markov. In contrast, evolution strategies depend on adaptive parameters and are not usually population-Markov.

Definition 10. An optimizer $\mathcal{G} \in \mathcal{PBO}_K$ is an *evolutionary algorithm* if it is a quasi-evolutionary algorithm with a masked crossover rule. Additionally, $\mathcal{G}$ is a *genetic algorithm* if it is also population-Markov.
This definition encompasses most traditional evolutionary algorithms and excludes more recent developments that still conform to the definition of a quasi-evolutionary algorithm as defined above. Again, a crossover rule of order one may be used, so that every quasi-evolutionary algorithm with a vacuous crossover rule is trivially an evolutionary algorithm.

Putting all of these pieces together, a basic genetic algorithm with single-point crossover, proportional selection, and a binary encoding can be written as

$$\mathcal{SGA}\langle p\rangle = (\mathcal{PS} \star ((\triangleleft\mathcal{PS}) \star \mathcal{SC})) \star \mathcal{B}\langle p\rangle, \tag{28}$$

which is Goldberg's simple genetic algorithm with a mutation rate of p [5]. The resulting algorithm is formally a genetic algorithm, since it is composed of a population-Markov selection rule, a recombination operator with masked crossover, and a mutation operator. Most standard genetic algorithms can be written down similarly by mixing and matching the components described in this section.

8. CONTINUITY OF OPTIMIZERS

The adopted formalism for stochastic optimizers is useful because it leads to general theoretical results. The characterization of optimizers as a closed, convex subset of a normed vector space in Section 5 is one such result. But many more results are also possible. For example, the theory allows one to state the conditions under which optimizers may be expected to have similar behavior on similar problems, i.e., the conditions under which they are continuous. Continuity is important because it determines when approximations of the fitness function or the optimizer may be used without a loss of performance. Such approximations are already used to optimize complex fitness functions more efficiently. The theory may also suggest that certain uncomputable optimizers may perform well, and continuity means that computable approximations will perform similarly. The section states several theorems about the continuity of genetic algorithms in particular. A few proofs are omitted; these proofs can be found in Chapter 5 of [11].

8.1 What is a Continuous Optimizer?

Optimizers are functions from a trajectory and a fitness function to a signed measure over the search space. Continuity answers the following two questions:

- Will an optimizer choose similar points when given similar evaluation histories?
- Will an optimizer choose similar points when given similar fitness functions?

The first question pertains to *continuity in trajectories*, and the second question to *continuity in objectives.*

Continuity is a topological concept. The most familiar type of topology is the metric topology, which induces the epsilon-delta definition of continuity. A function f that maps one metric space (X, d_X) to another metric space (Y, d_Y) is continuous if for every $\epsilon > 0$ and every point x there exists a $\delta = \delta(x) > 0$ such that for all y with $d_X(x, y) < \delta$, it holds that $d_Y(f(x), f(y)) < \epsilon$.

The search domain X is assumed to be metric from this point forward for simplicity, since most practical search domains are metric. A metric on the space of evaluation histories $\mathcal{T}[X]$ is then given by

$$d_\rho(t_1, t_2) = \big|\,|t_1| - |t_2|\,\big| + \sum_{i=1}^{|t_1|\wedge|t_2|} \rho\left(t_1^i, t_2^i\right), \tag{29}$$

where ρ is a metric on X, t_1^i is the ith element of t_1, and $|t_1|$ is the length of the trajectory t_1.

Definition 11. An optimizer $\mathcal{G} \in \mathcal{MF}[X]$ is *continuous in objectives* at f if for any sequence of fitness functions $\{f_n\}$, $f_n \to f$ implies $||\mathcal{G}[t,f] - \mathcal{G}[t,f_n]||_{\mathcal{M}} \to 0$.

Definition 12. An optimizer $\mathcal{G} \in \mathcal{MF}$ is *continuous in trajectories* at t if for every $\epsilon > 0$ there exists a $\delta > 0$ such that whenever $d_\rho(t,u) < \delta$ then $||\mathcal{G}[t,f] - \mathcal{G}[u,f]||_{\mathcal{M}} < \epsilon$.

If an optimizer is continuous in objectives, then it can be expected to perform similarly on similar problems. If an optimizer is continuous in trajectories, then it can be expected to make similar decisions on similar trajectories.

8.2 Continuity of Evolutionary Algorithms

In Section 6, a quasi-evolutionary algorithm was defined as a convolution $\mathcal{E} = \mathcal{S}\star\mathcal{R}\star\mathcal{V}$. Evolutionary algorithms can be continuous or discontinuous, depending on the details of the genetic operators. Mutation operators are independent of the fitness function and therefore trivially continuous in objectives. Typically, mutation operators are continuous in trajectories as well, as with Bernoulli or Gaussian mutation. Crossover rules are likewise independent of objectives and therefore continuous over objectives. Cases where evolutionary algorithms as a whole are continuous or discontinuous will be addressed with two general theorems in this subsection. These theorems demonstrate two distinct cases in which a convolution can be continuous. First, a convolution $\mathcal{A} \star \mathcal{B}$ is continuous if both optimizers are continuous at certain points. Second, a convolution may be continuous if the right side is continuous and the left side generates convergent samples.

In order to support the following theorem, the property of bounded magnitude is introduced. An optimizer $\mathcal{G} \in \mathcal{MF}$ is of *bounded magnitude* if there exists a number $M < \infty$ such that $||\mathcal{G}[t,f]||_{\mathcal{M}} \leq M$ for all t, f. Otherwise, an unbounded sequence could cause a discontinuity. This condition is satisfied trivially for any optimizer in $\mathcal{PF}$.

THEOREM 8.1. *Let $\mathcal{S}, \mathcal{V} \in \mathcal{MF}$. Then $\mathcal{S} \star \mathcal{V}$ is continuous in objectives (or trajectories) at t, f if both $\mathcal{S}$ and $\mathcal{V}$ are of bounded magnitude, $\mathcal{S}$ is continuous in objectives (or trajectories) at t, f, and for some $C \in \mathcal{B}_\tau$ with $|\mathcal{S}[t,f]|(C) = |\mathcal{S}[t,f]|(X)$, $\mathcal{V}$ is continuous in objectives (or trajectories) at $t \cup x, f$ for all $x \in C$.*

PROOF. Assume that $\mathcal{S}$ and $\mathcal{V}$ are continuous in both objectives and trajectories at t, f. Fix $\epsilon > 0$. Suppose

$||\mathcal{S}[u,g]||_{\mathcal{M}} \leq M < \infty$ and $||\mathcal{V}[u,g]||_{\mathcal{M}} \leq M$ for all u, g. Let $f_n \to f$, $t_n \to t$. Let $A \in \mathcal{B}_{\mathcal{T}}$. Then

$$
\begin{aligned}
&|\mathcal{S} \star \mathcal{V}[t_n, f_n](A) - \mathcal{S} \star \mathcal{V}[t,f](A)| \\
&= \left| \int_X \mathcal{V}[t_n \cup x, f_n](A) \mathcal{S}[t_n, f_n](dx) \right. \\
&\qquad \left. - \int_X \mathcal{V}[t \cup x, f](A) \mathcal{S}[t,f](dx) \right| \\
&\leq \left| \int_X \mathcal{V}[t_n \cup x, f_n](A) \mathcal{S}[t_n, f_n](dx) \right. \\
&\qquad \left. - \int_X \mathcal{V}[t \cup x, f](A) \mathcal{S}[t_n, f_n](dx) \right| \\
&\quad + \left| \int_X \mathcal{V}[t \cup x, f](A) \mathcal{S}[t_n, f_n](dx) \right. \\
&\qquad \left. - \int_X \mathcal{V}[t \cup x, f](A) \mathcal{S}[t,f](dx) \right| \\
&\leq \int_C |\mathcal{V}[t_n \cup x, f_n](A) - \mathcal{V}[t \cup x, f](A)| |\mathcal{S}[t_n, f_n](dx)| \\
&\quad + \int_X |\mathcal{V}[t \cup x, f](A)| |\mathcal{S}[t_n, f_n](dx) - \mathcal{S}[t,f](dx)| \quad (30) \\
&< \frac{\epsilon}{2} \frac{1}{M} |\mathcal{S}[t_n, f_n]|(C) + M |\mathcal{S}[t_n, f_n] - \mathcal{S}[t,f]|(X) \quad (31) \\
&< \frac{\epsilon}{2} + \frac{\epsilon}{2} = \epsilon.
\end{aligned}
$$

To obtain Equation 31, use the fact that $\mathcal{V}$ is continuous on the left side and the fact that $\mathcal{V}$ is of bounded magnitude on the right. To obtain Equation 32, note that $\mathcal{S}$ is bounded in magnitude by M and that $\mathcal{S}$ is continuous. For Equation 31, continuity is sufficient to imply that there exists an N independent of x such that

$$|\mathcal{V}[t_n \cup x, f_n](A) - \mathcal{V}[t \cup x, f](A)| < \frac{\epsilon}{2} \frac{1}{M}$$

for all $n > N$ because $d_\rho(t_n \cup x, t \cup x) = d_\rho(t_n, t)$ for all $x \in X$, using d_ρ from Equation 29. This justification can be extended to general topological spaces; the details are not included here.

The proof above holds for jointly continuous $\mathcal{S}$ and $\mathcal{V}$; continuity in either objectives or trajectories separately can be proven by repeating the equations above with $t_n = t$ or $f_n = f$ as needed. ☐

Theorem 8.1 can be applied to evolutionary algorithms to deduce continuity based on the continuity of the selection rules, the crossover rule, and the mutation operator. There is a problem with this approach, however, since most selection and crossover rules are discontinuous in some sense. This problem can be circumvented by using the concept of *sample convergence* instead.

Definition 13. An optimizer $\mathcal{G} \in \mathcal{MF}$ is *sample-convergent* in trajectories at t, f if

1. there is a trajectory $u_{t,f} \in \mathcal{T}[X]$ s.t. $\{y \in u_{t,f}\}$ has full measure on $\mathcal{G}[t,f]$ and $|\mathcal{G}[t,f]|(\{y\}) > 0$ for each $y \in u_{t,f}$,
2. $t_n \to t$ implies $\exists u_{t_n,f}$ as in the prior statement and $u_{t_n,f} \to u_{t,f}$, and
3. $t_n \to t$ implies $\mathcal{G}[t_n, f](\{u^i_{t_n,f}\}) \to \mathcal{G}[t,f](\{u^i_{t,f}\})$ for all $1 \leq i \leq |u_{t,f}|$.

If the above statements hold when $t_n \to t$ is replaced with $f_n \to f$, then $\mathcal{G}$ is sample-convergent in objectives at t, f.

A sample drawn from a sample-convergent optimizer converges along a sequence of trajectories or objectives. That is, if $Y_{t,f} \sim \mathcal{G}[t,f]$ for all t, f, then Y_{t_n,f_n} converges in distribution to $Y_{t,f}$ when $t_n, f_n \to t, f$. Sample convergence can make a convolution be continuous.

THEOREM 8.2. *Suppose $\mathcal{G} \in \mathcal{MF}$. If $\mathcal{G}$ can be written as $\mathcal{A} \star \mathcal{B}$ where $\mathcal{A}$ and $\mathcal{B}$ are both of bounded magnitude, $\mathcal{A}$ is sample convergent in objectives (or trajectories) at t, f with trajectory $u_{t,f}$ as above, and $\mathcal{B}$ is continuous in objectives (or trajectories) at $t \cup x, f$ for all $x \in u_{t,f}$, then $\mathcal{G}$ is continuous in objectives (or trajectories) at t, f.*

PROOF. Without loss of generality, suppose $\mathcal{A}$ is sample convergent in both objectives and trajectories at t, f and that $\mathcal{B}$ is continuous in both objectives and trajectories at t, f. Fix $\epsilon > 0$ and suppose $\mathcal{A} \leq M < \infty$ and $\mathcal{B} \leq M$. The optimizer $\mathcal{G}$ can be written as

$$\mathcal{G}[t,f](A) = \sum_{i=1}^{|u_{t,f}|} \mathcal{A}[t,f](\{u^i_{t,f}\})\ \mathcal{B}[t \cup u^i_{t,f}, f](A). \quad (32)$$

To reduce notation, let $N = |u_{t,f}|$, $p(i,t,f) = \mathcal{A}[t,f](\{u^i_{t,f}\})$, and $\nu_{i,t,f}(A) = \mathcal{B}[t \cup u^i_{t,f}, f](A)$. Then the above can be restated as

$$\mathcal{G}[t,f](A) = \sum_{i=1}^{N} p(i,t,f)\ \nu_{i,t,f}(A). \quad (33)$$

Suppose now that $t_n \to t$ and $f_n \to f$. Because $\mathcal{A}$ is sample convergent, it follows that $p(i, t_n, f_n) \to p(i,t,f)$. Also, $\nu_{i,t_n,f_n}(A) \to \nu_{i,t,f}$ since $\mathcal{B}$ is continuous. But then

$$
\begin{aligned}
&|\mathcal{G}[t,f](A) - \mathcal{G}[t_n, f_n](A)| \\
&\quad \leq \textstyle\sum_{i=1}^N |p(i,t,f)\nu_{i,t,f}(A) - p(i,t_n,f_n)\nu_{i,t_n,f_n}(A)| \\
&\quad \leq \textstyle\sum_{i=1}^N |p(i,t,f)\nu_{i,t,f}(A) - p(i,t,f)\nu_{i,t_n,f_n}(A)| \\
&\qquad + \sum_{i=1}^N |p(i,t,f)\nu_{i,t_n,f_n}(A) - p(i,t_n,f_n)\nu_{i,t_n,f_n}(A)| \\
&\quad = \textstyle\sum_{i=1}^N |p(i,t,f)|\,|\nu_{i,t,f}(A) - \nu_{i,t_n,f_n}(A)| \\
&\qquad + \sum_{i=1}^N |\nu_{i,t_n,f_n}(A)|\,|p(i,t,f) - p(i,t_n,f_n)| \\
&\quad \leq M \sum_{i=1}^N \left[\frac{\epsilon}{2NM} + \frac{\epsilon}{2NM}\right] = \epsilon \quad (34)
\end{aligned}
$$

where the next to last line follows from the convergence of p and ν mentioned above and from the bounded magnitude of $\mathcal{A}$ and $\mathcal{B}$. Thus $\mathcal{G}$ is continuous in both objectives and trajectories at t, f. To show $\mathcal{G}$ is only continuous in objectives or trajectories separately, repeat the above steps with $t_n = t$ or $f_n = f$. ☐

COROLLARY 8.3. *A quasi-evolutionary algorithm is continuous in objectives at t, f if its selection rules are sample-convergent in objectives at t, f.*

The next theorem states that masked crossover rules are sample-convergent if they have sample-convergent selection rules. Since most crossover rules are masked crossover rules, the continuity of most evolutionary algorithms depends only on the sample convergence of the selection rule.

THEOREM 8.4. *The convolution of a selection rule and a recombination operator with a masked crossover rule is sample-convergent in objectives (or trajectories) at t, f if its selection rules are also sample-convergent in objectives (or trajectories) at t, f.*

PROOF. Suppose X is a d-dimensional vector space, so that a masked crossover rule can be applied. Let $\mathcal{S}$ be a selection rule that is sample convergent in both trajectories and objectives. Let $\mathcal{R}$ be a recombination operator with a masked crossover rule. Then

$$\mathcal{S} \star \mathcal{R} = \mathcal{S} \star (\triangleleft \mathcal{S}_1 \star (\cdots \star (\triangleleft_{n-1} \mathcal{S}_{n-1} \star \mathcal{C} < \mathbb{P}_M >)))$$

for sample convergent selection rules $\mathcal{S}_1, \ldots, \mathcal{S}_{n-1}$ and a masked crossover rule $\mathcal{C} < \mathbb{P}_M >$ of order n. Assume for now that each selection rule is sample convergent in both objectives and trajectories at t, f. Let $\mathcal{S}_0 = \mathcal{S}$ to simplify the notation.

For all t, f there is a trajectory $u_{i,t,f}$ for each selection rule $\mathcal{S}_i$ with $i = 0, \ldots, n-1$ such that $\mathcal{S}_i[t, f](\{y \in u_{i,t,f}\}) = 1$. There are n^d possible crossover masks, and each selection rule can only select one of $|u_{i,t,f}|$ points. Thus there are exactly $n^d \prod_i |u_{i,t,f}| < \infty$ points that can result from recombination, and these points may be enumerated within a trajectory $\tilde{u}_{t,f}$, where the order of enumeration is independent of t and f. To be specific, for each position k in $\tilde{u}_{t,f}$ there is a crossover mask m^k and an index to a selected parent $p_{i,k}$ for each selection rule i such that m^k and $(p_{i,k})_{i=1}^n$ depend solely on the position k and not on t, f. Recalling Equation 23, $\tilde{u}_{t,f}^k = \sum_{i=1}^n m^k \otimes_i u_{i,t,f}^{p_{i,k}}$, and $\mathcal{S} \star \mathcal{R}[t, f](\{y \in \tilde{u}_{t,f}\}) = 1$.

Suppose $t_n \to t$ and $f_n \to f$. Then $u_{i,t_n,f_n} \to u_{i,t,f}$ for each selection rule $\mathcal{S}_i$. Let $x = \tilde{u}_{t,f}^k$, the kth element of the trajectory $\tilde{u}_{t,f}$. Then x is generated from a particular crossover mask m determined by the position k. Suppose m has the value j in the ℓth component, i.e. $m_\ell = j$. Then $x_\ell = \left(u_{j,t,f}^k\right)_\ell$. Let $x^n = \tilde{u}_{t_n,f_n}^k$. Then because the enumeration order was fixed, $x_\ell^n = \left(u_{j,t_n,f_n}^k\right)_\ell$. Since $u_{j,t_n,f_n} \to u_{j,t,f}$, it follows that $x_\ell^n \to x_\ell$. But k, j, and ℓ were arbitrary, so it follows that $\tilde{u}_{t_n,f_n} \to \tilde{u}_{t,f}$.

Again, suppose $t_n \to t$ and $f_n \to f$. Let m be the crossover mask for $u_{t,f}^k$, and let $y_i = u_{i,t,f}^{p_{i,k}}$ be the point selected on t, f by the ith selection rule at the kth position in the enumeration. Observe that

$$\mathcal{S} \star \mathcal{R}[t, f](\{\tilde{u}_{t,f}^k\}) = \mathbb{P}_M(m) \prod_i \mathcal{S}_i[t, f](\{y_i\}). \tag{35}$$

Let $y_i^n = u_{i,t_n,f_n}^{p_{i,k}}$ be the point selected on t_n, f_n by the ith selection rule at the kth position in the enumeration and note that (1) $y_i^n \to y_i$, (2) $\tilde{u}_{t_n,f_n}^k \to \tilde{u}_{t,f}^k$, and (3) the particular mask m is a function of the position k independent of t, f. Since $\mathbb{P}_M(m)$ is independent of t, f and $\mathcal{S}_i[t_n, f_n](\{y_i^n\}) \to \mathcal{S}_i[t, f](\{y_i\})$ for all i, it follows that $\mathcal{S} \star \mathcal{R}[t_n, f_n](\{\tilde{u}_{t_n,f_n}^k\}) \to \mathcal{S} \star \mathcal{R}[t, f](\{\tilde{u}_{t,f}^k\})$. Therefore $\mathcal{S} \star \mathcal{R}$ is sample convergent at t, f. To show that $\mathcal{S} \star \mathcal{R}$ is only convergent in either trajectories or objectives, repeat the above with $f_n = f$ or $t_n = t$. □

COROLLARY 8.5. *An evolutionary algorithm with a masked crossover rule is continuous in trajectories (or objectives) at t, f if its selection rules are sample convergent in trajectories (or objectives) at t, f and its mutation operator is continuous in trajectories (or objectives) at $t \cup x, f$ for all x generated by masked crossover of elements in t.*

As a final piece of the puzzle, proportional selection is sample-convergent on $\overline{C[X]}$ under certain conditions. [3] Recall that $\mathcal{PS}\langle g \rangle$ from Equation 21 is generalized proportional selection with a modulating function g. The theorem below implies that the simple genetic algorithm is continuous.

THEOREM 8.6. *Proportional selection with modulating function g is sample convergent on all trajectories and all objectives in $\overline{C[X]}$ if g is continuous in both arguments and for every pair t, f with $f \in \overline{C[X]}$, $h_k(u, \tilde{f}) = g(u, \tilde{f}(H(u)^{-1,k}))$ is bounded on some neighborhood of t, f for all $1 \leq k \leq K$.*

PROOF. To make the proof simpler, use unnormalized proportional selection,

$$\mathcal{UPS}{<}g{>}[t, f](B) = \sum_{k=1}^K g(t, f\left(H(t)^{-1,k}\right)) 1_B(H(t)^{-1,k}), \tag{36}$$

noting that $H(t)^{-1}$ is a sequence that may repeat points.

Suppose $t_n \to t$ and $f_n \to f$. Without loss of generality, suppose f_n is continuous, as we may, since continuous functions are dense in $\overline{C[X]}$. Clearly, the set $P_{t,f} = \{y \in H(t)^{-1}\}$ has full measure on $\mathcal{UPS}[t, f]$ for all t, f, and $H(t_n)^{-1} \to H(t)^{-1}$ in X^K (or in $\mathcal{T}[X]$). It remains to show that

$$\mathcal{UPS}[t_n, f_n](\left\{H(t_n)^{-1,k}\right\}) \to \mathcal{UPS}[t, f](\left\{H(t)^{-1,k}\right\})$$

for all k. The definitions imply

$$\begin{aligned} &|\mathcal{UPS}[t_n, f_n](\{H(t_n)^{-1,k}\}) - \mathcal{UPS}[t, f](\{H(t)^{-1,k}\})| \\ &= \left|g(t_n, f_n\left(H(t_n)^{-1,k}\right)) - g(t, f\left(H(t)^{-1,k}\right))\right|. \end{aligned} \tag{37}$$

Now f_n is continuous and $f_n \to f$, so for any $\epsilon > 0$,

$$\begin{aligned} &\left|f_n\left(H(t_n)^{-1,k}\right) - f\left(H(t)^{-1,k}\right)\right| \\ &\leq \left|f_n\left(H(t_n)^{-1,k}\right) - f_n\left(H(t)^{-1,k}\right)\right| \\ &\quad + \left|f_n\left(H(t)^{-1,k}\right) - f\left(H(t)^{-1,k}\right)\right| \\ &< \tfrac{\epsilon}{2} + \tfrac{\epsilon}{2} = \epsilon. \end{aligned} \tag{38}$$

Since g is continuous in both arguments, it follows that $\mathcal{UPS}$ is sample convergent at t, f. Because g is bounded near t, f, the desired conclusion follows by normalizing $\mathcal{UPS}$. □

COROLLARY 8.7. *The simple genetic algorithm of Equation 28 is jointly continuous in trajectories and objectives.*

PROOF. Recall that

$$\mathcal{SGA}{<}p{>} = (\mathcal{PS}{<}|x|{>} \star ((\triangleleft \mathcal{PS}{<}|x|{>}) \star \mathcal{SC})) \star \mathcal{B}{<}p{>},$$

where the objective is assumed to be negative (for minimization). The search space is $\{0,1\}^d$ with the discrete topology (i.e. all sets are open), and therefore $\overline{C[\{0,1\}^d]} = \mathbb{R}^X$. The function $g(t, x) = |x|$ is continuous. The fitness function f is bounded, since f can only take finitely many values on X. Fix $\epsilon > 0$. Then for any f, the set $N_\epsilon^f = \{u, \tilde{f} \mid \sup_{x \in X} |\tilde{f}(x) - f(x)| < \epsilon\}$ forms a neighborhood of t, f on which $\tilde{f}$ and therefore g is bounded, and hence the neighborhood requirement of Theorem 8.6 is satisfied. Thus $\mathcal{PS}{<}|x|{>}$ is sample convergent everywhere by Theorem 8.6. The Bernoulli mutation operator $\mathcal{B}{<}p{>}$ is jointly

[3] $\overline{C[X]} \subseteq \mathbb{R}^X$ consists of all continuous real functions and their pointwise limits, including functions with jump discontinuities or point discontinuities.

continuous. Single-point crossover $\mathcal{SC}$ is a masked crossover rule, so Corollary 8.5 implies that $\mathcal{SGA}$ is jointly continuous everywhere. □

Genetic algorithms in any space are jointly continuous on all trajectories and objectives in $\overline{C[X]}$ when they use masked crossover and proportional selection with a continuous modulating function. For example, a real-coded genetic algorithm with proportional selection, uniform crossover, and Gaussian mutation is continuous in this way.

Proportional selection is no longer commonly used as a selection rule; it has been replaced by rank-based methods such as tournament selection. Whereas proportional selection makes a genetic algorithm continuous, rank-based selection is discontinuous at some points. The following subsection identifies these discontinuities, leading up to a full characterization of when these selection rules are continuous.

8.3 Discontinuity of Some Methods

Sample convergence was used to show that many genetic algorithms are continuous on a large set of objectives. These results also have a converse; selection rules whose samples diverge are a source of discontinuities in the optimizer.

Definition 14. An optimizer $\mathcal{G} \in \mathcal{MF}$ is *sample-divergent* in trajectories at t, f if

1. there is a trajectory $u_{t,f} \in \mathcal{T}[X]$ s.t. $\{y \in u_{t,f}\}$ has full measure on $\mathcal{G}[t, f]$ and $\mathcal{G}[t, f](\{y\}) > 0$ for each $y \in u_{t,f}$,
2. $t_n \to t$ implies $\exists u_{t_n,f}$ as in the prior statement, and $u_{t_n,f} \to u_{t,f}$,
3. $t_n \to t$ implies $\mathcal{G}[t_n, f](\{u^i_{t_n,f}\}) \nrightarrow \mathcal{G}[t, f](\{u^i_{t,f}\})$ for some $1 \leq i \leq |u_{t,f}|$.

If the above statements hold when $t_n \to t$ is replaced with $f_n \to f$, then $\mathcal{G}$ is sample-divergent in objectives at t, f.

The first two properties of sample divergence are identical to those for sample-convergence, but the final properties are opposites. Any optimizer $\mathcal{G}$ together with any pair t, f that meets the first two requirements must be either sample-convergent or sample-divergent and cannot be both, since the trajectory with full measure must be unique.

THEOREM 8.8. *Suppose $\mathcal{G} \in \mathcal{MF}$. If $\mathcal{G}$ can be written as $\mathcal{A} \star \mathcal{B}$ where $\mathcal{A}$ and $\mathcal{B}$ are both of bounded magnitude, $\mathcal{A}$ is sample divergent in objectives (or trajectories) at t, f, and $\mathcal{B}$ is continuous in objectives (or trajectories) at t, f, then $\mathcal{G}$ is discontinuous in objectives (or trajectories) at t, f provided that for all $x \in u_t, f$ for $\mathcal{A}$, $\mathcal{B}[t \cup x, f] \neq 0$.*

PROOF. Without loss of generality, assume that $\mathcal{A}$ is sample divergent in both objectives and trajectories at t, f and that $\mathcal{B}$ is continuous in both objectives and trajectories at t, f. Adopt notation for $\mathcal{G}$ as in Equation 33. Suppose $\mathcal{A} \leq M < \infty$ and $\mathcal{B} \leq M$. Then there exist sequences $t_n \to t$ and $f_n \to f$ and some i such that $p(i, t_n, f_n) \nrightarrow p(i, t, f)$, i.e. there is some constant $c_1 > 0$ such that for any N, there exists $m > N$ with $|p(i, t_m, f_m) - p(i, t, f)| \geq c_1$. There is also a set $A \in \mathcal{B}_\tau$ such that $|\nu_{i,t,f}|(A) = c_2 > 0$, since $\mathcal{B}[t \cup u^i_{t,f}, f] \neq 0$. The following inequalities hold:

$$\begin{aligned}
||\mathcal{G}[t, f] - \mathcal{G}[t_n, f_n]||_{\mathcal{M}} &\geq |\mathcal{G}[t, f](A) - \mathcal{G}[t_n, f_n](A)| \\
&\geq |p(i, t, f)\nu_{i,t,f}(A) - p(i, t_n, f_n)\nu_{i,t_n,f_n}(A)| \\
&\geq |[p(i, t, f) - p(i, t_n, f_n)]\, \nu_{i,t,f}(A) \\
&\quad + p(i, t_n, f_n)\, [\nu_{i,t,f}(A) - \nu_{i,t_n,f_n}(A)]| . \qquad (39)
\end{aligned}$$

Because $\mathcal{A}$ is bounded by M, $|p(i, t, f)| \leq M$, and because $\mathcal{B}$ is continuous at t, f, there is some N_0 such that for $m > N_0$, $|\nu_{i,t,f}(A) - \nu_{i,t_m,f_m}(A)| < \frac{c_1 c_2}{2M}$. Therefore

$$|p(i, t, f)\, [\nu_{i,t,f}(A) - \nu_{i,t_m,f_m}(A)]| < \frac{c_1 c_2}{2}.$$

On the other hand, regardless of the value of N_0, m can be chosen so that $|p(i, t, f) - p(i, t_m, f_m)| \geq c_1$ and hence

$$|[p(i, t, f) - p(i, t_n, f_n)]\, \nu_{i,t,f}(A)| \geq c_1 c_2.$$

Consequently,

$$||\mathcal{G}[t, f] - \mathcal{G}[t_m, f_m]||_{\mathcal{M}} > c_1 c_2 - \frac{c_1 c_2}{2} = \frac{c_1 c_2}{2}, \qquad (40)$$

and this inequality holds for any value of $N \geq N_0$. Thus $||\mathcal{G}[t, f] - \mathcal{G}[t_n, f_n]||_{\mathcal{M}}$ does not converge, and $\mathcal{G}$ is discontinuous at t, f. □

Theorem 8.4 stated that a masked crossover rule preserves sample convergence from its selection rules. As an analogue, masked crossover also preserves sample divergence. The following Theorem and Corollary can be proven in a similar way to Theorem 8.4 and its corollaries, and so the proofs are omitted.

THEOREM 8.9. *A recombination operator with a masked crossover rule is sample-divergent in objectives (or trajectories) at t, f if all of its selection rules are sample-divergent in objectives (or trajectories) at t, f.*

COROLLARY 8.10. *An evolutionary algorithm with a masked crossover rule is discontinuous in objectives (or trajectories) at t, f if all of its selection rules are sample-divergent in objectives (or trajectories) at t, f and its mutation operator is continuous in objectives (or trajectories) at $t \cup x, f$ for all x generated by masked crossover of elements in t.*

Theorem 8.6 showed that generalized proportional selection is sample-convergent where the modulating function is continuous on the image of the fitness. Conversely, proportional selection is sample-divergent when the composition of the modulating function and the objective is discontinuous.

THEOREM 8.11. *Proportional selection with modulating function g is sample divergent in objectives (or trajectories) at t, f whenever $h_k(u, \tilde{f}) = g(u, \tilde{f}(H(u)^{-1,k}))$ is discontinuous in objectives (or trajectories) at t, f and bounded away from zero on some neighborhood of t, f for all $1 \leq k \leq K$, i.e., $|h_k(u, \tilde{f})| > c > 0$.*

PROOF. Suppose $t_n \to t$ and $f_n \to f$ but $h_k(t_n, f_n) \nrightarrow h_k(t, f)$. As in the proof of Theorem 8.6, use unnormalized proportional selection, $\mathcal{UPS}$. Also as in that proof, $\mathcal{UPS}$ meets the basic requirements of sample divergence (or convergence), i.e. $u_{t,f} = H(t)^{-1}$ and $P_{t,f} = \{y \in H(t)^{-1}\}$ has full measure. Let $x^n_k = H(t_n)^{-1,k}$. Then

$$\begin{aligned}
|\mathcal{UPS}[t_n, f_n](\{x^n_k\}) &- \mathcal{UPS}[t, f](\{x_k\})| \\
&= |h_k(t_n, f_n) - h_k(t, f)| . \qquad (41)
\end{aligned}$$

That is, $\mathcal{UPS}[t_n, f_n](\{x^n_k\}) \nrightarrow \mathcal{UPS}[t, f](\{x_k\})$. Because h_k is bounded away from zero, normalization yields that $\mathcal{PS}$ is sample divergent at t, f. □

Theorem 8.11 can be leveraged to conclude that tournament selection (and, by extension, any selection rule based on rank) is sample-divergent on the majority of objectives for trajectories that have distinct points with the same fitness.

Definition 15. A trajectory $t \in \mathcal{T}[X]$ is of *ambivalent fitness* at degree K on a fitness function f if there exist points $x, y \in H(t)^{-1}$ for population size K with $x \neq y$ but $f(x) = f(y)$. Otherwise, t is of *unambivalent fitness* at degree K on f. The trajectory t is ambivalent at full degree if $K = |t|$; the degree may be omitted if clear from the context.

THEOREM 8.12. *Tournament selection (Equation 22) with selection pressure $q \in [0, 1)$ is sample divergent in objectives at every objective on trajectories of ambivalent fitness at the degree of the selection rule.*

PROOF. Let $R(y, f, P)$ be the ranking function of Section 7. Tournament selection over the whole population is proportional selection with $h_k(u, \tilde{f})$ in the statement of Theorem 8.11 given by

$$h_k(u, \tilde{f}) = (1-q)^{R(H(u)^{-1,k}, \tilde{f}, H(u)^{-1})}. \quad (42)$$

This h_k is bounded away from zero everywhere, so Theorem 8.11 implies that tournament selection is sample divergent at the discontinuities of h_k. Now h_k is a continuous function of $R(H(u)^{-1,k}, \tilde{f}, H(u)^{-1})$, and thus its discontinuities are exactly the discontinuities of R.

Let f be any non-monotonic objective and let t be a trajectory of ambivalent fitness on f at the degree of the selection rule, so that there are two points y and z in $H(t)^{-1}$ with $y \neq z$ and $f(y) = f(z)$, where z occurs later in the population. Next, construct f_n so that $f_n(z) = f(z) + \frac{1}{n}$ and $f_n(x) = f(x)$ for all $x \neq z$. Then $f_n \to f$, and

$$R(z, f_n, H(t)^{-1}) - R(y, f_n, H(t)^{-1}) > 0$$

is a positive constant independent of n, i.e. y is ranked higher than z, and thus has a lower index in the ranked population. But according to the disambiguation rule in Section 7,

$$R(z, f, H(t)^{-1}) - R(y, f, H(t)^{-1}) < 0,$$

that is, y is ranked lower than z at the limit and has a higher index in the population. Therefore R is discontinuous in objectives at t, f, and by consequence tournament selection is discontinuous in objectives at t, f as well. If the tie-breaking procedure is reversed, the proof still holds by using $f_n(z) = f(z) - \frac{1}{n}$ instead. □

Trajectories of ambivalent fitness have measure zero in the optimization process generated by tournament selection, unless the fitness function has a plateau. Even on functions with many small plateaus, trajectories of ambivalent fitness will rarely be encountered. If trajectories of ambivalent fitness are avoided, then tournament selection is sample-convergent.

THEOREM 8.13. *Tournament selection is sample-convergent in objectives in $\overline{C[X]}$ at trajectories of unambivalent fitness.*

PROOF. As in the proof of Theorem 8.12, tournament and ranking selection are sample divergent at exactly the points where R is discontinuous. Let $f \in \overline{C[X]}$, and let t be a trajectory that is of unambivalent fitness on f at the degree of the selection rule. Assume $f_n \to f$. Then there is an N such that $R(x, f_n, H(t)^{-1}) = R(x, f, H(t)^{-1})$ for $n > N$, since the population size K is finite, and any finite set of points in $\mathbb{R}$ can be separated by disjoint open sets. But then R is continuous on f at t, and therefore tournament and ranking selection are sample convergent by Theorem 8.6 using h_k from the proof of Theorem 8.12. □

Thus a genetic algorithm with tournament selection is continuous almost surely on fitness functions without plateaus; the same fact holds for any rank-based selection mechanism, e.g. ranking selection or truncation selection. These facts provide a complete picture of exactly when common genetic algorithms can be expected to behave similarly on similar problems. This result is particularly useful, since it provides theoretical justification for methods that approximate fitness functions such as metamodeling or surrogates in evolutionary computation.

9. DISCUSSION AND FUTURE WORK

This paper presented a formal measure-theoretic approach that identifies iterative stochastic optimizers as a closed, convex subset of a normed vector space. This approach provides a rich setting within which powerful theorems about optimization methods can be proven. It has been shown in detail how genetic algorithms fit in to this framework. To demonstrate a first taste of what is possible using these theoretical tools, a full characterization of the continuity of genetic algorithms was provided.

These results are a promising beginning of what can potentially be proven with these tools. This formal framework can be used for many innovative tasks: to define and reason about explicit performance criteria; to prove generalized NFL theorems, including necessary and sufficient conditions for arbitrary fitness priors; and to establish rigorously a mathematical duality between problems and the optimizers. See [11] for a more detailed discussion of these matters.

The convexity of optimizer space as proven in this paper suggests that better performance on a particular problem may be achieved by blending two known optimizers convexly; this claim is supported by preliminary experiments [11]. The optimizer-to-objective duality that can be defined based on these results can be used as a starting point for meta-optimization or to examine the question of optimal optimization for a given problem class. These topics and others will be explored in future work.

10. CONCLUSION

Overall, a rigorous formal approach to optimization may lead to new optimization methods and new ways of configuring and improving existing methods. Such an approach can help to organize the profusion of new and diverse optimization methods as well as guide new research. The theory in this paper constitutes a first step towards these goals.

11. REFERENCES

[1] AUGER, A., AND TEYTAUD, O. Continuous lunches are free! In *Proceedings of the 9th Annual Conference on Genetic and Evolutionary Computation (GECCO-2007)* (New York, 2007), ACM Press.

[2] BILLINGSLEY, P. *Probability and Measure.* John Wiley, 1986.

[3] COHN, D. *Measure Theory.* Birkhauser, Boston, MA, 1980.

[4] EL-BELTAGY, M., NAIR, P. B., AND KEANE, A. J. Metamodeling techniques for evolutionary optimization of computationally expensive problems: Promises and limitations. In *GECCO'99* (1999), pp. 196–203.

[5] GOLDBERG, D. E. *Genetic Algorithms in Search, Optimization and Machine Learning.* Addison-Wesley Longman Publishing Co., Inc., Boston, MA, USA, 1989.

[6] HALMOS, P. *Measure Theory.* Springer-Verlag, New York, NY, 1974.

[7] JIN, Y. Surrogate-assisted evolutionary computation: Recent advances and future challenges. *Swarm and Evolutionary Computation 1*, 2 (2011), 61 – 70.

[8] KIRKPATRICK, S., GELATT, C. D., AND VECCHI, M. P. Optimization by simulated annealing. *Science 220*, 4598 (1983).

[9] LEHMAN, J., AND STANLEY, K. O. Abandoning objectives: Evolution through the search for novelty alone. *Evolutionary Computation 19*, 2 (2011).

[10] LOCKETT, A., AND MIIKKULAINEN, R. Real-space evolutionary annealing. In *Proceedings of the 2011 Genetic and Evolutionary Computation Conference (GECCO-2011)* (2011).

[11] LOCKETT, A. J. *General-Purpose Optimization Through Information Maximization.* PhD thesis, University of Texas at Austin, 2012.

[12] MUNKRES, J. R. *Topology.* Prentice Hall, Upper Saddle River, NJ, 2000.

[13] RADCLIFFE, N., AND SURRY, P. D. Fundamental limitations on search algorithms: Evolutionary computing in perspective. In *LECTURE NOTES IN COMPUTER SCIENCE 1000* (1995), Springer-Verlag, pp. 275–291.

[14] ROWE, J. E., VOSE, M. D., AND WRIGHT, A. H. Reinterpreting no free lunch. *Evolutionary Computation 17*, 1 (2009).

[15] SCHAUL, T., SUN, Y., WIERSTRA, D., GOMEZ, F., AND SCHMIDHUBER, J. Curiosity-Driven Optimization. In *IEEE Congress on Evolutionary Computation (CEC)* (2011).

[16] SCHUMACHER, C., VOSE, M. D., AND WHITLEY, L. D. The no free lunch and problem description length. In *Proceedings of the Genetic and Evolutionary Computation Conference (GECCO-2001* (2001), Morgan Kaufmann, pp. 565–570.

[17] VOSE, M. *The Simple Genetic Algorithm.* MIT Press, Cambridge, Massachusetts, 1999.

[18] VOSE, M. D. Random heuristic search. *Theoretical Computer Science 229* (1999), 103–142.

[19] WOLPERT, D. H., AND MACREADY, W. G. No free lunch theorems for optimization. *IEEE Transactions on Evolutionary Computation 1*, 1 (1997).

Runtime Analysis of Mutation-Based Geometric Semantic Genetic Programming on Boolean Functions

Alberto Moraglio & Andrea Mambrini
CERCIA, University of Birmingham
Birmingham B15 2TT, UK
a.moraglio@cs.bham.ac.uk
a.mambrini@cs.bham.ac.uk

Luca Manzoni
DISCo, University of Milano-Bicocca
20126 Milano, Italy
luca.manzoni@disco.unimib.it

ABSTRACT

Geometric Semantic Genetic Programming (GSGP) is a recently introduced form of Genetic Programming (GP), rooted in a geometric theory of representations, that searches *directly* the semantic space of functions/programs, rather than the space of their syntactic representations (e.g., trees) as in traditional GP. Remarkably, the fitness landscape seen by GSGP is *always* – for any domain and for any problem – unimodal with a linear slope by construction. This has two important consequences: (i) it makes the search for the optimum much easier than for traditional GP; (ii) it opens the way to analyse theoretically in a easy manner the optimisation time of GSGP in a *general setting*. The runtime analysis of GP has been very hard to tackle, and only simplified forms of GP on specific, unrealistic problems have been studied so far. We present a runtime analysis of GSGP with various types of mutations on the class of *all* Boolean functions.

Categories and Subject Descriptors

F.2.2 [**Analysis of Algorithms and Problem Complexity**]: Nonnumerical Algorithms and Problems

Keywords

Genetic programming, semantics, geometric crossover, runtime analysis, boolean functions

1. INTRODUCTION

Traditional Genetic Programming searches the space of functions/programs by using search operators that manipulate their syntactic representation, regardless of their actual semantics/behaviour. For instance, subtree swap crossover is used to recombine functions represented as parse trees, regardless of trees representing Boolean expressions, mathematical functions, or computer programs. Although this guarantees that offspring are always syntactically well-formed, it is unclear why such a blind syntactic search should work well for different problems and across domains.

In recent literature, there are a number of approaches that use the semantics of programs in various ways to guide the search of GP. Beadle & Johnson and Jackson use reduction to a canonical representation, in which individuals encoding the same function have a unique representation, to enforce semantic diversity throughout evolution, by creating semantically unique individuals in the initial population [3, 6], and by discarding offspring of crossover and mutation when semantically coinciding with their parents [2].

The semantics of a program can be directly and uniquely represented by enumerating the input-output pairs making up the computed function, or equivalently, by the vector of all output values of the program for a certain fixed order of all possible input values. Uy et al. [21] have proposed a probabilistic measure of semantic distance between individuals based on how their outputs differ for the same set of inputs sampled at random. This distance is then used to bias semantically the search operators: mutation rejects offspring that are not sufficiently semantically similar to the parent; crossover chooses only semantically similar subtrees to swap between parents.

Geometric crossover and geometric mutation [17, 13] are formal, representation-independent search operators that can be, in principle, instantiated to any search space and representation, once a notion of distance between individuals is provided. Simply stated, the offspring of geometric crossover are in the space-specific segment between parents, and the offspring of geometric mutation are in a space-specific ball around the parent. Many crossover and mutation operators across representations are geometric operators (w.r.t. some distance). Krawiec et al. [7, 8] have used a notion of semantic distance to propose a crossover operator for GP trees that is approximately a geometric crossover in the semantic space (i.e., a semantic geometric crossover). The operator was implemented approximately by using the traditional sub-tree swap crossover, generating a large number of offspring, and accepting only those offspring that were sufficiently "semantically intermediate" with respect to the parents. An analogous approach can be used to implement a semantic geometric mutation, with offspring lying in a small ball around the parent in the semantic space.

Whereas the semantically aware methods above are promising, as they have been shown to be better than traditional GP on a number of benchmark problems [3, 6, 21, 7], their

FOGA'13, January 16-20, 2013, Adelaide, Australia.

implementations are very wasteful as heavily based on trial-and-error: search operators are implemented via acting on the syntax of the parents to produce offspring, which are accepted only if some semantic criterion is satisfied. More importantly from a theoretical perspective, these implementations do not provide insights on how syntactic and semantic searches relate to each other. This drawback seems unavoidable. It was in fact believed [7, 8] that due to the complexity of the genotype-phenotype mapping in GP, a *direct* implementation of semantic operators that, acting on the syntax of the parent programs, produce offspring that are *guaranteed* to respect some semantic criterion/specification by construction, is probably impossible.

Geometric Semantic Genetic Programming [16, 15] is a form of genetic programming that uses semantic geometric crossover and semantic geometric mutation to search *directly* the semantic space of functions/programs. This is possible because, seen from a geometric viewpoint, the genotype-phenotype mapping of GP becomes *surprisingly easy*, and allows us to derive explicit algorithmic characterization of semantic geometric operators for different domains following a *simple formal recipe*, which was used to derive specific forms of GSGP for a number of classic GP domains (i.e, Boolean functions, arithmetic functions and classifiers).

The fitness landscape seen by the semantic geometric operators is *always* unimodal with a linear slope (cone landscape) by construction, as the fitness of an individual is its semantic distance to the optimum individual. This has the consequence that GP search on functions with semantic geometric operators is formally *equivalent* to a GA search on the corresponding output vectors with standard crossover and mutation operators. For example, for Boolean functions, GSGP search is equivalent to GA search on binary strings on the OneMax landscape, for *any* Boolean problem.

This equivalence suggests that GSGP performs better than standard GP. GSGP was compared with standard GP on several well-known problems across domains (finding Boolean functions, polynomial regressions, and classification tasks) and it consistently found much better solutions with the same budget of fitness evaluations [16, 15]. Furthermore, GSGP has been found more efficient and generalising better than standard GP on some initial studies on real-world problems [4].

Genetic programming has been hard to analyse from a theoretical point of view. The current literature on GP theory is heterogeneous. Perhaps the most developed theory of GP is the schema theory [9]. There is also some work on Markov models of GP search [12]. There are theory-laden methods to combat bloat based on an exact formalisation of the dynamics of average program size [20]. Other works focus on the analysis of some static structural features of the search space of GP programs (e.g., proportions of programs encoding the same function for different program sizes), and experimental hardness studies of fitness landscapes [9]. There is also some theoretical works on GP from a semantic perspective. In [19], a notion of geometric mutation based on a semantic distance was used to show that the No Free Lunch theorem does not apply to GP. Furthermore, the work [11] analyses traditional subtree crossover in terms of "semantic building blocks" in Boolean functions, reporting that most of the times this crossover does not make useful search in the semantic space.

Runtime analysis is the standard approach to analyse analytically algorithmic performance. In the last decade it has been applied, with an ever increasing success, to randomised search heuristics and it is establishing itself as a leading theory [18, 1]. Despite its success, the analysis is done on a per-algorithm-and-per-problem basis. Obtaining interesting, general runtime results holding on a large class of problems for non-trivial search algorithms would be a major progress. Due to the difficulty of analysing GP, there is only very initial work on its runtime analysis. Durrett et al. [5] present the runtime analysis of a mutation-based GP with a tree representation on very simplified problems, in which trees do not represent functions (i.e., objects that return different output values for different input values) but, rather, structures (i.e., objects whose fitness depends on some structural properties of the tree representation). This deviates quite significantly from the very essence of GP, which is about evolving functions.

GSGP is very attractive from a theoretical point of view. The equivalence of GSGP search to a GA search on cone landscapes opens the way to a rigorous theoretical analysis of the optimisation time of GSGP by simply extending known runtime results for GAs on OneMax-like problems. This analysis is not only relatively easy to obtain but it is also remarkably general, as it applies to all problems of a certain domain (e.g., all Boolean functions are seen as OneMax by GSGP). Furthermore, unlike existing runtime analysis for GP, the solutions of the problem considered are functions and not structures. Therefore, there is the potential to develop a general runtime analysis of GSGP on interesting problems. We start this line of theory and present a runtime analysis of GSGP with various types of mutations on the class of all Boolean functions.

Section 2 describes the theory of geometric semantic genetic programming framework. Section 3 introduces a number of mutation operators, and analyses their runtime. Section 4 reports experimental results comparing the various types of mutation on randomly generated problems. Section 5 presents conclusions and future work.

2. GEOMETRIC SEMANTIC GENETIC PROGRAMMING

Next, we describe the GSGP framework formally reporting and expanding on the relevant results from [16]. We first give abstract definitions of geometric semantic operators and their properties. Then we explain how to construct these operators in Section 2.2.

2.1 Abstract Geometric Semantic Search

A search operator $CX : S \times S \rightarrow S$ is a *geometric crossover* w. r. t. the metric d on S if for any choice of parents p_1 and p_2, any offspring $o = CX(p_1, p_2)$ is in the segment $[p_1, p_2]$ between parents, i.e., it holds that $d(p_1, o) + d(o, p_2) = d(p_1, p_2)$. A search operator $M : S \rightarrow S$ is a *geometric ϵ-mutation* w. r. t. the metric d if for any parent p, any of its offspring $o = M(p)$ is in the ball of radius ϵ centered in the parent, i.e., $d(o, p) \leq \epsilon$. Given a fitness function $f : S \rightarrow \mathbb{R}$, the geometric search operators induce or see the fitness landscape identified by the triple (f, S, d). Many well-known recombination operators across representations are geometric crossovers [13]. In particular for binary strings, any type of homologous crossover is a geometric crossover

w. r. t. Hamming distance (HD), and point mutation is geometric 1-mutation w. r. t. Hamming distance [13]. Geometric operators can also be derived for new spaces and representations by using in their definitions a distance based on a target representation (e.g., edit distance). If the distance between solutions is not directly linked to their representation, the geometric operators are well-defined in an abstract sense but their algorithmic description may be hard to derive.

For most applications, genetic programming can be seen as a supervised learning method. Given a training set made of fixed input-output pairs $T = \{(x_1, y_1), ..., (x_N, y_N)\}$ (i.e., fitness cases), a function $h : X \rightarrow Y$ within a certain fixed class H of functions (i.e., the search space specified by the chosen terminal and function sets) is sought that interpolates the known input-output pairs. I.e., for an optimal solution h it holds that $\forall (x_i, y_i) \in T : h(x_i) = y_i$. The fitness function $F_T : \mathrm{H} \rightarrow \mathbb{R}$ measures the error of a candidate solution h on the training set T. Compared to other learning methods, two distinctive features of GP are (i) it can be applied to learn virtually any type of functions, and (ii) it is a black-box method, as it does not need explicit knowledge of the training set, but only of the errors on the training set.

We define the *genotype-phenotype mapping* as the function $P : \mathrm{H} \rightarrow Y^{|X|}$ that maps a representation of a function h (i.e., its genotype) to the vector of the outcomes of the application of the function h to all possible input values in X (i.e., its phenotype), i.e., $P(h) = (h(x_1), ..., h(x_{|X|}))$. We can define a *partial* genotype-phenotype mapping by restricting the set of input values X to a given subset X' as follows: $P_{X'} : \mathrm{H} \rightarrow Y^{|X'|}$ with $P_{X'}(h) = (h(x_1), ..., h(x_{|X'|}))$ with $x_i \in X'$. Let $I = (x_1, ..., x_N)$ and $O = (y_1, ..., y_N)$ be the vectors obtained by splitting inputs and outputs of the pairs in the training set T. The output vector of a function h on the training inputs I is therefore given by its partial genotype-phenotype mapping $P_I(h)$ with input domain restricted to the training inputs I, i.e., $P_I(h) = (h(x_1), ..., h(x_N))$. The training set T identifies the partial genotype-phenotype mapping of the optimal solution h restricted to the training inputs I, i.e., $P_I(h) = O$.

Traditional measures of error of a function h on the training set T can be *interpreted as distance* between the target output vector O and the output vector $P_I(h)$ measured using some suitable metric D, i.e., $F_T(h) = D(O, P_I(h))$ (to minimise). For example, when the space H of functions considered is the class of Boolean functions, the input and output spaces are $X = \{0,1\}^n$ and $Y = \{0,1\}$, and the output vector is a binary vector of size $N = 2^n$ (i.e., Y^N). A suitable metric D to measure the error as a distance between binary vectors is the Hamming distance.

We define *semantic distance* SD between two functions $h_1, h_2 \in \mathrm{H}$ as the distance between their corresponding output vectors measured with the metric D used in the definition of the fitness function F_T, i.e., $SD(h_1, h_2) = D(P(h_1), P(h_2))$. The semantic distance SD is a genotypic distance induced from a phenotypic metric D, via the genotype-phenotype mapping P. As P is generally non-injective (i.e., different genotypes may have the same phenotype), SD is only a pseudometric (i.e., distinct functions can have distance zero). This naturally induces an equivalence relation on genotypes. Genotypes h_1 and h_2 belong to the same semantic class $\overline{h}$ iff their semantic distance is zero, i.e., $h_1, h_2 \in \overline{h}$ iff $SD(h_1, h_2) = 0$. Therefore the set of all genotypes H can be partitioned in equivalence classes, each one containing all genotypes in H with the same semantics. Let $\overline{H}$ be the set of all semantic classes of genotypes of H. The set of semantic classes $\overline{H}$ is by construction in one-to-one correspondence with the set of phenotypes (i.e., output vectors). Then, as D is a metric on the set of phenotypes, it is naturally inherited as a metric on the set $\overline{H}$ of semantic classes.

We define *semantic geometric crossover and mutation* as the instantiations of geometric crossover and geometric mutation to the space of functions H endowed with the distance SD. E.g., semantic geometric crossover SGX on Boolean functions returns offspring Boolean functions such that the output vectors of the offspring are in the Hamming segment between the output vectors of the parents (w. r .t. all $x_i \in X$). I.e., any offspring function $h_3 = SGX(h_1, h_2)$ of parent functions h_1 and h_2 meets the condition $SD(h_1, h_3) + SD(h_2, h_3) = SD(h_1, h_2)$ which for the specific case of Boolean functions becomes $HD(P(h_1), P(h_3)) + HD(P(h_2), P(h_3)) = HD(P(h_1), P(h_2))$. The geometric crossover SGX can be also seen as a geometric crossover on the space of semantic classes of functions $\overline{H}$ endowed with the metric D. From the definition of SGX above, it is evident that if $h_3 = SGX(h_1, h_2)$ then it holds that $h'_3 = SGX(h'_1, h'_2)$ for any $h'_1 \in \overline{h_1}, h'_2 \in \overline{h_2}, h'_3 \in \overline{h_3}$ because $P(h_1) = P(h'_1), P(h_2) = P(h'_2)$ and $P(h_3) = P(h'_3)$. In words, the result of the application of SGX depends only on the semantic classes of the parents $\overline{h_1}$, $\overline{h_2}$ and not directly on the parents' genotypes h_1, h_2, and the returned offspring can be any genotype h_3 belonging to the offspring semantic class $\overline{h_3}$. Therefore, SGX can be thought as searching directly the semantic space of functions.

When the training set covers all possible inputs, the *semantic fitness landscape* seen by an evolutionary algorithm with semantic geometric operators is, from the definition of semantic distance, a particularly nice type of unimodal landscape in which the fitness of a solution is its distance in the search space to the optimum [1] (i.e., a *cone landscape*). This observation is *remarkably general*, as it holds for any domain of application of GP (e.g., Boolean, Arithmetic, Program), any specific problem within a domain (e.g., Parity and Multiplexer problems in the Boolean domain) and for any choice of metric for the error function. Furthermore, there is some formal evidence [14] that EAs with geometric operators can optimise cone landscapes efficiently very generally for most metric. Naturally, in practice, the training set covers only a fraction of all possible input-output pairs of a function. This has the effect of *adding a particular form of neutrality* to the cone landscape, as only the part of the output vector of a function corresponding to the training set affects its fitness, the remaining large part is "inactive". The various forms of mutations that will be introduced and analysed in Section 3 have different strategies to cope with this form of neutrality and produce an efficient search.

GP search with geometric operators w. r .t. the semantic distance SD on the space of functions H is formally equivalent to EA search with geometric operators w. r .t. the distance D on the space of output vectors. This is because: (i) semantic classes of functions are in bijective correspondence with output vectors, as "functions with the same output vec-

[1] Notice that the optimum in the space of function classes is unique, as the output target vector is unique (since the training set is fixed prior to evolution), and it identifies uniquely the target function class.

tor" is the defining property of a semantic class of function; (ii) semantic geometric operators on functions are isomorphic to geometric operators on output vectors, as SD is induced from D via the genotype-phenotype mapping P (see also diagram (1) and explanation in the next section). Despite this formal equivalence, actually encoding a function in a EA using its output vector instead of, say, a parse tree, is futile: in the end we want to find a function represented in an *intensive form* that can represent concisely "interesting" functions and that allows for meaningful generalisation of the training set.

For the specific case of Boolean functions with n input variables and a single output variable, GSGP search with a training set of size N is equivalent to GA search with standard mutation and crossover on binary strings of length 2^n (i.e., the number of all possible inputs of n Boolean variables). When the training set covers all possible inputs, the fitness landscape seen by the GA is OneMax because minimising the error means minimising the Hamming distance between the output vector of candidate solutions and the target output vector, which is the same as minimising the number of wrong outputs, or equivalently as maximising the number of the right outputs, which on binary strings is equivalent to maximising the number of ones. When the training set covers only a subset of all possible inputs, the fitness landscape seen by the GA is OneMax on τ "active" bits that contribute to the fitness, and it is neutral on the remaining bits that do not affect the fitness. The position of the active bits are fixed but unknown, as we operate under the black-box scenario in which the algorithm cannot have direct knowledge of the training set but can only access the errors on the training set of candidate solutions via evaluation. Furthermore, *all Boolean functions are seen as equivalent* from GSGP search. This is because, whereas any distinct target training set gives rise to a different fitness landscape whose optimum is a different target string, any unbiased black-box search algorithm [10] does not assume a priori the knowledge of the location of the optimum and sees all these landscapes as equivalent.

2.2 Construction of Geometric Semantic Operators

The commutative diagram below illustrates the relationship between the semantic geometric crossover GX_{SD} on genotypes (e.g., trees) on the top, and the geometric crossover (GX_D) operating on the phenotypes (i.e., output vectors) induced by the genotype-phenotype mapping P, at the bottom. It holds that for any $T1, T2$ and $T3 = GX_{SD}(T1, T2)$ then $P(T3) = GX_D(P(T1), P(T2))$.

$$\begin{array}{ccccc} T1 & \times & T2 & \xrightarrow{GX_{SD}} & T3 \\ \downarrow{\scriptstyle P} & & \downarrow{\scriptstyle P} & & \downarrow{\scriptstyle P} \\ O1 & \times & O2 & \xrightarrow{GX_D} & O3 \end{array} \qquad (1)$$

The problem of finding an algorithmic characterization of semantic geometric crossover can be stated as follows: given a family of functions H, find a recombination operator GX_{SD} (unknown) acting on elements of H that induces via the genotype phenotype mapping P a geometric crossover GX_D (known) on output vectors. E.g., for the case of Boolean functions with fitness measure based on Hamming distance, output vectors are binary strings and GX_D is a mask-based crossover. We want to derive a recombination operator acting on Boolean functions that corresponds to a mask-based crossover on their output vectors. Note that there is a different type of semantic geometric crossover for each choice of space H and distance D. Consequently, there are different semantic crossovers for different GP domains. Furthermore, note that as the semantic crossover works directly on the semantic space of functions, *it does not matter how functions are actually represented* as the representation does not affect the search behaviour. For the sake of contrasting this framework with traditional GP, we will represent functions as trees.

DEFINITION 1. ***Boolean semantic crossover:*** *Given two parent functions* $T1, T2 : \{0,1\}^n \to \{0,1\}$, *the recombination SGXB returns the offspring Boolean function* $T3 = (T1 \wedge TR) \vee (\overline{TR} \wedge T2)$ *where* TR *is a randomly generated Boolean function (see Fig. 1).*

DEFINITION 2. ***Boolean semantic mutation:*** *Given a parent function* $T : \{0,1\}^n \to \{0,1\}$, *the mutation SGMB returns the offspring Boolean function* $TM = T \vee M$ *with probability* 0.5 *and* $TM = T \wedge \overline{M}$ *with probability* 0.5 *where* M *is a random minterm of all input variables.*

THEOREM 1. *SGXB is a semantic geometric crossover for the space of Boolean functions with fitness function based on Hamming distance, for any training set and any Boolean problem. SGMB is semantic 1-geometric mutations for Boolean functions with fitness function based on Hamming distance.*

The proof of the previous theorem can be found in [16]. In the following, we give an example to illustrate the theorem for the crossover. Let us consider the 3-parity problem, in which, we want to find a Boolean function $F(X_1, X_2, X_3)$ that returns 1 when an odd number of input variables is 1, 0 otherwise. Its truth table is in Table 1 (first 4 columns). As we have 3 input variables, there are 2^3 possible input combinations (first 3 columns of Table 1). In this example, we consider the training set to be made of all 8 entries of the truth table. However, normally the training set comprises only a small subset of all input-output pairs. The target output vector Y is the binary string 01101001 (column 4 of Table 1). For each tree representing a Boolean function, one can obtain its output vector by querying the tree with all possible input combinations. The output vectors of the trees in Figure 1 are in the last 4 columns of Table 1. The fitness $f(T)$ of a tree T (to minimise) is the Hamming distance between its output vector $P(T)$ and the target output vector Y (restricted to the outputs of the training set), e.g., the fitness of parent $T1$ is $f(T1) = HD(P(T1), Y) = HD(00000011, 01101001) = 4$. The semantic distance between two trees $T1$ and $T2$ is the Hamming distance between their output vectors $P(T1)$ and $P(T2)$, e.g., the semantic distance between parent trees $T1$ and $T2$ is $SD(T1, T2) = HD(P(T1), P(T2)) = HD(00000011, 01110111) = 4$. Let us now consider the relations between the output vectors of the trees in Table 1. The output vector of TR acts as a crossover mask to recombine the output vectors of $T1$ and $T2$ to produce the output vector of $T3$ (in $P(TR)$, a 1 indicates that $P(T3)$ gets a bit from $P(T1)$ for that position, and 0 that the bit to $P(T3)$ is from $P(T1)$). This crossover on output vectors is a geometric crossover w.r.t. Hamming

```
        AND              Crossover Scheme           Offspring
T1 =   /   \
      X1   X2                  OR                          OR
                              /  \                        /  \
        OR                 AND    AND                  AND    X3
T2 =   /  \        T3 =   /  \   /  \        =        /  \
      X2  X3             T1  TR NOT  T2             AND   NOT
                                 |                 /  \    |
        NOT                      TR               X1  X2   X3
TR =     |
        X3
```

Figure 1: T1 and T2 are parent functions and TR is a random function. The offspring T3 is obtained by substituting T1, T2 and TR in the crossover scheme and simplifying algebraically.

Table 1: Truth table of 3-parity problem (first 4 columns). Output vectors of trees in Figure 1 (last 4 columns): of parents T1 and T2, of random mask TR, and of offspring T3.

X_1	X_2	X_3	Y	$P(T1)$	$P(T2)$	$P(TR)$	$P(T3)$
0	0	0	0	0	0	1	0
0	0	1	1	0	1	0	1
0	1	0	1	0	1	1	0
0	1	1	0	0	1	0	1
1	0	0	1	0	0	1	0
1	0	1	0	0	1	0	1
1	1	0	0	1	1	1	1
1	1	1	1	1	1	0	1

distance, as $P(T3)$ is in the Hamming segment between $P(T1)$ and $P(T2)$ (i.e., it holds that $HD(P(T1), P(T3)) + HD(P(T3), P(T2)) = HD(P(T1), P(T2))$), as we can verify on the example:
$HD(00000011, 01010111) + HD(01010111, 01110111) = 3 + 1 = 4 = HD(00000011, 01110111)$. This shows that the crossover on trees in Figure 1 is a semantic geometric crossover w.r.t. Hamming distance.

Intuitively, the reason the theorem holds in general is that the crossover scheme in Figure 1 describes, using the language of Boolean functions, the selecting action of the recombination mask bit on the corresponding bits in the parents to determine the bit to assign to the offspring (i.e., it is a 1-bit multiplexer function piloted by the mask bit).

As the syntax of the offspring of semantic operators contain at least one parent, the size of individuals grows quickly in the number of generations. To keep their size manageable during evolution, we need to *simplify* offspring sufficiently and efficiently (not optimally, as that is NP-Hard on many domains) *without changing the computed function.* The search of semantic crossover and semantic mutation is completely unaffected by syntactic simplification, which can then be done at any moment and in any amount. For Boolean functions, there are quick function-preserving simplifiers. For the other domains, computer algebra system and formal methods can be used for these purpose.

3. RUNTIME ANALYSIS OF SEMANTIC MUTATIONS

We consider two families of semantic mutations, pointwise and blockwise mutations. They differ on the level of granularity of the changes to the output vector they can make. Pointwise mutations can change single entries independently. Blockwise mutations make the same change to entire blocks of entries.

3.1 Pointwise Mutations

We design semantic mutations that correspond to traditional mutations on the output vector. This will highlight a number of fundamental issues of semantic mutation and allow us to identify the requirements a semantic mutation should meet to be efficient.

Let us first consider the case in which the training set encompasses all possible input-output pairs of a Boolean function with n input variables. The size of the output vectors is $N = 2^n$, which is also the number of examples in the training set. A natural definition of *problem size* is the number of input variables n of the functions in the search space. Let us also assume that we have a GSGP (e.g., searching the space of functions represented as trees) that is exactly equivalent to a (1+1) EA (with mutation probability $1/N$) or to a RLS on the space of output vectors. The runtime of GSGP would be the same as of (1+1) EA or RLS on OneMax on the space of output vectors, which is $O(NlogN) = O(n2^n)$. This highlights a first issue: although the fitness landscape seen by GSGP is OneMax, since the size of the output vectors N is exponentially long in the problem size n, the runtime of GSGP is exponential.

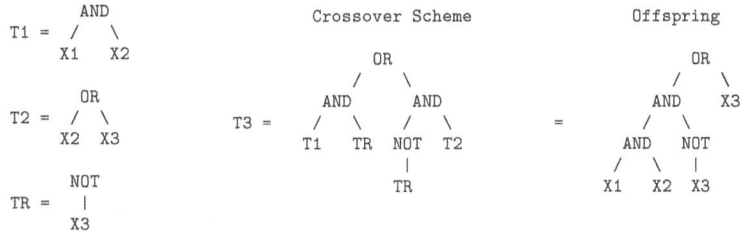

A second issue is that with an exponential size of the training set in n, each single fitness evaluation takes exponential time as it requires to evaluate all the outputs of a function against the target vector on exponentially many fitness cases. Naturally, in practice, the training set encompasses only a small fraction of all the input-output pairs of a function. To be able to evaluate the fitness of a function in polynomial time the size of the training set needs to be polynomial in n. In the following, we will consider the size of the training set (τ) to be linear in n (it is easy to extend the analysis to polynomial size of the training set). This transforms the problem seen by the EA on output vectors into a "sparse" version of OneMax in which most of vector entries are neutral, and the remaining entries, whose locations in the output vector are unknown, give each a unitary contribution to the fitness. Even with a training set of polynomial size, it is easy to see that both RLS and (1+1) EA (with mutation probability $1/N$) take exponential time to find the optimum. This is because at each generation the probability of mutating a non-neutral position of the output vector is exponentially small, hence it takes exponential time to get an improvement. What would it be then a mutation operator that gives rise to a polynomial runtime on the sparse OneMax problem?

3.1.1 Initialisation operator

Before attempting answering this question, let us consider another issue with semantic mutation. Can we *actually* implement semantic mutation operators corresponding to (1+1) EA and RLS *efficiently*? Even implementing the initialisation operator that generates a function uniformly at random in the sematic space takes exponential space and time most of the time! This is because it is equivalent to sampling its output vector uniformly at random, which is a random binary string exponentially long in n. From Kolmogorov complexity theory, we know that only a logarithmically small fraction of random binary strings can be compressed. So, most of the initial random functions are exponentially long and take exponential time to generate. Fortunately, the problem is easily solved by starting from an arbitrary initial solution which admits a short representation (e.g., the True function) rather than from a random one. This does not have a significant impact on the runtime, and on the runtime analysis that will be done w.r.t. the worst-case initial solution.

3.1.2 Point mutations

The original semantic mutation for Boolean functions [16] can be implemented efficiently, and it is reported below.

DEFINITION 3. ***Forcing point mutation:*** *Given a parent function $\mathcal{X} : \{0,1\}^n \to \{0,1\}$, the mutation returns the offspring Boolean function $\mathcal{X}' = \mathcal{X} \vee M$ with probability 0.5, and $\mathcal{X}' = \mathcal{X} \wedge \overline{M}$ with probability 0.5, where M is a random minterm of all input variables.*

Seen it on the output vectors, this operator forces to a random value exactly one randomly selected entry of the parent output vector. This is because adding ($\vee$) a minterm to a Boolean expression has the effect of forcing the corresponding single entry in the truth table to 1, and multiplying it ($\wedge$) by a negated minterm forces the corresponding entry to 0. This operator can be also rephrased as: it flips a randomly selected entry with probability 0.5 and it does not change anything with probability 0.5. So, it can be looked at as a semi-point mutation. Like point mutation, the runtime of GSGP with this operator is exponential.

The semantic mutation below (bit-flip point mutation) induces exactly point mutation on output vectors. This mutation can be seen as crossover of the parent with the negation of itself with a crossover mask which selects all bits but one from the parent.

DEFINITION 4. ***Bit-flip point mutation:*** *Given a parent function $\mathcal{X} : \{0,1\}^n \to \{0,1\}$ the mutation returns the offspring Boolean function $\mathcal{X}' = (\mathcal{X} \wedge \overline{M}) \vee (M \wedge \overline{\mathcal{X}})$, where M is a random minterm of all input variables.*

Seen it on the output vectors, this operator flips the output of the parent function corresponding to the combination of the input variables that makes the random minterm M true. Let us illustrate this mutation with an example. Let us consider the 2-parity problem, so $n = 2$ input variables. Its truth table is in Table 2, in the first three columns from left. Let us consider the following application of the bit-flip point mutation operator:

Table 2: First three columns from left: truth table of 2-parity problem with inputs X_1 and X_2, and output Y. Three rightmost columns: output vectors of the random minterm M, of the parent P and of the produced offspring O obtained by applying the bit-flip point mutation.

X_1	X_2	Y	M	P	O
1	1	0	**1**	**1**	**0**
1	0	1	0	1	1
0	1	1	0	1	1
0	0	0	0	0	0

Random minterm: M $= X_1 \wedge X_2$
Parent: P $= (X_1 \wedge X_2) \vee (X_1 \vee X_2)$
Offspring: $O = (P \wedge \overline{M}) \vee (\overline{P} \wedge M)$

The three rightmost columns of Table 2 report the corresponding output vector view of the application of the bit-flip point mutation above. Note that the output vector of the offspring is obtained by flipping the bit of the output vector of the parent corresponding to the '1' in the output vector of the random minterm (boldface in Table 2).

3.1.3 Bitwise mutation

Let us now consider bitwise mutation, which flips each bit independently with a certain probability. Before considering a semantic mutation that induces bitwise mutation on the output vectors, we show that bitwise mutation with an adequate mutation probability can lead to a polynomial runtime on the sparse OneMax with exponentially long chromosome.

THEOREM 2. *On the sparse OneMax problem with an exponentially long chromosome with $N = 2^n$ entries and with $\tau < N$ non-neutral entries, (1+1) EA with bitwise mutation with $p = \Omega(1/\tau)$ finds the optimum in time $O(\tau \log \tau)$. In particular, when τ is polynomial in n, the runtime is polynomial.*

PROOF. We define the potential k as the number of incorrect bits. At each iteration the potential decreases if an incorrect bit is flipped. This happens with probability

$$p_k > k\frac{1}{\tau}\left(1-\frac{1}{\tau}\right)^{N-1} > k\frac{1}{\tau}\left(1-\frac{1}{N}\right)^{N-1} > \frac{k}{e\tau}$$

Since the potential can decrease at most τ times and the expected time for the potential to decrease is $1/p_k$, the expected time to reach $k = 0$ (an finding the solution to the problem is)

$$E(T) = \sum_{i=0}^{\tau} 1/p_k = \sum_{i=0}^{\tau} \frac{e\tau}{i} = O(\tau \log \tau)$$

□

How can we implement a semantic mutation that corresponds to bitwise mutation with mutation probability p on the output vectors?

DEFINITION 5. ***Bitwise mutation:*** *Given a parent function $\mathcal{X} : \{0,1\}^n \to \{0,1\}$ the mutation do the following:*

- *Sample an integer number x from $x \sim Bin(p, N)$*

- *Generate x minterms uniformly at random without repetitions* $\{M_1, \cdots, M_x\}$
- *The offspring is* $\mathcal{X}' = (\mathcal{X} \wedge \overline{M}) \vee (M \wedge \overline{\mathcal{X}})$, *where* $M = M_1 \vee \cdots \vee M_x$.

Unfortunately, also this operator has a problem. Using a probability of mutation $p = \Omega(\frac{1}{\tau})$, which by theorem 2 makes the runtime of GSGP efficient for a training set size τ polynomial, this implementation becomes exponential in space hence in time because the expected number of minterms making up M is pN, which is exponential in n. So, by changing the probability p, what it is gained in terms of runtime of GSGP, it is then lost in terms of efficiency of the implementation of a single application of the mutation operator, and vice versa. The challenge is therefore finding a semantic mutation operator that, at the same time, (i) can be implemented efficiently and (ii) makes the runtime of GSGP polynomial in n for any Boolean problem. Does such operator even exist?

3.2 Blockwise Mutations

In this section, we consider four semantic mutations, which extend the forcing point mutation introduced in the previous section in different ways. The extension is obtained by replacing the mutating random minterm M with an *incomplete minterm* which may include only a subset of all the input variables. The four mutations differ on the family of incomplete minterms considered and their probability distributions. Like the forcing point mutation, these mutation operators can be implemented efficiently. The outstanding issue is therefore to see if they lead to a polynomial runtime for GSGP. Using an incomplete, rather than a full, minterm in the forcing mutation has the effect to force more than an entry of the output vector to the same value, i.e., it forces a block of entries to the same value, hence the name block mutations. These operators could work well on the sparse OneMax problem on exponentially long strings. As a first approximation, the idea behind these operators is that, by using sufficiently few variables in the incomplete minterm, the mutation would affect sufficiently many entries of the output vector, so that typically a non-neutral bit will be affected after a single application of the mutation operator. This, in effect, would be equivalent to searching the OneMax problem on the non-neutral entries, which are polynomially many, hence leading to a polynomial optimisation time. However, the analysis of block mutations is complicated by the fact that, unlike traditional mutations, they force *dependencies* between values at different entries of the string, as they cannot act separately on a single entry. In the following, we propose four block mutations that are analysable. These mutations are introduced in increasing order of the complexity of dependency between entries they produce.

3.2.1 Fixed Block Mutation

DEFINITION 6. ***Fixed Block Mutation (FBM):*** *Let us consider a* fixed *set of $v < n$ variables (fixed in some arbitrary way at the initialisation of the algorithm). FBM draws uniformly at random an incomplete minterm M comprising all fixed variables as a base for the forcing mutation.*

Fixing v of the n input variables induces a *partition* of the output vector into $b = 2^v$ blocks each covering 2^{n-v} entries of the output vector (which has a total of 2^n entries). There is a one-to-one correspondence between the set of all incomplete minterms M made up of the fixed v variables and the set of all the blocks partitioning the output vector. The effect of mutation FBM on the output vector is that of selecting one block uniformly at random and forcing all the entries belonging to the block to the same value, 0 or 1, selected at random with equal probability. Table 3 shows an example of application of FBM.

Table 3: Example of FBM. First four columns: truth table of 3-parity problem. Remaining columns: output vectors of the drawn random incomplete minterm $M = X_1 \wedge \overline{X_2}$, of the parent $P = X_2 \vee (X_1 \wedge \overline{X_2} \wedge X_3)$, and of the offspring $O = P \vee M = X_1 \wedge X_2$. Horizontal lines separate blocks of the partition of the output vectors obtained by fixing variables X_1 and X_2.

X_1	X_2	X_3	Y	M	P	O
0	0	0	0	0	0	0
0	0	1	1	0	0	0
0	1	0	1	0	1	1
0	1	1	0	0	1	1
1	0	0	1	**1**	**0**	**1**
1	0	1	0	**1**	**1**	**1**
1	1	0	0	0	1	1
1	1	1	1	0	1	1

GSGP with FBM is restricted to search the space of functions whose output vectors have the same output values for all entries of each block. This creates a difficulty: for some training sets of some Boolean problems, the optimal function satisfying the training set is not reachable for some choice of the fixed variables, as it lies outside the search space. This happens when at least two training examples with different outputs belong to the same block (e.g., in Table 3 the values of the entries in the first block of the optimum output vector Y are 0 and 1. This solution is therefore not reachable as reachable output vectors have both these entries set at zero or at one).

The particular settings of the analysis are as follows. We make the standard Machine Learning assumption that the training set T is sampled uniformly at random from the set of all input-output pairs of the Boolean problem P at hand. The training set is sampled only once, before the search for a function satisfying it has started, and, in particular, it remains unchanged during evolution. Therefore, from an optimisation viewpoint, the training set T defines the specific instance of the Boolean problem P being tackled by the search. The reachability of the optimum is uniquely determined when the training set T of a problem P is fixed, and when also the set V of variables inducing the partition of the output vector is fixed. We are interested in the worst-case probability across all Boolean problems that GSGP with FBM initialised with an arbitrary fixed set of variables V can reach the optimum on a training set sampled uniformly at random from the problem at hand [2]. Furthermore, when

[2]This is different from the traditional notion of probability of success of a search algorithm, as the source of the probabilistic outcome is the randomisation on the sampled

GSGP with FBM can reach the optimum, we are interested in an upper-bound w.r.t. all Boolean problems (any P) and all problem instances (any T of P) of the expected runtime to reach the optimum.

THEOREM 3. *For any Boolean problem P, given a training set T of size τ sampled uniformly at random on the set of all input-output pairs of P, GSGP with FBM with an arbitrarily fixed set of v variables finds the optimal Boolean function satisfying the training set T in time $O(b \log b)$, with probability $p \approx e^{-\frac{\tau^2}{2b}}$ for $b >> \tau$, where $b = 2^v$ is the number of blocks partitioning the output vector.*

PROOF. GSGP with FBM can reach the optimum provided that each distinct training example of the sampled training set T belongs to a distinct block. This holds irrespective of the prescribed output of the training examples, hence on any problem P. The optimum can be reached because with each training example in a different block, one application of FBM can flip independently the output value of each training example in the current solution. So, a function with any configuration of the outputs on the training set can be reached by the search.

The τ training examples are sampled uniformly at random on the set of all input-output pairs, i.e., uniformly on the output vector. The output vector is partitioned in b blocks of equal size. The probability of having each training example in a distinct block can be calculated by looking at it as a balls and bins process: blocks are bins of equal size, training examples are balls thrown uniformly at random on the bins. The probability of having at most one ball in each bin is the probability of throwing the first ball in an empty bin (1) times the probability of throwing the second ball in a bin left empty after the first throw ($(b-1)/b$), and so on, until all balls have been thrown. So we have:

$$P(b,\tau) = \prod_{i=1}^{\tau} \frac{b-(i-1)}{b}$$

When the number of bins is much larger than the number of balls, i.e., $b >> \tau$, $\frac{i-1}{b}$ is very small, as $e^x \approx 1 + x$ for x close to 0, then $P(b,\tau) \approx \prod_{i=1}^{\tau} e^{-\frac{i-1}{b}} = e^{-\frac{\tau(\tau-1)}{2b}} \approx e^{-\frac{\tau^2}{2b}}$.

When each example of the training set belongs to a distinct block, GSGP with FBM, which at each generation creates an offspring by forcing all the entries of an entire block to the same value, can modify independently each single output value of the current solution corresponding to an entry in the training set. This search is therefore equivalent to that of RLS with point forcing mutation on binary strings of length b on a sparse OneMax problem with τ non-neutral entries. As point forcing mutation makes no change half of the time, else it makes a point mutation, RLS with point forcing mutation takes twice the time of standard RLS with point mutation. With a routine argument, we obtain that the runtime of RLS on the sparse OneMax problem is $O(b \log \tau)$, which is bounded from above by $O(b \log b)$ as $b > \tau$. □

The number of blocks b partitioning the output vector is critical for the performance of the search. On one hand, from the theorem above, the runtime of GSGP with FBM becomes larger for a larger number of blocks. Therefore, we would like to have as few blocks as possible. On the other hand, the probability of success becomes higher as b gets larger [3]. So, in this respect, the more blocks the better. The number of blocks b is an indirect parameter of the algorithm that can be chosen by choosing the number v of variables in the initial fixed set, as $b = 2^v$. Furthermore, the number of blocks b should be chosen relative to the size of the training set τ (e.g., we must have $b \geq \tau$ to have enough bins to host all balls individually). The question is therefore if we can always choose the number of blocks relative to the number of training examples such that we have both a polynomial runtime and high probability of success. It turns out that this is always possible, as stated in the theorem below.

THEOREM 4. *Let us assume that the size of the training set τ is a polynomial n^c in the number of input variables n, with c a positive constant. Let us choose the number of fixed variables v logarithmic in n such that $v > 2c \log_2(n)$. Then, GSGP with FBM finds a function satisfying the training set in polynomial time with high probability of success, on any problem P, and training set T uniformly sampled from P.*

PROOF. The number of blocks $b = 2^v$ is then a polynomial in n with degree strictly larger than $2c$, i.e., $b = n^{2c+\epsilon}$ for some $\epsilon > 0$. From Theorem 3, we have a success probability of $p \approx e^{-\frac{\tau^2}{2b}} = e^{-\frac{n^{2c}}{2n^{2c+\epsilon}}} = e^{-\frac{1}{2}n^{-\epsilon}}$. As the argument of the exponent approaches 0 as n grows, we can use the expansion $e^x = 1 + x$ obtaining $p = 1 - \frac{1}{2}n^{-\epsilon}$, which tells us that the runtime holds with high probability for any $\epsilon > 0$. Again for Theorem 3 the running time is $O\left(n^{2c} \log n\right)$, that is polynomial in the size of the problem. □

3.2.2 Varying Block Mutation

The Fixed Block Mutation operator is an unnaturally "rigid" operator as it requires to fix a set of variables at the beginning of the search in some arbitrary way (e.g., selecting them at random), which are then used throughout evolution as sole components of the incomplete minterms used in the forcing mutation. On one hand, this operator is appealing because it fixes a partition structure on the output vectors that remains unchanged during evolution, and that makes it particularly suitable for theoretical analysis. On the other hand, fixing the partition structure may restrict the search space too much and make the the optimum function lie outside the search space, hence unreachable. In the following, we introduce a more "flexible" mutation operator that extends the Fixed Block Mutation, and enlarges its search space.

DEFINITION 7. ***Varying Block Mutation (VBM):*** *Let $v < n$ be a parameter. VBM draws uniformly at random an incomplete minterm M made of v of the n input variables as a base for the forcing mutation.*

The VBM operator can be thought as constructing an incomplete minterm in two stages. First, it draws uniformly at random v distinct variables from the set of n input variables to form a set V variables. Then, it draws uniformly at random an incomplete minterm M comprising all variables in V as a base for the forcing mutation. The effect on the

problem instance (i.e., sampled training set T from P), and not the randomisation of the search algorithm.

[3] This can be intuitively understood, as increasing the number of bins (i.e., blocks) while keeping the number of balls unchanged (i.e., training examples) increases the chance of getting each ball in a separate bin.

output vector of a single application of the VBM operator is, therefore, as follows: first, it draws uniformly at random a partitioning of the output vector with $b = 2^v$ blocks, each covering 2^{n-v} entries of the output vector; then, it selects one block of the current partitioning uniformly at random and it forces all the entries belonging to the block to the same value, 0 or 1, selected at random with equal probability.

Since when using VBM the partition structure on the output vector is not fixed, the search space seen by GSGP with this operator is larger than that with FBM, and in particular, the former search space covers completely the latter. The reason for that is that GSGP with VBM has always a chance to select the fixed variable set used by FBM to feed to VBM, and explore this part of the search space.

We say that an operator is *more expressive* than another when the search space covered by the former includes the search space covered by the latter. In this case VBM is more expressive than FBM. When the optimum of a certain Boolean problem is within the search space of a less expressive operator is also within the search space of a more expressive search operator, but the viceversa is not true in general. From its definition, the probability of success of an operator is higher than the probability of success of all operators less expressive than it. We say that an operator is completely expressive when its search space covers all solutions of all Boolean problems and all training sets, thus its probability of success is 1. Since VBM is more expressive than FBM its probability of success is higher. However, as FBM, also VBM is not able to always reach the optimum for any choice of Boolean problem and training set: there exists certain training set configurations such that for *all* partitionings induced by any choice of v input variables, there are always at least two training examples with different output values belonging to the same block.

PROPOSITION 1. *Consider GSGP with VBM using $v < n$. Then there exists a training set of size $\tau = n + 1$ of the Boolean parity problem on which this algorithm cannot find the optimum.*

PROOF. Consider the training set with input entries $\mathcal{T} = \{x \in \{0,1\}^n \mid \exists! i \in \{1,...,v\}\ x_i = 1\} \cup \{(0,\ldots,0)\}$ and as output values those of the parity problem (i.e., $(0\cdots,0)$ has output 0, while all the other vectors have output 1, as in Example 1).

Let M be an incomplete minterm of $v < n$ variables. If the all-zero vector satisfy M, then there exists a vector with output value 1 in $\mathcal{T}$ that satisfy M. Since VBM is a forcing mutation and every incomplete minterm that is satisfied by the all-zero vector is always satisfied also by another vector in τ with different output value, it is not possibile to obtain a perfect score on the training set τ. □

EXAMPLE 1. *We will illustrate the training set of Proposition 1 for $n = 3$ variables. In this case the training set is:*

	v_1	v_2	v_3	$f(v_1, v_2, v_3)$
$x_1 =$	0	0	0	0
$x_2 =$	1	0	0	1
$x_3 =$	0	1	0	1
$x_4 =$	0	0	1	1

where v_1, v_2, v_3 are variables and $x_1, \ldots, x_4$ elements of the training set. Note that for any choice of two variables we cannot separate x_1 from another element of the training set: with v_1 and v_2 we cannot separate x_1 and x_4, with v_1 and v_3 we cannot separate x_1 and x_3, and with v_2 and v_3 we cannot separate x_1 and x_2.

In the previous section, we have shown that GSGP with FBM, when it can reach the optimum, it finds it, quite remarkably, in polynomial time in the worst case w.r.t. all Boolean problems and training sets. Unfortunately, GSGP with VBM requires exponential time to find the optimum in the worst case.

PROPOSITION 2. *Consider GSGP with VBM using $v = c \log n < n$ variables for some constant $c > 0$. Then there exists a training set of size $\tau = n^c$ of the Boolean parity problem on which this algorithm needs superpolynomial time in n to find the optimum.*

PROOF. Consider the training set with input entries $\mathcal{T} = \{x \in \{0,1\}^n \mid \forall i \in \{v+1,...,n\}\ x_i = 0\}$ and as output values those of the parity problem (see Example 2). Note that the number of entries in the training set is $\tau = 2^v = n^c$.

For every selection of variables different from the first v variables, any incomplete minterm M made with those variables will be such that the subset $\mathcal{T}'$ of $\mathcal{T}$ of all train instances that satisfy M contains exactly $|\mathcal{T}'|/2$ instances with output value 1 and $|\mathcal{T}'|/2$ instances with output value 0. Since VBM is a forcing mutation, using M as the incomplete minterm for the mutation it is not possible to increase the fitness (i.e., if all output are forced to 1 then we obtain the incorrect value for half of the instances in $\mathcal{T}'$, the same if we force 0).

There is only one selection of variables that allows to increase the fitness (i.e., the first v variables). As the selection is uniform across all the subsets of v variables, in expectation only one step every $\binom{n}{v} \geq \left(\frac{n}{v}\right)^v = \frac{n^{c \log n}}{(c \log n)^{c \log n}}$ can produce an individual with a better fitness and that can be accepted by the mutation. □

EXAMPLE 2. *Consider the following training set in four variables:*

	v_1	v_2	v_3	v_4	$f(v_1, v_2, v_3, v_4)$
$x_1 =$	0	0	0	0	0
$x_2 =$	1	0	0	0	1
$x_3 =$	0	1	0	0	1
$x_4 =$	1	1	0	0	0

where $v_1, \ldots, v_4$ are variables and $x_1, \ldots, x_4$ elements of the training set. Note that the only choice of variables that allow us to select elements of the training set with equal output value (and thus increase the fitness) is $\{v_1, v_2\}$ However there are $\binom{4}{2} = 6$ different possible subsets of two variables. Hence the fitness increase just once every 6 generations, in expectation.

3.2.3 Fixed Alternative Block Mutation

In the following we introduce a mutation operator which is half-way between FBM and VBM, which has higher probability of success than FBM and finds the optimum in polynomial time in the worst case.

DEFINITION 8. ***Fixed Alternative Block Mutation (FABM):*** *Let $v < n$ be a parameter. Let us consider a* fixed *partition of the set of the n input variables (fixed in some* *arbitrary way at the initialisation of the algorithm) into n/v groups of v variables each. These groups of variables are the set of fixed alternatives of the mutation operator. FABM selects uniformly at random a group of variables among the fixed alternatives, and then draws uniformly at random an incomplete minterm M comprising all the variables in that group as a base for the forcing mutation.*

The FABM operator is half-way between FBM and VBM: as FBM, it fixes the choice of (groups of) variables at the initialisation, however, as VBM, it can use each time different (groups of) variables to construct the incomplete minterm to feed to the forcing mutation. From their definitions we have that FABM is more expressive than FBM, but less expressive than VBM. So, the probability of success of FABM is bounded below by the probability of success of FBM, and bounded above by the probability of success of VBM. We saw in the previous section that VBM is not completely expressive as there are some problems it cannot solve. Therefore, FABM is also not completely expressive as it is less expressive than VBM. The following theorem relates the performance of GSGP with FABM to those with FBM.

THEOREM 5. *For any Boolean problem of size n on which GSGP with FBM with v fixed variables finds an optimal solution with probability p in time T, GSGP with FABM with groups of v variables finds an optimal solution in time $T' = O\left(\frac{n}{v}T\right)$ with success probability $p' \geq 1-(1-p)^{n/v}$.*

PROOF. For GSGP with FABM with groups of v fixed variables, it holds that:

- if FBM finds the optimum for a given problem and training set then it exists a group of variables among the alternatives for which we can always improve any current non-optimal solution;
- the worst case happens when there is only one group of variables that can be used to improve on the current solution. In this case the runtime is n/v times slower than the runtime of GSGP with FBM as, in expectation, the algorithm can draw a group of variables that allows for an improvement only once every n/v trials. Thus the running time of GSGP with FABM is $T' = \frac{n}{v}T$.

GSGP with FABM tries to find the optimum using n/v disjoint groups of the input variables. The probability that the optimum cannot be found using any of those subsets is bounded above by $(1-p)^{n/v}$, thus the probability of success of FABM is $p' \geq 1-(1-p)^{n/v}$. □

As a corollary, as GSGP with FBM finds an optimal solution in polynomial time with high probability, GSGP with FABM finds it with higher probability and higher, but still polynomial, time.

3.2.4 Multiple Size Block Mutation

The block mutation operators considered so far cannot guarantee to find the optimum in all cases, but when they do they may find it in polynomial time. Instead, pointwise mutation operators can always find the optimum as they can act on the value of any entry of the output vector independently from any other entry. However, they need exponential time to find the optimum on any problem and any choice of training set. In the following, we introduce a mutation operator that combines both blockwise and pointwise mutations, which attempts to preserve the benefits of both.

DEFINITION 9. ***Multiple Size Block Mutation (MSBM):*** *The operator MSBM samples the number of variables v to consider uniformly at random between 0 and n. Then, it selects v variables at random from the set of n input variables, and it generates uniformly at random an incomplete minterm M using those variables, which is then used as a base for the forcing mutation.*

The effect on the output vectors of the feature of MSBM that the number of variable v is not fixed but it can be any number between 0 to n at each application is that the number of blocks partitioning the output vectors can vary from 1 block with 2^n entries to 2^n blocks with a single entry each. On one hand, as for pointwise mutation, this allows GSGP with MSBM to always reach the optimum as each single entry of the output vector can be acted upon independently by the mutation. On the other hand, GSGP with MSBM can solve efficiently any problem that can be solved efficiently by GSGP with the block mutation VBM. This is because MSBM can simulate VBM on v variables in time which is in the worst case n times larger (as the probability of selecting exactly v variables by MSBM is $1/n$). However, the time needed by GSGP with MSBM to reach an optimal solution can be exponential on some training set, as shown below.

PROPOSITION 3. *There exists a training set for which GSGP with MSBM takes expected exponential time to find the optimum.*

PROOF. Consider the training set with input entries $\mathcal{T} = \{x \in \{0,1\}^n \mid \exists! i \in \{1,...,v\}\ x_i = 1\} \cup \{(0,\ldots,0)\}$ and as output values those of the parity problem. Except for the all-zero vector, that has output value 0, all the others output values are 1 (See Example 1).

By the same reasoning as the proof of Proposition 1, the only way to reach the optimum is to obtain a minterm M that is satisfied by the all-zero vector and no other vector. Note that there exists only one minterm of n variables with this property.

Since there are 2^n complete minterm and we select each of them with equal probability, selecting the correct one requires an exponential number of trials in expectation. □

The training set of Example 1 is also a training set in which MSBM takes expected exponential time to find the optimum.

On Boolean problems whose solutions can be written as Boolean formulas with a small number of conjunctions, and each conjunction uses few variables, it is possible to find the optimum in polynomial time.

THEOREM 6. *Let ϕ be a DNF formula with $\alpha = Poly(n)$ conjunctions and every conjunction with at most $\beta = O(1)$ variables. Then ϕ can be obtained by GSGP with MSBM in expected polynomial time.*

PROOF. The time to select a correct conjunction is bounded by the number of conjunctions of β variables, i.e., by $\binom{n}{\beta}2^\beta = O(n^\beta 2^\beta)$ conjunctions, and the time to select the correct conjunction size, i.e., $O(n)$.

The action of selection preserves correctly selected conjunctions, thus α is only a multiplicative factor, since only

α conjunctions must be selected. Therefore, the time needed to reach the optimum is $O\left(\alpha n^{\beta+1}2^{\beta}\right)$. Since β is a constant and α is polynomial in n, the resulting time is polynomial in n. □

It is interesting to note that the previous result is independent from the choice of the training set, and it depends solely on the class of Boolean problem.

Note that for all the block mutation considered, the length of the Boolean function found as optimum is bounded above by the time complexity. In fact, as all the block mutations considered add a single (incomplete) minterm at each generation of GSGP, the number of minterms forming the optimum is bounded from above by the runtime, so it is polynomial. Thus, when the time complexity is polynomial, the length of the Boolean function found is also polynomial .

4. EXPERIMENTS

In this section, we present an experimental investigation of the time to reach the optimum and the success rate for GSGP with the four block mutations introduced in this paper. The theoretical analysis has focused on worst case analysis and asymptotic behaviour. The empirical investigation complements the theoretical one focusing instead on the average case for growing finite problem size.

A problem instance is a pair of a Boolean function P and a training set $\mathcal{T}$. We set the size of the training set τ equal to the number on input variables n of the Boolean function, i.e., the problem size. At each run, a randomly selected training set of a randomly selected function is generated and tested on GSGP with the four mutations. For each problem size from 8 to 48 with step 8, 100 runs were performed. For all mutations except MSBM, the number of variables selected was $v = 2\lceil\log_2 n\rceil$. We used a GP with population of one, initialised with a random minterm, mutation applied with probability 1, and the offspring replaced the parent only if it had better fitness (i.e., a higher number of correct outputs on the training set). A run was stopped when either the optimal solution was found or 10^5 generations had passed [4].

The results on the success rates for the different mutations is presented in Table 4. As for FBM, with the chosen v theory says that asymptotically GSGP has a constant probability of success different from 1. The fluctuations and deviations from constancy for growing problem size seen experimentally are due to the rounding in the used expression for v and to the fact that the theory does not apply for "small" problem size. As for both VBM and FABM, from theory we expect an asymptotical rate of convergence higher than for FBM. This is confirmed experimentally. It is also not surprising that the rate of convergence approaches 1 for increasing problem size for these two mutations, as the chosen v is a threshold point for the asymptotic behaviour of FBM between constant probability of success different from one, and probability of success one. As expected from the theory, MSBM converged to the optimum at all times given enough time.

[4]The choice of using a limit as high as 10^5 generations was due to the necessity to avoid stopping a run too early, thus decreasing our estimates of both the success rate and the expected time to reach an optimal solution. The value 10^5 was empirically chosen both to reach that goal and to allow a reasonable completion time for the experiments.

Table 4: Success rate of GSGP on random Boolean problems for different problem sizes and mutations.

	Problem Size					
	8	16	24	32	40	48
FBM	0.95	0.76	0.93	0.74	0.87	0.88
VBM	0.95	0.99	1.00	1.00	1.00	1.00
FABM	1.00	1.00	1.00	1.00	1.00	1.00
MSBM	1.00	1.00	1.00	1.00	1.00	1.00

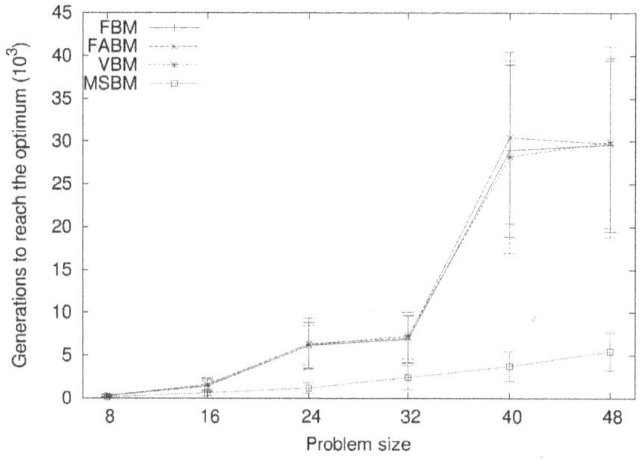

Figure 2: Average number of generations GSGP took to attain an optimal solution on random Boolean problems. The error bars represents one standard deviation above and below the average.

The results on the number of generations to reach an optimal solution are presented in Table 5. A plot of the optimisation time for increasing problem size is presented in Fig. 2. Experimentally FBM, VBM and FABM have very similar performance. The experiments estimate the average-case performance which draw quite a different picture from the worst-case performance determined theoretically in which FBM and FABM have a polynomial worst case, and VBM an exponential worst case. The rather non-smooth shape of the performance curves for these three mutations is caused by the rounding effect in the used expression for v. Furthermore, it is striking that MSBM performs significantly better than the other mutations, and, unlike those, MSBM seems to present a linear trend between optimisation time and problem size. Again, the experimental average-case picture is different from the theoretical one, which prescribes an exponential worst case for this mutation.

5. SUMMARY AND FUTURE WORK

Geometric semantic genetic programming searches directly the semantic space of functions. Seen from a geometric viewpoint, the genotype-phenotype mapping of GP becomes very simple, and allows us to derive explicit algorithmic characterizations of semantic operators for different domains. The search of GP with semantic operators on functions (genotypes) is formally equivalent to the search of a GA with standard search operators on their output vectors (phenotypes). Remarkably, the landscape seen by the equivalent GA, hence by GSGP, is always a cone by construction, for any problem and any domain. This, at the same time, makes the search

Table 5: **Minimum (min), median (med) and maximum (max) number of generations for GSGP to reach the optimum on random Boolean problems.**

		Problem Size					
		8	16	24	32	40	48
FBM	Min	34	294	1659	2353	14445	10434
	Med	207	1330	5862	6544	28456	27916
	Max	649	4959	14229	17068	69617	61842
VBM	Min	44	471	1815	1736	11970	11225
	Med	235	1531	5406	6432	29358	28437
	Max	759	3841	17355	22863	60965	56365
FABM	Min	18	438	2316	2289	9900	11901
	Med	254	1244	5756	6719	25827	28499
	Max	863	3925	13675	16792	81845	66043
MSBM	Min	5	117	182	477	1072	2291
	Med	115	547	1053	2222	3333	4928
	Max	450	2174	2677	8229	11907	14044

for the optimum much easier than for traditional GP, and it opens the way to analyse theoretically the runtime of GP in a *general settings* – an important open challenge – in an easy manner by extending known results for GA on one-max-like problems. In this paper, we have started this line of theory and presented a runtime analysis of GSGP with various types of mutation on the class of all Boolean functions.

There are a number of peculiar issues arising with GSGP, which required a careful design of mutation operators to obtain an efficient algorithm. The fitness landscape seen by GSGP is a heavily neutral extension of OneMax on exponentially long bit strings, in which only a polynomial number of entries contribute to the fitness. Standard GA mutation operators, i.e., point mutation and bitwise mutation, give rise to an exponential runtime. Furthermore, some semantic mutation operators do not admit an efficient implementation on Boolean functions (i.e., may require exponential time for generating a single offspring). Blockwise mutations are mutation operators that can be implemented efficiently and that at each application force a whole block of bits to a random value. We proposed four block mutations, two of which (i.e. FBM and FABM) reach the optimum in polynomial time with high probability on any Boolean problem. This is a *surprisingly general positive result* about the worst case performance of GSGP. Experimental results testing the average-case complexity of the block mutations have shown that one of the mutation (i.e. MSBM) seems, on the average case, much superior to the others, as it finds the optimum all the times and its runtime grows only linearly in the problem size.

There is plenty of future work. As training sets, which define specific problem instances, are sampled at random, it would be interesting to analyse theoretically the average-case complexity beside the worst-case as done in the current paper. We also would like to do further experimental investigations of GP with the new semantic operators on standard GP benchmarks, to see how they perform on more practical problems. As there are now a number of runtime results for GA with crossover, we intend to extend those to analyse GSGP with semantic crossover. At present, how functions trained by GP generalise on unseen inputs is a big mystery. As the effect of semantic operators on the output vectors is transparent, this may allow us to explicitly characterise the dependencies between training and testing sets reveling exactly what the inductive bias of GSGP is. Finally, we want to analyse GSGP on other domains. This seems to be within reach as, e.g., semantic operators for arithmetic functions and classifiers give rise to cone landscapes on real vectors and integer vectors, which have been studied already for traditional GA and ES, and whose analysis may be extended to GSGP.

6. ACKNOWLEDGEMENTS

The authors are grateful to Dirk Sudholt for helping check the proofs. Alberto Moraglio was supported by EPSRC grant EP/I010297/1.

7. REFERENCES

[1] A. Auger and B. Doerr, editors. *Theory of Randomized Search Heuristics – Foundations and Recent Developments.* World Scientific, 2011.

[2] L. Beadle and C. G. Johnson. Sematically driven crossover in genetic programming. In *Proc. of IEEE WCCI '08*, pages 111–116, 2008.

[3] L. Beadle and C. G. Johnson. Semantic analysis of program initialisation in genetic programming. *Genetic Programming and Evolvable Machines*, 10(3):307–337, 2009.

[4] M. Castelli, L. Manzoni, and L. Vanneschi. An efficient genetic programming system with geometric semantic operators and its application to human oral bioavailability prediction. Preprint arXiv:cs.NE/1208.2437v1, 2012.

[5] G. Durrett, F. Neumann, and U.-M. O'Reilly. Computational complexity analysis of simple genetic programming on two problems modeling isolated program semantics. In *Workshop on Foundations of Genetic Algorithms*, 2011.

[6] D. Jackson. Phenotypic diversity in initial genetic programming populations. In *Proc. of EuroGP 2010*, pages 98–109, 2010.

[7] K. Krawiec and P. Lichocki. Approximating geometric crossover in semantic space. In *Proc. of GECCO '09*, pages 987–994, 2009.

[8] K. Krawiec and B. Wieloch. Analysis of semantic modularity for genetic programming. *Foundations of Computing and Decision Sciences*, 34(4):265–285, 2009.

[9] W. Langdon and R. Poli. *Foundations of Genetic Programming.* Springer-Verlag, 2002.

[10] P. K. Lehre and C. Witt. Black-box search by unbiased variation. In *Proceedings of Genetic and Evolutionary Computation Conference*, 2010.

[11] N. F. McPhee, B. Ohs, and T. Hutchison. Semantic building blocks in genetic programming. In *European Conference on Genetic Programming*, 2008.

[12] B. Mitavskiy and J. Rowe. Some results about the markov chains associated to GPs and to general EAs. *Theoretical Computer Science*, 361(1):72–110, 2006.

[13] A. Moraglio. *Towards a Geometric Unification of Evolutionary Algorithms.* PhD thesis, University of Essex, 2007.

[14] A. Moraglio. Abstract convex evolutionary search. In *Workshop on the Foundations of Genetic Algorithms*, pages 151–162, 2011.

[15] A. Moraglio, K. Krawiec, and C. Johnson. Geometric semantic genetic programming. In *Workshop on Theory of Randomized Search Heuristics*, 2011.

[16] A. Moraglio, K. Krawiec, and C. Johnson. Geometric semantic genetic programming. In *Proceedings of Parallel Problem Solving from Nature*, 2012.

[17] A. Moraglio and R. Poli. Topological interpretation of crossover. In *Proc. of GECCO '04*, pages 1377–1388, 2004.

[18] F. Neumann and C. Witt. *Bioinspired Computation in Combinatorial Optimization – Algorithms and Their Computational Complexity*. Springer, 2010.

[19] R. Poli, M. Graff, and N. McPhee. Free lunches for function and program induction. In *Workshop on Foundations of Genetic Algorithms*, 2009.

[20] R. Poli and N. F. McPhee. Parsimony pressure made easy: Solving the problem of bloat in gp. In Y. Borenstein and A. Moraglio, editors, *Theory and Principled Methods for Designing Metaheuristics*, chapter 9. Springer, 2012.

[21] N. Q. Uy, N. X. Hoai, M. O'Neill, R. McKay, and E. Galván-López. Semantically-based crossover in genetic programming: Application to real-valued symbolic regression. *Genetic Programming and Evolvable Machines*, 12(2):91–119, 2011.

A Further Generalization of the Finite-Population Geiringer-like Theorem for POMDPs to Allow Recombination Over Arbitrary Set Covers

Boris Mitavskiy* and Jun He
Department of Computer Science
Aberystwyth University
Aberystwyth, SY23 3DB, U.K.
bom4@aber.ac.uk, jqh@aber.ac.uk

ABSTRACT

A popular current research trend deals with expanding the Monte-Carlo tree search sampling methodologies to the environments with uncertainty and incomplete information. Recently a finite population version of Geiringer theorem with nonhomologous recombination has been adopted to the setting of Monte-Carlo tree search to cope with randomness and incomplete information by exploiting the entrinsic similarities within the state space of the problem. The only limitation of the new theorem is that the similarity relation was assumed to be an equivalence relation on the set of states. In the current paper we lift this "curtain of limitation" by allowing the similarity relation to be modeled in terms of an arbitrary set cover of the set of state-action pairs.

Categories and Subject Descriptors

G.3 [**Probability and Statistics**]: Probabilistic algorithms; I.2.1 [**Artificial Intelligence**]: Games

Keywords

Geiringer Theorem, Evolutionary Algorithms, Non-homologous Recombination, Markov Chains, Lumping Quotients of Markov Chains,
Partially Observable Markov Decision Processes (POMDPs), Model-free Reinforcement Learning, Monte-Carlo Tree Search

*This work has been supported by EPSRC EP/I009809/1 "Evolutionary Approximation Algorithms for Optimization: Algorithm Design and Complexity Analysis" Grant.

FOGA'13, January 16-20, 2013, Adelaide, Australia.

1. INTRODUCTION

In recent years Monte-Carlo sampling methods, such as Monte Carlo tree search, have achieved tremendous success in model free reinforcement learning with, perhaps the most celebrated example, being the computer Go software that has beaten the top human player (see [2], for instance). Unlike the traditional techniques such as the mini-max method (that, by the way, have not succeeded for "Go"), Monte-Carlo Tree search (MCT) is based on running simulated self-plays, called "rollouts" until the end of the game when a terminal state with a known payoff has been encountered. A position in a game is represented by a state-action pair $\vec{s} = (s, \vec{\alpha})$ where $\vec{\alpha} = (\alpha_1, \alpha_2, \ldots, \alpha_{l(s)})$ is the collection of actions (or moves) available in a position s. The goal is to evaluate actions through back-propagation and averaging. Much effort in the current research is devoted to widening the range of applicability of the method in the environments with randomness and incomplete information. Recently, a finite population Geiringer Theorem with nonhomologous recombination has been adopted to the setting of Monte-Carlo tree search, based on which efficient parallel algorithms that exploit the intrinsic similarities within the state-action space to increase exponentially the size of a simulated sample of rollouts can be developed. The importance of similarity relations when coping with POMDPs is emphasized by other researchers, see, for instance, [4]. The main idea is that the algorithms sample directly from a long term probability distribution of repeated recombination applications defined in terms of the similarities. The only limitation of the new theorem is that the notion of similarity is limited to equivalence relations partitioning the set of state-action pairs. The current work lifts this "curtain of limitation" by allowing the similarity relation to be any set cover of the set of state-action pairs. The reader is strongly encouraged to familiarize themselves with the the first four sections of [7] prior to reading the current sequel paper, where a much more detailed introduction as well as mathematical support is provided.

2. MATHEMATICAL FRAMEWORK AND NOTATION

2.1 Set Cover of the State Space

Let S denote the set of states (enormous but finite in the current framework). Formally each state $\vec{s} \in S$ is an ordered pair $(s, \vec{\alpha})$ where $\vec{\alpha}$ is the set of actions an agent can possibly take when in the state $\vec{s}$. Let $\mathcal{C}$ denote an arbitrary set cover of S (i.e. $\mathcal{C} \subseteq \mathcal{P}(S)$ is a collection of subsets of S such that $\bigcup_{O \in \mathcal{C}} O = S$). Given a set $O \in \mathcal{C}$, for any two states $\vec{s}_1$ and $\vec{s}_2 \in O$ we will say that $\vec{s}_1$ and $\vec{s}_2$ are *O-similar states* and write $\vec{s}_1 \overset{O}{\sim} \vec{s}_2$. Intuitively, the sets O represent certain measure of similarity between the states $\vec{s}_1$ and $\vec{s}_2$. In practice, of course, if $\vec{s}_1 \overset{O}{\sim} \vec{s}_2$, the corresponding sets of actions $\vec{\alpha}_1$ and $\vec{\alpha}_2$ must be related in some kind of fashion: for instance, one may require that there are functions $f_{O, \vec{s}_1, \vec{s}_2} : \vec{\alpha}_1 \to \vec{\alpha}_2$ and $f_{O, \vec{s}_2, \vec{s}_1} : \vec{\alpha}_2 \to \vec{\alpha}_1$ that provide a natural similarity correspondence among the actions. Needless to say, the choice or design of such correspondences goes hand in hand with the choice or design of the set cover $\mathcal{C}$. In fact, there is a variety of ways in which this can be modeled depending on the specific applications. We leave the detailed investigations for future research.

Unlike the framework in [7], the current setting allows various degrees and types of similarity relations that are not limited to partitions of S induced by equivalence relations. Consider, for instance, a set covering induced by a distance function $d : S \times S \to [0, \infty)$ satisfying the usual axioms of a pseudo-metric: $\forall x, y, z \in S$ we have $d(x, x) = 0$, $d(x, y) = d(y, x)$ and $d(x, z) \leq d(x, y) + d(y, z)$. Such a pseudo-metric naturally induces a neighborhood structure on the set of states S: $\mathcal{C} = \{B(x, \epsilon) \mid x \in S \text{ and } \epsilon > 0\}$ where $B(x, \epsilon) = \{y \mid y \in S \text{ and } d(x, y) < \epsilon\}$ is a clopen ball[1]. Notice further that $\mathcal{C}$ has a number of subcovers such as, for instance, $\mathcal{C}_r = \{B(x, \epsilon) \mid x \in S \text{ and } r > \epsilon > 0\}$ where $r > 0$ and each one of these could be used in specific applications. As mentioned in the introduction, due to an overwhelming number of states as well as incomplete information and randomness, some sort of a coarse graining of the set of states is inevitable in applications. As pointed out in [7], the primary idea of the Geiringer-like theorems for decision making in the environments with randomness and incomplete information is to exploit the similarity relations on the set of states to estimate the average action payoffs based on an exponentially larger sample of rollouts than the one simulated at a relatively little computational expense. The version of the Geiringer-like theorem presented in this paper greatly expands the variety of the similarity relations that can be used in practice, thereby significantly widening the range and the flexibility of applications.

Just as in [7], a convenient way to represent a similarity relation $\mathcal{C}$ on a set of states S is to assign a positive integer to each similarity set $O \in \mathcal{C}$ in a one-to-one fashion. Each element of a set O labeled by an integer l is then uniquely determined by an additional alphabet symbol. Unlike the case in [7], it is possible for the same state to be labeled in a number of different ways as long as the corresponding integer labels differ. An example appears below.

Example 2.1. *A state space S consisting of 13 states and a set cover $\mathcal{C}$ consisting of 7 sets are pictured in figure 1. Notice that $\mathbf{1} = \{1a, 1b, 1c\}$, $\mathbf{3} = \{3a, 3b, 3c, 3d\}$, $\mathbf{2} = \mathbf{1} \cap \mathbf{3} = \{1a\} = \{2a\} = \{3a\}$, $\mathbf{5} = \{5a, 5b, 5c\}$, $\mathbf{6} = \{6a, 6b, 6c\}$, $\mathbf{4} = \mathbf{3} \cap \mathbf{6}$ consists of 2 elements that can be written as pictured on the Venn diagram on figure 1 and, finally, $\mathbf{7} = \{7a, 7b, 7c\}$. For $\mathbf{i} \neq \mathbf{j}$ we have $\mathbf{i} \cap \mathbf{j} = \emptyset$ unless $\{i, j\} = \{1, 3\}, \{1, 2\}, \{3, 2\}, \{3, 6\}, \{3, 4\}$ or $\{4, 6\}$.*

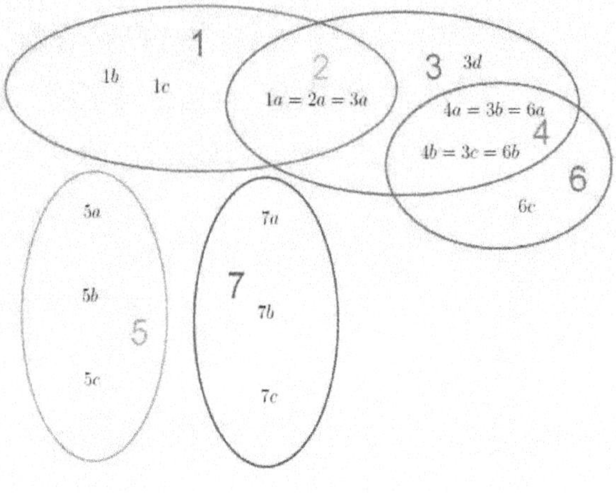

Figure 1: A set cover of a 13-element set of states consisting of 7 sets.

We end this section with a couple of simple definitions, the significance of which will become very clear in section 3.4, when we state the main theorem of the current article.

Definition 2.1. *Given a set of state-action pairs S and a set cover $\mathcal{C}$ of S, consider the relation $\backsim \subseteq S^2$ defined as $x \backsim y \iff \exists O \in \mathcal{C}$ such that x and $y \in O$ and notice that $\backsim$ is a symmetric and reflexive relation. We denote by $\overline{\mathcal{C}}$ the partition induced by the transitive closure of the relation $\backsim$, we will denote this equivalence relation (the transitive closure) by $\simeq$.*

Remark 2.1. *Apparently,*

$$\mathcal{C} = \overline{\mathcal{C}} \iff \mathcal{C} \text{ is a partition of } S \iff \backsim = \simeq .$$

An example below illustrates definition 2.1

Example 2.2. *Continuing with example 2.1, consider the 13-element set of state-action pairs and the set cover pictured on figure 1. Then the symmetric relation*

$$\backsim = \{(x, y) \mid i \in \mathbb{N} \text{ with } 1 \leq i \leq 7,\ x \in i \wedge y \in i\},$$

the partition $\overline{\mathcal{C}} = \{1 \cup 3 \cup 6, 5, 7\}$ and the equivalence relation $\simeq$ is the one corresponding to the partition $\overline{\mathcal{C}}$.

Definition 2.2. *Given any set $O \in \mathcal{C}$, we will say that the unique equivalence class in $\overline{\mathcal{C}}$, call it $\overline{O}$, that contains O is the expansion of the similarity set O.*

Example 2.3. *Continuing with examples 2.1 and 2.2, we have $\overline{1} = \overline{2} = \overline{3} = \overline{4} = \overline{6} = 1 \cup 3 \cup 6$ while $\overline{5} = 5$ and $\overline{7} = 7$.*

[1] Since the set S is finite, the pseudo-metric (i.e. the distance function) can take only finitely many values thereby inducing the discrete topology on the set S (see, for instance, [12] to learn about basic point-set topology). The induced topological space is then totally disconnected so that every open ball is also a closed ball, usually abbreviated as "clopen". In fact, in such a case it is sufficient to consider only integer-valued pseudo-metrics, yet depending on a specific application it may be sometimes more convenient to consider real or rational valued pseudo-metrics.

2.2 Rollouts and Recombination Operators

DEFINITION 2.3. *Suppose we are given a chance node $\vec{s} = (s, \vec{\alpha})$ and a sequence $\{\alpha_i\}_{i=1}^b$ of actions in $\vec{\alpha}$ (it is possible that $\alpha_i = \alpha_j$ for $i \neq j$). We may then call $\vec{s}$ a* root state, *or a* state in question, *the sequence $\{\alpha_i\}_{i=1}^b$, the* sequence of moves (actions) under evaluation *and the set of moves $\mathcal{A} = \{\alpha \mid \alpha = \alpha_i$ for some i with $1 \leq i \leq b\}$, the set of actions (or moves) under evaluation.*

DEFINITION 2.4. *A* rollout *with respect to the state in question $\vec{s} = (s, \vec{\alpha})$ and an action $\alpha \in \vec{\alpha}$ is a sequence of states following the action α and ending with a terminal label $f \in \Sigma$ where Σ is an arbitrary set of labels[2], which looks as $\{(\alpha, s_1, s_2, \ldots, s_{t-1}, f)\}$. For technical reasons which will become obvious later we will also require that $s_i \neq s_j$ for $i \neq j$ (it is possible and common to have $s_i \overset{O}{\backsim} s_j$ for various $O \in \mathcal{C}$ though). We will say that the total number of states in a rollout (which is $k-1$ in the notation of this definition) is the* height *of the rollout.*

REMARK 2.2. *Notice that in definition 2.4 we included only the initial move α made at the state in question (see definition 2.3) which is the move under evaluation (see definition 2.3). The moves between the intermediate states are chosen randomly or with respect to some dynamically updated distributions and are not evaluated so that there is no reason to consider them.*

A single rollout provides rather little information about an action particularly due to the combinatorial explosion in the branching factor of possible moves of the player and the opponents. Normally a large, yet comparable with total resource limitations, number of rollouts is thrown to evaluate the actions at various positions. The challenging question which the current work addresses is how one can take full advantage of the parallel sequence of rollouts. Since the main idea is motivated by Geiringer theorem which is originated from population genetics ([3]) and later has also been involved in evolutionary computation theory ([9], [5] and [6]) we shall exploit the terminology of the evolutionary computation community here.

DEFINITION 2.5. *Given a state in question $\vec{s} = (s, \vec{\alpha})$ and a sequence $\{\alpha_i\}_{i=1}^b$ of moves under evaluation (in the sense of definition 2.3) then a* population P *with respect to the state $\vec{s} = (s, \vec{\alpha})$ and the sequence $\{\alpha_i\}_{i=1}^b$ is a sequence of rollouts $P = \{r_i^{l(i)}\}_{i=1}^b$ where $r_i = \{(\alpha_i, s_1^i, s_2^i, \ldots, s_{l(i)-1}^i, f_i)\}$. Just as in definition 2.4 we will assume that $s_k^i \neq s_q^j$ whenever $i \neq j$ (which, in accordance with definition 2.4, is as strong as requiring that $s_k^i \neq s_q^j$ whenever $i \neq j$ or $k \neq q$)[3]*

[2]Intuitively, each terminal label in the set Σ represents a terminal state that we can assign a numerical value to via a function $\phi : \Sigma \to \mathbb{Q}$. The reason we introduce the set Σ of formal labels as opposed to requiring that each terminal label is a rational number straight away, is to avoid confusion in the upcoming definitions

[3]The last assumption that all the states in a population are formally distinct (although they may be similar with respect to various sets in $\mathcal{C}$) will be convenient later to extend the crossover operators from pairs to the entire populations. This assumption does make sense from the intuitive point of view as well since the exact state in most games involving randomness or incomplete information is simply unknown.

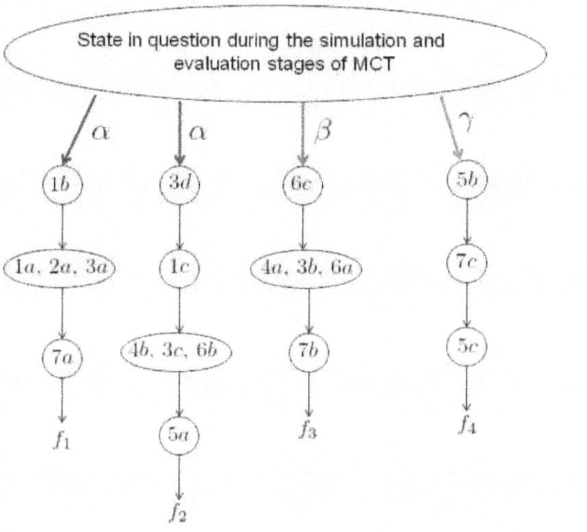

Figure 2: A population of 4 rollouts.

Moreover, we also assume that the terminal labels f_i are also all distinct within the same population, i.e. for $i \neq j$ the terminal labels $f_i \neq f_j$[4] In a very special case when ($\exists O \in \mathcal{C}$ such that $s_j^i \overset{O}{\backsim} s_k^q) \Longrightarrow (j = k)$ we will say that the population P is homologous. *Loosely speaking, a homologous population is one where similar states can not appear at different "heights".*

REMARK 2.3. *Each rollout $r_i^{l(i)}$ in definition 2.5 is started with the corresponding move α_i of the sequence of moves under evaluation (see definition 2.3). It is clear that if one were to permute the rollouts without changing the actual sequences of states the corresponding populations should provide identical values for the corresponding actions under evaluation. In fact, most authors in evolutionary computation theory (see [13], for instance) do assume that such populations are equivalent and deal with the corresponding equivalence classes of multisets corresponding to the individuals (these are sequences of rollouts). Nonetheless, when dealing with finite-population Geiringer-like theorems it is convenient for technical reasons (see also [5] and [6]) to assume the* ordered multiset model *i.e. the populations are considered formally* distinct *when the individuals are permuted. Incidentally, ordered multiset models are useful for other types of theoretical analysis in [10] and [11].*

EXAMPLE 2.4. *An example of a population of rollouts from the state space S described in example 2.1 with the set cover pictured in figure 1 appears in figure 2.*

The main idea is that the actions taken at similar states should be interchangeable with some probability depending on the similarity level for a number of reasons such as incomplete information or simply because they are randomly explored during the simulation stage of the MCT algorithm. In the language of evolutionary computing, such a swap of

[4]This assumption does not reduce any generality since one can choose an arbitrary (possibly a many to one) assignment function $\phi : \Sigma \to \mathbb{Q}$, yet the complexity of the statements of our main theorems will be mildly alleviated.

moves is called a crossover. Due to randomness or incomplete information (together with the various similarity relations which can be defined using the expert knowledge of a specific game being analyzed) in order to obtain the most out of a sample (population in our language) of the parallel rollouts it is desirable to explore all possible populations obtained by making various swaps of the corresponding rollouts in similar positions. Computationally this task seems expensive if one were to run the type of genetic programming described precisely below, yet, it turns out that we can predict exactly what the limiting outcome of this "mixing procedure" would be.[5] We now continue with the rigorous definitions of crossover. Crossover or recombination operators will be defined in terms of the similarities induced by the set cover much in the same way as it has been done in [7]. Nonetheless, here we are not limited to a single equivalence relation on the set of states, and many more recombination operators will be introduced depending on various similarity sets in $\mathcal{C}$. For this reason it is convenient to introduce the following notion:

DEFINITION 2.6. *Given a state $\vec{s} \in S$, we say that the collection of sets $\vec{s}(\mathcal{C}) = \{O \mid O \in \mathcal{C} \text{ and } \vec{s} \in O\}$ is the* collection of similarity sets of the state $\vec{s}$. *Given states $\vec{s}_1$ and $\vec{s}_2 \in S$ and a set $O \in \vec{s}_1(\mathcal{C}) \cap \vec{s}_2(\mathcal{C})$ we say that $(O, \vec{s}_1, \vec{s}_2)$ is a* recombination-compatible triple.

EXAMPLE 2.5. *Continuing with example 2.1, for the states* 1*b and* 3*a we have* $1b(\mathcal{C}) = \{\mathbf{1}\}$ *and* $3a(\mathcal{C}) = \{\mathbf{1}, \mathbf{2}, \mathbf{3}\}$ *so that* $(\mathbf{1}, 1b, 3a)$ *is a recombination-compatible triple while* $(\mathbf{2}, 1b, 3a)$ *is not.*

For every recombination compatible triple we can introduce the following two recombination operators:

DEFINITION 2.7. *Given two rollouts*

$$r_1 = (\alpha_1, \vec{s}_1, \vec{s}_2, \ldots, \vec{s}_{l(1)-1}, f)$$

and

$$r_2 = (\alpha_2, \vec{t}_1, \vec{t}_2, \ldots, \vec{t}_{l(2)-1}, g)$$

of lengths $k(1)$ and $k(2)$ respectively that share no state in common (i.e., as in definition 2.4,) there are two (non-homologous) crossover (or recombination) operators we introduce here. For a recombination-compatible triple $(O, \vec{u}, \vec{v})$ define the one-point non-homologous crossover *transformation as follows: $\chi_{O,\vec{u},\vec{v}}(r_1, r_2) = (\widehat{r}_1, \widehat{r}_2)$ where*

$$\widehat{r}_1 = (\alpha_1, \vec{s}_1, \vec{s}_2, \ldots, \vec{s}_{k-1}, \vec{t}_q, \vec{t}_{q+1}, \ldots, \vec{t}_{l(2)-1}, g)$$

and

$$\widehat{r}_2 = (\alpha_2, \vec{t}_1, \vec{t}_2, \ldots, \vec{t}_{q-1}, \vec{s}_k, \vec{s}_{k+1}, \ldots, \vec{s}_{l(1)-1}, f)$$

if [either ($\vec{s}_k = \vec{u}$ and $\vec{t}_q = \vec{v}$) or vise versa: ($\vec{s}_k = \vec{v}$ and $\vec{t}_q = \vec{u}$)] and $(\widehat{r}_1, \widehat{r}_2) = (r_1, r_2)$ otherwise.

Likewise, we introduce a single position swap crossover*: $\nu_{O,\vec{u},\vec{v}}(r_1, r_2) = (\widetilde{r}_1, \widetilde{r}_2)$ where*

$$\widetilde{r}_1 = (\alpha_1, \vec{s}_1, \vec{s}_2, \ldots, \vec{s}_{k-1}, \vec{t}_q, \vec{s}_{k+1}, \ldots, \vec{s}_{l(1)-1}, f)$$

while

$$\widetilde{r}_2 = (\alpha_2, \vec{t}_1, \vec{t}_2, \ldots, \vec{t}_{q-1}, \vec{s}_k, \vec{t}_{q+1}, \ldots, \vec{t}_{l(2)-1}, g)$$

if [either ($\vec{s}_k = \vec{u}$ and $\vec{t}_q = \vec{v}$) or vise versa: ($\vec{s}_k = \vec{v}$ and $\vec{t}_q = \vec{u}$)] and $(\widehat{r}_1, \widehat{r}_2) = (r_1, r_2)$ otherwise.

In addition, a singe swap crossover is defined not only on the pairs of rollouts but also on a single rollout swapping the positions of the O-similar states $\vec{u}$ and $\vec{v}$ in the analogous manner: If

$$r = (\alpha, \vec{s}_1, \ldots, \vec{s}_{j-1}, \vec{s}_j, \vec{s}_{j+1}, \ldots, \vec{s}_{k-1}, \vec{s}_k, \vec{s}_{k+1}, \ldots, \vec{s}_{l-1}, f)$$

and [either ($\vec{s}_k = \vec{u}$ and $\vec{s}_q = \vec{v}$) or vise versa: ($\vec{s}_k = \vec{v}$ and $\vec{s}_q = \vec{u}$)] then

$$\nu_{O,\vec{u},\vec{v}}(r) = (\alpha, \vec{s}_1, \ldots, \vec{s}_{j-1}, \vec{s}_k, \vec{s}_{j+1}, \ldots$$

$$\ldots, \vec{s}_{k-1}, \vec{s}_j, \vec{s}_{k+1}, \ldots, \vec{s}_{l-1}, f$$

if [either ($\vec{s}_j = \vec{u}$ and $\vec{s}_k = \vec{v}$) or vise versa: ($\vec{s}_j = \vec{v}$ and $\vec{t}_k = \vec{u}$)] and, of course, $\nu_{O,\vec{u},\vec{v}}(r)$ fixes r (i.e. $\nu_{O,\vec{u},\vec{v}}(r) = r$) otherwise.

REMARK 2.4. *Notice that definition 2.7 makes sense thanks to the assumption that no rollout contains an identical pair of states in definition 2.4.*

REMARK 2.5. *Intuitively, performing one point crossover means that the corresponding player might have changed their strategy in a similar situation due to randomness and a single swap crossover corresponds to the player not knowing the exact state they are in due to incomplete information, for instance.*

Just as in case of defining crossover operators for pairs of rollouts, thanks to the assumption that all the states in a population of rollouts are formally distinct (see definition 2.5), it is easy to extend definition 2.7 to the entire populations of rollouts. In view of remark 2.5, to get the most informative picture out of the sequence of parallel rollouts one would want to run the genetic programming routine without selection and mutation and using only the crossover operators specified above for as long as possible and then, in order to evaluate a certain move α, collect the weighted average of the terminal values (i. e. the values assigned to the terminal labels via some rational-valued assignment function) of all the rollouts starting with the move α which ever occurred in the process. We now describe precisely what the process is.

DEFINITION 2.8. *Given a population P and a transformation of the form $\chi_{O,\vec{u},\vec{v}}$, there exists at most one pair of distinct rollouts in the population P, namely the pair of rollouts r_1 and r_2 such that the state $\vec{u}$ appears in r_1 and the state $\vec{v}$ appears in r_2. If such a pair exists, then we define the recombination transformation $\chi_{O,\vec{u},\vec{v}}(P) = P'$ where P' is the population obtained from P by replacing the pair of rollouts (r_1, r_2) with the pair $\chi_{O,\vec{u},\vec{v}}(r_1, r_2)$ as in definition 2.7. In any other case we do not make any change, i.e. $\chi_{O,\vec{u},\vec{v}}(P) = P$. The transformation $\nu_{O,\vec{u},\vec{v}}(P)$ is defined in an entirely analogous manner with one more amendment: if the states $\vec{u}$ and $\vec{v}$ appear within the same individual (rollout), call it*

$$r = (\alpha, \vec{s}_1, \ldots, \vec{s}_2, \ldots, \vec{u}, \ldots, \vec{v}, \ldots, \vec{s}_{l-1}, f),$$

[5]In this paper we will need to "inflate" the population first and then take the limit of a sequence of these limiting procedures as the inflation factor increases. All of this will be rigorously presented and discussed in subsection 3.4; see also [7].

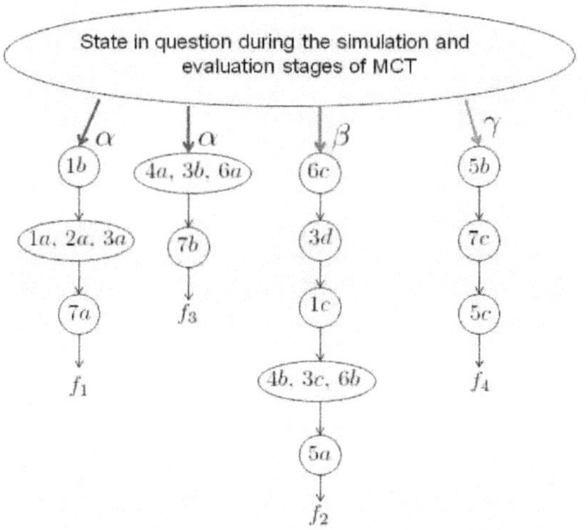

Figure 3: The population obtained after applying the crossover transformation in example 2.6 to the population displayed in figure 2.

and the state $\vec{u}$ precedes the state $\vec{v}$, then these states are interchanged obtaining the new rollout

$$r' = (\alpha, \vec{s}_1, \ldots, \vec{s}_2, \ldots, \vec{v}, \ldots, \vec{u}, \ldots, \vec{s}_{l-1}, f).$$

Of course, it could be that the state v precedes the state u instead, in which case the definition would be analogous: if

$$r = (\alpha, \vec{s}_1, \ldots, \vec{s}_2, \ldots, \vec{v}, \ldots, \vec{u}, \ldots, \vec{s}_{l-1}, f)$$

then replace the rollout r with the rollout

$$r' = (\alpha, \vec{s}_1, \ldots, \vec{s}_2, \ldots, \vec{u}, \ldots, \vec{v}, \ldots, \vec{s}_{l-1}, f).$$

EXAMPLE 2.6. *Continuing with example 2.4, applying the crossover transformation $\chi_{\mathbf{3},\, 3d,\, 3b}$ to the population we obtain the population on figure 3.*

REMARK 2.6. *It is very important for the main theorem of our paper that each of the crossover transformations $\chi_{O,\, \vec{u},\, \vec{v}}$ and $\nu_{O,\, \vec{u},\, \vec{v}}$ is a bijection on their common domain, that is the set of all populations of rollouts at the specified chance node. As a matter of fact, the reader can easily verify by direct computation from definitions 2.8 and 2.7 that each of the transformations $\chi_{O,\, \vec{u},\, \vec{v}}$ and $\nu_{O,\, \vec{u},\, \vec{v}}$ is an involution on its domain, i.e. $\forall\, O \in \mathcal{C}$ and $x,\, y \in O$ we have $\chi^2_{O,\, \vec{u},\, \vec{v}} = \nu^2_{O,\, \vec{u},\, \vec{v}} = \mathbf{1}$ where $\mathbf{1}$ is the identity transformation.*

3. GEIRINGER AND GEIRINGER-LIKE THEOREMS FOR POMDPS AND MCT.

3.1 The Main Idea Of the Current Work

Suppose a certain initial population of rollouts has been simulated during a simulation stage of the MCT. Although the rollouts have been simulated independently, similar states encountered during the simulations are likely to repeat in a number of settings. Assume now we were to run a GP (genetic programming) routine performing swaps (crossovers/recombinations) of rollouts in accordance with definitions 2.7 and 2.8 without any selection or mutation. Clearly the swaps correspond to potential populations of rollouts that could have been simulated just as likely, provided that something different in the environment (and/or opponent's hand) has taken place. Intuitively speaking, if we were to run the GP longer and longer time, we would be getting significantly more enriched information about potential outcomes and hence improve the quality of the payoff estimates. The central idea behind results such as the main theorem of this article (a special case where the similarity relation is an equivalence relation (i.e. $\mathcal{C}$ is a partition of S) has been established in [7]) is that one can actually anticipate the long term (or limiting) frequency of occurrence of various rollouts provided such a genetic programming routine has ran. This type of predictions is what the Geiringer-like theorems are about. In [5] a rather general simple and powerful theorem (named "finite population Geiringer theorem") has been established in the setting of Markov chains (populations being the states of the Markov chain: more on this in the next section) which tells us that under certain conditions that are satisfied by most recombination operators, the stationary distribution of this Markov chain is uniform. Furthermore, a methodology has been developed to derive what we call "Geiringer-like" theorems that address the limiting frequency of occurrence of various schemata (in our case subsets of rollouts: more on this in the upcoming subsection 3.4). Based on such a theorem it is not hard to invent efficient parallel dynamic algorithms that estimate the expected action payoff values based on the sample obtained after the entire "infinite time" run of the GP routine described above. It may be worthwhile to mention that "homologous recombination" (translating into the setting of MCT this would mean that the similarity classes may occur only at the same heights of the corresponding rollouts) versions of a Geiringer-like theorem have been obtained previously in the setting of genetic programming using the methodology appearing in [5] (see [6]). A version of Geiringer-like theorem with non-homologous recombination remained an open question and it has been established recently in [7] in a very similar setting as in the current article. While the Geiringer-like theorem in [7] is already rather interesting and powerful, it is limited to the case when the notion of similarity is measured via an equivalence relation, which does not allow any degree of similarity: any two states are either similar or not, but there is no way to judge how similar they are and every state (with the corresponding actions) of the same similarity class is evaluated indistinguishably. In the current article, we point out that this limitation can be easily alleviated to allow practically any notion of similarity among the states (i.e. an arbitrary set cover of the set of states) and, at the same time, the statement and the proof of the corresponding Geiringer like theorem are somewhat simplified. In the next section we will establish a generalization of the finite population Geiringer theorem for POMDPs in [7] that will allow us to derive the corresponding generalization of the Geiringer-like theorem of [7].

3.2 Specializing the Finite Population Geiringer Theorem to the setting of Monte Carlo Sampling for POMDPs

DEFINITION 3.1. *Let $\mathbf{n} = \{1, 2, \ldots, n\}$ denote the set of first n natural numbers. Consider any probability distribu-*

tion μ on the set of all finite sequences of crossover transformations $\mathcal{F} = \bigcup_{n=1}^{\infty} \mathcal{F}_n \cup \{\mathbf{1}\}$ where

$$\mathcal{F}_n = (\{\chi_{O,\,\vec{u},\,\vec{v}} \,|\, O \in \mathcal{C} \text{ and } \vec{u},\, \vec{v} \in O\} \cup$$

$$\cup \{\nu_{O,\,\vec{u},\,\vec{v}} \,|\, O \in \mathcal{C} \text{ and } \vec{u},\, \vec{v} \in O\})^{\mathbf{n}}$$

which assigns a positive probability to the singleton sequences[6] *and to the* identity element **1**. *(i.e. to every element of the subset $\mathcal{F}_1 \cup \{\mathbf{1}\}$. Given a sequence of transformations $\vec{\Theta} = \{\Theta_{O_j,\,\vec{u}_j,\,\vec{v}_j}\}_{j=1}^{n}$ where each Θ is either χ or ν (i.e. $\forall j$ either $\Theta_{O_j,\,\vec{u}_j,\,\vec{v}_j} = \chi_{O_j,\,\vec{u}_j,\,\vec{v}_j}$ or $\Theta_{O_j,\,\vec{u}_j,\,\vec{v}_j} = \nu_{O_j,\,\vec{u}_j,\,\vec{v}_j}$), consider the transformation*

$$\widetilde{\Theta} = \Theta_{O_n,\,\vec{u}_n,\,\vec{v}_n} \circ \Theta_{O_{n-1},\,\vec{u}_{n-1},\,\vec{v}_{n-1}} \circ \ldots \circ \Theta_{O_2,\,\vec{u}_2,\,\vec{v}_2} \circ \Theta_{O_1,\,\vec{u}_1,\,\vec{v}_1}$$

on the set of all populations starting at the specified chance node obtained by composing all the transformations in the sequence $\vec{\Theta}$. The identity element **1** *stands for the identity map on the set of all possible populations of rollouts. Now define the Markov transition Matrix M_μ on the set of all populations of rollouts (see definition 2.5) as follows: given populations X and Y of the same size k, the probability of obtaining the population Y from the population X after performing a single crossover stage, $p_{X \to Y} = \mu(\mathcal{S}_{X \to Y})$ where*

$$\mathcal{S}_{X \to Y} = \{\Gamma \,|\, \Gamma \in \mathcal{F} \text{ and } T(\Gamma)(X) = Y\}$$

where

$$T(\Gamma) = \begin{cases} \widetilde{\Theta} & \text{if } \Gamma = \vec{\Theta} \\ \text{The identity map} & \text{if } \Gamma = \mathbf{1}. \end{cases}$$

REMARK 3.1. *Evidently the map $T : \mathcal{F} \to P^P$ introduced at the end of definition 3.1 can be regarded as a random variable on the set $\mathcal{F}$ described at the beginning of definition 3.1 where P denotes the set of all populations of rollouts containing k individuals so that P^P is the set of all endomorphisms (functions with the same domain and codomain) on P and the probability measure μ_T on P^P is the "pushforward" measure induced by T, i.e. $\mu_T(S) = \mu(T^{-1}(S))$.*[7] *To alleviate the complexity of verbal (or written) presentation we will usually abuse the language and use the set $\mathcal{F}$ in place of P^P so that a transformation $F \in P^P$ is identified with the entire set $T^{-1}(F) \in \mathcal{F}$. For example,*

$$\text{if we write } \mu(\{F \,|\, F \in \mathcal{F} \text{ and } F(X) = Y\})$$

$$\text{we mean } \mu(\{\Gamma \,|\, \Gamma \in \mathcal{F} \text{ and } T(\Gamma)(X) = Y\}).$$

It may be worth pointing out that the set T^{-1} is not necessarily a singleton, i.e. the map T is usually not one-to-one (for instance, given any $O \in \mathcal{C}$ and any $\vec{u},\, \vec{v} \in O$ the sequence of the form $\vec{\Theta} = (\chi_{O,\,\vec{u},\,\vec{v}},\, \chi_{O,\,\vec{u},\,\vec{v}})$ or of the form $\vec{\Theta} = (\nu_{O,\,\vec{u},\,\vec{v}},\, \nu_{O,\,\vec{u},\,\vec{v}})$ both induce identity transformation on the set of populations of rollouts. Indeed, $\chi_{O,\,\vec{u},\,\vec{v}} \circ \chi_{O,\,\vec{u},\,\vec{v}} = \nu_{O,\,\vec{u},\,\vec{v}} \circ \nu_{O,\,\vec{u},\,\vec{v}} = \mathbf{1}$ since performing a swap at identical positions twice brings back the original population of rollouts.)

[6]This technical assumption may be altered in various manner as long as the induced Markov chain remains irreducible.
[7]The sigma algebra on P^P is the one generated by T with respect to the sigma-algebra that is originally chosen on $\mathcal{F}$, however in practical applications the sets involved are finite and so all the sigma-algebras can be safely assumed to be power sets.

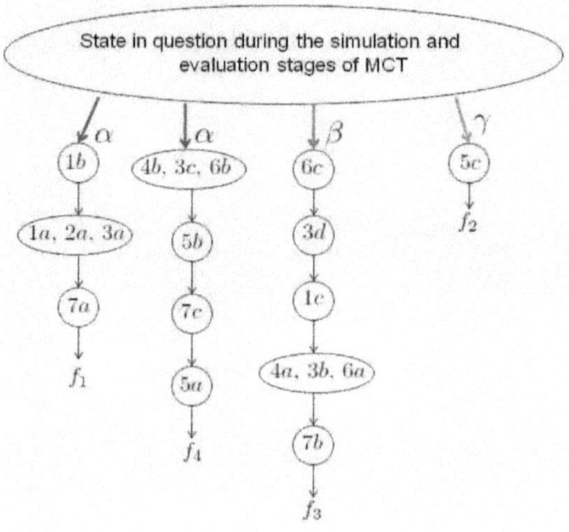

Figure 4: The population $R \sim Q \sim P$.

REMARK 3.2. *Notice that any concatenation of sequences in $\mathcal{F}$ (which is what corresponds to the composition of the corresponding functions) stays in $\mathcal{F}$. In other words, the family of maps induced by $\mathcal{F}$ is closed under composition.*

Of course, running the Markov process induced by the transition matrix in definition 3.1 infinitely long is impossible, but fortunately one does not have to do it. The central idea of the current paper is that the limiting outcome as time goes to infinity can be predicted exactly using the Geiringer-like theory and the desired evaluations of moves can be well-estimated at rather little computational cost in most cases. As pointed out in remark 3.1 above, each of the transformations $\Theta_{O,\,\vec{u},\,\vec{v}}$ is an involution and, in particular, is bijective. Therefore, every composition of these transformations is a bijection as well. We deduce, thereby, that the family $\mathcal{F}$ consists of bijections only (see remark 3.1). The finite population Geiringer theorem (see [5]) now applies and tells us the following:

DEFINITION 3.2. *Given populations P and Q of rollouts at a specified state in question as in definition 2.5, we say that $P \sim Q$ if there is a transformation $F \in \mathcal{F}$ such that $Q = F(P)$.*

EXAMPLE 3.1. *The populations P and Q and R displayed in figures* 2, 3 *and* 4 *respectively are equivalent in the sense of definition 3.2 since $Q = \chi_{\mathbf{3},\,3d,\,3b}(P)$, $R = \nu_{\mathbf{5},\,5a,\,5b} \circ \chi_{\mathbf{5},\,5a,\,5b} \circ \chi_{\mathbf{4},\,4a,\,4b}(Q)$*

THEOREM 3.1 (GEIRINGER THEOREM FOR POMDPS). *The relation $\sim$ introduced in definition 3.2 is an equivalence relation. Given a population P of rollouts at a specified state in question, the restriction of the Markov transition matrix introduced in definition 3.1 to the equivalence class $[P]$ of the population P under $\sim$ is a well-defined Markov transition matrix which induces an irreducible and aperiodic Markov chain on $[P]$ and the unique stationary distribution of this Markov chain is the uniform distribution on $[P]$.*[8]

[8]In fact, thanks to the application of the classical contrac-

Knowing that the limiting frequency of occurrence of a any two given populations Q_1 and $Q_2 \in [P]$ is the same, it is sometimes possible to compute the limiting frequency of occurrence of any specific rollout and even certain subsets of rollouts using the machinery developed in [5], [6] and enhanced further in [7].

To state and derive these "Geiringer-like" results we need to introduce the appropriate notions of schemata (see, for instance, [1] and [8]) here.

3.3 Schemata for MCT Algorithm

DEFINITION 3.3. *Given a state $(s, \vec{\alpha})$ in question (see definition 2.3), a rollout* Holland-Poli schema *is a sequence consisting of entries from the set* $\vec{\alpha} \cup \mathcal{C} \cup \{\#\} \cup \Sigma$ *of the form* $h = \{x_i\}_{i=1}^{k}$ *for some* $k \in \mathbb{N}$ *such that for* $k > 1$ *we have* $x_1 \in \vec{\alpha}$, $x_i \in \mathcal{C}$ *when* $1 < i < k$ *represents a similarity class of states, and* $x_k \in \{\#\} \cup \Sigma$ *could represent either a terminal label if it is a member of the set of terminal labels* Σ*, or any substring defining a valid rollout if it is a* $\#$ *sign.*[10] *For* $k = 1$ *there is a unique schema of the form* $\#$*. Every schema uniquely determines a set of rollouts* $R_h =$

$$\begin{cases} \{(x_1, \vec{s}_2, \vec{s}_3, \ldots, \vec{s}_{k-1}, x_k) \\ \mid \vec{s}_i \in x_i \textit{ for } 2 < i < k-1\} & \textit{if } k > 1 \textit{ and } x_k \in \Sigma \\ \\ \{(x_1, \vec{s}_2, \vec{s}_3, \ldots, \vec{s}_{k-1}, \\ \vec{t}_k, \vec{t}_{k+1}, \ldots, f) \\ \mid \vec{s}_i \in x_i \textit{ for } 2 < i < k-1, \vec{t}_j \in S\} & \textit{if } k > 1 \textit{ and } x_k = \# \\ \\ \textit{the entire set of all possible rollouts} & \textit{if } k = 1 \textit{ or,} \\ & \textit{equivalently, } h = \#. \end{cases}$$

which fit the schema in the sense mentioned above. We will often abuse the language and use the same word schema to mean either the schema h *as a formal sequence as above or schema as a set* R_h *of rollouts which fit the schema. For example, if* h *and* h^* *is a schema, we will write* $h \cap h^*$ *as a shorthand notation for* $R_h \cap R_{h^*}$ *where* $\cap$ *denotes the usual intersection of sets. Just as in definition 2.4, we will say that* $k-1$*, the number of states in the schema* h*, is the* height *of the schema* h*.*

EXAMPLE 3.2. *Continuing with example 2.1, consider the rollout Holland-Poli schema* $h = (\beta, 6, 3, 1, 4, \#)$*. Then the* 3rd *rollout in the population pictured in figure 4 starting with the action* β *fits the schema* h *while the rollout* $r = (\beta, 6c, 3a, 1c, 3a)$ *does not since* $3a = 1a = 2a \notin \mathbf{4}$ *(see figure 1).*

The notion of schema is useful for stating and proving Geiringer-like results largely thanks to the following notion of partial order.

DEFINITION 3.4. *Given schemata* h *and* g *we will write* $h > g$ *either if* $h = \#$ *and* $g \neq \#$ *or* $h = (x_1, x_2, x_3, \ldots, x_{k-1}, \#)$ *while* $g = (x_1, x_2, x_3, \ldots, x_{k-1}, y_k, y_{k+1}, \ldots, y_{l-1}, y_l)$ *where* y_l *could be either of the allowable values: a* $\#$ *or a terminal label* $f \in \Sigma$*. However, if* $y_l = \#$ *then we require that* $l > k$*.*

tion mapping principle[9] analyzed in section 6 of [7]) the stationary distribution is uniform in a rather strong sense as discussed in theorem 23 and example 24 of [7].

[10]This notion of a schema is somewhat of a mixture between Holland's and Poli's notions.

An obvious fact following immediately from definitions 3.3 and 3.4 is the following.

PROPOSITION 3.2. *Suppose we are given schemata* h *and* g*. Then* $h \geq g \Longrightarrow S_h \supseteq S_g$*.*

REMARK 3.3. *It may be worth pointing out that the converse of proposition 3.2 is false. Continuing with examples 2.1 and 3.2, consider, for instance, schemata* $h = (\beta, 6, 3, 1, 4, \#)$ *and* $g = (\beta, 6, 3, 1, 6, \#)$*. Evidently* $S_g \supset S_h$ *yet the schemata* h *and* g *are incomparable in the sense of definition 3.4. Fortunately, it is only proposition 3.2 (and not the converse) that's involved in deriving Geiringer-like theorems from theorem 3.1.*

3.4 The Statement of Geiringer-like Theorems for the POMDPs

In evolutionary computation Geiringer-like results address the limiting frequency of occurrence of a set of individuals fitting a certain schema (see [9], [5] and [6]). In this work our theory rests on the finite population model based on stationary distribution of the Markov chain of all populations potentially encountered in the process (see theorem 3.1). The "limiting frequency of occurrence" (rigorous definition appear in [7], [5] and [6]; an informal description is provided prior to the statement of the theorem in the current article) of a certain subset of individuals determined by a Holland-Poli schema h among all the populations in the equivalence class $[P]$ as time increases (i.e. as $t \to \infty$), where P is the initial population of rollouts, will be expressed solely in terms of the initial population P and schema h. These quantities are defined below.

DEFINITION 3.5. *For any action under evaluation* α*, let* $\alpha \downarrow (P) = \{\overline{O} \mid \overline{O} \in \overline{\mathcal{C}}$ *and at least one of the rollouts in the population* P *fits the Holland-Poli schema* $(\alpha, \overline{O}, \#)\}$*. Likewise, for an equivalence class* $\overline{O} \in \mathcal{C}$ *define a set valued function on the populations of size b, as* $\overline{O} \downarrow (P) = \{\overline{T} \mid \exists$ *states* $\vec{s} \in \overline{O}$*,* $\vec{t} \in \overline{T}$ *and a rollout* r *in the population* P *such that* $r = (\ldots, \vec{s}, \vec{t}, \ldots)\} \cup \{f \mid f \in \Sigma$ *and* $\exists$ *a state* $\vec{s} \in \overline{O}$ *and a rollout* r *in the population* P *such that* $r = (\ldots, \vec{s}, f)\}$*. In words,* $\overline{O} \downarrow (P)$ *is the collection of all equivalence classes in* $\overline{\mathcal{C}}$ *together with the terminal labels which appear after the states from the equivalence class* $\overline{O}$ *in at least one of the rollouts from the population* P*.*

As usual, we illustrate definition 3.5 with an example.

EXAMPLE 3.3. *Continuing with examples 2.1 and 2.4, from figure 2 we see that the states following the action* α *are of types* 1 *and* 3 *and both of these similarity classes belong to the equivalence class* $1 \cup 3 \cup 6$ *so that, according to definition 3.5,* $\alpha \downarrow (P) = \{1 \cup 3 \cup 6\}$*. The only state following the action* β *is of type* 6 *and the expansion of* 6 *is, again,* $1 \cup 3 \cup 6$*, so that* $\beta \downarrow (P) = \{1 \cup 3 \cup 6\}$*. The only state following the action* γ *is of type* 5 *and so* $\gamma \downarrow (P) = \{\overline{5}\} = \{5\}$*. Various states from every equivalence class in* $\overline{\mathcal{C}}$ *follow states of types* 1, 3 *and* 6*: for instance,* 1c *follows* 3d *and* 5a *follows* 3c *in the second rollout, while* 7a *follows* 1a *in the first rollout. No terminal label follows the equivalence class* $\{1 \cup 3 \cup 6\}$*. It follows then that* $1 \cup 3 \cup 6 \downarrow = \overline{\mathcal{C}}$*. The only similarity class following states from the equivalence class* $\overline{5} = 5$ *is* 7*. Terminal labels* f_2 *and* f_4 *follow states* 5a *in the second rollout and* 5c *in the* 4th *rollout. It follows than that* $5 \downarrow (P) = \{f_2, 7, f_4\}$*. Analogously,* $7 \downarrow (P) = \{f_1, f_3, 5\}$*.*

Definition 3.6. *Given a population P and equivalence classes $\overline{O} \in \overline{\mathcal{C}}$ and $\overline{T} \in \overline{O} \downarrow (P)$ let Order($\overline{O} \downarrow \overline{T}$, P) =*

$$= |\{((\overline{O}, a), (\overline{T}, b)) \mid \text{the segment } ((\overline{O}, a), (\overline{T}, b))$$

$$\text{appears in one of the rollouts in the population } P\}|.$$

Loosely speaking, Order($\overline{O} \downarrow \overline{T}$, P) is the total number of times the equivalence class $\overline{T}$ follows the equivalence class $\overline{O}$ within the population of rollouts P.

Let

$$Order(\overline{O} \downarrow P) = \sum_{\overline{T} \in \overline{O} \downarrow P} Order(\overline{O} \downarrow \overline{T}, P) + |\Sigma \cap (\overline{O} \downarrow \overline{T}, (P))|$$

denote the total number of states and terminal labels that follow the states from the equivalence class $\overline{O}$ in the population P.

Likewise, given a population of rollouts P, an action α under evaluation and an equivalence class $\overline{T} \in \alpha \downarrow (P)$, let

$$Order(\alpha \downarrow \overline{T}, P) = |\{(\alpha, (\overline{T}, b)) \mid \text{the segment } (\alpha, (\overline{T}, b))$$

$$\text{appears in one of the rollouts in the population } P\}|.$$

Alternatively, Order($\alpha \downarrow \overline{T}$, P) is the number of rollouts in the population P fitting the rollout Holland schema $(\alpha, \overline{T}, \#)$.

$$Order(\alpha \downarrow (P)) = \sum_{\overline{T} \in \overline{O} \downarrow P} Order(\overline{O} \downarrow \overline{T}, P)$$

denotes the total number of states that follow the action under evaluation α in the population P.

Example 3.4. *Continuing with example 3.3, for the population P pictured in figure 2 and the set cover $\mathcal{C}$ displayed via a Venn diagram on figure 1, recall that $\alpha \downarrow (P) = \beta \downarrow (P) = \{1 \cup 3 \cup 6\}$ and notice that the total number of states from the only equivalence class $1 \cup 3 \cup 6 \in \alpha \downarrow$ that follows the action α is 2: the state $1a = 2a = 3a$ in the first rollout and the state $1c$ following the state $3d$ in the second rollout; while the total number of states in the only equivalence class $1 \cup 3 \cup 6 \in \alpha \downarrow$ that follows the action β is 1: the state $6c$ in the 3rd rollout. Thus Order($\alpha \downarrow 1 \cup 3 \cup 6$, P) = Order($\alpha \downarrow (P)$) = 2 and Order($\beta \downarrow 1 \cup 3 \cup 6$, P) = Order($\beta \downarrow (P)$) = 1. Likewise, Order($\gamma \downarrow 5$, P) = Order($\gamma \downarrow (P)$) = 1. States from the equivalence class $1 \cup 3 \cup 6$ follow their own kind 4 times in the population P: $1a = 2a = 3a$ follows $1b$ in the first rollout, $1c$ follows $3d$ and $4b = 3c = 6b$ follows $1c$ in the second rollout, while $4a = 3b = 6a$ follows $6c$ in the third rollout so that Order($1 \cup 3 \cup 6 \downarrow 1 \cup 3 \cup 6$, P) = 4. The only state in the equivalence class 5 that follows a state from the equivalence class $1 \cup 3 \cup 6$ is $5a$ in the second rollout, following the state $4b = 3c = 6b \in 1 \cup 3 \cup 6$ so that Order($1 \cup 3 \cup 6 \downarrow 5$, P) = 1. There are 2 states from the equivalence class 7, namely $7a$ and $7b$, that follow the states from the equivalence class $1 \cup 3 \cup 6$, namely $1a = 2a = 3a$ and $4a = 3b = 6a$ respectively, in the first and the third rollouts of the population P so that Order($1 \cup 3 \cup 6 \downarrow 7$, P) = 2. No terminal label follows a state from the equivalence class $1 \cup 3 \cup 6$ and we deduce that Order($1 \cup 3 \cup 6 \downarrow (P)$) = $4 + 1 + 2 = 7$. Recalling that $5 \downarrow (P) = \{f_2, 7, f_4\}$ and observing that the only state in the equivalence class 7 that follows a state from the equivalence class 5, namely the state $5b$, is $7c$, while $|\Sigma \cap \{f_2, 7, f_4\}| = |\{f_2, f_4\}| = 2$ we deduce that Order($5 \downarrow 7$, P) = 1 and Order($5 \downarrow (P)$) = $1 + 2 = 3$. Likewise, the reader may compute the remaining numbers Order($7 \downarrow 5$, P) = 1 and Order($7 \downarrow (P)$) = $1 + 2 = 3$.*

Observe that applying any recombination transformation of the form $\chi_{O, \vec{s}, \vec{t}}$ or $\nu_{O, \vec{s}, \vec{t}}$ to a population P of rollouts neither removes any states from the population nor adds any new ones, and hence another important invariance property of the equivalent populations that opens the door for a lovely application of Markov inequality in the proof of the main theorem of the current article (see [7]) that follows from the same considerations is stated below.

Remark 3.4. *Given any population $Q \in [P]$, the total number of states in the population Q is the same as that in the population P. Apparently, as we already mentioned, the the total number of states in a population is the sum of the heights of all rollouts in that population (see definition 2.4 and 2.5). It follows then, that the sum of the heights of all rollouts within a population is an invariant quantity under the equivalence relation in definition 3.2. In other words, if $Q \sim P$ then the sum of the heights of the rollouts in the population Q is the same as the sum of the heights of the rollouts in the population P.*

There is yet one more important notion, namely that of the "limiting frequency of occurrence" of a schema as one runs the genetic programming routine with recombination only we need to introduce to state the Geiringer-like results of the current paper. A rigorous definition in the most general framework appears in [7], [5] and [6]. The description below is sufficient to understand the statement of finite population Geiringer-like theorems.

Informal Description of the Limiting Frequency of Occurrence: Given a schema h and a population P of size m, suppose we run the Markov process $\{X_n\}_{n=0}^{\infty}$ on the populations in the equivalence class $[P]$ of the initial population of rollouts P as in definition 3.1.[11] As discussed previously, this corresponds to "running the genetic programming routine forever" and each recombination models the changes in player's strategies due to incomplete information, randomness personality etc. Up to time t a total of $m \cdot t$ individuals (counting repetitions) have been encountered. Among these a certain number, say $h(t)$, fit the schema h in the sense of definition 3.3. We now let $\Phi(P, h, t) = \frac{h(t)}{m \cdot t}$ to be the proportion of these individuals fitting the schema h out of the total number of individuals encountered up to time t. Although it may be possible to derive the formulas for $\lim_{t \to \infty} \Phi(P, h, t)$ in the most general case when the initial population of rollouts P is non-homologous[12] (in other words when the states representing the same equivalence class may appear at various "heights" in the same population of rollouts: see definition 2.5), the formulas obtained in this manner would definitely be significantly more cumbersome and would not be as well suited for algorithm development[13] as the limiting result with respect to "inflating" the initial population P in the sense described below. Remarkably, the formula for the limiting result in the general non-homologous initial population case coincides with the one for the homologous populations.

---

[11] In fact, such Markov chains don't even have to be time homogenous: (see theorem 23 and example 24 of [7] for a detailed exposition.

[12] such exact formulas have been derived for the case of homologous recombination in the setting of GP: see [6]

[13] This is an open question, yet it's practical importance is highly unclear

DEFINITION 3.7. *Given a population* $P = \{r_i^{l(i)}\}_{i=1}^{b}$ *of rollouts in the sense of definition 2.5, where*

$$r_i = \{(\alpha_i, \vec{s}_1^{\,i}, \vec{s}_2^{\,i}, \ldots, \vec{s}_{l(i)-1}^{\,i}, f_i)\}$$

and a positive integer m*, we first increase the size of the set of states* S *by a factor of* m*: formally, we update the set of states as follows:*

$$S := S \times m = \{(\vec{s}, i) \mid \vec{s} \in S, i \in \mathbb{N} \text{ and } 1 \leq i \leq m\}.$$

Likewise, we also increase the terminal set of labels Σ *by a factor of* m *so that*

$$\Sigma := \Sigma \times m = \{(f, i) \mid f \in \Sigma, i \in \mathbb{N} \text{ and } 1 \leq i \leq m\}.$$

Certainly, the set cover $\mathcal{C}$ *of the original set* S *is naturally updated into the corresponding set cover of the updated set of states as*

$$\mathcal{C} := \{O \mid O := \{(\vec{s}, i) \mid \vec{s} \in O, i \in \mathbb{N} \text{ and } 1 \leq i \leq m\}\}$$

Now we let

$$P_m = \{r_{i,k}^{l(i)}\}_{1 \leq i \leq b \text{ and } 1 \leq k \leq m}$$

where

$$r_{i,k}^{l(i)} = \{(\alpha_i, (\vec{s}_1^{\,i}, k), (\vec{s}_2^{\,i}, k), \ldots, (\vec{s}_{l(i)-1}^{\,i}, k), (f_i, k))\}.$$

We will say that the population P_m *is an* inflation *of the population* P *by a factor of* m*.*

Essentially, a population P_m consists of m *formally distinct* copies of each rollout in the population P. Intuitively speaking, the stochastic information captured in the sample of rollouts comprising the population P_m (such as the frequency of obtaining a state in a similarity set O after a state in a similarity set T) is the same as the one contained within the population P emphasized by the factor of m. In fact, the following rather important obvious facts make some of this intuition precise:

PROPOSITION 3.3. *Given a population* P *of rollouts and a positive integer* m *consider the inflation of the population* P *by a factor of* m*,* P_m *as in definition 3.7. Then the following are true:*

$$\alpha \downarrow (P_m) = \alpha \downarrow (P),\ \overline{O} \downarrow (P_m) = \overline{O} \downarrow (P)$$

while

$$\text{Order}(\overline{O} \downarrow \overline{T}, P_m) = m \cdot \text{Order}(\overline{O} \downarrow \overline{T}, P),$$

$$\text{Numb}(\alpha, P_m) = m \cdot \text{Numb}(\alpha, P)$$

and

$$\text{Order}(\overline{O} \downarrow, P_m) = m \cdot \text{Order}(\overline{O} \downarrow, P) \quad (1)$$

For any population of rollouts Q *let* Total(Q) *denote the total number of states in the population* Q *which is, of course, the same thing as the sum of the heights of all rollouts in the population* Q*. Then, clearly,* Total$(P_m) = m \cdot$ Total(P)*. In the special case when* P *is a homologous population,* $\forall\, m \in \mathbb{N}$ *so is the population* P_m*.*

REMARK 3.5. *We will use the same Holland-Poli schema* $h = (\alpha, O_1, O_2, \ldots, O_{k-1}, f)$ *to model the corresponding sets of rollouts of the set of states* S *as of the set* S *inflated by a factor of* m*. Of course,* $S_h = S_h^m$ *where* S_h^m *is the set of states inflated by a factor of* m *just as in proposition 3.3 above. Furthermore, it is important to point out that in the statement of the theorem below we use the sets* O *from the initial (non-inflated, or, alternatively, inflated by a factor of* 1*) population to express the limiting frequency of occurrence.*

We are finally ready to state the main result of the current paper.

THEOREM 3.4 (THE GEIRINGER-LIKE THEOREM FOR MCT). *Repeat verbatim the assumptions of theorem 3.1*[14]*. Let*

$$h = (\alpha, O_1, O_2, \ldots, O_{k-1}, x_k)$$

where $x_k \in \{\#\} \cup \Sigma$ *be a given Holland-Poli schema. For* $m \in \mathbb{N}$ *consider the random variable* $\Phi(P_m, h, t)$ *described in the paragraph just above (alternatively, a rigorous definition in the most general framework appears in [7], [5] and [6]) with respect to the Markov process* X_n^m *where* m *indicates that the initial population of rollouts is the inflated population* P_m *as in definition 3.7. Then*

$$\lim_{m \to \infty} \lim_{t \to \infty} \Phi(P_m, h, t) = \frac{Numb(\alpha, P)}{b} \cdot \prod_{q=1}^{k-1} \frac{|O_q|}{|\overline{O_q}|} \times$$

$$\frac{\text{Order}(\alpha \downarrow \overline{O_1}, P)}{\text{Order}(\alpha \downarrow, P)} \cdot \prod_{q=1}^{k-1} \frac{\text{Order}(\overline{O_{q-1}} \downarrow \overline{O_q}, P)}{\text{Order}(\overline{O_{q-1}} \downarrow, P)} \cdot \text{LF}(P, h) \quad (2)$$

where

$$\text{LF}(P, h) = \begin{cases} 1 & \text{if } x_k = \# \\ 0 & \text{if } x_k = f \in \Sigma \text{ and } f \notin \overline{O_{k-1}} \downarrow (P) \\ \text{Fraction} & \text{if } x_k = f \in \Sigma \text{ and } f \in \overline{O_{k-1}} \downarrow_\Sigma (P) \end{cases}$$

where

$$\text{Fraction} = \frac{1}{\text{Order}(\overline{O_{k-1}} \downarrow, P)}$$

(we write "LF" as short for "Last Factor"). Furthermore, in the special case when the initial population P *is homologous (see definition 2.5), one does not need to take the limit as* $m \to \infty$ *in the sense that* $\lim_{t\to\infty} \Phi(P_m, h, t)$ *is a constant independent of* m *and its value is given by the right hand side of equation 2.*

REMARK 3.6. *Notice a simplification in the statement of theorem 3.4 here: unlike the case in [7], thanks to the assumption that the state space* S *contains no states that are not present in the initial population* P*, the denominators of the multiples in the right hand side of equation 2 are never* 0*. As mentioned before, this assumption does not reduce the generality since one can always shrink or enlarge the set of states* S *and modify the collection* $\mathcal{C}$ *of similarity sets according to the population of rollouts under consideration.*

EXAMPLE 3.5. *Continuing with examples 2.1, 2.4 and 3.4, consider the Holland-Poli rollout schema* $h = (\beta, 4, 7, 5, f_2)$*. Since the population* P *consists of exactly* 4 *rollouts,* $b = 4$ *and, since the action* β *occurs only once in the population* P*,* $Numb(\beta, P) = 1$*. Then, according to theorem 3.4, we have*

$$\lim_{m \to \infty} \lim_{t \to \infty} \Phi(P_m, h, t) = \frac{1}{4} \cdot \frac{|4|}{|1 \cup 3 \cup 6|} \cdot \frac{|7|}{|7|} \frac{|5|}{|5|} \times$$

[14]This theorem holds based on the same argument under the assumption of a more general theorem 23 of [7]

$$\times \frac{\text{Order}(\beta \downarrow (1 \cup 3 \cup 6),\, P)}{\text{Order}(\beta \downarrow (P))} \cdot \frac{\text{Order}((1 \cup 3 \cup 6) \downarrow 7,\, P)}{\text{Order}((1 \cup 3 \cup 6) \downarrow (P))} \times$$

$$\times \frac{\text{Order}(7 \downarrow 5,\, P)}{\text{Order}(7 \downarrow (P))} \cdot \frac{1}{\text{Order}(5 \downarrow (P))} =$$

after plugging in values from example 3.4
$$=$$

$$= \frac{1}{4} \cdot \frac{2}{7} \cdot 1 \cdot 1 \cdot 1 \cdot \frac{2}{7} \cdot \frac{1}{3} \cdot \frac{1}{3} = \frac{1}{441}.$$

3.5 Deriving Theorem 3.4 for the MCT algorithm

The crucial step in establishing theorem 3.4 has been the observation that recombination operators can be defined over arbitrary set cover of the set of state-action pairs in a bijective manner so that the general finite population Geiringer theorem in [5] (it is also presented and extended for non-homogenous time Markov processes in [7]) applies. This result is stated in theorem 3.1 of the current article. We now know that the stationary distribution of the Markov chain over the set of all populations started with an initial population P_m that's obtained by inflating a given population P by a factor of m, call it $[P_m]_{\mathcal{F}}$ (see subsection 3.2 for the detailed description of the family of recombination transformations $\mathcal{F}$ and the associated Markov chain), is the uniform distribution over $[P_m]$. At the same time, we may consider the family of recombination transformations $\overline{\mathcal{F}}$ defined with respect to the set cover $\overline{\mathcal{C}}$ in place of $\mathcal{C}$ (the details of how this is done are presented in subsection 3.2). Since $\overline{\mathcal{C}}$ is a partition of the set of states, we can now apply theorem 40 of [7] (the particular case of theorem 3.4) to deduce the following. Let $[P_m]_{\overline{\mathcal{F}}}$ denote the set of all populations that can be obtained from the population P_m after applying the transformations from the family $\overline{\mathcal{F}}$. Then, if

$$\bar{h} = (\alpha, \overline{O_1}, \overline{O_2}, \ldots, \overline{O_{k-1}}, x_k) \tag{3}$$

is a given Holland-Poli rollout schema, we have

$$\lim_{m \to \infty} \lim_{t \to \infty} \Phi(P_m, \bar{h}, t) =$$

$$= \frac{\text{Numb}(\alpha, P)}{b} \cdot \prod_{q=1}^{k-1} \frac{Order(\overline{O_{q-1}} \downarrow \overline{O_q},\, P)}{Order(\overline{O_{q-1}} \downarrow, P)} \cdot LF(P, h) \tag{4}$$

where

$$LF(P, h) = \begin{cases} 1 & \text{if } x_k = \# \\ 0 & \text{if } x_k = f \in \Sigma \text{ and } f \notin \overline{O_{k-1}} \downarrow (P) \\ Fraction & \text{if } x_k = f \in \Sigma \text{ and } f \in \overline{O_{k-1}} \downarrow_{\Sigma} (P) \end{cases}$$

and

$$Fraction = \frac{1}{Order(\overline{O_{k-1}} \downarrow, P)}$$

Although there is a formal difference between the sets of populations $[P_m]_{\mathcal{F}}$ and $[P_m]_{\overline{\mathcal{F}}}$ mainly due to distinct labeling policies, if we extend the notion of a Holland-Poli rollout schema in a natural way to the set of all possible rollouts from the populations in $[P_m]_{\mathcal{F}}$ so that a rollout r fits the schema $\bar{h}$ introduced in equation 3 if and only if it fits at least one schema of the form

$$h = (\alpha, T_1, T_2, \ldots, T_{k-1}, x_k)$$

where $\overline{T_i} = \overline{O_i}$ whenever $1 \leq i \leq k-1$ (In other wards, the set of rollouts defined by the schema $\bar{h}$ in equation 3 is the union of the sets of rollouts represented by the schemata the extension of the similarity classes of which are precisely the corresponding equivalence classes appearing in $\bar{h}$), then we claim that $\forall m \in \mathbb{N}$, the fraction of occurrence of the schema $\bar{h}$ in the set of populations $[P_m]_{\mathcal{F}}$ is the same as it is in the populations $[P_m]_{\overline{\mathcal{F}}}$ (of course, since the corresponding unique stationary distributions of the two Markov chains are uniform, it follows that $\forall m \in \mathbb{N}\ \lim_{t \to \infty} \Phi_{\mathcal{F}}(P_m, \bar{h}, t) = \lim_{t \to \infty} \Phi_{\overline{\mathcal{F}}}(P_m, \bar{h}, t)$). To see the assertion in the previous sentence, consider the functions $\phi_1 : [P_m]_{\mathcal{F}} \to P_m^{\text{EquivSchemata}}$ and $\phi_2 : [P_m]_{\overline{\mathcal{F}}} \to \overline{P}_m^{\text{EquivSchemata}}$ where the sets $P_m^{\text{EquivSchemata}}$ and $\overline{P}_m^{\text{EquivSchemata}}$ are obtained from the corresponding sets of populations in $[P_m]_{\mathcal{F}}$ and in $[P_m]_{\overline{\mathcal{F}}}$ respectively by replacing every label of the form $(O_1, O_2, \ldots, O_{l(\vec{u})}\ \vec{u})$ (where, of course, $O_i \in \{O \mid O \in \mathcal{C} \text{ and } \vec{u} \in O\}$) with the corresponding label $\overline{O_1}$ (notice that whenever $1 \leq i \leq l(\vec{u})$, we have $\overline{O_i} = \overline{O_1}$ since $\bigcap_{i=1}^{l(\vec{u})} O_i \supseteq \{\vec{u}\} \neq \emptyset$ so that all of the sets O_i are within the same equivalence class of the transitive closure of the symmetric and reflexive relation induced by the set cover $\mathcal{C}$). The functions ϕ_1 and ϕ_2 are, essentially, the "projections" onto the sets $P_m^{\text{EquivSchemata}}$ and $\overline{P}_m^{\text{EquivSchemata}}$: given a population $Q \in [P_m]_{\mathcal{F}}$ (or $Q \in [P_m]_{\overline{\mathcal{F}}}$), simply replace the labels of every rollout with the unique equivalence class label as described in the preceding sentence, thereby obtaining an element of $P_m^{\text{EquivSchemata}}$ (or $\overline{P}_m^{\text{EquivSchemata}}$). Notice that if we are given an initial population P of rollouts, the states can be labeled either according to the similarity relation $\mathcal{C}$ or $\overline{\mathcal{C}}$ on the set of states. While these populations are formally distinct (in terms of labeling only: one of them is considered to be an initial population in the set $[P_m]_{\mathcal{F}}$ while the other one is the corresponding initial population in the set $[P_m]_{\overline{\mathcal{F}}}$), let's call them P and $\overline{P}$, the corresponding images of these populations under the maps ϕ_1 and ϕ_2 are obviously identical. In fact, a lot more is true:

Lemma 3.5. *$\forall m \in \mathbb{N}$ we have*

$$P_m^{EquivSchemata} = \overline{P}_m^{EquivSchemata}$$

.

Proof. Since there are more possibilities for recombination when using the family of transformations $\overline{\mathcal{F}}$ rather than the family of transformations $\mathcal{F}$ that only allows immediate swaps of sub-rollouts at the states that are subsets of a particular similarity set $O \subseteq \overline{O}$, it is clear that

$$P_m^{\text{EquivSchemata}} \subseteq \overline{P}_m^{\text{EquivSchemata}}.$$

The reverse inclusion follows from the definition of the transitive closure of a symmetric and reflexive relation. In fact, as mentioned in the sentence preceding the statement of lemma 3.5,

$$P_m^{\text{EquivSchemata}} \cap \overline{P}_m^{\text{EquivSchemata}} \supseteq \{\phi_1(P_m) = \phi_2(\overline{P}_m)\} \neq \emptyset.$$

Since every population $U \in [P_m]_{\mathcal{F}}$ is obtained via a finite number of applications of the transformations of the form $\Theta_{\overline{O},\, \vec{u},\, \vec{v}} \in \overline{F}$ (see definition 3.1), by the principle of induction, it is sufficient to show that if we are given a population $Q \in [P_m]_{\mathcal{F}}$ with $\phi_1(Q) = \phi_2(\overline{Q})$, then $\forall$ transformation of the form $\Theta_{\overline{O},\, \vec{u},\, \vec{v}} \in \overline{F}$, $\exists$ a finite sequence $\{\Theta_{O_j,\, \vec{u}_j,\, \vec{v}_j}\}_{j=1}^{k}$ of crossover transformations in $\mathcal{F}$ such that $\phi_2\left(\Theta_{\overline{O},\,\vec{u},\,\vec{v}}(\overline{Q})\right) =$

$$\phi_1\left(\Theta_{O_k,\,\vec{u}_k,\,\vec{v}_k} \circ \Theta_{O_{k-1},\,\vec{u}_{k-1},\,\vec{v}_{k-1}} \circ \ldots \circ \Theta_{O_1,\,\vec{u}_1,\,\vec{v}_1}(Q)\right). \tag{5}$$

Since $\vec{u} \simeq \vec{v}$ (see definition 2.1 and remark 2.1), $\exists$ a sequence of similarity classes $O_1, O_2, \ldots, O_{l-1}, O_l \in \mathcal{O}$ with $\overline{O_1} = \overline{O}$ and a corresponding sequence of states $\vec{u} = \vec{u}_1, \vec{u}_2, \ldots, \vec{u}_l = \vec{v}$ with $\vec{u}_1 \in O_1$, and, whenever $1 < i \leq l$, $\vec{u}_i \in O_{i-1} \cap O_i$ (evidently, in this case, $\forall i$ with $1 \leq i \leq l$, we have $\overline{O_i} = \overline{O_1} = \overline{O}$). Observing that the function ϕ_1 (as well as ϕ_2, of course), is invariant under the applications of the single swap crossover transformations (recall definitions 2.7 and 2.8) we deduce that $\phi_1(Q) = \phi_1(Q_1)$ where

$$Q_1 = \nu_{O_{l-1},\,\vec{u}_l,\,\vec{u}_{l-1}} \circ \nu_{O_3,\,\vec{u}_4,\,\vec{u}_3} \circ \ldots \circ \nu_{O_2,\,\vec{u}_3,\,\vec{u}_2}(Q).$$

At the same time, the corresponding states $\vec{u}$ and $\vec{v}$ in the population Q_1 are O_1 similar (recall the beginning of section 2) so that $\phi_1\left(\Theta(O_1,\,\vec{u},\,\vec{v})\right)(Q_1) = \phi_2\left(\Theta_{\overline{O},\,\vec{u},\,\vec{v}}(\overline{Q})\right)$ thereby producing a desired sequence of crossover transformations for the equality in 5 to hold and finishing the argument. □

Evidently, the number of rollouts fitting the schema $\bar{h}$ in a population $Q \in [P_m]_{\mathcal{F}}$ is the same as that in the population $\phi_1(Q) \in P_m^{\text{EquivSchemata}}$ (in fact, this is precisely the way to count them, according to the way ϕ_1 is defined). Likewise, of course, the same holds for the population $\overline{Q} \in [\overline{P}_m]_{\overline{\mathcal{F}}}$: the number of rollouts fitting the schema $\bar{h}$ in the population $\overline{Q}$ is the same as the corresponding number in $\phi_2(\overline{Q}) \in \overline{P}_m^{\text{EquivSchemata}} = P_m^{\text{EquivSchemata}}$ according to lemma 3.5. Evidently, the total number of states fitting a given similarity class $O \in \mathcal{C}$ (as well as these fitting its expansion, $\overline{O}$) remains invariant after an application of any of the possible recombination transformations. Since the functions ϕ_1 and ϕ_2 are both invariant under the applications of the single-swap crossover transformations of the form $\nu_{O,\,\vec{u},\,\vec{u}}$, and, of course, every permutation is a composition of transpositions, for every population $H \in P_m^{\text{EquivSchemata}} = \overline{P}_m^{\text{EquivSchemata}}$ the size of the pre-image $\phi_1^{-1}(H) = \prod_{O\in\mathcal{C}}(m\cdot|O|)!$ while $\phi_2^{-1}(H) = \prod_{\overline{O}\in\overline{\mathcal{C}}}(m\cdot|\overline{O}|)!$, it follows, in particular, that $\exists\, k$ depending only on the inflation factor m, such that $\forall H \in P_m^{\text{EquivSchemata}} = \overline{P}_m^{\text{EquivSchemata}}$ we have $\phi_1^{-1}(H) = k\cdot\phi_2^{-1}(H)$. It is now apparent that the fraction of occurrence of rollouts fitting the schema $\bar{h}$ out of the total number of rollouts in $[P_m]$, is the same as that out of the total number of rollouts in $[\overline{P}_m]$ and is that out of $P_m^{\text{EquivSchemata}} = \overline{P}_m^{\text{EquivSchemata}}$. Thus, we have now shown the following intermediate fact:

LEMMA 3.6. *$\forall m \in \mathbb{N}$ we have*

$$\lim_{t\to\infty} \Phi_{\mathcal{F}}(P_m,\,\bar{h},\,t) = \lim_{t\to\infty} \Phi_{\overline{\mathcal{F}}}(\overline{P}_m,\,\bar{h},\,t)$$

so that, in particular, the equality in 4 holds.

The remaining part of the argument proceeds in a very similar manner as the proof of theorem 40 in [7].[15] Due to space limitations we provide only an outline of the argument reminding the cornerstones and the mathematical tools developed in [5] and largely enhanced in [7]. The first important step is the following fact (lemma 48 of [7]) that allows us to derive Geiringer-like results in terms of the fraction of populations where a rollout fitting a given schema h occurs in a specified position (say, the first individual) in the population out of the total number of populations in $[P_m]_{\mathcal{F}}$.

LEMMA 3.7. *Given a subset $S \subseteq \Omega$ of rollouts and an initial population of rollouts, P, under the assumptions of theorem 3.4, it is true that*

$$\lim_{t\to\infty} \Phi(S,\,P_m,\,t) = \frac{|\mathcal{V}(P_m,\,S)|}{|[P_m]_{\mathcal{F}}|}$$

where the set $\mathcal{V}(P_m,\,S)$ is the set of populations in $[P_m]_{\mathcal{F}}$ the first rollout of which, call it $r_1 \in S$.

In view of lemma 3.7, our goal is to estimate the ratio of the form $\frac{|\mathcal{V}(P_m,\,h)|}{|[P_m]_{\mathcal{F}}|}$ and, afterwards, to compute the limit as $m \to \infty$. We accomplish this task step by step: combining lemmas 3.6 and 3.7 we deduce that

$$\lim_{m\to\infty} \frac{|\mathcal{V}(P_m,\,\bar{h})|}{|[P_m]_{\mathcal{F}}|} =$$

$$= \frac{\text{Numb}(\alpha,\,P)}{b} \cdot \prod_{q=1}^{k-1} \frac{\mathit{Order}(\overline{O_{q-1}} \downarrow \overline{O_q},\,P)}{\mathit{Order}(\overline{O_{q-1}} \downarrow,\,P)} \cdot LF(P,h).$$

Certainly we can write

$$\bar{h} = h_0 \supseteq h_1 \supseteq \ldots \supseteq h_{k-1} = h$$

where

$$h_i = (\alpha,\,O_1,\,O_2,\ldots,O_{i-1},\,O_i,\,\overline{O_{i+1}},\,\overline{O_{i+2}},\ldots,\overline{O_{k-1}},\,x_k)$$

is the Holland-Poli schema with respect to the set cover $\mathcal{C}\cup\overline{\mathcal{C}}$. Now we can write

$$\frac{|\mathcal{V}(P_m,\,h)|}{|[P_m]_{\mathcal{F}}|} = \frac{|\mathcal{V}(P_m,\,h_{k-1})|}{|\mathcal{V}(P_m,\,h_{k-2})|}\cdot\frac{|\mathcal{V}(P_m,\,h_{k-2})|}{|\mathcal{V}(P_m,\,h_{k-3})|}\cdot\ldots\cdot\frac{|\mathcal{V}(P_m,\,h_0)|}{|[P_m]_{\mathcal{F}}|}$$

as a "telescoping" product so that

$$\lim_{m\to\infty} \frac{|\mathcal{V}(P_m,\,h)|}{|[P_m]_{\mathcal{F}}|} =$$

$$= \left(\prod_{i=1}^{k-2} \lim_{m\to\infty} \frac{|\mathcal{V}(P_m,\,h_{k-i})|}{|\mathcal{V}(P_m,\,h_{k-i+1})|}\right) \cdot \lim_{m\to\infty} \frac{|\mathcal{V}(P_m,\,\bar{h})|}{|[P_m]_{\mathcal{F}}|} =$$

$$= \left(\prod_{i=1}^{k-2} \lim_{m\to\infty} \frac{|\mathcal{V}(P_m,\,h_{k-i})|}{|\mathcal{V}(P_m,\,h_{k-i+1})|}\right) \times$$

$$\times \frac{\text{Numb}(\alpha,\,P)}{b} \cdot \prod_{q=1}^{k-1} \frac{\mathit{Order}(\overline{O_{q-1}} \downarrow \overline{O_q},\,P)}{\mathit{Order}(\overline{O_{q-1}} \downarrow,\,P)} \cdot LF(P,h). \tag{6}$$

and, thanks to equation 6, all that remains to establish theorem 3.4 at this point is to show that $\forall i \in \{1,\,2,\ldots,k-1\}$ we have

$$\lim_{m\to\infty} \frac{|\mathcal{V}(P_m,\,h_i)|}{|\mathcal{V}(P_m,\,h_{i-1})|} = \frac{|O_i|}{|\overline{O_{i-1}}|}. \tag{7}$$

The main tools involved in deriving equation 7, just as in establishing theorem 40 in [7], are the Markov inequality and the lumping quotients of Markov chains technique in the same way as in [7]. The lumping quotient method modified for specific applications such as in the current paper,

[15]Certainly, lemma 3.6 can be established by nearly repeating the derivation of theorem 40 in [7], yet the argument presented in the current paper is shorter.

is described in details in subsection 5.3 of [7]. Rather than estimating the ratio

$$R_i^m = \frac{|\mathcal{V}(P_m,\, h_i)|}{|\mathcal{V}(P_m,\, h_{i-1})|} \tag{8}$$

directly, it is more convenient to estimate the closely related ratio

$$\widetilde{R_i^m} = \frac{\mathcal{V}(P_m,\, h_i)}{\mathcal{V}(P_m,\, h_{i-1} \setminus h_i)}. \tag{9}$$

Indeed, an elementary algebraic manipulation shows that

$$R_i^m = \frac{1}{1 + \frac{1}{\widetilde{R_i^m}}}. \tag{10}$$

The way to estimate the ratio in equation 9, is to construct a Markov chain (possibly non-irreducible) having a symmetric Markov transition matrix, so that the uniform probability distribution is one of its stationary distributions, call it π_m^i on $\mathcal{V}(P_m,\, h_{i-1})$ and to express the ratio $\widetilde{R_i^m}$ in equation 9 in terms of the ratio of the corresponding probabilities under the uniform probability distribution π_m^i:

$$\widetilde{R_i^m} = \frac{\pi_m^i(\mathcal{V}(P_m,\, h_i))}{\pi_m^i(\mathcal{V}(P_m,\, h_{i-1} \setminus h_i))}.$$

We then make use of lemma 55 in subsection 5.3 of [7] to estimate the ratio $\widetilde{R_i^m}$ in terms of the ratios of the corresponding generalized transition probabilities between the subsets

$$\frac{(1-\delta)\lambda_1}{(1-\delta)\kappa_2 + \delta} \le \widetilde{R_i^m} = \frac{\pi_m^i\,(\mathcal{V}(P_m,\, h_i))}{\pi_m^i\,(\mathcal{V}(P_m,\, h_{i-1} \setminus h_i))} \le$$

$$\frac{(1-\delta)\kappa_1 + \delta}{(1-\delta)\lambda_2} \tag{11}$$

where λ_1, λ_2, κ_1 and κ_2 are the corresponding bounds on the appropriate generalized transition probabilities (see subsection 5.3 of [7] for details), while $0 < \delta \ll 1$ is an arbitrary given small constant and the inequality 11 holds $\forall\, m > M_\delta$. For the sake of completeness, lemma 55 of [7] is stated below.

LEMMA 3.8. *Let $\{p_{x \to y}\}_{x,\, y \in \mathcal{X}}$ denote a Markov transition matrix over a finite state space $\mathcal{X}$. Suppose π is a stationary distribution of this Markov chain (i.e. a fixed point of the associated Markov transition matrix) Suppose A and $B \subseteq \mathcal{X}$ is a complementary pair of subsets (i.e. $A \cap B = \emptyset$ and $A \cup B = \mathcal{X}$). Suppose further that $U \subseteq \mathcal{X}$ is such that*

$$\frac{\pi(U \cap A)}{\pi(A)} < \delta < 1 \text{ and } \frac{\pi(U \cap B)}{\pi(B)} < \delta < 1.$$

Assume now that we find constants λ_1, λ_2, κ_1 and κ_2 such that $\forall\, b \in U^c \cap B$ we have $\lambda_1 \le p_{b \to A} \le \kappa_1$ and $\forall\, a \in U^c \cap A$ we have $\lambda_2 \le p_{a \to B} \le \kappa_2$. (given a state $x \in \mathcal{X}$ and a subset $Y \in \mathcal{X}$, $p_{x \to y} = \sum_{y \in Y} p_{x \to y}$). Then we have

$$\frac{(1-\delta)\lambda_1}{(1-\delta)\kappa_2 + \delta} \le \frac{\pi(A)}{\pi(B)} \le \frac{(1-\delta)\kappa_1 + \delta}{(1-\delta)\lambda_2}$$

Since the argument proceeds along exactly the same steps and ideas as the proof of theorem 40 presented in section 5 of [7], we provide only a very rough and brief outline within a few sentences. The Markov chain on the state space $\mathcal{V}(P_m,\, h_{i-1})$ is constructed as follows: given a population $Q \in \mathcal{V}(P_m,\, h_{i-1})$, the first rollout of P fits the schema h_{i-1} (so that, in particular, the ith state of this rollout, call it $\vec{s} \in \overline{O_i}$). Let Mobile$(Q,\, i-1)$ denote the set of all states in $\overline{O_i}$ that do not appear within the first rollout in the population Q. Now select a state $\vec{t} \in \overline{O_i}$ uniformly at random and apply the one point crossover transformation $\chi_{\overline{O_i}, \vec{s}, \vec{t}}$ to the population Q, thereby obtaining a new population $\chi_{\overline{O_i}, \vec{s}, \vec{t}}(Q) \in \mathcal{V}(P_m,\, h_{i-1})$ that is different from Q if and only if $\vec{s} \in$ Mobile$(Q,\, i-1)$. Due to the fact that recombination is non-homologous (i.e. it may take place at distinct hight of various rollouts) the height of the first rollout may be arbitrarily large and, at first glance, it seems that the set Mobile$(Q,\, i-1)$ may vary in size greatly from population to population, nonetheless, we make a crucial observation that as the inflation factor $m \to \infty$, the sizes of each of the similarity sets $O \in \mathcal{C}$ and $\overline{O} \in \overline{\mathcal{C}}$ increase linearly by the factor of m in size, while the average height of the first rollout in a population stays constant and is the same as the average height of the population P (this is due to the fact that all recombination transformations preserve the total number of states within the population, and in particular, the average height of the population, and, at the same time, inflating a population by any factor $m \in \mathbb{N}$ also preserves the average height). A lovely application of the classical Markov inequality now shows that as the inflation factor $m \to \infty$, the probability that the first rollout contains a fixed (δ-size) fraction of states from any given similarity set $O \in \mathcal{C}$ (and, even more so, $\overline{O} \in \overline{\mathcal{C}}$) goes to 0 (all of the technical details are entirely analogous to the ones presented in section 5 of [7]). Now let $A = \mathcal{V}(P_m,\, h_i)$, $B = \mathcal{V}(P_m,\, h_{i-1} \setminus h_i)$ and, for a given $\delta > 0$ select $M \in \mathbb{N}$ large enough so that $\forall\, m > M$

$$\frac{\pi_m^i\left(\mathcal{V}(P_m,\, h_i) \cap U_m^{\delta \cdot const(i)}\right)}{\pi_m^i(\mathcal{V}(P_m,\, h_{i-1}))} < \delta \tag{12}$$

and

$$\frac{\pi_m^i\left(\mathcal{V}(P_m,\, h_{i-1} \setminus h_i) \cap U_m^{\delta \cdot const(i)}\right)}{\pi_m^i(\mathcal{V}(P_m,\, h_{i-1}))} < \delta \tag{13}$$

where $U_m^{\delta \cdot const(i)}$ denotes the set of all populations in $[P_m]_{\mathcal{F}}$ with the property that the height of the first rollout in such populations is at least $M = \frac{E(H_1)}{(const(i) \cdot \delta)^2}$ and H_1 denotes the random variable measuring the height of the first rollout in a population selected from the set $[P_m]_{\mathcal{F}}$ uniformly at random, while $const(i) > 0$ depends only on the schema h and the initial population P of rollouts.[16] It is easy to see from the construction of this auxiliary Markov chain, that the transition matrix $\{p_{Q \to R}\}_{Q \text{ and } R \in \mathcal{V}(P_m,\, h_{i-1})}$ is symmetric so that the uniform probability distribution π_m^i is a stationary distribution of this Markov chain, and, furthermore, $\forall$ population $Q \in \mathcal{V}(P_m,\, h_{i-1} \setminus h_i) \setminus U_m^{\delta \cdot const(i)}$ we have

$$\lambda_1 = \frac{|O_i| - \delta}{|\overline{O_i}|} =$$

$$= \frac{m \cdot |O_i| - m \cdot \delta}{m \cdot |\overline{O_i}|} \le \frac{m \cdot |O_i| - Mobile(Q,\, i-1)}{m \cdot |\overline{O_i}|} =$$

$$p_{Q \to \mathcal{V}(P_m,\, h_i)} \le \frac{m \cdot |O_i|}{m \cdot |\overline{O_i}|} = \frac{|O_i|}{|\overline{O_i}|} = \kappa_1 \tag{14}$$

[16] We invite the reader to study section 5 of [7] to understand how the constants $const(i) > 0$ are selected and why the inequalities 12 and 13 hold.

and, likewise, $\forall$ population $Q \in \mathcal{V}(P_m, h_i) \setminus U_m^{\delta \cdot const(i)}$ we have

$$\lambda_2 = \frac{|\overline{O_i}| - |O_i| - \delta}{|\overline{O_i}|} =$$

$$= \frac{m \cdot (|\overline{O_i}| - |O_i|) - m \cdot \delta}{m \cdot |\overline{O_i}|} = \frac{m \cdot (|\overline{O_i} \setminus O_i|) - m \cdot \delta}{m \cdot |\overline{O_i}|} \leq$$

$$\leq \frac{m \cdot (|\overline{O_i}| - |O_i|) - Mobile(Q,\, i-1)}{m \cdot |\overline{O_i}|} = p_{Q \to \mathcal{V}(P_m,\, h_i)} \leq$$

$$\leq \frac{m \cdot (|\overline{O_i}| - |O_i|)}{m \cdot |\overline{O_i}|} = \frac{|\overline{O_i}| - |O_i|}{|\overline{O_i}|} = \kappa_2 \tag{15}$$

so that lemma 3.8 immediately yields the bounds

$$\frac{\frac{|O_i| - \delta}{|\overline{O_i}|}(1-\delta)}{(1-\delta)\frac{|\overline{O_i}| - |O_i|}{|\overline{O_i}|} + \delta} \leq \frac{\pi_m^i\left(\mathcal{V}(P_m,\, h_i)\right)}{\pi_m^i\left(\mathcal{V}(P_m,\, h_{i-1} \setminus h_i)\right)} \leq$$

$$\frac{(1-\delta)\frac{|O_i|}{|\overline{O_i}|} + \delta}{(1-\delta)\frac{|\overline{O_i}| - |O_i| - \delta}{|\overline{O_i}|}} \tag{16}$$

Given any $\delta > 0$, the "sandwich" bounds in the inequality 16 hold for all sufficiently large m depending on the δ so that taking the limit of both sides as $\delta \to 0$ finally tells us that

$$\lim_{m \to \infty} \frac{|\mathcal{V}(P_m,\, h_i)|}{|\mathcal{V}(P_m,\, h_{i-1} \setminus h_i)|} =$$

$$= \lim_{m \to \infty} \frac{\pi_m^i\left(\mathcal{V}(P_m,\, h_i)\right)}{\pi_m^i\left(\mathcal{V}(P_m,\, h_{i-1} \setminus h_i)\right)} = \frac{|O_i|}{|\overline{O_i}| - |O_i|} \tag{17}$$

and equation 7 follows from equation 17 via equation 10 thereby finishing the proof of theorem 3.4.

4. CONCLUSIONS

In the current paper we have significantly generalized a novel version of a finite population Geiringer-like theorem with non-homologous recombination established in [7] by allowing similarity relations on the set of state-action pairs to be modeled in terms of arbitrary set covers of the state-action space (not necessarily partitions induced by equivalence relations). This raises questions regarding further potential applications of Geiringer-like theorems for decision making to the design, of novel algorithms for pay-off-based clustering.

5. REFERENCES

[1] J. Antonisse. A new interpretation of schema notation that overturns the binary encoding constraint. In *Procedings of the Third International Conference on Genetic Algorithms.*

[2] Chaslot, Saito, Bouzy, Uiterwijk, and van den Herik. Monte-carlo strategies for computer go. In *Procedings of the 18th Belgian-Dutch Conference on Artificial Intelligence.*

[3] H. Geiringer. On the probability of linkage in mendelian heredity. *Annals of Mathematical Statistics*, 15.

[4] Kee-Eung. Exploiting symmetries in pomdps for point-based algorithms. In *Proceedings of the 23rd national conference on Artificial intelligence.*

[5] B. Mitavskiy and J. Rowe. An extension of geiringer theorem for a wide class of evolutionary algorithms. *Evolutionary Computation*, 14(1):87–118.

[6] B. Mitavskiy and J. Rowe. A schema-based version of geiringer theorem for nonlinear genetic programming with homologous crossover. In *Foundations of Genetic Algorithms 8 (FOGA-2005)*, pages 156–175. Springer, lecture Notes in Computer Science 3469.

[7] B. Mitavskiy, J. Rowe, and C. Cannings. A version of geiringer-like theorem for decision making in the environments with randomness and incomplete information. *International Journal of Intelligent Computing and Cybernetics*, 5(1):36–90.

[8] R. Poli and B. Langdon. Schema theory for genetic programming with one-point crossover and point mutation. *Evolutionary Computation*, 6(3):231–252.

[9] S. C. W. A. Poli, R. and J. Rowe. A schema theory based extension of geiringer's theorem for linear gp and variable length gas under homologous crossover. In *Foundations of Genetic Algorithms 7 (FOGA-2003).*

[10] L. Schmitt. Theory of genetic algorithms. *Theoretical Computer Science*, 259.

[11] L. Schmitt. Theory of genetic algorithms. *Theoretical Computer Science*, 310.

[12] G. Simmons. *Introduction to Topology and Modern Analysis.* R.E. Krieger Pub. Co.

[13] M. Vose. *The simple genetic algorithm: foundations and theory.* MIT Press.

A Feature-Based Comparison of Local Search and the Christofides Algorithm for the Travelling Salesperson Problem

Samadhi Nallaperuma, Markus Wagner, Frank Neumann
Evolutionary Computation Group
School of Computer Science
The University of Adelaide
Adelaide, SA 5005, Australia

Bernd Bischl, Olaf Mersmann, Heike Trautmann
Statistics Faculty
TU Dortmund University
44221 Dortmund, Germany

ABSTRACT

Understanding the behaviour of well-known algorithms for classical NP-hard optimisation problems is still a difficult task. With this paper, we contribute to this research direction and carry out a feature based comparison of local search and the well-known Christofides approximation algorithm for the Traveling Salesperson Problem. We use an evolutionary algorithm approach to construct easy and hard instances for the Christofides algorithm, where we measure hardness in terms of approximation ratio. Our results point out important features and lead to hard and easy instances for this famous algorithm. Furthermore, our cross-comparison gives new insights on the complementary benefits of the different approaches.

Categories and Subject Descriptors

F.2 [**Theory of Computation**]: Analysis of Algorithms and Problem Complexity

General Terms

Theory, Algorithms, Performance

Keywords

Traveling Salesperson Problem, Approximation Algorithms, Local Search, Classification, Prediction, Feature Selection

1. INTRODUCTION

Our goal is to understand the performance of algorithms for hard optimisation problems such as the Travelling Salesperson Problem (TSP). This understanding is essential for algorithm design and automated algorithm selection. In both the artificial intelligence (AI) and operational research communities, this topic has become a major point of interest. Thus, various kinds of attempts have been made theoretically and empirically. Classical approaches taking a worst-case or an average-case perspective hardly capture what is happening for real instances. For a given instance I of a combinatorial optimisation problem, it is often hard to predict the performance of an algorithm A without running A on I.

Hyper heuristics in the optimisation domain and meta-learning in the machine learning domain focus on finding the conditions that determine algorithm performance in advance. Smith-Miles and Lopes [8] classify the research on problem hardness analysis into two different directions. The first direction is to consider the problem as a learning problem, where automatic algorithm selection [3] is done based on learned knowledge from previous algorithm performance. The second direction is to analyse the algorithms and problems theoretically [7, 10, 4] and experimentally [8] [13] to understand the reasons for performance on different problem instances. This understanding is the key to future algorithm design for more complex real world problems.

Our study considers both approaches, where we investigate the performance of important algorithms for the TSP on different instances. Heuristic methods are frequently used to tackle NP-hard combinatorial optimisation problems. Usually, they do not provide any performance guarantees. In contrast to this, approximation algorithms provide guarantees on the quality of a solution that is achieved by running the approximation algorithm. In this paper, we investigate which features make instances of the TSP hard or easy for the well-known Christofides approximation algorithm. Easy and hard instances for this algorithm are generated by an evolutionary algorithm (EA) presented in [6]. Furthermore, we examine the behaviour of a 2-Opt based local search algorithm on these instances and carry out a comparison to a well-known 2-Approximation algorithm.

Our results provide evidence on the capability of individual or combinations of features to classify instances into hard and easy ones. Some features like distance and minimum spanning tree statistics are more effective for this classification for the Christofides algorithm than others like convex hull or mode features. Combined with the analysis of the feature values of the instances of medium difficulty, an increased understanding of the individual feature influences on the approximation quality is provided. Results of the algorithm comparisons enable the analysis of relative strengths of the algorithms on each others' difficult instances as 2-Opt (the Christofides algorithm respectively) outperformed the

FOGA'13, January 16-20, 2013, Adelaide, Australia.

Christofides algorithm (2-Opt respectively) on its hard instances. These insights can be used to improve automatic algorithm selection and algorithm design.

The rest of the paper is organised as follows. In Section 2, we introduce the considered algorithms and the approach of selecting features that measure problem difficulty. In Section 3, we carry out the analysis of easy and hard instances for the Christofides algorithm. In Section 4, we compare the performance of different algorithms on their respective easy and hard instances. Finally, we conclude with some remarks.

2. PRELIMINARIES

The Travelling Salesperson Problem (TSP) is one of the most famous NP-hard combinatorial optimization problems. Given a set of n cities $\{1, \ldots, n\}$ and a distance matrix $d = (d_{i,j})$, $1 \leq i, j \leq n$, the goal is to compute a tour of minimal length that visits each city exactly once and returns to the origin. A tour that visits each city exactly once and return to the origin is frequently called a Hamiltonian cycle. Hamiltonian cycles for complete graphs can be represented as permutations of the n cities. For a given permutation $\pi = (x_1, \ldots, x_n)$ we denote by

$$c(\pi) = d_{x_n, x_1} + \sum_{i=1}^{n-1} d_{x_i, x_{i+1}}$$

the cost of the tour π.

A wide range of algorithms have been developed for the TSP including approximation algorithms and various heuristic approaches. The approximation ratio of an algorithm A for a given instance I is defined as

$$\alpha_A(I) = A(I)/OPT(I)$$

where $A(I)$ is the tour length produced by algorithm A for the given instance I, and $OPT(I)$ is the length of the shortest Hamiltonian cycle in I. An algorithm A is an r-approximation algorithm if for any valid input I, $\alpha_A(I) \leq r$ holds, i. e. the worst case instance can have an approximation ratio of at most r.

Different approximation algorithms have been developed for the TSP. We refer the reader to the book of Vazirani [12] for a comprehensive presentation. In general, the TSP is not only NP-hard but also hard to approximate. We will restrict ourselves to a subset of all TSPs, the class of Metric TSPs. Here the distances between the cities have to fulfill the triangle inequality

$$\forall i, j, k \in \{1, \ldots n\}\colon d_{ik} \leq d_{ij} + d_{jk}.$$

One of the most prominent approximation algorithms for the Metric TSP is the Christofides algorithm (see Algorithm 1), which achieves an approximation ratio of $3/2$. It starts by computing a minimum spanning tree T for the given input. Furthermore, a minimum weight matching M is computed on nodes that have odd degree in T. The graph obtained by combining the edges of T and M is used to compute an Euler tour which is then turned into a Hamiltonian cycle by using short-cuts.

A prominent special case of the Metric TSP is the Euclidean TSP. Here, cities are represented by points in the plane and distances are given by the Euclidean instances between these points. The Euclidean TSP is often considered in experimental investigations. Note, that the Euclidean TSP is still NP-hard but admits a PTAS [2]. However, this algorithm is not considered to be practical, instead we will investigate the performance of the Christofides algorithm on Euclidean instances of the TSP in greater detail by analyzing features of easy and hard instances.

Algorithm 1: Christofides $3/2$-approximation algorithm

input : Graph G
output: Hamiltonian cycle π

Compute a minimum spanning tree MST T of G.;
Find a minimum-weight perfect matching M on the set of nodes of T having an odd degree.;
Combine the edges of M and T to form the graph U.;
Create an Euler cycle S in U.;
Obtain a Hamiltonian cycle π from S by skipping already visited nodes.;
return π;

In practice, heuristic methods such as local search are frequently used to solve instances of the TSP. Our goal is to compare the Christofides algorithm to a standard local search algorithm based on the well-known 2-Opt operator. The complete local search algorithm is given Algorithm 2. It repeatedly checks whether the swapping of two edges in a tour results in a shorter tour. If no improvement can be found any more, the tour is called "2-Optimal" and the algorithm terminates. Note that in [6] a variant is used in which randomness is only induced by varying the initial tour, whereas the 2-opt algorithm is deterministic in always choosing the edge replacement resulting in the highest reduction of the current tour length.

2.1 Hard and easy instance generation

The most generic way to generate hard or easy instances is based on a feature set that is considered to determine problem hardness [9]. Hard or easy instances are generated by setting the values of these features to modify the problem difficulty level. Then algorithm performance is measured on these instances. Smith-Miles and Lopes [9] criticise this conventional approach. The two major drawbacks are the difficulty of generating diverse random instances and the restrictedness of randomly generated benchmark datasets in the spectrum of difficulty. Van Hemert [11] has proposed a different approach. His approach is based on an evolutionary algorithm that evolves instances based on the performance of the algorithm being investigated. After this study on the Lin-Kernighan algorithm [5], there were several more studies that used this approach to generate hard and easy instances for problems like the TSP [8, 6, 9]. Using an evolutionary algorithm, it is possible to evolve sets of extremely hard and easy instances by maximizing or minimizing the fitness (tour length) of each instance. This is essential to achieve diversity within the data set [9]. Therefore, we assume that an evolutionary algorithm based approach can generate a diverse set of easy and hard instances for approximation algorithms as well.

We measure the hardness of an instance I for a given algorithm A by the approximation ratio $\alpha_A(I)$. We drop the subscript A and write $\alpha(I)$ if it is clear which algorithm A is under investigation. Since we only consider deterministic approximation algorithms in this paper, we can obtain $A(I)$ by a single run of algorithm A on a given instance I. However, within the instance generation for 2-opt in [6] it is accounted for randomness by using several different ini-

Algorithm 2: 2-Opt algorithm

---

input : Graph G
output: Hamiltonian cycle π

1   Choose a π;
2   **while** *true* **do**
3   best improvement := 0;
4   **for** *i from 0 to number of cities* **do**
5       $x_i := i^{th}$ node in π;
6   **for** *j from i to number of cities* **do**
7         $x_j := j^{th}$ node in π;
8   improvement := $distance(\{x_i, x_{i+1}\})$ + $distance(\{x_j, x_{j+1}\}) - distance(\{x_i, x_j\}) - distance(\{x_{i+1}, x_{j+1}\})$;
9   **if** *improvement > best improvement* **then**
10           $\pi := \pi'$;
11   best improvement:=$c(\pi')$;
12   best current := i;
13   best other := j;
14   **if** *best improvment > 0* **then**
15   comment : swap edges and reverse the cities in between;
16   current:= best current + 1; other := best other;
17   **while** *current <= other* **do**
18   increment current; decrement other;
19   tmp := $\pi[current]$;
20         $\pi[current]$:= $\pi[other]$;
21         $\pi[other]$:= tmp;
22   **else**
23   break while-loop;
24   **return** π;

---

tial tours. $OPT(I)$ is obtained by using the exact TSP solver Concorde [1].

In order to evolve easy and hard instances for approximation algorithms, we use the evolutionary algorithm introduced by Mersmann et al. [6]. The search is guided by the approximation ratio of an instance, which is used as the fitness function in the evolutionary algorithm. It should be noted that this is in contrast to the approach proposed by van Hemert [11] who used algorithm runtime as a measure for the hardness of a particular problem instance. We maximize $\alpha(I)$ in order to generate hard instances and we minimize $\alpha(I)$ in order to generate easy instances for a given fixed algorithm A. For the analysis instance sizes of 25, 50, 100 and 200 nodes are investigated.

Our evolutionary algorithm uses two strategies to create new instances: (1) "local mutation" is performed by adding a small normal perturbation to the location (normalMutation), and (2) "global mutation" is carried out by replacing each coordinate of the city with a new uniform random value (uniformMutation). This later step was performed with a very low probability. The two sequential mutation strategies together enable small local as well as global structural changes in the offspring. The parameters of the evolutionary algorithm are set as follows: *population size* = 30, *generations* = 5000, *time limit* = 24h, *normalMutationRate* = 0.01, *uniformMutationRate* = 0.001, *cells* = 100, and the standard deviation of the normal distribution used in the normal- Mutation step equals *normalMutationSd* = 0.025. The parameter levels were

chosen based on initial experiments. For each combination of difficulty and input size, we run the evolutionary process 100 times with different initial populations in order to create a diverse set of hard and easy instances.

2.2   Investigated features

We study features that lead to easy and hard instances in a similar way as Mersmann et al. [6], including statistics based on the distance matrix, the minimum spanning tree, and the convex hull of the cities. The complete set of features is listed in the following.

Distance Features: Features based on summary statistics of the edge cost distribution such as the lowest, highest, mean and median edge costs, the proportion of edges with distances shorter than the mean distance, the fraction of distinct distances, the standard deviation of the distance matrix and the expected tour length for a random tour.

Mode Features: The number of modes of the edge, the cost distribution and related features such as the frequency and quantity of the modes, the mean of the modal values, and the number of modes of the edge cost distribution.

Cluster Features: These features assume that the existence and the number of node clusters relates to algorithm performance. In particular, the number of clusters and mean distances to cluster centroids are determined using different levels of reachability distances of the clustering algorithm GDB-SCAN.

Nearest Neighbour Distance Features: Features reflecting the uniformity of an instance such as the minimum, maximum, mean, median, standard deviation and the coefficient of variation of the normalised nearest neighbour distances of each node.

Centroid Features: The coordinates of the instance centroid together with the minimum, mean and maximum distance of the nodes from the centroid.

MST Features: Statistics that are related to the depth and the distances of the minimum spanning tree (MST). These include the minimum, mean, median, maximum and the standard deviation of the depth and distance values of the MST completed by the sum of the distances on the MST, normalised by diving it by the sum of all pair wise distances. This feature group represents the MST heuristic that provides an upper bound for the optimal tour, i.e. the solution of the MST heuristic is within a factor two of the optimal.

Angle Features: Statistics regarding the angles between a node and its two nearest neighbour nodes, i.e. the minimum, mean, median, maximum and the respective standard deviation.

Convex Hull Features: The area of the convex hull of the instance reflecting the spread of the instance in the plane and the fraction of nodes that define the convex hull.

Different TSP instance sizes are considered for the analysis. Cities are generated in $[0, 1]^2$ and placed on a discretised grid enabling cross comparison of features. Instances with varying difficulty levels in between easy and hard are generated by a sophisticated morphing strategy which includes a heuristic point matching strategy between easy and hard instances and computes convex combinations of the respective points of both instance classes. The instances of various difficulty levels will help to increase the understanding of the correlation between instance features, algorithm performance and problem difficulty.

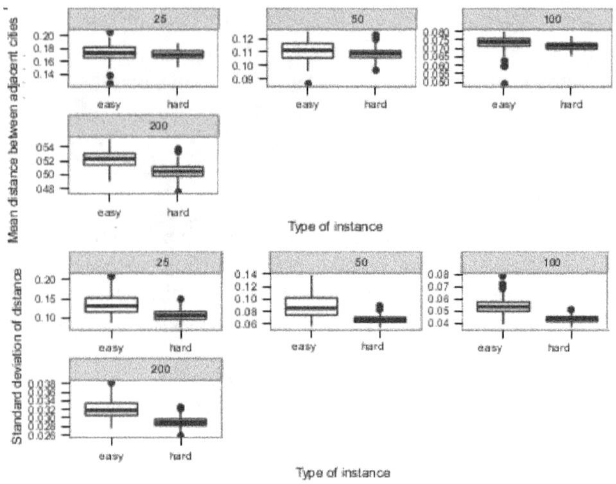

Figure 1: Boxplots of the mean (top) and standard deviations (bottom) of the tour length legs of the optimal tour, both for the evolved easy and hard instances for Christofides.

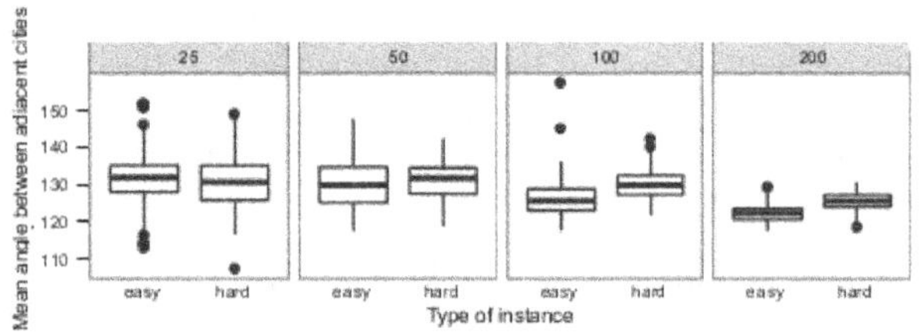

Figure 2: Boxplots of the mean values angle between adjacent cities on the optimal tour for Christofides.

3. ANALYSIS OF THE CHRISTOFIDES ALGORITHM

We now characterize instances of different difficulty for the Christofides algorithm. We start by examining hard and easy instances for the Christofides algorithm. The achieved approximation ratio is close to 1 for all the easy instances and roughly 1.4 for the hard instances. Later on, we morph easy instances into hard ones. The mean distances of the optimal tours of the easy instances are greater than those of the hard instances across all considered instance sizes. Similarly, the standard deviation of the distances of each leg of an optimal tour of the easy instances is considerably higher than for the hard instances. This does not change for increasing instance size (see Figure 1). It is observable that easy instances consist of small clusters of cities as opposed to a more uniform distribution for the hard instances.

As observed in Figure 2, the mean angle of successive tour legs of the easy instances are higher than those of the hard instances (when considering small instances), and lower for larger instance sizes. However, the differences in location are not statistically significant for the small instances. Nevertheless, the results for the larger instance sizes indicate that in this case the instances have higher angles than the easy ones.

Using the boxplots in Figures 1 and 2), we can identify individual features with the capability to differentiate easy from hard instances. This can be refined by using two features to classify instances as easy or hard. Examples for this are shown in Figure 3. There, the top figure shows a combination of distance (standard deviation) and angle (standard deviation) features, while the bottom figure shows a combination of MST (the standard deviation of the depth of MST) and centroid (maximum distance to the centroid) features. As observed in the previous boxplots, the angle features alone do not provide enough information for an accurate classification. Nevertheless, once combined with another features (such as distance), the angle features are capable of discerning easy from hard instances reasonably well. Similarly, two exemplary MST and centroid features are show in the bottom figure, to illustrate that these too can be used to build accurate classification rules.

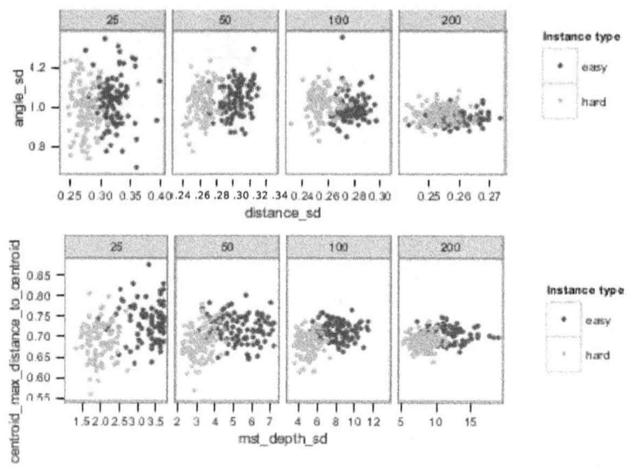

Figure 3: Scatterplots of exemplary feature combinations classifying easy and hard instances for Christofides.

3.1 Features of instances with different approximation ratios

We create instances with varying difficulty levels by forming convex combinations of easy and hard instances, a process we call morphing in the following. Then, the changes of the feature values with increasing difficulty level are studied in order to understand the influence of the different features on the approximation quality. Figures 9 to 13 show the approximation quality for the Christofides instances of all morphing sequences, for the various instance difficulty levels represented by α. Here, $\alpha \in \{0, 0.2, ..., 0.8, 1\}$ increases from hard to easy instances (left to right). In the following, we will discuss basic observations on the variation of the feature values from hard to easy instances for Christofides, with references to the previous observations on 2-Opt [6].

Figure 9 explains the variation of distance features with the instance difficulty for Christofides. The mean, median and the standard deviation of distances have inverse relationships with the instance difficulty. They decrease drastically when the approximation ratio increases. The maximum distance shows a similar pattern, yet does not have a dramatic change over increasing difficulty. Some features such as the minimum distance and the mean tour length do not exhibit a systematic relationship with increasing α. In most cases the variation of the feature over all values for α is larger for small instances than for larger instances. For example, the standard deviation of the distance for the smallest instance size varies within a range of 0.15 (from 0.25 to 0.4), where as for the largest instance size this range is only 0.05 (from 0.25 to 0.30). This pattern holds even for the features like the mean tour length, minimum and the distinct distance, which do not exhibit a strong relationship with increasing α. Compared to the feature values for 2-Opt [6], some features exhibit a stronger relationship with α for Christofides. For example, the median and the mean show stronger relationships with α for all instance sizes, where 2-Opt had the strong increasing pattern only for the smallest instance size. For the rest of the features, the pattern of this systematic nonlinear relationship is almost similar for both algorithms, in spite of slight differences in exact values of features. In contrast to the distance features, the cluster features shown in Figure 9 do not exhibit a strong systematic relationship with α. The cluster feature values for Christofides show patterns similar to 2-Opt [6], as well as having exact values also much closer to the values of 2-Opt's cluster features.

Figure 10 shows some evidence that the angle features do not have a strong systematic relationship between the feature value and the instance difficulty for Christofides like for 2-Opt [6]. Nevertheless, there is a slight variation observable in the standard deviation, minimum and the maximum angle features. There, feature values decrease (increase in minimum angle accordingly) until the medium difficulty level is reached, and then again increase slightly, over the increasing (decreasing in minimum angle accordingly) α. This provides a hint on the dominance of angle features for the instances with medium difficulty. Thus, we might use the angle features to identify instances with medium difficulty for the approximation algorithm, in spite of its inability to differentiate hard from easy instances. Interestingly, similar observation for the maximum angle feature can be made for 2-Opt as well.

Some of the features in the centroid feature group, like the maximum distance from centroid and the mean distance from centroid, provide a good representation of the instance difficulty, through the systematic nonlinear relationship with increasing feature values over α. However, it is observable that the exact centroid location alone does not provide any insight into the problem difficulty (see Figure 10). The highest range of feature values is observed for the mean distance to centroid in case of the smallest instance size, which is 0.2 (from 0.35 to 0.55). Similar nonlinear relationships are observed for centroid features for 2-Opt [6] also, with slight differences in the range of the feature values, such as a 0.3 to 0.7 range for centroid x for 2-Opt and 0.35 to 0.06 for Christofides.

The convex hull features also reflect an influence on the approximation ratio along α, although this is less prominent than in other feature groups (see Figure 11). Among the two features, only the area of the convex hull relates with instance difficulty, having increasing feature value with α, thus decreasing with the instance difficulty. In terms of the area of the convex hull, Christofides shows patterns inverse to those of 2-Opt [6], where the area grows with the instance difficulty. Moreover, the feature values for the points on the hull also increases over α for 2-Opt, while no such notable variation observed for Christofides.

As shown in Figure 11 mode features do not exhibit any correlation with the instance difficulty, having similar feature values over increasing α. The range of feature value is reduced with the instance size, similar to the convex full feature group. The pattern of variation in mode features for Christofides aligns well with that of 2-Opt [6], except for the mode quantity for larger instance sizes, where 2-Opt has feature values in 0.1 range and Christofides has in 0.01 range.

Strong systematic relationships can be detected for the MST features (see Figure 12). Among this feature group, features representing the depth of the spanning tree have stronger relationship with α than others. These include the depth mean, median, maximum and the depth's standard deviation. Considering the difference in scale, it is not possible to compare the exact values for the variation of feature values among features. However, it is observed visually, that a strong systematic relationship exists for the maximum distance feature, in the case of the smallest instance size. The distance features of the MST show relationships with increasing α, mostly for smaller instance sizes. An interesting observation in this group is that some features are more prominent for smaller instance sizes (distance maximum, distance standard deviation), while some are dominating for larger instance sizes (depth features). Furthermore, it is observed that the minimum statistics of both feature groups, distance and depth (minimum depth and minimum distance) do not indicate any relationship with α. When comparing this with the results for 2-Opt [6], Christofides shows similar patterns of the variation of the MST feature values with α, except for the depth features. There, Christofides shows more consistent relationship of increasing feature value with α for all instance sizes, whereas 2-Opt merely shows a slight variation for the largest instance size. Again, these depth feature values for the largest instance size are decreasing with α, in contrast to the increasing pattern of the Christofides algorithm.

The nearest neighbour distance feature group (see Figure 13) also shows relationships with α. Especially the standard deviation and the coefficient of variation provide stronger relationships than the maximum and the minimum statistics. The coefficient of variation exhibits the largest variation and influence of the feature values. This is observed for the smallest instance size. Instances for both 2-Opt [6] and Christofides algorithms exhibit similar patterns of (nonlinear) relationship of approximation ratio with feature levels, where some features like the median and the mean are decreasing with α, while others like the standard deviation and the coefficient of variation are increasing.

In summary, the variation of feature values over the difficulty level (α) is more prominent in some feature groups than the others. The distance, nearest neighbour, centroid and the MST feature groups have stronger systematic relationships with α than the angle, convex hull, cluster and the mode feature groups. It is observed that some features have greater variation with α than others, even within a single feature group. For example, the area of the convex hull increases drastically with α, while the number of points in the hull stays relatively steady. Interestingly, some features exhibit different tendencies for the smallest and highest instance size, such as the features reflecting the minimum distance to the centroid and mean of angles in Figure 10. This is due to the structural shapes of small and large instance classes. Generally, the standard deviations seem to have a larger influence than maximum and minimum statistics. However, in some feature groups like the MST and the nearest neighbour group, the maximum statistics also provide considerable variations of feature values over α. These values provide suggestions for the best features to estimate the problem difficulty for Christofides. Furthermore, these features are similar to the most prominent features for 2-Opt [6] to a considerable extent. Nevertheless, there exist differences in the strength of the relationships and the contrast patterns of some features

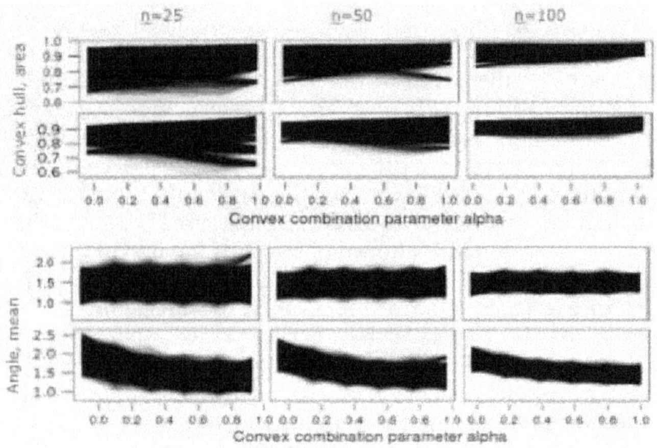

Figure 4: Some contrast patterns observed for Christofides (top) and 2-Opt (bottom)

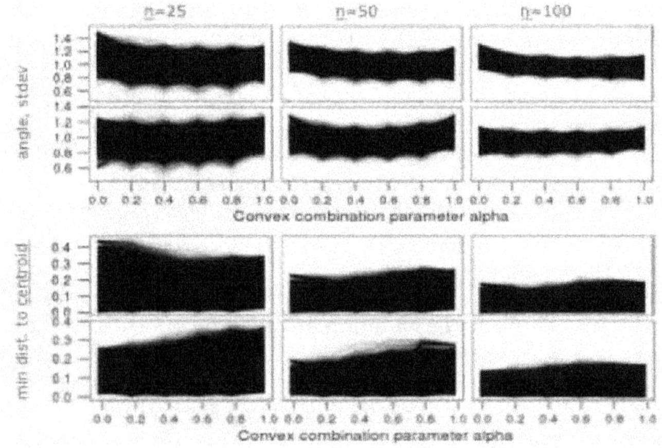

Figure 5: Some contrast patterns observed for 2-Approximation (top) and Christofides (bottom)

for the two algorithms such as the angle and the convex hull features (see Figure 4). As shown in Figure 5 such contrast patterns are also observed among the 2-Approximation and Christofides. This provides evidence on instance difficulty unique to the algorithm. Hence, we will further investigate this topic in next section, with the aim to identify complementary capabilities of the considered algorithms in this study.

4. PERFORMANCE COMPARISON OF LOCAL SEARCH AND APPROXIMATION ALGORITHMS

In this section, we consider algorithms with different underlying techniques, and we compare their relative performance on each others' difficult instances. We compare the Christofides algorithm, the 2-Opt local search algorithm studied in [6], and a well-known 2-Approximation algorithm. The 2-Approximation algorithm is similar to the Christofides algorithm but does not compute the minimum weight matching. Instead of this, it doubles the edges of the minimum spanning tree and uses the resulting graph to compute the Euler tour that is afterwards turned into a Hamiltonian cycle

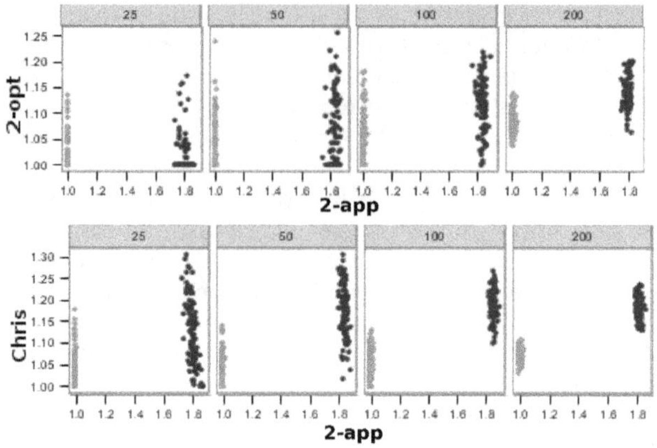

Figure 6: Performance of the 2-Opt algorithm (top) and Christofides algorithm (bottom) on the easy (grey) and hard (black) instances of the 2-Approximation algorithm.

by using short-cuts. A detailed description of this algorithm can be found in the textbook of Vazirani [12]. For the first test, these algorithms are considered pairwise, then run on each others' hard and easy instances, and the achieved approximation ratios are calculated. In this manner, it is possible to derive relative strengths and weaknesses of the considered algorithms by observing how well one algorithm performs in situations that are difficult for the others. Note that the three algorithms achieved approximation ratios close to 1 on their respective easy instances. On its hard instances, 2-Opt achieves ratios in the range from 1.15 to 1.3. The 2-Approximation algorithm achieves ratios of around 1.8 on its own hard instances, and the Christofides algorithm achieves ratios of roughly 1.4 on it own hard instances.

Our observations on the pair-wise comparison are as follows. As shown in Figure 6, both 2-Opt and Christofides algorithms perform better than the 2-Approximation algorithm on the hard instances generated by the 2-Approximation algorithm itself and worse on the easy ones. In the former case, for smaller instance sizes, 2-Opt achieves approximation ratios ranging from 1 to 1.2, and it slightly outperforms Christofides that achieves a range of 1 to 1.3. In contrast, for larger instance sizes, both algorithms have a similar performance with approximation ratios in a tighter range (1.1 to 1.2). As a general observation, 2-Opt and the Christofides algorithm perform similarly on the easy instances, despite the slight variations shown in the approximation values. The 2-Approximation algorithm obtains a better approximation ratio around 1, while the others range from 1 to 1.2 (see Figure 6).

As shown in Figure 7, both the 2-Approximation algorithm and the Christofides algorithm shows similar patterns of the achieved approximation ratios. For smaller instances, these values form straight lines for easy instances, and are scattered for hard instances. For the largest instances, two separate clusters are formed of the easy and hard instances. In the case of the hard 2-Opt instances, the ranges differ significantly for the two algorithms. There, the 2-Approximation algorithm obtains ratios ranging from 1 to 1.6, while the Christofides algorithm achieves a much smaller range from 1 to 1.2. Interestingly, the instances that are hard for 2-opt are not that hard for the Christofides algorithm (see bottom diagram in Figure 7): the approximation ratios obtained by 2-Opt on the hard instances vary from 1 to 1.3, whereas the range is

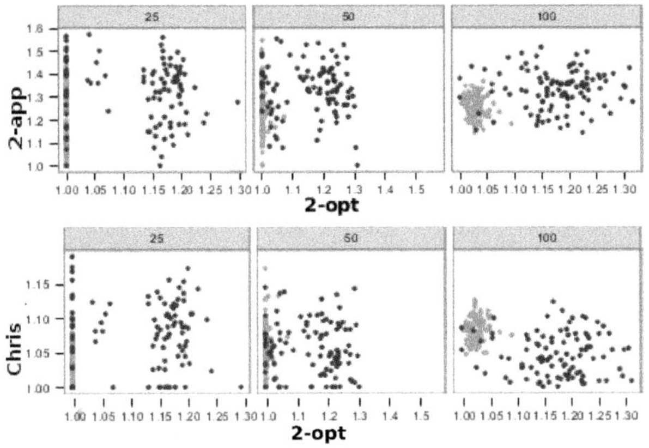

Figure 7: Performance of the 2-Approximation algorithm (top) and the Christofides algorithm (bottom) on the easy (grey) and hard (black) instances of 2-Opt algorithm.

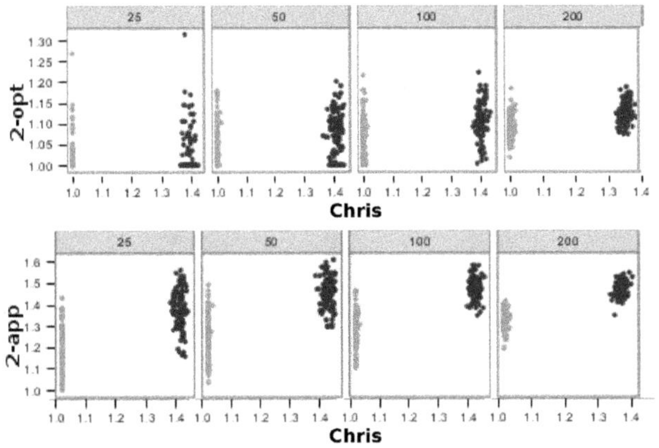

Figure 8: Performance of 2-Opt algorithm (top) and the 2-Approximation algorithm (bottom) on easy (grey) and hard (black) instances of Christofides algorithm.

1 to 1.15 for Christofides, and even just 1 to 1.1, for larger instances.

Figure 8 shows the results obtained by 2-Opt and the 2-Approximation algorithm on easy and hard Christofides instances. It can be observed that the Christofides algorithm itself has better performance for larger instance sizes than the 2-Approximation. This is more prominent in the case of hard instances where the clusters move to the upper right, with increasing instance size. Comparatively, 2-Opt achieves the best approximation values ranging from 1 to 1.3 for hard Christofides instances, the 2-Approximation algorithm (from 1.1 to 1.6) and Christofides (from 1.3 to 1.4). In contrast, Christofides achieves the best approximation ratios on its own easy instances (very close range around 1), whereas 2-Opt (from 1 to 1.2) and the 2-Approximation algorithm (from 1 to 1.5) cover wider ranges. For 2-Opt and the 2-Approximation algorithm these ranges get smaller with increasing instance size.

In summary it is observed that Christofides and 2-Opt algorithms surpass each other in the case of their own hard instances (see Figure 7 and 8), and this effect is more prominent in larger instance sizes. This implies that even though the hard instances of the different algorithms share some features, some other features are specific to each algorithm. For the easy instances, the generating algorithm generally performed best on its easy instances, and all algorithms achieve approximation ratios very close to 1. Considering hard instances only, the best approximation ratio is obtained by Christofides on the largest hard instances of 2-Opt (from 1 to 1.1). On the other hand, the worst approximation values for the hard instances are obtained for instances of the 2-Approximation algorithm by this algorithm itself, with values around 1.8. Both 2-Opt and Christofides algorithms compete with each other, having similar performances, while the 2-Approximation algorithm stays at a fair distance behind them. In general, these results imply that there are complementary capabilities of all the three algorithms on the difficult instances of each other. In addition, it becomes obvious that in general – as expected – hard and easy instances for a specific algorithm cannot be distinguished solely by means of the corresponding approximation ratios of the two remaining algorithms. The only slight exception is the 2-Approximation heuristic which allows for some conclusions regarding the approximation quality of the Christofides algorithm, especially for larger instance sizes.

5. CONCLUSIONS AND OUTLOOK

We used an evolutionary algorithm approach to generate easy and hard instances for the well-known Christofides and a 2-Approximation algorithm. Various features of easy and hard instances for the Christofides instances have been analysed in order to identify features for distinguishing the instance classes. Furthermore, the relationship of the feature values with the problem difficulty when moving from easy to hard instances has been examined which increased the understanding of underlying structures and relationships. Afterwards, we compared the Christofides, the 2-Approximation and a local search algorithm based on the 2-Opt operator by running the algorithms on each others' hard and easy instances. The results of this comparison of the hard instances point out complementary capabilities of the considered algorithms. Future work will be concentrated on feature based prediction of algorithm performance or the best suited algorithm for the analysed problem instances which will provide meaningful insights regarding algorithm design and especially the final goal of automated algorithm selection for given TSP instances.

References

[1] D. Applegate, W. J. Cook, S. Dash, and A. Rohe. Solution of a min-max vehicle routing problem. *INFORMS Journal on Computing*, 14(2):132–143, 2002.

[2] S. Arora. Polynomial time approximation schemes for euclidean traveling salesman and other geometric problems. *J. ACM*, 45(5):753–782, 1998.

[3] B. Bischl, O. Mersmann, H. Trautmann, and M. Preuß. Algorithm selection based on exploratory landscape analysis and cost-sensitive learning. In *Proceedings of the fourteenth international conference on Genetic and evolutionary computation conference*, GECCO '12. ACM, 2012.

[4] T. Kötzing, F. Neumann, H. Röglin, and C. Witt. Theoretical analysis of two aco approaches for the traveling salesman problem. *Swarm Intelligence*, pages 1–21, 2012.

[5] S. Lin and B. Kernighan. An effective heuristic algorithm for the traveling salesman problem. *Operations Research*, 21(1):498–516, 1973.

[6] O. Mersmann, B. Bischl, J. Bossek, H. Trautmann, M. Wagner, and F. Neumann. Local search and the traveling salesman problem: A feature-based characterization of problem hardness. In *Proceedings of the Learning and Intelligent Optimization Conference (LION)*, LNCS. Springer, 2012. http://arxiv.org/abs/1208.2318.

[7] F. Neumann and C. Witt. *Bioinspired Computation in Combinatorial Optimization – Algorithms and Their Computational Complexity*. Springer, 2010.

[8] K. Smith-Miles and L. Lopes. Measuring instance difficulty for combinatorial optimization problems. *Computers & OR*, 39(5):875–889, 2012.

[9] K. Smith-Miles, J. I. van Hemert, and X. Y. Lim. Understanding tsp difficulty by learning from evolved instances. In *LION*, pages 266–280, 2010.

[10] A. Sutton and F. Neumann. A parameterized runtime analysis of evolutionary algorithms for the euclidean traveling salesperson problem. In *Proceedings of Association of Advancements of Artificial Intelligence*. AAAI, 2012.

[11] J. I. van Hemert. Evolving combinatorial problem instances that are difficult to solve. *Evol. Comput.*, 14(4):433–462, Dec. 2006.

[12] V. V. Vazirani. *Approximation algorithms*. Springer, 2001.

[13] L. Xu, F. Hutter, H. H. Hoos, and K. Leyton-Brown. Satzilla: portfolio-based algorithm selection for sat. *J. Artif. Int. Res.*, 32(1):565–606, June 2008.

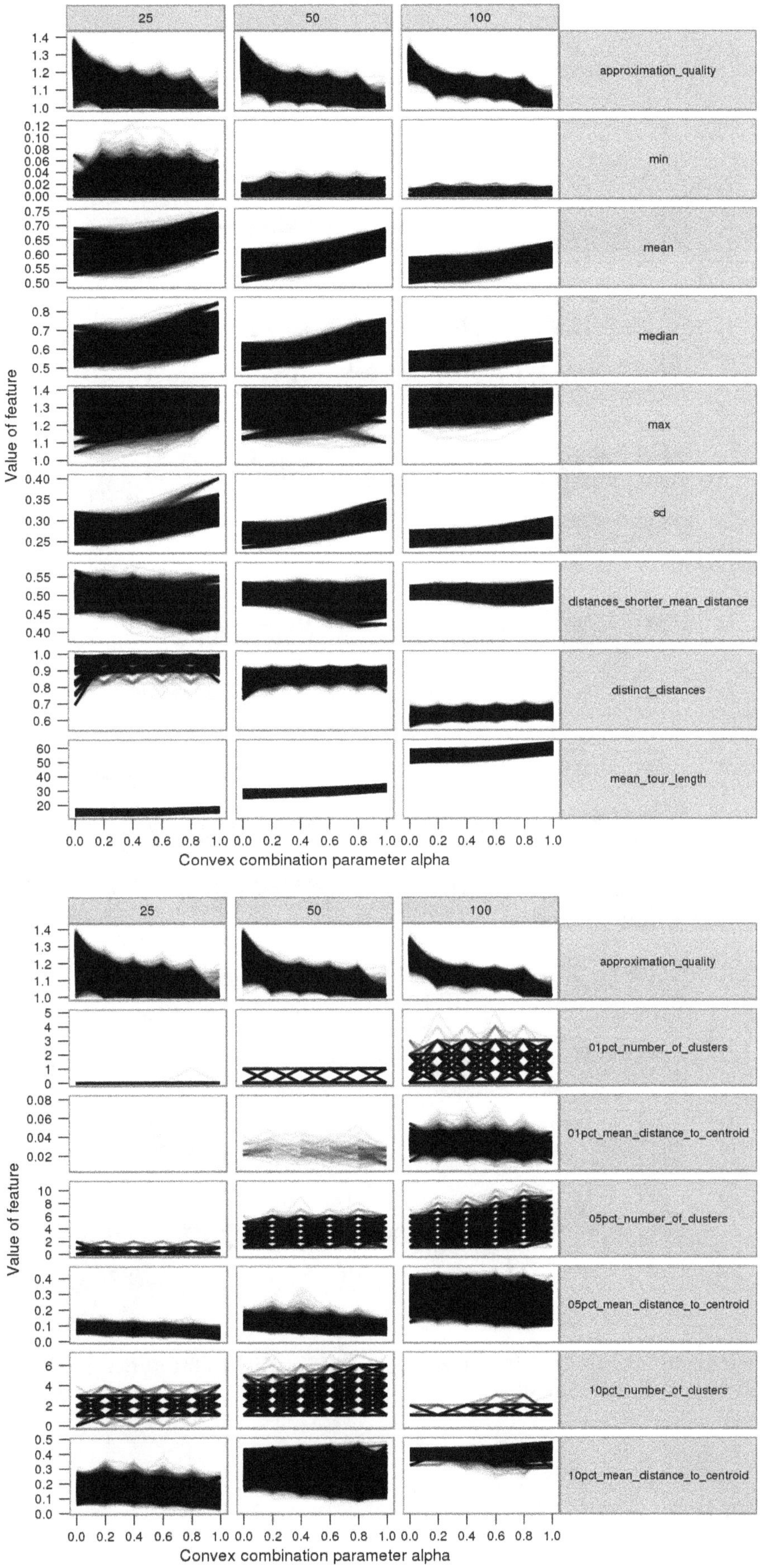

Figure 9: Distance features (top) and Cluster features (bottom): approximation quality and feature values for different α levels of all conducted morphing experiments for Christofides.

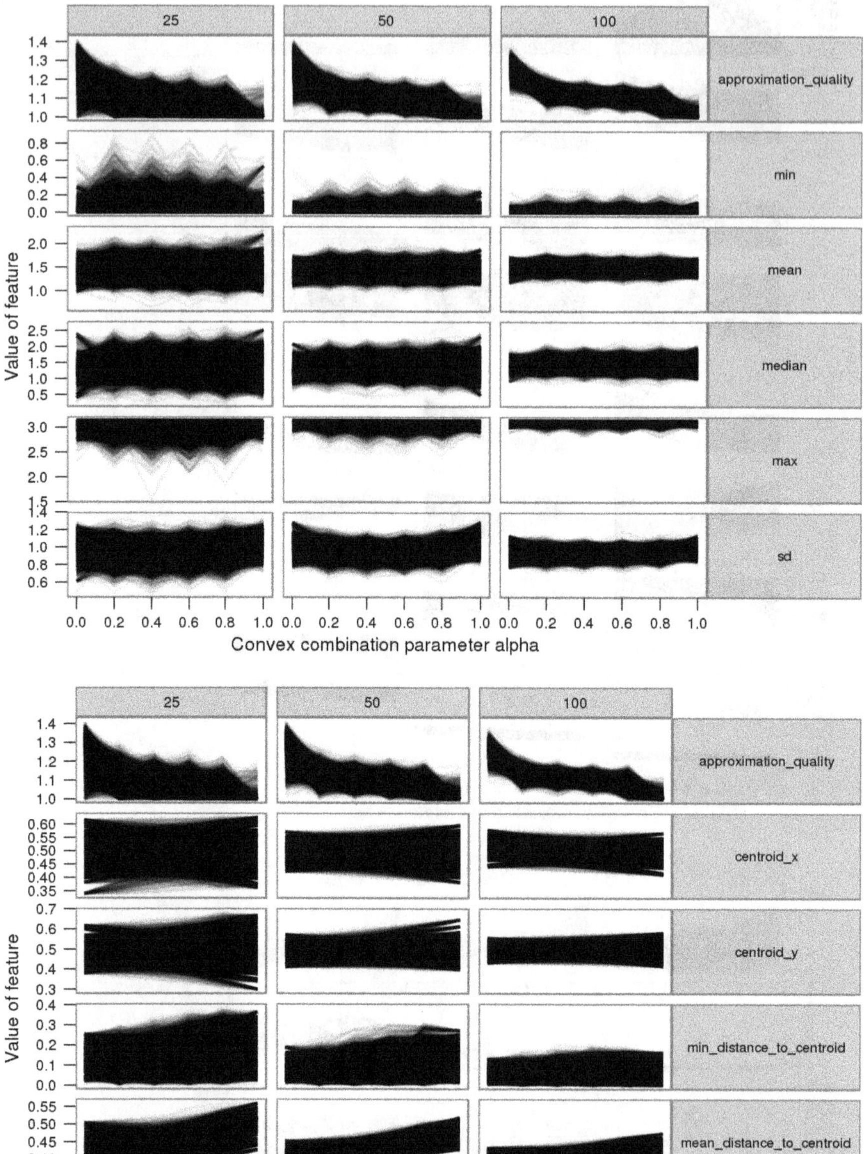

Figure 10: Angle (top) and Centroid Features (bottom): approximation quality and feature values for different α levels of all conducted morphing experiments for Christofides.

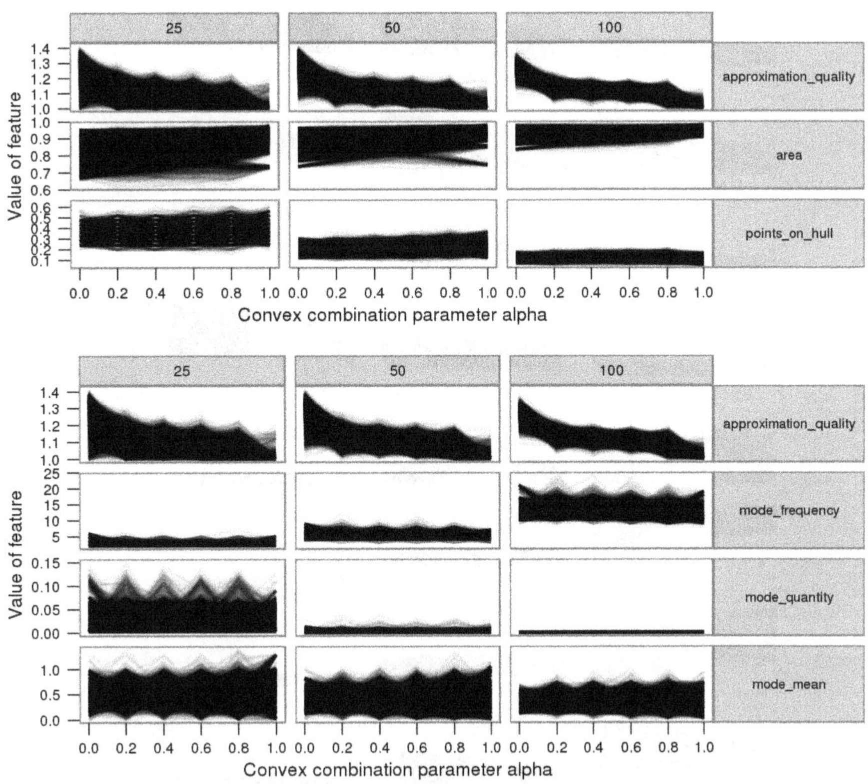

Figure 11: Convex Hull (top) and Mode (bottom) features: approximation quality and feature values for different α levels of all conducted morphing experiments for Christofides.

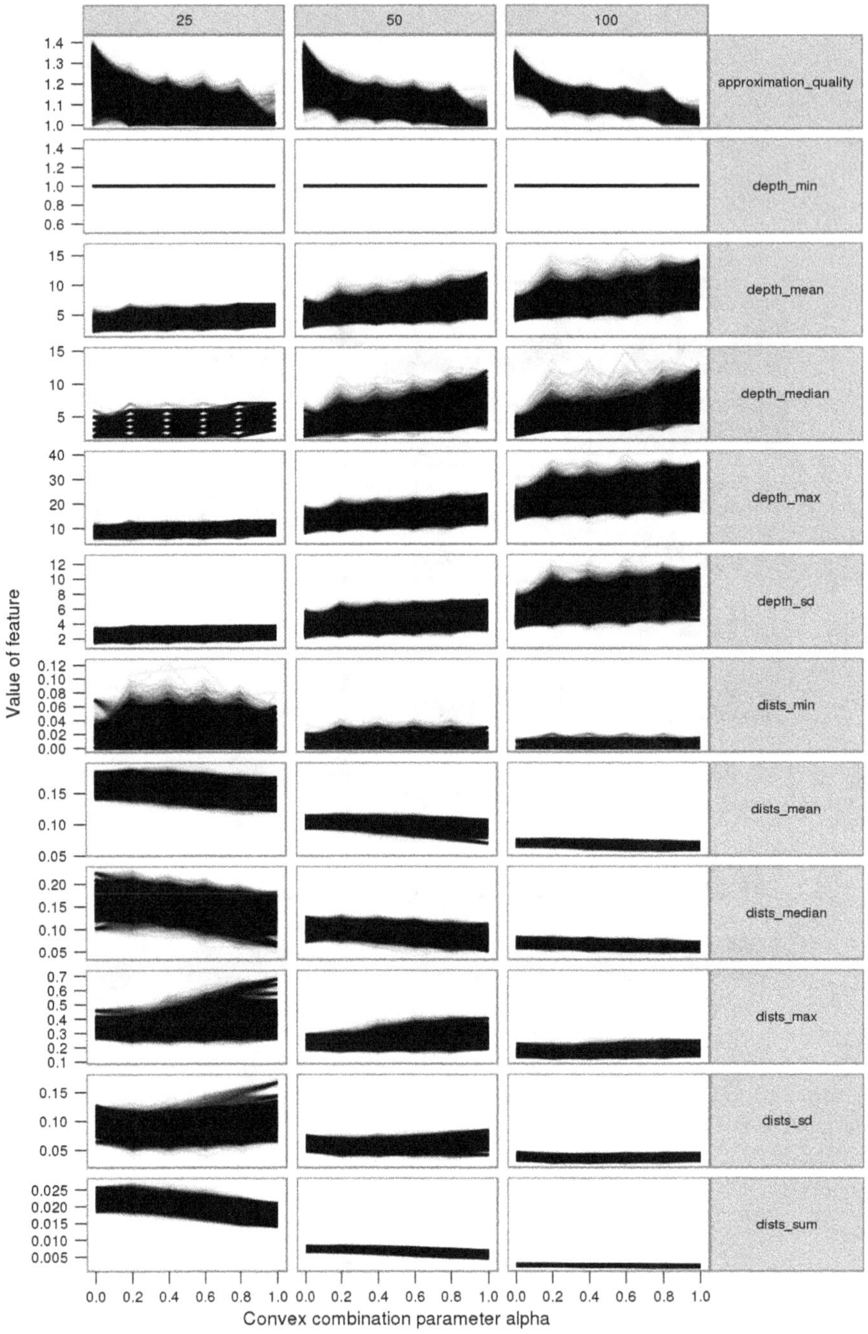

Figure 12: MST features: approximation quality and feature values for different α levels of all conducted morphing experiments for Christofides.

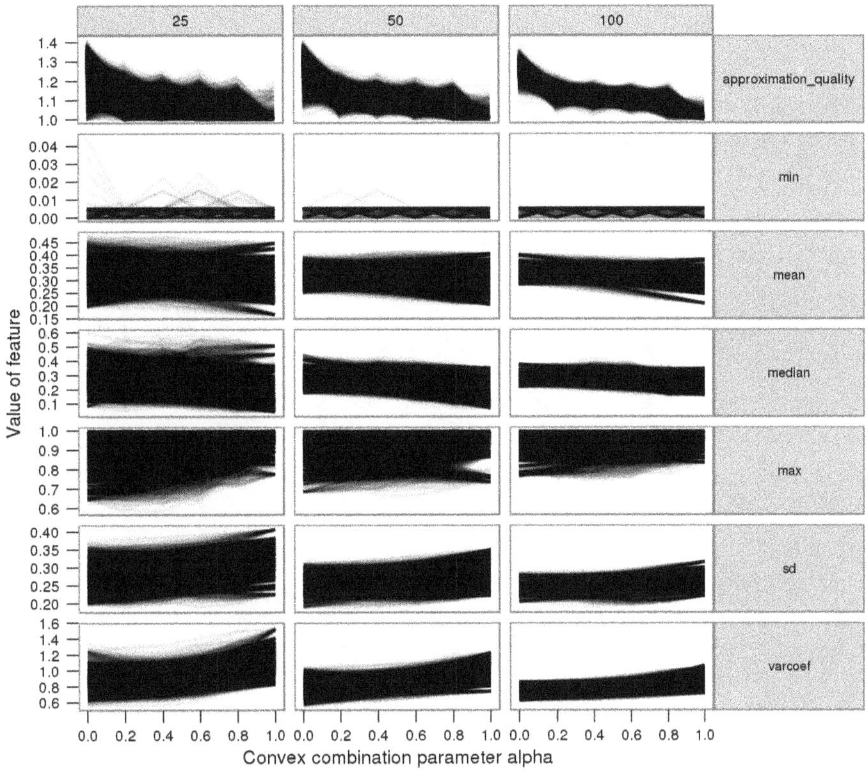

Figure 13: Nearest neighbour distance features: approximation quality and feature values for different α levels of all conducted morphing experiments for Christofides.

Single- and Multi-Objective Genetic Programming: New Bounds for Weighted ORDER and MAJORITY

Anh Nguyen
Evolutionary Computation Group
School of Computer Science
The University of Adelaide
Adelaide, SA 5005, Australia

Tommaso Urli
Dipartimento di Ingegneria Elettrica, Gestionale e Meccanica
Università degli Studi di Udine
33100 Udine, Italy

Markus Wagner
Evolutionary Computation Group
School of Computer Science
The University of Adelaide
Adelaide, SA 5005, Australia

ABSTRACT

We consolidate the existing computational complexity analysis of genetic programming (GP) by bringing together sound theoretical proofs and empirical analysis. In particular, we address computational complexity issues arising when coupling algorithms using variable length representation, such as GP itself, with different bloat-control techniques. In order to accomplish this, we first introduce several novel upper bounds for two single- and multi-objective GP algorithms on the generalised Weighted ORDER and MAJORITY problems. To obtain these, we employ well-established computational complexity analysis techniques such as fitness-based partitions, and for the first time, additive and multiplicative drift.

The bounds we identify depend on two measures, the maximum tree size and the maximum population size, that arise during the optimization run and that have a key relevance in determining the runtime of the studied GP algorithms. In order to understand the impact of these measures on a typical run, we study their magnitude experimentally, and we discuss the obtained findings.

Categories and Subject Descriptors

F.2 [**Theory of Computation**]: Analysis of Algorithms and Problem Complexity

General Terms

Theory, Algorithms, Performance

Keywords

Genetic Programming, Multi-objective Optimization, Theory, Runtime Analysis

1. INTRODUCTION

In the last decade, genetic programming (GP) has found various applications (see Poli et al., 2008) in a number of domains. As other paradigms based on variable length representation, however, GP can be subject to *bloating*. Bloating occurs when a solution's growth in complexity does not correspond to a growth in quality and causes the optimization process to diverge and slow down. Since bloat-control is a key factor to the efficient functioning of GP, its impact on the computational complexity has been studied already for simple problems, in Durrett et al. (2011) and Neumann (2012). The algorithms that have been considered are a stochastic hill-climber called (1+1)-GP, and a population-based multi-objective genetic programming algorithm called SMO-GP; the latter considers the trade-offs between solutions complexity C and fitness with respect to a problem F. These algorithms have been analysed on problems with isolated program semantics taken from Goldberg and O'Reilly (1998), namely ORDER and MAJORITY, which can be seen as the analogue of linear pseudo-Boolean functions Droste et al. (2002) that are known from the computational complexity analysis of evolutionary algorithms working with fixed length binary representations. Both problems are simple enough to be analysed thoroughly, and they represent different aspects of problems solved through genetic programming, that is, including components in the correct order (ORDER), and including the correct set of components in a solution (MAJORITY). Additional recent computational complexity results are those of Kötzing et al. (2012) on the MAX problem, and of Wagner and Neumann (2012) on the SORTING problem.

The results provided in Durrett et al. (2011); Neumann (2012) raise several questions that remain unanswered in both papers. In particular, for different combinations of algorithms and problems no (or no exact) runtime bounds are given. These works suggest that two measures, namely the maximum tree size T_{max} and the maximum population size P_{max} obtained during the run, play a role in determining the expected optimization time of the investigated algorithms. Urli et al. (2012) have made significant effort to study the order of growth of these quantities, and to conjecture runtime bounds for both problems. However, their results are based purely on extensive experimental investigations, potentially neglecting problematic cases. Even though Urli et al. (2012) conjecture runtimes based on their observations, the impact of both quantities on the runtime is still unclear from the theory side.

In this paper, we address these questions. We use multiplicative drift (Doerr et al., 2010) on the fitness values to bound the runtime of (1+1)-GP on the *Weighted* ORDER (WORDER) problem. Subsequently, we consider (1+1)-GP on the multi-objective formulations of WORDER, which considers the complexity as well. There, we apply drift analysis on the solution sizes in order to bound (with high probability) the maximum tree sizes encountered. Lastly, we consider the multi-objective SMO-GP algorithm, and bound the runtimes using fitness-based partitions. In the cases where T_{max} and P_{max} are part of the asymptotic bound, we augment the results with experimental observations.

Note that our investigations focus on the weighted variants WORDER and WMAJORITY, which both allow for exponentially many different fitness values. Very few runtime bounds were known for both problems so far.

The paper is structured as follows. In Section 2, we introduce the analysed problems and algorithms. In Section 3, we summarize the previous computational complexity results from Durrett et al. (2011); Neumann (2012). In Sections 4 and 5, we present several new theoretical upper bounds and we complement the analyses with experimental results whenever a term of the bound is not under the control of the user. In the final section, we summarise the existing known bounds and ours, and we point out open questions.

2. PRELIMINARIES

In our theoretical and experimental investigations, we will treat the algorithms and problems analyzed in Durrett et al. (2011); Neumann (2012). We consider tree-based genetic programming where a possible solution is represented by a syntax tree. The inner nodes of such a tree are labelled by function symbols from a set F and the leaves of the tree are labelled by terminals from a set T.

We examine the problems Weighted ORDER (WORDER) and Weighted MAJORITY (WMAJORITY). In these problems, the only function symbol is the join (denoted by J), which is binary. The terminal set is a set of $2n$ variables, where $\bar{x}_i$ is considered the complement of x_i. Hence, $F := \{J\}$, and $L := \{x_1, \bar{x}_1, x_2, \bar{x}_2, ..., x_n, \bar{x}_n\}$.

In WORDER and WMAJORITY, each variable x_i is assigned a weight $w_i \in \mathbb{R}$, $1 \leq i \leq n$ so that the variables can differ in their contributions to the fitness of a tree. Without loss of generality, we assume that $w_1 \geq w_2 \geq w_3 \geq \ldots \geq w_n > 0$. We get the ORDER and MAJORITY as specific cases of WORDER and WMAJORITY where $w_i = 1, 1 \leq i \leq n$.

For a given solution X, the fitness value is computed by parsing the represented tree inorder. For WORDER, the weight w_i of a variable x_i contributes to the fitness of X iff x_i is visited in the inorder parse before all the $\bar{x}_i$ in the tree. For WMAJORITY, the weight of x_i contributes to the fitness of X iff the number of occurrences of x_i in the tree is at least one and not less than the number of occurrence of $\bar{x}_i$ (see Figures 2 and 3). We call a variable redundant if it occurs multiple times in the tree; in this case the variable contributes only once to the fitness value. The goal of WORDER and WMAJORITY problems is to maximize their function values. We illustrate both problems by an example (see Figure 1).

MO-WORDER and MO-MAJORITY are variants of the above-described problems, which take the complexity C of a syntax tree (computed by the number of leaves of the tree) as the second objective:

- MO-WORDER (X) = (WORDER (X), C(X))
- MO-WMAJORITY (X) = (WMAJORITY (X), C(X))

Optimization algorithms can then use this to cope with the bloat problem: if two solutions have the same fitness value, then the solution of lower complexity can be preferred. In the special case, where $w_i = 1$ holds for all $1 \leq i \leq n$, we have the problems:

- MO-ORDER (X) = (ORDER (X), C(X))
- MO-MAJORITY (X) = (MAJORITY (X), C(X))

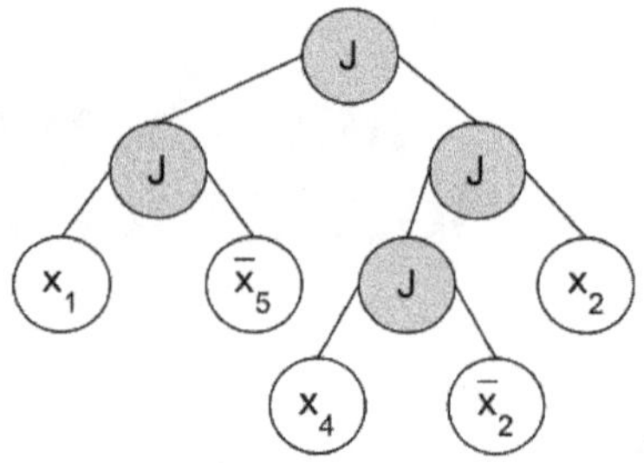

Figure 1: Example for evaluations according to WORDER and WMAJORITY. Let $n = 5$ and $w_1 = 15$, $w_2 = 14$, $w_3 = 12$, $w_4 = 7$, and $w_5 = 2$. For the shown tree X, we get (after inorder parsing) $l = (x_1, \bar{x}_5, x_4, \bar{x}_2, x_2)$. For WORDER, we get $S = (x_1, x_4)$ and WORDER$(X) = w_1 + w_4 = 22$. For WMAJORITY, we get $S = (x_1, x_4, x_2)$ and WMAJORITY$(X) = w_1 + w_4 + w_2 = 36$.

Input: a syntax tree X
Init: l an empty leaf list, S is an empty statement list.

1. Parse X inorder and insert each leaf at the rear of l as it is visited.
2. Generate S by parsing l front to rear and adding ("expressing") a leaf to S only if it or its complement are not yet in S (i.e. have not yet been expressed).
3. WORDER (X) = $\sum_{x_i \in S} w_i$

Figure 2: Computation of WORDER (X)

Input: a syntax tree X
Init: l an empty leaf list, S is an empty statement list.

1. Parse X inorder and insert each leaf at the rear of l as it is visited.
2. For $1 \leq i \leq n$, if count$(x_i \in l) \geq 1$ and count$(x_i \in l) \geq$ count$(\bar{x}_i \in l)$, add x_i to S
3. WMAJORITY (X) = $\sum_{x_i \in S} w_i$

Figure 3: Computation of WMAJORITY (X)

In this paper, all algorithms only use the mutation operator HVL-Prime to generate offspring. HVL-Prime produces a new tree by making changes to the original tree via three basic operators: insertion, deletion and substitution. A more detailed explanation of this operator can be found in Durrett et al. (2011). In each step of the algorithms, k mutations are applied to the selected solution. For the single-operation variants of the algorithms, $k = 1$ holds. For the multi-operation variants, the number of operations performed is drawn each time from the distribution $k = 1 + Pois(1)$, where $Pois(1)$ is the Poisson distribution with parameter 1.

3. THEORETICAL RESULTS

The computational complexity analysis of genetic programming analyses the expected number of fitness evaluations

F(X)	(1+1)-GP, F(X) Durrett et al. (2011)		(1+1)-GP, MO-F(X) Neumann (2012)		SMO-GP, MO-F(X) Neumann (2012)	
	k=1	k=1+Pois(1)	k=1	k=1+Pois(1)	k=1	k=1+Pois(1)
ORDER	$O(nT_{max})$	$O(nT_{max})$	$O(T_{init} + n \log n)$		$O(nT_{init} + n^2 \log n)$	
WORDER	?	?	$O(T_{init} + n \log n)$	?	$O(n^3)\star$	?
MAJORITY	$O(n^2 T_{max} \log n)$	?	$O(T_{init} + n \log n)$		$O(nT_{init} + n^2 \log n)$	
WMAJORITY	?	?	$O(T_{init} + n \log n)$		$O(n^3)\star$	?

Table 1: Computational complexity results from Durrett et al. (2011); Neumann (2012)

Mutate Y by applying HVL-Prime k times, In each time, randomly choose either insert, subsitute or delete.

- Insert: Choose a variable $u \in L$ uniformly at random and select a node $v \in Y$ uniformly at random. Replace v by a join node whose children are u and v, in which their orders are chosen randomly,
- Substitute: Replace a randomly chosen leaf $v \in Y$ by a randomly chosen leaf $u \in L$.
- Delete: Choose a leaf node $v \in Y$ randomly with parent p and sibling u. Replace p by u and delete p and u.

Figure 4: HVL-Prime mutation operator

until the algorithm has produced an optimal solution for the first time. This is called the *expected optimization time*. In the case of multi-objective optimization the definition of expected optimization time is slightly different and considers the number of fitness evaluations until the whole Pareto front, i.e. the set of optimal trade-offs between the objectives, has been computed.

The existing bounds from Durrett et al. (2011); Neumann (2012) are listed in Table 1. As it can be seen, all results for (1+1)-GP take into account tree sizes of some kind: either the maximum tree size T_{max} found during search or the initial tree T_{init} size play a role in determining the bound. While T_{init} is something which can be decided in advance, T_{max} is a result of the interactions between the fitness function, the set of mutations and the selection process. As mutations involve a degree of randomness, in some cases such a measure is very difficult to control.

A similar problem arises when dealing with multi-objective algorithms, such as SMO-GP. As we will see, the maximum population size reached during optimization, P_{max}, is a fundamental term in most bounds and it is again very difficult to tackle when a random number of mutations is involved. This is the paramount reason for which the only bounds for the single-mutation variant are known to date. Lastly, note that the upper bounds marked with $\star$ hold only if the algorithm has been initialized in the particular, i.e. non-redundant, way described in Neumann (2012).

Because of the direct relation between these measures and the bounds, investigating their magnitude is key to the fundamental understanding of the bounds meaning.

4. (1+1)-GP

The algorithm (1+1)-GP starts with an initial solution X, and in each generation a new offspring Y is produced by mutating X. Y replaces X if it is favoured by the selection mechanism. Different from WORDER and WMAJORITY where solutions of equal fitnesses can replace each other unconditionally, the selection on MO-WORDER and MO-WMAJORITY favours solutions with higher fitness value or smaller complexity value when two solutions have the same fitness value.

Algorithm 1: (1+1)-GP algorithm

1. Choose an initial solution X
2. Repeat
   - Set $Y := X$
   - Apply mutation to Y
   - If the selection favours Y over X then $X := Y$.

Let X, Y be the solutions and F be the fitness function in (1+1)-GP.

- (1+1)-GP on *F*: Favour Y over X iff $F(Y) \geq F(X)$
- (1+1)-GP on *MO-F*: Favour Y over X iff $(F(Y) > F(X)) \vee ((F(Y) = F(X)) \wedge ((C(Y) \leq C(X)))$

Figure 5: Selection mechanism of (1+1)-GP

However, since in MO-WORDER and MO-WMAJORITY, the complexity of a syntax tree is not taken into account, there is no mechanism for handling the bloat problem. Given the maximum tree size T_{max} for a run is unknown, it would be preferable to have runtime bounds based on the size of the initial tree T_{init}, which the user can control. Using a different approach in which the selection in Figure 4 is used, Neumann (2012) proved that the expected optimisation time for (1+1)-GP-single on both MO-WORDER and MO-WMAJORITY is $O(T_{init} + n \log n)$. In the following subsections, (1+1)-GP with one and more than one mutation in each step are correspondingly denoted by (1+1)-GP-single and (1+1)-GP-multi.

4.1 (1+1)-GP on F(X) Problems

In previous works, Durrett et al. (2011) showed that the upper bound of the expected run time for (1+1)-GP on ORDER is $O(nT_{max})$. First, we show that this bound immediately carries over for (1+1)-GP-single on WORDER.

THEOREM 1. *The expected optimization time of (1+1)-GP-single on WORDER is $O(nT_{max})$.*

PROOF. As (1+1)-GP-single performs only a single mutation operation at a time, it is not possible (1) to increase the

WORDER value of a tree and (2) to decrease the number of expressed variables at the same time. Hence, once a variable is expressed, it will stay expressed for the rest of the optimisation process. This, however, means that the weights associated to the variables are effectively irrelevant. Thus, the upper bound of the runtime is identical to that of (1+1)-GP-single on the unweighted ORDER, and the bound immediately carries over. □

The bound for the multi-operation variant is found by applying **Theorem 3** (multiplicative drift analysis) from Doerr et al. (2010), which is defined as follows.

THEOREM 2 (MULT. DRIFT, DOERR ET AL. (2010)). *Let $S \subseteq \mathbb{R}$ be a finite set of positive numbers with minimum s_{min}. Let $X^{(t)}{}_{t \in \mathbb{N}}$ be a sequence of random variables over $S \cup \{0\}$. Let T be the random variable that denotes the first point in time $t \in \mathbb{N}$ for which $X^{(t)} = 0$.*

Suppose that there exists a constant $\delta > 0$ such that

$$E\left[X^{(t)} - X^{(t+1)} | X^{(t)} = s\right] \geq \delta s \qquad (1)$$

holds for all $s \in S$ with $\Pr[X^t = s] > 0$. Then for all $s_0 \in S$ with $\Pr[X^{(0)} = s_0] > 0$,

$$E[T | X^{(0)} = s_0] \leq \frac{1 + \log(s_0/s_{min})}{\delta}. \qquad (2)$$

In the following theorem we employ Theorem 2 to provide an upper bound on the expected runtime of (1+1)-GP-multi, F(X) on WORDER when starting from any solution.

THEOREM 3. *The expected optimization time of (1+1)-GP-multi on WORDER is $O(nT_{max}(\log n + \log w_{max}))$.*

PROOF. In order to prove the stated bounds we need to instantiate Theorem 2 on our problem. The theorem is valid if we can identify a finite set $S \subseteq \mathbb{R}$ from which the random variables X^t are drawn. In our case the drift is defined on the (at most exponentially many) values of the fitness function. Also, since the result holds under the assumption that the underlying problem is a minimization problem, we first need to define an auxiliary problem WORDER$_{min}$ which get minimized whenever WORDER gets maximized

$$\text{WORDER}_{min}(x) = \sum_{i=1}^{n} w_i - \text{WORDER}(x).$$

Note that while WORDER(x) is the sum of the weights for the expressed variables in x, WORDER$_{min}(x)$ is the sum of the weights of the unexpressed variables. We also recall that ORDER(x) denotes the number of expressed variables in x.

Now, given a solution x^t at time t, let s_t = WORDER$_{min}(x^t)$ be the WORDER-value of this solution and $m = n -$ORDER(x^t) the number of unexpressed variables in x^t. Since an improvement can be done by inserting a non-expressed variables into the current tree, then the expected increment, i.e. the drift, of WORDER$_{min}$ is lower bounded by: $E\left[X^{(t)} - X^{(t+1)} | X^{(t)} = s_t\right] \geq \frac{\text{WORDER}_{min}(x^t)}{m} \cdot \frac{m}{6enT_{max}} = \frac{\text{WORDER}_{min}(x^t)}{6enT_{max}}$. since the probability of expressing any of the m unexpressed variables at the beginning of the tree is at least $\frac{m}{2n} \cdot \frac{1}{3eT_{max}} = \frac{m}{6enT_{max}}$ for both the single- and the multi-operation case, and the expected improvement when performing such step is $WORDER_{min}(x^t)/m$ (because the missing weights are distributed over m variables).

Given this drift, we have (in Theorem 2 terminology)

$$\delta = \frac{1}{6enT_{max}} \qquad s = \text{WORDER}_{min}(x^t).$$

Also, from the definition of WORDER, we have that $s_{min} = w_{min}$. From Theorem 2 follows that, for any initial value s_0 = WORDER$_{min}(x^0)$, we have

$$\begin{aligned} E[T|X^{(0)} = s_0] &\leq \left(1 + \ln\left(\frac{s_0}{w_{min}}\right)\right) \cdot \delta^{-1} \\ &\leq \left(1 + \ln\left(\frac{s_0}{w_{min}}\right)\right) \cdot 6enT_{max}. \end{aligned}$$

Since we are interested in an upper bound over the expected optimization time, we must consider starting from the worst possible initial solution, i.e. where none of the variables is expressed. Let w_{max} be the largest weight in the set, then the maximum distance from the optimal solution is $nw_{max} \geq s_0$. Hence we have

$$\begin{aligned} E[T] &\leq \left(1 + \ln\left(\frac{nw_{max}}{w_{min}}\right)\right) \cdot 6enT_{max} \\ &\leq (1 + \ln(nw_{max})) \cdot 6enT_{max} \\ &= O(nT_{max}\log(nw_{max})) = O(nT_{max}(\log n + \log w_{max})) \end{aligned}$$

which states that the expected optimization time T of (1+1)-GP, F(X) for WORDER$_{min}$, and hence for WORDER, starting from any solution is bounded by $O(nT_{max}(\log n + \log w_{max}))$. □

The dependence of this bound, and of the bound for ORDER introduced in Durrett et al. (2011), on T_{max} is easily explained by the fact that, in order to guarantee a single-step improvement, one must perform a beneficial insertion, i.e. one which expresses one of the unexpressed variables, at the beginning of the tree. This involves selecting one out of at most T_{max} nodes in the tree. Unfortunately, T_{max} can potentially grow arbitrarily large since $F(X)$ does not control solution complexity.

We have investigated this measure experimentally in order to understand what its typical magnitude is. The experiments were performed on AMD Opteron 250 CPUs (2.4GHz), on Debian GNU/Linux 5.0.8, with Java SE RE 1.6 and were given a maximum runtime of 3 hours and a budget of 10^9 evaluations. Furthermore, each experiment (involving two different initialization schemes, respectively with 0 and $2n$ leaves in the initial tree) has been repeated 400 times, which results in a standard error of the mean of $1/\sqrt{400} = 5\%$. The empirical distributions of maximum tree sizes for (1+1)-GP, $F(X)$ on all ORDER variants are shown as box-plots in Figure 6. The blue-toned line plots show the median T_{max} divided by n (solid line) and by $n\log(n)$ (dashed line); the nearly constant behaviour of the solid line suggests that T_{max} has typical a linear behaviour for all ORDER variants, at least for the tested values of n and the employed initialization schemes.

4.2 Algorithms on MO-F(X) Problems

For the multi-operation variants, a single HVL-Prime application can lead to more than a single mutation with constant probability. This would lead to the case where the complexity increase faster than the fitness value, i.e. an improvement on the fitness of the tree can be followed by multiple increase on the complexity. We start our analysis by showing an upper bound of the maximum tree size, T_{max}, during run

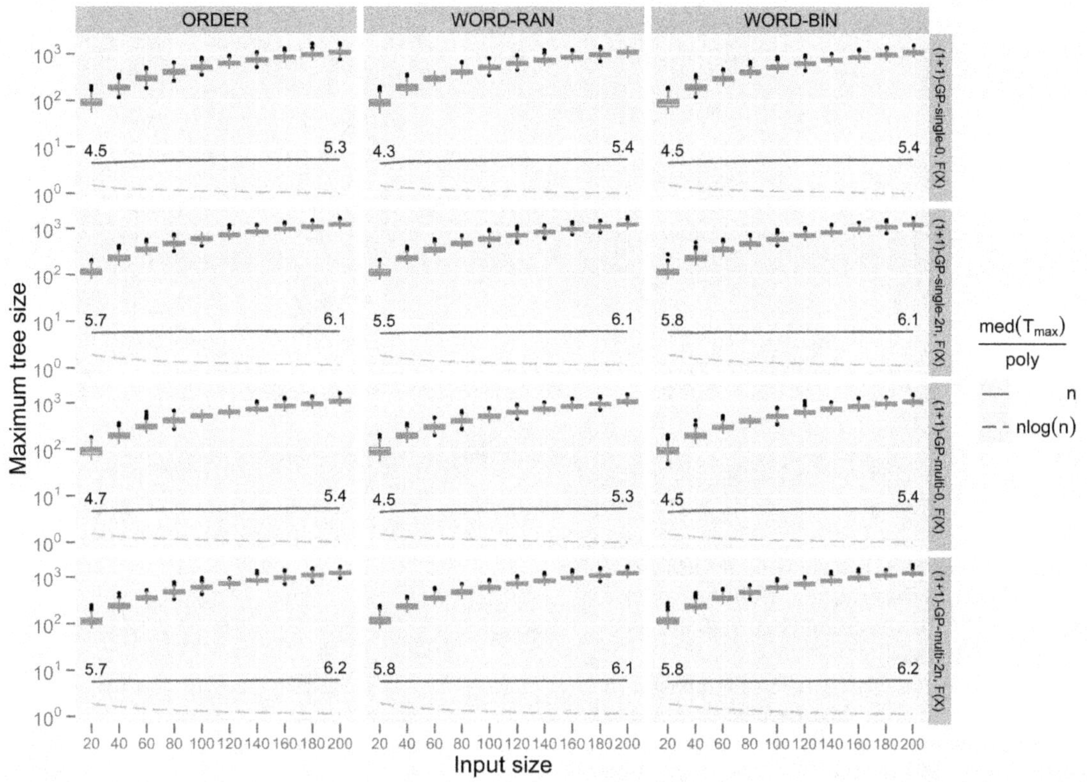

Figure 6: Distribution, as green box-plots, of the maximum tree sizes observed for (1+1)-GP, $F(X)$ on the ORDER variants. The blue-toned lines are the median T_{max} values divided by the corresponding polynomial (see the legend) and suggest the asymptotic behavior of the measure. In this case the almost horizontal line for n shows that the maximum tree size is very close to linear, at least for the tested input sizes.

time and then using that fact to bound the expected optimisation time of (1+1)-GP-multi on MO-WORDER.

THEOREM 4. *(Oliveto and Witt, 2011) Let $X_t, t \geq 0$, be the random variables describing a Markov process over a finite state space $S \subseteq \mathbb{R}_0^+$ and denote $\Delta_t(i) := (X_{t+1} - X_t \mid X_t = i)$ for $i \in S$ and $t \geq 0$. Suppose there exists an interval $[a, b]$ in the state space, two constants $\delta, \varepsilon > 0$ and, possibly depending on $l := b - a$, a function $r(l)$ satisfying $1 \leq r(l) = o(l/log(l))$ such that for all $t \geq 0$ the following two conditions hold:*

1. *$E(\Delta_t(i)) \geq \varepsilon$ for $a < i < b$,*
2. *$Prob(|\Delta_t(i)| \geq j) \leq \frac{r(l)}{(1+\delta)^j}$ for $i > a$ and $j \in \mathbb{N}_0$.*

Then there is a constant $c^* > 0$ such that for $T^* := \min\{t \geq 0 : X_t \leq a \mid X_0 \geq b\}$ it holds $Prob\left(T^* \leq 2^{c^* l/r(l)}\right) = 2^{-\Omega(l/r(l))}$. In the conference version, $r(l)$ was only allowed to be a constant, i.e., $r(l) = O(1)$. In this case, the last statement is simplified to

$$Prob(T^* \leq 2^{c^* l}) = 2^{-\Omega(l)}.$$

THEOREM 5. *Let $T_{init} \leq 19n$ be the complexity of the initial solution. Then, the maximum tree size encountered by (1+1)-GP-multi on MO-WORDER in less than exponential time is $20n$, with high probability.*

Note that the state space S (of the tree sizes) is finite for both problems, as at most 2^n fitness improvements are accepted. Thus, at most $2^n + 1$ different tree sizes can be attained.

PROOF. Theorem 4 was used to find the lower bound value of a function in less than exponential time. In case of finding the upper bound value of a function, condition 1 and 2 of Theorem 4 are then changed to :

1. $E(\Delta_t(i)) \leq -\varepsilon$ for $a < i < b$ and $\varepsilon > 0$,
2. $Prob(|\Delta_t(i)| \geq j) \leq \frac{r(l)}{(1+\delta)^j}$ for $i > a$ and $j \in \mathbb{N}_0$.

Let $a = 19n$, $b = 20n$, k be the number of expressed variables, and s be the number of leaves of the current tree. For condition 1 to hold, the expected drift of the size of a syntax tree in the interval $[a, b] = [19n, 20n]$ must be a negative constant. This is computed by

$$\begin{aligned} E(\Delta_t(i)) &= \sum_{j \in \mathbb{Z}} j \cdot P(\Delta_t(i) = j) \\ &= \sum_{j \in \mathbb{Z}, j<0} j \cdot P(\Delta_t(i) = j) + \sum_{j \in \mathbb{N}} j \cdot P(\Delta_t(i) = j) \\ &= \sum_{j \in \mathbb{N}} -j \cdot P(\Delta_t(i) = -j) + \sum_{j \in \mathbb{N}} j \cdot P(\Delta_t(i) = j) \end{aligned}$$

When $\Delta_t(i) = -j$ for $j \in \mathbb{N}$, then the tree size is reduced by j. We can find a lower bound to the expected decrease in size by observing that to obtain a reduction of $-j$, we can do in principle $t > j$ operations, out of which j must be deletions of redundant variables and the other $t - j$ must be neutral moves. Since we have three mutations with equal probability of being selected, there are at least to 3^{t-j} possible combinations of mutations that lead to a decrease of $-j$.

We know that among these, at least one is made of substitutions that don't decrease the fitness and the probability of obtaining it $1/3^{t-j}$. Let $s = cn$, $19 < c < 20$, then

$$\begin{aligned}
&\sum_{j\in\mathbb{N}} -j \cdot P(\Delta_t(i) = -j) \\
&\leq -\sum_{j\in\mathbb{N}} j \sum_{t=j}^{\infty} \left[\left(\frac{1}{3}\right)^j \binom{s-k}{j} \left(\frac{1}{s}\right)^j \cdot \frac{1}{3^{t-s}} \cdot Pois(x=t) \right] \\
&\leq -\sum_{j\in\mathbb{N}} j \sum_{t=j}^{\infty} \left[\left(\frac{1}{3}\right)^j \binom{s-k}{j} \left(\frac{1}{s}\right)^j \cdot \frac{1}{3^{t-s}} \cdot \frac{1}{et!} \right] \\
&\leq -\tfrac{1}{e} \sum_{j\in\mathbb{N}} j \left(\frac{1}{3}\right)^j \cdot \left(\frac{s-k}{j}\right)^j \cdot \left(\frac{1}{s}\right)^j \sum_{t=j}^{\infty} \left(\frac{1}{3^{t-s}} \cdot \frac{1}{t!}\right) \\
&\leq -\tfrac{1}{e} \sum_{j\in\mathbb{N}} j \left(\frac{1}{3}\right)^j \cdot \left(\frac{c-1}{c}\right)^j \cdot \left(\frac{1}{j}\right)^j \sum_{t=j}^{\infty} \left(\frac{1}{3^{t-s}} \cdot \frac{1}{t!}\right)
\end{aligned}$$

where $(1/3)^j$ comes from the fact that we need to perform j deletions, $(1/s)^j$ is related to selecting the right leaf over s leaves for j times and $\binom{s-k}{j}$ is the number of possible permutations of redundant variables.

When $\Delta_t(i) = j$ for $j \in \mathbb{N}$, the size of the tree increases. In order to provide a upper bound on the expected increase of the tree size, we need to consider all the possible combinations of t mutations which lead us to an increase of j. Since we need to increase the tree size by j, we need at least j insertions, thus the remaining $t - j$ mutations can be arranged in 3^{t-j} different ways. Note that this is an upper bound, as many of these combinations will not lead to an increase of j. This means that the probability to do a correct number of insertions is upper bounded by $\frac{3^{t-j}}{3^t} = \frac{1}{3^j}$. Also, in order to accept a larger tree size, the fitness must be increased as well. In the worst case, this can be accomplished by inserting one unexpressed variable in such a position that it increases the fitness of the tree size, an inserting $m - 1$ random variables in positions that don't decrease the fitness of the tree. Thus the expected increase in the tree size is

$$\begin{aligned}
&\sum_{j\in\mathbb{N}} j \cdot P(\Delta_t(i) = j) \\
&\leq \sum_{j\in\mathbb{N}} \left(j \cdot \frac{n-k}{2n} \cdot P_1 \cdot P_2 \sum_{t=j} Pois(x=t) \right) \\
&\leq \sum_{j\in\mathbb{N}} \left(j \cdot \frac{1}{3^j} \cdot \frac{1}{2} \sum_{t=j} \frac{1}{et!} \right) = \frac{1}{e} \sum_{j\in\mathbb{N}} \left(j \cdot \frac{1}{2} \cdot \frac{1}{3^j} \sum_{t=j} \frac{1}{t!} \right)
\end{aligned}$$

where the $(1/3)^j$ term comes from the fact that we want to do j insertions, $(n-k)/2n$ comes from the fact that we want to insert one of the unexpressed variables, P_1 comes from the fact that we want to insert the unexpressed variable in a position where it can determine an increase in the fitness, and $P_2^{(j-1)}$ comes from the fact that we want to put $j - 1$ (possibly redundant) random variables (whose probability 1 of being selected has been omitted) at any position in which they don't determine a decrease in the fitness. Also note that $P_1, P_2 \leq 1$ and $n - k/2n \leq 1/2$. Therefore, we have that

$$\begin{aligned}
E(\Delta_t(i)) &= \sum_{j\in\mathbb{N}} -j \cdot P(\Delta_t(i) = -j) + \sum_{j\in\mathbb{N}} j \cdot P(\Delta_t(i) = j) \\
&\leq -\frac{1}{e} \sum_{j\in\mathbb{N}} \left[\frac{j}{j!} \cdot \left(\frac{1}{3}\right)^j \cdot \left(\frac{1}{cn}\right)^j \cdot \left(\frac{(c-1)n}{j}\right)^j \cdot \right. \\
&\quad \left. \sum_{t=j}^{\infty} \left(\frac{1}{3^{t-s}} \cdot \frac{1}{t!}\right) \right] + \sum_{j\in\mathbb{N}} \left(j \cdot \frac{1}{2} \cdot \frac{1}{3^j} \cdot \frac{1}{e} \sum_{t=j} \frac{1}{t!} \right) \\
&= \frac{1}{e} \sum_{j\in\mathbb{N}} \left(\frac{j}{3^j} \cdot \left[\frac{1}{2} \left(\sum_{t=j} \frac{1}{t!} \right) - \frac{1}{j!} \cdot \left(\frac{c-1}{c}\right)^j \cdot \right. \right. \\
&\quad \left. \left. \frac{1}{j^j} \left(\frac{1}{j!} \frac{1}{3 \cdot (j+1)!} \right) \right] \right)
\end{aligned}$$

Let $A = \sum_{j\in\mathbb{N}} A_j$, where

$$A_j = \frac{j}{3^j} \cdot \left[\frac{1}{2} \sum_{t=j} \frac{1}{t!} - \left(\frac{c-1}{c}\right)^j \frac{1}{j^j} \sum_{t=j} \left(\frac{1}{3^{t-j}} \frac{1}{t!} \right) \right]$$

in which $\sum_{t=j} \left(\frac{1}{3^{t-j}} \frac{1}{t!}\right) \geq \left(\frac{1}{j!} \frac{1}{3\cdot(j+1)!}\right)$ for $19 < c < 20$, we have

$$\begin{aligned}
A_1 &< \frac{1}{3} \cdot \left(\frac{e-1}{2} - \frac{19}{20}(1 + 1/6) \right) = -0.083064 \\
A_2 &< \frac{2}{9} \cdot \left(\frac{e-2}{2} - \left(\frac{19}{20}\right)^2 \cdot \frac{1}{4}(1/2 + 1/18) \right) = 0.051954 \\
A_3 &< \frac{1}{9} \cdot \left(\frac{e-2-0.5}{2} - \left(\frac{19}{20}\right)^3 \cdot \frac{1}{27}(1/6 + 1/72) \right) \\
&= 0.011490
\end{aligned}$$

Hereby,

$$A = A_1 + A_2 + A_3 + \sum_{j\geq 4} A_j < -0.019620 + \sum_{j\geq 4} A_j.$$

However, since

$$\begin{aligned}
\sum_{j\geq 4} A_j &= \sum_{j\geq 4} \frac{j}{3^j} \cdot \left[\frac{1}{2} \sum_{t=j} \frac{1}{t!} - \left(\frac{c-1}{c}\right)^j \frac{1}{j^j} \sum_{t=j} \left(\frac{1}{3^{t-j}} \frac{1}{t!} \right) \right] \\
&< \sum_{j\geq 4} \frac{j}{3^j} \cdot \left(\frac{1}{2} \sum_{t=j} \frac{1}{t!} \right) \\
&< \sum_{j\geq 4} \frac{j}{3^j} \cdot \frac{e - 2 - 0.5 - 1/6}{2} \\
&< 0.025808 \cdot \sum_{j\geq 4} \frac{j}{3^j} \\
&\leq 0.025808 \cdot \frac{1/3}{(1 - 1/3)^2} = 0.019356
\end{aligned}$$

This gives us

$$\begin{aligned}
A &= A_1 + A_2 + A_3 + \sum_{j\geq 4} A_j \\
&= -0.000264
\end{aligned}$$

Therefore $E(\Delta_t(i)) = \frac{1}{e} \cdot A < 0$, and condition 1 holds.

For condition 2 to hold, in order to increase the number of nodes of the original tree by j, at least j insertions must be made. Thus, the probability that the tree size increases exactly by j is at most

$$P(\Delta_i = j) \le \frac{1}{e} \cdot \left(\frac{1}{2} \cdot \frac{1}{3^j} \sum_{t=j} \frac{1}{t!}\right)$$
$$\le \frac{1}{e} \cdot \frac{1}{3^j} \cdot \frac{1}{2} \cdot \sum_{t=j} \frac{1}{t!}$$
$$\le \frac{1}{3^j}$$

Hence,

$$P(\Delta_i \ge j) = \sum_{k=j}^{\infty} P(\Delta_i = k)$$
$$\le \sum_{k=j}^{\infty} \frac{1}{3^j} = \sum_{k=1}^{\infty} \frac{1}{3^j} - \sum_{k=1}^{j-1} \frac{1}{3^j}$$
$$= \sum_{k=0}^{\infty} \frac{1}{3^j} - 1 - \left[\sum_{k=0}^{j-1} \frac{1}{3^j} - 1\right]$$
$$= \frac{1}{1-1/3} - \frac{1-(1/3)^j}{1-1/3} = \frac{3}{2}\frac{1}{3^j}$$

In order to decrease the number of nodes of the original tree by j, at least j deletions must be made. Thus, the probability that the tree with size s and k expressed variables decreases exactly by j is at most

$$P(\Delta_i = -j) \le \sum_{t=j}^{\infty} \frac{1}{3^j} \cdot \frac{1}{s^j} \cdot \binom{s-k}{j} \cdot Pois(x=t)$$
$$= \sum_{t=j}^{\infty} \frac{1}{3^j} \cdot \frac{1}{s^j} \cdot \binom{s-k}{j} \cdot \frac{1}{et!}$$
$$= \frac{1}{3^j} \cdot \frac{1}{s^j} \cdot \binom{s-k}{j} \cdot \frac{1}{e} \sum_{t=j}^{\infty} \frac{1}{t!}$$
$$\le \frac{1}{3^j} \cdot \frac{1}{s^j} \frac{(s-k)!}{j! \cdot (s-k-j)!}$$
$$= \frac{1}{3^j} \cdot \frac{1}{s^j} \frac{(s-k)(s-k-1)....(s-k-j+1)}{j!}$$
$$< \frac{1}{3^j} \cdot \left(\frac{s-k}{s}\right)^j \cdot \frac{1}{j!} \le \frac{1}{3^j}$$

to $P(\Delta_i \ge j)$,

$$P(\Delta_i \le -j) \le \sum_{k=j}^{\infty} \frac{1}{3^j} = \frac{3}{2}\frac{1}{3^j}$$

We have

$$P(|\Delta_i| > j) = P(\Delta_i \ge j) + P(\Delta_i \le -j) = \frac{3}{3^j}$$

Let $r(l)$ be a constant and $\delta = 2$, then condition 2 holds. □

THEOREM 6. *Starting with an solution with initial size $T_{init} < 19n$, the optimization time of (1+1)-GP-multi on MO-ORDER is $O(n^2 \log n)$, with high probability.*

PROOF. This algorithm contains multiple phases. At each phase, there are two main tasks:

- Delete all the redundant variables in the current tree to obtain a non-redundant tree.
- Insert an unexpressed variable into the tree to improve the fitness

The algorithm terminates when all of n variables are expressed and the tree size is n. Let k_i, j_i be the number of the redundant and expressed variables of the solution at the beginning of phase i. The expected time T_i to delete all of the redundant variables at phase i is upper bounded by

$$T_i = \sum_{l=1}^{k_i} (\frac{1}{3e})^{-1} \cdot (\frac{l}{l+j_i})^{-1} \le 3e \sum_{l=1}^{k_i} \frac{l+n}{l}$$
$$\le 3e \sum_{l=1}^{n} \frac{l+n}{l} + 3e \sum_{l=n+1}^{k_i} \frac{l+n}{l}$$
$$\le 3e \sum_{l=1}^{n} \frac{l+n}{l} + 3e \sum_{l=n+1}^{k_i} 2$$
$$\le O(n \log n) + 2k_i$$

An unexpressed variable is then chosen and inserted in to the tree in any position to improve the fitness. The expected time to do such a step is $\frac{n-j_i}{6en}$. Therefore, the expected time for a single phase is $O(n \log n) + 2k_i + \frac{n-j_i}{6en}$.

The selection mechanism of (1+1)-GP on MO-F(X) problems does not accept any decrease in the fitness of the solution. Thus, j_i increases during the run time, which we can denote as $j_0 = 0 < j_1 = 1 < ... < j_{n-1} = n-1$. Since there are at most n variables that need to be inserted, there are at most n phases need to be done to obtain the optimal tree. The total runtime is then, with high probability, bounded by:

$$\sum_{j=0}^{n-1} O(n \log n) + 2k_i + \left(\frac{n-j}{6en}\right)^{-1}$$
$$\le O(n^2 \log n) + 2\sum_{j=0}^{n-1} E\left[T_{max}\right] + 6en \sum_{j=0}^{n-1} \frac{i}{n-j}$$
$$\le O(n^2 \log n) + 40n^2 + 6enO(\log n)$$
$$\le O(n^2 \log n)$$

After n phases, the current tree now has the highest fitness value. The last step now is to remove all of the redundant variables to obtain a tree with highest fitness and complexity value of n. Let s be the number of leaves, the expected time for this step is upper bounded by:

$$\sum_{s=n+1}^{4n} \left(\frac{1}{3e} \cdot \frac{s-n}{s}\right)^{-1} = 3e \sum_{j=1}^{3n} \frac{j+n}{j}$$
$$= 3e \sum_{j=1}^{n} \frac{j+n}{j} + 3e \sum_{j=n+1}^{2n} \frac{j+n}{j} + 3e \sum_{j=2n+1}^{3n} \frac{j+n}{j}$$
$$\le 3e \cdot \sum_{j=1}^{n} \frac{j+n}{j} + 3e \cdot \sum_{j=n+1}^{2n} 2 + 3e \sum_{j=2n+1}^{3n} \frac{3}{2}$$
$$= O(n \log n) + O(n)$$

Summing up the runtimes for all the tasks, the optimization time of (1+1)-GP-multi on MO-ORDER is $O(n^2 \log n)$ with high probability. □

5. MULTI-OBJECTIVE ALGORITHMS

In SMO-GP, the complexity $C(X)$ of a solution X is also taken into account and treated as equally important as the fitness value $F(X)$. The classical Pareto dominance relations are:

1. A solution X *weakly dominates* a solution Y (denoted by $X \succeq Y$) iff $(F(X) \geq F(Y) \wedge C(X) \leq C(Y))$.

2. A solution X *dominates* a solution Y (denoted by $X \succ Y$) iff $((X \succeq Y) \wedge (F(X) > F(Y) \vee C(X) < C(Y))$.

3. Two solutions X and Y are called *incomparable* iff neither $X \succeq Y$ nor $Y \succeq X$ holds.

A *Pareto optimal solution* is a solution that is not dominated by any other solution in the search space. All Pareto optimal solutions together form the Pareto optimal set, and the set of corresponding objective vectors forms the Pareto front. The classical goal in multi-objective optimization (here: of SMO-GP) is to compute for each objective vector of the Pareto front a Pareto optimal solution. Alternatively, if the Pareto front is too large, the goal then is to find a representative subset of the front, where the definition of 'representative' depends on the choice of the conductor.

SMO-GP starts with a single solution, and at all times keeps a population that contains only the non-dominated solutions among the set of solutions seen so far.

Algorithm 2: SMO-GP

1. Choose an initial solution X
2. Set $P := \{X\}$
3. repeat
   - Randomly choose $X \in P$
   - Set $Y := X$
   - Apply mutation to Y
   - If $\{Z \in P | Z \succ Y\} = \varnothing$ set $P := (P \backslash \{Z \in P | Y \succ Z\}) \cup \{Y\}$

In his paper, Neumann (2012) proved that the expected optimization time of SMO-GP-single and SMO-GP-multi on MO-ORDER and MO-MAJORITY is $O(nT_{init} + n^2 \log n)$. In the case of WORDER and WMAJORITY, the proven runtime bound of $O(n^3)$ (for both problems) requires that the algorithm is initialised with a non-redundant solution.

5.1 SMO-GP-single

If the initial solution is generated randomly, it is not likely to be a non-redundant one. In order to generalise the proof, we start the analysis by bounding the maximum tree size T_{max} based on the initial tree size T_{init} for SMO-GP-single. Using this result, we re-calculate the expected optimization time of SMO-GP-single on both MO-WORDER and MO-WMAJORITY, when using an arbitrary initial solution of size T_{init}.

THEOREM 7. *Let T_{init} be the tree size of initial solution. Then the population size of SMO-GP-single on MO-WORDER and MO-WMAJORITY until the empty tree included in the population is upper bounded by $T_{init} + n$ during the run of the algorithm.*

PROOF. When two solutions X, Y have the same complexity, the solution with higher fitness dominates the other one. Therefore, in the population where no solution is dominated by any other solutions, all the solutions have different complexities. Without loss of generality, assume that a solution X is selected for mutation and Y is the new solution. Then there are five ways to generate Y:

1. inserting an unexpressed variable, and thus increasing the complexity of the new solution by 1,

2. deleting an expressed variable, and thus decreasing the complexity of the new solution by 1,

3. deleting a redundant variable, and thus decreasing the complexity of the new solution by 1. As $F(X) = F(Y) \wedge C(X) > C(Y)$, X is then replaced by Y in the population,

4. inserting a redundant variable to X, thus generating a new solution with the same fitness and higher complexity, which is not accepted by SMO-GP-single,

5. substituting a variable x_i in X by another variable x_j.
   - If x_j is a non-redundant variable and $w_i < w_j$, $F(X) < F(Y) \wedge C(X) = C(Y)$, Y replaces X in the population
   - If x_j is a non-redundant variable and $w_i > w_j$, $F(X) > F(Y) \wedge C(X) = C(Y)$, Y is discarded.
   - If x_j is redundant variable, $F(X) > F(Y) \wedge C(X) = C(Y)$, Y is discarded.

As shown above, the number of redundant variables in the solution will not increase during the run of the algorithm. Let R_i be the number of redundant variables in solution i, then for all the solutions in the population holds $R_i \leq R_{init}$.

Let $X \in P$ be a solution in P and α_X be the number of expressed variables in X, then the complexity of X is $C(X) = R_X + \alpha_X$. Since $R_X \leq R_{init}$ and $\alpha_X \leq n$, the complexity of a solution in P is upper bounded by $R_{init} + n \leq T_{init} + n$.

The population size only increases when a new solution with different fitness is generated. This only happens when the complexity increases or decreases by 1. Because the highest complexity that a solution can reach is $T_{init} + n$, and because the empty tree can be in the population as well[1], the maximum size the population can reach is $T_{init} + n + 1$. □

LEMMA 1. *Starting with an arbitrary initial solution of size T_{init}, the expected time until the population of SMO-GP-single on MO-WORDER and MO-WMAJORITY contains the empty tree is $O(T_{init}^2 + nT_{init})$.*

PROOF. We will bound the time by repeated deletions of randomly chosen leaf nodes in the solutions of lowest complexity, until the empty tree has been reached. Let X be the solution in the population with the lowest complexity. The probability of choosing the lowest complexity solution X in the population is at least $\frac{1}{T_{init}+n+1}$, while the probability of making a deletion is $\frac{1}{3}$. In each step, because any variable in X can be deleted, the probability of choosing the correct variable is 1. The probability of deleting a variable in X at each step therefore is bounded from below by $\frac{1}{3} \cdot \frac{1}{T_{init}+n+1}$, and

[1] as the empty tree is Pareto optimal with $F(X) = C(X) = 0$

the expected time to do such a step is at most $3\cdot(T_{init}+n+1)$. Since T_{init} is the number of leaves in the initial tree, there are T_{init} repetitions required to delete all the variables. This implies that the expected time for the empty tree to be included in the population is upper bounded by

$$T_{init}\cdot 3\cdot(T_{init}+n+1)=O\left(T_{init}^2+nT_{init}\right) \quad \square$$

THEOREM 8. *Starting with a single arbitrary initial solution of size T_{init}, the expected optimization time of SMO-GP-single on MO-WORDER and MO-WMAJORITY is $O(T_{init}^2+n^2T_{init}+n^3)$.*

PROOF. In the following steps, we will bound the time needed to discover the whole Pareto front, once the empty solution is introduced into the population. As shown in Theorem 1, the empty tree is included in the population after $O(T_{init}^2+nT_{init})$ steps. The empty tree is now a Pareto optimal solution with complexity $C(X)=0$. Note that a solution of complexity j, $0\leq j\leq n$ is Pareto optimal in MO-WORDER and MO-MAJORITY, if it contains only the largest j variables.

Let us assume that the population contains all Pareto optimal solutions with complexities j, $0\leq j\leq i$. Then, a population which includes all Pareto optimal solutions with complexities j, $0\leq j\leq i+1$, can be achieved by producing a solution Y that is Pareto optimal and that has complexity $i+1$. Y can be obtained from a Pareto optimal solution X with $C(X)=i$ and $F(X)=\sum_{i=1}^{k}w_i$ by inserting the leaf x_{k+1} (with associated weight w_{k+1}) at any position. This operation produces from a solution of complexity i a solution of complexity $i+1$.

Based on this idea we can bound the expected optimization time once we can bound the probability for such steps to happen. Choosing X for mutation has the known probability of at least $\frac{1}{T_{init}+n+1}$ as the population size is upper bound by $T_{init}+n+1$. Next, the inserting operation of the mutation operator is chosen with probability $\frac{1}{3}$. As a specific element out of a total of n elements has to be inserted at a randomly chosen position, the probability to do so it $\frac{1}{n}$. Thus, the total probability of such a generation is lower bounded by $\frac{1}{T_{init}+n+1}\cdot\frac{1}{3}\cdot\frac{1}{n}$.

Now, we use the method of fitness-based partitions Wegener (2002) according to the $n+1$ different Pareto front sizes i. Thus, as there are only n Pareto-optimal improvements possible once the empty solution is introduced into the population, the expected time until all Pareto optimal solutions have been generated is:

$$\sum_{i=0}^{n-1}\left(\frac{1}{T_{init}+n+1}\cdot\frac{1}{3}\cdot\frac{1}{n}\right)^{-1}=3n^2(T_{init}+n+1)$$
$$=O(n^2T_{init}+n^3). \quad \square$$

Summing up the number of steps to generate the empty tree and all other Pareto optimal solutions, the expected optimisation time is $O(T_{init}^2+n^2T_{init}+n^3)$

5.2 SMO-GP-multi

In principle, when considering WORDER and WMAJORITY in SMO-GP, it is possible to generate an exponential number of trade-offs between solution fitness and complexity. For instance, if $w_i=2^{n-i}, 1\leq i\leq n$, then one can easily generate 2^n different individuals by considering different subsets of variables. These solutions are dominated by the true Pareto front, and our experimental analysis suggests that many of them get discarded early in the optimization process.

In this section, we employ the P_{max} measure collected in our experimental analysis (see Figure 7) to consolidate some of the theoretical bounds about WORDER and WMAJORITY presented in Neumann (2012) and introduce new bounds for their multi-operation variants.

LEMMA 2. *The expected time before SMO-GP, initialized with T_{init} leaves, adds the empty tree to its population is bound by $O(T_{init}P_{max})$.*

PROOF. If the empty tree is the initial solution, i.e. $T_{init}=0$, then Lemma 2 follows immediately.

If $T_{init}>0$, then we need to perform T_{init} deletions in order to reach the empty tree. Let X be the individual of lowest complexity, then the probability of selecting it for mutation is at least $1/P_{max}$. The probability of performing a single deletion is lower bounded by $\frac{1}{3e}$ for both the single- and the multi-operation variants of the HVL-Prime operator. Therefore, the total probability of selecting the solution of lowest complexity and deleting one of its nodes is $\Omega(1/P_{max})$, and the expected time to make such a step is $O(P_{max})$. Since we need to delete T_{init} leaves, the total expected time to add the empty tree to the population is bounded by the repeated deletion taking $O(T_{init}P_{max})$ steps. $\square$

Note that, contrary to Theorem 1, this lemma holds for both the single- and the multi-mutation variants of SMO-GP. However, this lemma depends on P_{max}, which is not under the control of the user.

We now state an upper bound for SMO-GP on WORDER and WMAJORITY in both single and multi-operation variants.

THEOREM 9. *The expected optimization time of SMO-GP on WORDER and WMAJORITY is $O(P_{max}(T_{init}+n^2))$.*

PROOF. This proof follows the structure of the proof of Theorem 8. First, due to Lemma 2 we can assume that we have added the empty tree to the population after $O(T_{init}P_{max})$ steps. We now recall that a solution of complexity j, $0\leq j\leq n$, is Pareto optimal for MO-WORDER and MO-WMAJORITY, if it contains, for the j largest weights, exactly one positive variable.

Similar to the second step of the proof of Theorem 8, we assume that the population already contains the i Pareto optimal solutions with complexities j, $0\leq j\leq i$. Then, a population which includes all Pareto optimal solutions with complexities j, $0\leq j\leq i+1$, can be achieved by producing a solution Y that is Pareto optimal and that has complexity $i+1$. Y can be obtained from a Pareto optimal solution X with $C(X)=i$ and $F(X)=\sum_{i=1}^{k}w_i$ by inserting the leaf x_{k+1} (with associated weight w_{k+1}) at any position. This operation produces from a solution of complexity i a solution of complexity $i+1$.

Again, based on this idea, we can bound the expected optimization time once we can bound the probability for such steps to happen. Choosing X for mutation is lower bounded by $1/P_{max}$, the inserting operation of the mutation operator is chosen with probability $1/3e$, and as a specific element out of a total of up to $2n$ elements has to be inserted at a randomly chosen position, the probability to do so it $1/2n$. Thus,

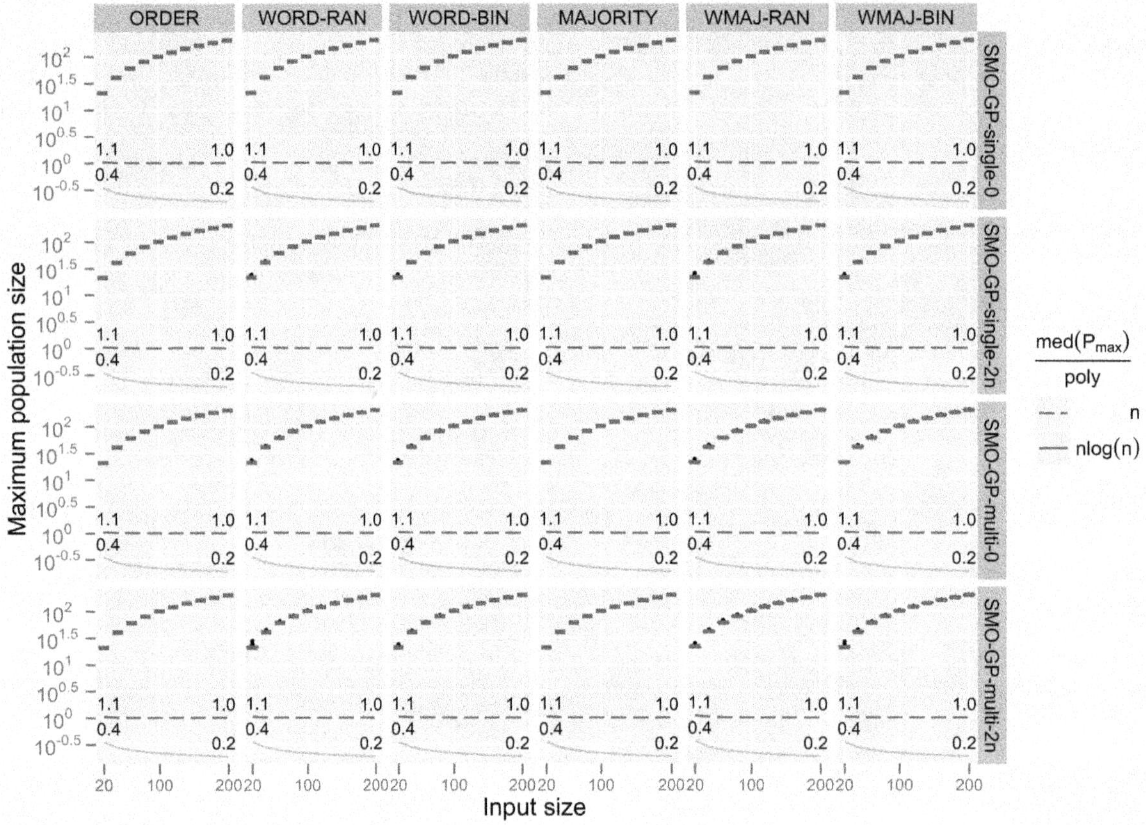

Figure 7: Maximum population size distributions (as box-plots) reached before finding an optimal solution in SMO-GP. The blue lines represent the medians divided by the corresponding polynomials and give an indication of the order of magnitude of the P_{max} measure.

the total probability of such a generation is lower bounded by $1/(6enP_{max})$.

Now, using the method of fitness-based partitions according to the $n+1$ different Pareto front sizes i, the expected time until all Pareto optimal solutions have been generated (once the empty tree was introduced) is bounded by

$$\sum_{i=0}^{n-1} \left(\frac{1}{P_{max}} \cdot \frac{1}{3e} \cdot \frac{1}{2n} \right)^{-1} = 6en^2 P_{max}$$
$$= O(n^2 P_{max}).$$

Therefore, the total expected optimization time when starting from an individual with T_{init} leaves is thus $O(T_{init}P_{max} + n^2 P_{max})$, which concludes the proof. □

As we mentioned before, to date there is no theoretical understanding about how P_{max} grows during an optimization run and, in principle, its order of growth could be exponential in n. For this reason, similarly to what we did for T_{max}, we have investigated this measure experimentally. The experimental setup is the same described previously, and the empirical distributions of P_{max} are shown as box-plots in Figure 7. The blue-toned line plots show the median P_{max} divided by n and $\log(n)$. Again, the nearly constant behavior of the solid line suggests a magnitude of P_{max} which is linearly dependent on n and, in general, very close to n as the factors, at most 1.1, suggest.

6. CONCLUSIONS

In this paper, we carried out theoretical investigations to complement the recent results on the runtime of two genetic programming algorithms (Durrett et al., 2011; Neumann, 2012; Urli et al., 2012). Crucial measures in the theoretical analyses are the maximum tree size T_{max} that is attained during the run of the algorithms, as well as the maximum population size P_{max} when dealing with multi-objective models.

We introduced several new bounds for different GP variants on the different versions of the problems WORDER and WMAJORITY. Tables 2 and 3 summarise our results and the existing known bounds on the investigated problems.

Despite the significant theoretical and experimental effort, the following open challenges still remain:

1. Almost no theoretical results for the multi-operation variants are known to date. A major reason for this is that it is not clear how to bound the number of accepted operations when employing the multi-operation variants on the weighted cases.

2. Of particular difficulty seems to be the problem to bound runtimes on WMAJORITY. There, in order to achieve a fitness increment, the incrementing operation needs to be preceded by a number of operations that reduce the difference in positive and negative occurrences of a variable. Said difference is currently difficult to control, as it can increase and decrease during a run.

3. Several bounds rely on T_{max} or P_{max} measures, which are not set in advance and whose probability to increase or decrease during the optimization is hard to predict. This is because their growth (or decrease) depends on the content of the individual and the content of the population at a specific time step. Solving these problems would allow bounds which only depend on parameters the user can initially set. Observe that limiting T_{max} and P_{max} is not an option, since we are considering variable length representation algorithms, and populations that represent *all* the trade-offs between objectives.

4. Finally, it is not known to date how tight these bounds are.

References

Doerr, B., Johannsen, D., and Winzen, C. (2010). Multiplicative drift analysis. In Pelikan, M. and Branke, J., editors, *GECCO*, pages 1449–1456. ACM.

Droste, S., Jansen, T., and Wegener, I. (2002). On the analysis of the (1+1) evolutionary algorithm. *Theoretical Computer Science*, 276:51–81.

Durrett, G., Neumann, F., and O'Reilly, U.-M. (2011). Computational complexity analysis of simple genetic programing on two problems modeling isolated program semantics. In *FOGA*, pages 69–80. ACM.

Goldberg, D. E. and O'Reilly, U.-M. (1998). Where does the good stuff go, and why? How contextual semantics influences program structure in simple genetic programming. In *EuroGP*, volume 1391 of *LNCS*, pages 16–36. Springer.

Kötzing, T., Sutton, A. M., Neumann, F., and O'Reilly, U.-M. (2012). The max problem revisited: the importance of mutation in genetic programming. In *Proceedings of the fourteenth international conference on Genetic and evolutionary computation conference*, GECCO '12, pages 1333–1340, New York, NY, USA. ACM.

Neumann, F. (2012). Computational complexity analysis of multi-objective genetic programming. In *Proceedings of the fourteenth international conference on Genetic and evolutionary computation conference*, GECCO '12, pages 799–806, New York, NY, USA. ACM.

Oliveto, P. S. and Witt, C. (2011). Simplified drift analysis for proving lower bounds in evolutionary computation. *Algorithmica*, 59(3):369–386.

Poli, R., Langdon, W. B., and McPhee, N. F. (2008). *A Field Guide to Genetic Programming*. lulu.com.

Urli, T., Wagner, M., and Neumann, F. (2012). Experimental supplements to the computational complexity analysis of genetic programming for problems modelling isolated program semantics. In *PPSN*. Springer. (to be published).

Wagner, M. and Neumann, F. (2012). Parsimony pressure versus multi-objective optimization for variable length representations. In *PPSN*. Springer. (to be published).

Wegener, I. (2002). Methods for the analysis of evolutionary algorithms on pseudo-Boolean functions. In *Evolutionary Optimization*, pages 349–369. Kluwer.

F(X)	(1+1)-GP, F(X)	
	k=1	k=1+Pois(1)
ORDER	$O(nT_{max})$ Durrett et al. (2011) $O(T_{init} + n \log n)$ Urli et al. (2012)	$O(nT_{max})$ Durrett et al. (2011) $O(T_{init} + n \log n)$ Urli et al. (2012)
WORDER	$O(nT_{max})$ ⋆ $O(T_{init} + n \log n)$ Urli et al. (2012)	$O(nT_{max}(\log n + \log w_{max}))$ ⋆ $O(T_{init} + n \log n)$ Urli et al. (2012)
MAJORITY	$O(n^2 T_{max} \log n)$ Durrett et al. (2011) $O(T_{init} + n \log n)$ Urli et al. (2012)	? $O(T_{init} + n \log n)$ Urli et al. (2012)
WMAJORITY	? $O(T_{init} + n \log n)$ Urli et al. (2012)	? $O(T_{init} + n \log n)$ Urli et al. (2012)
F(X)	(1+1)-GP, MO-F(X)	
	k=1	k=1+Pois(1)
ORDER	$O(T_{init} + n \log n)$Neumann (2012) $O(T_{init} + n \log n)$ Urli et al. (2012)	$O(n^2 \log n)$ ⋆ † $O(T_{init} + n \log n)$ Urli et al. (2012)
WORDER	$O(T_{init} + n \log n)$Neumann (2012) $O(T_{init} + n \log n)$ Urli et al. (2012)	? $O(T_{init} + n \log n)$ Urli et al. (2012)
MAJORITY	$O(T_{init} + n \log n)$Neumann (2012) $O(T_{init} + n \log n)$ Urli et al. (2012)	? $O(T_{init} + n \log n)$ Urli et al. (2012)
WMAJORITY	$O(T_{init} + n \log n)$Neumann (2012) $O(T_{init} + n \log n)$ Urli et al. (2012)	? $O(T_{init} + n \log n)$ Urli et al. (2012)

Table 2: Summary of our bounds (⋆) and the existing theoretical upper bounds from Table 1. The average-case conjectures from Urli et al. (2012) are listed to indicate tightness. Note that (?) mark the cases for which no theoretical bounds are known, and bounds marked with (†) require special initialisations.

F(X)	SMO-GP, MO-F(X)	
	k=1	k=1+Pois(1)
ORDER	$O(nT_{init} + n^2 \log n)$Neumann (2012) $O(nT_{init} + n^2 \log n)$ Urli et al. (2012)	$O(nT_{init} + n^2 \log n)$Neumann (2012) $O(nT_{init} + n^2 \log n)$ Urli et al. (2012)
WORDER	$O(T_{init}^2 + n^2 T_{init} + n^3)$ ⋆ $O(n^3)$ Neumann (2012) † $O(nT_{init} + n^2 \log n)$ Urli et al. (2012)	$O(T_{init} P_{max} + n^2 P_{max})$ ⋆ $O(nT_{init} + n^2 \log n)$ Urli et al. (2012)
MAJORITY	$O(nT_{init} + n^2 \log n)$Neumann (2012) $O(nT_{init} + n^2 \log n)$ Urli et al. (2012)	$O(nT_{init} + n^2 \log n)$Neumann (2012) $O(nT_{init} + n^2 \log n)$ Urli et al. (2012)
WMAJORITY	$O(T_{init}^2 + n^2 T_{init} + n^3)$ ⋆ $O(n^3)$ Neumann (2012) † $O(nT_{init} + n^2 \log n)$ Urli et al. (2012)	$O(T_{init} P_{max} + n^2 P_{max})$ ⋆ $O(nT_{init} + n^2 \log n)$ Urli et al. (2012)

Table 3: Summary of our bounds (⋆) and the existing theoretical upper bounds from Table 1. The average-case conjectures from Urli et al. (2012) are listed to indicate tightness. Note that the bounds marked with (†) require special initialisations.

Triple and Quadruple Comparison-Based Interactive Differential Evolution and Differential Evolution

Yan Pei
Graduate School of Design, Kyushu University
4-9-1, Shiobaru, Minami-ku
Fukuoka, 815-8540, Japan
peiyan@kyudai.jp

Hideyuki Takagi
Faculty of Design, Kyushu University
4-9-1, Shiobaru, Minami-ku
Fukuoka, 815-8540, Japan
takagi@design.kyushu-u.ac.jp

ABSTRACT

We propose a triple comparison and a quadruple comparison-based mechanism for enhancing differential evolution (DE), especially for interactive DE (IDE) where the method can be used to reduce IDE user fatigue. Besides the target vector and trial vector from normal DE, opposition vectors generated by opposition-based learning are used to determine offspring, and the best vector from among these three or four vectors becomes offspring for the next generation. We evaluate the proposed methods by comparing them with conventional IDE and conventional opposition-based IDE using a simulated IDE modeled using a four dimensional Gaussian mixture model. We also evaluate them in DE using 24 benchmark functions. The experiments show that our proposed methods can enhance IDE and DE search efficiently according to several evaluation indices. These include the converged fitness values after the same number of generations, converged fitness values after the same number of fitness calculations, fitness calculation cost, convergence success rates and acceleration rates.

Categories and Subject Descriptors

F.2 [**Analysis of Algorithms and Problem Complexity**]: Numerical Algorithms and Problems; H.1 [**Models and Principles**]: User/Machine Systems

Keywords

interactive differential evolution, differential evolution, opposition-based learning, triple comparison, quadruple comparison

1. INTRODUCTION

Interactive evolutionary computation (IEC) is an approach whereby such properties as human knowledge, experience, and preference are embedded into an optimization process, such that solutions are searched using a human evaluation-based system. By embedding the human being itself into an optimization system, EC techniques become applicable to tasks for which it is difficult to construct an evaluation system or measure the evaluations. For example, hearing-aid fitting [32] or cochlear implant fitting [10] are tasks well suited to an IEC approach because there is no way to measure how a human being hears sounds; the user's subjective response is the only measurable index. IEC has also been applied to artistic areas such as creating music or graphics, engineering areas such as sound and image processing, control and robotics, virtual reality, data mining, media database retrieval, and others, including geoscience, education, games, and many other tasks in various areas [28].

From a framework point of view, IEC can be realized with any evolutionary computation (EC) algorithm by replacing the fitness function with a human user. Several EC techniques are used in IEC, such as interactive genetic algorithms (IGA) [3], interactive genetic programming [25], interactive evolution strategy [4], human based-genetic algorithm [9], interactive particle swarm optimization [12], interactive differential evolution (IDE) [33], as discussed in this paper, and others. Evaluation noise due to human subjective evaluations cannot be avoided and EC algorithms that are sensitive to noise do not therefore show better performance when used as-is in IEC. From a practical point of view, when such noise-sensitive EC algorithms are used in IEC, it is necessary to add an algorithm for overcoming the noise-sensitivity [14].

There are many directions in IEC research, such as expanding the applications of IEC; expanding IEC frameworks [29]; applying IEC in a reverse engineering approach to analyze humans and thus advance [30]; accelerating IEC searches and improving IEC interfaces. The major remaining IEC problem is the problem of IEC user fatigue [28]. In addition to the previously mentioned acceleration and improvement of IEC interfaces, many approaches for reducing IEC user fatigue have been conducted. Some of these approaches improve methods of inputting fitness, use a combination of IEC and EC, allow users to intervene in EC searches, introduce IEC user evaluation models, construct new IEC frameworks, and introduce paired comparison-based fitness evaluation rather than evaluating all individuals at once.

This paper studies a method of reducing IEC user fatigue by accelerating the EC search. There have been several EC acceleration approaches proposed in the past, including a gradient method; a hill-climbing method; combining other meta-heuristic approaches [18]; and approximating the EC fitness landscape [7]. There are also several approaches of landscape approximation which have been investigated, in-

FOGA'13, January 16-20, 2013, Adelaide, Australia.

cluding a method approximating the landscape with a unimodal function and estimating the global optimum area that is defined as the area located around the global optimum [6, 31], accelerating the approximation by using a lower dimensional function [15, 16, 17, 21] and landscape approximation using the Fourier transform and estimating the global optimum area [19, 20].

In this paper, we propose and evaluate IEC acceleration methods that embed opposition-based learning (OBL) into differential evolution (DE). OBL is embedded into two stages of the DE: initial value determination and offspring generation, as discussed later in section 2. We propose the new methods for embedding OBL into IDE in section 3. The proposed methods demand triple or quadruple comparisons, and the IDE user fatigue for a single comparison stage is therefore greater than in the case of conventional paired comparison-based IDE. However, the proposed methods are based on the hypothesis that IDE user fatigue may not increase drastically when the number of comparing individuals is less than a memorable number, such as three individuals, and the thought that the total fatigue of a human user can be decreased by accelerating the IDE search. We evaluate the methods using an IDE simulation in section 4. The proposed methods can be used not only for IDE but also for DE, and we evaluate their performance as DE accelerators using 24 benchmark functions in section 5. Finally, we conclude this research and describe our future research directions in section 6.

2. CONVENTIONAL TECHNIQUES

2.1 Paired Comparison-Based Interactive Differential Evolution

In most instances of IEC, as typified by IGA, all individuals are presented to the IEC user and the user is then required to input a fitness evaluation for each of them. In the case where the individuals are still images, it is easy for an IEC user to compare them spatially and evaluate them. For this reason, most IEC approaches use this method of display and evaluation.

However, when the individuals are sounds or movies, an IEC user has to compare each individual with others held in their memory and the mental load and fatigue increase. It was been pointed out that humans possess limited memory and cannot process more than five to nine different items simultaneously [13]. The population sizes of many IEC systems frequently exceed this memory limitation, and displaying 10 to 20 sounds or movies to an IEC user is not practical.

Paired comparison-based IEC solves this problem by replacing the comparison of all individuals with paired comparisons and is thus expected to reduce IEC user fatigue. The first proposed approach is a tournament IGA [8, 11]. $N-1$ paired comparisons are iterated for N individuals per generation, and fitness values are calculated using the number of winnings and fitness differences between each pair. The disadvantage of tournament GA is that the obtained fitness necessarily includes noise because the tournament is not a round robin competition against the original GA algorithm. The noise influences the GA selection operation and results in reduced GA search performance.

Differential evolution (DE) is a type of population-based optimization algorithm [22, 26]. It searches for the global optimum using a differential vector between two individuals for which the length is in proportion to the distribution size of the individuals in general and for which each parent individual generates its offspring. The following description outlines the main steps of a DE implementation.

(1) Chose one individual to be the target vector. Select two other individuals as parameter vectors at random and derive a difference vector from them; the best individual from the rest of the individuals or another individual selected at random is the base vector.

(2) Create a mutant vector by adding a weighted differential vector to the base vector.

(3) Generate a trial vector by crossing the target vector and the mutant vector.

(4) Compare the target vector with the trial vector, and select whichever one is better as the offspring for the next generation.

(5) Go to (1) and generate other offspring until all individuals are processed using the same operations,. Then proceed with the next generation.

Paired comparison-based IDE [33] does not modify any parts of its algorithm because the algorithm already includes paired comparison by nature in step (4) of the above algorithm. Since pairs of individuals are presented to the IDE user for comparison without modifying the DE algorithm, the IDE is expected to be a promising IEC method.

2.2 Opposition-Based Learning

Opposition-based learning (OBL) [34] is used in machine learning [35] and to accelerate optimization searches (OBL optimization). Suppose that $x \in [a, b]$ is a real number, then the opposition point of x is given by $OP(x) = a + b - x$. By extending this idea to a multi-dimensional space, the opposition point, $OP(X)$, of a point on a n-dimensional real space, $X = (x_1, x_2, ..., x_n)$ $(x_i \in [a_i, b_i], i = 1, 2, ..., n;\ a_i, b_i \in R)$, is given by Eq.s (1) and (2).

$$OP(X) = \{OP(x_1), OP(x_2), ..., OP(x_n)\} \quad (1)$$

$$OP(x_i) = a_i + b_i - x_i \quad (2)$$

OBL optimization uses the opposition point to accelerate EC search, and two acceleration approaches are widely used: OBL-based initialization of individuals and OBL-based generation of offspring. The former generates opposite points for randomly generated individuals and chooses the better of the randomly generated individuals and their opposites as the initialized individuals for the first generation. When a population size is small, the risk becomes higher that randomly initialized individuals do not cover a search space evenly and are biased to certain areas and are trapped in a local minimum. The OBL-based initialization can reduce this risk and help EC to start its search from better subareas from the global viewpoint.

The latter switches between two strategies for generating offspring with a probability called the *jumping rate*; one strategy is to generate offspring based on normal EC operations and the other is to generate offspring by comparing pairs of parent individuals and their opposite points.

Acceleration approaches using opposition points are based on two hypotheses. One is that most population-based optimization methods are of a stochastic nature and when the search point is located far from the global optimum, the probability that the opposition point is better becomes high; another is that the probability of the search point or its opposite being better is usually equivalent.

OBL has been applied to several EC algorithms, and an opposite based differential evolution (OBDE) that embeds the two previously mentioned OBL techniques into a conventional DE was been proposed [24]. Since then, several further variations have also been proposed: OBDE applied to shuffled DE [1], generalized OBDE extended by introducing an opposite search space and four schemes for making the opposition point [36], a new DE applying an opposition operator for a mutant vector and leaving the winner to the next generation [5], and others.

In this paper, we propose new OBDE with the specific aim of accelerating IDE search without significantly increasing IDE user fatigue.

Table 1: Conventional paired comparison-based DE/IDE and proposed triple and quadruple comparison-based DE/IDE. Target-OB and trial-OB refer to the opposition vectors for target vectors and trial vectors. We use the center point of an individual distribution to calculate an opposition point.

conventional method #1	Ordinary DE [22] / paired comparison-based IDE [33] (pair comparison of a target vector and a trial vector).
conventional method #2	Switching between ordinary DE and paired comparison of a target vector and target-OB according to a jumping rate [24].
proposed method #1	Triple comparison-based DE among target, trial, and target-OB.
proposed method #2	Triple comparison-based DE among target, trial, trial-OB.
proposed method #3	Quadruple comparison-based DE among target, trial, target-OB, trial-OB.
proposed method #4	Triple comparison-based DE among target, trial, random.

3. PROPOSAL OF A NEW OBDE

Table 1 shows our proposed OBDE along with conventional methods for comparison. As the first OBL technique, using OBL for the initialization of individuals as mentioned in section 2.2, is applicable to all the methods compared in this paper, we only use the second OBL technique – opposition-based individual selection with jumping rate – for comparing with the proposed methods.

It is necessary to consider (a) the computational cost of a fitness value, (b) that of an introduced acceleration method, and (c) convergence speed when we use or develop EC acceleration methods. Since (c) has higher priority than (b) for tasks where (a) takes the most time, total time until convergence reaches the goal is frequently used as an evaluation index.

On the other hand, user fatigue is an important factor in the evaluation of IEC. When the mental demand for evaluating individuals is otherwise the same, we may say that the IEC user fatigue is in proportion to the total time until the IEC user finds a satisfactory individual. However, when the mental load for evaluating individuals is different due to different IEC interfaces, this relation is not always true. There are cases where IEC user fatigue becomes low thanks to easy evaluation even if total evaluation time until the goal is reached is long. Likewise there are opposite cases where IEC user fatigue can be lowered thanks to short total evaluation time even if the mental load for a single evaluation is high. We need to evaluate acceleration methods by analyzing the load of a single evaluation along with the convergence characteristics through IEC simulation, and after that we must conduct a human subjective evaluation to confirm the simulation results. This paper deals with the IEC simulation of the first stage.

Our idea is to use not only a target vector and a trial vector but also their opposition vectors at every comparison in the DE search. Our proposed method #1 functionally includes conventional method #2 because it conducts the comparison of a trial vector and its opposition vector as in the conventional method #2. For the same reason, we may say that proposed method #3 includes the proposed methods #1 and #2 functionally. In order to compare the effectiveness of the opposite mechanism, i.e., the proposed methods #1, #2 and #3, we also propose to use a random vector as a third vector to compare the optimization performance with proposed methods #1, #2 and #3, we refer to it as proposed method #4 in this paper.

When the proposed methods are applied to non-interactive DE, whereas conventional paired-comparison-based DE had twice the number of calculations, the proposed methods require three or four times the number of calculations. In other words, the calculation time of (a) mentioned above is 1.5 or 2.0 times that which is required for the conventional paired comparison DE case. The crux of our study into the application of the proposed methods for ordinary non-interactive DE is whether the acceleration performance gains of the proposed methods exceed the increased time required for their fitness calculations, allowing the total calculation time to be reduced.

The number of fitness calculations is not the final evaluation index for IDE because IDE user fatigue is not in proportion to it. Consider the case of user fatigue from choosing the best still image between two images or from among three or four images. The former must be less than the latter, but the mental load in the latter case is not 1.5 or 2.0 times that of the former. Even when the IDE requires the comparison of sounds or movies that we cannot compare spatially and simultaneously, the IDE user's mental load must increase, but the ratio will not necessarily increase by 1.5 or 2.0 times. Generally speaking, when the number of individual comparisons is within the number that an IDE user can memorize, IEC user fatigue is lower; when it exceeds the maximum memory capacity, user fatigue increases drastically. We focus on this fact in developing our proposed methods requiring triple and quadruple comparisons, and aim to reduce the total user fatigue by accelerating IDE search even if the user fatigue for each single comparison increases.

One mirror point for calculating opposition points is used in this paper. Reference [24], i.e. conventional method #2, uses the center gravity point of an individual distribution as the mirror point. This appears reasonable for narrowing the distribution of the opposition vectors according to the DE individual distribution.

4. IDE EXPERIMENTAL EVALUATIONS AND ANALYSIS

4.1 IDE User Model and Experimental Conditions

Experimental evaluations frequently require many repeated experiments under the same conditions, and in this case it is necessary to perform the evaluations using an IEC user model rather than with a real human IEC user. Our IEC user model [14] was designed based on the four following specifications: (1) the fitness landscape should be relatively simple, (2) the fitness landscape should be multimodal, (3) the landscape should have a big valley structure, and (4) the shape and complexity of the fitness landscape should be parametrically controllable. The rationale for (1) is that a human IEC user cannot distinguish differences less than the differential threshold of perceptions nevertheless he/she can obtain practical solutions. For (2), there are graphics, design, music, and others areas for which fitness values are high but their expressions are quite different. For (3), an IEC user can reach the global optimum area easily in spite of (2).

A Gaussian mixture model is used as the parametric IEC user evaluation model based on the assumption that IEC fitness landscapes are simple multimodal but have a roughly a big valley structure [14]. We can implement many IEC different user models by controlling averages, variances, and amplitudes of the multi-dimensional Gaussian functions.

We use Gaussian mixture models for evaluation in this section. Concretely, we combine four Gaussian functions ($k = 4$) and realize the characteristics expressed by Eq. (3) in 3 dimensions (3-D), 5-D, 7-D, and 10-D. Figure 1 is a 3-D representation of the 4-D Gaussian mixture model.

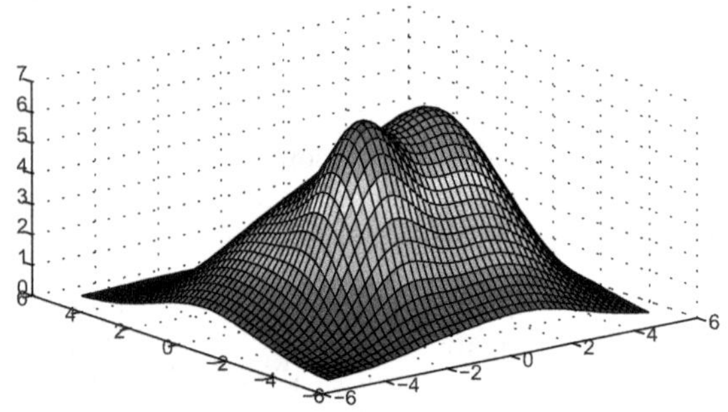

Figure 1: 3-D view of 4-D of a Gaussian mixture model.

$$GMM(\mathbf{x}) = \sum_{i=0}^{k} a_i \exp\left(-\sum_{j=0}^{n} \frac{(x_{ij} - \mu_{ij})^2}{2\sigma_{ij}^2}\right) \quad (3)$$

where

$$\sigma = \begin{pmatrix} 1.5 & 1.5 & 1.5 & 1.5 & 1.5 & 1.5 & 1.5 & 1.5 & 1.5 & 1.5 \\ 2 & 2 & 2 & 2 & 2 & 2 & 2 & 2 & 2 & 2 \\ 1 & 1 & 1 & 1 & 1 & 1 & 1 & 1 & 1 & 1 \\ 2 & 2 & 2 & 2 & 2 & 2 & 2 & 2 & 2 & 2 \end{pmatrix}$$

$$\mu = \begin{pmatrix} -1 & 1.5 & -2 & 2.5 & -1 & 1.5 & -2 & 2.5 & -1 & 1.5 \\ 0 & -2 & 3 & 1 & 0 & -2 & 3 & 1 & 0 & -2 \\ -2.5 & -2 & 1.5 & 3.5 & -2.5 & -2 & 1.5 & 3.5 & -2.5 & -2 \\ -2 & 1 & -1 & 3 & -2 & 1 & -1 & 3 & -2 & 1 \end{pmatrix}$$

$$a_i = (\ 3.1,\ \ 3.4,\ \ 4.1,\ \ 3.0\ )^T$$

The big difference between an IEC user model and ordinary fitness functions is in the implementation of (a) relative and (b) discrete fitness evaluations as are produced by a human user. Unlike a fitness function, a human IEC user compares given individuals in relative terms and does not produce an absolute fitness value. He or she also cannot give precise fitness values but rather can only rate according to discrete levels, e.g. 1 to 5 points, every generation, while ordinary fitness functions give continuous values. When the difference between individuals is less than the minimum discrete fitness range, i.e. an evaluation threshold, a human IEC user cannot distinguish the difference, and this becomes fitness noise that IEC user model should realize.

The IDE user simulation in this section randomly chooses either a trial vector or a target vector and leaves it as offspring in the next generation when the difference of their fitness values are less than a certain value to simulate the unavailability of a human IDE user's comparison; we set the difference threshold as 1/50 of the difference between the minimum and maximum fitness value in the population at each generation.

Experimental evaluations are conducted as follows. The four dimensional Gaussian mixture models are run for 1,000 generations. 30 trial runs of these searches with different initial search points are conducted. A Wilcoxon signed-rank test is applied at the 20th generation and the 1,000th generation to test for a significant difference between them.

IDE parameters are set as described in Table 2. Population size, 20, is decided upon to take match the sort of population size used in IEC experiments with a real human user.

Table 2: IDE experiment parameters setting

population size	20
search range of parameters	[−5.12, 5.12]
scale factor F	0.3
crossover rate	0.7
DE operation	DE/best/1/bin
max. search generation, MAX_{NFC}	1,000
dimensions of Gaussian mixture model, D	3,5,7,10
# of trial runs	30

4.2 Experimental Evaluation of the Proposed Methods

Comparisons between ordinary IDE and proposed method #1 are shown in Figure 2. They show how the proposed method converges faster than normal IDE at each generation.

Convergence comparisons with practical conditions, i.e. at the 20th generation with a population size of 20, are shown in Table 3(a). There was no significant difference between ordinary IDE and others for a 3-D Gaussian mixture model. However, convergence speed of the proposed methods became significantly faster than ordinary IDE as the task complexity increases, i.e. the dimensions of model functions increase. The proposed methods were superior to both conventional methods.

We can easily imagine the reason for the superiority from Figure 2. That is, for the simple 3 dimensional case, all methods converged sufficiently by the 20th generation that no significant difference could be observed. However, convergence at the 20th generation was still ongoing for the higher

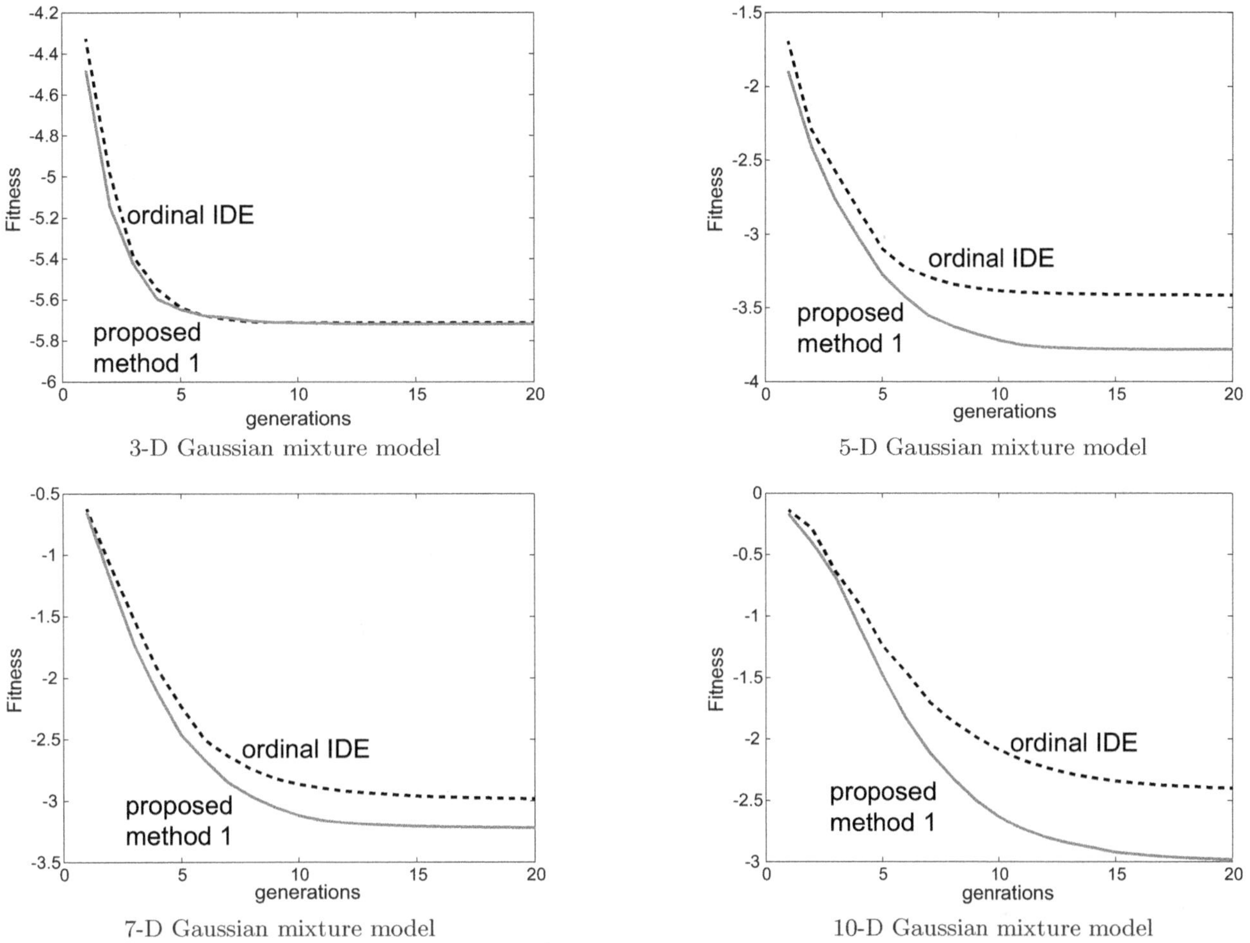

Figure 2: Average convergence curves for 30 trial runs with 3-D, 5-D, 7-D and 10-D Gaussian mixture models. Dot line and solid lines represent the conventional method #1 (ordinary IDE) and the proposed method #1, respectively.

dimensional Gaussian mixture models, and the convergence acceleration of the proposed methods became effective.

The evaluation results in Table 3(b) showed the same tendency as with Table 3(a) though the evaluation at the 1,000th generation is not realistic for IDE but should be considered in the evaluation conducted in section 5.

Comparisons using only Table 3(a) cannot be fair because proposed methods #1, #2, #3 and #4 are triple, triple, quadruple and triple comparison-based searches, respectively, while the two conventional methods are paired comparison-based ones. Table 4 is another evaluation that compares convergence at the same number of fitness calculations. Since conventional methods #1 and #2 calculate fitness 40 times (= 20 individuals × 2 for each paired comparison) per generation, 1200 and 1600 fitness calculations equate to the evaluations at the 30th and the 40th generations, respectively. Likewise, they correspond to the 20th, the 20th and the 28th generation for he triple comparison-based proposed methods #1, #2 and #4, and the 16th generation for the quadruple comparison-based proposed method #3.

The results here are the same as in Table 3; there is no significant difference between ordinary IDE and the others when the tasks are simple, such as with a 3-D Gaussian mixture model, and they have converged in early generations. On the other hand, the proposed methods converge significantly faster than conventional methods when the complexity of tasks increases, such as for the higher dimensional Gaussian mixture model.

4.3 Discussion on Convergence Characteristics

We applied a Wilcoxon-signed rank test for comparison of the proposed methods #1, #2 and #3 with #4 at 20th generation, 1000th generation, 1200th fitness calculation and 1600th fitness calculation. The results show only proposed method #3 outperforms significantly proposed method #4 in all cases with the 10-D Gaussian mixture model. There is not a significant difference between the three triple-comparison methods (proposed methods #1, #2 and #4) for the entire 4 Gaussian mixture models in all the cases.

The same statistical test is applied to compare proposed method #3 with proposed method #1 and #2. From the results, it is demonstrated that proposed method #3 performs significantly better than proposed method #1 and #2 in the

10-D Gaussian mixture model in 20th generation, 1000th generation, and 1600th fitness calculation.

We can draw some conclusions from the above observations. First, the triple-comparison mechanism using the random method offers the same enhancement to performance as the opposite method. Second, for the IDE case, the triple-comparison mechanism implemented by opposition does not show any advantages over randomness. Third, for the higher dimension problem (10-D Gaussian mixture model), proposed method #3, i.e., the quadruple-comparison method, significantly shows better performance than any other proposed methods.

Table 3: Average fitness values at the 20th and 1000th generation for 3-D, 5-D, 7-D, and 10-D Gaussian mixture models (pseudo-IDE users). Conventional method #2 is opposition-based generation jump with a jumping rate of 37% [24]. See details for the conventional and proposed methods in Table 1. Bold values and daggers mean that Wilcoxon sign-ranked tests showed significant differences between conventional method #1 and the proposed method and between conventional method #2 and the proposed method, respectively (p <0.05).

(a) Average fitness at the 20th generation.

method	3-D	5-D	7-D	10-D
conventional method #1	-5.71	-3.42	-2.98	-2.40
conventional method #2	-5.70	-3.46	-3.03	-2.48
IDE-proposed method #1	-5.72	**-3.78†**	**-3.22†**	**-2.98†**
IDE-proposed method #2	-5.73	**-3.57 †**	**-3.19 †**	**-2.87 †**
IDE-proposed method #3	-5.72	**-3.73†**	**-3.25†**	**-3.14†**
IDE-proposed method #4	-5.70	**-3.66†**	**-3.12**	**-2.93†**

(b) Average fitness at the 1,000th generation.

method	3-D	5-D	7-D	10-D
conventional method #1	-5.71	-3.42	-3.00	-2.44
conventional method #2	-5.70	-3.47	-3.04	-2.49
IDE-proposed method #1	-5.72†	**-3.78†**	**-3.22†**	**-3.00†**
IDE-proposed method #2	-5.73 †	**-3.62†**	**-3.24†**	**-2.93†**
IDE-proposed method #3	-5.72	**-3.73†**	**-3.25†**	**-3.18†**
IDE-proposed method #4	-5.70	**-3.66†**	**-3.13**	**-2.95†**

Table 4: Average fitness values when the number of fitness calculation reaches 1200 and 1600. For details, see the values indicated in bold or with daggers in Table 3 and those of the others in Table 1.

(a) Average fitness at the 1200th fitness calculation.

mrthod	3-D	5-D	7-D	10-D
conventional method #1	-5.71	-3.42	-2.99	-2.43
conventional method #2	-5.70	-3.47	-3.04	-2.49
IDE-proposed method #1	-5.72	**-3.78†**	**-3.22†**	**-2.99†**
IDE-proposed method #2	-5.73	**-3.57†**	**-3.20†**	**-2.89†**
IDE-proposed method #3	-5.72	**-3.73†**	**-3.22†**	**-3.08†**
IDE-proposed method #4	-5.70	**-3.66†**	**-3.13**	**-2.93†**

(b) Average fitness at the 1600th fitness calculation.

method	3-D	5-D	7-D	10-D
conventional method #1	-5.71	-3.42	-3.00	-2.43
conventional method #2	-5.70	-3.47	-3.04	-2.49
IDE-proposed method #1	-5.72	**-3.78†**	**-3.22†**	**-3.00†**
IDE-proposed method #2	-5.73	**-3.61†**	**-3.22 †**	**-2.92†**
IDE-proposed method #3	-5.72	**-3.73†**	**-3.25†**	**-3.14†**
IDE-proposed method #4	-5.70	**-3.66†**	**-3.13**	**-2.95†**

5. DE EXPERIMENTAL EVALUATIONS AND ANALYSIS

5.1 Test Functions and Experimental Conditions

We evaluate our proposed methods with 24 benchmark functions. Our proposed methods aim to reduce IDE user fatigue by accelerating IDE search even if user fatigue for a single comparison is increased. However, their use is not limited to IDE but rather they are applicable to any DE searches with a fitness function. We compare them with conventional methods of ordinary DE and OBDE using minimum optimization problems made by 24 benchmark functions [27]. Definitions, search ranges for optimization parameters, the global optimum values, and characteristics of the benchmark functions can be seen in Table 5.

Table 5: Twenty-four benchmark functions adopted from [27] are used in the experimental evaluations. (Uni=Unimodal, Mul=Multimodal, Rt=Rotated, GB=Global on Bounds, HC=Hybrid Composition, NM=Number Matrix, NS=Non-Separable, and S=Separable.)

No.	function	search range	optimum value	characteristics
F1	Sphere	[-100,100]	-450	Uni-S
F2	Schwefel 1.2	[-100,100]	-450	Uni-NS
F3	Elliptic	[-100,100]	-450	Uni-NS
F4	F2 with Noise	[-100,100]	-450	Uni-NS
F5	Schwefel 2.6 GB	[-100,100]	-310	Uni-NS
F6	Rosenbrock	[-100,100]	390	Mul-NS
F7	Griewank	[0,600]	-180	Mul-NS
F8	Ackley GB	[-32,32]	-140	Mul-NS
F9	Rastrigin	[-5,5]	-330	Mul-Sep
F10	Rt Rastrigin	[-5,5]	-330	Rt-Mul-NS
F11	Weierstrass	[-0.5,0.5]	90	Mul-NS
F12	Schwefel 2.13	[-100,100]	-460	Mul-NS
F13	Expanded F8F2	[-3,1]	-130	Mul-NS
F14	Scaffer F6	[-100,100]	-300	Mul-NS
F15	HC Function	[-5,5]	120	HC-S
F16	Rt HC F1	[-5,5]	120	Rt-HC-NS
F17	F16 with Noise	[-5,5]	120	Rt-HC-NS
F18	Rt HC F2	[-5,5]	10	Rt-HC-NS
F19	F18 with Basin	[-5,5]	10	Rt-HC-NS
F20	F18 with GB	[-5,5]	10	Rt-HC-NS
F21	Rt HC F3	[-5,5]	360	Rt-HC-NS
F22	F21 with NM	[-5,5]	360	Rt-HC-NS
F23	NC Rt F2	[-5,5]	360	HC-NS
F24	Rt HC F4	[-5,5]	260	Rt-HC-NS

Because there is no need to evaluate IDE user fatigue, as was done in 4, the evaluation indices used in this section for comparing our proposed method applied to DE are the number of fitness calculations (NFC) until the convergence threshold (CT) is reached and the success ratio (SR) for those that reach the CT. The lower NFC is, the faster convergence is.

Evaluations trial runs are 30, and the maximum generation is MAX_{NFC} =1,000. A successful convergence is counted when a convergence reaches the CT defined by Eq. (4). All benchmark functions are evaluated by an acceleration ratio, AR, too, to evaluate convergence speed. It is defined using NFC at the maximum generation, the 1,000th generation, in Eq. (7), and $AR > 1$ means that the proposed method converges faster than ordinary DE. Success ratio, SR, is defined by the number of trials that reached the convergence threshold, CT, in Eq. (6). Furthermore, average acceleration ratio and average success ratio are calculated and used for the final evaluation results.

$$converg.\,threshold,\ CT = average\,fitness\,of\,each\,method\,at\,MAX_{NFC} - th\,generation. \quad (4)$$

$$NFC = average\,\#\,of\,fitness\,calculation\,until\,convergence\,reaches\,CT. \quad (5)$$

$$success\,ratio,\ SR = \frac{\#\,of\,reached\,to\,CT}{\#\,of\,MAX_{NFC}} \quad (6)$$

$$acceleration\,ratio,\ AR = \frac{NFC_{ordinaryDE}}{NFC_{proposal}} \quad (7)$$

The DE experimental parameters are set as shown in Table 6. The evaluation is conducted under difficult search conditions; only 50 individuals are used to search 10-D functions for which search parameter ranges have been expanded.

Table 6: DE experiment parameters setting

population size	50
scale factor F	0.3
crossover rate	0.7
DE operations	DE/best/1/bin
max. search generation, MAX_{NFC}	1,000
convergence threshold, CT	CT in Table 7
dimensions of benchmark functions, D	10
# of trial runs	30

5.2 Evaluation of Proposed Methods

Convergence characteristics for the 24 benchmark functions are shown in Table 7. Numerical values in the table are the average fitness values over 30 trial runs at the 1,000th generation. Convergence thresholds, CT's, for convergence success ratio, SR, in Table 8 are also listed in this table. Comparisons of computational cost are listed in Table 8.

The proposed methods converged faster than the conventional methods at the same generation for all but a few functions. This effect cannot be observed for the F12 function, where all methods failed to approach its global optimum. The global optimum of the F12 function is −460, but the fitness values of all methods at the 1,000th generation are still large positive values, which means there was no convergence at all. It must be too difficult to search the 10-D F12 function with only 50 individuals. These methods have not reached the global optima of F15 - F24 functions at the 1,000th generation, but their average fitness values are close to the global optima and their convergence are largely better than that of the ordinary DE. As a general remark, the acceleration effectiveness of the proposed methods is significant except in the case of F12 and F18-F20, which proved to be too difficult for all the methods under the given experimental conditions.

Comparative evaluations of the computational costs, i.e. the number of fitness calculations, and the success ratios, SR, of reaching a convergence threshold, CT, are shown in Table 8. It is hard for the ordinary DE to search 10-D benchmark functions with only 50 individuals; the average SR for the 24 benchmark functions was 17%, and the SR of only 3 of the 24 functions exceeded 50%. The average SR of conventional method #2 was better than that of #1 and was 60%, but our proposed methods achieved around 60%-80%. They showed better performance for all benchmark functions except for the F12 and F18-F20 functions where none of the methods converged with the difficult experimental conditions given in this section.

The average number of fitness calculations, NFS, before reaching the convergence threshold, CT, was lower using our proposed methods than when using the conventional methods. Not only convergence evaluation at the same generation as shown in Table 7, but also NFS in Table 8 showed that the proposed methods reached the CT quickly with less computational cost. From these results, we can say that the proposed methods can realize an effective acceleration of convergence.

The generation number for when a DE search reaches the convergence threshold, CT, is calculated as:

$$generation\,\# = NFC/(population\ size \times p),$$

where p is the number of individuals being compared per comparison, and p = 2, 3, and 4 for paired comparison-based conventional methods #1 and #2, triple comparison-based proposed methods #1 #2 and #4, and quadruple comparison-based proposed method #3, respectively.

As a summary of the experimental results, all four kinds of our proposed methods #1 - #4 are better than or equal to the conventional methods for all 24 benchmark functions by number of fitness calculations, the success ratio for reaching a convergence threshold, acceleration ratio, and fitness value at each generation.

5.3 Discussion on Functional Inclusion and Convergence Characteristics

Although proposed method #1 includes the conventional method #2 and proposed method #3 includes the proposed methods #1 and #2 functionally as mentioned in section 3, methods which included the functionality of one or more methods did not always perform better than the method(s) they included, though they outperformed them in general. We now discuss this point in more detail.

The reason for this result is that it is not guaranteed that the continuous selection of the best individual at each comparison as *best-best-best* will become the total best; in other words, the principle of optimality [2] does not stand up in this case. Probabilistically speaking, it is expected that areas around better individuals are more likely to reach the global optimum than other areas. However, monotonicity, which is a requirement of the principle of optimality, does not stand up in multi-modal tasks, and it is not guaranteed that the areas where opposite vectors are chosen are advantageous to reach the global optimum even if the opposite vectors are the best among the triple or quadruple individuals used for comparison. Additionally, if a non-advantageous individual is chosen, subsequent selections will also be affected by this choice.

From these two points, when method A includes method B functionally, we can say that the method A is expected to converge faster than the method B probabilistically but this expectation is not guaranteed. For further investigation of the enhancement to performance among our pro-

Table 7: Average fitness values for the benchmark function, F1 – F24 at the 1,000th generation over 30 trial runs. Bold values and daggers mean that Wilcoxon sign-ranked tests showed significant differences between conventional method #1 and the proposed method and between conventional method #2 and the proposed method, respectively (p <0.05). *Conventional* and *proposal* mean respectively *conventional method* and *proposed method*.

method	F1	F2	F3	F4	F5	F6	F7	F8	F9	F10	F11	F12
conventional #1	-354.71	-250.18	192113.06	-141.32	2359.79	733669.47	-170.87	-119.60	-313.48	-302.79	95.21	3374.60
conventional #2	**-413.53**	**-359.01**	308946.65	**-448.03**	26.70	287810.81	**-179.41**	**-136.56**	**-320.56**	**-320.56**	**91.16**	18078.54
DE-proposal #1	**-440.88**†	**-438.45**†	67357.98	**-416.28**†	**-39.89**	**10528.84**†	**-179.74**†	**-137.68**†	**-323.89**†	**-323.89**†	**90.89**	12610.21
DE-proposal #2	**-444.75**†	**-441.15**†	**26538.41**†	**-433.12**†	**-127.78**†	**7668.20**†	**-179.84**†	**-138.29**†	**-323.44**†	**-323.44**†	**90.92**	13725.32
DE-proposal #3	**-447.59**†	**-440.02**†	**12532.29**†	**-443.62**†	**-120.31**†	**1042.11**†	**-179.87**†	**-138.72**†	**-324.02**†	**-324.02**†	**90.73**†	14801.29
DE-proposal #4	**-440.47**†	**-377.29**	70371.76†	**-418.67**†	**179.05**	**13491.41**†	**-179.76**†	**-138.23**†	**-321.11**	**-321.11**†	**90.63**	15473.06
CT	-423.66	-384.35	112976.69	-383.51	379.59	175701.81	-178.25	-134.85	-321.08	-319.30	91.59	13010.50
method	F13	F14	F15	F16	F17	F18	F19	F20	F21	F22	F23	F24
conventional #1	-127.92	-296.71	498.21	299.84	306.39	990.61	990.25	992.80	1463.61	1253.51	1546.75	1077.70
conventional #2	-128.18	**-297.98**	**158.22**	**158.22**	**157.13**	992.86	1006.69	1005.34	**414.45**	**414.45**	**400.56**	**911.72**
DE-proposal #1	**-128.99**†	**-298.90**†	**148.68**†	**148.68**†	**147.75**†	959.60	958.27	959.23	**403.18**†	**403.18**†	**385.85**†	**354.11**†
DE-proposal #2	**-129.09**†	**-298.97**†	**147.01**†	**147.01**†	**145.43**†	962.36	970.57	965.20	**400.62**†	**400.62**†	**386.21**†	**339.78**†
DE-proposal #3	**-129.06**†	**-299.01**†	**143.99**†	**143.99**†	**144.87**†	966.31	965.93	964.67	**398.10**†	**398.10**†	**384.86**†	**310.60**†
DE-proposal #4	**-129.23**†	**-298.85**†	**153.54**	**153.54**	**154.76**	936.51†	942.82†	935.39 †	**400.61**†	**400.61**†	**387.76**†	**381.16**†
CT	-128.75	-298.40	208.27	175.21	176.05	968.04	972.42	970.44	580.09	545.08	582.00	562.51

Table 8: Evaluation indices for 30 trial runs of benchmark functions, F1 – F24. See Eq.s (5), (6), and (7) for the # of fitness calculations, NFC, convergence success ratio, SR, and acceleration ratio, AR, respectively. *conventional* and *proposal* are defined as in the caption of Table 7.

	conventional #1 (DE)		conventional #2 (OBDE)			DE-proposal #1			DE-proposal #2			DE-proposal #3			DE-proposal #4		
function	NFC	SR	NFC	SR	AR	NFC	SR	AR	NFC	SR	AR	NFC	SR	AR	NFC	SR	AR
F1	60897	0.39	51644	0.62	1.18	16750	0.89	3.64	11585	0.92	5.26	2273	0.99	26.79	21595	0.86	2.82
F2	70757	0.29	65527	0.52	1.08	3040	0.98	23.28	2915	0.98	24.27	3993	0.98	17.72	56860	0.62	1.24
F3	38357	0.62	69391	0.49	0.55	31590	0.79	1.21	11665	0.92	3.29	2253	0.99	17.02	41370	0.72	0.93
F4	79197	0.21	8741	0.94	9.06	23085	0.85	3.43	13405	0.91	5.91	4040	0.98	19.60	34880	0.77	2.27
F5	86620	0.13	11047	0.92	7.84	7315	0.95	11.84	6985	0.95	12.40	3033	0.98	28.56	37010	0.75	2.34
F6	47300	0.53	15390	0.89	3.07	1520	0.99	31.12	1305	0.99	36.25	1593	0.99	29.69	6420	0.96	7.37
F7	83683	0.16	10791	0.92	7.75	1455	0.99	57.51	1380	0.99	60.64	1753	0.99	47.73	1510	0.99	55.42
F8	100000	0.00	28802	0.79	3.47	6455	0.96	15.49	1430	0.99	69.93	1880	0.99	53.19	1495	0.99	66.89
F9	86913	0.13	65710	0.52	1.32	29415	0.80	2.95	33680	0.78	2.58	39620	0.80	2.19	62675	0.58	1.39
F10	100000	0.00	38812	0.72	2.58	14655	0.90	6.82	18920	0.87	5.29	20167	0.90	4.96	47920	0.68	2.09
F11	100000	0.00	47352	0.65	2.11	36685	0.76	2.73	17260	0.88	5.79	22833	0.89	4.38	17320	0.88	5.77
F12	43357	0.57	92557	0.32	0.47	120095	0.20	0.36	119970	0.20	0.36	163673	0.18	0.26	136445	0.09	0.32
F13	67763	0.32	88169	0.36	0.77	37470	0.75	1.81	27450	0.82	2.47	49427	0.75	1.37	12735	0.92	5.32
F14	100000	0.00	101910	0.26	0.98	62850	0.58	1.59	38135	0.75	2.62	47420	0.76	2.11	49055	0.67	2.04
F15	100000	0.00	2069	0.98	48.34	2050	0.99	48.78	2050	0.99	48.78	3260	0.98	30.67	2225	0.99	44.94
F16	100000	0.00	7234	0.95	13.82	7680	0.95	13.02	7785	0.95	12.85	4580	0.98	21.83	8030	0.95	12.45
F17	100000	0.00	20600	0.85	4.85	3330	0.98	30.03	3260	0.98	30.67	5720	0.97	17.48	8540	0.94	11.71
F18	70373	0.30	105422	0.23	0.67	105405	0.30	0.67	95735	0.36	0.74	121227	0.39	0.58	85925	0.43	0.82
F19	67060	0.33	100891	0.26	0.66	95620	0.36	0.70	95580	0.36	0.70	127660	0.36	0.53	85935	0.43	0.78
F20	70370	0.30	105390	0.23	0.67	95640	0.36	0.74	90775	0.39	0.78	127753	0.36	0.55	85860	0.43	0.82
F21	100000	0.00	1238	0.99	80.80	800	0.99	125.00	755	0.99	132.45	947	1.00	105.63	875	0.99	114.29
F22	100000	0.00	1375	0.99	72.75	955	0.99	104.71	930	0.99	107.53	1200	0.99	83.33	1045	0.99	95.69
F23	100000	0.00	1196	0.99	83.58	695	1.00	143.88	590	1.00	169.49	807	1.00	123.97	735	1.00	136.05
F24	96700	0.03	51489	0.62	1.88	6845	0.95	14.13	11765	0.92	8.22	9060	0.95	10.67	16810	0.89	5.75
average		0.17		0.60	10.65		0.80	18.34		0.80	21.98		0.60	17.11		0.71	16.76

posed methods, we applied Wilcoxon signed rank test to compare the performance between proposed method #3 and proposed methods #1 and #2. The results show that proposed method #3 is significantly better than proposed methods #1 and #2 for F3, F6-F9, F11 and F24, and only worse than proposed methods #1 and #2 in F3. The experimental results in Tables 7 and 8 are consistent with this discussion.

The effectiveness of the third vector from the random mechanism and the opposition mechanism is compared by applying Wilcoxon signed rank test on the proposed method #1, #2, #3 and #4. The results show the proposed method #4 is significantly worse than the proposed method #1, #2 and #3 for most of the benchmark functions. This shows that the the third vector is more effective when selected from the opposition than at random, which also confirms the previous work in [23].

6. CONCLUSION AND FUTURE WORKS

We proposed new OBDE methods embedding opposition-based learning into DE and evaluated them. The proposed methods are triple and quadruple comparison-based methods. Fitness calculation cost per comparison is higher than ordinary DE and ordinary OBDE based on paired comparison. However, experimental evaluations using an IDE simulation and 24 benchmark functions showed better acceleration performance than conventional methods on converged fitness values at same generations, the number of fitness calculations, the success ratio for reaching a convergence threshold, and acceleration ratio.

There are many IDE tasks where the IDE user can memorize three or four individuals. In these cases, we expect that IDE user fatigue for our proposed methods will not become 1.5 or 2.0 times of that of paired comparison-based conventional methods. Taking account of their fast convergence performance and the non-proportional characteristics of IDE user fatigue, we conclude that the proposed methods are effective, especially for IDE.

We conducted simulation evaluations to compare the characteristics of several methods with multiple different initializations under the same experimental conditions. In the next step, we should quantitatively evaluate IDE user fatigue with the largest population size that a human being can memorize and collect basic experimental data together with the convergence experiment results in this paper. After that, we need to conduct human subjective tests with human IDE users, evaluate user fatigue and acceleration performance synthetically, and thus conclude our evaluation of methods proposed here.

Acknowledgment

This work was supported in part by the Grant-in-Aid for Scientific Research (23500279) and Kyushu University Fund. Yan Pei would like to thank the Yoshida Scholarship Foundation for its support of his doctoral research.

7. REFERENCES

[1] M. Ahandani and H. Alavi-Rad. Opposition-based learning in the shuffled differential evolution algorithm. *Soft Computing*, pages 1–35, 2012.

[2] R. Bellman. *Dynamic Programming*. Princeton University Press, 1957.

[3] R. Dawkins. *The Blind Watchmaker*. Essex: Longman, 1986.

[4] M. Herdy. Evolutionary optimisation based on subjective selection-evolving blends of coffee. In *5th Eourpean Cong. on Itellengt Techniques and Soft Computing (EUFIT'97)*, pages 640–644, Sept. 1997.

[5] G. Iacca, F. Neri, and E. Mininno. Opposition-based learning in compact differential evolution. In *Lecture Notes in Computer Science*, volume 6624, pages 264–273, 2011.

[6] T. Ingu and H. Takagi. Accelerating a ga convergence by fitting a single-peak function. In *IEEE Int. Conf. on Fuzzy Systems (FUZZ-IEEE'99)*, pages 1415–1420, Aug. 1999.

[7] Y. Jin. A comprehensive survey of fitness approximation in evolutionary computation. *Soft Computing*, 9(1):3–12, 2005.

[8] B. Johanson. Automated fitness raters for the gp-music system. Master's degree final project, Univ. of Birmingham, Sept. 1997.

[9] A. Kosorukoff. Human-based genetic algorithm. In *2001 IEEE Int. Conf. on Systems, Man and Cybernetic (SMC2001)*, pages 3464–3469, Oct. 2001.

[10] P. Legrand, C. Bourgeois-Republique, V. Pean, H. Cohen, Esther, J. Levy-Vehel, B. Frachet, E. Lutton, and P. Collet. Interactive evolution for cochlear implants fitting. *Genetic Programming and Evolvable Machines*, 8(4):319–354, 2007.

[11] I. S. Lim and D. Thalmann. Tournament selection for browsing temporal signals. In *ACM Symp. on Applied Computing (SAC2000)*, pages 570–573, Mar. 2000.

[12] J. Mader, J. Abonyi, and F. Szeifert. Interactive particle swarm optimization. In *Int. Conf. on Intelligent Systems Design and Applications (ISDA2005)*, pages 2314–319, Sept. 2005.

[13] A. Miller, George. The magical mumber seven, plus or minus two: Some limits on our capacity for processing information. *The Psychological Review*, 63:81–97, 1956.

[14] Y. Nakano and H. Takagi. Influence of quantization noise in fitness on the performance of interactive pso. In *IEEE Congress on Evolutionary Computation (CEC2009)*, pages 2146–2422, May. 2009.

[15] Y. Pei and H. Takagi. Accelerating evolutionary computation with elite obtained in projected one-dimensional spaces. In *5th Int. Conf. on Genetic and Evolutionary Computing*, pages 89–92, Aug./Sept. 2011.

[16] Y. Pei and H. Takagi. Comparative evaluations of evolutionary computation with elite obtained in reduced dimensional spaces. In *3rd Int. Conf. on Intelligent Networking and Collaborative Systems (INCoS2011)*, pages 35–40, Nov./Dec. 2011.

[17] Y. Pei and H. Takagi. Novel traveling salesman problem solution by accelerated evolutionary computation with approximated cost matrix in an industrial application. In *3rd Int. Conf. on Soft Computing and Pattern Recognition (SoCPaR2011)*, pages 39–44, Oct. 2011.

[18] Y. Pei and H. Takagi. A survey on accelerating evolutionary computation approaches. In *3rd Int. Conf. on Soft Computing and Pattern Recognition (SoCPaR2011)*, pages 201–206, Oct. 2011.

[19] Y. Pei and H. Takagi. Comparative study on fitness landscape approximation with fourier transform. In *Sixth Int. Conf. on Genetic and Evolutionary Computation (ICGEC2012)*, pages 400–403, Aug. 2012.

[20] Y. Pei and H. Takagi. Fourier analysis of the fitness landscape for evolutionary search acceleration. In *2012 IEEE Congress on Evolutionary Computation (IEEE CEC 2012)*, pages 2934–2940, Jun. 2012.

[21] Y. Pei, S. Zheng, Y. Tan, and H. Takagi. An empirical study on influence of approximation approaches to enhance fireworks algorithm. In *2012 IEEE Int. Conf. on Systems, Man, and Cybernetics (SMC2012)*, pages 1322–1327, Oct. 2012.

[22] K. Price, R. Storn, and J. Lampinen. *Differential Evolution: A Practical Approach to Global Optimization*. Springer-Verlag, Berlin, Germany, 2005.

[23] S. Rahnamayan, H. R. Tizhoosh, and M. Salama. Opposition versus randomness in soft computing techniques. *Applied Soft Computing*, 8(2):906–918, 2008.

[24] S. Rahnamayan, H. R. Tizhoosh, and M. M. Salama. Opposition-based differential evolution algorithms. *IEEE Trans. on Evolutionary Computation*, 12(1):64–79, Feb. 2008.

[25] K. Sims. Ariticial evolution for computer graphic. *Computer Graphics*, 25(4):319–328, Jul. 1991. Proc. of Siggraph 91.

[26] R. Storn and K. Price. Differential evolution - a simple and efficient heuristic for global optimization over continuous spaces. *Journal of Global Optimization*, 11:341–359, 1997.

[27] P. Suganthan, N. Hansen, J. Liang, K. Deb, Y. Chen, A. Auger, and S. Tiwari. Problem definitions and evaluation criteria for the cec 2005 special session on real-parameter optimization. Technical report, Nanyang Technological University, 2005.

[28] H. Takagi. Interactive evolutionary computation: Fusion of the capabilities of ec optimization and human evaluation. *Proceedings of the IEEE*, 89(9):1275–1296, 2001.

[29] H. Takagi. *in Aspects of Soft Computing, Intelligent Robotic and Control*, chapter New IEC Research and Framkworks, pages 65–78. Springer-Verlag, Berlin Heidelberg, 2009.

[30] H. Takagi. Interactive evolutionary computation for analyzing human aware mechanism. *Applied Computational Intelligence and Soft Computing*, 2012, 2012.

[31] H. Takagi, T. Ingu, and K. Ohnishi. Accelerating a ga convergence by fitting a single-peak function. *J. of Japan Society for Fuzzy Theory and Intelligent Informatics*, 15(2):219–229, 2003.

[32] H. Takagi and M. Ohsaki. Interactive evolutionary computation-based hearing-aid fitting. *IEEE Trans. on Evolutionary Computation*, 11(23):414–427, 2007.

[33] H. Takagi and D. Pallez. Paired comparison-based interactive differential evolution. In *The First World Congress on Nature and Biologically Inspired Computing (NaBIC2009)*, pages 375–480, Dec. 2009.

[34] H. R. Tizhoosh. Opposition-based learning: A new scheme for machine intelligence. In *Int. Conf. on Computational Intelligence for Modelling Control and Automation (CIMCA2005)*, volume I, pages 695–701, Nov. 2005.

[35] H. R. Tizhoosh. Reinforcement learning based on actions and opposite actions. In *ICGST Int. Conf. on Artificial Intelligence and Machine Learning (AIML-05)*, Dec. 2005.

[36] H. Wang, Z. Wu, and S. Rahnamayan. Enhanced opposition-based differential evolution for solving high-dimensional continuous optimization problems. *Soft Computing*, 15(11):2127–2140, Nov. 2011.

Noisy Optimization Complexity Under Locality Assumption

Jérémie Decock
TAO team
Inria Saclay IDF, UMR CNRS 8623
Université Paris-Sud, Orsay, France
jeremie.decock@inria.fr

Olivier Teytaud
TAO team
Inria Saclay IDF, UMR CNRS 8623
Université Paris-Sud, Orsay, France
olivier.teytaud@inria.fr

ABSTRACT

In spite of various recent publications on the subject, there are still gaps between upper and lower bounds in evolutionary optimization for noisy objective function. In this paper we reduce the gap, and get tight bounds within logarithmic factors in the case of small noise and no long-distance influence on the objective function.

Categories and Subject Descriptors

G.1.6 [**Mathematics of Computing**]: Numerical Analysis—*Optimization*

General Terms

Theory

Keywords

Noisy optimization; black box complexity model; local sampling

1. INTRODUCTION

Noisy optimization is the optimization of stochastic objective functions, i.e. the objective value $f(\boldsymbol{x}, \omega)$ depends on $\boldsymbol{x}$ and on a random variable ω. Equivalently, $f(\boldsymbol{x})$ is a random variable distributed as $f(\boldsymbol{x}, \omega)$. Often (yet not always, as risk considerations can be involved), the goal is to optimize the expected value, i.e. $\mathbb{E}_\omega f(\boldsymbol{x}, \omega)$ where $\mathbb{E}_\omega$ is the expectation with respect to ω. We here work on derivative-free noisy optimization, on a continuous domain $D = [0, 1]^d$; we assume that the optimum is unique, and the detailed setting below will assume that getting rid of tricky local optima is less important than handling noise properly.

In all the paper, we use $\tilde{O}(f(n))$ as a short notation for $O(f(n)\log(n))$. Section 1.1 presents our framework, and in particular the family of functions on which we show lower bounds (all families including this family are also concerned by the lower bounds). Section 1.2 discusses the context of our results, in particular the critical "locality" assumption, discussing whether an algorithm uses points far from the optimum or not for improving its convergence rate.

Then, Section 2 gives the mathematical formulation and the main lemmas. Section 3 is the main result.

1.1 Framework

There are many convergence rates known in numerical optimization, depending on assumptions (derivative-free[1] or not, comparison-based [2] or not, global[3] or not). Robustness to noise, even early in the origins of evolutionary computation[4], is cited as a strength of these algorithms. In spite of this strong interest for noise in evolutionary computation, complexity in the noisy case is less clear, because details on the assumption have a big impact on the performance[5, 6, 7, 8, 9, 10]; a main distinction being adaptive noise[11] (with small noise variance around the optimum) and additive noise[12] (with lower-bounded variance around the optimum). Also, defining convergence rates is more difficult when either the algorithm or the objective function has a random part, because the distance of $\boldsymbol{x}_n$ to the optimum $\boldsymbol{x}^*$ is not a constant (n being the nth objective function evaluation). Various convergence rates can be defined depending on the precise considered definition of convergence (we will not give too many details on this in this introduction, but our results will state precisely the definitions involved).

For example, the algorithm CLOP[13, 14] reaches a convergence $\|\boldsymbol{x}_n - \boldsymbol{x}^*\| = \tilde{O}(1/\sqrt{n})$on a wide range of symmetric objective functions, using regression; in a very structured case (when the family of functions is very well approximated by a known model), statistical tools (supervised machine learning) provide such fast rates, even on very flat functions.

An other example of algorithm for noisy optimization is R-EDA (Racing-based Estimation of Distribution Algorithm, [15, 16]). It considers a different definition of convergence (more on this later).R-EDA was proposed as a typical noisy optimization algorithm, easy to analyze and making a good approximation of real-world approaches[17]. The noisy optimization framework is described in Algorithm 1 and R-EDA is defined in Algorithm 2. For $\beta > 0$, the convergence rate is typically $\|\boldsymbol{x}_n - \boldsymbol{x}^*\| = \tilde{O}(1/n^{1/\beta})$ on the family of objective functions

$$F_{\beta,\gamma} = \{f_{\boldsymbol{x}^*,\beta,\gamma}(\boldsymbol{x}); \boldsymbol{x}^* \in D\}, \quad (1)$$

where $D = [0, 1]^d$ and

$$f_{\boldsymbol{x}^*,\beta,\gamma}(\boldsymbol{x}) = \mathcal{B}\left(\gamma\left(\frac{\|\boldsymbol{x} - \boldsymbol{x}^*\|}{\sqrt{d}}\right)^\beta + (1-\gamma)\right). \quad (2)$$

FOGA'13, January 16-20, 2013, Adelaide, Australia.

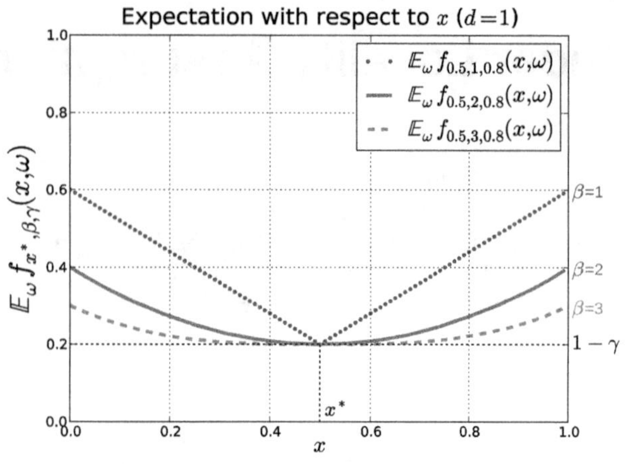

Figure 1: Expected values of $f_{x^*,\beta,\gamma}$ with respect to x, for $d = 1$ and with the optimal point $x^* = 0.5$, the noise level $\gamma = 0.8$ and β (the "flatness" of $\mathbb{E}f$ around x^*) equals to 1, 2 and 3.

Here $\mathcal{B}(p)$ states for a Bernoulli random variable with parameter p (i.e. equal to 1 with probability p and 0 otherwise). Fig. 1 show the expected values of $f_{x^*,\beta,\gamma}$ with respect to x for some set of parameters.

We will show in this paper that R-EDA is optimal within logarithmic factors for $F_{\beta,\gamma}$ under locality assumptions discussed below and for some values of γ (case with variance linearly decreasing as a function of expected fitness values).

Algorithm 2 R-EDA: algorithm for optimizing noisy fitness functions. *Bernstein* denotes a Bernstein race, as defined in Algorithm 3. The initial domain is $[\boldsymbol{x}_0^-, \boldsymbol{x}_0^+] \in \mathbb{R}^D$, δ is the confidence parameter. This algorithm goes back to [15, 16]. Please note that $\boldsymbol{x}_i^-$ and $\boldsymbol{x}_i^+$ are indexed by i, the iteration number, and not by the number of evaluations as in our convergence criteria.

$n \leftarrow 0$
while True **do**
  // Pick the coordinate with highest uncertainty
  $c_n = \arg\max_i (\boldsymbol{x}_n^+)_i - (\boldsymbol{x}_n^-)_i$
  $\delta_n^{\max} = (\boldsymbol{x}_n^+)_{c_n} - (\boldsymbol{x}_n^-)_{c_n}$
  for $i \in [[1,3]]$ **do**
    // Consider the middle point
    $\boldsymbol{x'}_n^i \leftarrow \frac{1}{2}(\boldsymbol{x}_n^- + \boldsymbol{x}_n^+)$
    // The c_n^{th} coordinate may take $3 \neq$ values
    $(\boldsymbol{x'}_n^i)_{c_n} \leftarrow (\boldsymbol{x}_n^-)_{c_n} + \frac{i-1}{2}(\boldsymbol{x}_n^+ - \boldsymbol{x}_n^-)_{c_n}$
  end for
  $(good_n, bad_n) = Bernstein(\boldsymbol{x'}_n^1, \boldsymbol{x'}_n^2, \boldsymbol{x'}_n^3, \frac{6\delta}{\pi^2(n+1)^2})$.
  // A good and a bad point
  Let H_n be the halfspace
  $\{\boldsymbol{x} \in \mathbb{R}^D; ||\boldsymbol{x} - good_n|| \leq ||\boldsymbol{x} - bad_n||\}$
  Split the domain: $[\boldsymbol{x}_{n+1}^-, \boldsymbol{x}_{n+1}^+] = H_n \cap [\boldsymbol{x}_n^-, \boldsymbol{x}_n^+]$
  $n \leftarrow n + 1$
end while

Algorithm 3 Bernstein race between 3 points. Eq. 3 is Bernstein's inequality to compute the precision for empirical estimates (see e.g. [18, p124]); $\hat{\sigma}_i$ is the empirical estimate of the standard deviation of point $\boldsymbol{x}_i$'s associated random variable $F_t(\boldsymbol{x}_i)$ (it is 0 in the first iteration, which does not alter the algorithm's correctness); $\hat{f}(\boldsymbol{x})$ is the average of the fitness measurements at $\boldsymbol{x}$.

Bernstein$(\boldsymbol{x}_1, \boldsymbol{x}_2, \boldsymbol{x}_3, \delta')$
$T = 0$
repeat
  $T \leftarrow T + 1$
  Evaluate the fitness of points $\boldsymbol{x}_1, \boldsymbol{x}_2, \boldsymbol{x}_3$ once, *i.e.* evaluate the noisy fitness at each of these points.
  Evaluate the precision:

$$\epsilon_{(T)} = 3\log\left(\frac{3\pi^2T^2}{6\delta'}\right)/T + \max_i \hat{\sigma}_i \sqrt{2\log\left(\frac{3\pi^2T^2}{6\delta'}\right)/T}. \quad (3)$$

until Two points $(good, bad)$ satisfy $\hat{f}(bad) - \hat{f}(good) \geq 2\epsilon$ — **return** $(good, bad)$

1.2 Symmetry assumptions and information theory

We pointed out above that the $\tilde{O}(1/\sqrt{n})$ is possible for algorithms (e.g. CLOP) using models which are very close to the real objective function (for example if we know that the fitness function is a Bernoulli as in Eq. 2). In these algorithms, the sampled point is not necessarily close to the optimum or to the current approximation of the optimum that the algorithm has. This is related to information theory: there are areas in which one gets more information than others, and points minimizing $\boldsymbol{x} \mapsto E_\omega f(\boldsymbol{x}, w)$ are not necessarily the most informative. Typically, when you have a relevant model of the objective function, you will learn more about the optimum by sampling maximum uncertainty points (i.e. points $\boldsymbol{x}$ such that $f(\boldsymbol{x}, \omega)$ has high variance), rather than by sampling points close to the optimum.

There are therefore two distinct strategies[1]:

- sampling close to the current estimation of the optimum;
- sampling maximum uncertainty areas.

As we have already said, getting knowledge on the objective function far from the current approximation of the optimum does not help for finding $\boldsymbol{x}^*$ if you have no model of the objective function (at least in a setting without tricky local optima). But, if you have a strong prior on the objective function, you can indeed sample only very far from the current estimation of the optimum, at locations where the objective function is less flat and from this sampling, you get knowledge on $\boldsymbol{x}^*$. Again, this leads to algorithms which sample much more far from the current approximation of the optimum than close to it.

[1]Interestingly there were debates on the mailing list dedicated to the BBOB noisy optimization testbeds because the designers of the testbeds assess the quality of optimization algorithms not from their estimation on the location of the optimum, but from the points they sample, which is clearly not fair for algorithms which are precisely based on estimating the optimum from points far from the optimum.

Algorithm 1 Noisy optimization framework. This is not an optimization algorithm; this just explains the framework of noisy optimization with Bernoulli random variables (the fitness function outputs 1 if random ($= \omega_n$) is less than $\mathbb{E}f_{\boldsymbol{x}^*,\beta,\gamma}(\boldsymbol{x}_{\boldsymbol{x}^*,n,\omega,\omega'})$). *Optimize* is an optimization algorithm taking as input a sequence of visited points, their binary noisy fitness values and an internal noise. It outputs a new point to be visited, looking for points $\boldsymbol{x}$ of the domain such that $f_{\boldsymbol{x}^*,\beta,\gamma}(\boldsymbol{x})$ is as small as possible.

Input:
ω the uniform noise of f,
ω' a random seed of the algorithm,
$\boldsymbol{x}^*$ the optimal point,
β and γ two fixed parameters of f.
Output:
$\boldsymbol{x}_{\boldsymbol{x}^*,n,\omega,\omega'}$ the estimation of the optimum.

for all $n = 1, 2, 3, \dots$ **do**
  $\boldsymbol{x}_{\boldsymbol{x}^*,n,\omega,\omega'} = \text{Optimize}(\boldsymbol{x}_{\boldsymbol{x}^*,1,\omega,\omega'}, \dots, \boldsymbol{x}_{\boldsymbol{x}^*,n-1,\omega,\omega'}, y_1, \dots, y_{n-1}, \omega')$
  if $\omega_n \leq \mathbb{E}f_{\boldsymbol{x}^*,\beta,\gamma}(\boldsymbol{x}_{\boldsymbol{x}^*,n,\omega,\omega'})$ **then**
    $y_n = 1$
  else
    $y_n = 0$
  end if
end for
return $\boldsymbol{x}_{\boldsymbol{x}^*,n,\omega,\omega'}$

These algorithms have two distinct steps:

- Exploration: choosing a point $\boldsymbol{x}_n$ for which they want to sample $f(\boldsymbol{x}_n)$.
- Recommendation: providing an estimate $\tilde{\boldsymbol{x}}_n^*$ of $\arg\min \mathbb{E}f$.

Nevertheless, various compromises are possible (for not relying too much on the model) between strategies relying only on maximum uncertainty (strongly trusting a model) and strategies relying only on sampling close to the estimation of the optimum; [19] is based on methods for choosing to which extent the model should be trusted.

So far, we have discussed the distinction between algorithms which samples close to the estimation of the optimum and those which samples at maximum uncertainty areas. But in this paper we will only consider the fastest theoretical convergence rates for algorithms which samples close to the estimation of the optimum. Formally speaking, we assume the following *locality assumption* for some $0 < \delta < 1/2$ and some constant $C(d) > 0$ depending on d only,

$$\forall f \in F, \forall i \leq n, \|\boldsymbol{x}_i - \boldsymbol{x}^*\| \leq \frac{C(d)}{i^\alpha}, \tag{4}$$

with probability at least $1 - \delta/2$; $\alpha > 0$ large implies that there is a fast convergence. This equation depends on n; in fact, the whole work would make sense with n replaced by ∞, but we can show our results for any n sufficiently large, so we keep this assumption under this form (the main theorem will assume this for all n, but results in it are derived for n sufficiently large).

Actually, convergence rates could be formalized differently. For example, we might consider that the rate is α if

$$\forall f \in F, \forall n, \|\boldsymbol{x}_{k_n} - \boldsymbol{x}^*\| \leq \frac{C(d)}{{k_n}^\alpha}. \tag{5}$$

for some increasing sequence k_n. This is a weaker assumption, because only $\boldsymbol{x}_i$ such that $\exists n; i = k_n$ have a fast rate; other points can be sampled anywhere in the domain without modifying the measure α of the convergence rate. For instance, the following algorithm satisfies Eq. 5 but not Eq. 4, for $0 < \alpha < 1/2$:

- define $k_n = n^2$;
- if i different from k_n for all n, then do *exploration* ($\boldsymbol{x}_i$ is uniformly drawn on the domain);
- otherwise, do *exploitation* ($\boldsymbol{x}_i$ is the maximum likelihood estimate of $\boldsymbol{x}^*$ given the $\boldsymbol{x}_i$ and their fitness evaluations).

Indeed, this algorithm is quite good for the objective function model that we have chosen (see Eq. 2); but it does not satisfy Eq.4 as some points are sampled far from the optimum. In fact the algorithm above can even be optimized by choosing $\boldsymbol{x}_i$, for exploration, at locations where it is most likely to help finding the optimum (this is active learning); see e.g. [20, 21]. Also, sometimes, the $\boldsymbol{x}_i$ for exploitation are computed, but not evaluated.

When designing a testbed for noisy optimization, this issue makes sense. Many optimization algorithms for noisy settings distinguish $\boldsymbol{x}_i$'s which are supposed to be good approximations of the optimum and $\boldsymbol{x}_i$'s which are sampled for gathering information about the optimum. If the testbed makes no difference between the two kinds of points, it implicitly assumes that sampling far from the optimum for gathering information is unlikely to be a good method. Rates reachable with no constraints are a well established part of the state of the art[22]; we here focus on rates which can be attained when focusing on Eq. 4 as a criterion for convergence. Importantly, this criterion is also relevant when all fitness values sampled are important; e.g. when improving, online, a production unit.

To sum up, the locality assumption (Eq.4) used to obtain our main result means that the algorithm has a given rate if and only if all its search points follow this rate; it is not allowed, for instance, to have one point out of two which is close to the optimum, and another far away in order to get some information which, for some reason, would help for the convergence. In other words, this assumption means that we consider rates that can be reached without relying on long distance correlations between fitness values. This is by no mean a negligible technical detail; as we have already said, there are fast algorithm which rely on sampling far from the optimum; these fast algorithms, however, can only be fast when there is a strong structure on the objective functions so that sampling far away can provide significant improvements on the convergence rate. This paper is devoted to showing bounds on rates for algorithms which do not use such sampling "far" from the current estimate of the optimum.

The results can therefore be viewed with two different complementary conclusions:

- either as the proof that fast rates (faster than the limits obtained in this paper) can only be obtained by sampling also far from the optimum;
- or as the proof that fast rates (faster than the limits obtained in this paper) are only possible for algorithm which assume some strong "flatness" of the objective function around the optimum, and these algorithms will not be so fast if we test them on other objective functions.

Under the locality assumption (Eq. 4), we show that for the family $F_{\beta,\gamma}$ of objective functions ($\gamma > 0$), α is necessarily less than or equal to $1/\beta$ - if the function is very flat around the optimum (β large), the convergence of algorithms sampling close to the optimum (Eq. 4) is necessarily slow ($\alpha \leq 1/\beta$ in Eq. 4). On the other hand, for $\beta = 2$, local algorithms (like R-EDA) have the same order as the rate reached by machine learning methods, and can even be better for $\beta = 1$, reaching $\tilde{O}(1/n)$ when $\beta = 1$ instead of $\tilde{O}(1/\sqrt{n})$ by max-uncertainty sampling.

2. MODELS AND LEMMAS

Algorithm 1 describes our framework. As introduced in section 1.2 (Eq. 4), we assume, for some $0 < \delta < 1/2$, the locality assumption

$$\forall f \in F, \forall i \leq n, \|\boldsymbol{x}_i - \boldsymbol{x}^*\| \leq \frac{C(d)}{i^\alpha}$$

with probability at least $1 - \delta/2$. This contains two important elements:

- there is an $\tilde{O}(1/n^\alpha)$ convergence to the optimum;
- there is no sampling far from the current estimate of the optimum.

This implies that the algorithm converges and does not sample far from its limit.

As already stated in Eq. 1 and 2, we also consider the family of functions

$$F = F_{\beta,\gamma} = \{f_{\boldsymbol{x}^*,\beta,\gamma}(\boldsymbol{x}) \ ; \ \boldsymbol{x}^* \in D\},$$

where

$$f_{\boldsymbol{x}^*,\beta,\gamma}(\boldsymbol{x}) = \mathcal{B}\left(\gamma\left(\frac{\|\boldsymbol{x}_n - \boldsymbol{x}^*\|}{\sqrt{d}}\right)^\beta + (1-\gamma)\right),$$

that is to say the random variable ω is uniform in $[0,1]$ and $f(\boldsymbol{x},\omega) = 1$ if and only if $\omega \leq \gamma\left(\frac{\|\boldsymbol{x}_n - \boldsymbol{x}^*\|}{\sqrt{d}}\right)^\beta + (1-\gamma)$ ($f(\boldsymbol{x},\omega) = 0$ otherwise).

Equation 2 and the locality assumption (Eq. 4) imply

$$\underbrace{\mathbb{E}f(\boldsymbol{x}^*)}_{1-\gamma} \leq \mathbb{E}f(\boldsymbol{x}_n) \leq \underbrace{\mathbb{E}f(\boldsymbol{x}^*)}_{1-\gamma} + \frac{\gamma}{d^{\beta/2}}\frac{C(d)^\beta}{n^{\alpha\beta}},$$

with probability at least $1-\delta/2$ and where $\mathbb{E}f(\boldsymbol{x})$ is a short notation for $\mathbb{E}_\omega f(\boldsymbol{x},\omega)$.

The nth function evaluation y_n is, by definition, at $\boldsymbol{x}_{\boldsymbol{x}^*,n,\omega,\omega'}$ which depends on $\boldsymbol{x}^*$ (which specifies the objective function), ω (which is the sequence of random variables ω of the stochasticity of the objective function), ω' (which is the sequence of random choices within the optimization algorithm, which might be stochastic). It also depends on β and γ, but these will be considered as fixed.

For short, we will note $X_{n,\Omega}$, with $\Omega = (\omega,\omega')$ the set of all the $\boldsymbol{x}_{\boldsymbol{x}^*,n,\omega,\omega'}$ for all $\boldsymbol{x}^*$, that is to say $X_{n,\Omega}$ is the set of all points which can be chose by the optimization algorithm *Optimize* for the nth point to sample if we consider a given noise and internal randomness.

To obtain our main result, we first need a combinatorial lemma as follows:

LEMMA 1. *The cardinality of $X_{n,\Omega}$ is at most 2^N, where N is the cardinality of*

$$\left\{1 \leq i \leq n \ ; \ \underbrace{\mathbb{E}f(\boldsymbol{x}^*)}_{1-\gamma} \leq \omega_i \leq \underbrace{\mathbb{E}f(\boldsymbol{x}^*)}_{1-\gamma} + \frac{\gamma}{d^{\beta/2}}\frac{C(d)^\beta}{i^{\alpha\beta}}\right\}.$$

PROOF. $\boldsymbol{x}_n$ is deterministic as a function of Ω and of the fitness values; so the possible values of $\boldsymbol{x}_{\boldsymbol{x}^*,n,\omega,\omega'}$ only depend on the 2^N possible values of the y_i for i in the set above. □

We also need the following

LEMMA 2. *Let N be the cardinality of*

$$\left\{1 \leq i \leq n \ ; \ \mathbb{E}f(\boldsymbol{x}^*) \leq \omega_i \leq \mathbb{E}f(\boldsymbol{x}^*) + \frac{\gamma}{d^{\beta/2}}\frac{C(d)^\beta}{i^{\alpha\beta}}\right\}.$$

Then, N has expectation at most

$$z = \frac{\gamma}{d^{\beta/2}}C(d)^\beta \sum_{i=1}^{n} i^{-\alpha\beta} \tag{6}$$

and variance also at most z.

which is an immediate consequence of the definition of N.

Lemma 2 and Chebyshev's inequality[23, 24, 25] ensure the following lemma:

LEMMA 3. *Consider $\delta \in [0,1]$. $N \leq z + \sqrt{z}(\delta/2)^{-1/2}$ with probability at least $1-\delta/2$.*

Lemmas 1 and 3 together imply that the cardinality of $X_{n,\Omega}$ is at most

$$2^{z+\frac{\sqrt{z}}{\sqrt{\delta/2}}} \tag{7}$$

with probability at least $1-\delta/2$.

3. MAIN RESULTS

THEOREM 1. *Assume that F is as proposed in Eq. 2 for some $1 > \gamma > 0$ and $\beta > 0$. Assume that Eq. 4 (locality assumption) holds for all $n \geq 1, d \geq 1$, and for some $C(d)$, $\delta < 1$, $\alpha > 0$, i.e.*

$$\forall f \in F, \forall i \leq n, \|\boldsymbol{x}_i - \boldsymbol{x}^*\| \leq \frac{C(d)}{i^\alpha},$$

with probability at least $1 - \delta/2$. Then $\alpha \leq 1/\beta$.

PROOF. Let us show that $\alpha\beta \leq 1$. In order to do so, let us assume, in order to get a contradiction, that $\alpha\beta > 1$; then, knowing convergence of Riemann series for $\alpha\beta > 1$

$$\sum_{i=1}^{n} \frac{1}{i^{\alpha\beta}} < \frac{\alpha\beta}{\alpha\beta - 1}$$

equation 6 leads to:

$$z \leq \frac{\gamma C(d)^\beta}{d^{\beta/2}} \frac{\alpha\beta}{\alpha\beta - 1} \text{ if } \alpha\beta > 1 \tag{8}$$

Consider any optimization algorithm (stochastic or not). Eq. 8 implies the finiteness of z, and therefore by Eq. 7 the finiteness of $X_{n,\Omega}$, bounded above by a constant C independent of n, with probability at least $1 - \delta/2$.

We will here use sets of points with lower bounded distance to each other; such sets are classical in statistics[26], and are now also used for building lower bounds based on information theory[27, 28].

Consider R a set of cardinality C' such that

$$\frac{C'}{C} > \frac{1 - \frac{\delta}{2}}{1 - \delta} \tag{9}$$

and such that two distinct elements of R are at distance greater than 2ϵ, with $\epsilon = C(d)/n^\alpha$, from each other; such a set certainly exists if n is large enough. A nice property of this set is that if the optimum $\boldsymbol{x}^*$ is uniformly drawn in R, then it can only be found with probability $1 - \delta/2$ and with precision $C(d)/n^\alpha$ if $X_{n,\Omega}$ contains one point close to r for a proportion at least $1 - \delta/2$ of points $r \in R$.

Consider $f_{\boldsymbol{x}^*} = f_{\boldsymbol{x}^*,\beta,\gamma}$ with $\boldsymbol{x}^*$ uniformly distributed in R. Then:

$$\begin{aligned}
& P(\|\boldsymbol{x}_n - \boldsymbol{x}^*\| \leq \epsilon) \\
\leq \; & \mathbb{E}_\Omega P_{\boldsymbol{x}^*}(\boldsymbol{x}^* \in \text{Enl}(X_{n,\Omega}, \epsilon)) \\
\leq \; & P(\#X_{n,\Omega} \leq C) P_{\boldsymbol{x}^*}(\boldsymbol{x}^* \in \text{Enl}(X_{n,\Omega}, \epsilon) | \#X_{n,\Omega} \leq C) \\
& + P(\#X_{n,\Omega} > C) \\
\leq \; & (1 - \frac{\delta}{2}) \frac{C}{C'} + \frac{\delta}{2} \\
< \; & 1 - \frac{\delta}{2}
\end{aligned}$$

where $\text{Enl}(U, \epsilon)$ is the ϵ-enlargement of U defined as:

$$\text{Enl}(U, \epsilon) = \{\boldsymbol{x}; \exists \boldsymbol{x}' \in U, \|\boldsymbol{x} - \boldsymbol{x}'\| \leq \epsilon\}.$$

This contradicts Eq. 4.

This concludes the proof of $\alpha\beta \leq 1$. □

4. CONCLUSION

Our results are based on the *locality assumption* (Eq. 4). They show tight results in some cases. The locality assumption is somewhat natural, as most evolution strategies (not all, but almost all) verify this assumption; for example, [29], one of the main evolutionary optimization convergence results, shows a linear convergence, with no sampling far away; [30], showing faster rates with surrogate models, also verifies this assumption; and polynomial rates in noisy optimization as in [14, 31] have the same property as well as many experimentally known rates [32]. Nonetheless, other assumptions leading to similar results (e.g. assumptions ensuring that points far from the optimum cannot help too much) are worth being investigated for clarifying the overall picture.

Basically, our results are about optimization tricks as follows: an optimization algorithm uses the *far sampling trick* if there is a clear distinction between the approximation of the optimum that they propose and the search points that they use for exploring the fitness function.

Our results can be seen either:

- As proofs that fast rates (faster than those in the tables below) are possible only if you assume that points far away from the optimum do bring information, by statistical model estimation, which are relevant for improving the rate (so that the "far sampling trick" can work).
- As proofs that algorithms which, like most evolutionary algorithms (but not all), do not sample far away from the optimum, can not be optimal when the function is "flat" enough around the optimum (there are algorithms and families of functions for which better rates are possible - which does not mean that algorithms which do not want to use the far sampling trick are necessarily bad algorithms).

The hot discussions on the BBOB mailing list, around the fact that the test beds should distinguish the search points used for approximating the optimum and the search points used for gathering information by sampling far away, suggest that this paper comes at the right moment for noisy optimization formal analysis.

Table 1 summarizes the state of the art; new result from this paper are in bold, and we emphasize cases in which a gap is known. We see that our results show the tightness in the case $\gamma = 1$ (small noise; the variance goes to zero around the optimum), and reduce the gap in the case $\gamma < 1$ (large noise). Our results also show that for fast rates, sampling far from the optimum is necessary; e.g. if $\beta = 4$, $\alpha = 1/2$ is possible only with sampling far from the optimum. Though, this is only possible if there are long range dependencies on the fitness function, so that such points far from the optimum can be used.

Further work

The locality assumption might be or might not be, depending on the application, a good idea. From many discussions around that, we believe that there is room for works like this one, in which a locality assumption prevents the use of information far from the optimum, reliable only when strong assumptions on the model are available. It is also a model which shows that some rates imply sampling far from the

"flatness" β	Proved rate for R-EDA in [16] ("flatness" on an envelope of the fitness function; the fitness function does not have to be flat around $\boldsymbol{x}^*$)	Lower bound in [16]	R-EDA experimental rate in [14] (on functions with invariances)	This paper (lower bound under locality assumption)	Rate for learnable cases
Framework $\gamma = 1$ (small noise)					
1	$\alpha \geq 1$	$\alpha \leq 1$	$\alpha = 1$	$\alpha \leq 1$	$\alpha = 1/2$
2	$\alpha \geq 1/2$	$\alpha \leq 1$	$\alpha = 1/2$	$\alpha \leq \mathbf{1/2}$	$\alpha = 1/2$
4	$\alpha \geq 1/4$	$\alpha \leq 1$	$\alpha = 1/4$	$\alpha \leq \mathbf{1/4}$	$\alpha = 1/2$
Framework $\gamma < 1$ (large noise)					
1	$\alpha \geq 1/2$	$\alpha \leq 1$	$\alpha = 1/2$	$\alpha \leq 1$	$\alpha = 1/2$
2	$\alpha \geq 1/4$	$\alpha \leq 1$	$\alpha = 1/4$	$\alpha \leq \mathbf{1/2}$	$\alpha = 1/2$
4	$\alpha \geq 1/8$	$\alpha \leq 1$	$\alpha = 1/8$	$\alpha \leq \mathbf{1/4}$	$\alpha = 1/2$

Table 1: This table summarizes the state of the art in terms of α for which $||\tilde{x}_n - \boldsymbol{x}^*|| = \tilde{O}(1/n^\alpha)$ is possible. Rates for E-EDA include functions which are not differentiable, and are just upper bounded by flat functions around x^* with β coefficient; see [14] for more details. Experimental rates for R-EDA are for functions with strong invariances/symmetries; see [14] for details. The last column presents results with $\alpha = 1/2$, corresponding to cases in which using statistical model estimation is possible: the limit case of infinite differentiability in [33, 34, 22], is also reached by quadratic logistic regression under parametric assumptions on the objective function[14]; assumptions are not directly comparable to those of the other columns. Lower bounds on the complexity (upper bounds on α) from this paper are under the additional assumption of local sampling.

optimum. Fast optimization algorithms might, as CLOP, be a compromise between sampling close to the optimum and sampling on areas of maximum uncertainty. Further investigations on intermediate models might be a good idea.

There is still a gap between the upper and the lower bound, for algorithms having the locality assumption, in the case $\gamma < 1$ (large noise), which is an immediate further work.

We consider noisy optimization in the case of local convergence; clearly, the global convergence case can also be interesting[35].

We did not compute exactly constants C and C'. Maybe it is possible to obtain more information on the constant in the convergence using detailed computations of C and C'.

Acknowledgments

We are grateful to the Dagstuhl seminar on Evolutionary Algorithms, to the Montefiore institute in University of Belgium in which author #2 had interesting discussions around noisy optimization. We are grateful to various members of the Tao team for interesting discussions, as well as discussions in the BBOB mailing list. We are grateful to European project MASH, FP7 program.

5. REFERENCES

[1] A. Conn, K. Scheinberg, and L. Toint, "Recent progress in unconstrained nonlinear optimization without derivatives," 1997. [Online]. Available: citeseer.ist.psu.edu/conn97recent.html

[2] B. Doerr and C. Winzen, "Towards a complexity theory of randomized search heuristics: Ranking-based black-box complexity," in *CSR*, ser. Lecture Notes in Computer Science, A. S. Kulikov and N. K. Vereshchagin, Eds., vol. 6651. Springer, 2011, pp. 15–28.

[3] S. Grünewälder, J.-Y. Audibert, M. Opper, and J. Shawe-Taylor, "Regret Bounds for Gaussian Process Bandit Problems," in *JMLR Workshop and Conference Proceedings : AISTATS 2010*, vol. 9, Chia Laguna Resort, Sardinia, Italie, 2010, pp. 273–280. [Online]. Available: http://hal-enpc.archives-ouvertes.fr/hal-00654517

[4] H.-P. Schwefel, *Numerical Optimization of Computer Models*. New-York: John Wiley & Sons, 1981, 1995 – 2nd edition.

[5] H.-G. Beyer, "Mutate large, but inherit small ! On the analysis of mutations in $(1, \lambda)$-ES with noisy fitness data," in *Proc. of the* 5th *Conference on Parallel Problems Solving from Nature*, T. Bäck, G. Eiben, M. Schoenauer, and H.-P. Schwefel, Eds. Springer Verlag, 1998, pp. 109–118.

[6] J. Fitzpatrick and J. Grefenstette, "Genetic algorithms in noisy environments, in machine learning: Special issue on genetic algorithms, p. langley, ed. dordrecht: Kluwer academic publishers, vol. 3, pp. 101 120," 1988.

[7] D. V. Arnold and H.-G. Beyer, "Local performance of the (1+1)-ES in a noisy environment," *IEEE Transactions on Evolutionary Computation*, vol. 6, no. 1, pp. 30–41, 2002.

[8] D. V. Arnold and H. georg Beyer, "Evolution strategies with cumulative step length adaptation on the noisy parabolic ridge," Tech. Rep., 2006.

[9] U. Hammel and T. Bäck, "Evolution strategies on noisy functions: How to improve convergence properties," in *Parallel Problem Solving From Nature*, ser. LNCS, Y. Davidor, H.-P. Schwefel, and R. Männer, Eds., vol. 866. Jerusalem: springer, 9–14Oct. 1994, pp. 159–168.

[10] J. M. Fitzpatrick and J. J. Grefenstette, "Genetic algorithms in noisy environments," *Machine Learning*, vol. 3, pp. 101–120, 1988.

[11] M. Jebalia and A. Auger, "On multiplicative noise models for stochastic search," in *Parallel Problem Solving From Nature*, dortmund Allemagne, 2008.

[Online]. Available:
http://hal.inria.fr/inria-00287725/en/

[12] O. Teytaud and A. Auger, "On the adaptation of the noise level for stochastic optimization," in *IEEE Congress on Evolutionary Computation*, Singapour, 2007. [Online]. Available: http://hal.inria.fr/inria-00173224/en/

[13] R. Coulom, "Clop: Confident local optimization for noisy black-box parameter tuning," in *ACG*, ser. Lecture Notes in Computer Science, H. J. van den Herik and A. Plaat, Eds., vol. 7168. Springer, 2011, pp. 146–157.

[14] R. Coulom, P. Rolet, N. Sokolovska, and O. Teytaud, "Handling expensive optimization with large noise," in *FOGA*, H.-G. Beyer and W. B. Langdon, Eds. ACM, 2011, pp. 61–68.

[15] P. Rolet and O. Teytaud, "Bandit-based estimation of distribution algorithms for noisy optimization: Rigorous runtime analysis," in *Proceedings of Lion4 (accepted); presented in TRSH 2009 in Birmingham*, 2009.

[16] ——, "Adaptive Noisy Optimization," in *EvoStar 2010*, Istambul, Turquie, Feb. 2010. [Online]. Available: http://hal.inria.fr/inria-00459017

[17] V. Heidrich-Meisner and C. Igel, "Uncertainty handling cma-es for reinforcement learning," in *GECCO*, F. Rothlauf, Ed. ACM, 2009, pp. 1211–1218.

[18] L. Devroye, L. Györfi, and G. Lugosi, *A probabilistic Theory of Pattern Recognition.* Springer, 1997.

[19] R. Coulom, P. Rolet, N. Sokolovska, and O. Teytaud, "Handling expensive optimization with large noise," in *FOGA*, H.-G. Beyer and W. B. Langdon, Eds. ACM, 2011, pp. 61–68.

[20] D. R. Jones, M. Schonlau, and W. J. Welch, "Efficient global optimization of expensive black-box functions," *J. of Global Optimization*, vol. 13, no. 4, pp. 455–492, 1998.

[21] J. Villemonteix, E. Vazquez, and E. Walter, "An informational approach to the global optimization of expensive-to-evaluate functions," *Journal of Global Optimization*, p. 26 pages, 09 2008. [Online]. Available: dx.doi.org/10.1007/s10898-008-9354-2 http://hal-supelec.archives-ouvertes.fr/hal-00354262/en/

[22] V. Fabian, "Stochastic approximation of minima with improved asymptotic speed," *Ann. Math. Statist.*, vol. 38, no. 1, pp. 191–200, 1967.

[23] L. Bienaymé, "Considérations à l'appui de la découverte de laplace," *Comptes Rendus de l'Académie des Sciences*, vol. 37, pp. 309–324, 1853.

[24] P. Chebyshev, "Sur les valeurs limites des integrales," *Math Pure Appl*, vol. 19, p. 157£160, 1874.

[25] A. Markov, "On certain applications of algebraic continued fractions," Ph.D. dissertation, St Petersburg, 2002.

[26] A. V. D. Vaart and J. Wellner, *Weak Convergence and Empirical Processes.* Springer series in statistics, 1996.

[27] O. Teytaud and S. Gelly, "General lower bounds for evolutionary algorithms," in 10th *International Conference on Parallel Problem Solving from Nature (PPSN 2006)*, 2006.

[28] H. Fournier and O. Teytaud, "Lower bounds for comparison based evolution strategies using vc-dimension and sign patterns," *Algorithmica*, vol. 59, no. 3, pp. 387–408, 2011.

[29] A. Auger, "Convergence results for (1,λ)-SA-ES using the theory of φ-irreducible Markov chains," *Theoretical Computer Science*, vol. 334, no. 1-3, pp. 35–69, 2005.

[30] A. Auger, M. Schoenauer, and O. Teytaud, "Local and global order 3/2 convergence of a surrogate evolutionnary algorithm," in *Gecco*, 2005, p. 8 p.

[31] D. V. Arnold and H.-G. Beyer, "Efficiency and mutation strength adaptation of the (mu/mui,lambda)-es in a noisy environment," in *Parallel Problem Solving from Nature*, ser. LNCS, M. S. et al., Ed., vol. 1917. springer, 2000, pp. 39–48.

[32] H.-G. Beyer, *The Theory of Evolution Strategies*, ser. Natural Computing Series. Springer, Heideberg, 2001.

[33] H. Chen, "Lower rate of convergence for locating a maximum of a function," *Ann. Statist.*, vol. 16, no. 3, pp. 1330–1334, 1988.

[34] J. Kiefer and J. Wolfowitz, "Stochastic estimation of the maximum of a regression function," *Annals of Mathematical Statistics*, vol. 23, no. 3, p. 462£466, 1952.

[35] E. Vazquez, J. Villemonteix, M. Sidorkiewicz, and E. Walter, "Global optimization based on noisy evaluations: an empirical study of two statistical approaches," *Journal of Global Optimization*, p. 17 pages, 2008. [Online]. Available: dx.doi.org/10.1007/s10898-008-9313-y http://hal-supelec.archives-ouvertes.fr/hal-00354656/en/

[36] H.-G. Beyer and W. B. Langdon, Eds., *Foundations of Genetic Algorithms, 11th International Workshop, FOGA 2011, Schwarzenberg, Austria, January 5-8, 2011, Proceedings.* ACM, 2011.

Author Index

Akimoto, Youhei 1
Berzan, Constantin 75
Beyer, Hans-Georg 11
Bischl, Bernd 147
Bresolin, Davide 25
Burjorjee, Keki M. 37
Decock, Jérémie 183
Doerr, Benjamin 51
Feldmann, Matthias 65
He, Jun 133
Hellwig, Michael 11
Hemberg, Erik 75
Jansen, Thomas 87
Jiménez, Fernando 25
Kötzing, Timo 65
Lehre, Per Kristian 97
Lockett, Alan J. 105
Mambrini, Andrea 119
Manzoni, Luca 119
Mersmann, Olaf 147
Miikkulainen, Risto 105
Mitavskiy, Boris 133
Moraglio, Alberto 119
Nallaperuma, Samadhi 147
Neumann, Frank 147
Nguyen, Anh 161
Oliveto, Pietro S. 87
Ollivier, Yann 1
O'Reilly, Una-May 75
Özcan, Ender 97
Pei, Yan 173
Sánchez, Gracia 25
Sciavicco, Guido 25
Sudholt, Dirk 51
Takagi, Hideyuki 173
Teytaud, Olivier 183
Trautmann, Heike 147
Urli, Tommaso 161
Veeramachaneni, Kalyan 75
Wagner, Markus 147, 161
Witt, Carsten 51
Zarges, Christine 87

www.ingramcontent.com/pod-product-compliance
Lightning Source LLC
Chambersburg PA
CBHW081525220326
41598CB00036B/6330